THEODORE ROOSEVELT

AN AUTOBIOGRAPHY

THE MACMILLAN COMPANY
NEW YORK · BOSTON · CHICAGO · DALLAS
ATLANTA · SAN FRANCISCO

MACMILLAN & CO., Limited
LONDON · BOMBAY · CALCUTTA
MELBOURNE

THE MACMILLAN CO. OF CANADA, Ltd.
TORONTO

From a painting by P. Laszlo.

PRESIDENT THEODORE ROOSEVELT IN HIS RIDING COSTUME.

Theodore Roosevelt

AN AUTOBIOGRAPHY

WITH ILLUSTRATIONS

London

MACMILLAN AND CO., Limited

NEW YORK: THE MACMILLAN COMPANY

1913

Norwood Press
J. S. Cushing Co. — Berwick & Smith Co.
Norwood, Mass., U.S.A.

FOREWORD

NATURALLY, there are chapters of my autobiography which cannot now be written.

It seems to me that, for the nation as for the individual, what is most important is to insist on the vital need of combining certain sets of qualities, which separately are common enough, and, alas, useless enough. Practical efficiency is common, and lofty idealism not uncommon; it is the combination which is necessary, and the combination is rare. Love of peace is common among weak, short-sighted, timid, and lazy persons; and on the other hand courage is found among many men of evil temper and bad character. Neither quality shall by itself avail. Justice among the nations of mankind, and the uplifting of humanity, can be brought about only by those strong and daring men who with wisdom love peace, but who love righteousness more than peace. Facing the immense complexity of modern social and industrial conditions, there is need to use freely and unhesitatingly the collective power of all of us; and yet no exercise of collective power will ever avail if the average individual does not keep his or her sense of personal duty, initiative, and responsibility. There is need to develop all the virtues that have the state for their sphere of action; but these virtues are as dust in a windy street unless back of them lie the strong and tender virtues of a family life based on the love of the one man for the one woman and on their joyous and fearless acceptance of their common obligation to the children that are theirs. There must be the keenest sense of duty, and with it must go the joy of living; there must be shame at the thought of shirking the hard work of the world, and at the same time delight in the many-sided beauty of life. With soul of flame and temper of steel we must act as our coolest judgment bids us. We must exercise the largest charity towards the wrong-doer that is compatible with relentless war against the wrong-doing. We must be just to others, generous to others, and yet we must realize that it is a shameful and a wicked thing not to withstand oppression with high heart and ready hand. With gentleness and tenderness there must go dauntless bravery and grim acceptance of labor and hardship and peril. All for each, and each for all, is a good motto; but only on condition that each works with might and main to so maintain himself as not to be a burden to others.

We of the great modern democracies must strive unceasingly to make our several countries lands in which a poor man who works hard can live comfortably and honestly, and in which a rich man cannot live dishonestly nor in slothful avoidance of duty; and yet we must judge rich man and poor man alike by a standard which rests on conduct and not on caste, and we must frown with the same stern severity on the mean and vicious envy which hates and would plunder a man because he is well off and on the brutal and selfish arrogance which looks down on and exploits the man with whom life has gone hard.

THEODORE ROOSEVELT.

Sagamore Hill, Oct. 1, 1913.

CONTENTS

ILLUSTRATIONS

ILLUSTRATIONS

ILLUSTRATIONS

THEODORE ROOSEVELT

AN AUTOBIOGRAPHY

THEODORE ROOSEVELT
AN AUTOBIOGRAPHY

CHAPTER I

BOYHOOD AND YOUTH

MY grandfather on my father's side was of almost purely Dutch blood. When he was young he still spoke some Dutch, and Dutch was last used in the services of the Dutch Reformed Church in New York while he was a small boy.

About 1644 his ancestor Klaes Martensen van Roosevelt came to New Amsterdam as a "settler" — the euphemistic name for an immigrant who came over in the steerage of a sailing ship in the seventeenth century instead of the steerage of a steamer in the nineteenth century. From that time for the next seven generations from father to son every one of us was born on Manhattan Island.

My father's paternal ancestors were of Holland stock; except that there was one named Waldron, a wheelwright, who was one of the Pilgrims who remained in Holland when the others came over to found Massachusetts, and who then accompanied the Dutch adventurers to New Amsterdam. My father's mother was a Pennsylvanian. Her forbears had come to Pennsylvania with William Penn, some in the same ship with him; they were of the usual type of the immigration of that particular place and time. They included Welsh and English Quakers, an Irishman, — with a Celtic name, and apparently not a Quaker, — and peace-loving Germans, who were among the founders of Germantown, having been driven from their Rhineland homes when the armies of Louis the Fourteenth ravaged the Palatinate;

and, in addition, representatives of a by-no-means altogether peaceful people, the Scotch Irish, who came to Pennsylvania a little later, early in the eighteenth century. My grandmother was a woman of singular sweetness and strength, the keystone of the arch in her relations with her husband and sons. Although she was not herself Dutch, it was she who taught me the only Dutch I ever knew, a baby song of which the first line ran, "Trippe troppa tronjes." I always remembered this, and when I was in East Africa it proved a bond of union between me and the Boer settlers, not a few of whom knew it, although at first they always had difficulty in understanding my pronunciation — at which I do not wonder. It was interesting to meet these men whose ancestors had gone to the Cape about the time that mine went to America two centuries and a half previously, and to find that the descendants of the two streams of emigrants still crooned to their children some at least of the same nursery songs.

Of my great-grandfather Roosevelt and his family life a century and over ago I know little beyond what is implied in some of his books that have come down to me — the Letters of Junius, a biography of John Paul Jones, Chief Justice Marshall's "Life of Washington." They seem to indicate that his library was less interesting than that of my wife's great-grandfather at the same time, which certainly included such volumes as the original *Edinburgh Review*, for we have them now on our own book-shelves. Of my grandfather Roosevelt my most vivid childish reminiscence is not something I saw, but a tale that was told me concerning him. In *his* boyhood Sunday was as dismal a day for small Calvinistic children of Dutch descent as if they had been of Puritan or Scotch Covenanting or French Huguenot descent — and I speak as one proud of his Holland, Huguenot, and Covenanting ancestors, and proud that the blood of that stark Puritan divine Jonathan Edwards flows in the veins of his children. One summer afternoon, after listening to an unusually long Dutch Reformed sermon for the second time that day, my grandfather, a small boy, running home before the congregation had dispersed, ran into a party of pigs, which then wandered free in New

York's streets. He promptly mounted a big boar, which no less promptly bolted and carried him at full speed through the midst of the outraged congregation.

By the way, one of the Roosevelt documents which came down to me illustrates the change that has come over certain aspects of public life since the time which pessimists term "the earlier and better days of the Republic." Old Isaac Roosevelt was a member of an Auditing Committee which shortly after the close of the Revolution approved the following bill:

The State of New York, to John Cape   *Dr.*

To a Dinner Given by His Excellency the Governor and Council to their Excellencies the Minnister of France and General Washington & Co.

1783

December

To 120 dinners at	48:	0:0
To 135 Bottles Madira	54:	0:0
" 36 ditto Port	10:	16:0
" 60 ditto English Beer	9:	0:0
" 30 Bouls Punch	9:	0:0
" 8 dinners for Musick . . .	1:	12:0
" 10 ditto for Sarvts	2:	0:0
" 60 Wine Glasses Broken . . .	4:	10:0
" 8 Cutt decanters Broken . .	3:	0:0
" Coffee for 8 Gentlemen . . .	1:	12:0
" Music fees &ca	8:	0:0
" Fruit & Nuts	5:	0:0

                       £156:10:0

By Cash . . . 100:16:0

                       55:14:0

WE a Committee of Council having examined the above account do certify it (amounting to one hundred and fifty-six Pounds ten Shillings) to be just.

December 17th 1783.

                     ISAAC ROOSEVELT
                     JAS. DUANE
                     EGBT. BENSON
                     FRED. JAY

Received the above Contents in full
New York 17th December 1783

                     JOHN CAPE

Think of the Governor of New York now submitting such a bill for such an entertainment of the French Ambassador and the President of the United States ! Falstaff's views of the proper proportion between sack and bread are borne out by the proportion between the number of bowls of punch and bottles of port, Madeira, and beer consumed, and the "coffee for eight gentlemen" — apparently the only ones who lasted through to that stage of the dinner. Especially admirable is the nonchalant manner in which, obviously as a result of the drinking of said bottles of wine and bowls of punch, it is recorded that eight cut-glass decanters and sixty wine-glasses were broken.

During the Revolution some of my forefathers, North and South, served respectably, but without distinction, in the army, and others rendered similar service in the Continental Congress or in various local legislatures. By that time those who dwelt in the North were for the most part merchants, and those who dwelt in the South, planters.

My mother's people were predominantly of Scotch, but also of Huguenot and English, descent. She was a Georgian, her people having come to Georgia from South Carolina before the Revolution. The original Bulloch was a lad from near Glasgow, who came hither a couple of centuries ago, just as hundreds of thousands of needy, enterprising Scotchmen have gone to the four quarters of the globe in the intervening two hundred years. My mother's great-grandfather, Archibald Bulloch, was the first Revolutionary "President" of Georgia. My grandfather, her father, spent the winters in Savannah and the summers at Roswell, in the Georgia uplands near Atlanta, finally making Roswell his permanent home. He used to travel thither with his family and their belongings in his own carriage, followed by a baggage wagon. I never saw Roswell until I was President, but my mother told me so much about the place that when I did see it I felt as if I already knew every nook and corner of it, and as it if were haunted by the ghosts of all the men and women who had lived there. I do not mean merely my own family, I mean the slaves. My mother and her sister, my aunt, used to tell us children all kinds of stories about the slaves. One

"My father, Theodore Roosevelt, was the best man I ever knew."

of the most fascinating referred to a very old darky called Bear Bob, because in the early days of settlement he had been partially scalped by a black bear.   Then there was Mom' Grace, who was for a time my mother's nurse, and whom I had supposed to be dead, but who greeted me when I did come to Roswell, very respectable, and apparently with years of life before her.   The two chief personages of the drama that used to be repeated to us were Daddy Luke, the Negro overseer, and his wife, Mom' Charlotte.   I never saw either Daddy Luke or Mom' Charlotte, but I inherited the care of them when my mother died.   After the close of the war they resolutely refused to be emancipated or leave the place.   The only demand they made upon us was enough money annually to get a new "critter," that is, a mule. With a certain lack of ingenuity the mule was reported each Christmas as having passed away, or at least as having become so infirm as to necessitate a successor — a solemn fiction which neither deceived nor was intended to deceive, but which furnished a gauge for the size of the Christmas gift.

My maternal grandfather's house was on the line of Sherman's march to the sea, and pretty much everything in it that was portable was taken by the boys in blue, including most of the books in the library.   When I was President the facts about my ancestry were published, and a former soldier in Sherman's army sent me back one of the books with my grandfather's name in it.   It was a little copy of the poems of "Mr. Gray" — an eighteenth-century edition printed in Glasgow.

On October 27, 1858, I was born at No. 28 East Twentieth Street, New York City, in the house in which we lived during the time that my two sisters and my brother and I were small children.   It was furnished in the canonical taste of the New York which George William Curtis described in the *Potiphar Papers*.   The black haircloth furniture in the dining-room scratched the bare legs of the children when they sat on it.   The middle room was a library, with tables, chairs, and bookcases of gloomy respectability.   It was without windows, and so was available only at night.   The front room, the parlor, seemed to us children to be a room of much splendor, but was open for general use only on Sunday evening or on rare occasions when there were parties. The Sunday evening family gathering was the redeeming feature in a day which otherwise we children did not enjoy — chiefly because we were all of us made to wear clean clothes and keep neat. The ornaments of that parlor I remember now, including the gas chandelier decorated with a great quantity of cut-glass prisms. These prisms struck me as possessing peculiar magnificence. One of them fell off one day, and I hastily grabbed it and stowed it away, passing several days of furtive delight in the treasure, a delight always alloyed with fear that I would be found out and convicted of larceny. There was a Swiss wood-carving representing a very big hunter on one side of an exceedingly small mountain, and a herd of chamois, disproportionately small for the hunter and large for the mountain, just across the ridge. This always fascinated us; but there was a small chamois kid for which we felt agonies lest the hunter might come on it and kill it. There was also a Russian moujik drawing a gilt sledge on a piece of malachite. Some one mentioned in my hearing that malachite was a valuable marble. This fixed in my mind that it was valuable exactly as diamonds are valuable. I accepted that moujik as a priceless work of art, and it was not until I was well in middle age that it occurred to me that I was mistaken.

Now and then we children were taken round to our grandfather's house; a big house for the New York of those days, on the corner of Fourteenth Street and Broadway, fronting Union Square. Inside there was a large hall running up to the roof; there was a tesselated black and white marble floor, and a circular staircase round the sides of the hall, from the top floor down. We children much admired both the tessellated floor and the circular staircase. I think we were right about the latter, but I am not so sure as to the tessellated floor.

The summers we spent in the country, now at one place, now at another. We children, of course, loved the country beyond anything. We disliked the city. We were always wildly eager to get to the country when spring came, and very sad when in the late fall the family moved back to town.   In the country we of course had all kinds of pets — cats, dogs, rabbits, a coon, and a sorrel Shetland pony named General Grant.   When my younger sister first heard of the real General Grant, by the way, she was much struck by the coincidence that some one should have given him the same name as the pony.   (Thirty years later my own children had *their* pony Grant.)   In the country we children ran barefoot much of the time, and the seasons went by in a round of uninterrupted and enthralling pleasures — supervising the haying and harvesting, picking apples, hunting frogs successfully and woodchucks unsuccessfully, gathering hickory-nuts and chestnuts for sale to patient parents, building wigwams in the woods, and sometimes playing Indians in too realistic manner by staining ourselves (and incidentally our clothes) in liberal fashion with poke-cherry juice. Thanksgiving was an appreciated festival, but it in no way came up to Christmas.   Christmas was an occasion of literally delirious joy.   In the evening we hung up our stockings — or rather the biggest stockings we could borrow from the grown-ups — and before dawn we trooped in to open them while sitting on father's and mother's bed; and the bigger presents were arranged, those for each child on its own table, in the drawing-room, the doors to which were thrown open after breakfast.   I never knew any one else have what seemed to me such attractive Christmases, and in the next generation I tried to reproduce them exactly for my own children.

My father, Theodore Roosevelt, was the best man I ever knew.   He combined strength and courage with gentleness, tenderness, and great unselfishness.   He would not tolerate in us children selfishness or cruelty, idleness, cowardice, or untruthfulness.   As we grew older he made us understand that the same standard of clean living was demanded for the boys as for the girls; that what was wrong in a woman could not be right in a man.   With great love and patience, and the most understanding sympathy and consideration, he combined insistence on discipline.   He never physically

"MY MOTHER, MARTHA BULLOCH, WAS A SWEET, GRACIOUS, BEAUTIFUL SOUTHERN
WOMAN, A DELIGHTFUL COMPANION AND BELOVED BY EVERYBODY."

punished me but once, but he was the only man of whom I was ever really afraid. I do not mean that it was a wrong fear, for he was entirely just, and we children adored him. We used to wait in the library in the evening until we could hear his key rattling in the latch of the front hall, and then rush out to greet him; and we would troop into his room while he was dressing, to stay there as long as we were permitted, eagerly examining anything which came out of his pockets which could be regarded as an attractive novelty. Every child has fixed in his memory various details which strike it as of grave importance. The trinkets he used to keep in a little box on his dressing-table we children always used to speak of as "treasures." The word, and some of the trinkets themselves, passed on to the next generation. My own children, when small, used to troop into my room while I was dressing, and the gradually accumulating trinkets in the "ditty-box" — the gift of an enlisted man in the navy — always excited rapturous joy. On occasions of solemn festivity each child would receive a trinket for his or her "very own." My children, by the way, enjoyed one pleasure I do not remember enjoying myself. When I came back from riding, the child who brought the bootjack would itself promptly get into the boots, and clump up and down the room with a delightful feeling of kinship with Jack of the seven-league strides.

The punishing incident I have referred to happened when I was four years old. I bit my elder sister's arm. I do not remember biting her arm, but I do remember running down to the yard, perfectly conscious that I had committed a crime. From the yard I went into the kitchen, got some dough from the cook, and crawled under the kitchen table. In a minute or two my father entered from the yard and asked where I was. The warm-hearted Irish cook had a characteristic contempt for "informers," but although she said nothing she compromised between informing and her conscience by casting a look under the table. My father immediately dropped on all fours and darted for me. I feebly heaved the dough at him, and, having the advantage of him because I could stand up under the table, got a fair

"I never saw Roswell until I was President."

start for the stairs, but was caught halfway up them.
The punishment that ensued fitted the crime, and I hope —
and believe — that it did me good.

I never knew any one who got greater joy out of living
than did my father, or any one who more whole-heartedly
performed every duty; and no one whom I have ever met
approached his combination of enjoyment of life and performance of duty. He and my mother were given to a hospitality that at that time was associated more commonly
with southern than northern households; and, especially
in their later years when they had moved up town, in the
neighborhood of Central Park, they kept a charming, open
house.

My father worked hard at his business, for he died when
he was forty-six, too early to have retired. He was interested in every social reform movement, and he did an
immense amount of practical charitable work himself. He
was a big, powerful man, with a leonine face, and his heart
filled with gentleness for those who needed help or protection, and with the possibility of much wrath against a bully
or an oppressor. He was very fond of riding both on the
road and across the country, and was also a great whip.
He usually drove four-in-hand, or else a spike team, that is,
a pair with a third horse in the lead. I do not suppose that
such a team exists now. The trap that he drove we always
called the high phaëton. The wheels turned under in front.
I have it yet. He drove long-tailed horses, harnessed loose
in light American harness, so that the whole rig had no possible resemblance to anything that would be seen now. My
father always excelled in improving every spare half-hour
or three-quarters of an hour, whether for work or enjoyment.
Much of his four-in-hand driving was done in the summer
afternoons when he would come out on the train from his
business in New York. My mother and one or perhaps
two of us children might meet him at the station. I can
see him now getting out of the car in his linen duster, jumping into the wagon, and instantly driving off at a rattling
pace, the duster sometimes bagging like a balloon. The
four-in-hand, as can be gathered from the above description,

did not in any way in his eyes represent possible pageantry. He drove it because he liked it. He was always preaching caution to his boys, but in this respect he did not practice his preaching overmuch himself; and, being an excellent whip, he liked to take chances. Generally they came out all right. Occasionally they did not; but he was even better at getting out of a scrape than into it. Once when we were driving into New York late at night the leaders stopped. He flicked them, and the next moment we could dimly make out that they had jumped. It then appeared that the street was closed and that a board had been placed across it, resting on two barrels, but without a lantern. Over this board the leaders had jumped, and there was considerable excitement before we got the board taken off the barrels and resumed our way. When in the city on Thanksgiving or Christmas, my father was very apt to drive my mother and a couple of friends up to the racing park to take lunch. But he was always back in time to go to the dinner at the Newsboys' Lodging-House, and not infrequently also to Miss Sattery's Night School for little Italians. At a very early age we children were taken with him and were required to help. He was a stanch friend of Charles Loring Brace, and was particularly interested in the Newsboys' Lodging-Houses and in the night schools and in getting the children off the streets and out on farms in the West. When I was President, the Governor of Alaska under me, Governor Brady, was one of these ex-newsboys who had been sent from New York out West by Mr. Brace and my father. My father was greatly interested in the societies to prevent cruelty to children and cruelty to animals. On Sundays he had a mission class. On his way to it he used to drop us children at our Sunday-school in Dr. Adams's Presbyterian Church on Madison Square; I remember hearing my aunt, my mother's sister, saying that when he walked along with us children he always reminded her of Greatheart in Bunyan. Under the spur of his example I taught a mission class myself for three years before going to college and for all four years that I was in college. I do not think I made much of a success of it. But the other day on getting out of a taxi in New York the chauffeur spoke to me and told me that he was one of my old Sunday-school pupils. I remembered him well, and was much pleased to find that he was an ardent Bull Mooser !

My mother, Martha Bulloch, was a sweet, gracious, beautiful Southern woman, a delightful companion and beloved by everybody. She was entirely "unreconstructed" to the day of her death.

"HER MOTHER, MY GRANDMOTHER, ONE OF THE DEAREST OLD LADIES, LIVED WITH US."

Her mother, my grandmother, one of the dearest of old ladies, lived with us, and was distinctly over-indulgent to us children, being quite unable to harden her heart towards us even when the occasion demanded it. Towards the close of the Civil War, although a very small boy, I grew to have a partial but alert understanding of the fact that the family were not one in their views about that conflict, my father being a strong Lincoln Republican ; and once, when I felt that I had been wronged by maternal discipline during the day, I attempted a partial vengeance by praying with loud fervor for the success of the Union arms, when we all came to say our prayers before my mother in the evening. She was not only a most devoted mother, but was also blessed with a strong sense of humor, and she was too much amused to punish me ; but I was warned not to repeat the offense, under penalty of my father's being informed — he being the dispenser of serious punishment.

Morning prayers were with my father. We used to stand at the foot of the stairs, and when father came down we called out, "I speak for you and the cubby-hole too!" There were three of us young children, and we used to sit with father on the sofa while he conducted morning prayers. The place between father and the arm of the sofa we called the "cubby-hole." The child who got that place we regarded as especially favored both in comfort and somehow or other in rank and title. The two who were left to sit on the much wider expanse of sofa on the other side of father were outsiders for the time being.

My aunt Anna, my mother's sister, lived with us. She was as devoted to us children as was my mother herself, and we were equally devoted to her in return. She taught us our lessons while we were little. She and my mother used to entertain us by the hour with tales of life on the Georgia plantations; of hunting fox, deer, and wildcat; of the long-tailed driving horses, Boone and Crockett, and of the riding horses, one of which was named Buena Vista in a fit of patriotic exaltation during the Mexican War; and of the queer goings-on in the Negro quarters. She knew all the "Br'er Rabbit" stories, and I was brought up on them. One of my uncles, Robert Roosevelt, was much struck with them, and took them down from her dictation, publishing them in *Harper's*, where they fell flat. This was a good many years before a genius arose who in "Uncle Remus" made the stories immortal.

My mother's two brothers, James Dunwoodie Bulloch and Irvine Bulloch, came to visit us shortly after the close of the war. Both came under assumed names, as they were among the Confederates who were at that time exempted from the amnesty. "Uncle Jimmy" Bulloch was a dear old retired sea-captain, utterly unable to "get on" in the worldly sense of that phrase, as valiant and simple and upright a soul as ever lived, a veritable Colonel Newcome. He was an Admiral in the Confederate navy, and was the builder of the famous Confederate war vessel *Alabama*. My uncle Irvine Bulloch was a midshipman on the *Alabama*, and fired the last gun discharged from her batteries

in the fight with the *Kearsarge*.   Both of these uncles lived
in Liverpool after the war.

My uncle Jimmy Bulloch was forgiving and just in reference to the Union forces, and could discuss all phases of the
Civil War with entire fairness and generosity.   But in English politics he promptly became a Tory of the most ultra-
conservative school.   Lincoln and Grant he could admire,
but he would not listen to anything in favor of Mr. Glad-

"Two Georgia Girls" — Martha Bulloch and Anna Bulloch.

stone.   The only occasions on which I ever shook his faith
in me were when I would venture meekly to suggest that
some of the manifestly preposterous falsehoods about Mr.
Gladstone could not be true.   My uncle was one of the best
men I have ever known, and when I have sometimes been
tempted to wonder how good people can believe of me the
unjust and impossible things they do believe, I have con-
soled myself by thinking of Uncle Jimmy Bulloch's perfectly
sincere conviction that Gladstone was a man of quite exceptional and nameless infamy in both public and private life.

I was a sickly, delicate boy, suffered much from asthma, and frequently had to be taken away on trips to find a place where I could breathe. One of my memories is of my father walking up and down the room with me in his arms at night when I was a very small person, and of sitting up in bed gasping, with my father and mother trying to help me. I went very little to school. I never went to the public schools, as my own children later did, both at the "Cove school" at Oyster Bay and at the "Ford school" in Washington. For a few months I attended Professor McMullen's school in Twentieth Street near the house where I was born, but most of the time I had tutors. As I have already said, my aunt taught me when I was small. At one time we had a French governess, a loved and valued "mam'selle," in the household.

When I was ten years old I made my first journey to Europe. My birthday was spent in Cologne, and in order to give me a thoroughly "party" feeling I remember that my mother put on full dress for my birthday dinner. I do not think I gained anything from this particular trip abroad. I cordially hated it, as did my younger brother and sister. Practically all the enjoyment we had was in exploring any ruins or mountains when we could get away from our elders, and in playing in the different hotels. Our one desire was to get back to America, and we regarded Europe with the most ignorant chauvinism and contempt. Four years later, however, I made another journey to Europe, and was old enough to enjoy it thoroughly and profit by it.

While still a small boy I began to take an interest in natural history. I remember distinctly the first day that I started on my career as zoölogist. I was walking up Broadway, and as I passed the market to which I used sometimes to be sent before breakfast to get strawberries I suddenly saw a dead seal laid out on a slab of wood. That seal filled me with every possible feeling of romance and adventure. I asked where it was killed, and was informed in the harbor. I had already begun to read some of Mayne Reid's books and other boys' books of adventure, and I felt that this seal brought all these adventures in realistic fashion before me. As long

c

as that seal remained there I haunted the neighborhood of the market day after day. I measured it, and I recall that, not having a tape measure, I had to do my best to get its girth with a folding pocket foot-rule, a difficult undertaking. I carefully made a record of the utterly useless measurements, and at once began to write a natural history of my own, on the strength of that seal. This, and subsequent natural histories, were written down in blank books in simplified spelling, wholly unpremeditated and unscientific. I had vague aspirations of in some way or another owning and preserving that seal, but they never got beyond the purely formless stage. I think, however, I did get the seal's skull, and with two of my cousins promptly started what we ambitiously called the "Roosevelt Museum of Natural History." The collections were at first kept in my room, until a rebellion on the part of the chambermaid received the approval of the higher authorities

"'MY UNCLE JIMMY' BULLOCH WAS A DEAR OLD RETIRED SEA-CAPTAIN—A VERITABLE COLONEL NEWCOME."

of the household and the collection was moved up to a kind of bookcase in the back hall upstairs. It was the ordinary small boy's collection of curios, quite incongruous and entirely valueless except from the standpoint of the boy himself. My father and mother encouraged me warmly in this, as they always did in anything that could give me wholesome pleasure or help to develop me.

The adventure of the seal and the novels of Mayne Reid

together strengthened my instinctive interest in natural history. I was too young to understand much of Mayne Reid, excepting the adventure part and the natural history part — these enthralled me. But of course my reading was not wholly confined to natural history. There was very little effort made to compel me to read books, my father and mother having the good sense not to try to get me to read anything I did not like, un-less it was in the way of study. I was given the chance to read books that they thought I ought to read, but if I did not like them I was then given some other good book that I did like. There were certain books that were *taboo*. For instance, I was not allowed to read dime novels. I obtained some surreptitiously and did read them, but I do not think that the enjoyment com-pensated for the feeling of guilt. I was also forbidden to read the only one of Ouida's books which I wished to read — "Under Two Flags." I did read it, nevertheless, with greedy and fierce hope of coming on something unhealthy; but as a matter of fact all the parts that might have seemed un-healthy to an older person made no impression on me what-ever. I simply enjoyed in a rather confused way the general adventures.

"My Uncle Irvine Bulloch was a mid-shipman on the *Alabama*, and fired the last gun discharged from her batter-ies in the fight with the *Kearsarge*."

I think there ought to be children's books. I think that the child will like grown-up books also, and I do not believe a child's book is really good unless grown-ups get something out of it. For instance, there is a book I did not have when

I was a child because it was not written. It is Laura E. Richards's "Nursery Rhymes." My own children loved them dearly, and their mother and I loved them almost equally; the delightfully light-hearted "Man from New Mexico who Lost his Grandmother out in the Snow," the adventures of "The Owl, the Eel, and the Warming-Pan," and the extraordinary genealogy of the kangaroo whose "father was a whale with a feather in his tail who lived in the Greenland sea," while "his mother was a shark who kept very dark in the Gulf of Caribee."

As a small boy I had *Our Young Folks*, which I then firmly believed to be the very best magazine in the world — a belief, I may add, which I have kept to this day unchanged, for I seriously doubt if any magazine for old or young has ever surpassed it. Both my wife and I have the bound volumes of *Our Young Folks* which we preserved from our youth. I have tried to read again the Mayne Reid books which I so dearly loved as a boy, only to find, alas! that it is impossible. But I really believe that I enjoy going over *Our Young Folks* now nearly as much as ever. "Cast Away in the Cold," "Grandfather's Struggle for a Homestead," "The William Henry Letters" and a dozen others like them were first-class, good healthy stories, interesting in the first place, and in the next place teaching manliness, decency, and good conduct. At the cost of being deemed effeminate, I will add that I greatly liked the girls' stories — "Pussy Willow" and "A Summer in Leslie Goldthwaite's Life," just as I worshiped "Little Men" and "Little Women" and "An Old-Fashioned Girl."

This enjoyment of the gentler side of life did not prevent my reveling in such tales of adventure as Ballantyne's stories, or Marryat's "Midshipman Easy." I suppose everybody has kinks in him, and even as a child there were books which I ought to have liked and did not. For instance, I never cared at all for the first part of "Robinson Crusoe" (and although it is unquestionably the best part, I do not care for it now); whereas the second part, containing the adventures of Robinson Crusoe, with the wolves in the Pyrenees, and out in the Far East, simply fascinated me. What I did like in the first part were the adventures before Crusoe finally reached his island, the fight with the Sallee Rover, and the allusion to the strange beasts at night taking their improbable bath in the ocean. Thanks to being already an embryo zoölogist, I disliked the "Swiss Family Robinson" because of the wholly impossible collection of animals met by that worthy family as they ambled inland from the wreck. Even in poetry it was the relation of adventures that most appealed to me as a boy. At a pretty early age I began to read certain books of poetry, notably Longfellow's poem, "The Saga of King Olaf," which absorbed me. This introduced me to Scandinavian literature; and I have never lost my interest in and affection for it.

Among my first books was a volume of a hopelessly unscientific kind by Mayne Reid, about mammals, illustrated with pictures no more artistic than but quite as thrilling as those in the typical school geography. When my father found how deeply interested I was in this not very accurate volume, he gave me a little book by J. G. Wood, the English writer of popular books on natural history, and then a larger one of his called "Homes Without Hands." Both of these were cherished possessions. They were studied eagerly; and they finally descended to my children. The "Homes Without Hands," by the way, grew to have an added association in connection with a pedagogical failure on my part. In accordance with what I believed was some kind of modern theory of making education interesting and not letting it become a task, I endeavored to teach my eldest small boy one or two of his letters from the title-page. As the letter "H" appeared in the title an unusual number of times, I selected that to begin on, my effort being to keep the small boy interested, not to let him realize that he was learning a lesson, and to convince him that he was merely having a good time. Whether it was the theory or my method of applying it that was defective I do not know, but I certainly absolutely eradicated from his brain any ability to learn what "H" was; and long after he had learned all the other letters of the alphabet in the old-fashioned way, he proved wholly unable to remember "H" under any circumstances.

Quite unknown to myself, I was, while a boy, under a hopeless disadvantage in studying nature. I was very near-sighted, so that the only things I could study were those I ran against or stumbled over. When I was about thirteen I was allowed to take lessons in taxidermy from a Mr. Bell, a tall, clean-shaven, white-haired old gentleman, as straight as an Indian, who had been a companion of Audubon's. He had a musty little shop, somewhat on the order of Mr. Venus's shop in "Our Mutual Friend," a little shop in which he had done very valuable work for science. This "vocational study," as I suppose it would be called by modern educators, spurred and directed my interest in collecting specimens for mounting and preservation. It was this summer that I got my first gun, and it puzzled me to find that my companions seemed to see things to shoot at which I could not see at all. One day they read aloud an advertisement in huge letters on a distant billboard, and I then realized that something was the matter, for not only was I unable to read the sign but I could not even see the letters. I spoke of this to my father, and soon afterwards got my first pair of spectacles, which literally opened an entirely new world to me. I had no idea how beautiful the world was until I got those spectacles. I had been a clumsy and awkward little boy, and while much of my clumsiness and awkwardness was doubtless due to general characteristics, a good deal of it was due to the fact that I could not see and yet was wholly ignorant that I was not seeing. The recollection of this experience gives me a keen sympathy with those who are trying in our public schools and elsewhere to remove the physical causes of deficiency in children, who are often unjustly blamed for being obstinate or unambitious, or mentally stupid.

This same summer, too, I obtained various new books on mammals and birds, including the publications of Spencer Baird, for instance, and made an industrious book-study of the subject. I did not accomplish much in outdoor study because I did not get spectacles until late in the fall, a short

time before I started with the rest of the family for a second
trip to Europe. We were living at Dobbs Ferry, on the
Hudson. My gun was a breech-loading, pin-fire double-
barrel, of French manufacture. It was an excellent gun for
a clumsy and often absent-minded boy. There was no
spring to open it, and if the mechanism became rusty it
could be opened with a brick without serious damage.
When the cartridges stuck they could be removed in the
same fashion. If they were loaded, however, the result was
not always happy, and I tattooed myself with partially un-
burned grains of powder more than once.

When I was fourteen years old, in the winter of '72 and '73,
I visited Europe for the second time, and this trip formed a
really useful part of my education. We went to Egypt,
journeyed up the Nile, traveled through the Holy Land and
part of Syria, visited Greece and Constantinople; and then
we children spent the summer in a German family in Dresden. My first real collecting as a student of natural history
was done in Egypt during this journey. By this time I had
a good working knowledge of American bird life from the
superficially scientific standpoint. I had no knowledge of
the ornithology of Egypt, but I picked up in Cairo a book
by an English clergyman, whose name I have now forgotten,
who described a trip up the Nile, and in an appendix to his
volume gave an account of his bird collection. I wish I
could remember the name of the author now, for I owe that
book very much. Without it I should have been collecting entirely in the dark, whereas with its aid I could generally
find out what the birds were. My first knowledge of Latin
was obtained by learning the scientific names of the birds
and mammals which I collected and classified by the aid of
such books as this one.

The birds I obtained up the Nile and in Palestine represented merely the usual boy's collection. Some years afterward I gave them, together with the other ornithological
specimens I had gathered, to the Smithsonian Institution in
Washington, and I think some of them also to the American
Museum of Natural History in New York. I am told that
the skins are to be found yet in both places and in other

public collections.   I doubt whether they have my original labels on them.   With great pride the directors of the "Roosevelt Muesum," consisting of myself and the two cousins aforesaid, had printed a set of Roosevelt Museum labels in pink ink preliminary to what was regarded as my adventurous trip to Egypt.   This bird-collecting gave what was really the chief zest to my Nile journey.   I was old enough and had read enough to enjoy the temples and the desert scenery and the general feeling of romance; but this in time would have palled if I had not also had the serious work of collecting and preparing my specimens.   Doubtless the family had their moments of suffering — especially on one occasion when a well-meaning maid extracted from my taxidermist's outfit the old tooth-brush with which I put on the skins the arsenical soap necessary for their preservation, partially washed it, and left it with the rest of my wash kit for my own personal use.   I suppose

THE PROPRIETOR OF THE "ROOSEVELT MU-
SEUM OF NATURAL HISTORY."

Theodore Roosevelt at the age of ten.

that all growing boys tend to be grubby; but the ornithological small boy, or indeed the boy with the taste for natural history of any kind, is generally the very grubbiest of all.   An added element in my case was the fact that while in Egypt I suddenly started to grow.   As there were no tailors up the Nile, when I got back to Cairo I needed a new outfit.   But there was one suit of clothes too good to throw away, which we kept for a "change," and which was known as my "Smike suit," because it left my wrists and ankles as bare as those of poor Smike himself.

When we reached Dresden we younger children were left

to spend the summer in the house of Herr Minckwitz, a member of either the Municipal or the Saxon Government — I have forgotten which. It was hoped that in this way we would acquire some knowledge of the German language and literature. They were the very kindest family imagi-

"THIS, AND SUBSEQUENT NATURAL HISTORIES, WERE WRITTEN DOWN IN BLANK BOOKS IN SIMPLIFIED SPELLING, WHOLLY UNPREMEDITATED AND UNSCIENTIFIC."

nable. I shall never forget the unwearied patience of the two daughters. The father and mother, and a shy, thin, student cousin who was living in the flat, were no less kind. Whenever I could get out into the country I collected specimens industriously and enlivened the household with hedgehogs and other small beasts and reptiles which persisted in escaping from partially closed bureau drawers. The two sons were fascinating students from the University of Leipsic, both of them belonging to dueling corps, and much scarred in consequence.   One, a famous swordsman, was called *Der Rothe Herzog* (the Red Duke), and the other was nicknamed *Herr Nasehorn* (Sir Rhinoceros) because the tip of his nose had been cut off in a duel and sewn on again. I learned a good deal of German here, in spite of myself, and above all I became fascinated with the Nibelungenlied. German prose never became really easy to me in the sense that French prose did, but for German poetry I cared as much as for English poetry.   Above all, I gained an impression of the German people which I never got over. From that time to this it would have been quite impossible to make me feel that the Germans were really foreigners. The affection, the *Gemüthlichkeit* (a quality which cannot be exactly expressed by any single English word), the capacity for hard work, the sense of duty, the delight in studying literature and science, the pride in the new Germany, the more than kind and friendly interest in three strange children — all these manifestations of the German character and of German family life made a subconscious impression upon me which I did not in the least define at the time, but which is very vivid still forty years later.

When I got back to America, at the age of fifteen, I began serious study to enter Harvard under Mr. Arthur Cutler, who later founded the Cutler School in New York.   I could not go to school because I knew so much less than most boys of my age in some subjects and so much more in others. In science and history and geography and in unexpected parts of German and French I was strong, but lamentably weak in Latin and Greek and mathematics.   My grandfather had made his summer home in Oyster Bay a number of years before, and my father now made Oyster Bay the summer home of his family also.   Along with my college preparatory studies I carried on the work of a practical student of natural history.   I worked with greater industry than either intelligence or success, and made very few additions to the sum of human knowledge; but to this day certain obscure ornithological publications may be found in which are recorded such items as, for instance, that on one occasion a fish-crow, and on another an Ipswich sparrow, were obtained by one Theodore Roosevelt, Jr., at Oyster Bay, on the shore of Long Island Sound.

In the fall of 1876 I entered Harvard, graduating in 1880. I thoroughly enjoyed Harvard, and I am sure it did me good, but only in the general effect, for there was very little in my actual studies which helped me in after life. More than one of my own sons have already profited by their friendship with certain of their masters in school or college. I certainly profited by my friendship with one of my tutors, Mr. Cutler; and in Harvard I owed much to the professor of English, Mr. A. S. Hill. Doubtless through my own fault, I saw almost nothing of President Eliot and very little of the professors. I ought to have gained much more than I did gain from writing the themes and forensics. My failure to do so may have been partly due to my taking no interest in the subjects. Before I left Harvard I was already writing one or two chapters of a book I afterwards published on the Naval War of 1812. Those chapters were so dry that they would have made a dictionary seem light reading by comparison. Still, they represented purpose and serious interest on my part, not the perfunctory effort to do well enough to get a certain mark; and corrections of them by a skilled older man would have impressed me and have commanded my respectful attention. But I was not sufficiently developed to make myself take an intelligent interest in some of the subjects assigned me — the character of the Gracchi, for instance. A very clever and studious lad would no doubt have done so, but I personally did not grow up to this particular subject until a good many years later. The frigate and sloop actions between the American and British sea-tigers of 1812 were much more within my grasp. I worked drearily at the Gracchi because I had to; my conscientious and much-to-be-pitied professor dragging me through the theme by main strength, with my feet firmly planted in dull and totally idea-proof resistance.

I had at the time no idea of going into public life, and I never studied elocution or practiced debating. This was a loss to me in one way. In another way it was not. Personally I have not the slightest sympathy with debating contests in which each side is arbitrarily assigned a given proposition and told to maintain it without the least reference to whether those maintaining it believe in it or not. I know that under our system this is necessary for lawyers, but I emphatically disbelieve in it as regards general discussion of political, social, and industrial matters. What we need is to turn out of our colleges young men with ardent convictions on the side of the right; not young men who can make a good argument for either right or wrong as their interest bids them. The present method of carrying on debates on such subjects as "Our Colonial Policy," or "The Need of a Navy," or "The Proper Position of the Courts in Constitutional Questions," encourages precisely the wrong attitude among those who take part in them. There is no effort to instill sincerity and intensity of conviction. On the contrary, the net result is to make the contestants feel that their convictions have nothing to do with their arguments. I am sorry I did not study elocution in college; but I am exceedingly glad that I did not take part in the type of debate in which stress is laid, not upon getting a speaker to think rightly, but on getting him to talk glibly on the side to which he is assigned, without regard either to what his convictions are or to what they ought to be.

I was a reasonably good student in college, standing just within the first tenth of my class, if I remember rightly; although I am not sure whether this means the tenth of the whole number that entered or of those that graduated. I was given a Phi Beta Kappa "key." My chief interests were scientific. When I entered college, I was devoted to out-of-doors natural history, and my ambition was to be a scientific man of the Audubon, or Wilson, or Baird, or Coues type — a man like Hart Merriam, or Frank Chapman, or Hornaday, to-day. My father had from the earliest days instilled into me the knowledge that I was to work and to make my own way in the world, and I had always supposed that this meant that I must enter business. But in my freshman year (he died when I was a sophomore) he told me that if I wished to become a scientific man I could do so. He explained that I must be sure that I really intensely desired to do scientific work, because if I went into it I must make it a serious career; that he had made enough money to enable me to take up such a career and do non-remunerative work of value *if I intended to do the very best work there was in me;* but that I must not dream of taking it up as a dilettante. He also gave me a piece of advice that I have always remembered, namely, that, if I was not going to earn money, I must even things up by not spending it. As he expressed it, I had to keep the fraction constant, and if I was not able to increase the numerator, then I must reduce the denominator. In other words, if I went into a scientific career, I must definitely abandon all thought of the enjoyment that could accompany a money-making career, and must find my pleasures elsewhere.

After this conversation I fully intended to make science my life-work. I did not, for the simple reason that at that time Harvard, and I suppose our other colleges, utterly ignored the possibilities of the faunal naturalist, the outdoor naturalist and observer of nature. They treated biology as purely a science of the laboratory and the microscope, a science whose adherents were to spend their time in the study of minute forms of marine life, or else in section-cutting and the study of the tissues of the higher organisms under the microscope. This attitude was, no doubt, in part due to the fact that in most colleges then there was a not always intelligent copying of what was done in the great German universities. The sound revolt against superficiality of study had been carried to an extreme; thoroughness in minutiæ as the only end of study had been erected into a fetish. There was a total failure to understand the great variety of kinds of work that could be done by naturalists, including what could be done by outdoor naturalists — the kind of work which Hart Merriam and his assistants in the Biological Survey have carried to such a high degree of perfection as regards North American mammals. In the entirely proper desire to be thorough and to avoid slipshod methods, the tendency was to treat as not serious, as unscientific, any kind of work that was not carried on with laborious minuteness in the laboratory. My taste was specialized in a totally different direction, and I had no more desire or ability to be a microscopist and section-cutter than to be a mathematician. Accordingly I abandoned all thought of becoming a scientist. Doubtless this meant that I really did not have the intense devotion to science which I thought I had; for, if I had possessed such devotion, I would have carved out a career for myself somehow without regard to discouragements.

As regards political economy, I was of course while in college taught the *laissez-faire* doctrines — one of them being free trade — then accepted as canonical. Most American boys of my age were taught both by their surroundings and by their studies certain principles which were very valuable from the standpoint of National interest, and certain others which were very much the reverse. The political economists were not especially to blame for this; it was the general attitude of the writers who wrote for us of that generation. Take my beloved *Our Young Folks*, the magazine of which I have already spoken, and which taught me much more than any of my text-books. Everything in this magazine instilled the individual virtues, and the necessity of character as the chief factor in any man's success — a teaching in which I now believe as sincerely as ever, for all the laws that the wit of man can devise will never make a man a worthy citizen unless he has within himself the right stuff, unless he has self-reliance, energy, courage, the power of insisting on his own rights and the sympathy that makes him regardful of the rights of others. All this individual morality I was taught by the books I read at home and the books I studied at Harvard. But there was almost no teaching of the need for collective action, and of the fact that in addition to, not as a substitute for, individual responsibility, there is a collective responsibility. Books such as Herbert Croly's "Promise of American Life" and Walter E. Weyl's "New Democracy" would generally at that time have been treated either as unintelligible or else as pure heresy.

The teaching which I received was genuinely democratic in one way. It was not so democratic in another. I grew into manhood thoroughly imbued with the feeling that a man must be respected for what he made of himself. But I had also, consciously or unconsciously, been taught that socially and industrially pretty much the whole duty of the man lay in thus making the best of himself; that he should be honest in his dealings with others and charitable in the old-fashioned way to the unfortunate; but that it was no part of his business to join with others in trying to make things better for the many by curbing the abnormal and excessive development of individualism in a few. Now I do not mean that this training was by any means all bad. On the contrary, the insistence upon individual responsibility was, and is, and always will be, a prime necessity. Teaching of the kind I absorbed from both my text-books and my surroundings is a healthy anti-scorbutic to the sentimentality which by complacently excusing the individual for all his shortcomings would finally hopelessly weaken the spring of moral purpose. It also keeps alive that virile vigor for the lack of which in the average individual no possible perfection of law or of community action can ever atone. But such teaching, if not corrected by other teaching, means acquiescence in a riot of lawless business individualism which would be quite as destructive to real civilization as the lawless military individualism of the Dark Ages. I left college and entered the big world owing more than I can express to the training I had received, especially in my own home; but with much else also to learn if I were to become really fitted to do my part in the work that lay ahead for the generation of Americans to which I belonged.

Bronze Cougar, by Alexander P. Proctor.

PRESENTED TO MR. ROOSEVELT BY THE "TENNIS CABINET."

CHAPTER II

THE VIGOR OF LIFE

LOOKING back, a man really has a more objective feeling about himself as a child than he has about his father or mother. He feels as if that child were not the present he, individually, but an ancestor; just as much an ancestor as either of his parents. The saying that the child is the father to the man may be taken in a sense almost the reverse of that usually given to it. The child is father to the man in the sense that his individuality is separate from the individuality of the grown-up into which he turns. This is perhaps one reason why a man can speak of his childhood and early youth with a sense of detachment.

Having been a sickly boy, with no natural bodily prowess, and having lived much at home, I was at first quite unable to hold my own when thrown into contact with other boys of rougher antecedents. I was nervous and timid. Yet from reading of the people I admired — ranging from the soldiers of Valley Forge, and Morgan's riflemen, to the heroes of my favorite stories — and from hearing of the feats performed by my Southern forefathers and kinsfolk, and from knowing my father, I felt a great admiration for men who were fearless and who could hold their own in the world, and I had a great desire to be like them. Until I was nearly fourteen I let this desire take no more definite shape than day-dreams. Then an incident happened that did me real good. Having an attack of asthma,

I was sent off by myself to Moosehead Lake. On the stage-coach ride thither I encountered a couple of other boys who were about my own age, but very much more competent and also much more mischievous. I have no doubt they were good-hearted boys, but they were boys ! They found that I was a foreordained and predestined victim, and industriously proceeded to make life miserable for me. The worst feature was that when I finally tried to fight them I discovered that either one singly could not only handle me with easy contempt, but handle me so as not to hurt me much and yet to prevent my doing any damage whatever in return.

The experience taught me what probably no amount of good advice could have taught me. I made up my mind that I must try to learn so that I would not again be put in such a helpless position ; and having become quickly and bitterly conscious that I did not have the natural prow-ess to hold my own, I decided that I would try to supply its place by training. Accordingly, with my father's hearty approval, I started to learn to box. I was a painfully slow and awkward pupil, and certainly worked two or three years before I made any perceptible improve-ment whatever. My first boxing-master was John Long, an ex-prize-fighter. I can see his rooms now, with col-ored pictures of the fights between Tom Hyer and Yankee Sullivan, and Heenan and Sayers, and other great events in the annals of the squared circle. On one occasion, to excite interest among his patrons, he held a series of "cham-pionship" matches for the different weights, the prizes being, at least in my own class, pewter mugs of a value, I should suppose, approximating fifty cents. Neither he nor I had any idea that I could do anything, but I was entered in the lightweight contest, in which it happened that I was pitted in succession against a couple of reedy striplings who were even worse than I was. Equally to their surprise and to my own, and to John Long's, I won, and the pewter mug became one of my most prized pos-sessions. I kept it, and alluded to it, and I fear bragged about it, for a number of years, and I only wish I knew

D

where it was now.   Years later I read an account of a little man who once in a fifth-rate handicap race won a worthless pewter medal and joyed in it ever after.   Well, as soon as I read that story I felt that that little man and I were brothers.

This was, as far as I remember, the only one of my exceedingly rare athletic triumphs which would be worth relating.   I did a good deal of boxing and wrestling in Harvard, but never attained to the first rank in either, even at my own weight.   Once, in the big contests in the Gym, I got either into the finals or semi-finals, I forgot which; but aside from this the chief part I played was to act as trial horse for some friend or classmate who did have a chance of distinguishing himself in the championship contests.

I was fond of horseback-riding, but I took to it slowly and with difficulty, exactly as with boxing.   It was a long time before I became even a respectable rider, and I never got much higher.   I mean by this that I never became a first-flight man in the hunting field, and never even approached the bronco-busting class in the West.   Any man, if he chooses, can gradually school himself to the requisite nerve, and gradually learn the requisite seat and hands, that will enable him to do respectably across country, or to perform the average work on a ranch.   Of my ranch experiences I shall speak later.   At intervals after leaving college I hunted on Long Island with the Meadowbrook hounds.   Almost the only experience I ever had in this connection that was of any interest was on one occasion when I broke my arm.   My purse did not permit me to own expensive horses.   On this occasion I was riding an animal, a buggy horse originally, which its owner sold because now and then it insisted on thoughtfully lying down when in harness.   It never did this under the saddle; and when he turned it out to grass it would solemnly hop over the fence and get somewhere where it did not belong.   The last trait was what converted it into a hunter. It was a natural jumper, although without any speed. On the hunt in question I got along very well until the pace winded my ex-buggy horse, and it turned a somersault over a fence. When I got on it after the fall I found I could not use my left arm. I supposed it was merely a strain. The buggy horse was a sedate animal which I rode with a snaffle. So we pounded along at the tail of the hunt, and I did not appreciate that my arm was broken for three or four fences. Then we came to a big drop, and the jar made the bones slip past one another so as to throw the hand out of position. It did not hurt me at all, and as the horse was as easy to sit as a rocking-chair, I got in at the death.

I think August Belmont was master of the hunt when the above incident occurred. I know he was master on another occasion on which I met with a mild adventure. On one of the hunts when I was out a man was thrown, dragged by one stirrup, and killed. In consequence I bought a pair of safety stirrups, which I used the next time I went out. Within five minutes after the run began I found that the stirrups were so very "safe" that they would not stay in at all. First one went off at one jump, and then the other at another jump — with a fall for me on each occasion. I hated to give up the fun so early, and accordingly finished the run without any stirrups. My horse never went as fast as on that run. Doubtless a first-class horseman can ride as well without stirrups as with them. But I was not a first-class horseman. When anything unexpected happened, I was apt to clasp the solemn buggy horse firmly with my spurred heels, and the result was that he laid himself out to do his best in the way of galloping. He speedily found that, thanks to the snaffle bit, I could not pull him in, so when we came to a down grade he would usually put on steam. Then if there was a fence at the bottom and he checked at all, I was apt to shoot forward, and in such event we went over the fence in a way that reminded me of Leech's picture, in *Punch*, of Mr. Tom Noddy and his mare jumping a fence in the following order: Mr. Tom Noddy, I; his mare, II. However, I got in at the death this time also.

I was fond of walking and climbing. As a lad I used to go to the north woods, in Maine, both in fall and winter.

There I made life friends of two men, Will Dow and Bill Sewall : I canoed with them, and tramped through the woods with them, visiting the winter logging camps on snow-shoes. Afterward they were with me in the West. Will Dow is dead. Bill Sewall was collector of customs under me, on the Aroostook border. Except when hunting I never did any mountaineering save for a couple of conventional trips up the Matterhorn and the Jungfrau on one occasion when I was in Switzerland.

I never did much with the shotgun, but I practiced a good deal with the rifle. I had a rifle range at Sagamore Hill, where I often took friends to shoot. Once or twice when I was visited by parties of released Boer prisoners, after the close of the South African War, they and I held shooting matches together. The best man with both pistol and rifle who ever shot there was Stewart Edward White. Among the many other good men was a stanch friend, Baron Speck von Sternberg, afterwards German Ambassador at Washington during my Presidency. He was a capital shot, rider, and walker, a devoted and most efficient servant of Germany, who had fought with distinction in the Franco-German War when barely more than a boy ; he was the hero of the story of "the pig dog" in Archibald Forbes's volume of reminiscences. It was he who first talked over with me the raising of a regiment of horse riflemen from among the ranchmen and cowboys of the plains. When Ambassador, the poor, gallant, tender-hearted fellow was dying of a slow and painful disease, so that he could not play with the rest of us, but the agony of his mortal illness never in the slightest degree interfered with his work. Among the other men who shot and rode and walked with me was Cecil Spring-Rice, who has just been appointed British Ambassador to the United States. He was my groomsman, my best man, when I was married — at St. George's, Hanover Square, which made me feel as if I were living in one of Thackeray's novels.

My own experience as regards marksmanship was much the same as my experience as regards horsemanship. There are men whose eye and hand are so quick and so sure that

"ANY MAN, IF HE CHOOSES, CAN GRADUALLY SCHOOL HIMSELF SO AS TO DO
RESPECTABLY ACROSS COUNTRY."

they achieve a perfection of marksmanship to which no
practice will enable ordinary men to attain. There are
other men who cannot learn to shoot with any accuracy at
all. In between come the mass of men of ordinary abilities who, if they choose resolutely to practice, can by sheer
industry and judgment make themselves fair rifle shots.
The men who show this requisite industry and judgment
can without special difficulty raise themselves to the second
class of respectable rifle shots; and it is to this class that I
belong. But to have reached this point of marksmanship
with the rifle at a target by no means implies ability to hit
game in the field, especially dangerous game. All kinds
of other qualities, moral and physical, enter into being a
good hunter, and especially a good hunter after dangerous
game, just as all kinds of other qualities in addition to skill
with the rifle enter into being a good soldier. With dangerous game, after a fair degree of efficiency with the rifle
has been attained, the prime requisites are cool judgment
and that kind of nerve which consists in avoiding being
rattled. Any beginner is apt to have "buck fever," and
therefore no beginner should go at dangerous game.

Buck fever means a state of intense nervous excitement
which may be entirely divorced from timidity. It may
affect a man the first time he has to speak to a large audience just as it affects him the first time he sees a buck or
goes into battle. What such a man needs is not courage
but nerve control, cool-headedness. This he can get only
by actual practice. He must, by custom and repeated
exercise of self-mastery, get his nerves thoroughly under
control. This is largely a matter of habit, in the sense of
repeated effort and repeated exercise of will power. If
the man has the right stuff in him, his will grows stronger
and stronger with each exercise of it — and if he has not the
right stuff in him he had better keep clear of dangerous
game hunting, or indeed of any other form of sport or work
in which there is bodily peril.

After he has achieved the ability to exercise wariness
and judgment and the control over his nerves *which will
make him shoot as well at the game as at a target*, he can begin

his essays at dangerous game hunting, and he will then find that it does not demand such abnormal prowess as the ousider is apt to imagine. A man who can hit a soda-water bottle at the distance of a few yards can brain a lion or a bear or an elephant at that distance, and if he cannot brain it when it charges he can at least bring it to a stand-still. All he has to do is to shoot as accurately as he would at a soda-water bottle; and to do this requires nerve, at least as much as it does physical address. Having reached this point, the hunter must not imagine that he is war-ranted in taking desperate chances. There are degrees in proficiency; and what is a warrantable and legitimate risk for a man to take when he has reached a certain grade of efficiency may be a foolish risk for him to take before he has reached that grade. A man who has reached the degree of proficiency indicated above is quite warranted in walking in at a lion at bay, in an open plain, to, say, within a hundred yards. If the lion has not charged, the man ought at that distance to knock him over and prevent his charging; and if the lion is already charging, the man ought at that dis-tance to be able to stop him. But the amount of prowess which warrants a man in relying on his ability to perform this feat does not by any means justify him in thinking that, for instance, he can crawl after a wounded lion into thick cover. I have known men of indifferent prowess to perform this latter feat successfully, but at least as often they have been unsuccessful, and in these cases the result has been unpleasant. The man who habitually follows wounded lions into thick cover must be a hunter of the highest skill, or he can count with certainty on an ultimate mauling.

The first two or three bucks I ever saw gave me buck fever badly, but after I had gained experience with ordinary game I never had buck fever at all with dangerous game. In my case the overcoming of buck fever was the result of conscious effort and a deliberate determination to over-come it. More happily constituted men never have to make this determined effort at all — which may perhaps show that the average man can profit more from my experiences than he can from those of the exceptional man.

I have shot only five kinds of animals which can fairly be called dangerous game — that is, the lion, elephant, rhinoceros, and buffalo in Africa, and the big grizzly bear a quarter of a century ago in the Rockies. Taking into account not only my own personal experience, but the experiences of many veteran hunters, I regard all the four African animals, but especially the lion, elephant, and buffalo, as much more dangerous than the grizzly. As it happened, however, the only narrow escape I personally ever had was from a grizzly, and in Africa the animal killed closest to me as it was charging was a rhinoceros — all of which goes to show that a man must not generalize too broadly from his own personal experiences. On the whole, I think the lion the most dangerous of all these five animals ; that is, I think that, if fairly hunted, there is a larger percentage of hunters killed or mauled for a given number of lions killed than for a given number of any one of the other animals. Yet I personally had no difficulties with lions. I twice killed lions which were at bay and just starting to charge, and I killed a heavy-maned male while it was in full charge. But in each instance I had plenty of leeway, the animal being so far off that even if my bullet had not been fatal I should have had time for a couple more shots. The African buffalo is undoubtedly a dangerous beast, but it happened that the few that I shot did not charge. A bull elephant, a vicious "rogue," which had been killing people in the native villages, did charge before being shot at. My son Kermit and I stopped it at forty yards. Another bull elephant, also unwounded, which charged, nearly got me, as I had just fired both cartridges from my heavy double-barreled rifle in killing the bull I was after — the first wild elephant I had ever seen. The second bull came through the thick brush to my left like a steam plow through a light snowdrift, everything snapping before his rush, and was so near that he could have hit me with his trunk. I slipped past him behind a tree. People have asked me how I felt on this occasion. My answer has always been that I suppose I felt as most men of like experience feel on such occasions. At such a moment a hunter is so very busy that he has no time to get frightened. He wants to get in his cartridges and try another shot.

Rhinoceros are truculent, blustering beasts, much the most stupid of all the dangerous game I know. Generally their attitude is one of mere stupidity and bluff. But on occasions they do charge wickedly, both when wounded and when entirely unprovoked. The first I ever shot I mortally wounded at a few rods' distance, and it charged with the utmost determination, whereat I and my companion both fired, and more by good luck than anything else brought it to the ground just thirteen paces from where we stood. Another rhinoceros may or may not have been meaning to charge me; I have never been certain which. It heard us and came at us through rather thick brush, snorting and tossing its head. I am by no means sure that it had fixedly hostile intentions, and indeed with my present experience I think it likely that if I had not fired it would have flinched at the last moment and either retreated or gone by me. But I am not a rhinoceros mind reader, and its actions were such as to warrant my regarding it as a suspicious character. I stopped it with a couple of bullets, and then followed it up and killed it. The skins of all these animals which I thus killed are in the National Museum at Washington.

But, as I said above, the only narrow escape I met with was not from one of these dangerous African animals, but from a grizzly bear. It was about twenty-four years ago. I had wounded the bear just at sunset, in a wood of lodge-pole pines, and, following him, I wounded him again, as he stood on the other side of a thicket. He then charged through the brush, coming with such speed and with such an irregular gait that, try as I would, I was not able to get the sight of my rifle on the brain-pan, though I hit him very hard with both the remaining barrels of my magazine Winchester. It was in the days of black powder, and the smoke hung. After my last shot, the first thing I saw was the bear's left paw as he struck at me, so close that I made a quick movement to one side. He was, however, prac-

tically already dead, and after another jump, and while
in the very act of trying to turn to come at me, he collapsed like a shot rabbit.

By the way, I had a most exasperating time trying to
bring in his skin. I was alone, traveling on foot with one
very docile little mountain mare for a pack pony. The
little mare cared nothing for bears or anything else, so there
was no difficulty in packing her. But the man without
experience can hardly realize the work it was to get that
bearskin off the carcass and then to pack it, wet, slippery,
and heavy, so that it would ride evenly on the pony. I was
at the time fairly well versed in packing with a "diamond
hitch," the standby of Rocky Mountain packers in my day;
but the diamond hitch is a two-man job; and even working
with a "squaw hitch," I got into endless trouble with that
wet and slippery bearskin. With infinite labor I would get
the skin on the pony and run the ropes over it until to all
seeming it was fastened properly. Then off we would
start, and after going about a hundred yards I would notice
the hide beginning to bulge through between two ropes.
I would shift one of them, and then the hide would bulge
somewhere else. I would shift the rope again; and still
the hide would flow slowly out as if it was lava. The first
thing I knew it would come down on one side, and the little
mare, with her feet planted resolutely, would wait for me
to perform my part by getting that bearskin back in its
proper place on the McClellan saddle which I was using as
a makeshift pack saddle. The feat of killing the bear the
previous day sank into nothing compared with the feat of
making the bearskin ride properly as a pack on the following
three days.

The reason why I was alone in the mountains on this
occasion was because, for the only time in all my experience,
I had a difficulty with my guide. He was a crippled old
mountain man, with a profound contempt for "tenderfeet,"
a contempt that in my case was accentuated by the fact
that I wore spectacles — which at that day and in that
region were usually held to indicate a defective moral
character in the wearer. He had never previously acted as

guide, or, as he expressed it, "trundled a tenderfoot," and though a good hunter, who showed me much game, our experience together was not happy. He was very rheumatic and liked to lie abed late, so that I usually had to get breakfast, and, in fact, do most of the work around camp. Finally one day he declined to go out with me, saying that he had a pain. When, that afternoon, I got back to camp, I speedily found what the "pain" was. We were traveling very light indeed, I having practically nothing but my buffalo sleeping-bag, my wash kit, and a pair of socks. I had also taken a flask of whisky for emergencies—although, as I found that the emergencies never arose and that tea was better than whisky when a man was cold or done out, I abandoned the practice of taking whisky on hunting trips twenty years ago. When I got back to camp the old fellow was sitting on a tree-trunk, very erect, with his rifle across his knees, and in response to my nod of greeting he merely leered at me. I leaned my rifle against a tree, walked over to where my bed was lying, and, happening to rummage in it for something, I found the whisky flask was empty. I turned on him at once and accused him of having drunk it, to which he merely responded by asking what I was going to do about it. There did not seem much to do, so I said that we would part company — we were only four or five days from a settlement — and I would go in alone, taking one of the horses. He responded by cocking his rifle and saying that I could go alone and be damned to me, but I could not take any horse. I answered "all right," that if I could not I could not, and began to move around to get some flour and salt pork. He was misled by my quietness and by the fact that I had not in any way resented either his actions or his language during the days we had been together, and did not watch me as closely as he ought to have done. He was sitting with the cocked rifle across his knees, the muzzle to the left. My rifle was leaning against a tree near the cooking things to his right. Managing to get near it, I whipped it up and threw the bead on him, calling, "Hands up!" He of course put up his hands, and then said, "Oh, come, I was only joking";

The Tennis Cabinet.

The names of those standing behind Mr. Roosevelt are, from left to right: Captain Archibald Butt; William Phillips, Assistant Secretary of State; Herbert Knox Smith, Commissioner of Corporations; Beekman Winthrop, Assistant Secretary of the Treasury; Gifford Pinchot, Chief of the Forestry Service; Lawrence O. Murray, Comptroller; Henry L. Stimson, District Attorney; Herbert Satterlee, Assistant Secretary of the Navy; John J. McIlhenny, Civil Service Commissioner; Judge John C. Rose; Truman H. Newberry, Secretary of the Navy; Mr. George Woodruff, Counsel to the Forestry Service; M. Jusserand, French Ambassador; Mr. C. E. Heffelinger; George von L. Meyer, Postmaster-General; Francis Leupp, Indian Commissioner; Mr. Justice Moody; James R. Garfield, Secretary of the Interior; Marshall Seth Bullock; Solicitor-General Hoyt; John C. Abernathy; Luther Kelly, Indian Agent; Robert Bacon, Secretary of State; C. P. Neill, Labor Commissioner; William D. Sewall, Collector of Customs; D. J. Keefe, Commissioner of Immigration; John C. O'Laughlin, Assistant Secretary of State; J. B. Reynolds; Dr. H. C. Pritchett; William Loeb, Jr., Secretary to the President.

to which I answered, "Well, I am not. Now straighten your legs and let your rifle go to the ground" He remonstrated, saying the rifle would go off, and I told him to let it go off. However, he straightened his legs in such fashion that it came to the ground without a jar. I then made him move back, and picked up the rifle. By this time he was quite sober, and really did not seem angry, looking at me quizzically. He told me that if I would give him back his rifle, he would call it quits and we could go on together. I did not think it best to trust him, so I told him that our hunt was pretty well through, anyway, and that I would go home. There was a blasted pine on the trail, in plain view of the camp, about a mile off, and I told him that I would leave his rifle at that blasted pine if I could see him in camp, but that he must not come after me, for if he did I should assume that it was with hostile intent and would shoot. He said he had no intention of coming after me; and as he was very much crippled with rheumatism, I did not believe he would do so.

Accordingly I took the little mare, with nothing but some flour, bacon, and tea, and my bed-roll, and started off. At the blasted pine I looked round, and as I could see him in camp, I left his rifle there. I then traveled till dark, and that night, for the only time in my experience, I used in camping a trick of the old-time trappers in the Indian days. I did not believe I would be followed, but still it was not possible to be sure, so, after getting supper, while my pony fed round, I left the fire burning, repacked the mare and pushed ahead until it literally became so dark that I could not see. Then I picketed the mare, slept where I was without a fire until the first streak of dawn, and then pushed on for a couple of hours before halting to take breakfast and to let the little mare have a good feed. No plainsman needs to be told that a man should not lie near a fire if there is danger of an enemy creeping up on him, and that above all a man should not put himself in a position where he can be ambushed at dawn. On this second day I lost the trail, and toward nightfall gave up the effort to find it, camped where I was, and went out to shoot a grouse for supper. It was while hunting in vain for a grouse that I came on the bear and killed it as above described.

When I reached the settlement and went into the store, the storekeeper identified me by remarking: "You're the tenderfoot that old Hank was trundling, ain't you?" I admitted that I was. A good many years later, after I had been elected Vice-President, I went on a cougar hunt in northwestern Colorado with Johnny Goff, a famous hunter and mountain man. It was midwinter. I was rather proud of my achievements, and pictured myself as being known to the few settlers in the neighborhood as a successful mountain-lion hunter. I could not help grinning when I found out that they did not even allude to me as the Vice-President-elect, let alone as a hunter, but merely as "Johnny Goff's tourist."

Of course during the years when I was most busy at serious work I could do no hunting, and even my riding was of a decorous kind. But a man whose business is sedentary should get some kind of exercise if he wishes to keep himself in as good physical trim as his brethren who do manual labor. When I worked on a ranch, I needed no form of exercise except my work, but when I worked in an office the case was different. A couple of summers I played polo with some of my neighbors. I shall always believe we played polo in just the right way for middle-aged men with stables of the general utility order. Of course it was polo which was chiefly of interest to ourselves, the only onlookers being the members of our faithful families. My two ponies were the only occupants of my stable except a cart-horse. My wife and I rode and drove them, and they were used for household errands and for the children, and for two afternoons a week they served me as polo ponies. Polo is a good game, infinitely better for vigorous men than tennis or golf or anything of that kind. There is all the fun of football, with the horse thrown in; and if only people would be willing to play it in simple fashion it would be almost as much within their reach as golf. But at Oyster Bay our great and permanent amusements were rowing and sailing; I do not care for the latter, and am fond of the former. I suppose it sounds archaic, but I cannot help thinking that the people with motor boats miss a great deal. If they would only keep to rowboats or canoes, and use oar or paddle themselves, they would get infinitely more benefit than by having their work done for them by gasoline. But I rarely took exercise merely as exercise. Primarily I took it because I liked it. Play should never be allowed to interfere with work ; and a life devoted merely to play is, of all forms of existence, the most dismal. But the joy of life is a very good thing, and while work is the essential in it, play also has its place.

When obliged to live in cities, I for a long time found that boxing and wrestling enabled me to get a good deal of exercise in condensed and attractive form. I was reluctantly obliged to abandon both as I grew older. I dropped the wrestling earliest. When I became Governor, the champion middleweight wrestler of America happened to be in Albany, and I got him to come round three or four afternoons a week. Incidentally I may mention that his presence caused me a difficulty with the Comptroller, who refused to audit a bill I put in for a wrestling-mat, explaining that I could have a billiard-table, billiards being recognized as a proper Gubernatorial amusement, but that a wrestling-mat symbolized something unusual and unheard of and could not be permitted. The middleweight champion was of course so much better than I was that he could not only take care of himself but of me too and see that I was not hurt — for wrestling is a much more violent amusement than boxing. But after a couple of months he had to go away, and he left as a substitute a good-humored, stalwart professional oarsman. The oarsman turned out to know very little about wrestling. He could not even take care of himself, not to speak of me. By the end of our second afternoon one of his long ribs had been caved in and two of my short ribs badly damaged, and my left shoulder-blade so nearly shoved out of place that it creaked. He was nearly as pleased as I was when I told him I thought we would "vote the war a failure" and abandon wrestling. After that I took up boxing again. While President I used to box with some of the aides, as well as play single-stick with General Wood. After a few years I had to abandon boxing as well as wrestling, for in one bout a young captain of artillery cross-countered me on the eye, and the blow smashed the little blood-vessels. Fortunately it was my left eye, but the sight has been dim ever since, and if it had been the right eye I should have been entirely unable to shoot. Accordingly I thought it better to acknowledge that I had become an elderly man and would have to stop boxing. I then took up jiu-jitsu for a year or two.

When I was in the Legislature and was working very hard, with little chance of getting out of doors, all the exercise I got was boxing and wrestling. A young fellow turned up who was a second-rate prize-fighter, the son of one of my old boxing teachers. For several weeks I had him come round to my rooms in the morning to put on the gloves with me for half an hour. Then he suddenly stopped, and some days later I received a letter of woe from him from the jail. I found that he was by profession a burglar, and merely followed boxing as the amusement of his lighter moments, or when business was slack.

Naturally, being fond of boxing, I grew to know a good many prize-fighters, and to most of those I knew I grew genuinely attached. I have never been able to sympathize with the outcry against prize-fighters. The only objection I have to the prize ring is the crookedness that has attended its commercial development. Outside of this I regard boxing, whether professional or amateur, as a first-class sport, and I do not regard it as brutalizing. Of course matches can be conducted under conditions that make them brutalizing. But this is true of football games and of most other rough and vigorous sports. Most certainly prize-fighting is not half as brutalizing or demoralizing as many forms of big business and of the legal work carried on in connection with big business. Powerful, vigorous men of strong animal development must have some way in which their animal spirits can find vent. When I was Police Commissioner I found (and Jacob Riis will back me up in this) that the establishment of a boxing club in a tough neighborhood always tended to do away with knifing and gun-fighting among the young fellows who would otherwise have been in murderous gangs. Many of these young fellows were not naturally criminals at all, but they had to have some outlet for their activities. In the same way I have always regarded boxing as a first-class sport to encourage in the Young Men's Christian Association. I do not like to see young Christians with shoulders that slope like a champagne bottle. Of course boxing should be encouraged in the army and navy. I was first drawn to two naval chaplains, Fathers Chidwick and Rainey, by finding that each of them had bought half a dozen sets of boxing-gloves and encouraged their crews in boxing.

When I was Police Commissioner, I heartily approved the effort to get boxing clubs started in New York on a clean basis. Later I was reluctantly obliged to come to the conclusion that the prize ring had become hopelessly debased and demoralized, and as Governor I aided in the passage of and signed the bill putting a stop to professional boxing for money. This was because some of the prize-fighters themselves were crooked, while the crowd of hangers-on who attended and made up and profited by the matches had placed the whole business on a basis of commercialism and brutality that was intolerable. I shall always maintain that boxing contests themselves make good, healthy sport. It is idle to compare them with bull-fighting; the torture and death of the wretched horses in bull-fighting is enough of itself to blast the sport, no matter how great the skill and prowess shown by the bull-fighters. Any sport in which the death and torture of animals is made to furnish pleasure to the spectators is debasing. There should always be the opportunity provided in a glove fight or bare-fist fight to stop it when one competitor is hopelessly outclassed or too badly hammered. But the men who take part in these fights are hard as nails, and it is not worth while to feel sentimental about their receiving punishment which as a matter of fact they do not mind. Of course the men who look on ought to be able to stand up with the gloves, or without them, themselves; I have scant use for the type

E

of sportsmanship which consists merely in looking on at the feats of some one else.

Some as good citizens as I know are or were prize-fighters. Take Mike Donovan, of New York. He and his family represent a type of American citizenship of which we have a right to be proud. Mike is a devoted temperance man, and can be relied upon for every movement in the interest of good citizenship. I was first intimately thrown with him when I was Police Commissioner. One evening he and I — both in dress suits — attended a temperance meeting of Catholic societies. It culminated in a lively set-to between myself and a Tammany Senator who was a very good fellow, but whose ideas of temperance differed radically from mine, and, as the event proved, from those of the majority of the meeting. Mike evidently regarded himself as my backer — he was sitting on the platform beside me — and I think felt as pleased and interested as if the set-to had been physical instead of merely verbal. Afterwards I grew to know him well both while I was Governor and while I was President, and many a time he came on and boxed with me.

Battling Nelson was another stanch friend, and he and I think alike on most questions of political and industrial life; although he once expressed to me some commiseration because, as President, I did not get anything like the money return for my services that he aggregated during the same term of years in the ring. Bob Fitzsimmons was another good friend of mine. He has never forgotten his early skill as a blacksmith, and among the things that I value and always keep in use is a penholder made by Bob out of a horseshoe, with an inscription saying that it is "Made for and presented to President Theodore Roosevelt by his friend and admirer, Robert Fitzsimmons." I have for a long time had the friendship of John L. Sullivan, than whom in his prime no better man ever stepped into the ring. He is now a Massachusetts farmer. John used occasionally to visit me at the White House, his advent always causing a distinct flutter among the waiting Senators and Congressmen. When I went to Africa he presented me with a gold-mounted rabbit's foot for luck. I carried it through my African trip; and I certainly had good luck.

On one occasion one of my prize-fighting friends called on me at the White House on business. He explained that he wished to see me alone, sat down opposite me, and put a very expensive cigar on the desk, saying, "Have a cigar." I thanked him and said I did not smoke, to which he responded, "Put it in your pocket." He then added, "Take another; put both in your pocket." This I accordingly did. Having thus shown at the outset the necessary formal courtesy, my visitor, an old and valued friend, proceeded to explain that a nephew of his had enlisted in the Marine Corps, but had been absent without leave, and was threatened with dishonorable discharge on the ground of desertion. My visitor, a good citizen and a patriotic American, was stung to the quick at the thought of such an incident occurring in his family, and he explained to me that it must not occur, that there must not be the disgrace to the family, although he would be delighted to have the offender "handled rough" to teach him a needed lesson; he added that he wished I would take him and handle him myself, for he knew that I would see that he "got all that was coming to him." Then a look of pathos came into his eyes, and he explained: "That boy I just cannot understand. He was my sister's favorite son, and I always took a special interest in him myself. I did my best to bring him up the way he ought to go. But there was just nothing to be done with him. His tastes were naturally low. He took to music!" What form this debasing taste for music assumed I did not inquire; and I was able to grant my friend's wish.

While in the White House I always tried to get a couple of hours' exercise in the afternoons — sometimes tennis, more often riding, or else a rough cross-country walk, perhaps down Rock Creek, which was then as wild as a stream in the White Mountains, or on the Virginia side along the Potomac. My companions at tennis or on these rides and walks we gradually grew to style the Tennis Cabinet; and then we extended the term to take in many of my old-time Western friends such as Ben Daniels, Seth Bullock, Luther Kelly, and others who had taken part with me in more serious outdoor adventures than walking and riding for pleasure. Most of the men who were oftenest with me on these trips — men like Major-General Leonard Wood; or Major-General Thomas Henry Barry; or Presley Marion Rixey, Surgeon-General of the Navy; or Robert Bacon, who was afterwards Secretary of State; or James Garfield, who was Secretary of the Interior; or Gifford Pinchot, who was chief of the Forest Service — were better men physically than I was; but I could ride and walk well enough for us all thoroughly to enjoy it. Often, especially in the winters and early springs, we would arrange for a point to point walk, not turning aside for anything — for instance, swimming Rock Creek or even the Potomac if it came in our way. Of course under such circumstances we had to arrange that our return to Washington should be when it was dark, so that our appearance might scandalize no one. On several occasions we thus swam Rock Creek in the early spring when the ice was floating thick upon it. If we swam the Potomac, we usually took off our clothes. I remember one such occasion when the French Ambassador, Jusserand, who was a member of the Tennis Cabinet, was along, and, just as we were about to get in to swim, somebody said, "Mr. Ambassador, Mr. Ambassador, you haven't taken off your gloves," to which he promptly responded, "I think I will leave them on; we might meet ladies!"

We liked Rock Creek for these walks because we could do so much scrambling and climbing along the cliffs; there was almost as much climbing when we walked down the Potomac to Washington from the Virginia end of the Chain Bridge. I would occasionally take some big-game friend from abroad, Selous or St. George Littledale or Captain Radclyffe or Paul Niedicke, on these walks. Once I invited an entire class of officers who were attending lectures at the War College to come on one of these walks; I chose a route which gave us the hardest climbing along the rocks and the deepest crossings of the creek; and my army friends enjoyed it hugely — being the right sort, to a man.

"ONCE I INVITED AN ENTIRE CLASS OF OFFICERS WHO WERE ATTENDING LECTURES AT THE WAR COLLEGE, TO COME ON ONE OF THESE WALKS. I CHOSE A ROUTE WHICH GAVE US THE HARDEST CLIMBING ALONG THE ROCKS AND THE DEEPEST CROSSING OF THE CREEK, AND MY ARMY FRIENDS ENJOYED IT HUGELY — BEING THE RIGHT SORT, TO A MAN."

On March 1, 1909, three days before leaving the Presidency, various members of the Tennis Cabinet lunched with me at the White House. "Tennis Cabinet" was an elastic term, and of course many who ought to have been at the lunch were, for one reason or another, away from Washington; but, to make up for this, a goodly number of out-of-town honorary members, so to speak, were present — for instance, Seth Bullock; Luther Kelly, better known as Yellowstone Kelly in the days when he was an army scout against the Sioux; and Abernathy, the wolf-hunter. At the end of the lunch Seth Bullock suddenly reached forward, swept aside a mass of flowers which made a centerpiece on the table, and revealed a bronze cougar by Proctor, which was a parting gift to me. The lunch party and the cougar were then photographed on the lawn.

Some of the younger officers who were my constant companions on these walks and rides pointed out to me the condition of utter physical worthlessness into which certain of the elder ones had permitted themselves to lapse, and the very bad effect this would certainly have if ever the army were called into service. I then looked into the matter for myself, and was really shocked at what I found. Many of the older officers were so unfit physically that their condition would have excited laughter, had it not been so serious, to think that they belonged to the military arm of the Government. A cavalry colonel proved unable to keep his horse at a smart trot for even half a mile, when I visited his post; a Major-General proved afraid even to let his horse canter, when he went on a ride with us; and certain otherwise good men proved as unable to walk as if they had been sedentary brokers. I consulted with men like Major-Generals Wood and Bell, who were themselves of fine physique, with bodies fit to meet any demand. It was late in my administration; and we deemed it best only to make a beginning — experience teaches the most inveterate reformer how hard it is to get a totally non-military nation to accept seriously any military improvement. Accordingly, I merely issued directions that each officer should prove his ability to walk fifty miles, or ride one hundred, in three days.

This is, of course, a test which many a healthy middle-aged woman would be able to meet. But a large portion of the press adopted the view that it was a bit of capricious tyranny on my part; and a considerable number of elderly officers, with desk rather than field experience, intrigued with their friends in Congress to have the order annulled. So one day I took a ride of a little over one hundred miles myself, in company with Surgeon-General Rixey and two other officers. The Virginia roads were frozen and in ruts, and in the afternoon and evening there was a storm of snow and sleet; and when it had been thus experimentally shown, under unfavorable conditions, how easy it was to do in one day the task for which the army officers were allowed three days, all open objection ceased. But some bureau chiefs still did as much underhanded work against the order as they dared, and it was often difficult to reach them. In the Marine Corps Captain Leonard, who had lost an arm at Tientsin, with two of his lieutenants did the fifty miles in one day; for they were vigorous young men, who laughed at the idea of treating a fifty-mile walk as over-fatiguing. Well, the Navy Department officials rebuked them, and made them take the walk over again in three days, on the ground that taking it in one day did not comply with the regulations! This seems unbelievable; but Leonard assures me it is true. He did not inform me at the time, being afraid to "get in wrong" with his permanent superiors. If I had known of the order, short work would have been made of the bureaucrat who issued it.[1]

[1] One of our best naval officers sent me the following letter, after the above had appeared: —

"I note in your Autobiography now being published in the *Outlook* that you refer to the reasons which led you to establish a physical test for the Army, and to the action you took (your 100-mile ride) to prevent the test being abolished. Doubtless you did not know the following facts:

"1. The first annual navy test of 50 miles in three days was subsequently reduced to 25 miles in two days in each quarter.

"2. This was further reduced to 10 miles each month, which is the present 'test,' and there is danger lest even this utterly insufficient test be abolished.

"I enclose a copy of a recent letter to the Surgeon General which will show our present deplorable condition and the worse condition into which we are slipping back.

"The original test of 50 miles in three days did a very great deal of good. It

In no country with an army worth calling such is there a chance for a man physically unfit to stay in the service.

decreased by thousands of dollars the money expended on street car fare, and by a much greater sum the amount expended over the bar. It eliminated a number of the wholly unfit; it taught officers to walk; it forced them to learn the care of their feet and that of their men; and it improved their general health and was rapidly forming a taste for physical exercise."

The enclosed letter ran in part as follows : —

"I am returning under separate cover 'The Soldier's Foot and the Military Shoe.'

"The book contains knowledge of a practical character that is valuable for the men who HAVE TO MARCH, WHO HAVE SUFFERED FROM FOOT TROUBLES, AND WHO MUST AVOID THEM IN ORDER TO ATTAIN EFFICIENCY.

"The words in capitals express, according to my idea, the gist of the whole matter as regards military men.

"The army officer whose men break down on test gets a black eye. The one whose men show efficiency in this respect gets a bouquet.

"To such men the book is invaluable. There is no danger that they will neglect it. They will actually learn it, for exactly the same reasons that our fellows learn the gunnery instructions — or did learn them before they were withdrawn and burned.

"B U T, I have not been able to interest a single naval officer in this fine book. They will look at the pictures and say it is a good book, but they won't read it. The marine officers, on the contrary, are very much interested, because they have to teach their men to care for their feet and they must know how to care for their own. But the naval officers feel no such necessity, simply because their men do not have to demonstrate their efficiency by practice marches, and they themselves do not have to do a stunt that will show up their own ignorance and inefficiency in the matter.

"For example, some time ago I was talking with some chaps about shoes — the necessity of having them long enough and wide enough, etc., and one of them said : 'I have no use for such shoes, as I never walk except when I have to, and any old shoes do for the 10-mile-a-month stunt,' so there you are !

"When the first test was ordered, Edmonston (Washington shoe man) told me that he sold more real walking shoes to naval officers in three months than he had in the three preceding years. I know three officers who lost both big-toe nails after the first test, and another who walked nine miles in practice with a pair of heavy walking shoes that were too small and was laid up for three days — could not come to the office. I know plenty of men who after the first test had to borrow shoes from larger men until their feet 'went down' to their normal size.

"This test may have been a bit too strenuous for old hearts (of men who had never taken any exercise), but it was excellent as a matter of instruction and training of handling feet — and in an emergency (such as we soon may have in Mexico) sound hearts are not much good if the feet won't stand.

"However, the 25-mile test in two days each quarter answered the same purpose, for the reason that 12½ miles will produce sore feet with bad shoes, and sore feet and lame muscles even with good shoes, if there has been no practice marching.

"It was the necessity of doing 12½ MORE MILES ON THE SECOND DAY WITH SORE FEET AND LAME MUSCLES that made 'em sit up and take notice — made 'em practice walking, made 'em avoid street cars, buy proper shoes, show some curiosity about sox and the care of the feet in general.

Our countrymen should understand that every army officer —and every marine officer—ought to be summarily removed from the service unless he is able to undergo far severer tests than those which, as a beginning, I imposed. To follow any other course is to put a premium on slothful incapacity, and to do the gravest wrong to the Nation.

I have mentioned all these experiences, and I could mention scores of others, because out of them grew my philosophy — perhaps they were in part caused by my philosophy — of bodily vigor as a method of getting that vigor of soul without which vigor of the body counts for nothing. The dweller in cities has less chance than the dweller in the country to keep his body sound and vigorous. But he can do so, if only he will take the trouble. Any young lawyer,

"All this passed out with the introduction of the last test of 10 miles a month. As one fellow said: 'I can do that in sneakers' — but he couldn't if the second day involved a tramp on the sore feet.

"The point is that whereas formerly officers had to practice walking a bit and give some attention to proper footgear, now they don't have to, and the natural consequence is that they don't do it.

"There are plenty of officers who do not walk any more than is necessary to reach a street car that will carry them from their residences to their offices. Some who have motors do not do so much. They take no exercise. They take cocktails instead and are getting beefy and 'ponchy,' and something should be done to remedy this state of affairs.

"It would not be necessary if service opinion required officers so to order their lives that it would be common knowledge that they were 'hard,' in order to avoid the danger of being selected out.

"We have no such service opinion, and it is not in process of formation. On the contrary, it is known that the 'Principal Dignitaries' unanimously advised the Secretary to abandon all physical tests. He, *a civilian*, was wise enough not to take the advice.

"I would like to see a test established that would oblige officers to take sufficient exercise to pass it without inconvenience. For the reasons given above, 20 miles in two days every other month would do the business, while 10 miles each month does not touch it, simply because nobody has to walk on 'next day' feet. As for the proposed test of so many hours 'exercise' a week, the flat foots of the pendulous belly muscles are delighted. They are looking into the question of pedometers, and will hang one of these on their wheezy chests and let it count every shuffling step they take out of doors.

"If we had an adequate test throughout 20 years, there would at the end of that time be few if any sacks of blubber at the upper end of the list; and service opinion against that sort of thing would be established."

These tests were kept during my administration. They were afterwards abandoned; not through perversity or viciousness; but through weakness, and inability to understand the need of preparedness in advance, if the emergencies of war are to be properly met, when, or if, they arrive.

shopkeeper, or clerk, or shop-assistant can keep himself in good condition if he tries. Some of the best men who have ever served under me in the National Guard and in my regiment were former clerks or floor-walkers. Why, Johnny Hayes, the Marathon victor, and at one time world champion, one of my valued friends and supporters, was a floor-walker in Bloomingdale's big department store. Surely with Johnny Hayes as an example, any young man in a city can hope to make his body all that a vigorous man's body should be.

I once made a speech to which I gave the title "The Strenuous Life." Afterwards I published a volume of essays with this for a title. There were two translations of it which always especially pleased me. One was by a Japanese officer who knew English well, and who had carried the essay all through the Manchurian campaign, and later translated it for the benefit of his countrymen. The other was by an Italian lady, whose brother, an officer in the Italian army who had died on duty in a foreign land, had also greatly liked the article and carried it round with him. In translating the title the lady rendered it in Italian as *Vigor di Vita*. I thought this translation a great improvement on the original, and have always wished that I had myself used "The Vigor of Life" as a heading to indicate what I was trying to preach, instead of the heading I actually did use.

There are two kinds of success, or rather two kinds of ability displayed in the achievement of success. There is, first, the success either in big things or small things which comes to the man who has in him the natural power to do what no one else can do, and what no amount of training, no perseverance or will power, will enable any ordinary man to do. This success, of course, like every other kind of success, may be on a very big scale or on a small scale. The quality which the man possesses may be that which enables him to run a hundred yards in nine and three-fifths seconds, or to play ten separate games of chess at the same time blindfolded, or to add five columns of figures at once without effort, or to write the "Ode to a Grecian Urn," or to deliver the

Gettysburg speech, or to show the ability of Frederick at Leuthen or Nelson at Trafalgar. No amount of training of body or mind would enable any good ordinary man to perform any one of these feats. Of course the proper performance of each implies much previous study or training, but in no one of them is success to be attained save by the altogether exceptional man who has in him the something additional which the ordinary man does not have.

This is the most striking kind of success, and it can be attained only by the man who has in him the quality which separates him in kind no less than in degree from his fellows. But much the commoner type of success in every walk of life and in every species of effort is that which comes to the man who differs from his fellows not by the kind of quality which he possesses but by the degree of development which he has given that quality. This kind of success is open to a large number of persons, if only they seriously determine to achieve it. It is the kind of success which is open to the average man of sound body and fair mind, who has no remarkable mental or physical attributes, but who gets just as much as possible in the way of work out of the aptitudes that he does possess. It is the only kind of success that is open to most of us. Yet some of the greatest successes in history have been those of this second class — when I call it second class I am not running it down in the least, I am merely pointing out that it differs in kind from the first class. To the average man it is probably more useful to study this second type of success than to study the first. From the study of the first he can learn inspiration, he can get uplift and lofty enthusiasm. From the study of the second he can, if he chooses, find out how to win a similar success himself.

I need hardly say that all the successes I have ever won have been of the second type. I never won anything without hard labor and the exercise of my best judgment and careful planning and working long in advance. Having been a rather sickly and awkward boy, I was as a young man at first both nervous and distrustful of my own prowess. I had to train myself painfully and laboriously not merely as regards my body but as regards my soul and spirit.

When a boy I read a passage in one of Marryat's books which always impressed me. In this passage the captain of some small British man-of-war is explaining to the hero how to acquire the quality of fearlessness. He says that at the outset almost every man is frightened when he goes into action, but that the course to follow is for the man to keep such a grip on himself that he can act just as if he was not frightened. After this is kept up long enough it changes from pretense to reality, and the man does in very fact become fearless by sheer dint of practicing fearlessness when he does not feel it. (I am using my own language, not Marryat's.) This was the theory upon which I went. There were all kinds of things of which I was afraid at first, ranging from grizzly bears to "mean" horses and gun-fighters; but by acting as if I was not afraid I gradually ceased to be afraid. Most men can have the same experience if they choose. They will first learn to bear themselves well in trials which they anticipate and which they school themselves in advance to meet. After a while the habit will grow on them, and they will behave well in sudden and unexpected emergencies which come upon them unawares.

It is of course much pleasanter if one is naturally fearless, and I envy and respect the men who are naturally fearless. But it is a good thing to remember that the man who does not enjoy this advantage can nevertheless stand beside the man who does, and can do his duty with the like efficiency, *if he chooses to*. Of course he must not let his desire take the form merely of a day-dream. Let him dream about being a fearless man, and the more he dreams the better he will be, always provided he does his best to realize the dream in practice. He can do his part honorably and well provided only he sets fearlessness before himself as an ideal, schools himself to think of danger merely as something to be faced and overcome, and regards life itself as he should regard it, not as something to be thrown away, but as a pawn to be promptly hazarded whenever the hazard is warranted by the larger interests of the great game in which we are all engaged.

CHAPTER III

PRACTICAL POLITICS

WHEN I left Harvard, I took up the study of law.
If I had been sufficiently fortunate to come under
Professor Thayer, of the Harvard Law School,
it may well be that I would have realized that the
lawyer can do a great work for justice and against legalism.
But, doubtless chiefly through my own fault, some of
the teaching of the law books and of the classroom seemed
to me to be against justice. The *caveat emptor* side of the
law, like the *caveat emptor* side of business, seemed to me
repellent; it did not make for social fair dealing. The
"let the buyer beware" maxim, when translated into actual
practice, whether in law or business, tends to translate itself
further into the seller making his profit at the expense of the
buyer, instead of by a bargain which shall be to the profit
of both. It did not seem to me that the law was framed to
discourage as it should sharp practice, and all other kinds
of bargains except those which are fair and of benefit to
both sides. I was young; there was much in the judgment
which I then formed on this matter which I should now
revise; but, then as now, many of the big corporation
lawyers, to whom the ordinary members of the bar then as
now looked up, held certain standards which were difficult
to recognize as compatible with the idealism I suppose
every high-minded young man is apt to feel. If I had been
obliged to earn every cent I spent, I should have gone whole-
heartedly into the business of making both ends meet,
and should have taken up the law or any other respectable
occupation — for I then held, and now hold, the belief that
a man's first duty is to pull his own weight and to take care

of those dependent upon him; and I then believed, and now believe, that the greatest privilege and greatest duty for any man is to be happily married, and that no other form of success or service, for either man or woman, can be wisely accepted as a substitute or alternative. But it happened that I had been left enough money by my father not to make it necessary for me to think solely of earning bread for myself and my family. I had enough to get bread. What I had to do, if I wanted butter and jam, was to provide the butter and jam, but to count their cost as compared with other things. In other words, I made up my mind that, while I must earn money, I could afford to make earning money the secondary instead of the primary object of my career. If I had had no money at all, then my first duty would have been to earn it in any honest fashion. As I had some money I felt that my need for more money was to be treated as a secondary need, and that while it was my business to make more money where I legitimately and properly could, yet that it was also my business to treat other kinds of work as more important than money-making.

Almost immediately after leaving Harvard in 1880 I began to take an interest in politics. I did not then believe, and I do not now believe, that any man should ever attempt to make politics his only career. It is a dreadful misfortune for a man to grow to feel that his whole livelihood and whole happiness depend upon his staying in office. Such a feeling prevents him from being of real service to the people while in office, and always puts him under the heaviest strain of pressure to barter his convictions for the sake of holding office. A man should have some other occupation — I had several other occupations — to which he can resort if at any time he is thrown out of office, or if at any time he finds it necessary to choose a course which will probably result in his being thrown out, unless he is willing to stay in at cost to his conscience.

At that day, in 1880, a young man of my bringing up and convictions could join only the Republican party, and join it I accordingly did. It was no simple thing to join it then. That was long before the era of ballot reform and the control of primaries; long before the era when we realized that the Government must take official notice of the deeds and acts of party organizations. The party was still treated as a private corporation, and in each district the organization formed a kind of social and political club. A man had to be regularly proposed for and elected into this club, just as into any other club. As a friend of mine picturesquely phrased it, I "had to break into the organization with a jimmy."

Under these circumstances there was some difficulty in joining the local organization, and considerable amusement and excitement to be obtained out of it after I had joined.

It was over thirty-three years ago that I thus became a member of the Twenty-first District Republican Association in the city of New York. The men I knew best were the men in the clubs of social pretension and the men of cultivated taste and easy life. When I began to make inquiries as to the whereabouts of the local Republican Association and the means of joining it, these men — and the big business men and lawyers also — laughed at me, and told me that politics were "low"; that the organizations were not controlled by "gentlemen"; that I would find them run by saloon-keepers, horse-car conductors, and the like, and not by men with any of whom I would come in contact outside; and, moreover, they assured me that the men I met would be rough and brutal and unpleasant to deal with. I answered that if this were so it merely meant that the people I knew did not belong to the governing class, and that the other people did — and that I intended to be one of the governing class; that if they proved too hard-bit for me I supposed I would have to quit, but that I certainly would not quit until I had made the effort and found out whether I really was too weak to hold my own in the rough and tumble.

The Republican Association of which I became a member held its meetings in Morton Hall, a large, barn-like room over a saloon. Its furniture was of the canonical kind: dingy benches, spittoons, a dais at one end with a table and chair and a stout pitcher for iced water, and on the walls pictures of General Grant, and of Levi P. Morton, to whose

generosity we owed the room. We had regular meetings
once or twice a month, and between times the place was
treated, at least on certain nights, as a kind of club-room.
I went around there often enough to have the men get
accustomed to me and to have me get accustomed
to them, so that we began to speak the same language,
and so that each could begin to live down in the
other's mind what Bret Harte has called "the defective
moral quality of being a stranger." It is not often that a
man can make opportunities for himself. But he can put
himself in such shape that when or if the opportunities come
he is ready to take advantage of them. This was what
happened to me in connection with my experiences in Morton
Hall. I soon became on good terms with a number of the
ordinary "heelers" and even some of the minor leaders.
The big leader was Jake Hess, who treated me with
rather distant affability. There were prominent lawyers
and business men who belonged, but they took little part
in the actual meetings. What they did was done elsewhere.
The running of the machine was left to Jake Hess and his
captains of tens and of hundreds.

Among these lesser captains I soon struck up a friendship
with Joe Murray, a friendship which is as strong now as it
was thirty-three years ago. He had been born in Ireland,
but brought to New York by his parents when he was three
or four years old, and, as he expressed it, "raised as a bare-
footed boy on First Avenue." When not eighteen he had
enlisted in the Army of the Potomac and taken part in the
campaign that closed the Civil War. Then he came back
to First Avenue, and, being a fearless, powerful, energetic
young fellow, careless and reckless, speedily grew to some
prominence as leader of a gang. In that district, and at that
time, politics was a rough business, and Tammany Hall
held unquestioned sway. The district was overwhelmingly
Democratic, and Joe and his friends were Democrats who on
election day performed the usual gang work for the local
Democratic leader, whose business it was to favor and
reward them in return. This same local leader, like many
other greater leaders, became puffed up by prosperity, and

forgot the instruments through which he had achieved prosperity. After one election he showed a callous indifference to the hard work of the gang and complete disregard of his before-election promises. He counted upon the resentment wearing itself out, as usual, in threats and bluster.

But Joe Murray was not a man who forgot. He explained to his gang his purposes and the necessity of being quiet. Accordingly they waited for their revenge until the next election day. They then, as Joe expressed it, decided "to vote furdest away from the leader" — I am using the language of Joe's youth — and the best way to do this was to vote the Republican ticket. In those days each party had a booth near the polling-place in each election district, where the party representative dispensed the party ballots. This had been a district in which, as a rule, very early in the day the Republican election leader had his hat knocked over his eyes and his booth kicked over and his ballots scattered; and then the size of the Democratic majority depended on an elastic appreciation of exactly how much was demanded from headquarters. But on this day things went differently. The gang, with a Roman sense of duty, took an active interest in seeing that the Republican was given his full rights. Moreover, they made the most energetic reprisals on their opponents, and as they were distinctly the tough and fighting element, justice came to her own with a whoop. Would-be repeaters were thrown out on their heads. Every person who could be cajoled or, I fear, intimidated, was given the Republican ticket, and the upshot was that at the end of the day a district which had never hitherto polled more than two or three per cent of its vote Republican broke about even between the two parties.

To Joe it had been merely an act of retribution in so far as it was not simply a spree. But the leaders at the Republican headquarters did not know this, and when they got over their paralyzed astonishment at the returns, they investigated to find out what it meant. Somebody told them that it represented the work of a young man named Joseph Murray. Accordingly they sent for him. The room in which they received him was doubtless some

F

JOSEPH MURRAY.

"By nature a straight man, as fearless and as stanchly loyal as any one whom I have ever met — a man to be trusted in any position demanding courage, integrity, and good faith."

place like Morton Hall, and the men who received him were akin to those who had leadership in Morton Hall; but in Joe's eyes they stood for a higher civilization, for opportunity, for generous recognition of successful effort — in short, for all the things that an eager young man desires. He was received and patted on the back by a man who was a great man to the world in which he lived. He was introduced to the audience as a young man whose achievement was such as to promise much for the future, and moreover he was given a place in the post-office — as I have said, this was long before the day of Civil Service Reform.

Now, to the wrong kind of man all this might have meant nothing at all. But in Joe Murray's case it meant everything. He was by nature as straight a man, as fearless and as stanchly loyal, as any one whom I have ever met, a man to be trusted in any position demanding courage, integrity, and good faith. He did his duty in the public service, and became devotedly attached to the organization which he felt had given him his chance in life. When I knew him he was already making his way up ; one of the proofs and evidences of which was that he owned a first-class racing trotter — "Alice Lane" — behind which he gave me more than one spin. During this first winter I grew to like Joe and his particular cronies. But I had no idea that they especially returned the liking, and in the first row we had in the organization (which arose over a movement, that I backed, to stand by a non-partisan method of street-cleaning) Joe and all his friends stood stiffly with the machine, and my side, the reform side, was left with only some half-dozen votes out of three or four hundred. I had expected no other outcome and took it good-humoredly, but without changing my attitude.

Next fall, as the elections drew near, Joe thought he would like to make a drive at Jake Hess, and after considerable planning decided that his best chance lay in the fight for the nomination to the Assembly, the lower house of the Legislature. He picked me as the candidate with whom he would be most likely to win; and win he did. It was not my fight, it was Joe's ; and it was to him that I owe my entry into politics. I had at that time neither the reputation nor the ability to have won the nomination for myself, and indeed never would have thought of trying for it.

Jake Hess was entirely good-humored about it. In spite of my being anti-machine, my relations with him had been friendly and human, and when he was beaten he turned in to help Joe elect me. At first they thought they would take me on a personal canvass through the saloons along Sixth Avenue. The canvass, however, did not last beyond the first saloon. I was introduced with proper solemnity to the saloon-keeper — a very important personage, for this was before the days when saloon-keepers became merely the mortgaged chattels of the brewers — and he began to cross-examine me, a little too much in the tone of one who was dealing with a suppliant for his favor. He said he expected that I would of course treat the liquor business fairly; to which I answered, none too cordially, that I hoped I should treat all interests fairly. He then said that he regarded the licenses as too high; to which I responded that I believed they were really not high enough, and that I should try to have them made higher. The conversation threatened to become stormy. Messrs. Murray and Hess, on some hastily improvised plea, took me out into the street, and then Joe explained to me that it was not worth my while staying in Sixth Avenue any longer, that I had better go right back to Fifth Avenue and attend to my friends there, and that he would look after my interests on Sixth Avenue. I was triumphantly elected.

Once before Joe had interfered in similar fashion and secured the nomination of an Assemblyman; and shortly after election he had grown to feel toward this Assemblyman that he must have fed on the meat which rendered Cæsar proud, as he became inaccessible to the ordinary mortals whose place of resort was Morton Hall. He eyed me warily for a short time to see if I was likely in this respect to follow in my predecessor's footsteps. Finding that I did not, he and all my other friends and supporters assumed toward me the very pleasantest attitude that it was possible to assume. They did not ask me for a thing. They accepted as a matter of course the view that I was absolutely straight and was trying to do the best I could in the Legislature. They desired nothing except that I should make a success, and they supported me with hearty enthusiasm. I am a little at a loss to know quite how to express the quality in my relationship with Joe Murray and my other friends of this period which rendered that relationship so beneficial to me. When I went into politics at this time I was not conscious of going in with the set purpose to benefit other people, but of getting for myself a privilege to which I was entitled in common with other people. So it was in my relationship with these men. If there had lurked in the innermost recesses of my mind anywhere the thought that I was in some way a patron or a benefactor, or was doing something

noble by taking part in politics, or that I expected the smallest
consideration save what I could earn on my own merits, I
am certain that somehow or other the existence of that feeling would have been known and resented. As a matter of
fact, there was not the slightest temptation on my part to
have any such feeling or any one of such feelings. I no
more expected special consideration in politics than I would
have expected it in the boxing ring. I wished to act squarely
to others, and I wished to be able to show that I could hold
my own as against others. The attitude of my new friends
toward me was first one of polite reserve, and then that
of friendly alliance. Afterwards I became admitted to
comradeship, and then to leadership. I need hardly say
how earnestly I believe that men should have a keen
and lively sense of their obligations in politics, of their
duty to help forward great causes, and to struggle for the
betterment of conditions that are unjust to their fellows, the
men and women who are less fortunate in life. But in addition to this feeling there must be a feeling of real fellowship
with the other men and women engaged in the same task,
fellowship of work, with fun to vary the work ; for unless there
is this feeling of fellowship, of common effort on an equal plane
for a common end, it will be difficult to keep the relations
wholesome and natural. To be patronized is as offensive
as to be insulted. No one of us cares permanently to have
some one else conscientiously striving to do him good ;
what we want is to work with that some one else for the good
of both of us — any man will speedily find that other people
can benefit him just as much as he can benefit them.

Neither Joe Murray nor I nor any of our associates at
that time were alive to social and industrial needs which
we now all of us recognize. But we then had very clearly
before our minds the need of practically applying certain
elemental virtues, the virtues of honesty and efficiency in
politics, the virtue of efficiency side by side with honesty
in private and public life alike, the virtues of consideration
and fair dealing in business as between man and man,
and especially as between the man who is an employer and
the man who is an employee. On all fundamental questions

Joe Murray and I thought alike.   We never parted company
excepting on the question of Civil Service Reform, where he
sincerely felt that I showed doctrinaire affinities, that I
sided with the pharisees.   We got back again into close
relations as soon as I became Police Commissioner under
Mayor Strong, for Joe was then made Excise Commissioner,
and was, I believe, the best Excise Commissioner the
city of New York ever had.   He is now a farmer, his
boys have been through Columbia College, and he and I
look at the questions, political, social, and industrial, which
confront us in 1913 from practically the same standpoint,
just as we once looked at the questions that confronted us
in 1881.

There are many debts that I owe Joe Murray, and some
for which he was only unconsciously responsible.   I do not
think that a man is fit to do good work in our American
democracy unless he is able to have a genuine fellow-feeling
for, understanding of, and sympathy with his fellow-Ameri-
cans, whatever their creed or their birthplace, the section
in which they live, or the work which they do, provided they
possess the only kind of Americanism that really counts,
the Americanism of the spirit.   It was no small help to me,
in the effort to make myself a good citizen and good American,
that the political associate with whom I was on closest and
most intimate terms during my early years was a man
born in Ireland, by creed a Catholic, with Joe Murray's
upbringing;   just as it helped me greatly at a later period
to work for certain vitally necessary public needs with Arthur
von Briesen, in whom the spirit of the "Acht-und-Vierziger"
idealists was embodied;   just as my whole life was influenced
by my long association with Jacob Riis, whom I am tempted
to call the best American I ever knew, although he was
already a young man when he came hither from Denmark.

I was elected to the Legislature in the fall of 1881, and found
myself the youngest man in that body.   I was reëlected the
two following years.   Like all young men and inexperienced
members, I had considerable difficulty in teaching myself
to speak.   I profited much by the advice of a hard-headed
old countryman — who was unconsciously paraphrasing

he abhorred corruption. He had thought much on political problems; he admired Alexander Hamilton as much as I did, being a strong believer in a powerful National government; and we both of us differed from Alexander Hamilton in being stout adherents of Abraham Lincoln's views wherever the rights of the people were concerned. Any man who has met with success, if he will be frank with himself, must admit that there has been a big element of fortune in the success. Fortune favored me, whereas her hand was heavy against Billy O'Neill. All his life he had to strive hard to wring his bread from harsh surroundings and a reluctant fate; if fate had been but a little kinder, I believe he would have had a great political career; and he would have done good service for the country in any position in which he might have been put.

There were other Republicans, like Isaac Hunt and Jonas van Duzer and Walter Howe and Henry Sprague, who were among my close friends and allies; and a gigantic one-eyed veteran of the Civil War, a gallant General, Curtis from St. Lawrence County; and a capital fellow, whom afterwards, when Governor, I put on the bench, Kruse, from Cattaraugus County. Kruse was a German by birth; as far as I know, the only German from Cattaraugus County at that time; and, besides being a German, he was also a Prohibitionist. Among the Democrats were Hamden Robb and Thomas Newbold, and Tom Welch of Niagara, who did a great service in getting the State to set aside Niagara Falls Park — after a discouraging experience with the first Governor before whom we brought the bill, who listened with austere patience to our arguments in favor of the State establishing a park, and then conclusively answered us by the question, "But, gentlemen, why should we spend the people's money when just as much water will run over the Falls without a park as with it?" Then there were a couple of members from New York and Brooklyn, Mike Costello and Pete Kelly.

Mike Costello had been elected as a Tammany man. He was as fearless as he was honest. He came from Ireland, and had accepted the Tammany Fourth of July orations

as indicating the real attitude of that organization towards
the rights of the people.   A month or two in Albany converted him to a profound distrust of applied Tammany
methods.   He and I worked hand in hand with equal indifference to our local machines.   His machine leaders
warned him fairly that they would throw him out at the
next election, which they did; but he possessed a seasoned-
hickory toughness of ability to contend with adverse circumstances, and kept his head well above water.   A better
citizen does not exist; and our friendship has never faltered.

Peter Kelly's fate was a tragedy.   He was a bright,
well-educated young fellow, an ardent believer in Henry
George.   At the beginning he and I failed to understand
each other or to get on together, for our theories of government were radically opposed. After a couple of months spent
in active contests with men whose theories had nothing
whatever to do with their practices, Kelly and I found in
our turn that it really did not make much difference what
our abstract theories were on questions that were not before
the Legislature, in view of the fact that on the actual matters before the Legislature, the most important of
which involved questions of elementary morality, we were
heartily at one.   We began to vote together and act together, and by the end of the session found that in all
practical matters that were up for action we thought together.   Indeed, each of us was beginning to change his
theories, so that even in theory we were coming closer
together.   He was ardent and generous; he was a young
lawyer, with a wife and children, whose ambition had
tempted him into politics, and who had been befriended
by the local bosses under the belief that they could count
upon him for anything they really wished.   Unfortunately,
what they really wished was often corrupt.   Kelly defied
them, fought the battles of the people with ardor and
good faith, and when the bosses refused him a renomination, he appealed from them to the people.   When we both
came up for reëlection, I won easily in my district, where
circumstances conspired to favor me; and Kelly, with
exactly the same record that I had, except that it was more

creditable because he took his stand against greater odds, was beaten in his district. Defeat to me would have meant merely chagrin; to Kelly it meant terrible material disaster. He had no money. Like every rigidly honest man, he had found that going into politics was expensive and that his salary as Assemblyman did not cover the financial outgo. He had lost his practice and he had incurred the ill will of the powerful, so that it was impossible at the moment to pick up his practice again; and the worry and disappointment affected him so much that shortly after election he was struck down by sickness. Just before Christmas some of us were informed that Kelly was in such financial straits that he and his family would be put out into the street before New Year. This was prevented by the action of some of his friends who had served with him in the Legislature, and he recovered, at least to a degree, and took up the practice of his profession. But he was a broken man. In the Legislature in which he served one of his fellow-Democrats from Brooklyn was the Speaker — Alfred C. Chapin, the leader and the foremost representative of the reform Democracy, whom Kelly zealously supported. A few years later Chapin, a very able man, was elected Mayor of Brooklyn on a reform Democratic ticket. Shortly after his election I was asked to speak at a meeting in a Brooklyn club at which various prominent citizens, including the Mayor, were present. I spoke on civic decency, and toward the close of my speech I sketched Kelly's career for my audience, told them how he had stood up for the rights of the people of Brooklyn, and how the people had failed to stand up for him, and the way he had been punished, precisely because he had been a good citizen who acted as a good citizen should act. I ended by saying that the reform Democracy had now come into power, that Mr. Chapin was Mayor, and that I very earnestly hoped recognition would at last be given to Kelly for the fight he had waged at such bitter cost to himself. My words created some impression, and Mayor Chapin at once said that he would take care of Kelly and see that justice was done him. I went home that evening much pleased. In the morning, at breakfast, I received a brief note from Chapin in these words: "It was nine last evening when you finished speaking of what Kelly had done, and when I said that I would take care of him. At ten last night Kelly died." He had been dying while I was making my speech, and he never knew that at last there was to be a tardy recognition of what he had done, a tardy justification for the sacrifices he had made. The man had fought, at heavy cost to himself and with entire disinterestedness, for popular rights; but no recognition for what he had done had come to him from the people, whose interest he had so manfully upheld.

Where there is no chance of statistical or mathematical measurement, it is very hard to tell just the degree to which conditions change from one period to another. This is peculiarly hard to do when we deal with such a matter as corruption. Personally I am inclined to think that in public life we are on the whole a little better and not a little worse than we were thirty years ago, when I was serving in the New York Legislature. I think the conditions are a little better in National, in State, and in municipal politics. Doubtless there are points in which they are worse, and there is an enormous amount that needs reformation. But it does seem to me as if, on the whole, things had slightly improved.

When I went into politics, New York City was under the control of Tammany, which was from time to time opposed by some other — and evanescent — city Democratic organization. The up-country Democrats had not yet fallen under Tammany sway, and were on the point of developing a big country political boss in the shape of David B. Hill. The Republican party was split into the Stalwart and Half-Breed factions. Accordingly neither party had one dominant boss, or one dominant machine, each being controlled by jarring and warring bosses and machines. The corruption was not what it had been in the days of Tweed, when outside individuals controlled the legislators like puppets. Nor was there any such centralization of the boss system as occurred later. Many of the members were under the control of local bosses or local machines. But the corrupt work was usually done through the members directly.

Of course I never had anything in the nature of legal proof of corruption, and the figures I am about to give are merely approximate. But three years' experience convinced me, in the first place, that there were a great many thoroughly corrupt men in the Legislature, perhaps a third of the whole number; and, in the next place, that the honest men outnumbered the corrupt men, and that, if it were ever possible to get an issue of right and wrong put vividly and unmistakably before them in a way that would arrest their attention and that would arrest the attention of their constituents, we could count on the triumph of the right. The trouble was that in most cases the issue was confused. To read some kinds of literature one would come to the conclusion that the only corruption in legislative circles was in the form of bribery by corporations, and that the line was sharp between the honest man who was always voting against corporations and the dishonest man who was always bribed to vote for them. My experience was the direct contrary of this. For every one bill introduced (not passed) corruptly to favor a corporation, there were at least ten introduced (not passed, and in this case not intended to be passed) to blackmail corporations. The majority of the corrupt members would be found voting for the blackmailing bills if they were not paid, and would also be found voting in the interests of the corporation if they were paid. The blackmailing, or, as they were always called, the "strike" bills, could themselves be roughly divided into two categories : bills which it would have been proper to pass, and those that it would not have been proper to pass. Some of the bills aimed at corporations were utterly wild and improper ; and of these a proportion might be introduced by honest and foolish zealots, whereas most of them were introduced by men who had not the slightest intention of passing them, but who wished to be paid not to pass them. The most profitable type of bill to the accomplished blackmailer, however, was a bill aimed at a real corporate abuse which the corporation, either from wickedness or folly, was unwilling to remedy.

Of the measures introduced in the interest of corporations there were also some that were proper and some that were improper. The corrupt legislators, the "black horse cavalry," as they were termed, would demand payment to vote as the corporations wished, no matter whether the bill was proper or improper. Sometimes, if the bill was a proper one, the corporation would have the virtue or the strength of mind to refuse to pay for its passage, and sometimes it would not.

A very slight consideration of the above state of affairs will show how difficult it was at times to keep the issue clear, for honest and dishonest men were continually found side by side voting now against and now for a corporation measure, the one set from proper and the other set from grossly improper motives. Of course part of the fault lay in the attitude of outsiders. It was very early borne in upon me that almost equal harm was done by indiscriminate defense of, and indiscriminate attack on, corporations. It was hard to say whether the man who prided himself upon always antagonizing the corporations, or the man who, on the plea that he was a good conservative, always stood up for them, was the more mischievous agent of corruption and demoralization.

In one fight in the House over a bill as to which there was a bitter contest between two New York City street railway organizations, I saw lobbyists come down on the floor itself and draw venal men out into the lobbies with almost no pretense of concealing what they were doing. In another case in which the elevated railway corporations of New York City, against the protest of the Mayor and the other local authorities, rushed through a bill remitting over half their taxes, some of the members who voted for the measure probably thought it was right; but every corrupt man in the House voted with them; and the man must indeed have been stupid who thought that these votes were given disinterestedly.

The effective fight against this bill for the revision of the elevated railway taxes — perhaps the most openly crooked measure which during my time was pushed at Albany — was

William O'Neill.   Mr. Spinney of the New York *Times*.   Theodore Roosevelt.
Isaac Hunt.   Walter Howe.

THEODORE ROOSEVELT AND A GROUP OF HIS FRIENDS, WHEN HE WAS A MEMBER OF THE
NEW YORK LEGISLATURE.

waged by Mike Costello and myself. We used to spend a good deal of time in industrious research into the various bills introduced, so as to find out what their authors really had in mind; this research, by the way, being highly unappreciated and much resented by the authors. In the course of his researches Mike had been puzzled by an unimportant bill, seemingly related to a Constitutional amendment, introduced by a local saloon-keeper, whose interests, as far as we knew, were wholly remote from the Constitution, or from any form of abstract legal betterment. However, the measure seemed harmless; we did not interfere; and it passed the House. Mike, however, followed its career in the Senate, and at the last moment, almost by accident, discovered that it had been "amended" by the simple process of striking out everything after the enacting clause and unobtrusively substituting the proposal to remit the elevated railway taxes! The authors of the change wished to avoid unseemly publicity; their hope was to slip the measure through the Legislature and have it instantly signed by the Governor, before any public attention was excited. In the Senate their plan worked to perfection. There was in the Senate no fighting leadership of the forces of decency; and for such leadership of the non-fighting type the representatives of corruption cared absolutely nothing. By bold and adroit management the substitution in the Senate was effected without opposition or comment. The bill (in reality, of course, an absolutely new and undebated bill) then came back to the House nominally as a merely amended measure, which, under the rules, was not open to debate unless the amendment was first by vote rejected. This was the great bill of the session for the lobby; and the lobby was keenly alive to the need of quick, wise action. No public attention whatever had so far been excited. Every measure was taken to secure immediate and silent action. A powerful leader, whom the beneficiaries of the bill trusted, a fearless and unscrupulous man, of much force and great knowledge of parliamentary law, was put in the chair. Costello and I were watched; and when for a moment we were out of the House, the bill was brought over from the

Senate, and the clerk began to read it, all the black horse cavalry, in expectant mood, being in their seats. But Mike Costello, who was in the clerk's room, happened to catch a few words of what was being read. In he rushed, despatched a messenger for me, and began a single-handed filibuster. The Speaker pro tem called him to order. Mike continued to speak and protest; the Speaker hammered him down; Mike continued his protests; the sergeant-at-arms was sent to arrest and remove him; and then I bounced in, and continued the protest, and refused to sit down or be silent. Amid wild confusion the amendment was declared adopted, and the bill was ordered engrossed and sent to the Governor. But we had carried our point. The next morning the whole press rang with what had happened; every detail of the bill, and every detail of the way it had been slipped through the Legislature, were made public. All the slow and cautious men in the House, who had been afraid of taking sides, now came forward in support of us. Another debate was held on the proposal to rescind the vote; the city authorities waked up to protest; the Governor refused to sign the bill. Two or three years later, after much litigation, the taxes were paid; in the newspapers it was stated that the amount was over $1,500,000. It was Mike Costello to whom primarily was due the fact that this sum was saved the public, and that the forces of corruption received a stinging rebuff. He did not expect recognition or reward for his services; and he got none. The public, if it knew of what he had done, promptly forgot it. The machine did not forget it, and turned him down at the next election.

One of the stand-by "strikes" was a bill for reducing the elevated railway fare, which at that time was ten cents, to five cents. In one Legislature the men responsible for the introduction of the bill suffered such an extraordinary change of heart that when the bill came up — being pushed by zealous radicals who really were honest — the introducers actually voted against it! A number of us who had been very doubtful about the principle of the bill voted for it simply because we were convinced that money was being used to stop it, and we hated to seem to side with the cor-

G

ruptionists.   Then there came a wave of popular feeling
in its favor, the bill was reintroduced at the next session,
the railways very wisely decided that they would simply
fight it on its merits, and the entire black horse cavalry
contingent, together with all the former friends of the measure, voted against it.   Some of us, who in our anger at the
methods formerly resorted to for killing the bill had voted for
it the previous year, with much heart-searching again
voted for it, as I now think unwisely; and the bill was
vetoed by the then Governor, Grover Cleveland.   I believe
the veto was proper, and those who felt as I did supported
the veto; for although it was entirely right that the fare
should be reduced to five cents, which was soon afterwards
done, the method was unwise, and would have set a mischievous precedent.

An instance of an opposite kind occurred in connection
with a great railway corporation which wished to increase
its terminal facilities in one of our great cities.   The representatives of the railway brought the bill to me and asked me
to look into it, saying that they were well aware that it
was the kind of bill that lent itself to blackmail, and that
they wished to get it through on its merits, and invited the
most careful examination.   I looked carefully into it, found
that the municipal authorities and the property-owners
whose property was to be taken favored it, and also found
that it was an absolute necessity from the standpoint of
the city no less than from the standpoint of the railway.
So I said I would take charge of it if I had guarantees that
no money should be used and nothing improper done in
order to push it.   This was agreed to.   I was then acting
as chairman of the committee before which the bill went.

A very brief experience proved what I had already been
practically sure of, that there was a secret combination of
the majority of the committee on a crooked basis.   On one
pretext or another the crooked members of the committee
held the bill up, refusing to report it either favorably or unfavorably.   There were one or two members of the committee who were pretty rough characters, and when I decided to force matters I was not sure that we would not have

trouble. There was a broken chair in the room, and I got a leg of it loose and put it down beside me where it was not visible, but where I might get at it in a hurry if necessary. I moved that the bill be reported favorably. This was voted down without debate by the " combine," some of whom kept a wooden stolidity of look, while others leered at me with sneering insolence. I then moved that it be reported unfavorably, and again the motion was voted down by the same majority and in the same fashion. I then put the bill in my pocket and announced that I would report it anyhow. This almost precipitated a riot, especially when I explained, in answer to statements that my conduct would be exposed on the floor of the Legislature, that in that case I should give the Legislature the reasons why I suspected that the men holding up all report of the bill were holding it up for purposes of blackmail. The riot did not come off; partly, I think, because the opportune production of the chair-leg had a sedative effect, and partly owing to wise counsels from one or two of my opponents.

Accordingly I got the bill reported to the Legislature and put on the calendar. But here it came to a dead halt. I think this was chiefly because most of the newspapers which noticed the matter at all treated it in such a cynical spirit as to encourage the men who wished to blackmail. These papers reported the introduction of the bill, and said that "all the hungry legislators were clamoring for their share of the pie"; and they accepted as certain the fact that there was going to be a division of "pie." This succeeded in frightening honest men, and also in relieving the rogues; the former were afraid they would be suspected of receiving money if they voted for the bill, and the latter were given a shield behind which to stand until they were paid. I was wholly unable to move the bill forward in the Legislature, and finally a representative of the railway told me that he thought he would like to take the bill out of my hands, that I did not seem able to get it through, and that perhaps some "older and more experienced" leader could be more successful. I was pretty certain what this meant, but of course I had no kind of proof, and moreover I was not in a position to say that I could promise success. Accordingly, the bill was given into the charge of a veteran, whom I believe to have been a personally honest man, but who was not inquisitive about the motives influencing his colleagues. This gentleman, who went by a nickname which I shall incorrectly call "the bald eagle of Weehawken," was efficient and knew his job. After a couple of weeks a motion to put the bill through was made by "the bald eagle"; the "black horse cavalry," whose feelings had undergone a complete change in the intervening time, voted unanimously for it, in company with all the decent members; and that was the end. Now here was a bit of work in the interest of a corporation and in the interest of a community, which the corporation at first tried honestly to have put through on its merits. The blame for the failure lay primarily in the supine indifference of the community to legislative wrong-doing, so long as only the corporations were blackmailed.

Except as above mentioned, I was not brought in contact with big business, save in the effort to impeach a certain judge. This judge had been used as an instrument in their business by certain of the men connected with the elevated railways and other great corporations at that time. We got hold of his correspondence with one of these men, and it showed a shocking willingness to use the judicial office in any way that one of the kings of finance of that day desired. He had actually held court in one of that financier's rooms. One expression in one of the judge's letters to this financier I shall always remember: "I am willing to go to the very verge of judicial discretion to serve your vast interests." The curious thing was that I was by no means certain that the judge himself was corrupt. He may have been; but I am inclined to think that, aside from his being a man of coarse moral fiber, the trouble lay chiefly in the fact that he had a genuine — if I had not so often seen it, I would say a wholly inexplicable — reverence for the possessor of a great fortune as such. He sincerely believed that business was the end of existence, and that judge and legislator alike should do whatever was necessary to favor it; and the bigger the business the more he desired to favor it. Big business of the kind that is allied with politics thoroughly appreciated the usefulness of such a judge, and every effort was strained to protect him. We fought hard — by "we" I mean some thirty or forty legislators, both Republicans and Democrats — but the "black horse cavalry," and the timid good men, and the dull conservative men, were all against us; and the vote in the Legislature was heavily against impeachment. The minority of the committee that investigated him, with Chapin at its head, recommended impeachment; the argument for impeachment before the committee was made by Francis Lynde Stetson.

It was my first experience of the kind. Various men whom I had known well socially and had been taught to look up to, prominent business men and lawyers, acted in a way which not only astounded me, but which I was quite unable to reconcile with the theories I had formed as to their high standing — I was little more than a year out of college at the time. Generally, as has been always the case since, they were careful to avoid any direct conversation with me on a concrete case of what we now call "privilege" in business and in politics, that is, of the alliance between business and politics which represents improper favors rendered to some men in return for improper conduct on the part of others being ignored or permitted.

One member of a prominent law firm, an old family friend, did, however, take me out to lunch one day, evidently for the purpose of seeing just what it was that I wished and intended to do. I believe he had a genuine personal liking for me. He explained that I had done well in the Legislature, that it was a good thing to have made the "reform play," that I had shown that I possessed ability such as would make me useful in the right kind of law office or business concern; but that I must not overplay my hand; that I had gone far enough, and that now was the time to leave politics and identify myself with the right kind of people, the people who would always in the long run control others and obtain the real rewards which were worth having. I asked him if that meant that I was to yield to the ring in politics. He answered somewhat impatiently that I was entirely mistaken (as in fact I was) about there being merely a political ring, of the kind of which the papers were fond of talking; that the " ring," if it could be called such — that is, the inner circle — included certain big business men, and the politicians, lawyers, and judges who were in alliance with and to a certain extent dependent upon them, and that the successful man had to win his success by the backing of the same forces, whether in law, business, or politics.

This conversation not only interested me, but made such an impression that I always remembered it, for it was the first glimpse I had of that combination between business and politics which I was in after years so often to oppose. In the America of that day, and especially among the people whom I knew, the successful business man was regarded by everybody as preëminently *the* good citizen.   The orthodox books on political economy, not only in America but in England, were written for his especial glorification.   The tangible rewards came to him, the admiration of his fellow-citizens of the respectable type was apt to be his, and the severe newspaper moralists who were never tired of denouncing politicians and political methods were wont to hold up "business methods" as the ideal which we were to strive to introduce into political life.   Herbert Croly, in "The Promise of American Life," has set forth the reasons why our individualistic democracy — which taught that each man was to rely exclusively on himself, was in no way to be interfered with by others, and was to devote himself to his own personal welfare — necessarily produced the type of business man who sincerely believed, as did the rest of the community, that the individual who amassed a big fortune was the man who was the best and most typical American.

In the Legislature the problems with which I dealt were mainly problems of honesty and decency and of legislative and administrative efficiency.   They represented the effort, the wise, the vitally necessary effort, to get efficient and honest government.   But as yet I understood little of the effort which was already beginning, for the most part under very bad leadership, to secure a more genuine social and

industrial justice.   Nor was I especially to blame for this.
The good citizens I then knew best, even when themselves
men of limited means — men like my colleague Billy O'Neill,
and my backwoods friends Sewall and Dow — were no
more awake than I was to the changing needs the changing
times were bringing.   Their outlook was as narrow as my
own, and, within its limits, as fundamentally sound.

I wish to dwell on the soundness of our outlook on life,
even though as yet it was not broad enough.   We were no
respecters of persons.   Where our vision was developed
to a degree that enabled us to see crookedness, we opposed it
whether in great or small.   As a matter of fact, we found
that it needed much more courage to stand up *openly* against
labor men when they were wrong than against capitalists
when they were wrong.   The sins against labor are usually
committed, and the improper services to capitalists are
usually rendered, behind closed doors.   Very often the
man with the moral courage to speak in the open against
labor when it is wrong is the only man anxious to do effective
work for labor when labor is right.

The only kinds of courage and honesty which are permanently useful to good institutions anywhere are those shown
by men who decide all cases with impartial justice on grounds
of conduct and not on grounds of class.   We found that in
the long run the men who in public blatantly insisted that
labor was never wrong were the very men who in private
could not be trusted to stand for labor when it was right.
We grew heartily to distrust the reformer who never denounced wickedness unless it was embodied in a rich man.
Human nature does not change; and that type of "reformer" is as noxious now as he ever was.   The loud-
mouthed upholder of popular rights who attacks wickedness
only when it is allied with wealth, and who never publicly
assails any misdeed, no matter how flagrant, if committed
nominally in the interest of labor, has either a warped mind or
a tainted soul, and should be trusted by no honest man.   It
was largely the indignant and contemptuous dislike aroused
in our minds by the demagogues of this class which then
prevented those of us whose instincts at bottom were sound

from going as far as we ought to have gone along the lines of governmental control of corporations and governmental interference on behalf of labor.

I did, however, have one exceedingly useful experience. A bill was introduced by the Cigar-Makers' Union to prohibit the manufacture of cigars in tenement-houses.   I was appointed one of a committee of three to investigate conditions in the tenement-houses and see if legislation should be had. Of my two colleagues on the committee, one took no interest in the measure and privately said he did not think it was right, but that he had to vote for it because the labor unions were strong in his district and he was pledged to support the bill.   The other, a sporting Tammany man who afterwards abandoned politics for the race-track, was a very good fellow.   He told me frankly that he had to be against the bill because certain interests which were all-powerful and with which he had dealings required him to be against it, but that I was a free agent, and that if I would look into the matter he believed I would favor the legislation.   As a matter of fact, I had supposed I would be against the legislation, and I rather think that I was put on the committee with that idea, for the respectable people I knew were against it; it was contrary to the principles of political economy of the *laissez faire* kind; and the business men who spoke to me about it shook their heads and said that it was designed to prevent a man doing as he wished and as he had a right to do with what was his own.

However, my first visits to the tenement-house districts in question made me feel that, whatever the theories might be, as a matter of practical common sense I could not conscientiously vote for the continuance of the conditions which I saw.   These conditions rendered it impossible for the families of the tenement-house workers to live so that the children might grow up fitted for the exacting duties of American citizenship.   I visited the tenement-houses once with my colleagues of the committee, once with some of the labor union representatives, and once or twice by myself.   In a few of the tenement-houses there were suites of rooms ample in number where the work on the tobacco

was done in rooms not occupied for cooking or sleeping or
living. In the overwhelming majority of cases, however,
there were one, two, or three room apartments, and the work
of manufacturing the tobacco by men, women, and children
went on day and night in the eating, living, and sleeping
rooms — sometimes in one room.   I have always remembered
one room in which two families were living.   On my inquiry
as to who the third adult male was I was told that he was a
boarder with one of the families.   There were several children, three men, and two women in this room.   The tobacco
was stowed about everywhere, alongside the foul bedding,
and in a corner where there were scraps of food.   The men,
women, and children in this room worked by day and far
on into the evening, and they slept and ate there.   They
were Bohemians, unable to speak English, except that one
of the children knew enough to act as interpreter.

Instead of opposing the bill I ardently championed it.
It was a poorly drawn measure, and the Governor, Grover
Cleveland, was at first doubtful about signing it.   The Cigar-
Makers' Union then asked me to appear before the Governor
and argue for it.   I accordingly did so, acting as spokesman
for the battered, undersized foreigners who represented the
Union and the workers.   The Governor signed the bill.
Afterwards this tenement-house cigar legislation was declared invalid by the Court of Appeals in the Jacobs decision.
Jacobs was one of the rare tenement-house manufacturers
of cigars who occupied quite a suite of rooms, so that in his
case the living conditions were altogether exceptional.
What the reason was which influenced those bringing the
suit to select the exceptional instead of the average worker
I do not know; of course such action was precisely the
action which those most interested in having the law broken
down were anxious to see taken.   The Court of Appeals
declared the law unconstitutional, and in their decision
the judges reprobated the law as an assault upon the "hallowed" influences of "home."   It was this case which first
waked me to a dim and partial understanding of the fact
that the courts were not necessarily the best judges of what
should be done to better social and industrial conditions.

The judges who rendered this decision were well-meaning men. They knew nothing whatever of tenement-house conditions; they knew nothing whatever of the needs, or of the life and labor, of three-fourths of their fellow-citizens in great cities. They knew legalism, but not life. Their choice of the words "hallowed" and "home," as applicable to the revolting conditions attending the manufacture of cigars in tenement-houses, showed that they had no idea what it was that they were deciding. Imagine the "hallowed" associations of a "home" consisting of one room where two families, one of them with a boarder, live, eat, and work! This decision completely blocked tenement-house reform legislation in New York for a score of years, and hampers it to this day. It was one of the most serious setbacks which the cause of industrial and social progress and reform ever received.

I had been brought up to hold the courts in especial reverence. The people with whom I was most intimate were apt to praise the courts for just such decisions as this, and to speak of them as bulwarks against disorder and barriers against demagogic legislation. These were the same people with whom the judges who rendered these decisions were apt to foregather at social clubs, or dinners, or in private life. Very naturally they all tended to look at things from the same standpoint. Of course it took more than one experience such as this Tenement Cigar Case to shake me out of the attitude in which I was brought up. But various decisions, not only of the New York court but of certain other State courts and even of the United States Supreme Court, during the quarter of a century following the passage of this tenement-house legislation, did at last thoroughly wake me to the actual fact. I grew to realize that all that Abraham Lincoln had said about the Dred Scott decision could be said with equal truth and justice about the numerous decisions which in our own day were erected as bars across the path of social reform, and which brought to naught so much of the effort to secure justice and fair dealing for workingmen and workingwomen, and for plain citizens generally.

Some of the wickedness and inefficiency in public life

"REFORM WITHOUT BLOODSHED."

A cartoon by Thomas Nast in *Harper's Weekly*, of April 19, 1884, entitled "Governor Cleveland and Theodore Roosevelt at their work."

was then displayed in simpler fashion than would probably now be the case. Once or twice I was a member of committees which looked into gross and widely ramifying governmental abuses. On the whole, the most important part I played was in the third Legislature in which I served, when I acted as chairman of a committee which investigated various phases of New York City official life.

The most important of the reform measures our committee recommended was the bill taking away from the Aldermen their power of confirmation over the Mayor's appointments. We found that it was possible to get citizens interested in the character and capacity of the head of the city, so that they would exercise some intelligent interest in his conduct and qualifications. But we found that as a matter of fact it was impossible to get them interested in the Aldermen and other subordinate officers. In actual practice the Aldermen were merely the creatures of the local ward bosses or of the big municipal bosses, and where they controlled the appointments the citizens at large had no chance whatever to make their will felt. Accordingly we fought for the principle, which I believe to be of universal application, that what is needed in our popular government is to give plenty of power to a few officials, and to make these few officials genuinely and readily responsible to the people for the exercise of that power. Taking away the confirming power of the Board of Aldermen did not give the citizens of New York good government. We knew that if they chose to elect the wrong kind of Mayor they would have bad government, no matter what the form of the law was. But we did secure to them the chance to get good government if they desired, and this was impossible as long as the old system remained. The change was fought in the way in which all similar changes always are fought. The corrupt and interested politicians were against it, and the battle-cries they used, which rallied to them most of the unthinking conservatives, were that we were changing the old constitutional system, that we were defacing the monuments of the wisdom of the founders of the government, that we were destroying that distinction between legislative and executive power which was the bulwark of our liberties, and that we were violent and unscrupulous radicals with no reverence for the past.

Of course the investigations, disclosures, and proceedings of the investigating committee of which I was chairman brought me into bitter personal conflict with very powerful financiers, very powerful politicians, and with certain newspapers which these financiers and politicians controlled. A number of able and unscrupulous men were fighting, some for their financial lives, and others to keep out of unpleasantly close neighborhood to State's prison. This meant that there were blows to be taken as well as given. In such political struggles, those who went in for the kind of thing that I did speedily excited animosities among strong and cunning men who would stop at little to gratify their animosity. Any man engaged in this particular type of militant and practical reform movement was soon made to feel that he had better not undertake to push matters home unless his own character was unassailable. On one of the investigating committees on which I served there was a countryman, a very able man, who, when he reached New York City, felt as certain Americans do when they go to Paris — that the moral restraints of his native place no longer applied. With all his ability, he was not shrewd enough to realize that the Police Department was having him as well as the rest of us carefully shadowed. He was caught red-handed by a plain-clothes man doing what he had no business to do; and from that time on he dared not act save as those who held his secret permitted him to act. Thenceforth those officials who stood behind the Police Department had one man on the committee on whom they could count. I never saw terror more ghastly on a strong man's face than on the face of this man on one or two occasions when he feared that events in the committee might take such a course as to force him into a position where his colleagues would expose him even if the city officials did not. However, he escaped, for we were never able to get the kind of proof which would warrant our asking for the action in which this man could not have joined.

Traps were set for more than one of us, and if we had walked into these traps our public careers would have ended, at least so far as following them under the conditions which alone make it worth while to be in public life at all. A man can of course hold public office, and many a man does hold public office, and lead a public career of a sort, even if there are other men who possess secrets about him which he cannot afford to have divulged. But no man can lead a public career really worth leading, no man can act with rugged independence in serious crises, nor strike at great abuses, nor afford to make powerful and unscrupulous foes, if he is himself vulnerable in his private character. Nor will clean conduct by itself enable a man to render good service. I have always been fond of Josh Billings's remark that "it is much easier to be a harmless dove than a wise serpent." There are plenty of decent legislators, and plenty of able legislators; but the blamelessness and the fighting edge are not always combined. Both qualities are necessary for the man who is to wage active battle against the powers that prey. He must be clean of life, so that he can laugh when his public or his private record is searched; and yet being clean of life will not avail him if he is either foolish or timid. He must walk warily and fearlessly, and while he should never brawl if he can avoid it, he must be ready to hit hard if the need arises. Let him remember, by the way, that the unforgivable crime is soft hitting. Do not hit at all if it can be avoided; but *never* hit softly.

Like most young men in politics, I went through various oscillations of feeling before I "found myself." At one period I became so impressed with the virtue of complete independence that I proceeded to act on each case purely as I personally viewed it, without paying any heed to the principles and prejudices of others. The result was that I speedily and deservedly lost all power of accomplishing anything at all; and I thereby learned the invaluable lesson that in the practical activities of life no man can render the highest service unless he can act in combination with his fellows, which means a certain amount of give-and-take between him and them. Again, I at one period began to believe that I had a future before me, and that it behooved me to be very far-sighted and scan each action carefully with a view to its possible effect on that future. This speedily made me useless to the public and an object of aversion to myself; and I then made up my mind that I would try not to think of the future at all, but would proceed on the assumption that each office I held would be the last I ever should hold, and that I would confine myself to trying to do my work as well as possible while I held that office. I found that for me personally this was the only way in which I could either enjoy myself or render good service to the country, and I never afterwards deviated from this plan.

As regards political advancement the bosses could of course do a good deal. At that time the warring Stalwart and Half-Breed factions of the Republican party were supporting respectively President Arthur and Senator Miller. Neither side cared for me. The first year in the Legislature I rose to a position of leadership, so that in the second year, when the Republicans were in a minority, I received the minority nomination for Speaker, although I was still the youngest man in the House, being twenty-four years old. The third year the Republicans carried the Legislature, and the bosses at once took a hand in the Speakership contest. I made a stout fight for the nomination, but the bosses of the two factions, the Stalwarts and the Half-Breeds, combined and I was beaten. I was much chagrined for the moment. But the fact that I had fought hard and efficiently, even though defeated, and that I had made the fight single-handed, with no machine back of me, assured my standing as floor leader. My defeat in the end materially strengthened my position, and enabled me to accomplish far more than I could have accomplished as Speaker. As so often, I found that the titular position was of no consequence; what counted was the combination of the opportunity with the ability to accomplish results. The achievement was the all-important thing; the position, whether titularly high or low, was of consequence only in so far as it widened the chance for achievement. After the session closed four of us who looked at politics from the same standpoint and were known as Independent or Anti-Machine Republicans were sent by the State Convention as delegates-at-large to the Republican National Convention of 1884, where I advocated, as vigorously as I knew how, the nomination of Senator George F. Edmunds. Mr. Edmunds was defeated and Mr. Blaine nominated. Mr. Blaine was clearly the choice of the rank and file of the party; his nomination was won in fair and aboveboard fashion, because the rank and file of the party stood back of him; and I supported him to the best of my ability in the ensuing campaign.

The Speakership contest enlightened me as regards more things than the attitude of the bosses. I had already had some exasperating experiences with the "silk stocking" reformer type, as Abraham Lincoln called it, the gentlemen who were very nice, very refined, who shook their heads over political corruption and discussed it in drawing-rooms and parlors, but who were wholly unable to grapple with real men in real life. They were apt vociferously to demand "reform" as if it were some concrete substance, like cake, which could be handed out at will, in tangible masses, if only the demand were urgent enough. These parlor reformers made up for inefficiency in action by zeal in criticising; and they delighted in criticising the men who really were doing the things which they said ought to be done, but which they lacked the sinewy power to do. They often upheld ideals which were not merely impossible but highly undesirable, and thereby played into the hands of the very politicians to whom they professed to be most hostile. Moreover, if they believed that their own interests, individually or as a class, were jeoparded, they were apt to show no higher standards than did the men they usually denounced.

One of their shibboleths was that the office should seek the man and not the man the office. This is entirely true of certain offices at certain times. It is entirely untrue when the circumstances are different. It would have been unnecessary and undesirable for Washington to have sought the Presidency. But if Abraham Lincoln had not sought the Presidency he never would have been nominated. The objection in such a case as this lies not to seeking the office, but to seeking it in any but an honorable and proper manner. The effect of the shibboleth in question is usually merely to put a premium on hypocrisy, and therefore to favor the creature who is willing to rise by hypocrisy. When I ran for Speaker, the whole body of machine politicians was against me, and my only chance lay in arousing the people in the different districts. To do this I had to visit the districts, put the case fairly before the men whom I saw, and make them understand that I was really making a fight and would stay in the fight to the end. Yet there were reformers who shook their heads and deplored my "activity" in the canvass. Of course the one thing which corrupt machine politicians most desire is to have decent men frown on the activity, that is, on the efficiency, of the honest man who genuinely wishes to reform politics.

If efficiency is left solely to bad men, and if virtue is confined solely to inefficient men, the result cannot be happy. When I entered politics there were, as there always had been — and as there always will be — any number of bad men in politics who were thoroughly efficient, and any number of good men who would like to have done lofty things in politics but who were thoroughly inefficient. If I wished to accomplish anything for the country, my business was to combine decency and efficiency; to be a thoroughly practical man of high ideals who did his best to reduce those ideals to actual practice. This was my ideal, and to the best of my ability I strove to live up to it.

To a young man, life in the New York Legislature was always interesting and often entertaining. There was always a struggle of some kind on hand. Sometimes it was on a naked question of right and wrong. Sometimes it was on a question of real constructive statesmanship. Moreover, there were all kinds of humorous incidents, the humor being usually of the unconscious kind. In one session of the Legislature the New York City Democratic representatives were split into two camps, and there were two rivals for leadership. One of these was a thoroughly good-hearted, happy-go-lucky person who was afterwards for several

H

years in Congress. He had been a local magistrate and was called Judge. Generally he and I were friendly, but occasionally I did something that irritated him. He was always willing to vote for any other member's bill himself, and he regarded it as narrow-minded for any one to oppose one of his bills, especially if the opposition was upon the ground that it was unconstitutional — for his views of the Constitution were so excessively liberal as to make even me feel as if I belonged to the straitest sect of strict constructionists. On one occasion he had a bill to appropriate money, with obvious impropriety, for the relief of some miscreant whom he styled "one of the honest yeomanry of the State." When I explained to him that it was clearly unconstitutional, he answered, "Me friend, the Constitution don't touch little things like that," and then added, with an ingratiating smile, "Anyhow, I'd never allow the Constitution to come between friends." At the time I was looking over the proofs of Mr. Bryce's "American Commonwealth," and I told him the incident. He put it into the first edition of the "Commonwealth"; whether it is in the last edition or not, I cannot say.

On another occasion the same gentleman came to an issue with me in a debate, and wound up his speech by explaining that I occupied what "lawyers would call a quasi position on the bill." His rival was a man of totally different type, a man of great natural dignity, also born in Ireland. He had served with gallantry in the Civil War. After the close of the war he organized an expedition to conquer Canada. The expedition, however, got so drunk before reaching Albany that it was there incarcerated in jail, whereupon its leader abandoned it and went into New York politics instead. He was a man of influence, and later occupied in the Police Department the same position as Commissioner which I myself at one time occupied. He felt that his rival had gained too much glory at my expense, and, walking over with ceremonious solemnity to where the said rival was sitting close beside me, he said to him : "I would like you to know, Mr. Cameron [Cameron, of course, was not the real name], that Mr. Roosevelt knows more law in a wake than

you do in a month; and, more than that, Michael Cameron,
what do you mane by quoting Latin on the floor of this
House when you don't know the alpha and omayga of the
language?"

There was in the Legislature, during the deadlock above
mentioned, a man whom I will call Brogan. He looked like
a serious elderly frog. I never heard him speak more than
once. It was before the Legislature was organized, or had
adopted any rules; and each day the only business was
for the clerk to call the roll. One day Brogan suddenly
rose, and the following dialogue occurred:

Brogan. Misther Clu-r-r-k!

The Clerk. The gentleman from New York.

Brogan. I rise to a point of ordher under the rules!

The Clerk. There are no rules.

Brogan. Thin I object to them!

The Clerk. There are no rules to object to.

Brogan. Oh! [nonplussed; but immediately recovering
himself]. Thin I move that they be amended until there
ar-r-re!

The deadlock was tedious; and we hailed with joy such
enlivening incidents as the above.

During my three years' service in the Legislature I worked
on a very simple philosophy of government. It was that
personal character and initiative are the prime requisites in
political and social life. It was not only a good but an
absolutely indispensable theory as far as it went; but
it was defective in that it did not sufficiently allow
for the need of collective action. I shall never forget
the men with whom I worked hand in hand in these
legislative struggles, not only my fellow-legislators, but
some of the newspaper reporters, such as Spinney and
Cunningham; and then in addition the men in the various
districts who helped us. We had made up our minds that
we must not fight fire with fire, that on the contrary the
way to win out was to equal our foes in practical efficiency
and yet to stand at the opposite plane from them in applied
morality.

It was not always easy to keep the just middle, especially

when it happened that on one side there were corrupt and unscrupulous demagogues, and on the other side corrupt and unscrupulous reactionaries. Our effort was to hold the scales even between both. We tried to stand with the cause of righteousness even though its advocates were anything but righteous. We endeavored to cut out the abuses of property, even though good men of property were misled into upholding those abuses. We refused to be frightened into sanctioning improper assaults upon property, although we knew that the champions of property themselves did things that were wicked and corrupt. We were as yet by no means as thoroughly awake as we ought to have been to the need of controlling big business and to the damage done by the combination of politics with big business. In this matter I was not behind the rest of my friends; indeed, I was ahead of them, for no serious leader in political life then appreciated the prime need of grappling with these questions. One partial reason — not an excuse or a justification, but a partial reason — for my slowness in grasping the importance of action in these matters was the corrupt and unattractive nature of so many of the men who championed popular reforms, their insincerity, and the folly of so many of the actions which they advocated. Even at that date I had neither sympathy with nor admiration for the man who was merely a money king, and I did not regard the "money touch," when divorced from other qualities, as entitling a man to either respect or consideration. As recited above, we did on more than one occasion fight battles, in which we neither took nor gave quarter, against the most prominent and powerful financiers and financial interests of the day. But most of the fights in which we were engaged were for pure honesty and decency, and they were more apt to be against that form of corruption which found its expression in demagogy than against that form of corruption which defended or advocated privilege. Fundamentally, our fight was part of the eternal war against the Powers that Prey; and we cared not a whit in what rank of life these powers were found.

To play the demagogue for purposes of self-interest is a

cardinal sin against the people in a democracy, exactly as to play the courtier for such purposes is a cardinal sin against the people under other forms of government. A man who stays long in our American political life, if he has in his soul the generous desire to do effective service for great causes, inevitably grows to regard himself merely as one of many instruments, all of which it may be necessary to use, one at one time, one at another, in achieving the triumph of those causes; and whenever the usefulness of any one has been exhausted, it is to be thrown aside. If such a man is wise, he will gladly do the thing that is next, when the time and the need come together, without asking what the future holds for him. Let the half-god play his part well and manfully, and then be content to draw aside when the god appears. Nor should he feel vain regrets that to another it is given to render greater services and reap a greater reward. Let it be enough for him that he too has served, and that by doing well he has prepared the way for the other man who can do better.

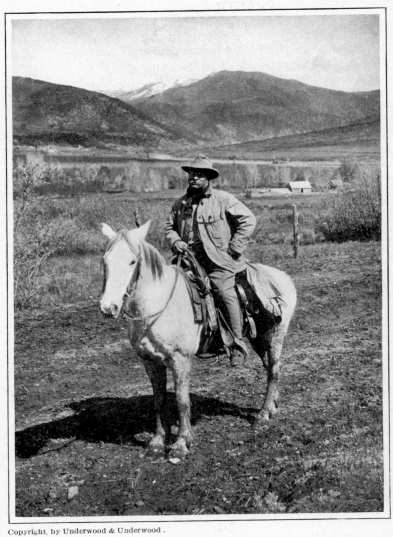

PRESIDENT ROOSEVELT RETURNING FROM THE BEAR HUNT, NEWCASTLE, COLORADO, IN 1905.

CHAPTER IV

IN COWBOY LAND

THOUGH I had previously made a trip into the then Territory of Dakota, beyond the Red River, it was not until 1883 that I went to the Little Missouri, and there took hold of two cattle ranches, the Chimney Butte and the Elkhorn.

It was still the Wild West in those days, the Far West, the West of Owen Wister's stories and Frederic Remington's drawings, the West of the Indian and the buffalo-hunter, the soldier and the cow-puncher. That land of the West has gone now, "gone, gone with lost Atlantis," gone to the isle of ghosts and of strange dead memories. It was a land of vast silent spaces, of lonely rivers, and of plains where the wild game stared at the passing horseman. It was a land of scattered ranches, of herds of long-horned cattle, and of reckless riders who unmoved looked in the eyes of life or of death. In that land we led a free and hardy life, with horse and with rifle. We worked under the scorching midsummer sun, when the wide plains shimmered and wavered in the heat; and we knew the freezing misery of riding night guard round the cattle in the late fall round-up. In the soft springtime the stars were glorious in our eyes each night before we fell asleep; and in the winter we rode through blinding blizzards, when the driven snow-dust burnt our faces. There were monotonous days, as we guided the trail cattle or the beef herds, hour after hour, at the slowest of walks; and minutes or hours teeming with excitement as we stopped stampedes or swam the herds across rivers treacherous with quicksands or brimmed with running ice. We knew toil and hardship and hunger and thirst; and we

103

saw men die violent deaths as they worked among the horses and cattle, or fought in evil feuds with one another; but we felt the beat of hardy life in our veins, and ours was the glory of work and the joy of living.

It was right and necessary that this life should pass, for the safety of our country lies in its being made the country of the small home-maker. The great unfenced ranches, in the days of "free grass," necessarily represented a temporary stage in our history. The large migratory flocks of sheep, each guarded by the hired shepherds of absentee owners, were the first enemies of the cattlemen; and owing to the way they ate out the grass and destroyed all other vegetation, these roving sheep bands represented little of permanent good to the country. But the homesteaders, the permanent settlers, the men who took up each his own farm on which he lived and brought up his family, these represented from the National standpoint the most desirable of all possible users of, and dwellers on, the soil. Their advent meant the breaking up of the big ranches; and the change was a National gain, although to some of us an individual loss.

I first reached the Little Missouri on a Northern Pacific train about three in the morning of a cool September day in 1883. Aside from the station, the only building was a ramshackle structure called the Pyramid Park Hotel. I dragged my duffle-bag thither, and hammered at the door until the frowsy proprietor appeared, muttering oaths. He ushered me upstairs, where I was given one of the fourteen beds in the room which by itself constituted the entire upper floor. Next day I walked over to the abandoned army post, and, after some hours among the gray log shacks, a ranchman who had driven into the station agreed to take me out to his ranch, the Chimney Butte ranch, where he was living with his brother and their partner.

The ranch was a log structure with a dirt roof, a corral for the horses near by, and a chicken-house jabbed against the rear of the ranch house. Inside there was only one room, with a table, three or four chairs, a cooking-stove, and three bunks. The owners were Sylvane and Joe Ferris and

A REUNION.

"Twenty-nine years later my four friends of that night (of bobcats and old sledge) were delegates to the First Progressive National Convention at Chicago." — Mr. Roosevelt, seated. From left to right, J. A. Ferris, S. M. Ferris, W. J. Merrifield, G. W. Meyer.

William J. Merrifield. Later all three of them held my commissions while I was President. Merrifield was Marshal of Montana, and as Presidential elector cast the vote of that State for me in 1904; Sylvane Ferris was Land Officer in North Dakota, and Joe Ferris Postmaster at Medora. There was a fourth man, George Meyer, who also worked for me later. That evening we all played old sledge round the table, and at one period the game was interrupted by a frightful squawking outside which told us that a bobcat had made a raid on the chicken-house.

After a buffalo hunt with my original friend, Joe Ferris, I entered into partnership with Merrifield and Sylvane Ferris, and we started a cow ranch, with the maltese cross brand — always known as "maltee cross," by the way, as the general impression along the Little Missouri was that "maltese" must be a plural. Twenty-nine years later my four friends of that night were delegates to the First Progressive National Convention at Chicago. They were among my most constant companions for the few years next succeeding the evening when the bobcat interrupted the game of old sledge. I lived and worked with them on the ranch, and with them and many others like them on the round-up; and I brought out from Maine, in order to start the Elkhorn ranch lower down the river, my two backwoods friends Sewall and Dow. My brands for the lower ranch were the elkhorn and triangle.

I do not believe there ever was any life more attractive to a vigorous young fellow than life on a cattle ranch in those days. It was a fine, healthy life, too; it taught a man self-reliance, hardihood, and the value of instant decision — in short, the virtues that ought to come from life in the open country. I enjoyed the life to the full. After the first year I built on the Elkhorn ranch a long, low ranch house of hewn logs, with a veranda, and with, in addition to the other rooms, a bedroom for myself, and a sitting-room with a big fire-place. I got out a rocking-chair — I am very fond of rocking-chairs — and enough books to fill two or three shelves, and a rubber bathtub so that I could get a bath. And then I do not see how any one could have lived more comfortably. We had buffalo robes and bearskins of our own killing. We always kept the house clean — using the word in a rather large sense. There were at least two rooms that were always warm, even in the bitterest weather; and we had plenty to eat. Commonly the mainstay of every meal was game of our own killing, usually antelope or deer, sometimes grouse or ducks, and occasionally, in the earlier days, buffalo or elk. We also had flour and bacon, sugar, salt, and canned tomatoes. And later, when some of the men married and brought out their wives, we had all kinds of good things, such as jams and jellies made from the wild plums and the buffalo berries, and potatoes from the forlorn little garden patch. Moreover, we had milk. Most ranchmen at that time never had milk. I knew more than one ranch with ten thousand head of cattle where there was not a cow that could be milked. We made up our minds that we would be more enterprising. Accordingly, we started to domesticate some of the cows. Our first effort was not successful, chiefly because we did not devote the needed time and patience to the matter. And we found that to race a cow two miles at full speed on horseback, then rope her, throw her, and turn her upside down to milk her, while exhilarating as a pastime, was not productive of re-sults. Gradually we accumulated tame cows, and, after we had thinned out the bobcats and coyotes, more chickens.

The ranch house stood on the brink of a low bluff over-looking the broad, shallow bed of the Little Missouri, through which at most seasons there ran only a trickle of water, while in times of freshet it was filled brimful with the boiling, foaming, muddy torrent. There was no neighbor for ten or fifteen miles on either side of me. The river twisted down in long curves between narrow bottoms bordered by sheer cliff walls, for the Bad Lands, a chaos of peaks, plateaus, and ridges, rose abruptly from the edges of the level, tree-clad, or grassy, alluvial meadows. In front of the ranch-house veranda was a row of cottonwood trees with gray-green leaves which quivered all day long if there was a breath of air. From these trees came the far-away, melancholy cooing of mourning doves, and little owls perched in them and called tremulously at night. In the long summer afternoons we would sometimes sit on the piazza, when there was no work to be done, for an hour or two at a time, watching the cattle on the sand-bars, and the sharply channeled and strangely carved amphitheater of cliffs across the bottom opposite; while the vultures wheeled overhead, their black shadows gliding across the glaring white of the dry river-bed. Sometimes from the ranch we saw deer, and once when we needed meat I shot one across the river as I stood on the piazza. In the winter, in the days of iron cold, when everything was white under the snow, the river lay in its bed fixed and immovable as a bar of bent steel, and then at night wolves and lynxes traveled up and down it as if it had been a highway passing in front of the ranch house. Often in the late fall or early winter, after a hard day's hunting, or when returning from one of the winter line camps, we did not reach the ranch until hours after sunset; and after the weary tramping in the cold it was keen pleasure to catch the first red gleam of the fire-lit windows across the snowy wastes.

The Elkhorn ranch house was built mainly by Sewall and Dow, who, like most men from the Maine woods, were mighty with the ax. I could chop fairly well for an amateur, but I could not do one-third the work they could. One day when we were cutting down the cottonwood trees, to begin our building operations, I heard some one ask Dow what the total cut had been, and Dow, not realizing that I was within hearing, answered: "Well, Bill cut down fifty-three, I cut forty-nine, and the boss he beavered down seventeen." Those who have seen the stump of a tree which has been gnawed down by a beaver will understand the exact force of the comparison.

In those days on a cow ranch the men were apt to be away on the various round-ups at least half the time. It was interesting and exciting work, and except for the lack of sleep on the spring and summer round-ups it was not exhausting work; compared to lumbering or mining or blacksmithing, to sit in the saddle is an easy form of labor. The ponies were of course grass-fed and unshod. Each man had his own string of nine or ten. One pony would be used for the morning work, one for the afternoon, and neither would again be used for the next three days. A separate pony was kept for night riding.

The spring and early summer round-ups were especially for the branding of calves. There was much hard work and some risk on a round-up, but also much fun. The meeting-place was appointed weeks beforehand, and all the ranchmen of the territory to be covered by the round-up sent their representatives. There were no fences in the West that I knew, and their place was taken by the cowboy and the branding-iron. The cattle wandered free. Each calf was branded with the brand of the cow it was following. Sometimes in winter there was what we called line riding; that is, camps were established and the line riders traveled a definite beat across the desolate wastes of snow, to and fro from one camp to another, to prevent the cattle from drifting. But as a rule nothing was done to keep the cattle in any one place. In the spring there was a general round-up in each locality. Each outfit took part in its own round-up, and all the outfits of a given region combined to send representatives to the two or three round-ups that covered the neighborhoods near by into which their cattle might drift. For example, our Little Missouri round-up generally worked down the river from a distance of some fifty or sixty miles above my ranch towards the Kildeer Mountains, about the same distance below. In addition we would usually send representatives to the Yellowstone round-up, and to the round-up along the upper Little Missouri; and, moreover, if we heard that cattle had drifted, perhaps toward the Indian reservation southeast of us, we would send a wagon and rider after them.

At the meeting-point, which might be in the valley of a half-dry stream, or in some broad bottom of the river itself, or perchance by a couple of ponds under some queerly shaped butte that was a landmark for the region round about, we would all gather on the appointed day. The chuck-wagons, containing the bedding and food, each drawn by four horses and driven by the teamster cook, would come jolting and rattling over the uneven sward. Accompanying each wagon were eight or ten riders, the cow-punchers, while their horses, a band of a hundred or so, were driven by the two herders, one of whom was known as the day wrangler and one as the night wrangler. The men were lean, sinewy fellows, accustomed to riding half-broken horses at any speed over any country by day or by night. They wore flannel shirts, with loose handkerchiefs knotted round their necks, broad hats, high-heeled boots with jingling spurs, and sometimes leather shaps, although often they merely had their trousers tucked into the tops of their high boots. There was a good deal of rough horse-play, and, as with any other gathering of men or boys of high animal spirits, the horse-play sometimes became very rough indeed; and as the men usually carried revolvers, and as there were occasionally one or two noted gun-fighters among them, there was now and then a shooting affray. A man who was a coward or who shirked his work had a bad time, of course; a man could not afford to let himself be bullied or treated as a butt; and, on the other hand, if he was "looking for a fight," he was certain to find it. But my own experience was that if a man did not talk until his associates knew him well and liked him, and if he did his work, he never had any difficulty in getting on. In my own round-up district I speedily grew to be friends with most of the men. When I went among strangers I always had to spend twenty-four hours in living down the fact that I wore spectacles, remaining as long as I could judiciously deaf to any side remarks about "four eyes," unless it became evident that my being quiet was misconstrued and that it was better to bring matters to a head at once.

If, for instance, I was sent off to represent the Little Missouri brands on some neighboring round-up, such as the Yellowstone, I usually showed that kind of diplomacy which consists in not uttering one word that can be avoided. I would probably have a couple of days' solitary ride, mounted on one horse and driving eight or ten others before me, one of them carrying my bedding. Loose horses drive best at a trot, or canter, and if a man is traveling alone in this fashion it is a good thing to have them reach the

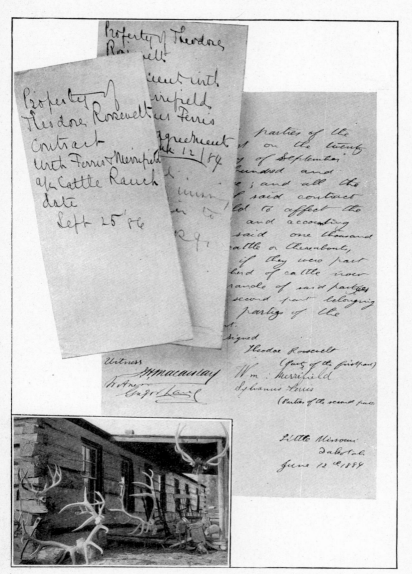

THE ELKHORN RANCH HOUSE AND THE DEEDS OF PURCHASE.

camp ground sufficiently late to make them desire to feed and sleep where they are until morning. In consequence I never spent more than two days on the journey from whatever the point was at which I left the Little Missouri, sleeping the one night for as limited a number of hours as possible.

As soon as I reached the meeting-place I would find out the wagon to which I was assigned. Riding to it, I turned my horses into the saddle-band and reported to the wagon boss, or, in his absence, to the cook — always a privileged character, who was allowed and expected to order men around. He would usually grumble savagely and profanely about my having been put with his wagon, but this was merely conventional on his part; and if I sat down and said nothing he would probably soon ask me if I wanted anything to eat, to which the correct answer was that I was not hungry and would wait until meal-time. The bedding rolls of the riders would be strewn round the grass, and I would put mine down a little outside the ring, where I would not be in any one's way, with my six or eight branding-irons beside it. The men would ride in, laughing and talking with one another, and perhaps nodding to me. One of their number, usually the wagon foreman, might put some question to me as to what brands I represented, but no other word would be addressed to me, nor would I be expected to volunteer any conversation. Supper would consist of bacon, Dutch oven bread, and possibly beef; once I won the good graces of my companions at the outset by appearing with two antelope which I had shot. After supper I would roll up in my bedding as soon as possible, and the others would follow suit at their pleasure.

At three in the morning or thereabouts, at a yell from the cook, all hands would turn hurriedly out. Dressing was a simple affair. Then each man rolled and corded his bedding — if he did not, the cook would leave it behind and he would go without any for the rest of the trip — and came to the fire, where he picked out a tin cup, tin plate, and knife and fork, helped himself to coffee and to whatever food there was, and ate it standing or squatting as best suited him. Dawn was probably breaking by this time, and the trampling of

unshod hoofs showed that the night wrangler was bringing
in the pony herd. Two of the men would then run ropes
from the wagon at right angles to one another, and into this
as a corral the horses would be driven. Each man might
rope one of his own horses, or more often point it out to the
most skillful roper of the outfit, who would rope it for him
— for if the man was an unskillful roper and roped the
wrong horse or roped the horse in the wrong place there was
a chance of the whole herd stampeding. Each man then
saddled and bridled his horse. This was usually followed
by some resolute bucking on the part of two or three of the
horses, especially in the early days of each round-up. The
bucking was always a source of amusement to all the men
whose horses did not buck, and these fortunate ones would
gather round giving ironical advice, and especially adjuring
the rider not to "go to leather" — that is, not to steady
himself in the saddle by catching hold of the saddle-horn.

As soon as the men had mounted, the whole outfit started
on the long circle, the morning circle. Usually the ranch
foreman who bossed a given wagon was put in charge of the
men of one group by the round-up foreman ; he might keep
his men together until they had gone some ten or fifteen
miles from camp, and then drop them in couples at different
points. Each couple made its way toward the wagon,
gathering all the cattle it could find. The morning's ride
might last six or eight hours, and it was still longer before
some of the men got in. Singly and in twos and threes they
appeared from every quarter of the horizon, the dust rising
from the hoofs of the steers and bulls, the cows and calves,
they had collected. Two or three of the men were left to
take care of the herd while the others changed horses, ate a
hasty dinner, and then came out to the afternoon work.
This consisted of each man in succession being sent into the
herd, usually with a companion, to cut out the cows of his
brand or brands which were followed by unbranded calves,
and also to cut out any mavericks or unbranded yearlings.
We worked each animal gently out to the edge of the herd,
and then with a sudden dash took it off at a run. It was
always desperately anxious to break back and rejoin the

I

herd.   There was much breakneck galloping and twisting
and turning before its desire was thwarted and it was driven
to join the rest of the cut — that is, the other animals which
had been cut out, and which were being held by one or two
other men.   Cattle hate being alone, and it was no easy
matter to hold the first one or two that were cut out; but

THE COW-PUNCHERS.

"The men were lean, sinewy fellows, accustomed to riding half-broken horses, at any
speed, over any country, by day or by night."

soon they got a little herd of their own, and then they were
contented.   When the cutting out had all been done, the
calves were branded, and all misadventures of the "calf
wrestlers," the men who seized, threw, and held each calf
when roped by the mounted roper, were hailed with yelling
laughter.   Then the animals which for one reason or another it was desired to drive along with the round-up were
put into one herd and left in charge of a couple of night

guards, and the rest of us would loaf back to the wagon for supper and bed.

By this time I would have been accepted as one of the rest of the outfit, and all strangeness would have passed off, the attitude of my fellow cow-punchers being one of friendly forgiveness even toward my spectacles. Night guards for the cattle herd were then assigned by the captain of the wagon, or perhaps by the round-up foreman, according to the needs of the case, the guards standing for two hours at a time from eight in the evening till four in the morning. The first and last watches were preferable, because sleep was not broken as in both of the other two. If things went well, the cattle would soon bed down and nothing further would occur until morning, when there was a repetition of the work, the wagon moving each day eight or ten miles to some appointed camping-place.

Each man would picket his night horse near the wagon, usually choosing the quietest animal in his string for that purpose, because to saddle and mount a "mean" horse at night is not pleasant. When utterly tired, it was hard to have to get up for one's trick at night herd. Nevertheless, on ordinary nights the two hours round the cattle in the still darkness were pleasant. The loneliness, under the vast empty sky, and the silence, in which the breathing of the cattle sounded loud, and the alert readiness to meet any emergency which might suddenly arise out of the formless night, all combined to give one a sense of subdued interest. Then, one soon got to know the cattle of marked individuality, the ones that led the others into mischief; and one also grew to recognize the traits they all possessed in common, and the impulses which, for instance, made a whole herd get up towards midnight, each beast turning round and then lying down again. But by the end of the watch each rider had studied the cattle until it grew monotonous, and heartily welcomed his relief guard. A newcomer, of course, had any amount to learn, and sometimes the simplest things were those which brought him to grief.

One night early in my career I failed satisfactorily to identify the direction in which I was to go in order to reach the night herd.   It was a pitch-dark night.   I managed to get started wrong, and I never found either the herd or the wagon again until sunrise, when I was greeted with withering scorn by the injured cow-puncher, who had been obliged to stand double guard because I failed to relieve him.

There were other misadventures that I met with where the excuse was greater. The punchers on night guard usually rode round the cattle in reverse directions; calling and singing to them if the beasts seemed restless, to keep them quiet.   On rare occasions something happened that made the cattle stampede, and then the duty of the riders was to keep with them as long as possible and try gradually to get control of them.

One night there was a heavy storm, and all of us who were at the wagons were obliged to turn out hastily to help the night herders. After a while there was a terrific peal of thunder, the lightning struck right by the herd, and away all the beasts went, heads and horns and tails in the air.   For a minute or two I could make out nothing except the dark forms of the beasts running on every side of me, and I should have been very sorry if my horse had stumbled, for those behind would have trodden me down.   Then the herd split, part going to one side, while the other part seemingly kept straight ahead, and I galloped as hard as ever beside them. I was trying to reach the point — the leading animals — in order to turn them, when suddenly there was a tremendous splashing in front.   I could dimly make out that the cattle immediately ahead and to one side of me were disappearing, and the next moment the horse and I went off a cut bank into the Little Missouri.   I bent away back in the saddle, and though the horse almost went down he just recovered himself, and, plunging and struggling through water and quicksand, we made the other side.   Here I discovered that there was another cowboy with the same part of the herd that I was with; but almost immediately we separated.   I galloped hard through a bottom covered with big cottonwood trees, and stopped the part of the herd that I was with, but very soon they broke on me again, and repeated this twice. Finally toward morning the few I had left came to a halt.

It had been raining hard for some time. I got off my horse and leaned against a tree, but before long the infernal cattle started on again, and I had to ride after them. Dawn came soon after this, and I was able to make out where I was and head the cattle back, collecting other little bunches as I went. After a while I came on a cowboy on foot carrying his saddle on his head. He was my companion of the previous night. His horse had gone full speed into a tree and killed itself, the man, however, not being hurt. I could not help him, as I had all I could do to handle the cattle. When I got them to the wagon, most of the other men had already come in and the riders were just starting on the long circle. One of the men changed my horse for me while I ate a hasty breakfast, and then we were off for the day's work.

As only about half of the night herd had been brought back, the circle riding was particularly heavy, and it was ten hours before we were back at the wagon. We then changed horses again and worked the whole herd until after sunset, finishing just as it grew too dark to do anything more. By this time I had been nearly forty hours in the saddle, changing horses five times, and my clothes had thoroughly dried on me, and I fell asleep as soon as I touched the bedding. Fortunately some men who had gotten in late in the morning had had their sleep during the daytime, so that the rest of us escaped night guard and were not called until four next morning. Nobody ever gets enough sleep on a round-up.

The above was the longest number of consecutive hours I ever had to be in the saddle. But, as I have said, I changed horses five times, and it is a great lightening of labor for a rider to have a fresh horse. Once when with Sylvane Ferris I spent about sixteen hours on one horse, riding seventy or eighty miles. The round-up had reached a place called the ox-bow of the Little Missouri, and we had to ride there, do some work around the cattle, and ride back.

Another time I was twenty-four hours on horseback in company with Merrifield without changing horses. On this occasion we did not travel fast. We had been coming back with the wagon from a hunting trip in the Big Horn Mountains. The team was fagged out, and we were tired of walking at a snail's pace beside it. When we reached country that the driver thoroughly knew, we thought it safe to leave him, and we loped in one night across a distance which it took the wagon the three following days to cover. It was a beautiful moonlight night, and the ride was delightful. All day long we had plodded at a walk, weary and hot. At supper time we had rested two or three hours, and the tough little riding horses seemed as fresh as ever. It was in September. As we rode out of the circle of the firelight, the air was cool in our faces. Under the bright moonlight, and then under the starlight, we loped and cantered mile after mile over the high prairie. We passed bands of antelope and herds of long-horn Texas cattle, and at last, just as the first red beams of the sun flamed over the bluffs in front of us, we rode down into the valley of the Little Missouri, where our ranch house stood.

I never became a good roper, nor more than an average rider, according to ranch standards. Of course a man on a ranch has to ride a good many bad horses, and is bound to encounter a certain number of accidents, and of these I had my share, at one time cracking a rib, and on another occasion the point of my shoulder. We were hundreds of miles from a doctor, and each time, as I was on the round-up, I had to get through my work for the next few weeks as best I could, until the injury healed of itself. When I had the opportunity I broke my own horses, doing it gently and gradually and spending much time over it, and choosing the horses that seemed gentle to begin with. With these horses I never had any difficulty. But frequently there was neither time nor opportunity to handle our mounts so elaborately. We might get a band of horses, each having been bridled and saddled two or three times, but none of them having been broken beyond the extent implied in this bridling and saddling. Then each of us in succession would choose a horse (for his string), I as owner of the ranch being given the first choice on each round, so to speak. The first time I was ever on a round-up Sylvane Ferris, Merrifield, Meyer, and I each chose his string in this fashion. Three or four of the animals I got were not easy to ride. The effort both to ride them and to look as if I enjoyed doing so, on some cool morning when my grinning cowboy friends had gathered round "to see whether the high-headed bay could buck the boss off," doubtless was of benefit to me, but lacked much of being enjoyable. The time I smashed my rib I was bucked off on a stone. The time I hurt the point of my shoulder I was riding a big, sulky horse named Ben Butler, which went over backwards with me. When we got up it still refused to go anywhere; so, while I sat it, Sylvane Ferris and George Meyer got their ropes on its neck and dragged it a few hundred yards, choking but stubborn, all four feet firmly planted and plowing the ground. When they released the ropes it lay down and wouldn't get up. The round-up had started; so Sylvane gave me his horse, Baldy, which sometimes bucked but never went over backwards, and he got on the now rearisen Ben Butler. To my discomfiture Ben started quietly beside us, while Sylvane remarked, "Why, there's nothing the matter with this horse; he's a plumb gentle horse." Then Ben fell slightly behind and I heard Sylvane again, "That's all right! Come along! Here, you! Go on, you! Hi, hi, fellows, help me out! he's lying on me!" Sure enough, he was; and when we dragged Sylvane from under him the first thing the rescued Sylvane did was to execute a war-dance, spurs and all, on the iniquitous Ben. We could do nothing with him that day; subsequently we got him so that we could ride him; but he never became a nice saddle-horse.

As with all other forms of work, so on the round-up, a man of ordinary power, who nevertheless does not shirk things merely because they are disagreeable or irksome, soon earns his place. There were crack riders and ropers who, just because they felt such overweening pride in their own prowess, were not really very valuable men. Continually on the circles a cow or a calf would get into some thick patch of bulberry bush and refuse to come out; or when it was getting late we would pass some bad lands that would probably not contain cattle, but might; or a steer would turn fighting mad, or a calf grow tired and want to lie down. If in such a case the man steadily persists in doing the unattractive thing, and after two hours of exasperation and harassment does finally get the cow out, and keep her out, of the bulberry bushes, and drives her to the wagon, or finds some animals that have been passed by in the fourth or fifth patch of bad lands he hunts through, or gets the calf up on his saddle and takes it in anyhow, the foreman soon grows to treat him as having his uses and as being an asset of worth in the round-up, even though neither a fancy roper nor a fancy rider.

When at the Progressive Convention last August, I met George Meyer for the first time in many years, and he recalled to me an incident on one round-up where we happened to be thrown together while driving some cows and calves to camp. When the camp was only just across the river, two of the calves positively refused to go any further. He took one of them in his arms, and after some hazardous maneuvering managed to get on his horse, in spite of the objections of the latter, and rode into the river. My calf was too big for such treatment, so in despair I roped it, intending to drag it over. However, as soon as I roped it, the calf started bouncing and bleating, and, owing to some lack of dexterity on my part, suddenly swung round the rear of the horse, bringing the rope under his tail. Down went the tail tight, and the horse "went into figures," as the cow-puncher phrase of that day was. There was a cut bank about four feet high on the hither side of the river, and over this the horse bucked. We went into the water with a splash. With a "pluck" the calf followed, described a parabola in the air, and landed beside us. Fortunately, this took the rope out from under the horse's tail, but left him thoroughly frightened. He could not do much bucking in the stream, for there were one or two places where we had to swim, and the shallows were either sandy or muddy; but across we went, at speed, and the calf made a wake like Pharaoh's army in the Red Sea.

On several occasions we had to fight fire. In the geography books of my youth prairie fires were always portrayed as taking place in long grass, and all living things ran before them. On the Northern cattle plains the grass was never long enough to be a source of danger to man or beast. The fires were nothing like the forest fires in the Northern woods. But they destroyed large quantities of

On the Long Circle.

feed, and we had to stop them where possible. The process we usually followed was to kill a steer, split it in two lengthwise, and then have two riders drag each half-steer, the rope of one running from his saddle-horn to the front leg, and that of the other to the hind leg. One of the men would spur this horse over or through the line of fire, and the two would then ride forward, dragging the steer bloody side downward along the line of flame, men following on foot with slickers or wet horse-blankets to beat out any flickering blaze that was still left. It was exciting work, for the fire and the twitching and plucking of the ox carcass over the uneven ground maddened the fierce little horses so that it was necessary to do some riding in order to keep them to their work. After a while it also became very exhausting, the thirst and fatigue being great, as, with parched lips and blackened from head to foot, we toiled at our task.

In those years the Stockman's Association of Montana was a powerful body. I was the delegate to it from the Little Missouri. The meetings that I attended were held in Miles City, at that time a typical cow town. Stockmen of all kinds attended, including the biggest men in the stock business, men like old Conrad Kohrs, who was and is the finest type of pioneer in all the Rocky Mountain country; and Granville Stewart, who was afterwards appointed Minister by Cleveland, I think to the Argentine; and "Hashknife" Simpson, a Texan who had brought his cattle, the Hashknife brand, up the trail into our country. He and I grew to be great friends. I can see him now the first time we met, grinning at me as, none too comfortable, I sat a half-broken horse at the edge of a cattle herd we were working. His son Sloan Simpson went to Harvard, was one of the first-class men in my regiment, and afterwards held my commission as Postmaster at Dallas.

At the stockmen's meeting in Miles City, in addition to the big stockmen, there were always hundreds of cowboys galloping up and down the wide dusty streets at every hour of the day and night. It was a picturesque sight during the three days the meetings lasted. There was always at least one big dance at the hotel. There were few dress suits, but there was perfect decorum at the dance, and in the square dances most of the men knew the figures far better than I did. With such a crowd in town, sleeping accommodations of any sort were at a premium, and in the hotel there were two men in every bed. On one occasion I had a roommate whom I never saw, because he always went to bed much later than I did and I always got up much earlier than he did. On the last day, however, he rose at the same time and I saw that he was a man I knew named Carter, and nicknamed "Modesty" Carter. He was a stalwart, good-looking fellow, and I was sorry when later I heard that he had been killed in a shooting row.

When I went West, the last great Indian wars had just come to an end, but there were still sporadic outbreaks here and there, and occasionally bands of marauding young braves were a menace to outlying and lonely settlements. Many of the white men were themselves lawless and brutal, and prone to commit outrages on the Indians. Unfortunately, each race tended to hold all the members of the other race responsible for the misdeeds of a few, so that the crime of the miscreant, red or white, who committed the original outrage too often invited retaliation upon entirely innocent people, and this action would in its turn arouse bitter feeling which found vent in still more indiscriminate retaliation. The first year I was on the Little Missouri some Sioux bucks ran off all the horses of a buffalo-hunter's outfit. One of the buffalo-hunters tried to get even by stealing the horses of a Cheyenne hunting party, and when pursued made for a cow camp, with, as a result, a long-range skirmish between the cowboys and the Cheyennes. One of the latter was wounded; but this particular wounded man seemed to have more sense than the other participants in the chain of wrong-doing, and discriminated among the whites. He came into our camp and had his wound dressed.

A year later I was at a desolate little mud road ranch on the Deadwood trail. It was kept by a very capable and very forceful woman, with sound ideas of justice and abundantly well able to hold her own. Her husband was a worthless devil, who finally got drunk on some whisky he obtained from an outfit of Missouri bull-whackers — that is, freighters, driving ox wagons. Under the stimulus of the whisky he picked a quarrel with his wife and attempted to beat her. She knocked him down with a stove-lid lifter, and the admiring bull whackers bore him off, leaving the lady in full possession of the ranch. When I visited her she had a man named Crow Joe working for her, a slab-sided, shifty-eyed person who later, as I heard my foreman explain, "skipped the country with a bunch of horses." The mistress of the ranch made first-class buckskin shirts of great durability.

The one she made for me, and which I used for years, was used by one of my sons in Arizona a couple of winters ago.   I had ridden down into the country after some lost horses, and visited the ranch to get her to make me the buck-skin shirt in question.   There were, at the moment, three Indians there, Sioux, well behaved and self-respecting, and she explained to me that they had been resting there waiting for dinner, and that a white man had come along and tried to run off their horses.   The Indians were on the lookout, however, and, running out, they caught the man ; but, after retaking their horses and depriving him of his gun, they let him go.   "I don't see why they let him go," exclaimed my hostess.   "I don't believe in stealing Indians' horses any more than white folks' ; so I told 'em they could go along and hang him — I'd never cheep.   Anyhow, I won't charge them anything for their dinner," concluded my hostess. She was in advance of the usual morality of the time and place, which drew a sharp line between stealing citizens' horses and stealing horses from the Government or the Indians.

A fairly decent citizen, Jap Hunt, who long ago met a violent death, exemplified this attitude towards Indians in some remarks I once heard him make.   He had started a horse ranch, and had quite honestly purchased a number of broken-down horses of different brands, with the view of doctoring them and selling them again.   About this time there had been much horse-stealing and cattle-killing in our Territory and in Montana, and under the direction of some of the big cattle-growers a committee of vigilantes had been organized to take action against the rustlers, as the horse thieves and cattle thieves were called.   The vigilantes, or stranglers, as they were locally known, did their work thor-oughly ; but, as always happens with bodies of the kind, toward the end they grew reckless in their actions, paid off private grudges, and hung men on slight provocation. Riding into Jap Hunt's ranch, they nearly hung him be-cause he had so many horses of different brands.   He was finally let off.   He was much upset by the incident, and explained again and again,   "The idea of saying that I

was a horse thief! Why, I never stole a horse in my life
— leastways from a white man.   I don't count Indians nor
the Government, of course." Jap had been reared among
men still in the stage of tribal morality, and while they recognized their obligations to one another, both the Government and the Indians seemed alien bodies, in regard to which
the laws of morality did not apply.

On the other hand, parties of savage young bucks would
treat lonely settlers just as badly, and in addition sometimes
murder them.   Such a party was generally composed of
young fellows burning to distinguish themselves.   Some
one of their number would have obtained a pass from the
Indian Agent allowing him to travel off the reservation,
which pass would be flourished whenever their action was
questioned by bodies of whites of equal strength.   I once
had a trifling encounter with such a band.   I was making
my way along the edge of the bad lands, northward from
my lower ranch, and was just crossing a plateau when five
Indians rode up over the further rim.   The instant they saw
me they whipped out their guns and raced full speed at me,
yelling and flogging their horses.   I was on a favorite horse,
Manitou, who was a wise old fellow, with nerves not to be
shaken by anything.   I at once leaped off him and stood
with my rifle ready.

It was possible that the Indians were merely making a
bluff and intended no mischief.   But I did not like their
actions, and I thought it likely that if I allowed them to
get hold of me they would at least take my horse and rifle,
and possibly kill me.   So I waited until they were a hundred
yards off and then drew a bead on the first.   Indians — and,
for the matter of that, white men — do not like to ride in on
a man who is cool and means shooting, and in a twinkling
every man was lying over the side of his horse, and all five
had turned and were galloping backwards, having altered
their course as quickly as so many teal ducks.

After this one of them made the peace sign, with his
blanket first, and then, as he rode toward me, with his open
hand.   I halted him at a fair distance and asked him what
he wanted.   He exclaimed, "How! Me good Injun, me

good Injun," and tried to show me the dirty piece of paper on which his agency pass was written. I told him with sincerity that I was glad that he was a good Indian, but that he must not come any closer. He then asked for sugar and tobacco. I told him I had none. Another Indian began slowly drifting toward me in spite of my calling out to keep back, so I once more aimed with my rifle, whereupon both Indians slipped to the other side of their horses and galloped off, with oaths that did credit to at least one side of their acquaintance with English. I now mounted and pushed over the plateau on to the open prairie. In those days an Indian, although not as good a shot as a white man, was infinitely better at crawling under and taking advantage of cover; and the worst thing a white man could do was to get into cover, whereas out in the open if he kept his head he had a good chance of standing off even half a dozen assailants. The Indians accompanied me for a couple of miles. Then I reached the open prairie, and resumed my northward ride, not being further molested.

In the old days in the ranch country we depended upon game for fresh meat. Nobody liked to kill a beef, and although now and then a maverick yearling might be killed on the round-up, most of us looked askance at the deed, because if the practice of beef-killing was ever allowed to start, the rustlers — the horse thieves and cattle thieves — would be sure to seize on it as an excuse for general slaughter. Getting meat for the ranch usually devolved upon me. I almost always carried a rifle when I rode, either in a scabbard under my thigh, or across the pommel. Often I would pick up a deer or antelope while about my regular work, when visiting a line camp or riding after the cattle. At other times I would make a day's trip after them. In the fall we sometimes took a wagon and made a week's hunt, returning with eight or ten deer carcasses, and perhaps an elk or a mountain sheep as well. I never became more than a fair hunter, and at times I had most exasperating experiences, either failing to see game which I ought to have seen, or committing some blunder in the stalk, or failing to kill when I fired. Looking back, I am inclined to say that if I had any good quality as a hunter it was that of perseverance. "It is dogged that does it" in hunting as in many other things. Unless in wholly exceptional cases, when we were very hungry, I never killed anything but bucks.

Occasionally I made long trips away from the ranch and among the Rocky Mountains with my ranch foreman Merrifield; or in later years with Tazewell Woody, John Willis, or John Goff. We hunted bears, both the black and the grizzly, cougars and wolves, and moose, wapiti, and white goat. On one of these trips I killed a bison bull, and I also killed a bison bull on the Little Missouri some fifty miles south of my ranch on a trip which Joe Ferris and I took together. It was rather a rough trip. Each of us carried only his slicker behind him on the saddle, with some flour and bacon done up in it. We met with all kinds of misadventures. Finally one night, when we were sleeping by a slimy little prairie pool where there was not a stick of wood, we had to tie the horses to the horns of our saddles; and then we went to sleep with our heads on the saddles. In the middle of the night something stampeded the horses, and away they went, with the saddles after them. As we jumped to our feet Joe eyed me with an evident suspicion that I was the Jonah of the party, and said: "O Lord! *I've* never done anything to deserve this. Did *you* ever do anything to deserve this?"

In addition to my private duties, I sometimes served as deputy sheriff for the northern end of our county. The sheriff and I crisscrossed in our public and private relations. He often worked for me as a hired hand at the same time that I was his deputy. His name, or at least the name he went by, was Bill Jones, and as there were in the neighborhood several Bill Joneses — Three Seven Bill Jones, Texas Bill Jones, and the like — the sheriff was known as Hell Roaring Bill Jones. He was a thorough frontiersman, excellent in all kinds of emergencies, and a very game man. I became much attached to him. He was a thoroughly good citizen when sober, but he was a little wild when drunk. Unfortunately, toward the end of his life he got to drinking very heavily. When, in 1905, John Burroughs and I visited the Yellowstone Park, poor Bill Jones, very much down in the world, was driving a team in Gardiner outside the park. I had looked forward to seeing him, and he was equally anxious to see me. He kept telling his cronies of our intimacy and of what we were going to do together, and then got drinking; and the result was that by the time I reached Gardiner he had to be carried out and left in the sage-brush.

SHERIFF DUTY.

"When I served as deputy sheriff for the northern end of our county."

When I came out of the park, I sent on in advance to tell them to be sure to keep him sober, and they did so. But it was a rather sad interview. The old fellow had gone to pieces, and soon after I left he got lost in a blizzard and was dead when they found him.

Bill Jones was a gun-fighter and also a good man with his fists. On one occasion there was an election in town. There had been many threats that the party of disorder would import section hands from the neighboring railway stations to down our side. I did not reach Medora, the forlorn little cattle town which was our county seat, until the election was well under way. I then asked one of my friends if there had been any disorder. Bill Jones was standing by. "Disorder hell!" said my friend. "Bill Jones just stood there with one hand on his gun and the other pointing over toward the new jail whenever any man who didn't have a right to vote came near the polls. There was only one of them tried to vote, and Bill knocked him down. Lord!" added my friend, meditatively, "the way that man fell!" "Well," struck in Bill Jones, "if he hadn't fell I'd have walked round behind him to see what was propping him up!"

In the days when I lived on the ranch I usually spent most of the winter in the East, and when I returned in the early spring I was always interested in finding out what had happened since my departure. On one occasion I was met by Bill Jones and Sylvane Ferris, and in the course of our conversation they mentioned "the lunatic." This led to a question on my part, and Sylvane Ferris began the story: "Well, you see, he was on a train and he shot the newsboy. At first they weren't going to do anything to him, for they thought he just had it in for the newsboy. But then somebody said, 'Why, he's plumb crazy, and he's liable to shoot any of *us*!' and then they threw him off the train. It was here at Medora, and they asked if anybody would take care of him, and Bill Jones said he would, because he was the sheriff and the jail had two rooms, and he was living in one and would put the lunatic in the other." Here Bill Jones interrupted: "Yes, and more fool me! I wouldn't take charge of another lunatic if the whole county asked me. Why" (with the air of a man announcing an astounding discovery), "that lunatic didn't have his right senses! He wouldn't eat, till me and Snyder got him down on the shavings and *made* him eat." Snyder was a huge, happy-go-lucky, kind-hearted Pennsylvania Dutchman, and was Bill Jones's chief deputy. Bill continued: "You know, Snyder's soft-hearted, he is. Well, he'd think that lunatic looked peaked, and he'd take him out for an airing. Then the boys would get joshing him as to how much start he could give

K

him over the prairie and catch him again." Apparently
the amount of the start given the lunatic depended upon the
amount of the bet to which the joshing led up. I asked Bill
what he would have done if Snyder hadn't caught the
lunatic. This was evidently a new idea, and he responded
that Snyder always did catch him. "Well, but suppose
he hadn't caught him?" "Well," said Bill Jones, "if
Snyder hadn't caught the lunatic, I'd have whaled hell out of
Snyder!"

Under these circumstances Snyder ran his best and always did catch the patient. It must not be gathered from
this that the lunatic was badly treated. He was well
treated. He became greatly attached to both Bill Jones
and Snyder, and he objected strongly when, after the frontier
theory of treatment of the insane had received a full trial,
he was finally sent off to the territorial capital. It was
merely that all the relations of life in that place and day were
so managed as to give ample opportunity for the expression
of individuality, whether in sheriff or ranchman. The
local practical joker once attempted to have some fun at
the expense of the lunatic, and Bill Jones described the result.
"You know Bixby, don't you? Well," with deep disapproval, "Bixby thinks he is funny, he does. He'd come
and he'd wake that lunatic up at night, and I'd have to get
up and soothe him. I fixed Bixby all right, though. I
fastened a rope on the latch, and next time Bixby came I let
the lunatic out on him. He 'most bit Bixby's nose off. I
learned Bixby!"

Bill Jones had been unconventional in other relations
besides that of sheriff. He once casually mentioned to me
that he had served on the police force of Bismarck, but he
had left because he "beat the Mayor over the head with his
gun one day." He added: "The Mayor, he didn't mind it,
but the Superintendent of Police said he guessed I'd better
resign." His feeling, obviously, was that the Superintendent
of Police was a martinet, unfit to take large views of life.

It was while with Bill Jones that I first made acquaintance
with Seth Bullock. Seth was at that time sheriff in the
Black Hills district, and a man he had wanted — a horse

thief — I finally got, I being at the time deputy sheriff two or three hundred miles to the north. The man went by a nickname which I will call "Crazy Steve"; a year or two afterwards I received a letter asking about him from his uncle, a thoroughly respectable man in a Western State; and later this uncle and I met at Washington when I was President and he a United States Senator. It was some time after "Steve's" capture that I went down to Dead-wood on business, Sylvane Ferris and I on horseback, while Bill Jones drove the wagon. At a little town, Spearfish, I think, after crossing the last eighty or ninety miles of gumbo prairie, we met Seth Bullock. We had had rather a rough trip, and had lain out for a fortnight, so I suppose we looked somewhat unkempt. Seth received us with rather distant courtesy at first, but unbent when he found out who we were, remarking, "You see, by your looks I thought you were some kind of a tin-horn gambling outfit, and that I might have to keep an eye on you!" He then inquired after the capture of "Steve" — with a little of the air of one sportsman when another has shot a quail that either might have claimed — "My bird, I believe?" Later Seth Bullock became, and has ever since remained, one of my stanchest and most valued friends. He served as Marshal for South Dakota under me as President. When, after the close of my term, I went to Africa, on getting back to Europe I cabled Seth Bullock to bring over Mrs. Bullock and meet me in London, which he did; by that time I felt that I just had to meet my own people, who spoke my neighborhood dialect.

When serving as deputy sheriff I was impressed with the advantage the officer of the law has over ordinary wrong-doers, provided he thoroughly knows his own mind. There are exceptional outlaws, men with a price on their heads and of remarkable prowess, who are utterly indifferent to taking life, and whose warfare against society is as open as that of a savage on the war-path. The law officer has no advantage whatever over these men save what his own prowess may — or may not — give him. Such a man was Billy the Kid, the notorious man-killer and desperado of

New Mexico, who was himself finally slain by a friend of mine, Pat Garrett, whom, when I was President, I made collector of customs at El Paso. But the ordinary criminal, even when murderously inclined, feels just a moment's hesitation as to whether he cares to kill an officer of the law engaged in his duty. I took in more than one man who was probably a better man than I was with both rifle and revolver; but in each case I knew just what I wanted to do, and, like David Harum, I "did it first," whereas the fraction of a second that the other man hesitated put him in a position where it was useless for him to resist.

I owe more than I can ever express to the West, which of course means to the men and women I met in the West. There were a few people of bad type in my neighborhood — that would be true of every group of men, even in a theological seminary — but I could not speak with too great affection and respect of the great majority of my friends, the hard-working men and women who dwelt for a space of perhaps a hundred and fifty miles along the Little Missouri. I was always as welcome at their houses as they were at mine. Everybody worked, everybody was willing to help everybody else, and yet nobody asked any favors. The same thing was true of the people whom I got to know fifty miles east and fifty miles west of my own range, and of the men I met on the round-ups. They soon accepted me as a friend and fellow-worker who stood on an equal footing with them, and I believe that most of them have kept their feeling for me ever since. No guests were ever more welcome at the White House than these old friends of the cattle ranches and the cow camps — the men with whom I had ridden the long circle and eaten at the tail-board of a chuck-wagon — whenever they turned up at Washington during my Presidency. I remember one of them who appeared at Washington one day just before lunch, a huge, powerful man who, when I knew him, had been distinctly a fighting character. It happened that on that day another old friend, the British Ambassador, Mr. Bryce, was among those coming to lunch. Just before we went in I turned to my cow-puncher friend and said to him with great solemnity,

"Remember, Jim, that if you shot at the feet of the British Ambassador to make him dance, it would be likely to cause international complications"; to which Jim responded with unaffected horror, "Why, Colonel, I shouldn't think of it, I shouldn't think of it!"

Not only did the men and women whom I met in the cow country quite unconsciously help me, by the insight which working and living with them enabled me to get into the mind and soul of the average American of the right type, but they helped me in another way. I made up my mind that the men were of just the kind whom it would be well to have with me if ever it became necessary to go to war. When the Spanish War came, I gave this thought practical realization.

Fortunately, Wister and Remington, with pen and pencil, have made these men live as long as our literature lives. I have sometimes been asked if Wister's "Virginian" is not overdrawn; why, one of the men I have mentioned in this chapter was in all essentials the Virginian in real life, not only in his force but in his charm. Half of the men I worked with or played with and half of the men who soldiered with me afterwards in my regiment might have walked out of Wister's stories or Remington's pictures.

There were bad characters in the Western country at that time, of course, and under the conditions of life they were probably more dangerous than they would have been elsewhere. I hardly ever had any difficulty, however. I never went into a saloon, and in the little hotels I kept out of the bar-room unless, as sometimes happened, the bar-room was the only room on the lower floor except the dining-room. I always endeavored to keep out of a quarrel until self-respect forbade my making any further effort to avoid it, and I very rarely had even the semblance of trouble.

Of course amusing incidents occurred now and then. Usually these took place when I was hunting lost horses, for in hunting lost horses I was ordinarily alone, and occasionally had to travel a hundred or a hundred and fifty miles away from my own country. On one such occasion I reached a little cow town long after dark, stabled my horse in an empty outbuilding, and when I reached the hotel was informed in response to my request for a bed that I could have the last one left, as there was only one other man in it. The room to which I was shown contained two double beds;

"SETH BULLOCK BECAME, AND HAS EVER SINCE REMAINED, ONE OF MY STANCHEST AND MOST VALUED FRIENDS."

one contained two men fast asleep, and the other only one man, also asleep. This man proved to be a friend, one of the Bill Joneses whom I have previously mentioned. I undressed according to the fashion of the day and place, that is, I put my trousers, boots, shaps, and gun down beside the

bed, and turned in. A couple of hours later I was awakened
by the door being thrown open and a lantern flashed in my
face, the light gleaming on the muzzle of a cocked .45.
Another man said to the lantern-bearer. "It ain't him";
the next moment my bedfellow was covered with two guns,
and addressed, "Now, Bill, don't make a fuss, but come
along quiet." "I'm not thinking of making a fuss," said
Bill. "That's right," was the answer; "we're your friends;
we don't want to hurt you; we just want you to come along,
you know why." And Bill pulled on his trousers and boots
and walked out with them. Up to this time there had not
been a sound from the other bed. Now a match was
scratched, a candle lit, and one of the men in the other bed
looked round the room. At this point I committed the
breach of etiquette of asking questions. "I wonder why
they took Bill," I said. There was no answer, and I repeated, "I wonder why they took Bill." "Well," said the
man with the candle, dryly, "I reckon they wanted him,"
and with that he blew out the candle and conversation
ceased. Later I discovered that Bill in a fit of playfulness
had held up the Northern Pacific train at a near-by station
by shooting at the feet of the conductor to make him dance.
This was purely a joke on Bill's part, but the Northern
Pacific people possessed a less robust sense of humor, and
on their complaint the United States Marshal was sent after
Bill, on the ground that by delaying the train he had interfered with the mails.

The only time I ever had serious trouble was at an even
more primitive little hotel than the one in question. It was
also on an occasion when I was out after lost horses. Below
the hotel had merely a bar-room, a dining-room, and a lean-
to kitchen; above was a loft with fifteen or twenty beds in it.
It was late in the evening when I reached the place. I heard
one or two shots in the bar-room as I came up, and I disliked going in. But there was nowhere else to go, and it was
a cold night. Inside the room were several men, who, including the bartender, were wearing the kind of smile worn
by men who are making believe to like what they don't like.
A shabby individual in a broad hat with a cocked gun in

each hand was walking up and down the floor talking with strident profanity. He had evidently been shooting at the clock, which had two or three holes in its face.

He was not a "bad man" of the really dangerous type, the true man-killer type, but he was an objectionable creature, a would-be bad man, a bully who for the moment was having things all his own way. As soon as he saw me he hailed me as "Four eyes," in reference to my spectacles, and said, "Four eyes is going to treat." I joined in the laugh and got behind the stove and sat down, thinking to escape notice. He followed me, however, and though I tried to pass it off as a jest this merely made him more offensive, and he stood leaning over me, a gun in each hand, using very foul language. He was foolish to stand so near, and, moreover, his heels were close together, so that his position was unstable. Accordingly, in response to his reiterated command that I should set up the drinks, I said, "Well, if I've got to, I've got to," and rose, looking past him.

As I rose, I struck quick and hard with my right just to one side of the point of his jaw, hitting with my left as I straightened out, and then again with my right. He fired the guns, but I do not know whether this was merely a convulsive action of his hands or whether he was trying to shoot at me. When he went down he struck the corner of the bar with his head. It was not a case in which one could afford to take chances, and if he had moved I was about to drop on his ribs with my knees; but he was senseless. I took away his guns, and the other people in the room, who were now loud in their denunciation of him, hustled him out and put him in a shed. I got dinner as soon as possible, sitting in a corner of the dining-room away from the windows, and then went upstairs to bed where it was dark so that there would be no chance of any one shooting at me from the outside. However, nothing happened. When my assailant came to, he went down to the station and left on a freight.

As I have said, most of the men of my regiment were just such men as those I knew in the ranch country; indeed, some of my ranch friends were in the regiment — Fred

Herrig, the forest ranger, for instance, in whose company I shot my biggest mountain ram. After the regiment was disbanded the careers of certain of the men were diversified by odd incidents. Our relations were of the friendliest, and, as they explained, they felt "as if I was a father" to them. The manifestations of this feeling were sometimes less attractive than the phrase sounded, as it was chiefly used by the few who were behaving like very bad children indeed. The great majority of the men when the regiment disbanded took up the business of their lives where they had dropped it a few months previously, and these men merely tried to help me or help one another as the occasion arose; no man ever had more cause to be proud of his regiment than I had of mine, both in war and in peace. But there was a minority among them who in certain ways were unsuited for a life of peaceful regularity, although often enough they had been first-class soldiers.

It was from these men that letters came with a stereotyped opening which always caused my heart to sink — "Dear Colonel: I write you because I am in trouble." The trouble might take almost any form. One correspondent continued: "I did not take the horse, but they say I did." Another complained that his mother-in-law had put him in jail for bigamy. In the case of another the incident was more markworthy. I will call him Gritto. He wrote me a letter beginning: "Dear Colonel: I write you because I am in trouble. I have shot a lady in the eye. But, Colonel, I was not shooting at the lady. I was shooting at my wife," which he apparently regarded as a sufficient excuse as between men of the world. I answered that I drew the line at shooting at ladies, and did not hear any more of the incident for several years.

Then, while I was President, a member of the regiment, Major Llewellyn, who was Federal District Attorney under me in New Mexico, wrote me a letter filled, as his letters usually were, with bits of interesting gossip about the comrades. It ran in part as follows: "Since I last wrote you Comrade Ritchie has killed a man in Colorado. I understand that the comrade was playing a poker game, and the

man sat into the game and used such language that Comrade
Ritchie had to shoot.   Comrade Webb has killed two men
in Beaver, Arizona.   Comrade Webb is in the Forest Service, and the killing was in the line of professional duty.   I
was out at the penitentiary the other day and saw Comrade
Gritto, who, you may remember, was put there for shooting
his sister-in-law [this was the first information I had had as
to the identity of the lady who was shot in the eye].   Since
he was in there Comrade Boyne has run off to old Mexico
with his (Gritto's) wife, and the people of Grant County
think he ought to be let out."   Evidently the sporting instincts of the people of Grant County had been roused, and
they felt that, as Comrade Boyne had had a fair start, the
other comrade should be let out in order to see what would
happen.

The men of the regiment always enthusiastically helped
me when I was running for office.   On one occasion Buck
Taylor, of Texas, accompanied me on a trip and made a
speech for me.   The crowd took to his speech from the
beginning and so did I, until the peroration, which ran as
follows :   "My fellow-citizens, vote for my Colonel ! vote for
my Colonel ! *and he will lead you, as he led us, like sheep to the
slaughter!*"   This hardly seemed a tribute to my military
skill ; but it delighted the crowd, and as far as I could tell
did me nothing but good.

On another tour, when I was running for Vice-President,
a member of the regiment who was along on the train got into
a discussion with a Populist editor who had expressed an
unfavorable estimate of my character, and in the course of
the discussion shot the editor — not fatally.   We had to
leave him to be tried, and as he had no money I left him
$150 to hire counsel — having borrowed the money from
Senator Wolcott, of Colorado, who was also with me.   After
election I received from my friend a letter running : "Dear
Colonel : I find I will not have to use that $150 you lent me,
as we have elected our candidate for District Attorney.
So I have used it to settle a horse transaction in which I
unfortunately became involved."   A few weeks later,
however, I received a heartbroken letter setting forth the

THE BRONCHO BUSTER, BY FREDERIC REMINGTON.

Presented to Colonel Roosevelt on September 15, 1898, by his regiment at Camp Wikoff, Montauk Point, where the Rough Riders were disbanded at the close of the Spanish-American War.

fact that the District Attorney — whom he evidently felt to be a cold-blooded formalist — had put him in jail. Then the affair dropped out of sight until two or three years later, when as President I visited a town in another State, and the leaders of the delegation which received me included both my correspondent and the editor, now fast friends, and both of them ardent supporters of mine.

At one of the regimental reunions a man, who had been an excellent soldier, in greeting me mentioned how glad he was that the judge had let him out in time to get to the reunion. I asked what was the matter, and he replied with some surprise : "Why, Colonel, don't you know I had a difficulty with a gentleman, and . . . er . . . well, I killed the gentleman. But you can see that the judge thought it was all right or he wouldn't have let me go." Waiving the latter point, I said : "How did it happen ? How did you do it ?" Misinterpreting my question as showing an interest only in the technique of the performance, the ex-puncher replied : "With a .38 on a .45 frame, Colonel." I chuckled over the answer, and it became proverbial with my family and some of my friends, including Seth Bullock. When I was shot at Milwaukee, Seth Bullock wired an inquiry to which I responded that it was all right, that the weapon was merely "a .38 on a .45 frame." The telegram in some way became public, and puzzled outsiders. By the way, both the men of my regiment and the friends I had made in the old days in the West were themselves a little puzzled at the interest shown in my making my speech after being shot. This was what they expected, what they accepted as the right thing for a man to do under the circumstances, a thing the nonperformance of which would have been discreditable rather than the performance being creditable. They would not have expected a man to leave a battle, for instance, because of being wounded in such fashion ; and they saw no reason why he should abandon a less important and less risky duty.

One of the best soldiers of my regiment was a huge man whom I made marshal of a Rocky Mountain State. He had spent his hot and lusty youth on the frontier during its viking age, and at that time had naturally taken part in incidents which seemed queer to men "accustomed to die decently of zymotic diseases." I told him that an effort would doubtless be made to prevent his confirmation by the Senate, and therefore that I wanted to know all the facts in his case. Had he played faro? He had; but it was when everybody played faro, and he had never played a brace game. Had he killed anybody? Yes, but it was in Dodge City on occasions when he was deputy marshal or town marshal, at a time when Dodge City, now the most peaceful of communities, was the toughest town on the continent, and crowded with man-killing outlaws and road agents; and he produced telegrams from judges of high character testifying to the need of the actions he had taken. Finally I said: "Now, Ben, how did you lose that half of your ear?" To which, looking rather shy, he responded: "Well, Colonel, it was bit off." "How did it happen, Ben?" "Well, you see, I was sent to arrest a gentleman, and him and me mixed it up, and he bit off my ear." "What did you do to the gentleman, Ben?" And Ben, looking more coy than ever, responded: "Well, Colonel, we broke about even!" I forebore to inquire what variety of mayhem he had committed on the "gentleman." After considerable struggle I got him confirmed by the Senate, and he made one of the best marshals in the entire service, exactly as he had already made one of the best soldiers in the regiment; and I never wish to see a better citizen, nor a man in whom I would more implicitly trust in every way.

When, in 1900, I was nominated for Vice-President, I was sent by the National Committee on a trip into the States of the high plains and the Rocky Mountains. These had all gone overwhelmingly for Mr. Bryan on the free-silver issue four years previously, and it was thought that I, because of my knowledge of and acquaintanceship with the people, might accomplish something towards bringing them back into line. It was an interesting trip, and the monotony usually attendant upon such a campaign of political speaking was diversified in vivid fashion by occasional hostile audiences. One or two of the meetings ended in riots.

One meeting was finally broken up by a mob; everybody fought so that the speaking had to stop. Soon after this we reached another town where we were told there might be trouble. Here the local committee included an old and valued friend, a "two-gun" man of repute, who was not in the least quarrelsome, but who always kept his word. We marched round to the local opera-house, which was packed with a mass of men, many of them rather rough-looking. My friend the two-gun man sat immediately behind me, a gun on each hip, his arms folded, looking at the audience; fixing his gaze with instant intentness on any section of the house from which there came so much as a whisper. The audience listened to me with rapt attention. At the end, with a pride in my rhetorical powers which proceeded from a misunderstanding of the situation, I remarked to the chairman: "I held that audience well; there wasn't an interruption." To which the chairman replied: "Interruption? Well, I guess not! Seth had sent round word that if any son of a gun peeped he'd kill him!"

There was one bit of frontier philosophy which I should like to see imitated in more advanced communities. Certain crimes of revolting baseness and cruelty were never forgiven. But in the case of ordinary offenses, the man who had served his term and who then tried to make good was given a fair chance; and of course this was equally true of the women. Every one who has studied the subject at all is only too well aware that the world offsets the readiness with which it condones a crime for which a man escapes punishment, by its unforgiving relentlessness to the often far less guilty man who *is* punished, and who therefore has made his atonement. On the frontier, if the man honestly tried to behave himself there was generally a disposition to give him fair play and a decent show. Several of the men I knew and whom I particularly liked came in this class. There was one such man in my regiment, a man who had served a term for robbery under arms, and who had atoned for it by many years of fine performance of duty. I put him in a high official position, and no man under me rendered better service to the State, nor was there any man whom, as soldier, as civil officer, as citizen, and as friend, I valued and respected — and now value and respect — more.

Now I suppose some good people will gather from this that I favor men who commit crimes. I certainly do not favor them. I have not a particle of sympathy with the sentimentality — as I deem it, the mawkishness — which overflows with foolish pity for the criminal and cares not at all for the victim of the criminal. I am glad to see wrongdoers punished. The punishment is an absolute necessity from the standpoint of society; and I put the reformation of the criminal second to the welfare of society. But I do desire to see the man or woman who has paid the penalty and who wishes to reform given a helping hand — surely every one of us who knows his own heart must know that he too may stumble, and should be anxious to help his brother or sister who has stumbled. When the criminal has been punished, if he then shows a sincere desire to lead a decent and upright life, he should be given the chance, he should be helped and not hindered; and if he makes good, he should receive that respect from others which so often aids in creating self-respect — the most invaluable of all possessions.

CHAPTER V

APPLIED IDEALISM

IN the spring of 1889 I was appointed by President Harrison Civil Service Commissioner. For nearly five years I had not been very active in political life; although I had done some routine work in the organization and had made campaign speeches, and in 1886 had run for Mayor of New York against Abram S. Hewitt, Democrat, and Henry George, Independent, and had been defeated.

THEODORE ROOSEVELT.
Civil Service Commissioner.

I served six years as Civil Service Commissioner — four years under President Harrison and then two years under President Cleveland. I was treated by both Presidents with the utmost consideration. Among my fellow-Commissioners there was at one time ex-Governor Hugh Thompson, of South Carolina, and at another time John R. Proctor, of Kentucky. They were Democrats and ex-Confederate soldiers. I became deeply attached to both, and we stood shoulder to shoulder in every contest in which the Commission was forced to take part.

Civil Service Reform had two sides. There was, first, the effort to secure a more efficient administration of the public service, and, second, the even more important effort to withdraw the administrative offices of the Government from the domain of spoils politics, and thereby cut out of American political life a fruitful source of corruption and degradation. The spoils theory of politics is that public office is so much plunder which the victorious political party is entitled to appropriate to the use of its adherents. Under this system the work of the Government was often done well even in those days, when Civil Service Reform was only an experiment, because the man running an office if himself an able and far-sighted man, knew that inefficiency in administration would be visited on his head in the long run, and therefore insisted upon most of his subordinates doing good work ; and, moreover, the men appointed under the spoils system were necessarily men of a certain initiative and power, because those who lacked these qualities were not able to shoulder themselves to the front. Yet there were many flagrant instances of inefficiency, where a powerful chief quartered friend, adherent, or kinsman upon the Government. Moreover, the necessarily haphazard nature of the employment, the need of obtaining and holding the office by service wholly unconnected with official duty, inevitably tended to lower the standard of public morality, alike among the office-holders and among the politicians who rendered party service with the hope of reward in office. Indeed, the doctrine that "To the victor belong the spoils," the cynical battle-cry of the spoils politician in America for the sixty years preceding my own entrance into public life, is so nakedly vicious that few right-thinking men of trained mind defend it. To appoint, promote, reduce, and expel from the public service, letter-carriers, stenographers, women typewriters, clerks, because of the politics of themselves or their friends, without regard to their own service, is, from the standpoint of the people at large, as foolish and degrading as it is wicked.

Such being the case, it would seem at first sight extraordinary that it should be so difficult to uproot the system. Unfortunately, it was permitted to become habitual and traditional in American life, so that the conception of public office as something to be used primarily for the good of the dominant political party became ingrained in the mind of

L

the average American, and he grew so accustomed to the whole process that it seemed part of the order of nature. Not merely the politicians but the bulk of the people accepted this in a matter-of-course way as the only proper attitude. There were plenty of communities where the citizens themselves did not think it natural, or indeed proper, that the Post-Office should be held by a man belonging to the defeated party. Moreover, unless both sides were forbidden to use the offices for purposes of political reward, the side that did use them possessed such an advantage over the other that in the long run it was out of the question for the other not to follow the bad example that had been set. Each party profited by the offices when in power, and when in opposition each party insincerely denounced its opponents for doing exactly what it itself had done and intended again to do.

It was necessary, in order to remedy the evil, both gradually to change the average citizen's mental attitude toward the question, and also to secure proper laws and proper administration of the laws. The work is far from finished even yet. There are still masses of office-holders who can be used by an unscrupulous Administration to debauch political conventions and fraudulently overcome public sentiment, especially in the "rotten borough" districts — those where the party is not strong, and where the office-holders in consequence have a disproportionate influence. This was done by the Republican Administration in 1912, to the ruin of the Republican party. Moreover, there are numbers of States and municipalities where very little has as yet been done to do away with the spoils system. But in the National Government scores of thousands of offices have been put under the merit system, chiefly through the action of the National Civil Service Commission.

The use of Government offices as patronage is a handicap difficult to overestimate from the standpoint of those who strive to get good government. Any effort for reform of any sort, National, State, or municipal, results in the reformers immediately finding themselves face to face with an organized band of drilled mercenaries who are paid out of the public chest to train themselves with such skill that ordinary good citizens when they meet them at the polls are in much the position of militia matched against regular troops.   Yet these citizens themselves support and pay their opponents in such a way that they are drilled to overthrow the very men who support them.   Civil Service Reform is designed primarily to give the average American citizen a fair chance in politics, to give to this citizen the same weight in politics that the "ward heeler" has.

Patronage does not really help a party.   It helps the bosses to get control of the machinery of the party — as in 1912 was true of the Republican party — but it does not help the party.   On the average, the most sweeping party victories in our history have been won when the patronage was against the victors.   All that the patronage does is to help the worst element in the party retain control of the party organization.   Two of the evil elements in our Government against which good citizens have to contend are, 1, the lack of continuous activity on the part of these good citizens themselves, and, 2, the ever-present activity of those who have only an evil self-interest in political life. It is difficult to interest the average citizen in any particular movement to the degree of getting him to take an efficient part in it.   He wishes the movement well, but he will not, or often cannot, take the time and the trouble to serve it efficiently; and this whether he happens to be a mechanic or a banker, a telegraph operator or a storekeeper.   He has his own interests, his own business, and it is difficult for him to spare the time to go around to the primaries, to see to the organization, to see to getting out the vote — in short, to attend to all the thousand details of political management.

On the other hand, the spoils system breeds a class of men whose financial interest it is to take this necessary time and trouble.   They are paid for so doing, and they are paid out of the public chest.   Under the spoils system a man is appointed to an ordinary clerical or ministerial position in the municipal, Federal, or State government, not primarily because he is expected to be a good servant, but because he has rendered help to some big boss or to the henchman of some big boss. His stay in office depends not upon how he performs service, but upon how he retains his influence in the party. This necessarily means that his attention to the interests of the public at large, even though real, is secondary to his devotion to his organization, or to the interest of the ward leader who put him in his place. So he and his fellows attend to politics, not once a year, not two or three times a year, like the average citizen, but every day in the year. It is the one thing that they talk of, for it is their bread and butter. They plan about it and they scheme about it. They do it because it is their business. I do not blame them in the least. I blame us, the people, for we ought to make it clear as a bell that the business of serving the people in one of the ordinary ministerial Government positions, which have nothing to do with deciding the policy of the Government, should have no necessary connection with the management of primaries, of caucuses, and of nominating conventions. As a result of our wrong thinking and supineness, we American citizens tend to breed a mass of men whose interests in governmental matters are often adverse to ours, who are thoroughly drilled, thoroughly organized, who make their livelihood out of politics, and who frequently make their livelihood out of bad politics. They know every little twist and turn, no matter how intricate, in the politics of their several wards, and when election day comes the ordinary citizen who has merely the interest that all good men, all decent citizens, should have in political life, finds himself as helpless before these men as if he were a solitary volunteer in the presence of a band of drilled mercenaries on a field of battle. There are a couple of hundred thousand Federal offices, not to speak of State and municipal offices. The men who fill these offices, and the men who wish to fill them, within and without the dominant party for the time being, make a regular army, whose interest it is that the system of bread-and-butter politics shall continue. Against their concrete interest we have merely the generally unorganized sentiment of the community in favor of putting things on a decent basis. The large number of men who believe vaguely in good are pitted against the smaller but still larger number of men whose interest it often becomes to act very concretely and actively for evil; and it is small wonder that the struggle is doubtful.

During my six years' service as Commissioner the field of the merit system was extended at the expense of the spoils system so as to include several times the number of offices that had originally been included. Generally this was done by the introduction of competitive entrance examinations; sometimes, as in the Navy-Yards, by a system of registration. This of itself was good work.

Even better work was making the law efficient and genuine where it applied. As was inevitable in the introduction of such a system, there was at first only partial success in its application. For instance, it applied to the ordinary employees in the big custom-houses and post-offices, but not to the heads of these offices. A number of the heads of the offices were slippery politicians of a low moral grade, themselves appointed under the spoils system, and anxious, directly or indirectly, to break down the merit system and to pay their own political debts by appointing their henchmen and supporters to the positions under them. Occasionally these men acted with open and naked brutality. Ordinarily they sought by cunning to evade the law. The Civil Service Reformers, on the other hand, were in most cases not much used to practical politics, and were often well-nigh helpless when pitted against veteran professional politicians. In consequence I found at the beginning of my experiences that there were many offices in which the execution of the law was a sham. This was very damaging, because it encouraged the politicians to assault the law everywhere, and, on the other hand, made good people feel that the law was not worth while defending.

The first effort of myself and my colleagues was to secure the genuine enforcement of the law. In this we succeeded after a number of lively fights. But of course in these fights we were obliged to strike a large number of influential politicians, some of them in Congress, some of them the supporters and backers of men who were in Congress. Accord-

ingly we soon found ourselves engaged in a series of contests
with prominent Senators and Congressmen.   There were a
number of Senators and Congressmen — men like Congressman (afterwards Senator) H. C. Lodge, of Massachusetts;
Senator Cushman K. Davis, of Minnesota ; Senator Orville
H. Platt, of Connecticut ; Senator Cockrell, of Missouri ;
Congressman (afterwards President) McKinley, of Ohio,
and Congressman Dargan, of South Carolina — who abhorred the business of the spoilsman, who efficiently and
resolutely championed the reform at every turn, and without whom the whole reform would certainly have failed.
But there were plenty of other Senators and Congressmen
who hated the whole reform and everything concerned with
it and everybody who championed it ; and sometimes, to
use a legal phrase, their hatred was for cause, and sometimes
it was peremptory — that is, sometimes the Commission
interfered with their most efficient, and incidentally most
corrupt and unscrupulous, supporters, and at other times,
where there was no such interference, a man nevertheless
had an innate dislike of anything that tended to decency in
government.   These men were always waging war against
us, and they usually had the more or less open support of a
certain number of Government officials, from Cabinet officers
down.   The Senators and Congressmen in question opposed
us in many different ways.   Sometimes, for instance, they
had committees appointed to investigate us — during my
public career without and within office I grew accustomed to
accept appearances before investigating committees as part
of the natural order of things.   Sometimes they tried to cut
off the appropriation for the Commission.

Occasionally we would bring to terms these Senators or
Congressmen who fought the Commission by the simple
expedient of not holding examinations in their districts.
This always brought frantic appeals from their constituents,
and we would explain that unfortunately the appropriations
had been cut, so that we could not hold examinations in
every district, and that obviously we could not neglect the
districts of those Congressmen who believed in the reform
and therefore in the examinations.   The constituents then

turned their attention to the Congressman, and the result was that in the long run we obtained sufficient money to enable us to do our work. On the whole, the most prominent leaders favored us. Any man who is the head of a big department, if he has any fitness at all, wishes to see that department run well; and a very little practical experience shows him that it cannot be run well if he must make his appointments to please spoilsmongering politicians. As with almost every reform that I have ever undertaken, most of the opposition took the guise of shrewd slander. Our opponents relied chiefly on downright misrepresentation of what it was that we were trying to accomplish, and of our methods, acts, and personalities. I had more than one lively encounter with the authors and sponsors of these misrepresentations, which at the time were full of interest to me. But it would be a dreary thing now to go over the record of exploded mendacity, or to expose the meanness and malice shown by some men of high official position. A favorite argument was to call the reform Chinese, because the Chinese had constructed an inefficient governmental system based in part on the theory of written competitive examinations. The argument was simple. There had been written examinations in China; it was proposed to establish written examinations in the United States; therefore the proposed system was Chinese. The argument might have been applied still further. For instance, the Chinese had used gunpowder for centuries; gunpowder is used in Springfield rifles; therefore Springfield rifles were Chinese. One argument is quite as logical as the other. It was impossible to answer every falsehood about the system. But it was possible to answer certain falsehoods, especially when uttered by some Senator or Congressman of note. Usually these false statements took the form of assertions that we had asked preposterous questions of applicants. At times they also included the assertion that we credited people to districts where they did not live; this simply meaning that these persons were not known to the active ward politicians of those districts.

One opponent with whom we had a rather lively tilt was

a Republican Congressman from Ohio, Mr. Grosvenor, one of the floor leaders. Mr. Grosvenor made his attack in the House, and enumerated our sins in picturesque rather than accurate fashion. There was a Congressional committee investigating us at the time, and on my next appearance before them I asked that Mr. Grosvenor be requested to meet me before the committee. Mr. Grosvenor did not take up the challenge for several weeks, until it was announced that I was leaving for my ranch in Dakota; whereupon, deeming it safe, he wrote me a letter expressing his ardent wish that I should appear before the committee to meet him. I promptly canceled my ticket, waited, and met him. He proved to be a person of happily treacherous memory, so that the simple expedient of arranging his statements in pairs was sufficient to reduce him to confusion. For instance, he had been trapped into making the unwary remark, "I do not want to repeal the Civil Service Law, and I never said so." I produced the following extract from one of his speeches: "I will vote not only to strike out this provision, but I will vote to repeal the whole law." To this he merely replied that there was "no inconsistency between those two statements." He asserted that "Rufus P. Putnam, fraudulently credited to Washington County, Ohio, never lived in Washington County, Ohio, or in my Congressional district, or in Ohio as far as I know." We produced a letter which, thanks to a beneficent Providence, he had himself written about Mr. Rufus P. Putnam, in which he said: "Mr. Rufus P. Putnam is a legal resident of my district and has relatives living there now." He explained, first, that he had not written the letter; second, that he had forgotten he had written the letter; and, third, that he was grossly deceived when he wrote it. He said: "I have not been informed of one applicant who has found a place in the classified service from my district." We confronted him with the names of eight. He looked them over and said, "Yes, the eight men are living in my district as now constituted," but added that his district had been gerrymandered so that he could no longer tell who did and who didn't live in it. When I started further to question him, he accused me of a lack of humor in not appreciating that his statements were made "in a jesting way," and then announced that "a Congressman making a speech on the floor of the House of Representatives was perhaps in a little different position from a witness on the witness stand" — a frank admission that he did not consider exactitude of statement necessary when he was speaking as a Congressman. Finally he rose with great dignity and said that it was his "constitutional right" not to be questioned elsewhere as to what he said on the floor of the House of Representatives; and accordingly he left the delighted committee to pursue its investigations without further aid from him.

A more important opponent was the then Democratic leader of the Senate, Mr. Gorman. In a speech attacking the Commission Mr. Gorman described with moving pathos how a friend of his, "a bright young man from Baltimore," a Sunday-school scholar, well recommended by his pastor, wished to be a letter-carrier; and how he went before us to be examined. The first question we asked him, said Mr. Gorman, was the shortest route from Baltimore to China, to which the "bright young man" responded that he didn't want to go to China, and had never studied up that route. Thereupon, said Mr. Gorman, we asked him all about the steamship lines from the United States to Europe, then branched him off into geology, tried him in chemistry, and finally turned him down.

Apparently Mr. Gorman did not know that we kept full records of our examinations. I at once wrote to him stating that I had carefully looked through all our examination papers and had not been able to find one question even remotely resembling any of these questions which he alleged had been asked, and that I would be greatly obliged if he would give me the name of the "bright young man" who had deceived him.

However, that "bright young man" remained permanently without a name. I also asked Mr. Gorman, if he did not wish to give us the name of his informant, to give us the date of the examination in which he was supposed to have

taken part; and I offered, if he would send down a representative to look through our files, to give him all the aid
we could in his effort to discover any such questions.   But
Mr. Gorman, not hitherto known as a sensitive soul, expressed himself as so shocked at the thought that the ve-
racity of the "bright young man" should be doubted that
he could not bring himself to answer my letter.   So I made
a public statement to the effect that no such questions had
ever been asked.   Mr. Gorman brooded over this; and
during the next session of Congress he rose and complained
that he had received a very "impudent" letter from me
(my letter was a respectful note calling attention to the fact
that, if he wished, he could by personal examination satisfy
himself that his statements had no foundation in fact).   He
further stated that he had been "cruelly" called to account
by me because he had been endeavoring to right a "great
wrong" that the Civil Service Commission had committed;
but he never, then or afterwards, furnished any clue to the
identity of that child of his fondest fancy, the bright
young man without a name.[1]
   The incident is of note chiefly as shedding light on the
mental make-up of the man who at the time was one of the
two or three most influential leaders of the Democratic
party.   Mr. Gorman had been Mr. Cleveland's party
manager in the Presidential campaign, and was the Democratic leader in Congress.   It seemed extraordinary that
he should be so reckless as to make statements with no
foundation in fact, which he might have known that I would
not permit to pass unchallenged.   Then, as now, the ordinary newspaper, in New York and elsewhere, was quite
as reckless in its misstatements of fact about public men and
measures; but for a man in Mr. Gorman's position of responsible leadership such action seemed hardly worth while.
However, it is at least to be said for Mr. Gorman that he
was not trying by falsehood to take away any man's character.   It would be well for writers and speakers to bear in

   [1] This is a condensation of a speech I at the time made to the St. Louis Civil
Service Reform Association.   Senator Gorman was then the Senate leader of the
party that had just been victorious in the Congressional elections.

mind the remark of Pudd'nhead Wilson to the effect that while there are nine hundred and ninety-nine kinds of falsehood, the only kind specifically condemned in Scripture, just as murder, theft, and adultery are condemned, is bearing false witness against one's neighbor.

One of the worst features of the old spoils system was the ruthless cruelty and brutality it so often bred in the treatment of faithful public servants without political influence. Life is hard enough and cruel enough at best, and this is as true of public service as of private service. Under no system will it be possible to do away with all favoritism and brutality and meanness and malice. But at least we can try to minimize the exhibition of these qualities. I once came across a case in Washington which very keenly excited my sympathy. Under an Administration prior to the one with which I was connected a lady had been ousted from a Government position. She came to me to see if she could be reinstated. (This was not possible, but by active work I did get her put back in a somewhat lower position, and this only by an appeal to the sympathy of a certain official.) She was so pallid and so careworn that she excited my sympathy and I made inquiries about her. She was a poor woman with two children, a widow. She and her two children were in actual want. She could barely keep the two children decently clad, and she could not give them the food growing children need. Three years before she had been employed in a bureau in a department of Washington, doing her work faithfully, at a salary of about $800. It was enough to keep her and her two children in clothing, food, and shelter. One day the chief of the bureau called her up and told her he was very sorry that he had to dismiss her. In great distress she asked him why; she thought that she had been doing her work satisfactorily. He answered her that she had been doing well, and that he wished very much that he could keep her, that he would do so if he possibly could, but that he could not; for a certain Senator, giving his name, a very influential member of the Senate, had demanded her place for a friend of his who had influence. The woman told the bureau chief that it meant turning her out to starve. She had been thirteen or fourteen years in the public service; she had lost all touch with her friends in her native State; dismissal meant absolute want for her

MARK HANNA.

"A man of rugged sincerity of purpose, of great courage and loyalty, and of unswerving devotion to the interests of the Nation and the people as he saw those interests."

and her children. On this the chief, who was a kind man, said he would not have her turned out, and sent her back to her work.

But three weeks afterwards he called her up again and

told her he could not say how sorry he was, but the thing had to be done. The Senator had been around in person to know why the change had not been made, and had told the chief that he would be himself removed if the place were not given him. The Senator was an extremely influential man. His wants had to be attended to, and the woman had to go. And go she did, and turned out she was, to suffer with her children and to starve outright, or to live in semi-starvation, just as might befall. I do not blame the bureau chief, who hated to do what he did, although he lacked the courage to refuse ; I do not even very much blame the Senator, who did not know the hardship that he was causing, and who had been calloused by long training in the spoils system; but this system, a system which permits and encourages such deeds, is a system of brutal iniquity.

Any man accustomed to dealing with practical politics can with difficulty keep a straight face when he reads or listens to some of the arguments advanced against Civil Service Reform. One of these arguments, a favorite with machine politicians, takes the form of an appeal to "party loyalty" in filling minor offices. Why, again and again these very same machine politicians take just as good care of henchmen of the opposite party as of those of their own party. In the underworld of politics the closest ties are sometimes those which knit together the active professional workers of opposite political parties. A friend of mine in the New York Legislature — the hero of the alpha and omega incident — once remarked to me : "When you have been in public life a little longer, Mr. Roosevelt, you will understand that there are no politics in politics." In the politics to which he was referring this remark could be taken literally.

Another illustration of this truth was incidentally given me, at about the same time, by an acquaintance, a Tammany man named Costigan, a good fellow according to his lights. I had been speaking to him of a fight in one of the New York downtown districts, a Democratic district in which the Republican party was in a hopeless minority, and, moreover, was split into the Half-Breed and Stalwart factions.

It had been an interesting fight in more than one way.   For instance, the Republican party, at the general election, polled something like five hundred and fifty votes, and yet at the primary the two factions polled seven hundred and twenty-five all told.   The sum of the parts was thus considerably greater than the whole.   There had been other little details that made the contest worthy of note.   The hall in which the primary was held had been hired by the Stalwarts from a conscientious gentleman.   To him the Half-Breeds applied to know whether they could not hire the hall away from their opponents, and offered him a substantial money advance.   The conscientious gentleman replied that his word was as good as his bond, that he had hired the hall to the Stalwarts, and that it must be theirs. But he added that he was willing to hire the doorway to the Half-Breeds if they paid him the additional sum of money they had mentioned.   The bargain was struck, and the meeting of the hostile hosts was spirited, when the men who had rented the doorway sought to bar the path of the men who had rented the hall.   I was asking my friend Costigan about the details of the struggle, as he seemed thoroughly acquainted with them, and he smiled good-naturedly over my surprise at there having been more votes cast than there were members of the party in the whole district.   Said I, "Mr. Costigan, you seem to have a great deal of knowledge about this; how did it happen?"   To which he replied, "Come now, Mr. Roosevelt, you know it's the same gang that votes in *all* the primaries."

So much for most of the opposition to the reform.   There was, however, some honest and at least partially justifiable opposition both to certain of the methods advocated by Civil Service Reformers and to certain of the Civil Service Reformers themselves.   The pet shibboleths of the opponents of the reform were that the system we proposed to introduce would give rise to mere red-tape bureaucracy, and that the reformers were pharisees.   Neither statement was true.   Each statement contained some truth.

If men are not to be appointed by favoritism, wise or unwise, honest or dishonest, they must be appointed in some

automatic way, which generally means by competitive examination.   The easiest kind of competitive examination is
an examination in writing.   This is entirely appropriate
for certain classes of work, for lawyers, stenographers, typewriters, clerks, mathematicians, and assistants in an as-
tronomical observatory, for instance.   It is utterly inap-
propriate for carpenters, detectives, and mounted cattle
inspectors along the Rio Grande — to instance three types
of employment as to which I had to do battle to prevent
well-meaning bureaucrats from insisting on written competitive entrance examinations.   It would be quite possible
to hold a very good competitive examination for mounted
cattle inspectors by means of practical tests in brand reading
and shooting with rifle and revolver, in riding "mean"
horses and in roping and throwing steers.   I did my best to
have examinations of this kind instituted, but my proposal
was of precisely the type which most shocks the routine
official mind, and I was never able to get it put into practical
effect.

The important point, and the point most often forgotten
by zealous Civil Service Reformers, was to remember that
the routine competitive examination was merely a means to
an end.   It did not always produce ideal results.   But it
was normally better than a system of appointments for
spoils purposes; it sometimes worked out very well indeed;
and in most big governmental offices it not only gave satisfactory results, but was the only system under which good
results could be obtained.   For instance, when I was Police
Commissioner we appointed some two thousand policemen
at one time.   It was utterly impossible for the Commissioners each to examine personally the six or eight thousand
applicants.   Therefore they had to be appointed either on
the recommendation of outsiders or else by written competitive examination.   The latter method — the one we
adopted — was infinitely preferable.   We held a rigid physical and moral pass examination, and then, among those
who passed, we held a written competitive examination, requiring only the knowledge that any good primary common
school education would meet — that is, a test of ordinary

intelligence and simple mental training. Occasionally a man who would have been a good officer failed, and occasionally a man who turned out to be a bad officer passed; but, as a rule, the men with intelligence sufficient to enable them to answer the questions were of a type very distinctly above that of those who failed.

The answers returned to some of the questions gave an illuminating idea of the intelligence of those answering them. For instance, one of our questions in a given examination was a request to name five of the New England States. One competitor, obviously of foreign birth, answered: "England, Ireland, Scotland, Whales, and Cork." His neighbor, who had probably looked over his shoulder but who had North of Ireland prejudices, made the same answer except that he substituted Belfast for Cork. A request for a statement as to the life of Abraham Lincoln elicited, among other less startling pieces of information, the fact that many of the applicants thought that he was a general in the Civil War; several thought that he was President of the Confederate States; three thought he had been assassinated by Jefferson Davis, one by Thomas Jefferson, one by Garfield, several by Guiteau, and one by Ballington Booth — the last representing a memory of the fact that he had been shot by a man named Booth, to whose surname the writer added the name with which he was most familiar in connection therewith. A request to name five of the States that seceded in 1861 received answers that included almost every State in the Union. It happened to be at the time of the silver agitation in the West, and the Rocky Mountain States accordingly figured in a large percentage of the answers. Some of the men thought that Chicago was on the Pacific Ocean. Others, in answer to a query as to who was the head of the United States Government, wavered between myself and Recorder Goff; one brilliant genius, for inscrutable reasons, placed the leadership in the New York Fire Department. Now of course some of the men who answered these questions wrong were nevertheless quite capable of making good policemen; but it is fair to assume that on the average the candidate who has a rudimentary knowledge of the government, geography, and history of his country is a little better fitted, in point of intelligence, to be a policeman than the one who has not.

Therefore I felt convinced, after full experience, that as regards very large classes of public servants by far the best way to choose the men for appointment was by means of written competitive examination. But I absolutely split off from the bulk of my professional Civil Service Reform friends when they advocated written competitive examinations for promotion. In the Police Department I found these examinations a serious handicap in the way of getting the best men promoted, and never in any office did I find that the written competitive promotion examination did any good. The reason for a written competitive entrance examination is that it is impossible for the head of the office, or the candidate's prospective immediate superior, himself to know the average candidate or to test his ability. But when once in office the best way to test any man's ability is by long experience in seeing him actually at work. His promotion should depend upon the judgment formed of him by his superiors.

So much for the objections to the examinations. Now for the objections to the men who advocated the reform. As a rule these men were high-minded and disinterested. Certain of them, men like the leaders in the Maryland and Indiana Reform Associations, for instances, Messrs. Bonaparte and Rose, Foulke and Swift, added common sense, broad sympathy, and practical efficiency to their high-mindedness. But in New York, Philadelphia, and Boston there really was a certain mental and moral thinness among very many of the leaders in the Civil Service Reform movement. It was this quality which made them so profoundly antipathetic to vigorous and intensely human people of the stamp of my friend Joe Murray — who, as I have said, always felt that my Civil Service Reform affiliations formed the one blot on an otherwise excellent public record. The Civil Service Reform movement was one from above downwards, and the men who took the lead in it were not men who as a rule possessed a very profound sym-

M

pathy with or understanding of the ways of thought and life of their average fellow-citizen.   They were not men who themselves desired to be letter-carriers or clerks or policemen, or to have their friends appointed to these positions.   Having no temptation themselves in this direction, they were eagerly anxious to prevent other people getting such appointments as a reward for political services.   In this they were quite right.   It would be impossible to run any big public office to advantage save along the lines of the strictest application of Civil Service Reform principles ; and the system should be extended throughout our governmental service far more widely than is now the case.

But there are other and more vital reforms than this. Too many Civil Service Reformers, when the trial came, proved tepidly indifferent or actively hostile to reforms that were of profound and far-reaching social and industrial consequence.   Many of them were at best lukewarm about movements for the improvement of the conditions of toil and life among men and women who labor under hard surroundings, and were positively hostile to movements which curbed the power of the great corporation magnates and directed into useful instead of pernicious channels the activities of the great corporation lawyers who advised them.

Most of the newspapers which regarded themselves as the especial champions of Civil Service Reform and as the highest exponents of civic virtue, and which distrusted the average citizen and shuddered over the "coarseness" of the professional politicians, were, nevertheless, given to vices even more contemptible than, although not so gross as, those they denounced and derided.   Their editors were refined men of cultivated tastes, whose pet temptations were backbiting, mean slander, and the snobbish worship of anything clothed in wealth and the outward appearances of conventional respectability.   They were not robust or powerful men ; they felt ill at ease in the company of rough, strong men ; often they had in them a vein of physical timidity.   They avenged themselves to themselves for an uneasy subconsciousness of their own shortcomings by sitting in cloistered — or, rather, pleasantly upholstered — seclusion, and sneering at and lying about men who made them feel uncomfortable. Sometimes these were bad men, who made them feel uncomfortable by the exhibition of coarse and repellent vice; and sometimes they were men of high character, who held ideals of courage and of service to others, and who looked down and warred against the shortcomings of swollen wealth, and the effortless, easy lives of those whose horizon is bounded by a sheltered and timid respectability. These newspapers, owned and edited by these men, although free from the repulsive vulgarity of the yellow press, were susceptible to influence by the privileged interests, and were almost or quite as hostile to manliness as they were to unrefined vice — and were much more hostile to it than to the typical shortcomings of wealth and refinement. They favored Civil Service Reform; they favored copyright laws, and the removal of the tariff on works of art; they favored all the proper (and even more strongly all the improper) movements for international peace and arbitration; in short, they favored all good, and many goody-goody, measures so long as they did not cut deep into social wrong or make demands on National and individual virility. They opposed, or were lukewarm about, efforts to build up the army and the navy, for they were not sensitive concerning National honor; and, above all, they opposed every non-milk-and-water effort, however sane, to change our social and economic system in such a fashion as to substitute the ideal of justice towards all for the ideal of kindly charity from the favored few to the possibly grateful many.

Some of the men foremost in the struggle for Civil Service Reform have taken a position of honorable leadership in the battle for those other and more vital reforms. But many of them promptly abandoned the field of effort for decency when the battle took the form, not of a fight against the petty grafting of small bosses and small politicians — a vitally necessary battle, be it remembered — but of a fight against the great intrenched powers of privilege, a fight to secure justice through the law for ordinary men and women, instead of leaving them to suffer cruel injustice either because the law failed to protect them or because it was twisted from its legitimate purposes into a means for oppressing them.

One of the reasons why the boss so often keeps his hold, especially in municipal matters, is, or at least has been in the past, because so many of the men who claim to be reformers have been blind to the need of working in human fashion for social and industrial betterment. Such words as "boss" and "machine" now imply evil, but both the implication the words carry and the definition of the words themselves are somewhat vague. A leader is necessary; but his opponents always call him a boss. An organization is necessary; but the men in opposition always call it a machine. Nevertheless, there is a real and deep distinction between the leader and the boss, between organizations and machines. A political leader who fights openly for principles, and who keeps his position of leadership by stirring the consciences and convincing the intellects of his followers, so that they have confidence in him and will follow him because they can achieve greater results under him than under any one else, is doing work which is indispensable in a democracy. The boss, on the other hand, is a man who does not gain his power by open means, but by secret means, and usually by corrupt means. Some of the worst and most powerful bosses in our political history either held no public office or else some unimportant public office. They made no appeal either to intellect or conscience. Their work was done behind closed doors, and consisted chiefly in the use of that greed which gives in order that in return it may get. A boss of this kind can pull wires in conventions, can manipulate members of the Legislature, can control the giving or withholding of office, and serves as the intermediary for bringing together the powers of corrupt politics and corrupt business. If he is at one end of the social scale, he may through his agents traffic in the most brutal forms of vice and give protection to the purveyors of shame and sin in return for money bribes. If at the other end of the scale, he may be the means of securing favors from high public officials, legislative or executive, to great industrial interests; the transaction being sometimes a naked matter of bargain and sale, and sometimes being carried on in such manner that both parties thereto can more or less successfully disguise it to their consciences as in the public interest. The machine is simply another name for the kind of organization which is certain to grow up in a party or section of a party controlled by such bosses as these and by their henchmen, whereas, of course, an effective organization of decent men is essential in order to secure decent politics.

If these bosses were responsible for nothing but pure wickedness, they would probably last but a short time in any community. And, in any event, if the men who are horrified by their wickedness were themselves as practical and as thoroughly in touch with human nature, the bosses would have a short shrift. The trouble is that the boss does understand human nature, and that he fills a place which the reformer cannot fill unless he likewise understands human nature. Sometimes the boss is a man who cares for political power purely for its own sake, as he might care for any other hobby; more often he has in view some definitely selfish object such as political or financial advancement. He can rarely accomplish much unless he has another side to him. A successful boss is very apt to be a man who, in addition to committing wickedness in his own interest, also does look after the interests of others, even if not from good motives. There are some communities so fortunate that there are very few men who have private interests to be served, and in these the power of the boss is at a minimum. There are many country communities of this type. But in communities where there is poverty and ignorance, the conditions are ripe for the growth of a boss. Moreover, wherever big business interests are liable either to be improperly favored or improperly discriminated against and blackmailed by public officials — and the result is just as vicious in one case as in the other — the boss is almost certain to develop. The best way of getting at this type of boss is by keeping the public conscience aroused and alert, so that it will tolerate neither improper attack upon, nor improper favoritism towards, these corporations, and will quickly punish any public servant guilty of either.

There is often much good in the type of boss, especially common in big cities, who fulfills towards the people of his district in rough and ready fashion the position of friend and protector. He uses his influence to get jobs for young men who need them. He goes into court for a wild young fellow who has gotten into trouble. He helps out with cash or credit the widow who is in straits, or the breadwinner who is crippled or for some other cause temporarily out of work. He organizes clambakes and chowder parties and picnics, and is consulted by the local labor leaders when a cut in wages is threatened. For some of his constituents he does proper favors, and for others wholly improper favors; but he preserves human relations with all. He may be a very bad and very corrupt man, a man whose action in blackmailing and protecting vice is of far-reaching damage to his constituents. But these constituents are for the most part men and women who struggle hard against poverty and with whom the problem of living is very real and very close. They would prefer clean and honest government, if this clean and honest government is accompanied by human sympathy, human understanding. But an appeal made to them for virtue in the abstract, an appeal made by good men who do not really understand their needs, will often pass quite unheeded, if on the other side stands the boss, the friend and benefactor, who may have been guilty of much wrong-doing in things that they are hardly aware concern them, but who appeals to them, not only for the sake of favors to come, but in the name of gratitude and loyalty, and above all of understanding and fellow-feeling. They have a feeling of clan-loyalty to him; his and their relations may be substantially those which are right and proper among primitive people still in the clan stage of moral development. The successful fight against this type of vicious boss, and the type of vicious politics which produces it, can be made only by men who have a genuine fellow-feeling for and understanding of the people for and with whom they are to work, and who in practical fashion seek their social and industrial benefit.

There are communities of poor men, whose lives are hard, in which the boss, though he would be out of place in a more advanced community, if fundamentally an honest man, meets a real need which would otherwise not be met. Because of his limitations in other than purely local matters it may be our duty to fight such a boss; but it may also be our duty to recognize, within his limitations, both his sincerity and his usefulness.

Yet again even the boss who really is evil, like the business man who really is evil, may on certain points be sound, and be doing good work. It may be the highest duty of the patriotic public servant to work with the big boss or the big business man on these points, while refusing to work with him on others. In the same way there are many self-styled reformers whose conduct is such as to warrant Tom Reed's bitter remark, that when Dr. Johnson defined patriotism as the last refuge of a scoundrel he was ignorant of the infinite possibilities contained in the word reform. Yet, none the less, it is our duty to work for the reforms these men champion, without regard to the misconduct of the men themselves on other points. I have known in my life many big business men and many big political bosses who often or even generally did evil, but who on some occasions and on certain issues were right. I never hesitated to do battle against these men when they were wrong; and, on the other hand, as long as they were going my way I was glad to have them do so. To have repudiated their aid when they were right and were striving for a right end, and for what was of benefit to the people — no matter what their motives may have been — would have been childish, and moreover would have itself been misconduct against the people.

My duty was to stand with every one while he was right, and to stand against him when he went wrong; and this I have tried to do as regards individuals and as regards groups of individuals. When a business man or labor leader, politician or reformer, is right, I support him; when he goes wrong, I leave him. When Mr. Lorimer upheld the war for the liberation of Cuba, I supported him; when he became United States Senator by improper methods, I opposed him.

The principles or methods which the Socialists advocate and which I believe to be in the interest of the people I support, and those which I believe to be against the interest of the people I oppose.   Moreover, when a man has done evil, but changes, and works for decency and righteousness, and when, as far as I can see, the change is real and the man's conduct sincere, then I welcome him and work heartily with him, as an equal with an equal.   For thirty years after the Civil War the creed of mere materialism was rampant in both American politics and American business, and many, many strong men, in accordance with the prevailing commercial and political morality, did things for which they deserve blame and condemnation; but if they now sincerely change, and strive for better things, it is unwise and unjust to bar them from fellowship.   So long as they work for evil, smite them with the sword of the Lord and of Gideon!   When they change and show their faith by their works, remember the words of Ezekiel: "If the wicked will turn from all the sins he has committed, and keep all my statutes, and do that which is lawful and right, he shall surely live, he shall not die.   All his transgressions that he hath committed, they shall not be mentioned unto him : in his righteousness that he hath done he shall live.   Have I any pleasure at all that the wicked should die? saith the Lord God; and not that he should return from his ways and live?"

Every man who has been in practical politics grows to realize that politicians, big and little, are no more all of them bad than they are all of them good.   Many of these men are very bad men indeed, but there are others among them — and some among those held up to special obloquy, too — who, even although they may have done much that is evil, also show traits of sterling worth which many of their critics wholly lack.   There are few men for whom I have ever felt a more cordial and contemptuous dislike than for some of the bosses and big professional politicians with whom I have been brought into contact.   On the other hand, in the case of some political leaders who were most bitterly attacked as bosses, I grew to know certain sides of their characters which inspired in me a very genuine regard and respect.

To read much of the assault on Senator Hanna, one would have thought that he was a man incapable of patriotism or of far-sighted devotion to the country's good. I was brought into intimate contact with him only during the two and a half years immediately preceding his death. I was then President, and perforce watched all his actions at close range. During that time he showed himself to be a man of rugged sincerity of purpose, of great courage and loyalty, and of unswerving devotion to the interests of the Nation and the people as he saw those interests. He was as sincerely desirous of helping laboring men as of helping capitalists. His ideals were in many ways not my ideals, and there were points where both by temperament and by conviction we were far apart. Before this time he had always been unfriendly to me; and I do not think he ever grew to like me, at any rate not until the very end of his life. Moreover, I came to the Presidency under circumstances which, if he had been a smaller man, would inevitably have thrown him into violent antagonism to me. He was the close and intimate friend of President McKinley. He was McKinley's devoted ally and follower, and his trusted adviser, who was in complete sympathy with him. Partly because of this friendship, his position in the Senate and in the country was unique.

With McKinley's sudden death Senator Hanna found himself bereft of his dearest friend, while I, who had just come to the Presidency, was in his view an untried man, whose trustworthiness on many public questions was at least doubtful. Ordinarily, as has been shown, not only in our history, but in the history of all other countries, in countless instances, over and over again, this situation would have meant suspicion, ill will, and, at the last, open and violent antagonism. Such was not the result, in this case, primarily because Senator Hanna had in him the quality that enabled him to meet a serious crisis with dignity, with power, and with disinterested desire to work for the common good. Within a few days of my accession he called on me, and with entire friendliness and obvious sincerity, but also with entire self-respect, explained that he mourned McKinley as probably no other man did; that he had not been especially my friend, but that he wished me to understand that thence-forward, on every question where he could conscientiously support me, I could count upon his giving me as loyal aid as it was in his power to render. He added that this must not be understood as committing him to favor me for nomination and election, because that matter must be left to take care of itself as events should decide; but that, aside from this, what he said was to be taken literally; in other words, he would do his best to make my Administration a success by supporting me heartily on every point on which he conscientiously could, and that this I could count upon. He kept his word absolutely. He never became especially favorable to my nomination; and most of his close friends became bitterly opposed to me and used every effort to persuade him to try to bring about my downfall. Most men in his position would have been tempted to try to make capital at my expense by antagonizing me and discrediting me so as to make my policies fail, just for the sake of making them fail. Senator Hanna, on the contrary, did everything possible to make them succeed. He kept his word in the letter and the spirit, and on every point on which he felt conscientiously able to support me he gave me the heartiest and most effective support, and did all in his power to make my Administration a success; and this with no hope of any reward for himself, of any gratitude from me, or of any appreciation by the public at large, but solely because he deemed such action necessary for the well-being of the country as a whole.

My experience with Senator Quay was similar. I had no personal relations with him before I was President, and knew nothing of him save by hearsay. Soon after I became President, Senator Quay called upon me, told me he had known me very slightly, that he thought most men who claimed to be reformers were hypocrites, but that he deemed me sincere, that he thought conditions had become such that aggressive courage and honesty were necessary in order to remedy them, that he believed I intended to be a good and efficient President, and that to the best of his ability he would support me in making my Administration a success.

He kept his word with absolute good faith. He had been in the Civil War, and was a medal of honor man; and I think my having been in the Spanish War gave him at the outset a kindly feeling toward me. He was also a very well-read man — I owe to him, for instance, my acquaintance with the writings of the Finnish novelist Topelius. Not only did he support me on almost every public question in which I was most interested — including, I am convinced, every one on which he felt he conscientiously could do so — but he also at the time of his death gave a striking proof of his disinterested desire to render a service to certain poor people, and this under conditions in which not only would he never know if the service were rendered but in which he had no reason to expect that his part in it would ever be made known to any other man.

Quay was descended from a French voyageur who had some Indian blood in him. He was proud of this Indian blood, took an especial interest in Indians, and whenever Indians came to Washington they always called on him. Once during my Administration a delegation of Iroquois came over from Canada to call on me at the White House. Their visit had in it something that was pathetic as well as amusing. They represented the descendants of the Six Nations, who fled to Canada after Sullivan harried their towns in the Revolutionary War. Now, a century and a quarter later, their people thought that they would like to come back into the United States; and these representatives had called upon me with the dim hope that perhaps I could give their tribes land on which they could settle. As soon as they reached Washington they asked Quay to bring them to call on me, which he did, telling me that of course their errand was hopeless and that he had explained as much to them, but that they would like me to extend the courtesy of an interview. At the close of the interview, which had been conducted with all the solemnities of calumet and wampum, the Indians filed out. Quay, before following them, turned to me with his usual emotionless face and said, "Good-by, Mr. President; this reminds one of the Flight of a Tartar Tribe, doesn't it?" I answered, "So you're fond of De Quincey,

Senator ?" to which Quay responded, "Yes; always liked De Quincey; good-by." And away he went with the tribesmen, who seemed to have walked out of a remote past.

Quay had become particularly concerned about the Delawares in the Indian Territory. He felt that the Interior Department did not do them justice. He also felt that his colleagues of the Senate took no interest in them. When in the spring of 1904 he lay in his house mortally sick, he sent me word that he had something important to say to me, and would have himself carried round to see me. I sent back word not to think of doing so, and that on my way back from church next Sunday I would stop in and call on him. This I accordingly did. He was lying in his bed, death written on his face. He thanked me for coming, and then explained that, as he was on the point of death and knew he would never return to Washington — it was late spring and he was about to leave — he wished to see me to get my personal promise that, after he died, I would myself look after the interests of the Delaware Indians. He added that he did not trust the Interior Department — although he knew that I did not share his views on this point — and that still less did he believe that any of his colleagues in the Senate would exert themselves in the interests of the Delawares, and that therefore he wished my personal assurance that I would personally see that no injustice was done them. I told him I would do so, and then added, in rather perfunctory fashion, that he must not take such a gloomy view of himself, that when he got away for the summer I hoped he would recover and be back all right when Congress opened. A gleam came into the old fighter's eyes and he answered: "No, I am dying, and you know it. I don't mind dying; but I do wish it were possible for me to get off into the great north woods and crawl out on a rock in the sun and die like a wolf !"

I never saw him again. When he died I sent a telegram of sympathy to his wife. A paper which constantly preached reform, and which kept up its circulation by the no less constant practice of slander, a paper which in theory condemned all public men who violated the eighth commandment, and in

practice subsisted by incessant violation of the ninth, assailed
me for sending my message to the dead man's wife.   I knew
the editors of this paper, and the editor who was their predecessor.   They had led lives of bodily ease and the avoidance of bodily risk; they earned their livelihood by the
practice of mendacity for profit; and they delivered malig-

MATTHEW STANLEY QUAY.

" In his youth he freely risked his life for a great ideal, and when death was already clutching his breast he spent almost his last breath in serving humble and friendless people
whom he had served with disinterested loyalty."

nant judgment on a dead man who, whatever his faults,
had in his youth freely risked his life for a great ideal, and
who when death was already clutching his breast had spent
almost his last breath on behalf of humble and friendless
people whom he had served with disinterested loyalty.

There is no greater duty than to war on the corrupt and
unprincipled boss, and on the corrupt and unprincipled
business man; and for the matter of that, on the corrupt

and unprincipled labor leader also, and on the corrupt and unprincipled editor, and on any one else who is corrupt and unprincipled. But where the conditions are such, whether in politics or in business, that the great majority of men have behaved in a way which is gradually seen to be improper, but which at one time did not conflict with the generally accepted morality, then the warfare on the system should not include warfare on the men themselves, unless they decline to amend their ways and to dissociate themselves from the system. There are many good, unimaginative citizens who in politics or in business act in accordance with accepted standards, in a matter-of-course way, without questioning these standards; until something happens which sharply arouses them to the situation, whereupon they try to work for better things. The proper course in such event is to let bygones be bygones, and if the men prove by their actions the sincerity of their conversion, heartily to work with them for the betterment of business and political conditions.

By the time that I was ending my career as Civil Service Commissioner I was already growing to understand that mere improvement in political conditions by itself was not enough. I dimly realized that an even greater fight must be waged to improve economic conditions, and to secure social and industrial justice, justice as between individuals and justice as between classes. I began to see that political effort was largely valuable as it found expression and resulted in such social and industrial betterment. I was gradually puzzling out, or trying to puzzle out, the answers to various questions — some as yet unsolvable to any of us, but for the solution of which it is the bounden duty of all of us to work. I had grown to realize very keenly that the duty of the Government to protect women and children must be extended to include the protection of all the crushable elements of labor. I saw that it was the affair of all our people to see that justice obtained between the big corporation and its employees, and between the big corporation and its smaller rivals, as well as its customers and the general public. I saw that it was the affair of all of us, and not only of the employer, if dividends went up and wages went down ; that it was to the interest of all of us that a full share of the benefit of improved machinery should go to the workman who used the machinery ; and also that it was to the interest of all of us that each man, whether brain worker or hand worker, should do the best work of which he was capable, and that there should be some correspondence between the value of the work and the value of the reward. It is these and many similar questions which in their sum make up the great social and industrial problems of to-day, the most interesting and important of the problems with which our public life must deal.

In handling these problems I believe that much can be done by the Government. Furthermore, I believe that, after all that the Government can do has been done, there will remain as the most vital of all factors the individual character of the average man and the average woman. No governmental action can do more than supplement individual action. Moreover, there must be collective action of kinds distinct from governmental action. A body of public opinion must be formed, must make itself felt, and in the end transform, and be transformed by, the gradual raising of individual standards of conduct.

It is curious to see how difficult it is to make some men understand that insistence upon one factor does not and must not mean failure fully to recognize other factors. The selfish individual needs to be taught that we must now shackle cunning by law exactly as a few centuries back we shackled force by law. Unrestricted individualism spells ruin to the individual himself. But so does the elimination of individualism, whether by law or custom. It is a capital error to fail to recognize the vital need of good laws. It is also a capital error to believe that good laws will accomplish anything unless the average man has the right stuff in him. The toiler, the manual laborer, has received less than justice, and he must be protected, both by law, by custom, and by the exercise of his right to increase his wage ; and yet to decrease the quantity and quality of his work will work only evil. There must be a far greater meed of respect and reward for the hand worker than we now give him, if our society is to be put on a sound basis; and this respect and reward cannot be given him unless he is as ambitious to do the best possible work as is the highest type of brain worker, whether doctor or writer or artist. There must be a raising of standards, and not a leveling down to the standard of the poorest and most inefficient. There is urgent need of intelligent governmental action to assist in making the life of the man who tills the soil all that it should be, and to see that the manual worker gets his full share of the reward for what he helps produce; but if either farmer, mechanic, or day laborer is shiftless or lazy, if he shirks downright hard work, if he is stupid or self-indulgent, then no law can save him, and he must give way to a better type.

I suppose that some good people will misunderstand what I say, and will insist on taking only half of it as representing the whole. Let me repeat. When I say, that, even after we have all the good laws necessary, the chief factor in any given man's success or failure must be that man's own character, it must not be inferred that I am in the least minimizing the importance of these laws, the real and vital need for them. The struggle for individual advancement and development can be brought to naught, or indefinitely retarded, by the absence of law or by bad law. It can be immeasurably aided by organized effort on the part of the State. Collective action and individual action, public law and private character, are both necessary. It is only by a slow and patient inward transformation such as these laws aid in bringing about that men are really helped upward in their struggle for a higher and a fuller life. Recognition of individual character as the most important of all factors does not mean failure fully to recognize that we must have good laws, and that we must have our best men in office to enforce these laws. The Nation collectively will in this way be able to be of real and genuine service to each of us individually; and, on the other hand, the wisdom of the collective action will mainly depend on the high individual average of citizenship.

The relationship of man and woman is the fundamental

relationship that stands at the base of the whole social structure. Much can be done by law towards putting women on
a footing of complete and entire equal rights with man —
including the right to vote, the right to hold and use property,
and the right to enter any profession she desires on the same
terms as the man. Yet when this has been done it will
amount to little unless on the one hand the man himself
realizes his duty to the woman, and unless on the other
hand the woman realizes that she has no claim to rights
unless she performs the duties that go with those rights and
that alone justify her in appealing to them. A cruel, selfish,
or licentious man is an abhorrent member of the community; but, after all, his actions are no worse in the long run
than those of the woman who is content to be a parasite on
others, who is cold, selfish, caring for nothing but frivolous
pleasure and ignoble ease. The law of worthy effort, the
law of service for a worthy end, without regard to whether
it brings pleasure or pain, is the only right law of life, whether
for man or for woman. The man must not be selfish; nor,
if the woman is wise, will she let the man grow selfish, and
this not only for her own sake but for his. One of the
prime needs is to remember that almost every duty is composed of two seemingly conflicting elements, and that over-
insistence on one, to the exclusion of the other, may defeat
its own end. Any man who studies the statistics of the
birth-rate among the native Americans of New England, or
among the native French of France, needs not to be told
that when prudence and forethought are carried to the point
of cold selfishness and self-indulgence, the race is bound to
disappear. Taking into account the women who for good
reasons do not marry, or who when married are childless or
are able to have but one or two children, it is evident that
the married woman able to have children must on an average
have four or the race will not perpetuate itself. This is the
mere statement of a self-evident truth. Yet foolish and
self-indulgent people often resent this statement as if it
were in some way possible by denunciation to reverse the
facts of nature; and, on the other hand, improvident and
shiftless people, inconsiderate and brutal people, treat the

N

statement as if it justified heads of families in having enormous numbers of badly nourished, badly brought up, and badly cared for children for whom they make no effort to provide.   A man must think well before he marries.   He must be a tender and considerate husband and realize that there is no other human being to whom he owes so much of love and regard and consideration as he does to the woman who with pain bears and with labor rears the children that are his.   No words can paint the scorn and contempt which must be felt by all right-thinking men, not only for the brutal husband, but for the husband who fails to show full loyalty and consideration to his wife.   Moreover, he must work, he must do his part in the world.   On the other hand, the woman must realize that she has no more right to shirk the business of wifehood and motherhood than the man has to shirk his business as breadwinner for the household. Women should have free access to every field of labor which they care to enter, and when their work is as valuable as that of a man it should be paid as highly.   Yet normally for the man and the woman whose welfare is more important than the welfare of any other human beings, the woman must remain the housemother, the homekeeper, and the man must remain the breadwinner, the provider for the wife who bears his children and for the children she brings into the world.   No other work is as valuable or as exacting for either man or woman; it must always, in every healthy society, be for both man and woman the prime work, the most important work; normally all other work is of secondary importance, and must come as an addition to, not a substitute for, this primary work.   The partnership should be one of equal rights, one of love, of self-respect and unselfishness, above all a partnership for the performance of the most vitally important of all duties.   The performance of duty, and not an indulgence in vapid ease and vapid pleasure, is all that makes life worth while.

Suffrage for women should be looked on from this standpoint.   Personally I feel that it is exactly as much a "right" of women as of men to vote.   But the important point with both men and women is to treat the exercise of the

JANE ADDAMS.

Copyright by Falk.
MARY ANTIN.

FRANCES KELLOR.

"I always favored Woman's Suffrage, but only tepidly, until my association with women like Jane Addams and Frances Kellor, who desired it as one means of enabling them to render better and more efficient service, changed me into a zealous instead of a luke-warm adherent of the cause, in spite of the fact that a few of the best women of the same type, women like Mary Antin, did not favor the movement."

suffrage as a duty, which, in the long run, must be well performed to be of the slightest value. I always favored woman's suffrage, but only tepidly, until my association with women like Jane Addams and Frances Kellor, who desired it as one means of enabling them to render better and more efficient service, changed me into a zealous instead of a lukewarm adherent of the cause — in spite of the fact that a few of the best women of the same type, women like Mary Antin, did not favor the movement. A vote is like a rifle: its usefulness depends upon the character of the user. The mere possession of the vote will no more benefit men and women not sufficiently developed to use it than the possession of rifles will turn untrained Egyptian fellaheen into soldiers. This is as true of woman as of man — and no more true. Universal suffrage in Hayti has not made the Haytians able to govern themselves in any true sense; and woman suffrage in Utah in no shape or way affected the problem of polygamy. I believe in suffrage for women in America, because I think they are fit for it. I believe for women, as for men, more in the duty of fitting one's self to do well and wisely with the ballot than in the naked right to cast the ballot.

I wish that people would read books like the novels and stories, at once strong and charming, of Henry Bordeaux, books like Kathleen Norris's "Mother," and Cornelia Comer's "Preliminaries," and would use these, and other such books, as tracts, now and then! Perhaps the following correspondence will give a better idea than I can otherwise give of the problems that in everyday life come before men and women, and of the need that the man shall show himself unselfish and considerate, and do his full share of the joint duty:

January 3, 1913.

Colonel Theodore Roosevelt:

Dear Sir — I suppose you are willing to stand sponsor for the assertion that the women of the country are not doing their duty unless they have large families. I wonder if you know the real reason, after all. Society and clubs are held largely to blame, but society really takes in so few people, after all. I thought, when I got married at twenty, that it was the proper thing to have a family, and, as we had very little of this world's goods, also thought it the thing to do all the necessary work for them. I have had nine children, did all my own work, including washing, ironing, house-cleaning, and the care of the little ones as they came along, which was about every two years; also sewed everything they wore, including trousers for the boys and caps and jackets for the girls while little. I also helped them all in their school work, and started them in music, etc. But as they grew older I got behind the times. I never belonged to a club or a society or lodge, nor went to any one's house scarcely; there wasn't time. In consequence, I knew nothing that was going on in the town, much less the events of the country, and at the same time my husband kept growing in wisdom and knowledge, from mixing with men and hearing topics of the times discussed. At the beginning of our married life I had just as quick a mind to grasp things as he did, and had more school education, having graduated from a three years' high school. My husband more and more declined to discuss things with me; as he said, "I didn't know anything about it." When I'd ask, he'd say, "Oh, you wouldn't understand if I'd tell you." So here I am, at forty-five years, hopelessly dull and uninteresting, while he can mix with the brightest minds in the country as an equal. He's a strong Progressive man, took very active part in the late campaign, etc. I am also Progressive, and tried my best, after so many years of shut-in life, to grasp the ideas you stood for, and read everything I could find during the summer and fall. But I've been out of touch with people too long now, and my husband would much rather go and talk to some woman who hasn't had any children, because she *knows things* (I am not specifying any particular woman). I simply bore him to death because I'm not interesting. Now, tell me, how was it my fault? I was only doing what I thought was my duty. No woman can keep up with things who never talks with any one but young children. As soon as my children grew up they took the same attitude as their father, and frequently say, "Oh, mother doesn't know." They look up to and admire their father because he's a man of the world and knows how to act when he goes out. How can I urge my daughters now to go and raise large families? It means by the time you have lost your figure and charm for them they are all ashamed of you. Now, as a believer in woman's rights, do a little talking to the men as to their duties to their wives, or else refrain from urging us women to have children. I am only one of thousands of middle-class respectable women who give their lives to raise a nice family, and then who become bitter from the injustice done us. Don't let this go into the waste-basket, but think it over. Yours respectfully, ————.

New York, January 11, 1913.

My Dear Mrs. ————:

Most certainly your letter will not go into the waste-paper basket. I shall think it over and show it to Mrs. Roosevelt. Will you let me say, in the first place, that a woman who can write such a letter is certainly not "hopelessly dull and uninteresting"! If the facts are as you state, then I do not wonder that you feel bitterly and that you feel that the gravest kind of injustice has been done you. I have always tried to insist to men that they should do their duty to the women even more than the women to them. Now I hardly like to write specifically about your husband, because you might not like it yourself. It seems to me almost incredible that any man who is the husband of a woman who has borne him nine children should not feel that they and he are lastingly her debtors. You say that you have had nine children, that you did all your own work, including washing, ironing, house-cleaning, and the care of the little ones as they came along; that you sewed everything they wore, including trousers for the boys and caps and jackets for the girls while little; that you helped them all in their school work and started them in music; but that as they grew older you got behind the times, that you never belonged to a club or society or lodge, nor went to any one's house, as you hardly had time to do so; and that in consequence your husband outgrew you, and that your children look up to him and not to you and feel that they have outgrown you. If these facts are so, you have done a great and wonderful work, and the only explanation I can possibly give of the attitude you describe on the part of your husband and children is that they do not understand what it is that you have done. I emphatically believe in unselfishness, but I also believe that it is a mistake to let other people grow selfish, even when the other people are husband and children.

Now, I suggest that you take your letter to me, of which I send you back a copy, and this letter, and then select out of your family the one with whom you feel most sympathy, whether it is your husband or one of your children. Show the two letters to him or her, and then have a frank talk about the matter. If any man, as you say, becomes ashamed of his wife because she has lost her figure in bearing his children, then that man is a hound and has every cause to be ashamed of himself. I am sending you a little book called "Mother," by Kathleen Norris, which will give you my views on the matter. Of course there are base and selfish men, just as there are, although I believe in smaller number, base and selfish women. Man and woman alike should profit by the teachings in such a story as this of "Mother."

Sincerely yours,
THEODORE ROOSEVELT.

January 21, 1913.

Colonel Theodore Roosevelt:

My dear Sir — Your letter came as a surprise, for I wasn't expecting an answer. The next day the book came, and I thank you for your ready sympathy and understanding. I feel as though you and Mrs. Roosevelt would think I was hardly loyal to my husband and children; but knowing of no other way to bring the idea which was so strong in my mind to your notice, I told my personal story. If it will, in a small measure, be the means of helping some one else by molding public opinion, through you, I shall be content. You have helped me more than you know. Just having you interested is as good as a tonic, and braces me up till I feel as though I shall refuse to be "laid on the shelf." . . . To think that you'd bother to send me a book. I shall always treasure it both for the text of the book and the sender. I read it with absorbing interest. The mother was so splendid. She was ideal. The situations are so startlingly real, just like what happens here every day with variations. —— ——.

A narrative of facts is often more convincing than a homily; and these two letters of my correspondent carry their own lesson.

Parenthetically, let me remark that whenever a man thinks that he has outgrown the woman who is his mate, he will do well carefully to consider whether his growth has not been downward instead of upward, whether the facts are not merely that he has fallen away from his wife's standard of refinement and of duty.

CHAPTER VI

THE NEW YORK POLICE

IN the spring of 1895 I was appointed by Mayor Strong Police Commissioner, and I served as President of the Police Commission of New York for the two following years. Mayor Strong had been elected Mayor the preceding fall, when the general anti-Democratic wave of that year coincided with one of the city's occasional insurrections of virtue and consequent turning out of Tammany from municipal control. He had been elected on a non-partisan ticket — usually (although not always) the right kind of ticket in municipal affairs, provided it represents not a bargain among factions but genuine non-partisanship with the genuine purpose to get the right men in control of the city government on a platform which deals with the needs of the average men and women, the men and women who work hard and who too often live hard. I was appointed with the distinct understanding that I was to administer the Police Department with entire disregard of partisan politics, and only from the standpoint of a good citizen interested in promoting the welfare of all good citizens. My task, therefore, was really simple. Mayor Strong had already offered me the Street-Cleaning Department. For this work I did not feel that I had any especial fitness. I resolutely refused to accept the position, and the Mayor ultimately got a far better man for his purpose in Colonel George F. Waring. The work of the Police Department, however, was in my line, and I was glad to undertake it.

The man who was closest to me throughout my two years in the Police Department was Jacob Riis. By this time, as I have said, I was getting our social, industrial, and political needs into pretty fair perspective. I was still ignorant of the extent to which big men of great wealth played a mischievous part in our industrial and social life,

JACOB A. RIIS.

"He and I looked at life and its problems from substantially the same standpoint. Our ideals and principles and purposes, and our beliefs as to the methods necessary to realize them, were alike."

but I was well awake to the need of making ours in good faith both an economic and an industrial as well as a political democracy.   I already knew Jake Riis, because his book

"How the Other Half Lives" had been to me both an enlight-
enment and an inspiration for which I felt I could never be
too grateful. Soon after it was written I had called at his
office to tell him how deeply impressed I was by the book,
and that I wished to help him in any practical way to try
to make things a little better. I have always had a horror
of words that are not translated into deeds, of speech that
does not result in action — in other words, I believe in real-
izable ideals and in realizing them, in preaching what can
be practiced and then in practicing it. Jacob Riis had
drawn an indictment of the things that were wrong, pitifully
and dreadfully wrong, with the tenement homes and the
tenement lives of our wage-workers. In his book he had
pointed out how the city government, and especially those
connected with the departments of police and health, could
aid in remedying some of the wrongs.

As President of the Police Board I was also a member
of the Health Board. In both positions I felt that with
Jacob Riis's guidance I would be able to put a goodly number of his principles into actual effect. He and I looked at
life and its problems from substantially the same standpoint.
Our ideals and principles and purposes, and our beliefs
as to the methods necessary to realize them, were alike.
After the election in 1894 I had written him a letter which
ran in part as follows:

It is very important to the city to have a business man's
Mayor, but it is more important to have a workingman's
Mayor; and I want Mr. Strong to be that also. . . . It is an
excellent thing to have rapid transit, but it is a good deal
more important, if you look at matters with a proper perspective, to have ample playgrounds in the poorer quarters
of the city, and to take the children off the streets so as to
prevent them growing up toughs. In the same way it is an
admirable thing to have clean streets; indeed, it is an essential thing to have them; but it would be a better thing to
have our schools large enough to give ample accommodation to all who should be pupils and to provide them with
proper playgrounds.

And I added, while expressing my regret that I had not been able to accept the street-cleaning commissionership, that "I would have been delighted to smash up the corrupt contractors and put the street-cleaning force absolutely out of the domain of politics."

This was nineteen years ago, but it makes a pretty good platform in municipal politics even to-day — smash corruption, take the municipal service out of the domain of politics, insist upon having a Mayor who shall be a working-man's Mayor even more than a business man's Mayor, and devote all the attention possible to the welfare of the children.

Therefore, as I viewed it, there were two sides to the work : first, the actual handling of the Police Department; second, using my position to help in making the city a better place in which to live and work for those to whom the conditions of life and labor were hardest. The two problems were closely connected; for one thing never to be forgotten in striving to better the conditions of the New York police force is the connection between the standard of morals and behavior in that force and the general standard of morals and behavior in the city at large. The form of government of the Police Department at that time was such as to make it a matter of extreme difficulty to get good results. It represented that device of old-school American political thought, the desire to establish checks and balances so elaborate that no man shall have power enough to do anything very bad. In practice this always means that no man has power enough to do anything good, and that what is bad is done anyhow.

In most positions the "division of powers" theory works unmitigated mischief. The only way to get good service is to give somebody power to render it, facing the fact that power which will enable a man to do a job well will also necessarily enable him to do it ill if he is the wrong kind of man. What is normally needed is the concentration in the hands of one man, or of a very small body of men, of ample power to enable him or them to do the work that is necessary; and then the devising of means to hold these men fully responsible for the exercise of that power by the people. This of course means that, if the people are willing to see power misused, it will be misused. But it also means that if, as we hold, the people are fit for self-government — if, in other words, our talk and our institutions are not shams — we will get good government. I do not contend that my theory will automatically bring good government. I do contend that it will enable us to get as good government as we deserve, and that the other way will not.

The then government of the Police Department was so devised as to render it most difficult to accomplish anything good, while the field for intrigue and conspiracy was limitless. There were four Commissioners, two supposed to belong to one party and two to the other, although, as a matter of fact, they never divided on party lines. There was a Chief, appointed by the Commissioners, but whom they could not remove without a regular trial subject to review by the courts of law. This Chief and any one Commissioner had power to hold up most of the acts of the other three Commissioners. It was made easy for the four Commissioners to come to a deadlock among themselves; and if this danger was avoided, it was easy for one Commissioner, by intriguing with the Chief, to bring the other three to a standstill. The Commissioners were appointed by the Mayor, but he could not remove them without the assent of the Governor, who was usually politically opposed to him. In the same way the Commissioners could appoint the patrolmen, but they could not remove them, save after a trial which went up for review to the courts.

As was inevitable under our system of law procedure, this meant that the action of the court was apt to be determined by legal technicalities. It was possible to dismiss a man from the service for quite insufficient reasons, and to provide against the reversal of the sentence, if the technicalities of procedure were observed. But the worst criminals were apt to be adroit men, against whom it was impossible to get legal evidence which a court could properly consider in a criminal trial (and the mood of the court might be to treat the case as if it were a criminal trial), although it was easy to get evidence which would render it not merely justifiable but necessary for a man to remove them from his private employ — and surely the public should be as well treated as a private employer. Accordingly, most of the worst men put out were reinstated by the courts; and when the Mayor attempted to remove one of my colleagues who made it his business to try to nullify the work done by the rest of us, the Governor sided with the recalcitrant Commissioner and refused to permit his removal.

Nevertheless, an astounding quantity of work was done in reforming the force. We had a good deal of power, anyhow; we exercised it to the full; and we accomplished some things by assuming the appearance of a power which we did not really possess.

The first fight I made was to keep politics absolutely out of the force; and not only politics, but every kind of improper favoritism. Doubtless in making thousands of appointments and hundreds of promotions there were men who contrived to use influence of which I was ignorant. But these cases must have been few and far between. As far as was humanly possible, the appointments and promotions were made without regard to any question except the fitness of the man and the needs of the service. As Civil Service Commissioner I had been instructing heads of departments and bureaus how to get men appointed without regard to politics, and assuring them that by following our methods they would obtain first-class results. As Police Commissioner I was able practically to apply my own teachings.

The appointments to the police force were made as I have described in the last chapter. We paid not the slightest attention to a man's politics or creed, or where he was born, so long as he was an American citizen; and on an average we obtained far and away the best men that had ever come into the Police Department. It was of course very difficult at first to convince both the politicians and the people that we really meant what we said, and that every one really would have a fair trial. There had been in previous years the most widespread and gross corruption in connection

with every activity in the Police Department, and there
had been a regular tariff for appointments and promotions.
Many powerful politicians and many corrupt outsiders
believed that in some way or other it would still be possible
to secure appointments by corrupt and improper methods,
and many good citizens felt the same conviction. I endeavored to remove the impression from the minds of both sets of
people by giving the widest publicity to what we were doing
and how we were doing it, by making the whole process
open and aboveboard, and by making it evident that we
would probe to the bottom every charge of corruption.

For instance, I received visits at one time from a Catholic
priest, and at another time from a Methodist clergyman,
who had parishoners who wished to enter the police force,
but who did not believe they could get in save by the payment of money or through political pressure. The priest
was running a temperance lyceum in connection with his
church, and he wished to know if there would be a chance
for some of the young men who belonged to that lyceum.
The Methodist clergyman came from a little patch of old
native America which by a recent extension had been taken
within the limits of the huge, polyglot, pleasure-loving city.
His was a small church, most of the members being ship-
wrights, mechanics, and sailormen from the local coasters.
In each case I assured my visitor that we wanted on the force
men of the exact type which he said he could furnish. I
also told him that I was as anxious as he was to find out if
there was any improper work being done in connection with
the examinations, and that I would like him to get four or
five of his men to take the examinations without letting me
know their names. Then, whether the men failed or succeeded, he and I would take their papers and follow them
through every stage so that we could tell at once whether
they had been either improperly favored or improperly
discriminated against. This was accordingly done, and in
each case my visitor turned up a few weeks later, his face
wreathed in smiles, to say that his candidates had passed
and that everything was evidently all straight. During
my two years as President of the Commission I think I

appointed a dozen or fifteen members of that little Methodist congregation, and certainly twice that number of men from the temperance lyceum of the Catholic church in question. They were all men of the very type I most wished to see on the force — men of strong physique and resolute temper, sober, self-respecting, self-reliant, with a strong wish to improve themselves.

Otto Raphael.

"A young Jew who had recently, by an exhibition of marked pluck and bodily prowess, saved some women and children from a burning building."

Occasionally I would myself pick out a man and tell him to take the examination. Thus one evening I went down to speak in the Bowery at the Young Men's Institute, a branch of the Young Men's Christian Association, at the request of Mr. Cleveland H. Dodge. While there he told me he wished to show me a young Jew who had recently, by an exhibition of marked pluck and bodily prowess, saved some women and children from a burning building. The young Jew, whose name was Otto Raphael, was brought up to see me; a powerful fellow, with good-humored, intelligent face. I asked him about his education, and told him to try the examination. He did, passed, was appointed, and made an admirable officer; and he and all his family, wherever

they may dwell, have been close friends of mine ever since.
Otto Raphael was a genuine East Sider. He and I were
both "straight New York," to use the vernacular of our
native city. To show our community of feeling and our
grasp of the facts of life, I may mention that we were almost
the only men in the Police Department who picked Fitzsimmons as a winner against Corbett. Otto's parents had
come over from Russia, and not only in social standing but
in pay a policeman's position meant everything to him.
It enabled Otto to educate his little brothers and sisters
who had been born in this country, and to bring over from
Russia two or three kinsfolk who had perforce been left
behind.

Rather curiously, it was by no means as easy to keep
politics and corruption out of the promotions as out of the
entrance examinations. This was because I could take
complete charge of the entrance examinations myself; and,
moreover, they were largely automatic. In promotions,
on the other hand, the prime element was the record and
capacity of the officer, and for this we had largely to rely
upon the judgment of the man's immediate superiors. This
doubtless meant that in certain cases that judgment was
given for improper reasons.

However, there were cases where I could act on personal
knowledge. One thing that we did was to endeavor to recognize gallantry. We did not have to work a revolution in
the force as to courage in the way that we had to work a
revolution in honesty. They had always been brave in
dealing with riotous and violent criminals. But they had
gradually become very corrupt. Our great work, therefore,
was the stamping out of dishonesty, and this work we did
thoroughly, so far as the ridiculous bi-partisan law under
which the Department was administered would permit.
But we were anxious that, while stamping out what was
evil in the force, we should keep and improve what was good.
While warring on dishonesty, we made every effort to
increase efficiency. It has unfortunately been shown by
sad experience that at times a police organization which is
free from the taint of corruption may yet show itself weak

o

in some great crisis or unable to deal with the more dangerous kinds of criminals. This we were determined to prevent.

Our efforts were crowned with entire success. The improvement in the efficiency of the force went hand in hand with the improvement in its honesty. The men in uniform and the men in plain clothes — the detectives — did better work than ever before. The aggregate of crimes where punishment followed the commission of the crime increased, while the aggregate of crimes where the criminal escaped punishment decreased. Every discredited politician, every sensational newspaper, and every timid fool who could be scared by clamor was against us. All three classes strove by every means in their power to show that in making the force honest we had impaired its efficiency; and by their utterances they tended to bring about the very condition of things against which they professed to protest. But we went steadily along the path we had marked out. The fight was hard, and there was plenty of worry and anxiety, but we won. I was appointed in May, 1895. In February, 1897, three months before I resigned to become Assistant Secretary of the Navy, the Judge who charged the Grand Jury of New York County was able to congratulate them on the phenomenal decrease in crime, especially of the violent sort. This decrease was steady during the two years. The police, after the reform policy was thoroughly tried, proved more successful than ever before in protecting life and property and in putting down crime and criminal vice.

The part played by the recognition and reward of actual personal prowess among the members of the police force in producing this state of affairs was appreciable, though there were many other factors that combined to bring about the betterment. The immense improvement in discipline by punishing all offenders without mercy, no matter how great their political or personal influence; the resolute warfare against every kind of criminal who had hitherto been able corruptly to purchase protection; the prompt recognition of ability even where it was entirely unconnected with personal prowess — all these were elements which had enormous weight in producing the change. Mere courage and daring, and the rewarding of courage and daring, cannot supply the lack of discipline, of ability, of honesty. But they are of vital consequence, nevertheless. No police force is worth anything if its members are not intelligent and honest; but neither is it worth anything unless its members are brave, hardy, and well disciplined.

We showed recognition of daring and of personal prowess in two ways: first, by awarding a medal or a certificate in remembrance of the deed; and, second, by giving it weight in making any promotion, especially to the lower grades. In the higher grades — in all promotions above that of sergeant, for instance — resolute and daring courage cannot normally be considered as a factor of determining weight in making promotions; rather is it a quality the lack of which unfits a man for promotion. For in the higher places we must assume the existence of such a quality in any fit candidate, and must make the promotion with a view to the man's energy, executive capacity, and power of command. In the lower grades, however, marked gallantry should always be taken into account in deciding among different candidates for any given place.

During our two years' service we found it necessary over a hundred times to single out men for special mention because of some feat of heroism. The heroism usually took one of four forms: saving somebody from drowning, saving somebody from a burning building, stopping a runaway team, or arresting some violent lawbreaker under exceptional circumstances. To illustrate our method of action, I will take two of the first promotions made after I became Commissioner. One case was that of an old fellow, a veteran of the Civil War, who was at the time a roundsman. I happened to notice one day that he had saved a woman from drowning, and had him summoned so that I might look into the matter. The old fellow brought up his record before me, and showed not a little nervousness and agitation; for it appeared that he had grown gray in the service, had performed feat after feat of heroism, but had no political backing of any account. No heed had ever been paid him.

He was one of the quiet men who attend solely to duty, and although a Grand Army man, he had never sought to use influence of any kind. Now, at last, he thought there was a chance for him. He had been twenty-two years on the force, and during that time had saved some twenty-five persons from death by drowning, varying the performance two or three times by saving persons from burning buildings. Twice Congress had passed laws especially to empower the then Secretary of the Treasury, John Sherman, to give him a medal for distinguished gallantry in saving life. The Life-Saving Society had also given him its medal, and so had the Police Department. There was not a complaint in all his record against him for any infraction of duty, and he was sober and trustworthy. He was entitled to his promotion; and he got it, there and then. It may be worth mentioning that he kept on saving life after he was given his sergeantcy. On October 21, 1896, he again rescued a man from drowning. It was at night, nobody else was in the neighborhood, and the dock from which he jumped was in absolute darkness, and he was ten minutes in the water, which was very cold. He was fifty-five years old when he saved this man. It was the twenty-ninth person whose life he had saved during his twenty-three years' service in the Department.

The other man was a patrolman whom we promoted to roundsman for activity in catching a burglar under rather peculiar circumstances. I happened to note his getting a burglar one week. Apparently he had fallen into the habit, for he got another next week. In the latter case the burglar escaped from the house soon after midnight, and ran away toward Park Avenue, with the policeman in hot chase. The New York Central Railroad runs under Park Avenue, and there is a succession of openings in the top of the tunnel. Finding that the policeman was gaining on him, the burglar took a desperate chance and leaped down one of these openings, at the risk of breaking his neck. Now the burglar was running for his liberty, and it was the part of wisdom for him to imperil life or limb; but the policeman was merely doing his duty, and nobody could have blamed him for not

taking the jump. However, he jumped; and in this particular case the hand of the Lord was heavy upon the unrighteous. The burglar had the breath knocked out of him, and
the "cop" didn't. When his victim could walk, the officer
trotted him around to the station-house; and a week after
I had the officer up and promoted him, for he was sober,
trustworthy, and strictly attentive to duty.

Now I think that any decent man of reasonable intelligence
will agree that we were quite right in promoting men in
cases like these, and quite right in excluding politics from
promotions. Yet it was because of our consistently acting
in this manner, resolutely warring on dishonesty and on that
peculiar form of baseness which masquerades as "practical"
politics, and steadily refusing to pay heed to any consideration except the good of the service and the city, and the
merits of the men themselves, that we drew down upon our
heads the bitter and malignant animosity of the bread-
and-butter spoils politicians. They secured the repeal of
the Civil Service Law by the State Legislature. They
attempted and almost succeeded in the effort to legislate
us out of office. They joined with the baser portion of the
sensational press in every species of foul, indecent falsehood
and slander as to what we were doing. They attempted
to seduce or frighten us by every species of intrigue and
cajolery, of promise of political reward and threat of political
punishment. They failed in their purpose. I believe in
political organizations, and I believe in practical politics.
If a man is not practical, he is of no use anywhere. But
when politicians treat practical politics as foul politics, and
when they turn what ought to be a necessary and useful
political organization into a machine run by professional
spoilsmen of low morality in their own interest, then it is
time to drive the politician from public life, and either to
mend or destroy the machine, according as the necessity may
determine.

We promoted to roundsman a patrolman, with an already
excellent record, for gallantry shown in a fray which resulted
in the death of his antagonist. He was after a gang of
toughs who had just waylaid, robbed, and beaten a man.

They scattered and he pursued the ringleader. Running hard, he gained on his man, whereupon the latter suddenly turned and fired full in his face. The officer already had his revolver drawn, and the two shots rang out almost together. The policeman was within a fraction of death, for the bullet from his opponent's pistol went through his helmet and just broke the skin of his head. His own aim was truer, and the man he was after fell dead, shot through the heart. I may explain that I have not the slightest sympathy with any policy which tends to put the policeman at the mercy of a tough, or which deprives him of efficient weapons. While Police Commissioner we punished any brutality by the police with such immediate severity that all cases of brutality practically came to an end. No decent citizen had anything to fear from the police during the two years of my service. But we consistently encouraged the police to prove that the violent criminal who endeavored to molest them or to resist arrest, or to interfere with them in the discharge of their duty, was himself in grave jeopardy; and we had every "gang" broken up and the members punished with whatever severity was necessary. Of course where possible the officer merely crippled the criminal who was violent.

One of the things that we did while in office was to train the men in the use of the pistol. A school of pistol practice was established, and the marksmanship of the force was wonderfully improved. The man in charge of the school was a roundsman, Petty, whom we promoted to sergeant. He was one of the champion revolver shots of the country, and could hit just about where he aimed. Twice he was forced to fire at criminals who resisted arrest, and in each case he hit his man in the arm or leg, simply stopping him without danger to his life.

In May, 1896, a number of burglaries occurred far uptown, in the neighborhood of One Hundred and Fifty-sixth Street and Union Avenue. Two officers were sent out each night to patrol the streets in plain clothes. About two o'clock on the morning of May 8 they caught a glimpse of two men loitering about a large corner house, and determined to make them explain their actions. In order to cut off their escape,

one officer went down one street and one the other. The
first officer, whose name was Ryan, found the two men at the
gateway of the side entrance of the house, and hailed to
know what they were doing. Without answering, they
turned and ran toward Prospect Avenue, with Ryan in close
pursuit. After running about one hundred feet, one of them
turned and fired three shots at Ryan, but failed to hit him.
The two then separated, and the man who had done the
shooting escaped. The other man, whose name proved to
be O'Connor, again took to his heels, with Ryan still after
him ; they turned the corner and met the other officer, whose
name was Reid, running as hard as he could toward the shooting. When O'Connor saw himself cut off by Reid, he fired
at his new foe, the bullet cutting Reid's overcoat on the left
shoulder. Reid promptly fired in return, his bullet going
into O'Connor's neck and causing him to turn a complete
somersault. The two officers then cared for their prisoner
until the ambulance arrived, when he was taken to the
hospital and pronounced mortally wounded. His companion
was afterward caught, and they turned out to be the very
burglars for whom Reid and Ryan had been on the lookout.

In December, 1896, one of our officers was shot. A row
occurred in a restaurant, which ended in two young toughs
drawing their revolvers and literally running amuck, shooting two or three men. A policeman, attracted by the noise,
ran up and seized one of them, whereupon the other shot
him in the mouth, wounding him badly. Nevertheless,
the officer kept his prisoner and carried him to the station-
house. The tough who had done the shooting ran out and
was seized by another officer. The tough fired at him, the
bullet passing through the officer's overcoat, but he was
promptly knocked down, disarmed, and brought to the
station-house. In this case neither policeman used his
revolver, and each brought in his man, although the latter
was armed and resisted arrest, one of the officers taking in
his prisoner after having been himself severely wounded.
A lamentable feature of the case was that this same officer
was a man who, though capable of great gallantry, was also
given to shirking his work, and we were finally obliged to

A Squad of Mounted Police.

dismiss him from the force, after passing over two or three glaring misdeeds in view of his record for courage.

We promoted another man on account of finding out accidentally that he had performed a notable feat, which he had forborne even to mention, so that his name never came on the roll of honor. Late at night, while patrolling a lonely part of his post, he came upon three young toughs who had turned highwaymen and were robbing a peddler. He ran in at once with his night-stick, whereupon the toughs showed fight, and one of them struck at him with a bludgeon, breaking his left hand. The officer, however, made such good use of his night-stick that he knocked down two of his assailants, whereupon the third ran away, and he brought both of his prisoners to the station-house. Then he went round to the hospital, had his broken hand set in plaster, and actually reported for duty at the next tour, without losing one hour. He was a quiet fellow, with a record free from complaints, and we made him roundsman.

The mounted squad have, of course, many opportunities to distinguish themselves in stopping runaways. In May, 1895, a mounted policeman named Heyer succeeded in stopping a runaway at Kingsbridge under rather noteworthy circumstances. Two men were driving in a buggy, when the horse stumbled, and in recovering himself broke the headstall, so that the bridle fell off. The horse was a spirited trotter, and at once ran away at full speed. Heyer saw the occurrence, and followed at a run. When he got alongside the runaway he seized him by the forelock, guided him dexterously over the bridge, preventing him from running into the numerous wagons that were on the road, and finally forced him up a hill and into a wagon-shed. Three months later this same officer saved a man from drowning.

The members of the bicycle squad, which was established shortly after we took office, soon grew to show not only extraordinary proficiency on the wheel, but extraordinary daring. They frequently stopped runaways, wheeling alongside of them, and grasping the horses while going at full speed; and, what was even more remarkable, they managed not only to overtake but to jump into the vehicle and capture, on two or three different occasions, men who were guilty of reckless driving, and who fought violently in resisting arrest. They were picked men, being young and active, and any feat of daring which could be accomplished on the wheel they were certain to accomplish.

Three of the best riders of the bicycle squad, whose names and records happen to occur to me, were men of the three ethnic strains most strongly represented in the New York police force, being respectively of native American, German, and Irish parentage.

The German was a man of enormous power, and he was able to stop each of the many runaways he tackled without losing his wheel. Choosing his time, he would get alongside the horse and seize the bit in his left hand, keeping his right on the crossbar of the wheel. By degrees he then got the animal under control. He never failed to stop it, and he never lost his wheel. He also never failed to overtake any "scorcher," although many of these were professional riders who deliberately violated the law to see if they could not get away from him; for the wheelmen soon get to know the officers whose beats they cross.

The Yankee, though a tall, powerful man and a very good rider, scarcely came up to the German in either respect; he possessed exceptional ability, however, as well as exceptional nerve and coolness, and he also won his promotion. He stopped about as many runaways; but when the horse was really panic-stricken he usually had to turn his wheel loose, getting a firm grip on the horse's reins and then kicking his wheel so that it would fall out of the way of injury from the wagon. On one occasion he had a fight with a drunken and reckless driver who was urging to top speed a spirited horse. He first got hold of the horse, whereupon the driver lashed both him and the beast, and the animal, already mad with terror, could not be stopped. The officer had of course kicked away his wheel at the beginning, and after being dragged along for some distance he let go the beast and made a grab at the wagon. The driver hit him with his whip, but he managed to get in, and after a vigorous tussle overcame his man, and disposed of him by getting him down and sitting on him. This left his hands free for the reins. By degrees he got the horse under control, and drove the wagon round to the station-house, still sitting on his victim. "I jounced up and down on him to keep him quiet when he turned ugly," he remarked to me parenthetically. Having disposed of the wagon, he took the man round to the court, and on the way the prisoner suddenly sprang on him and tried to throttle him. Convinced at last that patience had ceased to be a virtue, he quieted his assailant with a smash on the head that took all the fight out of him until he was brought before the judge and fined. Like the other "bicycle cops," this officer made a number of arrests of criminals, such as thieves, highwaymen, and the like, in addition to his natural prey — scorchers, runaways, and reckless drivers.

The third member of the trio, a tall, sinewy man with flaming red hair, which rather added to the terror he inspired in evil-doers, was usually stationed in a tough part of the city, where there was a tendency to crimes of violence, and incidentally an occasional desire to harass wheelmen. The officer was as good off his wheel as on it, and he speedily established perfect order on his beat, being always willing to "take chances" in getting his man. He was no respecter of persons, and when it became his duty to arrest a wealthy man for persistently refusing to have his carriage lamps lighted after nightfall, he brought him in with the same indifference that he displayed in arresting a street-corner tough who had thrown a brick at a wheelman.

Occasionally a policeman would perform work which ordinarily comes within the domain of the fireman. In November, 1896, an officer who had previously saved a man from death by drowning added to his record by saving five persons from burning. He was at the time asleep, when he was aroused by a fire in a house a few doors away. Running over the roofs of the adjoining houses until he reached the burning building, he found that on the fourth floor the flames had cut off all exit from an apartment in which there were four women, two of them over fifty, and one of the others with a six-months-old baby. The officer ran down to the adjoining house, broke open the door of the apartment on the same floor — the fourth — and crept out on the coping, less than three inches wide, that ran from one house to the other. Being a large and very powerful and active man, he managed to keep hold of the casing of the window with one hand, and with the other to reach to the window of the apartment where the women and child were. The firemen appeared, and stretched a net underneath. The crowd that was looking on suddenly became motionless and silent. Then, one by one, he drew the women out of their window, and, holding them tight against the wall, passed them into the other window. The exertion in such an attitude was great, and he strained himself badly ; but he possessed a practical mind, and as soon as the women were saved he began a prompt investigation of the cause of the fire, and arrested two men whose carelessness, as was afterward proved, caused it.

Now and then a man, though a brave man, proved to be slack or stupid or vicious, and we could make nothing out of him ; but hardihood and courage were qualities upon which we insisted and which we rewarded. Whenever I see the police force attacked and vilified, I always remember my association with it. The cases I have given above are merely instances chosen almost at random among hundreds of others. Men such as those I have mentioned have the right stuff in them ! If they go wrong, the trouble is with the system, and therefore with us, the citizens, for permitting the system to go unchanged. The conditions of New York life are such as to make the police problem therein more difficult than in any other of the world's great capitals. I am often asked if policemen are honest. I believe that the great majority of them want to be honest and will be honest whenever they are given the chance. The New York police force is a body thoroughly representative of the great city itself. As I have said above, the predominant ethnic strains in it are, first, the men of Irish birth or parentage, and, following these, the native Americans, usually from the country districts, and the men of German birth or parentage. There are also Jews, Scandinavians, Italians,

Slavs, and men of other nationalities. All soon become welded into one body. They are physically a fine lot. Moreover, their instincts are right; they are game, they are alert and self-reliant, they prefer to act squarely if they are allowed so to act. All that they need is to be given the chance to prove themselves honest, brave, and self-respecting.

The law at present is much better than in our day, so far as governing the force is concerned. There is now a single Commissioner, and the Mayor has complete power over him. The Mayor, through his Commissioner, now has power to keep the police force on a good level of conduct if with resolution and common sense he insists on absolute honesty within the force and at the same time heartily supports it against the criminal classes. To weaken the force in its dealings with gangs and toughs and criminals generally is as damaging as to permit dishonesty, and, moreover, works towards dishonesty. But while under the present law very much improvement can be worked, there is need of change of the law which will make the Police Commissioner a permanent, non-partisan official, holding office so long as he proves thoroughly fit for the job, completely independent of the politicians and privileged interests, and with complete power over the force. This means that there must be the right law, and the right public opinon back of the law.

The many-sided ethnic character of the force now and then gives rise to, or affords opportunity for, queer happenings. Occasionally it enables one to meet emergencies in the best possible fashion. While I was Police Commissioner an anti-Semitic preacher from Berlin, Rector Ahlwardt, came over to New York to preach a crusade against the Jews. Many of the New York Jews were much excited and asked me to prevent him from speaking and not to give him police protection. This, I told them, was impossible; and if possible would have been undesirable because it would have made him a martyr. The proper thing to do was to make him ridiculous. Accordingly I detailed for his protection a Jew sergeant and a score or two of Jew policemen. He made his harangue against the Jews under the active protection of some forty policemen, every one of them a Jew! It was the most effective possible answer; and incidentally it was an object-lesson to our people, whose greatest need it is to learn that there must be no division by class hatred, whether this hatred be that of creed against creed, nationality against nationality, section against section, or men of one social or industrial condition against men of another social and industrial condition. We must ever judge each individual on his own conduct and merits, and not on his membership in any class, whether that class be based on theological, social, or industrial considerations.

Among my political opponents when I was Police Commissioner was the head of a very influential local Democratic organization. He was a State Senator usually known as Big Tim Sullivan. Big Tim represented the morals of another era; that is, his principles and actions were very much those of a Norman noble in the years immediately succeeding the Battle of Hastings. (This will seem flattery only to those who are not acquainted with the real histories and antecedents of the Norman nobles of the epoch in question.) His application of these eleventh-century theories to our nineteenth-century municipal democratic conditions brought him into sharp contact with me, and with one of my right-hand men in the Department, Inspector John McCullough. Under the old dispensation this would have meant that his friends and kinsfolk were under the ban.

Now it happened that in the Department at that time there was a nephew or cousin of his, Jerry D. Sullivan. I found that Jerry was an uncommonly good man, a conscientious, capable officer, and I promoted him. I do not know whether Jerry or Jerry's cousin (Senator Sullivan) was more astonished. The Senator called upon me to express what I am sure was a very genuine feeling of appreciation. Poor Jerry died, I think of consumption, a year or two after I left the Department. He was promoted again after I left, and he then showed that he possessed the very rare quality of gratitude, for he sent me a telegram dated January 15, 1898, running as follows: "Was made

sergeant to-day. I thank you for all in my first advancement." And in a letter written to me he said: "In the
future, as in the past, I will endeavor at all times to perform my duty honestly and fearlessly, and never cause
you to feel that you were mistaken in me, so that you will
be justly proud of my record." The Senator, though politically opposed to me, always kept a feeling of friendship
for me after this incident. He served in Congress while
I was President.

The police can be used to help all kinds of good purposes.
When I was Police Commissioner much difficulty had been
encountered in locating illegal and fraudulent practitioners
of medicine. Dr. Maurice Lewi called on me, with a letter
from James Russell Parsons, the Secretary of the Board of
Regents at Albany, and asked me if I could not help. After
questioning him I found that the local authorities were
eager to prosecute these men, but could not locate them;
and I made up my mind I would try my hand at it. Accordingly, a sealed order was sent to the commanding officer
of each police precinct in New York, not to be opened until
just before the morning roll call, previous to the police
squad going on duty. This order required that, immediately
upon reaching post, each patrolman should go over his
beat and enter upon a sheet of paper, provided for that purpose, the full name and address of every doctor sign there
appearing. Immediately upon securing this information,
the patrolman was instructed to return the sheet to the officer in charge of the precinct. The latter in turn was instructed to collect and place in one large envelope and to
return to Police Headquarters all the data thus received.
As a result of this procedure, within two hours the prosecuting officials of the city of New York were in possession
of the name and address of every person in New York who
announced himself as a physician; and scores of pretended
physicians were brought to book or driven from the city.

One of the perennially serious and difficult problems,
and one of the chief reasons for police blackmail and corruption, is to be found in the excise situation in New York.
When I was Police Commissioner, New York was a city

with twelve or fifteen thousand saloons, with a State law which said they should be closed on Sundays, and with a local sentiment which put a premium on violating the law by making Sunday the most profitable day in the week to the saloon-keeper who was willing to take chances. It was this willingness to take chances that furnished to the corrupt politician and the corrupt police officer their opportunities.

There was in New York City a strong sentiment in favor of honesty in politics; there was also a strong sentiment in favor of opening the saloons on Sundays; and, finally, there was a strong sentiment in favor of keeping the saloons closed on Sunday. Unfortunately, many of the men who favored honest government nevertheless preferred keeping the saloons open to having honest government; and many others among the men who favored honest government put it second to keeping the saloons closed. Moreover, among the people who wished the law obeyed and the saloons closed there were plenty who objected strongly to every step necessary to accomplish the result, although they also insisted that the result should be accomplished.

Meanwhile the politicians found an incredible profit in using the law as a club to keep the saloons in line; all except the biggest, the owners of which, or the owners of the breweries back of which, sat in the inner councils of Tammany, or controlled Tammany's allies in the Republican organization. The police used the partial and spasmodic enforcement of the law as a means of collecting blackmail. The result was that the officers of the law, the politicians, and the saloon-keepers became inextricably tangled in a network of crime and connivance at crime. The most powerful saloon-keepers controlled the politicians and the police, while the latter in turn terrorized and blackmailed all the other saloon-keepers. It was not a case of non-enforcement of the law. The law was very actively enforced, but it was enforced with corrupt discrimination.

It is difficult for men who have not been brought into contact with that side of political life which deals with the underworld to understand the brazen openness with which this blackmailing of lawbreakers was carried out. A further very dark fact was that many of the men responsible for putting the law on the statute-books in order to please one element of their constituents, also connived at or even profited by the corrupt and partial non-enforcement of the law in order to please another set of their constituents, or to secure profit for themselves. The organ of the liquor-sellers at that time was the *Wine and Spirit Gazette*. The editor of this paper believed in selling liquor on Sunday, and felt that it was an outrage to forbid it. But he also felt that corruption and blackmail made too big a price to pay for the partial non-enforcement of the law. He made in his paper a statement, the correctness of which was never questioned, which offers a startling commentary on New York politics of that period. In this statement he recited the fact that the system of blackmail had been brought to such a state of perfection, and had become so oppressive to the liquor dealers themselves, that they communicated at length on the subject with Governor Hill (the State Democratic boss) and then with Mr. Croker (the city Democratic boss). Finally the matter was formally taken up by a committee of the Central Association of Liquor Dealers in an interview they held with Mr. Martin, my Tammany predecessor as President of the police force. In matter-of-course way the editor's statement continues: "An agreement was made between the leaders of Tammany Hall and the liquor dealers according to which the monthly blackmail paid to the force should be discontinued in return for political support." Not only did the big bosses, State and local, treat this agreement, and the corruption to which it was due, as normal and proper, but they never even took the trouble to deny what had been done when it was made public. Tammany and the police, however, did not fully live up to the agreement; and much discrimination of a very corrupt kind, and of a very exasperating kind to liquor-sellers who wished to be honest, continued in connection with the enforcing of the law.

In short, the agreement was kept only with those who had "pull." These men with "pull" were benefited when their

P

rivals were bullied and blackmailed by the police. The police, meanwhile, who had bought appointment or promotion, and the politicians back of them, extended the blackmailing to include about everything from the pushcart peddler and the big or small merchant who wished to use the sidewalk illegally for his goods, up to the keepers of the brothel, the gambling-house, and the policy-shop. The total blackmail ran into millions of dollars. New York was a wide-open town. The big bosses rolled in wealth, and the corrupt policemen who ran the force lost all sense of decency and justice. Nevertheless, I wish to insist on the fact that the honest men on the patrol posts, "the men with the night-sticks," remained desirous to see honesty obtain, although they were losing courage and hope.

This was the situation that confronted me when I came to Mulberry Street. The saloon was the chief source of mischief. It was with the saloon that I had to deal, and there was only one way to deal with it. That was to enforce the law. The howl that rose was deafening. The professional politicians raved. The yellow press surpassed themselves in clamor and mendacity. A favorite assertion was that I was enforcing a "blue" law, an obsolete law that had never before been enforced. As a matter of fact, I was only enforcing honestly a law that had hitherto been enforced dishonestly. There was very little increase in the number of arrests made for violating the Sunday law. Indeed, there were weeks when the number of arrests went down. The only difference was that there was no protected class. Everybody was arrested alike, and I took especial pains to see that there was no discrimination, and that the big men and the men with political influence were treated like every one else. The immediate effect was wholly good. I had been told that it was not possible to close the saloons on Sunday and that I could not succeed. However, I did succeed. The warden of Bellevue Hospital reported, two or three weeks after we had begun, that for the first time in its existence there had not been a case due to a drunken brawl in the hospital all Monday. The police courts gave the same testimony, while savings banks recorded

increased deposits and pawnshops hard times. The most
touching of all things was the fact that we received letters,
literally by the hundred, from mothers in tenement-houses
who had never been allowed to take their children to the
country in the wide-open days, and who now found their
husbands willing to take them and their families for an
outing on Sunday. Jake Riis and I spent one Sunday from
morning till night in the tenement districts, seeing for ourselves what had happened.

During the two years that we were in office things never
slipped back to anything like what they had been before.
But we did not succeed in keeping them quite as highly
keyed as during these first weeks. As regards the Sunday-
closing law, this was partly because public sentiment was
not really with us. The people who had demanded honesty,
but who did not like to pay for it by the loss of illegal pleasure, joined the openly dishonest in attacking us. Moreover, all kinds of ways of evading the law were tried, and
some of them were successful. The statute, for instance,
permitted any man to take liquor with meals. After two
or three months a magistrate was found who decided judi-
cially that seventeen beers and one pretzel made a meal —
after which decision joy again became unconfined in at least
some of the saloons, and the yellow press gleefully announced
that my "tyranny" had been curbed. But my prime
object, that of stopping blackmail, was largely attained.

All kinds of incidents occurred in connection with this
crusade. One of them introduced me to a friend who
remains a friend yet. His name was Edward J. Bourke.
He was one of the men who entered the police force through
our examinations shortly after I took office. I had summoned twenty or thirty of the successful applicants to let
me look over them; and as I walked into the hall, one of
them, a well-set-up man, called out sharply to the others,
"Gangway," making them move to one side. I found he
had served in the United States navy. The incident was
sufficient to make me keep him in mind. A month later I
was notified by a police reporter, a very good fellow, that
Bourke was in difficulties, and that he thought I had better

look into the matter myself, as Bourke was being accused by certain very influential men of grave misconduct in an arrest he had made the night before. Accordingly, I took the matter up personally. I found that on the new patrolman's beat the preceding night — a new beat — there was a big saloon run by a man of great influence in political circles known as "King" Calahan. After midnight the saloon was still running in full blast, and Bourke, stepping inside, told Calahan to close up. It was at the time filled with "friends of personal liberty," as Governor Hill used at that time, in moments of pathos, to term everybody who regarded as tyranny any restriction on the sale of liquor. Calahan's saloon had never before in its history been closed, and to have a green cop tell him to close it

CAPTAIN EDWARD J. BOURKE.

"'King' Calahan's saloon had never before in its history been closed, and to have a green cop tell him to close seemed to him so incredible that he regarded it merely as a bad jest."

seemed to him so incredible that he regarded it merely as a bad jest. On his next round Bourke stepped in and repeated the order. Calahan felt that the jest had gone too far, and by way of protest knocked Bourke down. This was an error of judgment on his part, for when Bourke arose he knocked down Calahan. The two then grappled and fell on the floor, while the "friends of personal liberty" danced around the fight and endeavored to stamp on everything they thought wasn't Calahan. However, Bourke, though pretty roughly handled, got his man and shut the saloon. When he appeared against the lawbreaker in court next day, he found the court-room crowded with influential Tammany Hall politicians, backed by one or two Republican leaders of the same type; for Calahan was a baron of the under-world, and both his feudal superiors and his feudal inferiors gathered to the rescue. His backers in court included a Congressman and a State Senator, and so deep-rooted was the police belief in "pull" that his own superiors had turned against Bourke and were preparing to sacrifice him. Just at this time I acted on the information given me by my newspaper friend by starting in person for the court. The knowledge that I knew what was going on, that I meant what I said, and that I intended to make the affair personal, was all that was necessary. Before I reached the court all effort to defend Calahan had promptly ceased, and Bourke had come forth triumphant. I immediately pro-moted him to roundsman. He is a captain now. He has been on the force ever since, save that when the Spanish War came he obtained a holiday without pay for six months and reëntered the navy, serving as gun captain in one of the gunboats, and doing his work, as was to be expected, in first-rate fashion, especially when under fire.

Let me again say that when men tell me that the police are irredeemably bad I remember scores and hundreds of cases like this of Bourke, like the case I have already men-tioned of Raphael, like the other cases I have given above. It is useless to tell me that these men are bad. They are naturally first-rate men. There are no better men any-where than the men of the New York police force; and when they go bad it is because the system is wrong, and because they are not given the chance to do the good work they can do and would rather do. I never coddled these men. I punished them severely whenever I thought their conduct required it. All I did was to try to be just; to reward them when they did well; in short, to act squarely by them. I believe that, as a whole, they liked me. When, in 1912,

I ran for President on the Progressive ticket, I received a number of unsigned letters inclosing sums of money for the campaign. One of these inclosed twenty dollars. The writer, who did not give his name, said that he was a policeman, that I had once had him before me on charges, and had fined him twenty dollars; that, as a matter of fact, he had not committed the offense for which I fined him, but that the evidence was such that he did not wonder that I had been misled, and never blamed me for it, because I had acted squarely and had given honest and decent men a chance in the Police Department; and that now he inclosed a twenty-dollar bill, the amount of the fine inflicted on him so many years before. I have always wished I knew who the man was.

The disciplinary courts were very interesting. But it was extraordinarily difficult to get at the facts in the more complicated cases — as must always be true under similar circumstances; for ordinarily it is necessary to back up the superior officer who makes the charge, and yet it is always possible that this superior officer is consciously or unconsciously biased against his subordinate.

In the courts the charges were sometimes brought by police officers and sometimes by private citizens. In the latter case we would get queer insights into twilight phases of New York life. It was necessary to be always on our guard. Often an accusation would be brought against the policeman because he had been guilty of misconduct. Much more often the accusation merely meant that the officer had incurred animosity by doing his duty. I remember one amusing case where the officer was wholly to blame but had acted in entire good faith.

One of the favorite and most demoralizing forms of gambling in New York was policy-playing. The policy slips consisted of papers with three rows of figures written on them. The officer in question was a huge pithecoid lout of a creature, with a wooden face and a receding forehead, and his accuser whom he had arrested the preceding evening was a little grig of a red-headed man, obviously respectable, and almost incoherent with rage. The anger of the little red-headed man was but natural, for he had just come out from a night in the station-house. He had been arrested late in the evening on suspicion that he was a policy-player, because of the rows of figures on a piece of paper which he had held in his hand, and because at the time of his arrest he had just stepped into the entrance of the hall of a tenement-house in order to read by lamplight. The paper was produced in evidence. There were the three rows of figures all right, but, as the accuser explained, hopping up and down with rage and excitement, they were all of them the numbers of hymns. He was the superintendent of a small Sunday-school. He had written down the hymns for several future services, one under the other, and on the way home was stopping to look at them, under convenient lamp-posts, and finally by the light of the lamp in a tenement-house hallway; and it was this conduct which struck the sagacious man in uniform as "suspicious."

One of the saddest features of police work is dealing with the social evil, with prostitutes and houses of ill fame. In so far as the law gave me power, I always treated the men taken in any raid on these houses precisely as the women were treated. My experience brought me to the very strong conviction that there ought not to be any toleration by law of the vice. I do not know of any method which will put a complete stop to the evil, but I do know certain things that ought to be done to minimize it. One of these is treating men and women on an exact equality for the same act. Another is the establishment of night courts and of special commissions to deal with this special class of cases. Another is that suggested by the Rev. Charles Stelzle, of the Labor Temple — to publish conspicuously the name of the owner of any property used for immoral purposes, after said owner has been notified of the use and has failed to prevent it. Another is to prosecute the keepers and backers of brothels, men and women, as relentlessly and punish them as severely as pickpockets and common thieves. They should never be fined; they should be imprisoned. As for the girls, the very young ones and first offenders should be put in the charge of probation officers or sent to reformatories, and the large percentage of feeble-minded girls and of incorrigible girls and women should be sent to institutions created for them. We would thus remove from this hideous commerce the articles of commerce. Moreover, the Federal Government must in ever-increasing measure proceed against the degraded promoters of this commercialism, for their activities are inter-State, and the Nation can often deal with them more effectively than the States; although, as public sentiment becomes aroused, Nation, State, and municipality will all coöperate towards the same end of rooting out the traffic. But the prime need is to raise the level of individual morality; and, moreover, to encourage early marriages, the single standard of sexmorality, and a strict sense of reciprocal conjugal obligation. The women who preach late marriages are by just so much making it difficult to better the standard of chastity.

As regards the white slave traffic, the men engaged in it, and the women too, are far worse criminals than any ordinary murderers can be. For them there is need of such a law as that recently adopted in England through the efforts of Arthur Lee, M.P., a law which includes whipping for the male offenders. There are brutes so low, so infamous, so degraded and bestial in their cruelty and brutality, that the only way to get at them is through their skins. Sentimentality on behalf of such men is really almost as unhealthy and wicked as the criminality of the men themseves. My experience is that there should be no toleration of any "tenderloin" or "red light" district, and that, above all, there should be the most relentless war on commercialized vice. The men who profit and make their living by the depravity and the awful misery of other human beings stand far below any ordinary criminals, and no measures taken against them can be too severe.

As for the wretched girls who follow the dreadful trade in question, a good deal can be done by a change in economic conditions. This ought to be done. When girls are paid wages inadequate to keep them from starvation, or to permit them to live decently, a certain proportion are forced by

their economic misery into lives of vice. The employers
and all others responsible for these conditions stand on a
moral level not far above the white slavers themselves.
But it is a mistake to suppose that either the correction of
these economic conditions or the abolition of the white
slave trade will wholly correct the evil or will even reach the
major part of it. The economic factor is very far from
being the chief factor in inducing girls to go into this dreadful life. As with so many other problems, while there must
be governmental action, there must also be strengthening of
the average individual character in order to achieve the
desired end. Even where economic conditions are bad,
girls who are both strong and pure will remain unaffected
by temptations to which girls of weak character or lax
standards readily yield. Any man who knows the wide
variation in the proportions of the different races and nationalities engaged in prostitution must come to the conclusion
that it is out of the question to treat economic conditions as
the sole conditions or even as the chief conditions that determine this question. There are certain races — the Irish
are honorably conspicuous among them — which, no matter
what the economic pressure, furnish relatively few inmates
of houses of ill fame. I do not believe that the differences
are due to permanent race characteristics; this is shown
by the fact that the best settlement houses find that practically all their "long-term graduates," so to speak, all the
girls that come for a long period under their influence, no
matter what their race or national origin, remain pure.
In every race there are some naturally vicious individuals
and some weak individuals who readily succumb under economic pressure. A girl who is lazy and hates hard work,
a girl whose mind is rather feeble, who is of "subnormal
intelligence," as the phrase now goes, or a girl who craves
cheap finery and vapid pleasure, is always in danger. A
high ideal of personal purity is essential. Where the same
pressure under the same economic conditions has tenfold
the effect on one set of people that it has on another, it is
evident that the question of moral standards is even more
important than the question of economic standards, very

important though this question is. It is important for us to remember that the girl ought to have the chance, not only for the necessaries of life, but for innocent pleasure ; and that even more than the man she must not be broken by over-work, by excessive toil. Moreover, public opinion and the law should combine to hunt down the "flagrant man swine" who himself hunts down poor or silly or unprotected girls. But we must not, in foolish sentimentality, excuse the girl from her duty to keep herself pure. Our duty to achieve the same moral level for the two sexes must be performed by raising the level for the man, not by lowering it for the woman ; and the fact that society must recognize its duty in no shape or way relieves, not even to the smallest degree, the individual from doing his or her duty. Sentimentality which grows maudlin on behalf of the willful prostitute is a curse ; to confound her with the entrapped or coerced girl, the real white slave, is both foolish and wicked. There are evil women just as there are evil men, naturally depraved girls just as there are naturally depraved young men ; and the right and wise thing, the just thing, to them, and the generous thing to innocent girls and decent men, is to wage stern war against the evil creatures of both sexes.

In company with Jacob Riis, I did much work that was not connected with the actual discipline of the force or indeed with the actual work of the force. There was one thing which he and I abolished — police lodging-houses, which were simply tramp lodging-houses, and a fruitful encouragement to vagrancy. Those who read Mr. Riis's story of his own life will remember the incidents that gave him from actual personal experience his horror of these tramp lodging-houses. As member of the Health Board I was brought into very close relations with the conditions of life in the tenement-house districts. Here again I used to visit the different tenement-house regions, usually in company with Riis, to see for myself what the conditions were. It was largely this personal experience that enabled me while on the Health Board to struggle not only zealously, but with reasonable efficiency and success, to improve conditions. We did our share in making forward strides in the matter of housing the working people of the city with some regard to decency and comfort.

The midnight trips that Riis and I took enabled me to see what the Police Department was doing, and also gave me personal insight into some of the problems of city life. It is one thing to listen in perfunctory fashion to tales of overcrowded tenements, and it is quite another actually to

THEODORE ROOSEVELT AND THE CHILDREN OF THE TENEMENT.

see what that overcrowding means, some hot summer night, by even a single inspection during the hours of darkness. There was a very hot spell one midsummer while I was Police Commissioner, and most of each night I spent walking through the tenement-house districts and visiting police stations to see what was being done. It was a tragic week. We did everything possible to alleviate the suffering. Much of it was heartbreaking, especially the gasping misery of the little children and of the worn-out mothers. Every resource of the Health Department, of the Police Department, and even the Fire Department (which flooded the hot streets) was taxed in the effort to render service. The heat killed such multitudes of horses that the means at our disposal for removing the poor dead beasts proved quite inadequate, although every nerve was strained to the limit. In consequence we received scores of complaints from persons before whose doors dead horses had remained, festering in the heat, for two or three days. One irascible man sent us furious denunciations, until we were at last able to send a big dray to drag away the horse that lay dead before his shop door. The huge dray already contained eleven other dead horses, and when it reached this particular door it broke down, and it was hours before it could be moved. The unfortunate man who had thus been cursed with a granted wish closed his doors in despair and wrote us a final pathetic letter in which he requested us to remove either the horses or his shop, he didn't care which.

I have spoken before of my experience with the tenement-house cigar factory law which the highest court of New York State declared unconstitutional. My experience in the Police Department taught me that not a few of the worst tenement-houses were owned by wealthy individuals, who hired the best and most expensive lawyers to persuade the courts that it was "unconstitutional" to insist on the betterment of conditions. These business men and lawyers were very adroit in using a word with fine and noble associations to cloak their opposition to vitally necessary movements for industrial fair play and decency. They made it evident that they valued the Constitution, not as a help to righteousness, but as a means for thwarting movements against unrighteousness. After my experience with them I became more set than ever in my distrust of those men, whether business men or lawyers, judges, legislators, or executive officers, who seek to make of the Constitution a fetich for the prevention of the work of social reform, for the prevention of work in the interest of those men, women, and children on whose behalf we should be at liberty to employ freely every governmental agency.

Occasionally during the two years we had to put a stop

to riotous violence, and now and then on these occasions some of the labor union leaders protested against the actions of the police.   By this time I was becoming a strong believer in labor unions, a strong believer in the rights of labor. For that very reason I was all the more bound to see that lawlessness and disorder were put down, and that no rioter was permitted to masquerade under the guise of being a friend of labor or a sympathizer with labor.   I was scrupulous to see that the labor men had fair play ; that, for instance, they were allowed to picket just so far as under the law picketing could be permitted, so that the strikers had ample opportunity peacefully to persuade other labor men not to take their places.   But I made it clearly and definitely understood that under no circumstances would I permit violence or fail to insist upon the keeping of order.   If there were wrongs, I would join with a full heart in striving to have them corrected.   But where there was violence all other questions had to drop until order was restored.   This is a democracy, and the people have the power, if they choose to exercise it, to make conditions as they ought to be made, and to do this strictly within the law ; and therefore the first duty of the true democrat, of the man really loyal to the principles of popular government, is to see that law is enforced and order upheld.   It was a peculiar gratification to me that so many of the labor leaders with whom I was thrown in contact grew cordially to accept this view. When I left the Department, several called upon me to say how sorry they were that I was not to continue in office. One, the Secretary of the Journeyman Bakers' and Confectioners' International Union, Henry Weismann, wrote me expressing his regret that I was going, and his appreciation as a citizen of what I had done as Police Commissioner ; he added : "I am particularly grateful for your liberal attitude toward organized labor, your cordial championship of those speaking in behalf of the toilers, and your evident desire to do the right thing as you saw it at whatever cost."

Some of the letters I received on leaving the Department were from unexpected sources.   Mr. E. L. Godkin, an editor who in international matters was not a patriotic man, wrote protesting against my taking the Assistant-Secretaryship of the Navy, and adding: "I have a concern, as the Quakers say, to put on record my earnest belief that in New York you are doing the greatest work of which any American to-day is capable, and exhibiting to the young men of the country the spectacle of a very important office administered by a man of high character in the most efficient way amid a thousand difficulties. As a lesson in politics I cannot think of anything more instructive."

About the same time I had a letter from Mr. (afterwards Ambassador) James Bryce, also expressing regret that I was leaving the Police Department, but naturally with much more appreciation of the work that was to be done in the Navy Department. This letter I quote, with his permission, because it conveys a lesson to those who are inclined always to think that the conditions of the present time are very bad. It was written July 7, 1897. Mr. Bryce spoke of the possibility of coming to America in a month or so, and continued: "I hope I may have a chance of seeing you if I do get over, and of drawing some comfort from you as regards your political phenomena, which, so far as I can gather from those of your countrymen I have lately seen, furnish some good opportunities for a persistent optimist like myself to show that he is not to be lightly discouraged. Don't suppose that things are specially 'nice,' as a lady would say, in Europe either. They are not." Mr. Bryce was a very friendly and extraordinarily competent observer of things American; and there was this distinct note of discouragement about our future in the intimate letter he was thus sending. Yet this was at the very time when the United States was entering on a dozen years during which our people accomplished more good, and came nearer realizing the possibilities of a great, free, and conscientious democracy, than during any other dozen years in our history, save only the years of Lincoln's Presidency and the period during which the Nation was founded.

CHAPTER VII

THE WAR OF AMERICA THE UNREADY

I SUPPOSE the United States will always be unready for war, and in consequence will always be exposed to great expense, and to the possibility of the gravest calamity, when the Nation goes to war. This is no new thing. Americans learn only from catastrophes and not from experience.

There would have been no war in 1812 if, in the previous decade, America,

A SPANISH CANNON ON THE LAWN AT SAGAMORE.

instead of announcing that "peace was her passion," instead of acting on the theory that unpreparedness averts war, had been willing to go to the expense of providing a fleet of a score of ships of the line. However, in that case, doubtless the very men who in the actual event deplored the loss of life and waste of capital which their own supineness had brought about would have loudly inveighed against the "excessive and improper cost of armaments"; so it all came to about the same thing in the end.

There is no more thoroughgoing international Mrs. Gummidge, and no more utterly useless and often utterly mischievous citizen, than the peace-at-any-price, universal-arbitration type of being, who is always complaining either about war or else about the cost of the armaments which act as the insurance against war. There is every reason why we should try to limit the cost of armaments, as these tend to grow excessive, but there is also every reason to remember

223

that in the present stage of civilization a proper armament is the surest guarantee of peace — and is the only guarantee that war, if it does come, will not mean irreparable and overwhelming disaster.

In the spring of 1897 President McKinley appointed me Assistant Secretary of the Navy. I owed the appointment chiefly to the efforts of Senator H. C. Lodge of Massachusetts, who doubtless was actuated mainly by his long and close friendship for me, but also — I like to believe — by his keen interest in the navy. The first book I had ever published, fifteen years previously, was "The History of the Naval War of 1812"; and I have always taken the interest in the navy which every good American ought to take. At the time I wrote the book, in the early eighties, the navy had reached its nadir, and we were then utterly incompetent to fight Spain or any other power that had a navy at all. Shortly afterwards we began timidly and hesitatingly to build up a fleet. It is amusing to recall the roundabout steps we took to accomplish our purpose. In the reaction after the colossal struggle of the Civil War our strongest and most capable men had thrown their whole energy into business, into money-making, into the development, and above all the exploitation and exhaustion at the most rapid rate possible, of our natural resources — mines, forests, soil, and rivers. These men were not weak men, but they permitted themselves to grow shortsighted and selfish; and while many of them down at the bottom possessed the fundamental virtues, including the fighting virtues, others were purely of the glorified huckster or glorified pawnbroker type — which when developed to the exclusion of everything else makes about as poor a national type as the world has seen. This unadulterated huckster or pawnbroker type is rarely keenly sympathetic in matters of social and industrial justice, and is usually physically timid and likes to cover an unworthy fear of the most just war under high-sounding names.

It was reënforced by the large mollycoddle vote — the people who are soft physically and morally, or who have a twist in them which makes them acidly cantankerous and unpleasant as long as they can be so with safety to their bodies. In addition there are the good people with no imagination and no foresight, who think war will not come, but that if it does come armies and navies can be improvised — a very large element, typified by a Senator I knew personally who, in a public speech, in answer to a question as to what we would do if America were suddenly assailed by a first-class military power, answered that "we would build a battle-ship in every creek." Then, among the wise and high-minded people who in self-respecting and genuine fashion strive earnestly for peace, there are the foolish fanatics always to be found in such a movement and always discrediting it — the men who form the lunatic fringe in all reform movements.

All these elements taken together made a body of public opinion so important during the decades immediately succeeding the Civil War as to put a stop to any serious effort to keep the Nation in a condition of reasonable military preparedness. The representatives of this opinion then voted just as they now do when they vote against battle-ships or against fortifying the Panama Canal. It would have been bad enough if we had been content to be weak, and, in view of our weakness, not to bluster. But we were not content with such a policy. We wished to enjoy the incompatible luxuries of an unbridled tongue and an unready hand. There was a very large element which was ignorant of our military weakness, or, naturally enough, unable to understand it; and another large element which liked to please its own vanity by listening to offensive talk about foreign nations. Accordingly, too many of our politicians, especially in Congress, found that the cheap and easy thing to do was to please the foolish peace people by keeping us weak, and to please the foolish violent people by passing denunciatory resolutions about international matters — resolutions which would have been improper even if we had been strong. Their idea was to please both the mollycoddle vote and the vote of the international tail-twisters by upholding, with pretended ardor and mean intelligence, a National policy of peace with insult.

Q

I abhor unjust war.   I abhor injustice and bullying by the strong at the expense of the weak, whether among nations or individuals.   I abhor violence and bloodshed.   I believe that war should never be resorted to when, or so long as, it is honorably possible to avoid it.   I respect all men and women who from high motives and with sanity and self-respect do all they can to avert war.   I advocate preparation for war in order to avert war; and I should never advocate war unless it were the only alternative to dishonor.   I describe the folly of which so many of our people were formerly guilty, in order that we may in our own day be on our guard against similar folly.

We did not at the time of which I write take our foreign duties seriously, and as we combined bluster in speech with refusal to make any preparation whatsoever for action, we were not taken seriously in return.   Gradually a slight change for the better occurred, the writings of Captain Mahan playing no small part therein.   We built some modern cruisers to start with; the people who felt that battle-ships were wicked compromising with their misguided consciences by saying that the cruisers could be used "to protect our commerce" — which they could not be, unless they had battle-ships to back them.   Then we attempted to build more powerful fighting vessels, and as there was a section of the public which regarded battle-ships as possessing a name immorally suggestive of violence, we compromised by calling the new ships armored cruisers, and making them combine with exquisite nicety all the defects and none of the virtues of both types.   Then we got to the point of building battle-ships.   But there still remained a public opinion, as old as the time of Jefferson, which thought that in the event of war all our problem ought to be one of coast defense, that we should do nothing except repel attack; an attitude about as sensible as that of a prize-fighter who expected to win by merely parrying instead of hitting.   To meet the susceptibilities of this large class of well-meaning people, we provided for the battle-ships under the name of "coast defense battle-ships"; meaning thereby that we did not make them quite as seaworthy as they ought to have been, or with quite as much coal capacity as they ought to have had. Then we decided to build real battle-ships. But there still remained a lingering remnant of public opinion that clung to the coast defense theory, and we met this in beautiful fashion by providing for "sea-going coast defense battle-ships" — the fact that the name was a contradiction in terms being of very small consequence compared to the fact that we did thereby get real battle-ships.

Our men had to be trained to handle the ships singly and in fleet formation, and they had to be trained to use the new weapons of precision with which the ships were armed. Not a few of the older officers, kept in the service under our foolish rule of pure seniority promotion, were not competent for the task; but a proportion of the older officers were excellent, and this was true of almost all the younger officers. They were naturally first-class men, trained in the admirable naval school at Annapolis. They were overjoyed that at last they were given proper instruments to work with, and they speedily grew to handle these ships individually in the best fashion. They were fast learning to handle them in squadron and fleet formation; but when the war with Spain broke out, they had as yet hardly grasped the principles of modern scientific naval gunnery.

Soon after I began work as Assistant Secretary of the Navy I became convinced that the war would come. The revolt in Cuba had dragged its weary length until conditions in the island had become so dreadful as to be a standing disgrace to us for permitting them to exist. There is much that I sincerely admire about the Spanish character; and there are few men for whom I have felt greater respect than for certain gentlemen of Spain whom I have known. But Spain attempted to govern her colonies on archaic principles which rendered her control of them incompatible with the advance of humanity and intolerable to the conscience of mankind. In 1898 the so-called war in Cuba had dragged along for years with unspeakable horror, degradation, and misery. It was not "war" at all, but murderous oppression. Cuba was devastated.

During those years, while we continued at "peace," several hundred times as many lives were lost, lives of men, women, and children, as were lost during the three months' "war" which put an end to this slaughter and opened a career of peaceful progress to the Cubans.   Yet there were misguided professional philanthropists who cared so much more for names than for facts that they preferred a "peace" of continuous murder to a "war" which stopped the murder and brought real peace.   Spain's humiliation was certain, anyhow; indeed, it was more certain without war than with it, for she could not permanently keep the island, and she minded yielding to the Cubans more than yielding to us.   Our own direct interests were great, because of the Cuban tobacco and sugar, and especially because of Cuba's relation to the projected Isthmian canal.   But even greater were our interests from the standpoint of humanity. Cuba was at our very doors.   It was a dreadful thing for us to sit supinely and watch her death agony.   It was our duty, even more from the standpoint of National honor than from the standpoint of National interest, to stop the devastation and destruction.   Because of these considerations I favored war; and to-day, when in retrospect it is easier to see things clearly, there are few humane and honorable men who do not believe that the war was both just and necessary.

The big financiers and the men generally who were susceptible to touch on the money nerve, and who cared nothing for National honor if it conflicted even temporarily with business prosperity, were against the war.   The more fatuous type of philanthropist agreed with them.   The newspapers controlled by, or run in the interests of, these two classes deprecated war, and did everything in their power to prevent any preparation for war.   As a whole the people in Congress were at that time (and are now) a shortsighted set as regards international matters.   There were a few men, Senators Cushman K. Davis,[1] for instance, and John Morgan,

[1] In a letter written me just before I became Assistant Secretary, Senator Davis unburdened his mind about one of the foolish "peace" proposals of that period; his letter running in part: "I left the Senate Chamber about three o'clock this

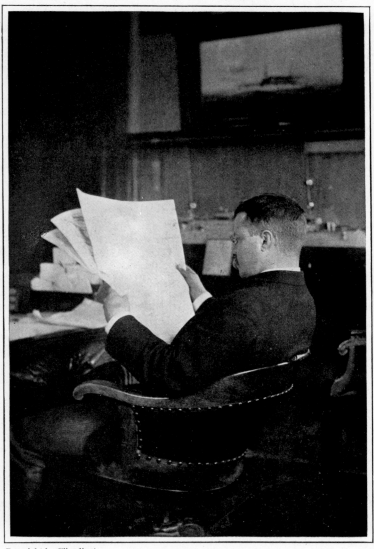

MR. ROOSEVELT AT HIS DESK WHEN ASSISTANT SECRETARY OF THE NAVY.

who did look ahead ; and Senator H. C. Lodge, who through-out his quarter of a century of service in the Senate and House has ever stood foremost among those who uphold with farsighted fearlessness and strict justice to others our national honor and interest ; but most of the Congressmen were content to follow the worst of all possible courses, that is, to pass resolutions which made war more likely, and yet to decline to take measures which would enable us to meet the war if it did come.

However, in the Navy Department we were able to do a good deal, thanks to the energy and ability of some of the bureau chiefs, and to the general good tone of the service. I soon found my natural friends and allies in such men as Evans, Taylor, Sampson, Wainwright, Brownson, Schroeder, Bradford, Cowles, Cameron Winslow, O'Neil, and others like them. I used all the power there was in my office to aid these men in getting the material ready. I also tried to gather from every source information as to who the best men were to occupy the fighting positions.

Sound naval opinion was overwhelmingly in favor of Dewey to command one squadron. I was already watching him, for I had been struck by an incident in his past career. It was at a time when there was threat of trouble with Chile. Dewey was off the Argentine, and was told to get ready to move to the other coast of South America. If the move became necessary, he would have to have coal, and yet if he

afternoon when there was going on a deal of mowing and chattering over the treaty by which the United States is to be bound to arbitrate its sovereign functions — for policies are matters of sovereignty. . . . The aberrations of the social move-ment are neither progress nor retrogression. They represent merely a local and temporary sagging of the line of the great orbit. Tennyson knew this when he wrote that fine and noble 'Maud.' I often read it, for to do so does me good." After quoting one of Poe's stories the letter continues : "The world will come out all right. Let him who believes in the decline of the military spirit observe the boys of a common school during the recess or the noon hour. Of course when American patriotism speaks out from its rank and file and demands action or ex-pression, and when, thereupon, the 'business man,' so called, places his hand on his stack of reds as if he feared a policeman were about to disturb the game, and protests until American patriotism ceases to continue to speak as it had started to do — why, you and I get mad, and I swear. I hope you will be with us here after March 4. We can then pass judgment together on the things we don't like, and together indulge in hopes that I believe are prophetic."

did not make the move, the coal would not be needed.   In
such a case a man afraid of responsibility always acts rigidly
by the regulations and communicates with the Department
at home to get authority for everything he does ; and therefore he usually accomplishes nothing whatever, but is able
to satisfy all individuals with red-tape minds by triumphantly pointing out his compliance with the regulations.
In a crisis, the man worth his salt is the man who meets
the needs of the situation in whatever way is necessary.
Dewey purchased the coal and was ready to move at once if
need arose.   The affair blew over; the need to move did
not occur ; and for some time there seemed to be a chance
that Dewey would get into trouble over having purchased
the coal, for our people are like almost all other peoples in
requiring responsible officers under such conditions to decide
at their own personal peril, no matter which course they
follow.   However, the people higher up ultimately stood by
Dewey.

The incident made me feel that here was a man who could
be relied upon to prepare in advance, and to act promptly,
fearlessly, and on his own responsibility when the emergency arose.   Accordingly I did my best to get him put in
command of the Asiatic fleet, the fleet where it was most
essential to have a man who would act without referring
things back to the home authorities.   An officer senior to
him, of the respectable commonplace type, was being pushed
by certain politicians who I knew had influence with the
Navy Department and with the President.   I would have
preferred to see Dewey get the appointment without appealing to any politician at all.   But while this was my preference, the essential thing was to get him the appointment.
For a naval officer to bring pressure to get himself a soft
and easy place is unpardonable ; but a large leniency should
be observed toward the man who uses influence only to
get himself a place in the picture near the flashing of the
guns.   There was a Senator, Proctor of Vermont, who I
knew was close to McKinley, and who was very ardent for
the war, and desirous to have it fought in the most efficient
fashion.   I suggested to Dewey that he should enlist the

services of Senator Proctor, which was accordingly done. In a fortunate hour for the Nation, Dewey was given command of the Asiatic squadron.

When the Maine was blown up in Havana Harbor, war became inevitable. A number of the peace-at-any-price men of course promptly assumed the position that she had blown herself up; but investigation showed that the explosion was from outside. And, in any event, it would have been impossible to prevent war. The enlisted men of the navy, who often grew bored to the point of desertion in peace, became keyed up to a high pitch of efficiency, and crowds of fine young fellows, from the interior as well as from the seacoast, thronged to enlist. The navy officers showed alert ability and unwearied industry in getting things ready. There was one deficiency, however, which there was no time to remedy, and of the very existence of which, strange to say, most of our best men were ignorant. Our navy had no idea how low our standard of marksmanship was. We had not realized that the modern battle-ship had become such a complicated piece of mechanism that the old methods of training in marksmanship were as obsolete as the old muzzle-loading broadside guns themselves. Almost the only man in the navy who fully realized this was our naval attaché at Paris, Lieutenant Sims. He wrote letter after letter pointing out how frightfully backward we were in marksmanship. I was much impressed by his letters; but Wainwright was about the only other man who was. And as Sims proved to be mistaken in his belief that the French had taught the Spaniards how to shoot, and as the Spaniards proved to be much worse even than we were, in the service generally Sims was treated as an alarmist. But although I at first partly acquiesced in this view, I grew uneasy when I studied the small proportion of hits to shots made by our vessels in battle. When I was President I took up the matter, and speedily became convinced that we needed to revolutionize our whole training in marksmanship. Sims was given the lead in organizing and introducing the new system; and to him more than to any other one man was due the astonishing progress made by our fleet in this respect, a progress which made the fleet, gun for gun, at least three times as effective, in point of fighting efficiency, in 1908, as it was in 1902. The shots that hit are the shots that count !

Like the people, the Government was for a long time unwilling to prepare for war, because so many honest but misguided men believed that the preparation itself tended to bring on the war. I did not in the least share this feeling, and whenever I was left as Acting Secretary I did everything in my power to put us in readiness. I knew that in the event of war Dewey could be slipped like a wolf-hound from a leash; I was sure that if he were given half a chance he would strike instantly and with telling effect; and I made up my mind that all I could do to give him that half-chance should be done. I was in the closest touch with Senator Lodge throughout this period, and either consulted him about or notified him of all the moves I was taking. By the end of February I felt it was vital to send Dewey (as well as each of our other commanders who were not in home waters) instructions that would enable him to be in readiness for immediate action. On the afternoon of Saturday, February 25, when I was Acting Secretary, Lodge called on me just as I was preparing the order, which (as it was addressed to a man of the right stamp) was of much importance to the subsequent operations. Admiral Dewey speaks of the incident as follows, in his autobiography :

"The first real step [as regards active naval preparations] was taken on February 25, when telegraphic instructions were sent to the Asiatic, European, and South Atlantic squadrons to rendezvous at certain convenient points where, should war break out, they would be most available.

"The message to the Asiatic squadron bore the signature of that Assistant Secretary who had seized the opportunity while Acting Secretary to hasten preparations for a conflict which was inevitable. As Mr. Roosevelt reasoned, precautions for readiness would cost little in time of peace, and yet would be invaluable in case of war. His cablegram was as follows :

"'Washington, February 25, '98.

"'*Dewey, Hong Kong:*

"'Order the squadron, except the Monocacy, to Hong Kong. Keep full of coal. In the event of declaration of war Spain, your duty will be to see that the Spanish squadron does not leave the Asiatic coast, and then offensive operations in Philippine Islands. Keep Olympia until further orders.   ROOSEVELT.'

"(The reference to keeping the Olympia until further orders was due to the fact that I had been notified that she would soon be recalled to the United States.)"

All that was needed with Dewey was to give him the chance to get ready, and then to strike, without being hampered by orders from those not on the ground. Success in war depends very largely upon choosing a man fit to exercise such powers, and then giving him the powers.

It would be instructive to remember, if only we were willing to do so, the fairly comic panic which swept in waves over our seacoast, first when it became evident that war was about to be declared, and then when it was declared. The public waked up to the sufficiently obvious fact that the Government was in its usual state — perennial unreadiness for war. Thereupon the people of the seaboard district passed at one bound from unreasoning confidence that war never could come to unreasoning fear as to what might happen now that it had come. That acute philosopher Mr. Dooley proclaimed that in the Spanish War we were in a dream, but that the Spaniards were in a trance. This just about summed up the facts. Our people had for decades scoffed at the thought of making ready for possible war. Now, when it was too late, they not only backed every measure, wise and unwise, that offered a chance of supplying a need that ought to have been met before, but they also fell into a condition of panic apprehension as to what the foe might do.

For years we had been saying, just as any number of our people now say, that no nation would venture to attack us. Then when we did go to war with an exceedingly feeble nation, we, for the time being, rushed to the other extreme of feeling, and attributed to this feeble nation plans of offensive warfare which it never dreamed of making, and which, if made, it would have been wholly unable to execute.   Some of my readers doubtless remember the sinister intentions and unlimited potentialities for destruction with which the fertile imagination of the yellow press endowed the armored cruiser Viscaya when she appeared in American waters just before war was declared.   The state of nervousness along much of the seacoast was funny in view of the lack of foundation for it ; but it offered food for serious thought as to what would happen if we ever became engaged with a serious foe.

The Governor of one State actually announced that he would not permit the National Guard of that State to leave its borders, the idea being to retain it against a possible Spanish invasion.   So many of the business men of the city of Boston took their securities inland to Worcester that the safe deposit companies of Worcester proved unable to take care of them.   In my own neighborhood on Long Island clauses were gravely put into leases to the effect that if the property were destroyed by the Spaniards the lease should lapse.   As Assistant Secretary of the Navy I had every conceivable impossible request made to me.   Members of Congress who had actively opposed building any navy came clamorously around to ask each for a ship for some special purpose of protection connected with his district. It seems incredible, but it is true, that not only these Congressmen but the Chambers of Commerce and Boards of Trade of different coast cities all lost their heads for the time being, and raised a deafening clamor and brought every species of pressure to bear on the Administration to get it to adopt the one most fatal course — that is, to distribute the navy, ship by ship, at all kinds of points and in all kinds of ports with the idea of protecting everything everywhere, and thereby rendering it absolutely certain that even the Spanish fleet, poor though it was, would be able to pick up our own navy ship by ship in detail.   One Congressman besought me for a ship to protect Jekyll Island, off the coast of Georgia, an island which derived its sole consequence because it contained the winter homes of certain millionaires. A lady whose husband occupied a very influential position, and who was normally a most admirable and sensible woman, came to insist that a ship should be anchored off a huge seaside hotel because she had a house in the neighborhood.

There were many such instances. One stood out above the others. A certain seaboard State contained in its Congressional delegation one of the most influential men in the Senate, and one of the most influential men in the lower house. These two men had been worse than lukewarm about building up the navy, and had scoffed at the idea of there ever being any danger from any foreign power. With the advent of war the feelings of their constituents, and therefore their own feelings, suffered an immediate change, and they demanded that a ship be anchored in the harbor of their city as a protection. Getting no comfort from me, they went "higher up," and became a kind of permanent committee in attendance upon the President. They were very influential men in the Houses, with whom it was important for the Administration to keep on good terms; and, moreover, they possessed a pertinacity as great as the widow who won her case from the unjust judge. Finally the President gave in and notified me to see that a ship was sent to the city in question. I was bound that, as long as a ship had to be sent, it should not be a ship worth anything. Accordingly a Civil War Monitor, with one smooth-bore gun, manned by a crew of about twenty-one naval militia, was sent to the city in question, under convoy of a tug. It was a hazardous trip for the unfortunate naval militiamen, but it was safely accomplished; and joy and peace descended upon the Senator and the Congressman, and upon the President whom they had jointly harassed. Incidentally, the fact that the protecting war-vessel would not have been a formidable foe to any antagonists of much more modern construction than the galleys of Alcibiades seemed to disturb nobody.

This was one side of the picture. The other side was that the crisis at once brought to the front any amount of latent fighting strength. There were plenty of Congressmen who showed cool-headed wisdom and resolution. The plain people, the men and women back of the persons who lost their heads, set seriously to work to see that we did whatever was necessary, and made the job a thorough one. The young men swarmed to enlist. In time of peace it had been difficult to fill the scanty regular army and navy, and there were innumerable desertions; now the ships and regiments were over-enlisted, and so many deserters returned in order to fight that it became difficult to decide what to do with them. England, and to a less degree Japan, were friendly. The great powers of Continental Europe were all unfriendly. They jeered at our ships and men, and with fatuous partisanship insisted that the Spaniards would prove too much for our "mercenaries" because we were a commercial people of low ideals who could not fight, while the men whom we attempted to hire for that purpose were certain to run on the day of battle.

Among my friends was the then Army Surgeon Leonard Wood. He was a surgeon. Not having an income, he had to earn his own living. He had gone through the Harvard Medical School, and had then joined the army in the Southwest as a contract doctor. He had every physical, moral, and mental quality which fitted him for a soldier's life and for the exercise of command. In the inconceivably wearing and harassing campaigns against the Apaches he had served nominally as a surgeon, really in command of troops, on more than one expedition. He was as anxious as I was that if there were war we should both have our part in it. I had always felt that if there were a serious war I wished to be in a position to explain to my children why I did take part in it, and not why I did not take part in it. Moreover, I had very deeply felt that it was our duty to free Cuba, and I had publicly expressed this feeling; and when a man takes such a position, he ought to be willing to make his words good by his deeds unless there is some very strong reason to the contrary. He should pay with his body.

As soon as war was upon us, Wood and I began to try for a chance to go to the front. Congress had authorized the raising of three National Volunteer Cavalry regiments, wholly apart from the State contingents. Secretary Alger of the War Department was fond of me personally, and Wood was his family doctor. Alger had been a gallant soldier in the Civil War, and was almost the only member of the Administration who felt all along that we would have to go to war with Spain over Cuba. He liked my attitude in the matter, and because of his remembrance of his own experiences he sympathized with my desire to go to the front. Accordingly he offered me the command of one of the regiments. I told him that after six weeks' service in the field I would feel competent to handle the regiment, but that I would not know how to equip it or how to get it into the first action; but that Wood was entirely competent at once to take command, and that if he would make Wood colonel I would accept the lieutenant-colonelcy. General Alger thought this an act of foolish self-abnegation on my part — instead of its being, what it was, the wisest act I could have performed. He told me to accept the colonelcy, and that he would make Wood lieutenant-colonel, and that Wood would do the work anyway; but I answered that I did not wish to rise on any man's shoulders; that I hoped to be given every chance that my deeds and abilities warranted; but that I did not wish what I did not earn, and that above all I did not wish to hold any position where any one else did the work. He laughed at me a little and said I was foolish, but I do not think he really minded, and he promised to do as I wished. True to his word, he secured the appointment of Wood as colonel and of myself as lieutenant-colonel of the First United States Volunteer Cavalry. This was soon nicknamed, both by the public and by the rest of the army, the Rough Riders, doubtless because the bulk of the men were from the Southwestern ranch country and were skilled in the wild horsemanship of the great plains.

Wood instantly began the work of raising the regiment. He first assembled several old non-commissioned officers of experience, put them in office, and gave them blanks for requisitions for the full equipment of a cavalry regiment. He selected San Antonio as the gathering-place, as it

THE COLONEL OF THE ROUGH RIDERS.

240 THEODORE ROOSEVELT — AN AUTOBIOGRAPHY

was in a good horse country, near the Gulf from some port on which we would have to embark, and near an old arsenal and an old army post from which we got a good deal of stuff — some of it practically condemned, but which we found serviceable at a pinch, and much better than nothing. He organized a horse board in Texas, and began purchasing all horses that were not too big and were sound. A day or two after he commissioned he wrote out in the office of the Secretary of War, under his authority, telegrams to the Governors of Arizona, New Mexico, Oklahoma, and Indian Territory, in substance as follows :

The President desires to raise —— volunteers in your Territory to form part of a regiment of mounted riflemen to be commanded by Leonard Wood, Colonel ; Theodore Roosevelt, Lieutenant-Colonel. He desires that the men selected should be young, sound, good shots and good riders, and that you expedite by all means in your power the enrollment of these men.

(Signed) R. A. ALGER, Secretary of War.

As soon as he had attended to a few more odds and ends he left Washington, and the day after his arrival in San Antonio the troops began to arrive.

For several weeks before I joined the regiment, to which Wood went ahead of me, I continued as Assistant Secretary of the Navy, trying to get some coherence of plan between the War Department and the Navy Department ; and also being used by Wood to finish getting the equipment for the regiment. As regards finding out what the plans of the War Department were, the task was simple. They had no plans. Even during the final months before the outbreak of hostilities very little was done in the way of efficient preparation. On one occasion, when every one knew that the declaration of war was sure to come in a few days, I went on military business to the office of one of the highest line generals of the army, a man who at that moment ought to have been working eighteen hours out of the twenty-four on the vital problems ahead of him. What he was actually doing was trying on a new type of smart-looking uniform on certain enlisted men; and he called me in to ask my advice as to the position of the pockets in the blouse, with a view to making it look attractive. An aide of this general — funnily enough a good fighting man in actual service — when I consulted him as to what my uniform for the campaign should be, laid special stress upon my purchasing a pair of black top boots for full dress, explaining that they were very effective on hotel piazzas and in parlors. I did not intend to be in any hotel if it could possibly be avoided; and as things turned out, I had no full-dress uniform, nothing but my service uniform, during my brief experience in the army.

I suppose that war always does bring out what is highest and lowest in human nature. The contractors who furnish poor materials to the army or the navy in time of war stand on a level of infamy only one degree above that of the participants in the white slave traffic themselves. But there is conduct far short of this which yet seems inexplicable to any man who has in him any spirit of disinterested patriotism combined with any power of imagination. Respectable men, who I suppose lack the imagination thoroughly to realize what they are doing, try to make money out of the Nation's necessities in war at the very time that other men are making every sacrifice, financial and personal, for the cause. In the closing weeks of my service as Assistant Secretary of the Navy we were collecting ships for auxiliary purposes. Some men, at cost to their own purses, helped us freely and with efficiency; others treated the affair as an ordinary business transaction; and yet others endeavored, at some given crisis when our need was great, to sell us inferior vessels at exorbitant prices, and used every pressure, through Senators and Congressmen, to accomplish their ends. In one or two cases they did accomplish them too, until we got a really first-class board established to superintend such purchases. A more curious experience was in connection with the point chosen for the starting for the expedition against Cuba. I had not supposed that any

R

human being could consider this matter save from the stand-point of military need.   But one morning a very wealthy and influential man, a respectable and upright man according to his own lights, called on me to protest against our choice of Tampa, and to put in a plea for a certain other port, *on the ground that his railroad was entitled to its share of the profit for hauling the army and equipment!*   I happened to know that at this time this very man had kinsfolk with the army, who served gallantly, and the circumstances of his coming to me were such as to show that he was not acting secretly, and had no idea that there was anything out of the way in his proposal.   I think the facts were merely that he had been trained to regard business as the sole object in life, and that he lacked the imagination to enable him to understand the real nature of the request that he was making;   and, moreover, he had good reason to believe that one of his business competitors had been unduly favored.

The War Department was in far worse shape than the Navy Department.   The young officers turned out from West Point are precisely as good as the young officers turned out from Annapolis, and this always has been true.   But at that time (something has been done to remedy the worst conditions since), and ever since the close of the Civil War, the conditions were such that after a few years the army officer stagnated so far as his profession was concerned. When the Spanish War broke out the navy really was largely on a war footing, as any navy which is even respectably cared for in time of peace must be.   The admirals, captains, and lieutenants were continually practicing their profession in almost precisely the way that it has to be practiced in time of war.   Except actually shooting at a foe, most of the men on board ship went through in time of peace practically all that they would have to go through in time of war.   The heads of bureaus in the Navy Department were for the most part men who had seen sea service, who expected to return to sea service, and who were preparing for needs which they themselves knew by experience.   Moreover, the civilian head of the navy had to provide for keeping the ships in a state of reasonable efficiency, and Congress could not hope-

lessly misbehave itself about the navy without the fact at
once becoming evident.

All this was changed so far as the army was concerned.
Not only was it possible to decrease the efficiency of the army
without being called to account for it, but the only way in
which the Secretary of War could gain credit for himself or
the Administration was by economy, and the easiest way to
economize was in connection with something that would not
be felt unless war should arise.   The people took no interest
whatever in the army; demagogues clamored against it,
and, inadequate though it was in size, insisted that it should
be still further reduced.   Popular orators always appealed
to the volunteers; the regulars had no votes and there was
no point in politicians thinking of them.   The chief activity
shown by Congressmen about the army was in getting special
army posts built in places where there was no need for them.
Even the work of the army in its campaigns against the
Indians was of such a character that it was generally performed by small bodies of fifty or a hundred men.   Until a
man ceased being a lieutenant he usually had plenty of professional work to attend to and was employed in the field,
and, in short, had the same kind of practice that his brother
in the navy had, and he did his work as well.   But once past
this stage he had almost no opportunity to perform any work
corresponding to his rank, and but little opportunity to
do any military work whatsoever.   The very best men,
men like Lawton, Young, Chaffee, Hawkins, and Sumner,
to mention only men under or beside whom I served, remained good soldiers, soldiers of the best stamp, in spite of
the disheartening conditions.   But it was not to be expected
that the average man could continue to grow when every
influence was against him.   Accordingly, when the Spanish
War suddenly burst upon us, a number of inert elderly
captains and field officers were, much against their own
wishes, suddenly pitchforked into the command of regiments,
brigades, and even divisions and army corps.   Often these
men failed painfully.   This was not their fault; it was the
fault of the Nation, that is, the fault of all of us, of you, my
reader, and of myself, and of those like us, because we had

permitted conditions to be such as to render these men unfit for command.   Take a stout captain of an out-of-the way two-company post, where nothing in the world ever occurred even resembling military action, and where the only military problem that really convulsed the post to its foundations was the quarrel between the captain and the quartermaster as to how high a mule's tail ought to be shaved (I am speaking of an actual incident).   What could be expected of such a man, even though thirty-five years before he had been a gallant second lieutenant in the Civil War, if, after this intervening do-nothing period, he was suddenly put in command of raw troops in a midsummer campaign in the tropics ?

The bureau chiefs were for the most part elderly incompetents, whose idea was to do their routine duties in such way as to escape the censure of routine bureaucratic superiors and to avoid a Congressional investigation.   They had not the slightest conception of preparing the army for war.   It was impossible that they could have any such conception. The people and the Congress did not wish the army prepared for war ; and those editors and philanthropists and peace advocates who felt vaguely that if the army were incompetent their principles were safe, always inveighed against any proposal to make it efficient, on the ground that this showed a natural bloodthirstiness in the proposer.   When such were the conditions, it was absolutely impossible that either the War Department or the army could do well in the event of war.   Secretary Alger happened to be Secretary when war broke out, and all the responsibility for the shortcomings of the Department were visited upon his devoted head.   He was made the scapegoat for our National shortcomings. The fault was not his ; the fault and responsibility lay with us, the people, who for thirty-three years had permitted our representatives in Congress and in National executive office to bear themselves so that it was absolutely impossible to avoid the great bulk of all the trouble that occurred, and of all the shortcomings of which our people complained, during the Spanish War.   The chief immediate cause was the condition of red-tape bureaucracy which existed in the War

Department at Washington, which had prevented any good organization or the preparation of any good plan of operation for using our men and supplies. The recurrence of these conditions, even though in somewhat less aggravated form, in any future emergency is as certain as sunrise unless we bring about the principle of a four years' detail in the staff corps — a principle which Congress has now for years stubbornly refused to grant.

There are nations who only need to have peaceful ideals inculcated, and to whom militarism is a curse and a misfortune. There are other nations, like our own, so happily situated that the thought of war is never present to their minds. They are wholly free from any tendency improperly to exalt or to practice militarism. These nations should never forget that there must be military ideals no less than peaceful ideals. The exaltation of Nogi's career, set forth so strikingly in Stanley Washburn's little volume on the great Japanese warrior, contains much that is especially needed for us of America, prone as we are to regard the exigencies of a purely commercial and industrial civilization as excusing us from the need of admiring and practicing the heroic and warlike virtues.

Our people are not military. We need normally only a small standing army; but there should be behind it a reserve of instructed men big enough to fill it up to full war strength, which is over twice the peace strength. Moreover, the young men of the country should realize that it is the duty of every one of them to prepare himself so that in time of need he may speedily become an efficient soldier — a duty now generally forgotten, but which should be recognized as one of the vitally essential parts of every man's training.

In endeavoring to get the "Rough Riders" equipped I met with some experiences which were both odd and instructive. There were not enough arms and other necessaries to go round, and there was keen rivalry among the intelligent and zealous commanders of the volunteer organizations as to who should get first choice. Wood's experience was what enabled us to equip ourselves in short order. There was another cavalry organization whose commander was at the

War Department about this time, and we had been eyeing him with much alertness as a rival.   One day I asked him what his plans were about arming and drilling his troops, who were of precisely the type of our own men.   He answered that he expected "to give each of the boys two revolvers and a lariat, and then just turn them loose."   I reported the conversation to Wood, with the remark that

COLONEL THEODORE ROOSEVELT AND A GROUP OF ROUGH RIDERS.

we might feel ourselves safe from rivalry in that quarter; and safe we were.

In trying to get the equipment I met with checks and rebuffs, and in return was the cause of worry and concern to various bureau chiefs who were unquestionably estimable men in their private and domestic relations, and who doubtless had been good officers thirty years before, but who were as unfit for modern war as if they were so many smoothbores.   One fine old fellow did his best to persuade us to take black powder rifles, explaining with paternal indulgence that no one yet really knew just what smokeless powder might do, and that there was a good deal to be said in favor of having smoke to conceal us from the enemy. I saw this pleasing theory actually worked out in practice later on, for the National Guard regiments with us at Santiago had black powder muskets, and the regular artillery black powder guns, and they really might almost as well have replaced these weapons by crossbows and mangonels. We succeeded, thanks to Wood, in getting the same cavalry carbines that were used by the regulars. We were determined to do this, not only because the weapons were good, but because this would in all probability mean that we were brigaded with the regular cavalry, which it was certain would be sent immediately to the front for the fighting.

There was one worthy bureau chief who was continually refusing applications of mine as irregular. In each case I would appeal to Secretary Alger — who helped me in every way — and get an order from him countenancing the irregularity. For instance, I found out that as we were nearer the July date than the January date for the issuance of clothing, and as it had long been customary to issue the winter clothing in July, so as to give ample leisure for getting it to all the various posts, it was therefore solemnly proposed to issue this same winter clothing to us who were about to start for a summer campaign in the tropics. This would seem incredible to those who have never dealt with an inert officialdom, a red-tape bureaucracy, but such is the fact. I rectified this and got an order for khaki clothing. We were then told we would have to advertise thirty days for horses. This meant that we would have missed the Santiago expedition. So I made another successful appeal to the Secretary. Other difficulties came up about wagons, and various articles, and in each case the same result followed. On the last occasion, when I came up in triumph with the needed order, the worried office head, who bore me no animosity, but who did feel that fate had been very unkind, threw himself back in his chair and exclaimed with a sigh: "Oh, dear! I had this office running in such good shape — and then along came the war and upset everything !" His feeling was that war was an illegitimate interruption to the work of the War Department.

There were of course department heads and bureau chiefs and assistants who, in spite of the worthlessness of the system, and of the paralyzing conditions that had prevailed, remained first-class men. An example of these was Commissary-General Weston. His energy, activity, administrative efficiency, and common sense were supplemented by an eager desire to help everybody do the best that could be done. Both in Washington and again down at Santiago we owed him very much. When I was President, it was my good fortune to repay him in part our debt, which means the debt of the people of the country, by making him a major-general.

The regiment assembled at San Antonio. When I reached there, the men, rifles, and horses, which were the essentials, were coming in fast, and the saddles, blankets, and the like were also accumulating. Thanks to Wood's exertions, when we reached Tampa we were rather better equipped than most of the regular regiments. We adhered strictly to field equipment, allowing no luxuries or anything else unnecessary, and so we were able to move off the field when ordered, with our own transportation, leaving nothing behind.

I suppose every man tends to brag about his regiment; but it does seem to me that there never was a regiment better worth bragging about than ours. Wood was an exceptional commander, of great power, with a remarkable gift for organization. The rank and file were as fine natural fighting men as ever carried a rifle or rode a horse in any country or any age. We had a number of first-class young fellows from the East, most of them from colleges like Harvard, Yale, and Princeton; but the great majority of the men were Southwesterners, from the then territories of Oklahoma, Indian Territory, Arizona, and New Mexico. They were accustomed to the use of firearms, accustomed to taking care of themselves in the open; they were intelligent and self-reliant; they possessed hardihood and endurance and physical prowess; and, above all, they had

the fighting edge, the cool and resolute fighting temper.
They went into the war with full knowledge, having deliberately counted the cost.   In the great majority of cases each
man was chiefly anxious to find out what he should do to
make the regiment a success.   They bought, first and last,
about 800 copies of the cavalry drill regulations and studied
them industriously.   Such men were practically soldiers to
start with, in all the essentials.   It is small wonder that
with them as material to work upon the regiment was raised,
armed, equipped, drilled, sent on trains to Tampa, embarked,
disembarked, and put through two victorious offensive —
not defensive — fights in which a third of the officers and
one-fifth of the men were killed or wounded, all within sixty
days.   It is a good record, and it speaks well for the men of
the regiment; and it speaks well for Wood

Wood was so busy getting the regiment ready that when I
reached San Antonio he turned most of the drilling of it
over to me.   This was a piece of great good fortune for me,
and I drilled the men industriously, mounted and unmounted.
I had plenty to learn, and the men and the officers even
more; but we went at our work with the heartiest good will.
We speedily made it evident that there was no room and no
mercy for any man who shirked any duty, and we accomplished good results.   The fact is that the essentials of drill
and work for a cavalry or an infantry regiment are easy to
learn, which of course is not true for the artillery or the engineers or for the navy.   The reason why it takes so long to
turn the average civilized man into a good infantryman or

---

[1] To counterbalance the newspapers which ignorantly and indiscriminately
praised all the volunteers there were others whose blame was of the same intelligent
quality.   The New York *Evening Post*, on June 18, gave expression to the following gloomy foreboding: "Competent observers have remarked that nothing more
extraordinary has been done than the sending to Cuba of the First United States
Volunteer Cavalry, known as the 'rough riders.'   Organized but four weeks, barely
given their full complement of officers, and only a week of regular drill, these men
have been sent to the front before they have learned the first elements of soldiering
and discipline, or have even become acquainted with their officers.   In addition
to all this, like the regular cavalry, they have been sent with only their carbines
and revolvers to meet an enemy armed with long-range rifles.   There have been
few cases of such military cruelty in our military annals."   A week or so after this
not wholly happy prophecy was promulgated, the "cruelty" was consummated,
first at Las Guasimas and then in the San Juan fighting.

cavalryman is because it takes a long while to teach the average untrained man how to shoot, to ride, to march, to take care of himself in the open, to be alert, resourceful, cool, daring, and resolute, to obey quickly, as well as to be willing, and to fit himself, to act on his own responsibility. If he already possesses these qualities, there is very little difficulty in making him a soldier; all the drill that is necessary to enable him to march and to fight is of a simple character. Parade ground and barrack square maneuvers are of no earthly consequence in real war. When men can readily change from line to column, and column to line, can form front in any direction, and assemble and scatter, and can do these things with speed and precision, they have a fairly good grasp of the essentials. When our regiment reached Tampa it could already be handled creditably at fast gaits, and both in mass and extended formations, mounted and dismounted.

I had served three years in the New York National Guard, finally becoming a captain. This experience was invaluable to me. It enabled me at once to train the men in the simple drill without which they would have been a mob; for although the drill requirements are simple, they are also absolutely indispensable. But if I had believed that my experience in the National Guard had taught me all that there was to teach about a soldier's career, it would have been better for me not to have been in it at all. There were in the regiment a number of men who had served in the National Guard, and a number of others who had served in the Regular Army. Some of these latter had served in the field in the West under campaign conditions, and were accustomed to long marches, privation, risk, and unexpected emergencies. These men were of the utmost benefit to the regiment. They already knew their profession, and could teach and help the others. But if the man had merely served in a National Guard regiment, or in the Regular Army at some post in a civilized country where he learned nothing except what could be picked up on the parade ground, in the barracks, and in practice marches of a few miles along good roads, then it depended purely upon his own good sense whether he had been helped or hurt by the experience.

If he realized that he had learned only five per cent of his profession, that there remained ninety-five per cent to accomplish before he would be a good soldier, why, he had profited immensely.

To start with five per cent handicap was a very great
advantage; and if the man was really a good man, he could
not be overtaken. But if the man thought that he had
learned all about the profession of a soldier because he had
been in the National Guard or in the Regular Army under
the conditions I have described, then he was actually of less
use than if he had never had any military experience at
all. Such a man was apt to think that nicety of alignment,
precision in wheeling, and correctness in the manual of arms
were the ends of training and the guarantees of good soldier-
ship, and that from guard mounting to sentry duty everything in war was to be done in accordance with what he
had learned in peace. As a matter of fact, most of what he
had learned was never used at all, and some of it had to
be unlearned. The one thing, for instance, that a sentry
ought never to do in an actual campaign is to walk up and
down a line where he will be conspicuous. His business is to
lie down somewhere off a ridge crest where he can see any
one approaching, but where a man approaching cannot
see him. As for the ceremonies, during the really hard part
of a campaign only the barest essentials are kept.

Almost all of the junior regular officers, and many of the
senior regular officers, were fine men. But, through no fault
of their own, had been forced to lead lives that fairly paralyzed their efficiency when the strain of modern war came
on them. The routine elderly regular officer who knew
nothing whatever of modern war was in most respects nearly
as worthless as a raw recruit. The positions and commands
prescribed in the text-books were made into fetishes by some
of these men, and treated as if they were the ends, instead
the not always important means by which the ends were
to be achieved. In the Cuban fighting, for instance, it
would have been folly for me to have taken my place in
the rear of the regiment, the canonical text-book position.
My business was to be where I could keep most command

over the regiment, and, in a rough-and-tumble, scrambling fight in thick jungle, this had to depend upon the course of events, and usually meant that I had to be at the front. I saw in that fighting more than one elderly regimental commander who unwittingly rendered the only service he could render to his regiment by taking up his proper position several hundred yards in the rear when the fighting began; for then the regiment disappeared in the jungle, and for its good fortune the commanding officer never saw it again until long after the fight was over.

After one Cuban fight a lieutenant-colonel of the regulars, in command of a regiment, who had met with just such an experience and had rejoined us at the front several hours after the close of the fighting, asked me what my men were doing when the fight began. I answered that they were following in trace in column of twos, and that the instant the shooting began I deployed them as skirmishers on both sides of the trail. He answered triumphantly, "You can't deploy men as skirmishers from column formation"; to which I responded, "Well, I did, and, what is more, if any captain had made any difficulty about it, I would have sent him to the rear." My critic was quite correct from the parade ground standpoint. The prescribed orders at that time were to deploy the column first into a line of squads at correct intervals, and then to give an order which, if my memory serves correctly, ran: "As skirmishers, by the right and left flanks, at six yards, take intervals, march." The order I really gave ran more like this: "Scatter out to the right there, quick, you! scatter to the left! look alive, look alive!" And they looked alive, and they scattered, and each took advantage of cover, and forward went the line.

Now I do not wish what I have said to be misunderstood. If ever we have a great war, the bulk of our soldiers will not be men who have had any opportunity to train soul and mind and body so as to meet the iron needs of an actual campaign. Long continued and faithful drill will alone put these men in shape to begin to do their duty, and failure to recognize this on the part of the average man will mean laziness and folly and not the possession of efficiency. Moreover, if men have been trained to believe, for instance, that they can "arbitrate questions of vital interest and national honor," if they have been brought up with flabbiness of moral fiber as well as flabbiness of physique, then there will be need of long and laborious and faithful work to give the needed tone to mind and body.   But if the men have in them the right stuff, it is not so very difficult.

At San Antonio we entrained for Tampa.   In various sociological books by authors of Continental Europe, there are jeremiads as to the way in which service in the great European armies, with their minute and machine-like efficiency and regularity, tends to dwarf the capacity for individual initiative among the officers and men.   There is no such danger for any officer or man of a volunteer organization in America when our country, with playful light-heartedness, has pranced into war without making any preparation for it.   I know no larger or finer field for the display of an advanced individualism than that which opened before us as we went from San Antonio to Tampa, camped there, and embarked on a transport for Cuba. Nobody ever had any definite information to give us, and whatever information we unearthed on our own account was usually wrong.   Each of us had to show an alert and not overscrupulous self-reliance in order to obtain food for his men, provender for his horses, or transportation of any kind for any object.   One lesson early impressed on me was that if I wanted anything to eat it was wise to carry it with me ; and if any new war should arise, I would earnestly advise the men of every volunteer organization always to proceed upon the belief that their supplies will not turn up, and to take every opportunity of getting food for themselves.

Tampa was a scene of the wildest confusion.   There were miles of tracks loaded with cars of the contents of which nobody seemed to have any definite knowledge.   General Miles, who was supposed to have supervision over everything, and General Shafter, who had charge of the expedition, were both there.   But, thanks to the fact that nobody had had any experience in handling even such a small force as ours — about 17,000 men — there was no semblance of order.

Wood and I were bound that we should not be left behind when the expedition started. When we were finally informed that it was to leave next morning, we were ordered to go to a certain track to meet a train. We went to the track, but the train never came. Then we were sent to another track to meet another train. Again it never came. However, we found a coal train, of which we took possession, and the conductor, partly under duress and partly in a spirit of friendly helpfulness, took us down to the quay.

All kinds of other organizations, infantry and cavalry, regular and volunteer, were arriving at the quay and wandering around it, and there was no place where we could get any specific information as to what transport we were to have. Finally Wood was told to "get any ship you can get which is not already assigned." He borrowed without leave a small motor boat, and commandeered the transport Yucatan. When asked by the captain what his authority was, he reported that he was acting "by orders of General Shafter," and directed the ship to be brought to the dock. He had already sent me word to be ready, as soon as the ship touched the pier, to put the regiment aboard her. I found that she had already been assigned to a regular regiment, and to another volunteer regiment, and as it was evident that not more than half of the men assigned to her could possibly get on, I was determined that we should not be among the men left off. The volunteer regiment offered a comparatively easy problem. I simply marched my men past them to the allotted place and held the gangway. With the regulars I had to be a little more diplomatic, because their commander, a lieutenant-colonel, was my superior in rank, and also doubtless knew his rights. He sent word to me to make way, to draw my regiment off to one side, and let his take possession of the gangway. I could see the transport coming in, and could dimly make out Wood's figure thereon. Accordingly I played for time. I sent respectful requests through his officers to the commander of the regulars, entered into parleys, and made protestations, until the transport got near enough so that by yelling at the top of my voice I was able to get into a — highly constructive — communication with Wood. What he was saying I had no idea, but he was evidently speaking, and on my own responsibility I translated it into directions to hold the gangway, and so informed the regulars that I was under the orders of my superior and of a ranking officer, and — to my great regret, etc., etc. — could not give way as they desired. As soon as the transport was fast we put our men aboard at the double. Half of the regular regiment got on, and the other half and the other volunteer regiment went somewhere else.

We were kept several days on the transport, which was jammed with men, so that it was hard to move about on the deck. Then the fleet got under way, and we steamed slowly down to Santiago. Here we disembarked, higgledy-piggledy, just as we had embarked. Different parts of different outfits were jumbled together, and it was no light labor afterwards to assemble the various batteries. For instance, one transport had guns, and another the locks for the guns ; the two not getting together for several days after one of them had been landed. Soldiers went here, provisions there ; and who got ashore first largely depended upon individual activity. Fortunately for us, my former naval aide, when I had been Assistant Secretary of the Navy, Lieutenant-Commander Sharp, a first-class fellow, was there in command of a little ship to which I had succeeded in getting him appointed before I left the Navy Department. He gave us a black pilot, who took our transport right in shore, the others following like a flock of sheep ; and we disembarked with our rifles, ammunition belts, and not much else. In theory it was out of our turn, but if we had not disembarked then, Heaven only knows when our turn would have come, and we did not intend to be out of the fighting if we could help it. I carried some food in my pockets, and a light waterproof coat, which was my sole camp equipment for the next two or three days. Twenty-four hours after getting ashore we marched from Daiquiri, where we had landed, to Siboney, also on the coast, reaching it during a terrific downpour of rain. When this was over, we built a fire, dried our clothes, and ate whatever we had brought with us.

We were brigaded with the First and Tenth Regular
Cavalry, under Brigadier-General Sam Young. He was a
fine type of the American regular. Like General Chaffee,
another of the same type, he had entered the army in the
Civil War as a private. Later, when I was President, it
was my good fortune to make each of them in succession
Lieutenant-General of the army of the United States. When
General Young retired and General Chaffee was to take his
place, the former sent to the latter his three stars to wear on
his first official presentation, with a note that they were from
"Private Young to Private Chaffee." The two fine old
fellows had served in the ranks, one in the cavalry, one in
the infantry, in their golden youth, in the days of the great
war nearly half a century before ; each had grown gray in a
lifetime of honorable service under the flag, and each closed
his active career in command of the army. General Young
was one of the few men who had given and taken wounds with
the saber. He was an old friend of mine, and when in
Washington before starting for the front he told me that if
we got in his brigade he would put us into the fighting all
right. He kept his word.

General Young had actively superintended getting his
two regular regiments, or at least a squadron of each, off
the transports, and late that night he sent us word that he
had received permission to move at dawn and strike the
Spanish advance position. He directed us to move along
a ridge trail with our two squadrons (one squadron having
been left at Tampa), while with the two squadrons of regulars,
one of the First and one of the Tenth, under his personal
supervision, he marched up the valley trail. Accordingly
Wood took us along the hill trail early next morning, till
we struck the Spaniards, and began our fight just as the
regulars began the fight in the valley trail.

It was a mountainous country covered with thick jungle,
a most confusing country, and I had an awful time trying
to get into the fight and trying to do what was right when in
it ; and all the while I was thinking that I was the only man
who did not know what I was about, and that all the others
did — whereas, as I found out later, pretty much everybody

else was as much in the dark as I was.   There was no surprise; we struck the Spaniards exactly where we had
expected; then Wood halted us and put us into the fight
deliberately and in order.   He ordered us to deploy alter-
nately by troops to the right and left of the trail, giving our
senior major, Brodie, a West Pointer and as good a soldier
as ever wore a uniform, the left wing, while I took the right
wing.   I was told if possible to connect with the regulars who
were on the right.   In theory this was excellent, but as
the jungle was very dense the first troop that deployed to
the right vanished forthwith, and I never saw it again until
the fight was over — having a frightful feeling meanwhile
that I might be court-martialed for losing it.   The next
troop deployed to the left under Brodie.   Then the third
came along, and I started to deploy it to the right as before.

By the time the first platoon had gotten into the jungle
I realized that it likewise would disappear unless I kept
hold of it.   I managed to keep possession of the last platoon.
One learns fast in a fight, and I marched this platoon and my
next two troops in column through the jungle without any
attempt to deploy until we got on the firing line.   This
sounds simple.   But it was not.   I did not know when
I had gotten on the firing line !   I could hear a good deal
of firing, some over to my right at a good distance, and the
rest to the left and ahead.   I pushed on, expecting to strike
the enemy somewhere between.

Soon we came to the brink of a deep valley.   There was a
good deal of cracking of rifles way off in front of us, but as
they used smokeless powder we had no idea as to exactly
where they were, or who they were shooting at.   Then it
dawned on us that we were the target.   The bullets began
to come overhead, making a sound like the ripping of a silk
dress, with sometimes a kind of pop; a few of my men fell,
and I deployed the rest, making them lie down and get
behind trees.   Richard Harding Davis was with us, and as
we scanned the landscape with our glasses it was he who
first pointed out to us some Spaniards in a trench some
three-quarters of a mile off.   It was difficult to make them
out.   There were not many of them.   However, we finally

s

did make them out, and we could see their conical hats, for the trench was a poor one. We advanced, firing at them, and drove them off.

What to do then I had not an idea. The country in front fell away into a very difficult jungle-filled valley. There was nothing but jungle all around, and if I advanced I was afraid I might get out of touch with everybody and not be going in the right direction. Moreover, as far as I could see, there was now nobody in front who was shooting at us, although some of the men on my left insisted that our own men had fired into us — an allegation which I soon found was almost always made in such a fight, and which in this case was not true. At this moment some of the regulars appeared across the ravine on our right. The first thing they did was to fire a volley at us, but one of our first sergeants went up a tree and waved a guidon at them and they stopped. Firing was still going on to our left, however, and I was never more puzzled to know what to do. I did not wish to take my men out of their position without orders, for fear that I might thereby be leaving a gap if there was a Spanish force which meditated an offensive return. On the other hand, it did not seem to me that I had been doing enough fighting to justify my existence, and there was obviously fighting going on to the left. I remember that I kept thinking of the refrain of the fox-hunting song, "Here's to every friend who struggled to the end"; in the hunting field I had always acted on this theory, and, no matter how discouraging appearances might be, had never stopped trying to get in at the death until the hunt was actually over; and now that there was work, and not play, on hand, I intended to struggle as hard as I knew how not to be left out of any fighting into which I could, with any possible propriety, get.

So I left my men where they were and started off at a trot toward where the firing was, with a couple of orderlies to send back for the men in case that proved advisable. Like most tyros, I was wearing my sword, which in thick jungle now and then got between my legs — from that day on it always went corded in the baggage. I struck the

trail, and began to pass occasional dead men. Pretty
soon I reached Wood and found, much to my pleasure, that
I had done the right thing, for as I came up word was
brought to him that Brodie had been shot, and he at once
sent me to take charge of the left wing. It was more open
country here, and at least I was able to get a glimpse of my
own men and exercise some control over them. There
was much firing going on, but for the life of me I could not
see any Spaniards, and neither could any one else. Finally
we made up our minds that they were shooting at us from a
set of red-tiled ranch buildings a good way in front, and
these I assaulted, finally charging them. Before we came
anywhere near, the Spaniards, who, as it proved, really
were inside and around them, abandoned them, leaving a
few dead men.

By the time I had taken possession of these buildings all
firing had ceased everywhere. I had not the faintest idea what
had happened : whether the fight was over ; or whether this
was merely a lull in the fight ; or where the Spaniards were ;
or whether we might be attacked again ; or whether we ought
ourselves to attack somebody somewhere else. I got my
men in order and sent out small parties to explore the
ground in front, who returned without finding any foe.
(By this time, as a matter of fact, the Spaniards were in
full retreat.) Meanwhile I was extending my line so as to
get into touch with our people on the right. Word was
brought to me that Wood had been shot — which fortunately
proved not to be true — and as, if this were so, it meant
that I must take charge of the regiment, I moved over
personally to inquire. Soon I learned that he was all
right, that the Spaniards had retreated along the main road,
and that Colonel Wood and two or three other officers
were a short distance away. Before I reached them I
encountered a captain of the Ninth Cavalry, very glum
because his troopers had not been up in time to take part in
the fight, and he congratulated me — with visible effort ! —
upon my share in our first victory. I thanked him cordially, not confiding in him that till that moment I myself
knew exceeding little about the victory ; and proceeded to

where Generals Wheeler, Lawton, and Chaffee, who had just come up, in company with Wood, were seated on a bank. They expressed appreciation of the way that I had handled my troops, first on the right wing and then on the left!

Copyright, by Underwood & Underwood.

GENERAL JOSEPH WHEELER, IN THE FOREGROND, COMMANDER OF THE LEFT WING OF THE ARMY BEFORE SAN JUAN HILL. FROM LEFT TO RIGHT: MAJOR GEORGE M. DUNN, COLONEL BRODIE, CHAPLAIN BROWN, LEONARD WOOD, AND COLONEL THEODORE ROOSEVELT.

As I was quite prepared to find I had committed some awful sin, I did my best to accept this in a nonchalant manner, and not to look as relieved as I felt. As throughout the morning I had preserved a specious aspect of wisdom, and had commanded first one and then the other wing, the

fight was really a capital thing for me, for practically all
the men had served under my actual command, and thenceforth felt an enthusiastic belief that I would lead them
aright.

It was a week after this skirmish before the army made
the advance on Santiago. Just before this occurred General
Young was stricken down with fever. General Wheeler,
who had commanded the Cavalry Division, was put in
general charge of the left wing of the army, which fought
before the city itself. Brigadier-General Sam Sumner,
an excellent officer, who had the second cavalry brigade,
took command of the cavalry division, and Wood took
command of our brigade, while, to my intense delight,
I got my regiment. I therefore had command of the regiment before the stiffest fighting occurred. Later, when
Wood was put in command in Santiago, I became the
brigade commander.

Late in the evening we camped at El Poso. There were
two regular officers, the brigade commander's aides, Lieutenants A. L. Mills and W. E. Shipp, who were camped by
our regiment. Each of my men had food in his haversack,
but I had none, and I would have gone supperless to bed
if Mills and Shipp had not given me out of their scanty
stores a big sandwich, which I shared with my orderly,
who also had nothing. Next morning my body servant
Marshall, an ex-soldier of the Ninth (Colored) Cavalry, a
fine and faithful fellow, had turned up and I was able in my
turn to ask Mills and Shipp, who had eaten all their food
the preceding evening, to take breakfast with me. A few
hours later gallant Shipp was dead, and Mills, an exception-
ally able officer, had been shot through the head from side to
side, just back of the eyes; yet he lived, although one eye
was blinded, and before I left the Presidency I gave him
his commission as Brigadier-General.

Early in the morning our artillery began firing from the
hill-crest immediately in front of where our men were
camped. Several of the regiment were killed and wounded
by the shrapnel of the return fire of the Spaniards. One
of the shrapnel bullets fell on my wrist and raised a bump

as big as a hickory nut, but did not even break the skin. Then we were marched down from the hill on a muddy road through thick jungle towards Santiago. The heat was great, and we strolled into the fight with no definite idea on the part of any one as to what we were to do or what would happen. There was no plan that our left wing was to make a serious fight that day; and as there were no plans, it was naturally exceedingly hard to get orders, and each of us had to act largely on his own responsibility.

Lawton's infantry division attacked the little village of El Caney, some miles to the right. Kent's infantry division and Sumner's dismounted cavalry division were supposed to retain the Spanish army in Santiago until Lawton had captured El Caney. Spanish towns and villages, however, with their massive buildings, are natural fortifications, as the French found in the Peninsular War, and as both the French and our people found in Mexico. The Spanish troops in El Caney fought very bravely, as did the Spanish troops in front of us, and it was late in the afternoon before Lawton accomplished his task.

Meanwhile we of the left wing had by degrees become involved in a fight which toward the end became not even a colonel's fight, but a squad leader's fight. The cavalry division was put at the head of the line. We were told to march forward, cross a little river in front, and then, turning to the right, march up alongside the stream until we connected with Lawton. Incidentally, this movement would not have brought us into touch with Lawton in any event. But we speedily had to abandon any thought of carrying it out. The maneuver brought us within fair range of the Spanish intrenchments along the line of hills which we called the San Juan Hills, because on one of them was the San Juan blockhouse. On that day my regiment had the lead of the second brigade, and we marched down the trail following in trace behind the first brigade. Apparently the Spaniards could not make up their minds what to do as the three regular regiments of the first brigade crossed and defiled along the other bank of the stream, but when our regiment was crossing they began to fire at us.

Under this flank fire it soon became impossible to continue the march. The first brigade halted, deployed, and finally began to fire back. Then our brigade was halted. From time to time some of our men would fall, and I sent repeated word to the rear to try to get authority to attack the hills in front. Finally General Sumner, who was fighting the division in fine shape, sent word to advance. The word was brought to me by Mills, who said that my orders were to support the regulars in the assault on the hills, and that my objective would be the red-ti ed ranch-house in front, on a hill which we afterwards christened Kettle Hill. I mention Mills saying this because it was exactly the kind of definite order the giving of which does so much to insure success in a fight, as it prevents all obscurity as to what is to be done. The order to attack did not reach the first brigade until after we ourselves reached it, so that at first there was doubt on the part of their officers whether they were at liberty to join in the advance.

I had not enjoyed the Guasimas fight at all, because I had been so uncertain as to what I ought to do. But the San Juan fight was entirely different. The Spaniards had a hard position to attack, it is true, but we could see them, and I knew exactly how to proceed. I kept on horseback, merely because I found it difficult to convey orders along the line, as the men were lying down; and it is always hard to get men to start when they cannot see whether their comrades are also going. So I rode up and down the lines, keeping them straightened out, and gradually worked through line after line until I found myself at the head of the regiment. By the time I had reached the lines of the regulars of the first brigade I had come to the conclusion that it was silly to stay in the valley firing at the hills, because that was really where we were most exposed, and that the thing to do was to try to rush the intrenchments. Where I struck the regulars there was no one of superior rank to mine, and after asking why they did not charge, and being answered that they had no orders, I said I would give the order. There was naturally a little reluctance shown by the elderly officer in command to accept my order, so I said, "Then let my men through, sir," and I marched through, followed by my grinning men. The younger officers and the enlisted men of the regulars jumped up and joined us. I waved my hat, and we went up the hill with a rush. Having taken it, we looked across at the Spaniards in the trenches under the San Juan blockhouse to our left, which Hawkins's brigade was assaulting. I ordered our men to open fire on the Spaniards in the trenches.

Memory plays funny tricks in such a fight, where things happen quickly, and all kinds of mental images succeed one another in a detached kind of way, while the work goes on. As I gave the order in question there slipped through my mind Mahan's account of Nelson's orders that each ship as it sailed forward, if it saw another ship engaged with an enemy's ship, should rake the latter as it passed. When Hawkins's soldiers captured the blockhouse, I, very much elated, ordered a charge on my own hook to a line of hills still farther on. Hardly anybody heard this order, however; only four men started with me, three of whom were shot. I gave one of them, who was only wounded, my canteen of water, and ran back, much irritated that I had not been followed — which was quite unjustifiable, because I found that nobody had heard my orders. General Sumner had come up by this time, and I asked his permission to lead the charge. He ordered me to do so, and this time away we went, and stormed the Spanish intrenchments. There was some close fighting, and we took a few prisoners. We also captured the Spanish provisions, and ate them that night with great relish. One of the items was salted flying-fish, by the way. There were also bottles of wine, and jugs of fiery spirit, and as soon as possible I had these broken, although not before one or two of my men had taken too much liquor. Lieutenant Howze, of the regulars, an aide of General Sumner's, brought me an order to halt where I was; he could not make up his mind to return until he had spent an hour or two with us under fire. The Spaniards attempted a counter-attack in the middle of the afternoon, but were driven back without effort, our men laughing and cheering as they rose to fire; because hitherto they had been assaulting breastworks, or lying still under artillery fire, and they were glad to get a chance to shoot at the Spaniards in the open. We lay on our arms that night and as we were drenched with sweat, and had no blankets save a few we took from the dead Spaniards, we found even the tropic night chilly before morning came.

During the afternoon's fighting, while I was the highest officer at our immediate part of the front, Captains Boughton and Morton of the regular cavalry, two as fine officers as any man could wish to have beside him in battle, came along the firing line to tell me that they had heard a rumor that we might fall back, and that they wished to record their emphatic protest against any such course. I did not believe there was any truth in the rumor, for the Spaniards were utterly incapable of any effective counter-attack. However, late in the evening, after the fight, General Wheeler visited us at the front, and he told me to keep myself in readiness, as at any moment it might be decided to fall back. Jack Greenway was beside me when General Wheeler was speaking. I answered, "Well, General, I really don't know whether we would obey an order to fall back. We can take that city by a rush, and if we have to move out of here at all I should be inclined to make the rush in the right direction." Greenway nodded an eager assent. The old General, after a moment's pause, expressed his hearty agreement, and said that he would see that there was no falling back. He had been very sick for a couple of days, but, sick as he was, he managed to get into the fight. He was a gamecock if every there was one, but he was in very bad physical shape on the day of the fight. If there had been any one in high command to supervise and press the attack that afternoon, we would have gone right into Santiago. In my part of the line the advance was halted only because we received orders not to move forward, but to stay on the crest of the captured hill and hold it.

We are always told that three-o'clock-in-the-morning courage is the most desirable kind. Well, my men and the regulars of the cavalry had just that brand of courage. At about three o'clock on the morning after the first fight, shooting began in our front and there was an alarm of a Spanish advance. I was never more pleased than to see the way in which the hungry, tired, shabby men all jumped up and ran forward to the hill-crest, so as to be ready for the attack; which, however, did not come. As soon as the sun rose the Spaniards again opened upon us with artillery. A shell burst between Dave Goodrich and myself, blacking us with powder, and killing and wounding several of the men immediately behind us.

Next day the fight turned into a siege; there were some stirring incidents; but for the most part it was trench work. A fortnight later Santiago surrendered. Wood won his brigadier-generalship by the capital way in which he handled his brigade in the fight, and in the following siege. He was put in command of the captured city; and in a few days I succeeded to the command of the brigade.

The health of the troops was not good, and speedily became very bad. There was some dysentery, and a little yellow fever; but most of the trouble was from a severe form of malarial fever. The Washington authorities had behaved better than those in actual command of the expedition at one crisis. Immediately after the first days' fighting around Santiago the latter had hinted by cable to Washington that they might like to withdraw, and Washington had emphatically vetoed the proposal. I record this all the more gladly because there were not too many gleams of good sense shown in the home management of the war; although I wish to repeat that the real blame for this rested primarily with us ourselves, the people of the United States, who had for years pursued in military matters a policy that rendered it certain that there would be ineptitude and failure in high places if ever a crisis came. After the siege the people in Washington showed no knowledge whatever of the conditions around Santiago, and proposed to keep the army there. This would have meant that at least three-fourths of the men would either have died or have been permanently invalided, as a virulent form of malaria was widespread, and there was a steady growth of dysentery and other complaints. No object of any kind was to be gained by keeping the army in or near the captured city. General Shafter tried his best to get the Washington authorities to order the army home. As he failed to accomplish anything, he called a council of the division and brigade commanders and the chief medical officers to consult over the situation.

Although I had command of a brigade, I was only a colonel, and so I did not intend to attend, but the General informed me that I was particularly wanted, and accordingly I went. At the council General Shafter asked the medical authorities as to conditions, and they united in informing him that they were very bad, and were certain to grow much worse; and that in order to avoid frightful ravages from disease, chiefly due to malaria, the army should be sent back at once to some part of the northern United States. The General then explained that he could not get the War Department to understand the situation; that he could not get the attention of the public; and that he felt that there should be some authoritative publication which would make the War Department take action before it was too late to avert the ruin of the army. All who were in the room expressed their agreement.

Then the reason for my being present came out. It was explained to me by General Shafter, and by others, that as I was a volunteer officer and intended immediately to return to civil life, I could afford to take risks which the regular army men could not afford to take and ought not to be expected to take, and that therefore I ought to make the publication in question; because to incur the hostility of the War Department would not make any difference to me, whereas it would be destructive to the men in the regular army, or to those who hoped to get into the regular army. I thought this true, and said I would write a letter or make a statement which could then be published. Brigadier-General Ames, who was in the same postion that I was, also announced that he would make a statement.

When I left the meeting it was understood that I was to make my statement as an interview in the press; but Wood, who was by that time Brigadier-General commanding the city of Santiago, gave me a quiet hint to put my statement in the form of a letter to General Shafter, and this I

accordingly did.   When I had written my letter, the correspondent of the Associated Press, who had been informed
by others of what had occurred, accompanied me to General
Shafter.   I presented the letter to General Shafter, who
waved it away and said: "I don't want to take it; do
whatever you wish with it."   I, however, insisted on handing
it to him, whereupon he shoved it toward the correspondent
of the Associated Press, who took hold of it, and I released
my hold.   General Ames made a statement direct to the
correspondent, and also sent a cable to the Assistant Secretary of the Navy at Washington, a copy of which he gave
to the correspondent.   By this time the other division and
brigade commanders who were present felt that they had
better take action themselves.   They united in a round
robin to General Shafter, which General Wood dictated,
and which was signed by Generals Kent, Bates, Chaffee,
Sumner, Ludlow, Ames, and Wood, and by myself.   General
Wood handed this to General Shafter, and it was made
public by General Shafter precisely as mine was made
public.[1]   Later I was much amused when General Shafter
stated that he could not imagine how my letter and the round
robin got out !   When I saw this statement, I appreciated
how wise Wood had been in hinting to me not to act on the
suggestion of the General that I should make a statement to
the newspapers, but to put my statement in the form of a
letter to him as my superior officer, a letter which I delivered to him.   Both the letter and the round robin were
written at General Shafter's wish, and at the unanimous
suggestion of all the commanding and medical officers of
the Fifty Army Corps, and both were published by General
Shafter.

In a regiment the prime need is to have fighting men;
the prime virtue is to be able and eager to fight with the

[1] General Wood writes me : "The representative of the Associated Press was
very anxious to get a copy of this despatch or see it, and I told him it was impossible
for him to have it or see it.   I then went in to General Shafter and stated the case
to him, handing him the despatch, saying, 'The matter is now in your hands.'   He,
General Shafter, then said, 'I don't care whether this gentleman has it or not,'
and I left then.   When I went back the General told me he had given the Press
representative a copy of the despatch, and that he had gone to the office with it."

utmost effectiveness. I have never believed that this was incompatible with other virtues. On the contrary, while there are of course exceptions, I believe that on the average the best fighting men are also the best citizens. I do not believe that a finer set of natural soldiers than the men of my regiment could have been found anywhere, and they were first-class citizens in civil life also. One fact may perhaps be worthy of note. Whenever we were in camp and so fixed that we could have regular meals, we used to have a general officers' mess, over which I of course presided. During our entire service there was never a foul or indecent word uttered at the officers' mess — I mean this literally; and there was very little swearing — although now and then in the fighting, if there was a moment when swearing seemed to be the best method of reaching the heart of the matter, it was resorted to.

The men I cared for most in the regiment were the men who did the best work; and therefore my liking for them was obliged to take the shape of exposing them to most fatigue and hardship, of demanding from them the greatest service, and of making them incur the greatest risk. Once I kept Greenway and Goodrich at work for forty-eight hours, without sleeping, and with very little food, fighting and digging trenches. I freely sent the men for whom I cared most, to where death might smite them; and death often smote them — as it did the two best officers in my regiment, Allyn Capron and Bucky O'Neil. My men would not have respected me had I acted otherwise. Their creed was my creed. The life even of the most useful man, of the best citizen, is not to be hoarded if there be need to spend it. I felt, and feel, this about others; and of course also about myself. This is one reason why I have always felt impatient contempt for the effort to abolish the death penalty on account of sympathy with criminals. I am willing to listen to arguments in favor of abolishing the death penalty so far as they are based purely on grounds of public expediency, although these arguments have never convinced me. But inasmuch as, without hesitation, in the performance of duty, I have again and again sent good and gallant and upright men to die, it seems to me the height of a folly both mischievous and mawkish to contend that criminals who have deserved death should nevertheless be allowed to shirk it.   No brave and good man can properly shirk death; and no criminal who has earned death should be allowed to shirk it.

One of the best men with our regiment was the British military attaché, Captain Arthur Lee, an old friend.   The other military attachés were herded together at headquarters and saw little.   Captain Lee, who had known me in Washington, escaped and stayed with the regiment.   We grew to feel that he was one of us, and made him an honorary member. There were two other honorary members.   One was Richard Harding Davis, who was with us continually and who performed valuable service on the fighting line.   The other was a regular officer, Lieutenant Parker, who had a battery of gatlings.   We were with this battery throughout the San Juan fighting, and we grew to have the strongest admiration for Parker as a soldier and the strongest liking for him as a man.   During our brief campaign we were closely and intimately thrown with various regular officers of the type of Mills, Howze, and Parker.   We felt not merely fondness for them as officers and gentlemen, but pride in them as Americans.   It is a fine thing to feel that we have in the army and in the navy modest, efficient, gallant gentlemen of this type, doing such disinterested work for the honor of the flag and of the Nation.   No American can overpay the debt of gratitude we all of us owe to the officers and enlisted men of the army and of the navy.

Of course with a regiment of our type there was much to learn both among the officers and the men.   There were all kinds of funny incidents.   One of my men, an ex-cowpuncher and former round-up cook, a very good shot and rider, got into trouble on the way down on the transport. He understood entirely that he had to obey the officers of his own regiment, but, like so many volunteers, or at least like so many volunteers of my regiment, he did not understand that this obligation extended to officers of other regiments.   One of the regular officers on the transport ordered him to do something which he declined to do. When the officer told him to consider himself under arrest, he responded by offering to fight him for a trifling consideration. He was brought before a court martial which sentenced him to a year's imprisonment at hard labor with dishonorable discharge, and the major-general commanding the division approved the sentence.

We were on the transport. There was no hard labor to do; and the prison consisted of another cow-puncher who kept guard over him with his carbine, evidently divided in his feelings as to whether he would like most to shoot him or to let him go. When we landed, somebody told the prisoner that I intended to punish him by keeping him with the baggage. He at once came to me in great agitation, saying: "Colonel, they say you're going to leave me with the baggage when the fight is on. Colonel, if you do that, I will never show my face in Arizona again. Colonel, if you will let me go to the front, I promise I will obey any one you say; any one you say, Colonel," with the evident feeling that, after this concession, I could not, as a gentleman, refuse his request. Accordingly I answered: "Shields, there is no one in this regiment more entitled to be shot than you are, and you shall go to the front." His gratitude was great, and he kept repeating, "I'll never forget this, Colonel, never." Nor did he. When we got very hard up, he would now and then manage to get hold of some flour and sugar, and would cook a doughnut and bring it round to me, and watch me with a delighted smile as I ate it. He behaved extremely well in both fights, and after the second one I had him formally before me and remitted his sentence — something which of course I had not the slightest power to do, although at the time it seemed natural and proper to me.

When we came to be mustered out, the regular officer who was doing the mustering, after all the men had been discharged, finally asked me where the prisoner was. I said, "What prisoner?" He said, "The prisoner, the man who was sentenced to a year's imprisonment with hard labor and dishonorable discharge." I said, "Oh! I pardoned him"; to which he responded, "I beg your pardon; you did what?"

This made me grasp the fact that I had exceeded authority, and I could only answer, "Well, I did pardon him, anyhow, and he has gone with the rest"; whereupon the mustering-out officer sank back in his chair and remarked, "He was sentenced by a court martial, and the sentence was approved by the major-general commanding the division. You were a lieutenant-colonel, and you pardoned him. Well, it was nervy, that's all I'll say."

The simple fact was that under the circumstances it was necessary for me to enforce discipline and control the

On the Firing Line.

regiment, and therefore to reward and punish individuals in whatever way the exigencies demanded. I often explained to the men what the reasons for an order were, the first time it was issued, if there was any trouble on their part in understanding what they were required to do. They were very intelligent and very eager to do their duty, and I hardly ever had any difficulty the second time with them. If, however, there was the slightest willful shirking of duty or insubordination, I punished instantly and mercilessly, and the whole regiment cordially backed me up. To have punished men for faults and shortcomings which they had no opportunity to know were such would have been as unwise as to have permitted any of the occasional bad characters to exercise the slightest license. It was a regiment which was sensitive about its dignity and was very keenly alive to justice and to courtesy, but which cordially approved absence of mollycoddling, insistence upon the performance of duty, and summary punishment of wrong-doing.

In the final fighting at San Juan, when we captured one of the trenches, Jack Greenway had seized a Spaniard, and shortly afterwards I found Jack leading his captive round with a string. I told him to turn him over to a man who had two or three other captives, so that they should all be taken to the rear. It was the only time I ever saw Jack look aggrieved. "Why, Colonel, can't I keep him for myself?" he asked, plaintively. I think he had an idea that as a trophy of his bow and spear the Spaniard would make a fine body servant.

One reason that we never had the slightest trouble in the regiment was because, when we got down to hard pan, officers and men shared exactly alike. It is all right to have differences in food and the like in times of peace and plenty, when everybody is comfortable. But in really hard times officers and men must share alike if the best work is to be done. As long as I had nothing but two hardtacks, which was the allowance to each man on the morning after the San Juan fight, no one could complain; but if I had had any private little luxuries the men would very naturally have realized keenly their own shortages.

Soon after the Guasimas fight we were put on short commons; and as I knew that a good deal of food had been landed and was on the beach at Siboney, I marched thirty or forty of the men down to see if I could not get some and bring it up. I finally found a commissary officer, and he asked me what I wanted, and I answered, anything he had. So he told me to look about for myself. I found a number of sacks of beans, I think about eleven hundred pounds, on the beach; and told the officer that I wanted eleven hundred pounds of beans. He produced a book of regulations, and showed me the appropriate section and subdivision which announced that beans were issued only for the officers' mess. This did me no good, and I told him so.

T

He said he was sorry, and I answered that he was not as sorry as I was. I then "studied on it," as Br'er Rabbit would say, and came back with a request for eleven hundred pounds of beans for the officers' mess. He said, "Why, Colonel, your officers can't eat eleven hundred pounds of beans," to which I responded, "You don't know what appetites my officers have." He then said he would send the requisition to Washington. I told him I was quite willing, so long as he gave me the beans. He was a good fellow, so we finally effected a working compromise — he got the requisition and I got the beans, although he warned me that the price would probably be deducted from my salary.

Under some regulation or other only the regular supply trains were allowed to act, and we were supposed not to have any horses or mules in the regiment itself. This was very pretty in theory; but, as a matter of fact, the supply trains were not numerous enough. My men had a natural genius for acquiring horseflesh in odd ways, and I continually found that they had staked out in the brush various captured Spanish cavalry horses and Cuban ponies and abandoned commissary mules. Putting these together, I would organize a small pack train and work it industriously for a day or two, until they learned about it at headquarters and confiscated it. Then I would have to wait for a week or so until my men had accumulated some more ponies, horses, and mules, the regiment meanwhile living in plenty on what we had got before the train was confiscated.

All of our men were good at accumulating horses, but within our own ranks I think we were inclined to award the palm to our chaplain. There was not a better man in the regiment than the chaplain, and there could not have been a better chaplain for our men. He took care of the sick and the wounded, he never spared himself, and he did every duty. In addition, he had a natural aptitude for acquiring mules, which made some admirer, when the regiment was disbanded, propose that we should have a special medal struck for him, with, on the obverse, "A Mule passant and Chaplain regardant." After the surrender of Santiago, a

Philadelphia clergyman whom I knew came down to General Wheeler's headquarters, and after visiting him announced that he intended to call on the Rough Riders, because he knew their colonel. One of General Wheeler's aides, Lieutenant Steele, who liked us both individually and as a regiment, and who appreciated some of our ways, asked the clergyman, after he had announced that he knew Colonel Roosevelt, "But do you know Colonel Roosevelt's regiment?" "No," said the clergyman. "Very well, then, let me give you a piece of advice. When you go down to see the Colonel, don't let your horse out of your sight; and if the chaplain is there, don't get off the horse!"

We came back to Montauk Point and soon after were disbanded. We had been in the service only a little over four months. There are no four months of my life to which I look back with more pride and satisfaction. I believe most earnestly and sincerely in peace, but as things are yet in this world the nation that cannot fight, the people that have lost the fighting edge, that have lost the virile virtues, occupy a position as dangerous as it is ignoble. The future greatness of America in no small degree depends upon the possession by the average American citizen of the qualities which my men showed when they served under me at Santiago.

Moreover, there is one thing in connection with this war which it is well that our people should remember, our people who genuinely love the peace of righteousness, the peace of justice — and I would be ashamed to be other than a lover of the peace of righteousness and of justice. The true preachers of peace, who strive earnestly to bring nearer the day when peace shall obtain among all peoples, and who really do help forward the cause, are men who never hesitate to choose righteous war when it is the only alternative to unrighteous peace. These are the men who, like Dr. Lyman Abbott, have backed every genuine movement for peace in this country, and who nevertheless recognized our clear duty to war for the freedom of Cuba.

But there are other men who put peace ahead of righteousness, and who care so little for facts that they treat fantastic declarations for immediate universal arbitration as being valuable, instead of detrimental, to the cause they profess to champion, and who seek to make the United States impotent for international good under the pretense of making us impotent for international evil. All the men of this kind, and all of the organizations they have controlled, since we began our career as a nation, all put together, have not accomplished one hundredth part as much for both peace and righteousness, have not done one hundredth part as much either for ourselves or for other peoples, as was accomplished by the people of the United States when they fought the war with Spain and with resolute good faith and common sense worked out the solution of the problems which sprang from the war.

Our army and navy, and above all our people, learned some lessons from the Spanish War, and applied them to our own uses. During the following decade the improvement in our navy and army was very great; not in material only, but also in personnel, and, above all, in the ability to handle our forces in good-sized units. By 1908, when our battle fleet steamed round the world, the navy had become in every respect as fit a fighting instrument as any other navy in the world, fleet for fleet. Even in size there was but one nation, England, which was completely out of our class; and in view of our relations with England and all the English-speaking peoples, this was of no consequence. Of our army, of course, as much could not be said. Nevertheless the improvement in efficiency was marked. Our artillery was still very inferior in training and practice to the artillery arm of any one of the great Powers such as Germany, France, or Japan — a condition which we only then began to remedy. But the workmanlike speed and efficiency with which the expedition of some 6000 troops of all arms was mobilized and transported to Cuba during the revolution of 1908 showed that, as regards our cavalry and infantry, we had at least reached the point where we could assemble and handle in first-rate fashion expeditionary forces. This is mighty little to boast of, for a Nation of our wealth and population; it is not pleasant to compare it with the extraordinary feats of contemporary Japan and the Balkan peoples; but, such as it is, it represents a long stride in advance over conditions as they were in 1898.

APPENDIX A

There was a sequel to the "round robin" incident which caused a little stir at the moment; Secretary Alger had asked me to write him freely from time to time. Accordingly, after the surrender of Santiago, I wrote him begging that the cavalry division might be put into the Porto Rican fighting, preparatory to what we supposed would be the big campaign against Havana in the fall. In the letter I extolled the merits of the Rough Riders and of the Regulars, announcing with much complacency that each of our regiments was worth "three of the National Guard regiments, armed with their archaic black powder rifles."[1] Secretary Alger believed, mistakenly, that I had made public the round robin, and was naturally irritated, and I suddenly received from him a published telegram, not alluding to the round robin incident, but quoting my reference to the comparative merits of the cavalry regiments and the National Guard regiments and rebuking me for it. The publication of the extract from my letter was not calculated to help me secure the votes of the National Guard if I ever became a candidate for office. However, I did not mind the matter much, for I had at the time no idea of being a candidate for anything — while in the campaign I ate and drank and thought and dreamed regiment and nothing but regiment, until I got the brigade, and then I devoted all my thoughts to handling the brigade. Anyhow, there was nothing I could do about the matter. When our transport reached Montauk Point, an army officer came aboard and before doing anything else handed me a sealed letter from the Secretary of War which ran as follows: —

WAR DEPARTMENT,
WASHINGTON,
August 10, 1898.

DEAR COL. ROOSEVELT:

You have been a most gallant officer and in the battle before Santiago showed superb soldierly qualities. I would rather add

---

[1] I quote this sentence from memory; it is substantially correct.

to, than detract from, the honors you have so fairly won, and I wish you all good things. In a moment of aggravation under great stress of feeling, first because I thought you spoke in a disparaging manner of the volunteers (probably without intent, but because of your great enthusiasm for your own men) and second that I believed your published letter would embarrass the Department I sent you a telegram which with an extract from a private letter of yours I gave to the press. I would gladly recall both if I could, but unable to do that I write you this letter which I hope you will receive in the same friendly spirit in which I send it. Come and see me at a very early day. No one will welcome you more heartily than I.

Yours very truly,

(Signed) R. A. ALGER.

I thought this a manly letter, and paid no more heed to the incident; and when I was President, and General Alger was Senator from Michigan, he was my stanch friend and on most matters my supporter.

APPENDIX B

THE SAN JUAN FIGHT

The San Juan fight took its name from the San Juan Hill or hills — I do not know whether the name properly belonged to a line of hills or to only one hill.

To compare small things with large things, this was precisely as the Battle of Gettysburg took its name from the village of Gettysburg, where only a small part of the fighting was done; and the Battle of Waterloo from the village of Waterloo, where none of the fighting was done. When it became the political interest of certain people to endeavor to minimize my part in the Santiago fighting (which was merely like that of various other squadron, battalion and regimental commanders) some of my opponents laid great stress on the alleged fact that the cavalry did not charge up San Juan Hill. We certainly charged some hills; but I did not ask their names before charging them. To say that the Rough Riders and the cavalry division, and among other people myself, were not in the San Juan fight is precisely like saying that the men who made Pickett's Charge, or the men who fought at Little Round Top and Culps Hill, were not at Gettysburg; or that Picton and the Scotch Greys and the French and English guards were not at

Waterloo. The present Vice-President of the United States in the campaign last year was reported in the press as repeatedly saying that I was not in the San Juan fight. The documents following herewith have been printed for many years, and were accessible to him had he cared to know or to tell the truth.

These documents speak for themselves. The first is the official report issued by the War Department. From this it will be seen that there were in the Santiago fighting thirty infantry and cavalry regiments represented. Six of these were volunteer, of which one was the Rough Riders. The other twenty-four were regular regiments. The percentage of loss of our regiment was about seven times as great as that of the other five volunteer regiments. Of the twenty-four regular regiments, twenty-two suffered a smaller percentage of loss than we suffered. Two, the Sixth United States Infantry and the Thirteenth United States Infantry, suffered a slightly greater percentage of loss — twenty-six per cent and twenty-three per cent as against twenty-two per cent.

(CONGRESSIONAL RECORD, 55TH CONGRESS, THIRD SESSION, VOLUME 32, PART II, PAGE 1250)

NOMINATIONS BY THE PRESIDENT

To be Colonel by Brevet

Lieutenant-Colonel Theodore Roosevelt, First Volunteer Cavalry, for gallantry in battle, La Guasima, Cuba, June 24, 1898.

To be Brigadier-General by Brevet

Lieutenant-Colonel Theodore Roosevelt, First Volunteer Cavalry, for gallantry in battle, Santiago de Cuba, July 1, 1898. (Nominated for brevet colonel, to rank from June 24, 1898.)

FORT SAN JUAN, CUBA,
July 17, 1898.

THE ADJUTANT-GENERAL UNITED STATES ARMY,
Washington, D. C.
(Through military channels)

SIR: I have the honor to invite attention to the following list of officers and enlisted men who specially distinguished themselves in the action at Las Guasimas, Cuba, June 24, 1898.

These officers and men have been recommended for favorable consideration by their immediate commanding officers in their respective reports, and I would respectfully urge that favorable action be taken.

OFFICERS

. . . . . .

In First United States Volunteer Cavalry — Colonel Leonard Wood, Lieutenant-Colonel Roosevelt.

. . . . .

Respectfully,
JOSEPH WHEELER,
Major-General United States Volunteers, Commanding.

HEADQUARTERS SECOND CAVALRY BRIGADE,
CAMP NEAR SANTIAGO DE CUBA, CUBA,
June 29, 1898.
THE ADJUTANT-GENERAL CAVALRY DIVISION.

SIR: By direction of the major-general commanding the Cavalry Division, I have the honor to submit the following report of the engagement of a part of this brigade with the enemy at Guasimas, Cuba, on June 24th, accompanied by detailed reports from the regimental and other commanders engaged, and a list of the killed and wounded:

. . . . . .

I cannot speak too highly of the efficient manner in which Colonel Wood handled his regiment, and of his magnificent behavior on the field. The conduct of Lieutenant-Colonel Roosevelt, as reported to me by my two aides, deserves my highest commendation. Both Colonel Wood and Lieutenant-Colonel Roosevelt disdained to take advantage of shelter or cover from the enemy's fire while any of their men remained exposed to it — an error of judgment, but happily on the heroic side.

. . . . . .

Very respectfully,
S. B. M. YOUNG,
Brigadier General United States Volunteers, Commanding.

HEADQUARTERS FIRST DIVISION SECOND ARMY CORPS
CAMP MACKENZIE, GA.,
December 30, 1898.
ADJUTANT-GENERAL,
Washington, D. C.

SIR: I have the honor to recommend Hon. Theodore Roosevelt, late Colonel First United States Volunteer Cavalry, for a medal of honor, as a reward for conspicuous gallantry at the battle of San Juan, Cuba, on July 1, 1898.

Colonel Roosevelt by his example and fearlessness inspired his men, and both at Kettle Hill and the ridge known as San Juan he led his command in person. I was an eye-witness of Colonel Roosevelt's action.

As Colonel Roosevelt has left the service, a Brevet Commission is of no particular value in his case.

Very respectfully,
SAMUEL S. SUMNER,
Major-General United States Volunteers.

WEST POINT, N. Y.,
December 17, 1898.

MY DEAR COLONEL: I saw you lead the line up the first hill — you were certainly the first officer to reach the top — and through your efforts, and your personally jumping to the front, a line more or less thin, but strong enough to take it, was led by you to the San Juan or first hill. In this your life was placed in extreme jeopardy, as you may recall, and as it proved by the number of dead left in that vicinity. Captain Stevens, then of the Ninth Cavalry, now of the Second Cavalry, was with you, and I am sure he recalls your gallant conduct. After the line started on the advance from the first hill, I did not see you until our line was halted, under a most galling fire, at the extreme front, where you afterwards entrenched. I spoke to you there and gave instructions from General Sumner that the position was to be held and that there would be no further advance till further orders. You were the senior officer there, took charge of the line, scolded me for having my horse so high upon the ridge; at the same time you were exposing yourself most conspicuously, while adjusting the line, for the example was necessary, as was proved when several colored soldiers — about eight or ten, Twenty-fourth Infantry, I think — started at a run to the rear to assist a wounded colored soldier, and you drew your revolver and put a short and effective stop to such apparent stampede — it quieted them. That position was hot, and now I marvel at your escaping there. . . .

Very sincerely yours,
ROBERT L. HOWZE.

WEST POINT, N. Y.,
December 17, 1898.

I hereby certify that on July 1, 1898, Colonel (then Lieutenant-Colonel) Theodore Roosevelt, First Volunteer Cavalry, distinguished himself through the action, and on two occasions during the battle when I was an eye-witness, his conduct was most conspicuous and clearly distinguished above other men, as follows:

1. At the base of San Juan, or first hill, there was a strong wire fence, or entanglement, at which the line hesitated under a galling fire, and where the losses were severe. Colonel Roosevelt jumped through the fence and by his enthusiasm, his example and courage succeeded in leading to the crest of the hill a line sufficiently strong to capture it. In this charge the Cavalry Brigade suffered its greatest loss, and the Colonel's life was placed in extreme jeopardy, owing to the conspicuous position he took in leading the line, and being the first to reach the crest of that hill, while under heavy fire of the enemy at close range.

2. At the extreme advanced position occupied by our lines, Colonel Roosevelt found himself the senior, and under his instructions from General Sumner to hold that position. He displayed the greatest bravery and placed his life in extreme jeopardy by unavoidable exposure to severe fire while adjusting and strengthening the line, placing the men in positions which afforded best protection, etc., etc. His conduct and example steadied the men, and on one occasion by severe but unnecessary measures prevented a small detachment from stampeding to the rear. He displayed the most conspicuous gallantry, courage and coolness, in performing extraordinarily hazardous duty.

ROBERT L. HOWZE,
Captain A. A. G., U. S. V.
(First Lieutenant Sixth United States Cavalry)

To THE ADJUTANT-GENERAL UNITED STATES ARMY,
Washington, D. C.

HEADQUARTERS UNITED STATES MILITARY ACADEMY,
WEST POINT, N. Y.,
April 5, 1899.

LIEUTENANT-COLONEL W. H. CARTER,
Assistant Adjutant-General United States Army,
Washington, D. C.

SIR: In compliance with the request, contained in your letter of April 30th, of the Board convened to consider the awarding of brevets, medals of honor, etc., for the Santiago Campaign, that I state any facts, within my knowledge as Adjutant-General of the Brigade in which Colonel Theodore Roosevelt served, to aid the Board in determining, in connection with Colonel Roosevelt's application for a medal of honor, whether his conduct at Santiago was such as to distinguish him above others, I have the honor to submit the following:

My duties on July 1, 1898, brought me in constant observation of and contact with Colonel Roosevelt from early morning until shortly before the climax of the assault of the Cavalry Division on the San Juan Hill — the so-called Kettle Hill. During this time, while under the enemy's artillery fire at El Poso, and while on the march from El Poso by the San Juan ford to the point from which his regiment moved to the assault — about two miles, the greater part under fire — Colonel Roosevelt was conspicuous above any others I observed in his regiment in the zealous performance of duty, in total disregard of his personal danger and in his eagerness to meet the enemy. At El Poso, when the enemy opened on that place with artillery fire, a shrapnel bullet grazed and bruised one of Colonel Roosevelt's wrists. The incident did not lessen his hazardous exposure, but he continued so exposed until he had placed his command under cover. In moving to the assault of San Juan Hill, Colonel Roosevelt was most conspicuously brave, gallant and indifferent to his own safety. He, in the open, led his regiment; no officer could have set a more striking example to his men or displayed greater intrepidity.

Very respectfully,
Your obedient servant,
A. L. MILLS,
Colonel United States Army, Superintendent.

HEADQUARTERS DEPARTMENT OF SANTIAGO DE CUBA,
SANTIAGO DE CUBA,
December 30, 1898.

TO THE ADJUTANT-GENERAL, UNITED STATES ARMY,
Washington, D. C.

SIR: I have the honor to make the following statement relative to the conduct of Colonel Theodore Roosevelt, late First United States Volunteer Cavalry, during the assault upon San Juan Hill, July 1, 1898.

I have already recommended this officer for a medal of honor, which I understand has been denied him, upon the ground that my previous letter was too indefinite. I based my recommendation upon the fact that Colonel Roosevelt, accompanied only by four or five men, led a very desperate and extremely gallant charge on San Juan Hill, thereby setting a splendid example to the troops and encouraging them to pass over the open country intervening between their position and the trenches of the enemy. In leading this charge, he started off first, as he supposed, with quite a following of men, but soon discovered that he was alone. He then returned and gathered up a few men and led them to the charge, as above stated. The charge in itself was an extremely gallant one, and the example set a most inspiring one to the troops in that part of the line, and while it is perfectly true that everybody finally went up the hill in good style, yet there is no doubt that the magnificent example set by Colonel Roosevelt had a very encouraging effect and had great weight in bringing up the troops behind him. During the assault, Colonel Roosevelt was the first to reach the trenches in his part of the line and killed one of the enemy with his own hand.

I earnestly recommend that the medal be conferred upon Colonel Roosevelt, for I believe that he in every way deserves it, and that his services on the day in question were of great value and of a most distinguished character.

Very respectfully,
LEONARD WOOD,
Major-General, United States Volunteers.
Commanding Department of Santiago de Cuba.

HUNTSVILLE, ALA.,
January 4, 1899.

THE ADJUTANT-GENERAL, UNITED STATES ARMY,
Washington, D. C.

SIR: I have the honor to recommend that a "Congressional Medal of Honor" be given to Theodore Roosevelt (late Colonel First Volunteer Cavalry), for distinguished conduct and conspicuous bravery in command of his regiment in the charge on San Juan Hill, Cuba, July 1, 1898.

In compliance with G. O. 135, A. G. O. 1898, I enclose my certificate showing my personal knowledge of Colonel Roosevelt's conduct.   Very respectfully,

C. J. STEVENS,
Captain Second Cavalry.

I hereby certify that on July 1, 1898, at the battle of San Juan, Cuba, I witnessed Colonel (then Lieutenant-Colonel) Roosevelt, First Volunteer Cavalry, United States of America, mounted, leading his regiment in the charge on San Juan. By his gallantry and strong personality he contributed most materially to the success of the charge of the Cavalry Division up San Juan Hill.

Colonel Roosevelt was among the first to reach the crest of the hill, and his dashing example, his absolute fearlessness and gallant leading rendered his conduct conspicuous and clearly distinguished above other men.

C. J. STEVENS,
Captain Second Cavalry.
(*Late First Lieutenant Ninth Cavalry.*)

YOUNG'S ISLAND, S. C.,
December 28, 1898.

TO THE ADJUTANT-GENERAL, UNITED STATES ARMY.
Washington, D. C.

SIR: Believing that information relating to superior conduct on the part of any of the higher officers who participated in the Spanish-American War (and which information may not have been given) would be appreciated by the Department over which you preside, I have the honor to call your attention to the part borne by Colonel Theodore Roosevelt, of the late First United States Volunteer Cavalry, in the battle of July 1st last. I do this not only because I think you ought to know, but because his regiment as a whole were very proud of his splendid actions that day and believe they call for that most coveted distinction of the American officer, the Medal of Honor. Held in support, he brought his regiment, at exactly the right time, not only up to the line of regulars, but went through them and headed, on horseback, the charge on Kettle Hill; this being done on his own initiative, the regulars as well as his own men following. He then headed the charge on the next hill, both regulars and the First United States Volunteer Cavalry following. He was so near the intrenchments on the second hill, that he shot and killed with a revolver one of the enemy before they broke completely. He then led the cavalry on the chain of hills overlooking Santiago, where he remained in charge of all the cavalry that was at the extreme front for the rest of that day and night. His unhesitating gallantry in taking the initiative against intrenchments lined by men armed with rapid fire guns certainly won him the highest consideration and admiration of all who witnessed his conduct throughout that day.

What I here write I can bear witness to from personally having seen.   Very respectfully,
                                    M. J. JENKINS,
                    Major Late First United States Cavalry.

PRESCOTT, A. T.,
December 25, 1898.

I was Colonel Roosevelt's orderly at the battle of San Juan Hill, and from that time on until our return to Montauk Point. I was with him all through the fighting, and believe I was the only man who was always with him, though during part of the time Lieutenants Ferguson and Greenwald were also close to him. He led our regiment forward on horseback until he came to the men of the Ninth Cavalry lying down. He led us through these and they got up and joined us. He gave the order to charge on Kettle Hill, and led us on horseback up the hill, both Rough Riders and the Ninth Cavalry. He was the first on the hill, I being very nearly alongside of him. Some Spanish riflemen were coming out of the intrenchments and he killed one with his revolver. He took the men on to the crest of the hill and bade them begin firing on the blockhouse on the hill to our left, the one the infantry were attacking. When we took it, he gave the order to charge, and led the troops on Kettle Hill forward against the blockhouse on our front. He then had charge of all the cavalry on the hills overlooking

Santiago, where we afterwards dug our trenches. He had command that afternoon and night, and for the rest of the time commanded our regiment at this point.

Yours very truly,
H. P. BARDSHAR.

CAMBRIDGE, MD.,
March 27, 1902.

THEODORE ROOSEVELT, *President of the United States.*
   Washington, D. C.

DEAR SIR: At your request, I send you the following extracts from my diary, and from notes taken on the day of the assault on San Juan. I kept in my pocket a small pad on which incidents were noted daily from the landing until the surrender. On the day of the fight notes were taken just before Grimes fired his first gun, just after the third reply from the enemy — when we were massed in the road about seventy paces from Grimes' guns, and when I was beginning to get scared and to think I would be killed — at the halt just before you advanced, and under the shelter of the hills in the evening. Each time that notes were taken, the page was put in an envelope addressed to my wife. At the first chance they were mailed to her, and on my arrival in the United States the story of the fight, taken from these notes, was entered in the diary I keep in a book. I make this lengthy explanation that you may see that everything put down was fresh in my memory.

I quote from my diary: "The tension on the men was great. Suddenly a line of men appeared coming from our right. They were advancing through the long grass, deployed as skirmishers and were under fire. At their head, or rather in front of them and leading them, rode Colonel Roosevelt. He was very conspicuous, mounted as he was. The men were the 'Rough Riders,' so-called. I heard some one calling to them not to fire into us, and seeing Colonel Carrol, reported to him, and was told to go out and meet them, and caution them as to our position, we being between them and the enemy. I did so, speaking to Colonel Roosevelt. I also told him we were under orders not to advance, and asked him if he had received any orders. He replied that he was going to charge the Spanish trenches. I told this to Colonel Carrol, and to Captain Dimmick, our squadron commander. A few moments after the word passed down that our left (Captain Taylor) was about to charge. Captain McBlain called out, 'we must go in with those troops; we must support Taylor.' I called this to Captain Dimmick, and he gave the order to assault."

"The cheer was taken up and taken up again, on the left, and in the distance it rolled on and on. And so we started. Colonel Roosevelt, of the Rough Riders, started the whole movement on the left, which was the first advance of the assault."

The following is taken from my notes and was hastily jotted down on the field: "The Rough Riders came in line — Colonel Roosevelt said he would assault — Taylor joined them with his troop — McBlain called to Dimmick, 'let us go, we must go to support them.' Dimmick said all right — and so, with no orders, we went in."

I find many of my notes are illegible from perspiration. My authority for saying Taylor went in with you, "joined with his troop" was the word passed to me and repeated to Captain Dimmick that Taylor was about to charge with you. I could not see his troop. I have not put it in my diary, but in another place I have noted that Colonel Carrol, who was acting as brigade commander, told me to ask you if you had any orders.

I have the honor to be,

Very respectfully,
Your obedient servant,
HENRY ANSON BARBER,
Captain Twenty-Eighth Infantry,
(formerly of Ninth Cavalry).

HEADQUARTERS PACIFIC DIVISION,
SAN FRANCISCO, CAL.,
May 11, 1905.

DEAR MR. PRESIDENT: As some discussion has arisen in the public prints regarding the battle of San Juan, Cuba, July 1, 1898, and your personal movements during that day have been the subject of comment, it may not be amiss in me to state some facts coming under my personal observation as Commanding General of the Cavalry Division, of which your regiment formed a part. It will, perhaps, be advisable to show first how I came to be in command, in order that my statement may have due weight as an authoritative statement of facts: I was placed in command of the Cavalry Division on the afternoon of June 30th by General Shafter; the assignment was made owing to the severe illness of General Wheeler, who was the permanent commander of said Division. Brigadier General Young, who commanded the Second

U

Cavalry Brigade, of which your regiment — the First Volunteer Cavalry — formed a part, was also very ill, and I found it necessary to relieve him from command and place Colonel Wood, of the Rough Riders, in command of the Brigade; this change placed you in command of your regiment.

The Division moved from its camp on the evening of June 30th, and bivouacked at and about El Poso. I saw you personally in the vicinity of El Poso, about 8 A.M., July 1st. I saw you again on the road leading from El Poso to the San Juan River; you were at the head of your regiment, which was leading the Second Brigade, and immediately behind the rear regiment of the First Brigade. My orders were to turn to the right at San Juan River and take up a line along that stream and try and connect with General Lawton, who was to engage the enemy at El Caney. On reaching the river we came under the fire of the Spanish forces posted on San Juan Ridge and Kettle Hill. The First Brigade was faced to the front in line as soon as it had cleared the road, and the Second Brigade was ordered to pass in rear of the first and face to the front when clear of the First Brigade. This movement was very difficult, owing to the heavy undergrowth, and the regiments became more or less tangled up, but eventually the formation was accomplished, and the Division stood in an irregular line along the San Juan River, the Second Brigade on the right. We were subjected to a heavy fire from the forces on San Juan Ridge and Kettle Hill; our position was untenable, and it became necessary to assault the enemy or fall back. Kettle Hill was immediately in front of the Cavalry, and it was determined to assault that hill. The First Brigade was ordered forward, and the Second Brigade was ordered to support the attack; personally, I accompanied a portion of the Tenth Cavalry, Second Brigade, and the Rough Riders were to the right. This brought your regiment to the right of the house which was at the summit of the hill. Shortly after I reached the crest of the hill you came to me, accompanied, I think, by Captain C. J. Stevens, of the Ninth Cavalry. We were then in a position to see the line of intrenchments along San Juan Ridge, and could see Kent's Infantry Division engaged on our left, and Hawkins' assault against Fort San Juan. You asked me for permission to move forward and assault San Juan Ridge. I gave you the order in person to move forward, and I saw you move forward and assault San Juan Ridge with your regiment and portions of the First and Tenth Cavalry belonging to your Brigade. I held a portion of the Second Brigade as a reserve on Kettle Hill, not knowing what force the enemy might have in reserve behind the ridge. The First Brigade also moved forward and assaulted the ridge to the right of Fort San Juan. There was a small lake between Kettle Hill and San Juan Ridge, and in moving forward your command passed to the right of this lake. This brought you opposite a house on San Juan Ridge — not Fort San Juan proper, but a frame house surrounded by an earthwork. The enemy lost a number of men at this point, whose bodies lay in the trenches. Later in the day I rode along the line, and, as I recall it, a portion of the Tenth Cavalry was immediately about this house, and your regiment occupied an irregular semi-circular position along the ridge and immediately to the right of the house. You had pickets out to your front; and several hundred yards to your front the Spaniards had a heavy outpost occupying a house, with rifle pits surrounding it. Later in the day, and during the following day, the various regiments forming the Division were rearranged and brought into tactical formation, the First Brigade on the left and immediately to the right of Fort San Juan, and the Second Brigade on the right of the First.

This was the position occupied by the Cavalry Division until the final surrender of the Spanish forces, on July 17, 1898.

In conclusion allow me to say, that I saw you, personally, at about 8 A.M., at El Poso; later, on the road to San Juan River; later, on the summit of Kettle Hill, immediately after its capture by the Cavalry Division. I saw you move forward with your command to assault San Juan Ridge, and I saw you on San Juan Ridge, where we visited your line together, and you explained to me the disposition of your command.

I am, sir, with much respect,
Your obedient servant,
SAMUEL S. SUMNER,
Major-General United States Army.

THEODORE ROOSEVELT, GOVERNOR OF NEW YORK STATE.

CHAPTER VIII

THE NEW YORK GOVERNORSHIP

IN September, 1898, the First Volunteer Cavalry, in company with most of the rest of the Fifth Army Corps, was disembarked at Montauk Point. Shortly after it was disbanded, and a few days later, I was nominated for Governor of New York by the Republican party. Timothy L. Woodruff was nominated for Lieutenant-Governor. He was my stanch friend throughout the term of our joint service.

The previous year, the machine or standpat Republicans, who were under the domination of Senator Platt, had come to a complete break with the anti-machine element over the New York mayoralty. This had brought the Republican party to a smash, not only in New York City, but in the State, where the Democratic candidate for Chief Judge of the Court of Appeals, Alton B. Parker, was elected by sixty or eighty thousand majority. Mr. Parker was an able man, a lieutenant of Mr. Hill's, standing close to the conservative Democrats of the Wall Street type. These conservative Democrats were planning how to wrest the Democratic party from the control of Mr. Bryan. They hailed Judge Parker's victory as a godsend. The Judge at once loomed up as a Presidential possibility, and was carefully groomed for the position by the New York Democratic machine, and its financial allies in the New York business world.

The Republicans realized that the chances were very much against them. Accordingly the leaders were in a chastened mood and ready to nominate any candidate with whom they thought there was a chance of winning. I was the only possibility, and, accordingly, under pressure from certain of the leaders who recognized this fact, and who responded to popular pressure, Senator Platt picked me for the nomination. He was entirely frank in the matter. He made no pretense that he liked me personally; but he deferred to the judgment of those who insisted that I was the only man who could be elected, and that therefore I had to be nominated.

Foremost among the leaders who pressed me on Mr. Platt (who "pestered" him about me, to use his own words) were Mr. Quigg, Mr. Odell — then State Chairman of the Republican organization, and afterwards Governor — and Mr. Hazel, now United States Judge. Judge Hazel did not know me personally, but felt that the sentiment in his city, Buffalo, demanded my nomination, and that the then Republican Governor, Mr. Black, could not be reëlected. Mr. Odell, who hardly knew me personally, felt the same way about Mr. Black's chances, and, as he had just taken the State Chairmanship, he was very anxious to win a victory. Mr. Quigg knew me quite well personally; he had been in touch with me for years, while he was a reporter on the *Tribune*, and also when he edited a paper in Montana; he had been on good terms with me while he was in Congress and I was Civil Service Commissioner, meeting me often in company with my especial cronies in Congress — men like Lodge, Speaker Tom Reed, Greenhalge, Butterworth, and Dolliver — and he had urged my appointment as Police Commissioner on Mayor Strong.

It was Mr. Quigg who called on me at Montauk Point to sound me about the Governorship; Mr. Platt being by no means enthusiastic over Mr. Quigg's mission, largely because he disapproved of the Spanish War and of my part in bringing it about. Mr. Quigg saw me in my tent, in which he spent a couple of hours with me, my brother-in-law, Douglas Robinson, being also present. Quigg spoke very frankly to me, stating that he earnestly desired to see me nominated and believed that the great body of Republican voters in the State so desired, but that the organization and the State Convention would finally do what Senator Platt desired. He said that county leaders were already coming to

Senator Platt, hinting at a close election, expressing doubt of Governor Black's availability for reëlection, and asking why it would not be a good thing to nominate me; that now that I had returned to the United States this would go on more and more all the time, and that he (Quigg) did not wish that these men should be discouraged and be sent back to their localities to suppress a rising sentiment in my favor. For this reason he said that he wanted from me a plain statement as to whether or not I wanted the nomination, and as to what would be my attitude toward the organization in the event of my nomination and election, whether or not I would "make war" on Mr. Platt and his friends, or whether I would confer with them and with the organization leaders generally, and give fair consideration to their point of view as to party policy and public interest. He said he had not come to make me any offer of the nomination, and had no authority to do so, nor to get any pledges or promises. He simply wanted a frank definition of my attitude towards existing party conditions.

To this I replied that I should like to be nominated, and if nominated would promise to throw myself into the campaign with all possible energy. I said that I should not make war on Mr. Platt or anybody else if war could be avoided; that what I wanted was to be Governor and not a faction leader; that I certainly would confer with the organization men, as with everybody else who seemed to me to have knowledge of and interest in public affairs, and that as to Mr. Platt and the organization leaders, I would do so in the sincere hope that there might always result harmony of opinion and purpose; but that while I would try to get on well with the organization, the organization must with equal sincerity strive to do what I regarded as essential for the public good; and that in every case, after full consideration of what everybody had to say who might possess real knowledge of the matter, I should have to act finally as my own judgment and conscience dictated and administer the State government as I thought it ought to be administered. Quigg said that this was precisely what he supposed I would say, that it was all anybody could expect, and that he would state it to Senator Platt precisely as I had put it to him, which he accordingly did; and, throughout my term as Governor, Quigg lived loyally up to our understanding.[1]

After being nominated, I made a hard and aggressive campaign through the State. My opponent was a respectable man, a judge, behind whom stood Mr. Croker, the boss of Tammany Hall. My object was to make the people understand that it was Croker, and not the nominal candidate, who was my real opponent; that the choice lay between Crokerism and myself. Croker was a powerful and truculent man, the autocrat of his organization, and of a domineering nature. For his own reasons he insisted upon Tammany's turning down an excellent Democratic judge who was a candidate for reëlection. This gave me my chance. Under my attack, Croker, who was a stalwart fighting man and who would not take an attack tamely, himself came to the front. I was able to fix the contest in the public mind as one between himself and myself; and, against all probabilities, I won by the rather narrow margin of eighteen thousand plurality.

As I have already said, there is a lunatic fringe to every reform movement. At least nine-tenths of all the sincere reformers supported me; but the ultra-pacificists, the so-called anti-imperialists, or anti-militarists, or peace-at-any-price men, preferred Croker to me; and another knot of extremists who had at first ardently insisted that I must be "forced" on Platt, as soon as Platt supported me themselves opposed me *because* he supported me. After election John Hay wrote me as follows: "While you are Governor, I believe the party can be made solid as never before. You have already shown that a man may be absolutely honest and yet practical; a reformer by instinct and a wise politician; brave, bold, and uncompromising, and yet not a wild ass of the desert. The exhibition made by the professional

---

[1] In a letter to me Mr. Quigg states, what I had forgotten, that I told him to tell the Senator that while I would talk freely with him, and had no intention of becoming a factional leader with a personal organization, yet that I must have direct personal relations with everybody, and get their views at first hand whenever I so desired, because I could not have one man speaking for all.

independents in voting against you for no reason on earth
except that somebody else was voting for you, is a lesson
that is worth its cost."

At that time boss rule was at its very zenith.   Mr. Bryan's
candidacy in 1896 on a free silver platform had threatened
such frightful business disaster as to make the business men,
the wage-workers, and the professional classes generally,
turn eagerly to the Republican party.   East of the Mississippi the Republican vote for Mr. McKinley was larger by
far than it had been for Abraham Lincoln in the days when
the life of the Nation was at stake.   Mr. Bryan championed
many sorely needed reforms in the interest of the plain
people; but many of his platform proposals, economic and
otherwise, were of such a character that to have put them
into practice would have meant to plunge all our people
into conditions far worse than any of those for which he
sought a remedy.   The free silver advocates included sincere
and upright men who were able to make a strong case for
their position; but with them and dominating them were
all the believers in the complete or partial repudiation of
National, State, and private debts; and not only the business men but the workingmen grew to feel that under these
circumstances too heavy a price could not be paid to avert
the Democratic triumph.   The fear of Mr. Bryan threw
almost all the leading men of all classes into the arms of
whoever opposed him.

The Republican bosses, who were already very powerful,
and who were already in fairly close alliance with the privileged interests, now found everything working to their
advantage.   Good and high-minded men of conservative
temperament in their panic played into the hands of the
ultra-reactionaries of business and politics.   The alliance
between the two kinds of privilege, political and financial,
was closely cemented; and wherever there was any attempt
to break it up, the cry was at once raised that this merely
represented another phase of the assault on National honesty
and individual and mercantile integrity.   As so often happens, the excesses and threats of an unwise and extreme
radicalism had resulted in immensely strengthening the

position of the beneficiaries of reaction. This was the era when the Standard Oil Company achieved a mastery of Pennsylvania politics so far-reaching and so corrupt that it is difficult to describe it without seeming to exaggerate.

In New York State, United States Senator Platt was the absolute boss of the Republican party. "Big business" was back of him; yet at the time this, the most important element in his strength, was only imperfectly understood. It was not until I was elected Governor that I myself came to understand it. We were still accustomed to talking of the "machine" as if it were something merely political, with which business had nothing to do. Senator Platt did not use his political position to advance his private fortunes — therein differing absolutely from many other political bosses. He lived in hotels and had few extravagant tastes. Indeed, I could not find that he had any tastes at all except for politics, and on rare occasions for a very dry theology wholly divorced from moral implications. But big business men contributed to him large sums of money, which enabled him to keep his grip on the machine and secured for them the help of the machine if they were threatened with adverse legislation. The contributions were given in the guise of contributions for campaign purposes, of money for the good of the party; when the money was contributed there was rarely talk of specific favors in return.[1] It was simply put into Mr. Platt's hands and treated by him as in the campaign chest. Then he distributed it in the districts where it was most needed by the candidates and organization leaders. Ordinarily no pledge was required from the latter to the bosses, any more than it was required by the business men from Mr. Platt or his lieutenants. No pledge was needed. It was all a "gentlemen's understanding." As the Senator

---

[1] Each nation has its own pet sins to which it is merciful and also sins which it treats as most abhorrent. In America we are peculiarly sensitive about big money contributions for which the donors expect any reward. In England, where in some ways the standard is higher than here, such contributions are accepted as a matter of course, nay, as one of the methods by which wealthy men obtain peerages. It would be well-nigh an impossibility for a man to secure a seat in the United States Senate by mere campaign contributions, in the way that seats in the British House of Lords have often been secured without any scandal being caused thereby.

once said to me, if a man's character was such that it was
necessary to get a promise from him, it was clear proof that
his character was such that the promise would not be worth
anything after it was made.

It must not be forgotten that some of the worst practices of
the machine in dealings of this kind represented merely
virtues in the wrong place, virtues wrenched out of proper
relation to their surroundings.   A man in a doubtful district
might win only because of the help Mr. Platt gave him;
he might be a decent young fellow without money enough
to finance his own campaign, who was able to finance it only
because Platt of his own accord found out or was apprised
of his need and advanced the money.   Such a man felt
grateful, and, because of his good qualities, joined with the
purely sordid and corrupt heelers and crooked politicians to
become part of the Platt machine.   In his turn Mr. Platt was
recognized by the business men, the big contributors, as an
honorable man; not only a man of his word, but a man who,
whenever he received a favor, could be trusted to do his best
to repay it on any occasion that arose.   I believe that
usually the contributors, and the recipient, sincerely felt
that the transaction was proper and subserved the cause of
good politics and good business; and, indeed, as regards
the major part of the contributions, it is probable that this
was the fact, and that the only criticism that could properly
be made about the contributions was that they were not
made with publicity — and at that time neither the parties
nor the public had any realization that publicity was necessary, or any adequate understanding of the dangers of the
"invisible empire" which throve by what was done in
secrecy.   Many, probably most, of the contributors of this
type never wished anything personal in exchange for their
contributions, and made them with sincere patriotism, desiring in return only that the Government should be conducted on a proper basis.   Unfortunately, it was, in practice, exceedingly difficult to distinguish these men from the
others who contributed big sums to the various party
bosses with the expectation of gaining concrete and personal
advantages (in which the bosses shared) at the expense of the

general public.   It was very hard to draw the line between these two types of contributions.

There was but one kind of money contribution as to which it seemed to me absolutely impossible for either the contributor or the recipient to disguise to themselves the evil meaning of the contribution.   This was where a big corporation contributed to both political parties.   I knew of one such case where in a State campaign a big corporation which had many dealings with public officials frankly contributed in the neighborhood of a hundred thousand dollars to one campaign fund and fifty thousand dollars to the campaign fund of the other side — and, I believe, made some further substantial contributions in the same ratio of two dollars to one side for every one dollar given to the other. The contributors were Democrats, and the big contributions went to the Democratic managers.   The Republican was elected, and after his election, when a matter came up affecting the company, in which its interests were hostile to those of the general public, the successful candidate, then holding a high State office, was approached by his campaign managers and the situation put frankly before him. He was less disturbed than astonished, and remarked, "Why, I thought So-and-so and his associates were Democrats and subscribed to the Democratic campaign fund." "So they did," was the answer; "they subscribed to them twice as much as they subscribed to us, but if they had had any idea that you intended doing what you now say you will do, they would have subscribed it all to the other side, and more too."   The State official in his turn answered that he was very sorry if any one had subscribed under a misapprehension, that it was no fault of his, for he had stated definitely and clearly his position, that he of course had no money wherewith himself to return what without his knowledge had been contributed, and that all he could say was that any man who had subscribed to his campaign fund under the impression that the receipt of the subscription would be a bar to the performance of public duty was sadly mistaken.

The control by Mr. Platt and his lieutenants over the organization was well-nigh complete.   There were splits among the bosses, and insurgent movements now and then, but the ordinary citizens had no control over the political machinery except in a very few districts.   There were, however, plenty of good men in politics, men who either came from districts where there was popular control, or who represented a genuine aspiration towards good citizenship on the part of some boss or group of bosses, or else who had been nominated frankly for reasons of expediency by bosses whose attitude towards good citizenship was at best one of Gallio-like indifference.   At the time when I was nominated for Governor, as later when Mr. Hughes was nominated and renominated for Governor, there was no possibility of securing the nomination unless the bosses permitted it.   In each case the bosses, the machine leaders, took a man for whom they did not care, because he was the only man with whom they could win.   In the case of Mr. Hughes there was of course also the fact of pressure from the National Administration.   But the bosses were never overcome in a fair fight, when they had made up their minds to fight, until the Saratoga Convention in 1910, when Mr. Stimson was nominated for Governor.

Senator Platt had the same inborn capacity for the kind of politics which he liked that many big Wall Street men have shown for not wholly dissimilar types of finance.   It was his chief interest, and he applied himself to it unremittingly. He handled his private business successfully; but it was politics in which he was absorbed, and he concerned himself therewith every day in the year.   He had built up an excellent system of organization, and the necessary funds came from corporations and men of wealth who contributed as I have described above.   The majority of the men with a natural capacity for organization leadership of the type which has generally been prevalent in New York politics turned to Senator Platt as their natural chief and helped build up the organization, until under his leadership it became more powerful and in a position of greater control than any other Republican machine in the country, excepting in Pennsylvania.   The Democratic machines in some of the big cities, as in New York and Boston, and the country

Democratic machine of New York under David B. Hill, were probably even more efficient, representing an even more complete mastery by the bosses, and an even greater degree of drilled obedience among the henchmen. It would be an entire mistake to suppose that Mr. Platt's lieutenants were either all bad men or all influenced by unworthy motives. He was constantly doing favors for men. He had won the gratitude of many good men. In the country districts especially, there were many places where his machine included the majority of the best citizens, the leading and substantial citizens, among the inhabitants. Some of his strongest and most efficient lieutenants were disinterested men of high character.

There had always been a good deal of opposition to Mr. Platt and the machine, but the leadership of this opposition was apt to be found only among those whom Abraham Lincoln called the "silk stockings," and much of it excited almost as much derision among the plain people as the machine itself excited anger or dislike. Very many of Mr. Platt's opponents really disliked him and his methods, for æsthetic rather than for moral reasons, and the bulk of the people half-consciously felt this and refused to submit to their leadership. The men who opposed him in this manner were good citizens according to their lights, prominent in the social clubs and in philanthropic circles, men of means and often men of business standing. They disliked coarse and vulgar politicians, and they sincerely reprobated all the shortcomings that were recognized by, and were offensive to, people of their own caste. They had not the slightest understanding of the needs, interests, ways of thought, and convictions of the average small man; and the small man felt this, although he could not express it, and sensed that they were really not concerned with his welfare, and that they did not offer him anything materially better from his point of view than the machine.

When reformers of this type attempted to oppose Mr. Platt, they usually put up either some rather inefficient, well-meaning person, who bathed every day, and didn't steal, but whose only good point was "respectability,"

and who knew nothing of the great fundamental questions
looming before us; or else they put up some big business
man or corporation lawyer who was wedded to the gross
wrong and injustice of our economic system, and who neither
by personality nor by programme gave the ordinary plain
people any belief that there was promise of vital good to
them in the change. The correctness of their view was
proved by the fact that as soon as fundamental economic
and social reforms were at stake the æsthetic, as distinguished
from the genuinely moral, reformers, for the most part
sided with the bosses against the people.

When I became Governor, the conscience of the people
was in no way or shape aroused, as it has since become
roused. The people accepted and practiced in a matter-of-
course way as quite proper things which they would not now
tolerate. They had no definite and clearly outlined conception of what they wished in the way of reform. They
on the whole tolerated, and indeed approved of, the machine;
and there had been no development on any considerable
scale of reformers with the vision to see what the needs of
the people were, and the high purpose sanely to achieve
what was necessary in order to meet these needs. I knew
both the machine and the silk-stocking reformers fairly well,
from many years' close association with them. The machine
as such had no ideals at all, although many of the men composing it did have. On the other hand, the ideals of very
many of the silk-stocking reformers did not relate to the
questions of real and vital interest to our people; and,
singularly enough, in international matters, these same silk-
stockings were no more to be trusted than the average ignorant demagogue or shortsighted spoils politicians. I felt
that these men would be broken reeds to which to trust in
any vital contest for betterment of social and industrial
conditions.

I had neither the training nor the capacity that would have
enabled me to match Mr. Platt and his machine people on
their own ground. Nor did I believe that the effort to
build up a machine of my own under the then existing conditions would meet the needs of the situation so far as the peo-

ple were concerned. I therefore made no effort to create
a machine of my own, and consistently adopted the plan of
going over the heads of the men holding public office and of
the men in control of the organization, and appealing directly
to the people behind them. The machine, for instance, had
a more or less strong control over the great bulk of the
members of the State Legislature; but in the last resort the
people behind these legislators had a still greater control
over them. I made up my mind that the only way I could
beat the bosses whenever the need to do so arose (and unless
there was such need I did not wish to try) was, not by attempting to manipulate the machinery, and not by trusting
merely to the professional reformers, but by making my appeal as directly and as emphatically as I knew how to the
mass of voters themselves, to the people, to the men who if
waked up would be able to impose their will on their representatives. My success depended upon getting the people
in the different districts to look at matters in my way, and
getting them to take such an active interest in affairs as to
enable them to exercise control over their representatives.

There were a few of the Senators and Assemblymen whom
I could reach by seeing them personally and putting before
them my arguments; but most of them were too much
under the control of the machine for me to shake them loose
unless they knew that the people were actively behind
me. In making my appeal to the people as a whole I was
dealing with an entirely different constituency from that
which, especially in the big cities, liked to think of itself as
the "better element," the particular exponent of reform and
good citizenship. I was dealing with shrewd, hard-headed,
kindly men and women, chiefly concerned with the absorbing
work of earning their own living, and impatient of fads, who
had grown to feel that the associations with the word "reformer" were not much better than the associations with the
word "politician." I had to convince these men and women
of my good faith, and, moreover, of my common sense and
efficiency. They were most of them strong partisans, and an
outrage had to be very real and very great to shake them
even partially loose from their party affiliations. Moreover,

they took little interest in any fight of mere personalities. They were not influenced in the least by the silk-stocking reform view of Mr. Platt. I knew that if they were persuaded that I was engaged in a mere faction fight against him, that it was a mere issue between his ambition and mine, they would at once become indifferent, and my fight would be lost.

But I felt that I could count on their support wherever I could show them that the fight was not made just for the sake of the row, that it was not made merely as a factional contest against Senator Platt and the organization, but was waged from a sense of duty for real and tangible causes such as the promotion of governmental efficiency and honesty, and forcing powerful moneyed men to take the proper attitude toward the community at large. They stood by me when I insisted upon having the canal department, the insurance department, and the various departments of the State Government run with efficiency and honesty; they stood by me when I insisted upon making wealthy men who owned franchises pay the State what they properly ought to pay; they stood by me when, in connection with the strikes on the Croton Aqueduct and in Buffalo, I promptly used the military power of the State to put a stop to rioting and violence.

In the latter case my chief opponents and critics were local politicians who were truckling to the labor vote; but in all cases coming under the first two categories I had serious trouble with the State leaders of the machine. I always did my best, in good faith, to get Mr. Platt and the other heads of the machine to accept my views, and to convince them, by repeated private conversations, that I was right. I never wantonly antagonized or humiliated them. I did not wish to humiliate them or to seem victorious over them; what I wished was to secure the things that I thought it essential to the men and women of the State to secure. If I could finally persuade them to support me, well and good; in such case I continued to work with them in the friendliest manner.

If after repeated and persistent effort I failed to get them

x

to support me, then I made a fair fight in the open, and in a majority of cases I carried my point and succeeded in getting through the legislation which I wished.   In theory the Executive has nothing to do with legislation.   In practice, as things now are, the Executive is or ought to be peculiarly representative of the people as a whole.   As often as not the action of the Executive offers the only means by which the people can get the legislation they demand and ought to have.   Therefore a good executive under the present conditions of American political life must take a very active interest in getting the right kind of legislation, in addition to performing his executive duties with an eye single to the public welfare.   More than half of my work as Governor was in the direction of getting needed and important legislation.   I accomplished this only by arousing the people, and riveting their attention on what was done.

Gradually the people began to wake up more and more to the fact that the machine politicians were not giving them the kind of government which they wished.   As this waking up grew more general, not merely in New York or any other one State, but throughout most of the Nation, the power of the bosses waned.   Then a curious thing happened.   The professional reformers who had most loudly criticized these bosses began to change toward them.   Newspaper editors, college presidents, corporation lawyers, and big business men, all alike, had denounced the bosses and had taken part in reform movements against them so long as these reforms dealt only with things that were superficial, or with fundamental things that did not affect themselves and their associates.   But the majority of these men turned to the support of the bosses when the great new movement began clearly to make itself evident as one against privilege in business no less than against privilege in politics, as one for social and industrial no less than for political righteousness and fair dealing.   The big corporation lawyer who had antagonized the boss in matters which he regarded as purely political stood shoulder to shoulder with the boss when the movement for betterment took shape in direct attack on the combination of business with politics and with the judiciary which has done so much to enthrone privilege in the economic world.

The reformers who denounced political corruption and fraud when shown at the expense of their own candidates by machine ward heelers of a low type hysterically applauded similar corrupt trickery when practiced by these same politicians against men with whose political and industrial programme the reformers were not in sympathy. I had always been instinctively and by nature a democrat, but if I had needed conversion to the democratic ideal here in America the stimulus would have been supplied by what I saw of the attitude, not merely of the bulk of the men of greatest wealth, but of the bulk of the men who most prided themselves upon their education and culture, when we began in good faith to grapple with the wrong and injustice of our social and industrial system, and to hit at the men responsible for the wrong, no matter how high they stood in business or in politics, at the bar or on the bench. It was while I was Governor, and especially in connection with the franchise tax legislation, that I first became thoroughly aware of the real causes of this attitude among the men of great wealth and among the men who took their tone from the men of great wealth.

Very soon after my victory in the race for Governor I had one or two experiences with Senator Platt which showed in amusing fashion how absolute the rule of the boss was in the politics of that day. Senator Platt, who was always most kind and friendly in his personal relations with me, asked me in one day to talk over what was to be done at Albany. He had the two or three nominal heads of the organization with him. They were his lieutenants, who counseled and influenced him, whose advice he often followed, but who, when he had finally made up his mind, merely registered and carried out his decrees. After a little conversation the Senator asked if I had any member of the Assembly whom I wished to have put on any committee, explaining that the committees were being arranged. I answered no, and expressed my surprise at what he had said, because I had not understood the Speaker who appointed the committees had himself been agreed upon by the members-elect.   "Oh !" responded the Senator, with a tolerant smile, "He has not been chosen yet, but of course whoever we choose as Speaker will agree beforehand to make the appointments we wish." I made a mental note to the effect that if they attempted the same process with the Governor-elect they would find themselves mistaken.

In a few days the opportunity to prove this arrived. Under the preceding Administration there had been grave scandals about the Erie Canal, the trans-State Canal, and these scandals had been one of the chief issues in the campaign for the Governorship.   The construction of this work was under the control of the Superintendent of Public Works. In the actual state of affairs his office was by far the most important office under me, and I intended to appoint to it some man of high character and capacity who could be trusted to do the work not merely honestly and efficiently, but without regard to politics.   A week or so after the Speakership incident Senator Platt asked me to come and see him (he was an old and physically feeble man, able to move about only with extreme difficulty).

On arrival I found the Lieutenant-Governor elect, Mr. Woodruff, who had also been asked to come.   The Senator informed me that he was glad to say that I would have a most admirable man as Superintendent of Public Works, as he had just received a telegram from a certain gentleman, whom he named, saying that he would accept the position ! He handed me the telegram.   The man in question was a man I liked ; later I appointed him to an important office in which he did well.   But he came from a city along the line of the canal, so that I did not think it best that he should be appointed anyhow ; and, moreover, what was far more important, it was necessary to have it understood at the very outset that the Administration was my Administration and was no one else's but mine.   So I told the Senator very politely that I was sorry, but that I could not appoint his man.   This produced an explosion, but I declined to lose my temper, merely repeating that I must decline to accept any man chosen for me, and that I must choose the man myself.

Although I was very polite, I was also very firm, and Mr. Platt and his friends finally abandoned their position.

I appointed an engineer from Brooklyn, a veteran of the Civil War, Colonel Partridge, who had served in Mayor Low's administration. He was an excellent man in every way. He chose as his assistant, actively to superintend the work, a Cornell graduate named Elon Hooker, a man with no political backing at all, picked simply because he was the best equipped man for the place. The office, the most important office under me, was run in admirable fashion throughout my Administration; I doubt if there ever was an important department of the New York State Government run with a higher standard of efficiency and integrity.

But this was not all that had to be done about the canals. Evidently the whole policy hitherto pursued had been foolish and inadequate. I appointed a first-class non-partisan commission of business men and expert engineers who went into the matter exhaustively, and their report served as the basis upon which our entire present canal system is based. There remained the question of determining whether the canal officials who were in office before I became Governor, and whom I had declined to reappoint, had been guilty of any action because of which it would be possible to proceed against them criminally or otherwise under the law. Such criminal action had been freely charged against them during the campaign by the Democratic (including the so-called mugwump) press. To determine this matter I appointed two Democratic lawyers, Messrs. Fox and MacFarlane (the latter Federal District Attorney for New York under President Cleveland), and put the whole investigation in their hands. These gentlemen made an exhaustive investigation lasting several months. They reported that there had been grave delinquency in the prosecution of the work, delinquency which justified public condemnation of those responsible for it (who were out of office), but that there was no ground for criminal prosecution. I laid their report before the Legislature with a message in which I said: "There is probably no lawyer of high standing in the State who, after studying the report of counsel in this case and the testimony taken by the investigating commission, would disagree with them as to the impracticability of a successful prosecution. Under such circumstances the one remedy was a thorough change in the methods and management. This change has been made."

When my successor in the Governorship took office, Colonel Partridge retired, and Elon Hooker, finding that he could no longer act with entire disregard of politics and with an eye single to the efficiency of the work, also left. A dozen years later — having in the meantime made a marked success in a business career — he became the Treasurer of the National Progressive party.

My action in regard to the canals, and the management of his office, the most important office under me, by Colonel Partridge, established my relations with Mr. Platt from the outset on pretty nearly the right basis. But, besides various small difficulties, we had one or two serious bits of trouble before my duties as Governor ceased. It must be remembered that Mr. Platt was to all intents and purposes a large part of, and sometimes a majority of, the Legislature. There were a few entirely independent men such as Nathaniel Elsberg, Regis Post, and Alford Cooley, in each of the two houses; the remainder were under the control of the Republican and Democratic bosses, but could also be more or less influenced by an aroused public opinion. The two machines were apt to make common cause if their vital interests were touched. It was my business to devise methods by which either the two machines could be kept apart or else overthrown if they came together.

My desire was to achieve results, and not merely to issue manifestoes of virtue. It is very easy to be efficient if the efficiency is based on unscrupulousness, and it is still easier to be virtuous if one is content with the purely negative virtue which consists in not doing anything wrong, but being wholly unable to accomplish anything positive for good. My favorite quotation from Josh Billings again applies: It is so much easier to be a harmless dove than a wise serpent. My duty was to combine both idealism and efficiency. At that time the public conscience was still dormant as regards many species of political and business misconduct, as to which during the next decade it became sensitive. I had to work with the tools at hand and to take into account the feeling of the people, which I have already described. My aim was persistently to refuse to be put in a position where what I did would seem to be a mere faction struggle against Senator Platt. My aim was to make a fight only when I could so manage it that there could be no question in the minds of honest men that my prime purpose was not to attack Mr. Platt or any one else except as a necessary incident to securing clean and efficient government.

In each case I did my best to persuade Mr. Platt not to oppose me. I endeavored to make it clear to him that I was not trying to wrest the organization from him; and I always gave him in detail the reasons why I felt I had to take the position I intended to adopt. It was only after I had exhausted all the resources of my patience that I would finally, if he still proved obstinate, tell him that I intended to make the fight anyhow. As I have said, the Senator was an old and feeble man in physique, and it was possible for him to go about very little. Until Friday evening he would be kept at his duties at Washington, while I was in Albany. If I wished to see him it generally had to be at his hotel in New York on Saturday, and usually I would go there to breakfast with him. The one thing I would not permit was anything in the nature of a secret or clandestine meeting. I always insisted on going openly. Solemn reformers of the tom-fool variety, who, according to their custom, paid attention to the name and not the thing, were much exercised over my "breakfasting with Platt." Whenever I breakfasted with him they became sure that the fact carried with it some sinister significance. The worthy creatures never took the trouble to follow the sequence of facts and events for themselves. If they had done so they would have seen that any series of breakfasts with Platt always meant that I was going to do something he did not like, and that I was trying, courteously and frankly, to reconcile him to it. My object was to make it as easy as possible for him to come with me. As long as there was no clash between us there was no object in my seeing him; it was only when the clash came or was imminent that I had to see him.   A series of breakfasts was always the prelude to some active warfare.[1]   In every instance I substantially carried my point, although in some cases not in exactly the way in which I had originally hoped.

Copyright by Pach Brothers.

WILLIAM LOEB, JR.

"Mr. Loeb gave me much information about various improper practices in the insurance business."

There were various measures to which he gave a grudging and querulous assent without any break being threatened.   I secured the reënactment of the Civil Service Law, which under my predecessor had very foolishly been repealed.   I secured a mass of labor legislation, including the enactment of laws to increase the number of factory inspectors, to create a Tenement-House Commission (whose findings resulted in further and excellent legislation to improve housing conditions), to regulate and improve sweatshop labor, to make the eight-hour and prevailing rate of wages law effective, to secure the genuine enforcement of the act relating to the hours of railway workers, to compel railways to equip freight trains with air-brakes, to regulate the working hours of women and protect both women and children from

[1] To illustrate my meaning I quote from a letter of mine to Senator Platt of December 13, 1899.   He had been trying to get me to promote a certain Judge X over the head of another Judge Y.   I wrote: "There is a strong feeling among the judges and the leading members of the bar that Judge Y ought not to have Judge X jumped over his head, and I do not see my way clear to doing it.   I am inclined to think that the solution I mentioned to you is the solution I shall have to adopt. Remember the breakfast at Douglas Robinson's at 8:30."

dangerous machinery, to enforce good scaffolding provisions for workmen on buildings, to provide seats for the use of waitresses in hotels and restaurants, to reduce the hours of labor for drug-store clerks, to provide for the registration of laborers for municipal employment. I tried hard but failed to secure an employers' liability law and the state control of employment offices. There was hard fighting over some of these bills, and, what was much more serious, there was effort to get round the law by trickery and by securing its inefficient enforcement. I was continually helped by men with whom I had gotten in touch while in the Police Department; men such as James Bronson Reynolds, through whom I first became interested in settlement work on the East Side. Once or twice I went suddenly down to New York City without warning any one and traversed the tenement-house quarters, visiting various sweat-shops picked at random. Jake Riis accompanied me; and as a result of our inspection we got not only an improvement in the law but a still more marked improvement in its administration. Thanks chiefly to the activity and good sense of Dr. John H. Pryor, of Buffalo, and by the use of every pound of pressure which as Governor I could bring to bear in legitimate fashion — including a special emergency message — we succeeded in getting through a bill providing for the first State hospital for incipient tuberculosis. We got valuable laws for the farmer; laws preventing the adulteration of food products (which laws were equally valuable to the consumer), and laws helping the dairyman. In addition to labor legislation I was able to do a good deal for forest preservation and the protection of our wild life. All that later I strove for in the Nation in connection with Conservation was foreshadowed by what I strove to obtain for New York State when I was Governor; and I was already working in connection with Gifford Pinchot and Newell. I secured better administration, and some improvement in the laws themselves. The improvement in administration, and in the character of the game and forest wardens, was secured partly as the result of a conference in the executive chamber which I held with forty of the best guides and woodsmen of the Adirondacks.

As regards most legislation, even that affecting labor and the forests, I got on fairly well with the machine. But on the two issues in which "big business" and the kind of politics which is allied to big business were most involved we clashed hard — and clashing with Senator Platt meant clashing with the entire Republican organization, and with the organized majority in each house of the Legislature. One clash was in connection with the Superintendent of Insurance, a man whose office made him a factor of immense importance in the big business circles of New York. The then incumbent of the office was an efficient man, the boss of an up-State county, a veteran politician and one of Mr. Platt's right-hand men. Certain investigations which I made — in the course of the fight — showed that this Superintendent of Insurance had been engaged in large business operations in New York City. These operations had thrown him into a peculiarly intimate business contact of one sort and another with various financiers with whom I did not deem it expedient that the Superintendent of Insurance, while such, should have any intimate and secret money-making relations. Moreover, the gentleman in question represented the straitest sect of the old-time spoils politicians. I therefore determined not to reappoint him. Unless I could get his successor confirmed, however, he would stay in under the law, and the Republican machine, with the assistance of Tammany, expected to control far more than a majority of all the Senators.

Mr. Platt issued an ultimatum to me that the incumbent must be reappointed or else that he would fight, and that if he chose to fight the man would stay in anyhow because I could not oust him — for under the New York Constitution the assent of the Senate was necessary not only to appoint a man to office but to remove him from office. As always with Mr. Platt, I persistently refused to lose my temper, no matter what he said — he was much too old and physically feeble for there to be any point of honor in taking up any of his remarks — and I merely explained good-humoredly that I had made up my mind and that the gentleman in question would not be retained. As for not being able to get his sucon conduct. I was therefore very glad to see Perkins and get a new point of view. I went over the matter with a great deal of care and at considerable length, and after we had thrashed the matter out pretty fully and Perkins had laid before me in detail the methods employed by Austria, Germany, Switzerland, and other European countries to handle their large insurance companies, I took the position that there undoubtedly were evils in the insurance business, but that they did not consist in insuring people's lives, for that certainly was not an evil; and I did not see how the real evils could be eradicated by limiting or suppressing a company's ability to protect an additional number of lives with insurance. I therefore announced that I would not favor a bill that limited volume of business, and would not sign it if it were passed; but that I favored legislation that would make it impossible to place, through agents, policies that were ambiguous and misleading, or to pay exorbitant prices to agents for business, or to invest policy-holders' money in improper securities, or to give power to officers to use the company's funds for their own personal profit. In reaching this determination I was helped by Mr. Loeb, then merely a stenographer in my office, but who had already attracted my attention both by his efficiency and by his loyalty to his former employers, who were for the most part my political opponents. Mr. Loeb gave me much information about various improper practices in the insurance business. I began to gather data on the subject, with the intention of bringing about corrective legislation, for at that time I expected to continue in office as Governor. But in a few weeks I was nominated as Vice-President, and my successor did nothing about the matter.

So far as I remember, this was the first time the question of correcting evils in a business by limiting the volume of business to be done was ever presented to me, and my decision in the matter was on all fours with the position I have always since taken when any similar principle was involved. At the time when I made my decision about the Limitation Bill, I was on friendly terms with the Mutual and Equitable people who were back of it, whereas I did not know Mr.

McCall at all, and Mr. Perkins only from hearing him discuss the bill.

An interesting feature of the matter developed subsequently. Five years later, after the insurance investigations took place, the Mutual Life strongly urged the passage of a Limitation Bill, and, because of the popular feeling developed by the exposure of the improper practices of the companies, this bill was generally approved. Governor Hughes adopted the suggestion, such a bill was passed by the Legislature, and Governor Hughes signed it. This bill caused the three great New York companies to reduce markedly the volume of business they were doing; it threw a great many agents out of employment, and materially curtailed the foreign business of the companies — which business was bringing annually a considerable sum of money to this country for investment.

GEORGE PERKINS.

"I got Mr. Perkins to serve on the Palisade Park Commission . . . to save the Palisades from vandalism."

In short, the experiment worked so badly that before Governor Hughes went out of office one of the very last bills he signed was one that permitted the life insurance companies to increase their business each year by an amount representing a certain percentage of the business they had previously done. This in practice, within a few years, practically annulled the Limitation Bill that had been previously passed. The experiment of limiting the size of business, of legislating against it merely because it was big, had been tried, and had failed so completely that the authors of the bill had themselves in effect repealed it. My action in refusing to try the experiment had been completely justified.

As a sequel to this incident I got Mr. Perkins to serve on the Palisade Park Commission. At the time I was taking active part in the effort to save the Palisades from vandalism and destruction by getting the States of New York and New Jersey jointly to include them in a public park. It is not easy to get a responsible and capable man of business to undertake such a task, which is unpaid, which calls on his part for an immense expenditure of time, money, and energy, which offers no reward of any kind, and which entails the certainty of abuse and misrepresentation. Mr. Perkins accepted the position, and has filled it for the last thirteen years, doing as disinterested, efficient, and useful a bit of public service as any man in the State has done throughout these thirteen years.

The case of most importance in which I clashed with Senator Platt related to a matter of fundamental governmental policy, and was the first step I ever took toward bringing big corporations under effective governmental control. In this case I had to fight the Democratic machine as well as the Republican machine, for Senator Hill and Senator Platt were equally opposed to my action, and the big corporation men, the big business men back of both of them, took precisely the same view of these matters without regard to their party feelings on other points. What I did convulsed people at that time, and marked the beginning of the effort, at least in the Eastern states, to make the great corporations really responsible to popular wish and governmental command. But we have gone so far past the stage in which we then were that now it seems well-nigh incredible that there should have been any opposition at all to what I at that time proposed.

The substitution of electric power for horse power in the street car lines of New York offered a fruitful chance for the most noxious type of dealing between business men and politicians. The franchises granted by New York were granted without any attempt to secure from the grantees returns, in the way of taxation or otherwise, for the value received. The fact that they were thus granted by improper favoritism, a favoritism which in many cases was unques-

Y

322 THEODORE ROOSEVELT—AN AUTOBIOGRAPHY

tionably secured by downright bribery, led to all kinds of
trouble. In return for the continuance of these improper
favors to the corporations the politicians expected improper
favors in the way of excessive campaign contributions, often
contributed by the same corporation at the same time to
two opposing parties. Before I became Governor a bill
had been introduced into the New York Legislature to tax
the franchises of these street railways. It affected a large
number of corporations, but particularly those in New York
and Buffalo. It had been suffered to slumber undisturbed,
as none of the people in power dreamed of taking it seriously,
and both the Republican and Democratic machines were
hostile to it. Under the rules of the New York Legislature
a bill could always be taken up out of its turn and passed if
the Governor sent in a special emergency message on its
behalf.

After I was elected Governor I had my attention directed
to the franchise tax matter, looked into the subject, and
came to the conclusion that it was a matter of plain decency
and honesty that these companies should pay a tax on their
franchises, inasmuch as they did nothing that could be considered as service rendered the public in lieu of a tax. This
seemed to me so evidently the common-sense and decent
thing to do that I was hardly prepared for the storm of
protest and anger which my proposal aroused. Senator
Platt and the other machine leaders did everything to get
me to abandon my intention. As usual, I saw them, talked
the matter all over with them, and did my best to convert
them to my way of thinking. Senator Platt, I believe, was
quite sincere in his opposition. He did not believe in popular rule, and he did believe that the big business men were
entitled to have things their way. He profoundly distrusted
the people — naturally enough, for the kind of human nature with which a boss comes in contact is not of an exalted
type. He felt that anarchy would come if there was any
interference with a system by which the people in mass
were, under various necessary cloaks, controlled by the
leaders in the political and business worlds. He wrote me
a very strong letter of protest against my attitude, expressed

in dignified, friendly, and temperate language, but using one word in a curious way.   This was the word "altruistic." He stated in his letter that he had not objected to my being independent in politics, because he had been sure that I had the good of the party at heart, and meant to act fairly and honorably; but that he had been warned, before I became a candidate, by a number of his business friends that I was a dangerous man because I was "altruistic," and that he now feared that my conduct would justify the alarm thus expressed.   I was interested in this, not only because Senator Platt was obviously sincere, but because of the way in which he used "altruistic" as a term of reproach, as if it was Communistic or Socialistic — the last being a word he did use to me when, as now and then happened, he thought that my proposals warranted fairly reckless vituperation. Senator Platt's letter ran in part as follows:

"When the subject of your nomination was under consideration, there was one matter that gave me real anxiety. I think you will have no trouble in appreciating the fact that it was *not* the matter of your independence.   I think we have got far enough along in our political acquaintance for you to see that my support in a convention does not imply subsequent 'demands,' nor any other relation that may not reasonably exist for the welfare of the party. . . . The thing that did bother me was this: I had heard from a good many sources that you were a little loose on the relations of capital and labor, on trusts and combinations, and, indeed, on those numerous questions which have recently arisen in politics affecting the security of earnings and the right of a man to run his own business in his own way, with due respect of course to the Ten Commandments and the Penal Code.   Or, to get at it even more clearly, I understood from a number of business men, and among them many of your own personal friends, that you entertained various altruistic ideas, all very well in their way, but which before they could safely be put into law needed very profound consideration. . . .   You have just adjourned a Legislature which created a good opinion throughout the State.

I congratulate you heartily upon this fact because I sincerely believe, as everybody else does, that this good impression exists very largely as a result of your personal influence in the Legislative chambers. But at the last moment, and to my very great surprise, you did a thing which has caused the business community of New York to wonder how far the notions of Populism, as laid down in Kansas and Nebraska, have taken hold upon the Republican party of the State of New York."

In my answer I pointed out to the Senator that I had as Governor unhesitatingly acted, at Buffalo and elsewhere, to put down mobs, without regard to the fact that the professed leaders of labor furiously denounced me for so doing; but that I could no more tolerate wrong committed in the name of property than wrong committed against property. My letter ran in part as follows : "I knew that you had just the feelings that you describe; that is, apart from my 'impulsiveness,' you felt that there was a justifiable anxiety among men of means, and especially men representing large corporate interests, lest I might feel too strongly on what you term the 'altruistic' side in matters of labor and capital and as regards the relations of the State to great corporations. . . . I know that when parties divide on such issues [as Bryanism] the tendency is to force everybody into one of two camps, and to throw out entirely men like myself, who are as strongly opposed to Populism in every stage as the greatest representative of corporate wealth, but who also feel strongly that many of these representatives of enormous corporate wealth have themselves been responsible for a portion of the conditions against which Bryanism is in ignorant revolt. I do not believe that it is wise or safe for us as a party to take refuge in mere negation and to say that there are no evils to be corrected. It seems to me that our attitude should be one of correcting the evils and thereby showing that, whereas the Populists, Socialists, and others really do not correct the evils at all, or else only do so at the expense of producing others in aggravated form, on the contrary we Republicans hold the just balance and set ourselves as resolutely against improper corporate influence on the one hand as against demagogy and mob rule on the other. I understand perfectly that such an attitude of moderation is apt to be misunderstood when passions are greatly excited and when victory is apt to rest with the extremists on one side or the other; yet I think it is in the long run the only wise attitude. . . . I appreciate absolutely [what Mr. Platt had said] that any applause I get will be too evanescent for a moment's consideration. I appreciate absolutely that the people who now loudly approve of my action in the franchise tax bill will forget all about it in a fortnight, and that, on the other hand, the very powerful interests adversely affected will always remember it. . . . [The leaders] urged upon me that I personally could not afford to take this action, for under no circumstances could I ever again be nominated for any public office, as no corporation would subscribe to a campaign fund if I was on the ticket, and that they would subscribe most heavily to beat me; and when I asked if this were true of Republican corporations, the cynical answer was made that the corporations that subscribed most heavily to the campaign funds subscribed impartially to both party organizations. Under all these circumstances, it seemed to me there was no alternative but to do what I could to secure the passage of the bill."

These two letters, written in the spring of 1899, express clearly the views of the two elements of the Republican party, whose hostility gradually grew until it culminated, thirteen years later. In 1912 the political and financial forces of which Mr. Platt had once been the spokesman, usurped the control of the party machinery and drove out of the party the men who were loyally endeavoring to apply the principles of the founders of the party to the needs and issues of their own day.

I had made up my mind that if I could get a show in the Legislature the bill would pass, because the people had become interested and the representatives would scarcely dare to vote the wrong way. Accordingly, on April 27, 1899, I sent a special message to the Assembly, certifying that the emergency demanded the immediate passage of the bill. The machine leaders were bitterly angry, and the Speaker actually tore up the message without reading it to the Assembly. That night they were busy trying to arrange some device for the defeat of the bill — which was not difficult, as the session was about to close. At seven the next morning I was informed of what had occurred. At eight I was in the Capitol at the Executive chamber, and sent in another special message, which opened as follows: "I learn that the emergency message which I sent last evening to the Assembly on behalf of the Franchise Tax Bill has not been read. I therefore send hereby another message on the subject. I need not impress upon the Assembly the need of passing this bill at once." I sent this message to the Assembly, by my secretary, William J. Youngs, afterwards United States District Attorney of Kings, with an intimation that if this were not promptly read I should come up in person and read it. Then, as so often happens, the opposition collapsed and the bill went through both houses with a rush. I had in the House stanch friends, such as Regis Post and Alford Cooley, men of character and courage, who would have fought to a finish had the need arisen.

My troubles were not at an end, however. The bill put the taxation in the hands of the local county boards, and as the railways sometimes passed through several different counties, this was inadvisable. It was the end of the session, and the Legislature adjourned. The corporations affected, through various counsel, and the different party leaders of both organizations, urged me not to sign the bill, laying especial stress on this feature, and asking that I wait until the following year, when a good measure could be put through with this obnoxious feature struck out. I had thirty days under the law in which to sign the bill. If I did not sign it by the end of that time it would not become a law. I answered my political and corporation friends by telling them that I agreed with them that this feature was wrong, but that I would rather have the bill with this feature than not have it at all; and that I was not willing to trust to what might be done a year later. Therefore, I explained, I would reconvene the Legislature in special session, and if the legislators chose to amend the bill by placing the power of taxation in the State instead of in the county or municipality, I would be glad; but that if they failed to amend it, or amended it improperly, I would sign the original bill and let it become law as it was.

When the representatives of Mr. Platt and of the corporations affected found they could do no better, they assented to this proposition. Efforts were tentatively made to outwit me, by inserting amendments that would nullify the effect of the law, or by withdrawing the law when the Legislature convened; which would at once have deprived me of the whip hand. On May 12 I wrote Senator Platt, outlining the amendments I desired, and said: "Of course it must be understood that I will sign the present bill if the proposed bill containing the changes outlined above fails to pass." On May 18 I notified the Senate leader, John Raines, by telegram: "Legislature has no power to withdraw the Ford bill. If attempt is made to do so, I will sign the bill at once." On the same day, by telegram, I wired Mr. Odell concerning the bill the leaders were preparing: "Some provisions of bill very objectionable. I am at work on bill to show you to-morrow. The bill must not contain greater changes than those outlined in my message." My wishes were heeded, and when I had reconvened the Legislature it amended the bill as I outlined in my message; and in its amended form the bill became law.

There promptly followed something which afforded an index of the good faith of the corporations that had been protesting to me. As soon as the change for which they had begged was inserted in the law, and the law was signed, they turned round and refused to pay the taxes; and in the lawsuit that followed, they claimed that the law was unconstitutional, because it contained the very clause which they had so clamorously demanded. Senator David B. Hill had appeared before me on behalf of the corporations to argue for the change; and he then appeared before the courts to make the argument on the other side. The suit was carried through to the Supreme Court of the United States, which declared the law constitutional during the time that I was President.

One of the painful duties of the chief executive in States like New York, as well as in the Nation, is the refusing of pardons. Yet I can imagine nothing more necessary from the standpoint of good citizenship than the ability to steel one's heart in this matter of granting pardons. The pressure is always greatest in two classes of cases : first, that where capital punishment is inflicted; second, that where the man is prominent socially and in the business world, and where in consequence his crime is apt to have been one concerned in some way with finance.

As regards capital cases, the trouble is that emotional men and women always see only the individual whose fate is up at the moment, and neither his victim nor the many millions of unknown individuals who would in the long run be harmed by what they ask. Moreover, almost any criminal, however brutal, has usually some person, often a person whom he has greatly wronged, who will plead for him. If the mother is alive she will always come, and she cannot help feeling that the case in which she is so concerned is peculiar, that in this case a pardon should be granted. It was really heartrending to have to see the kinsfolk and friends of murderers who were condemned to death, and among the very rare occasions when anything governmental or official caused me to lose sleep were the times when I had to listen to some poor mother making a plea for a criminal so wicked, so utterly brutal and depraved, that it would have been a crime on my part to remit his punishment.

On the other hand, there were certain crimes where requests for leniency merely made me angry. Such crimes were, for instance, rape, or the circulation of indecent literature, or anything connected with what would now be called the "white slave" traffic, or wife murder, or gross cruelty to women and children, or seduction and abandonment, or the action of some man in getting a girl whom he had seduced to commit abortion. I am speaking in each instance of cases that actually came before me, either while I was Governor or

while I was President. In an astonishing number of these
cases men of high standing signed petitions or wrote letters
asking me to show leniency to the criminal. In two or three
of the cases — one where some young roughs had committed
rape on a helpless immigrant girl, and another in which a
physician of wealth and high standing had seduced a girl and
then induced her to commit abortion — I rather lost my
temper, and wrote to the individuals who had asked for the
pardon, saying that I extremely regretted that it was not in
my power to increase the sentence. I then let the facts be
made public, for I thought that my petitioners deserved
public censure. Whether they received this public censure
or not I did not know, but that my action made them very
angry I do know, and their anger gave me real satisfaction.
The list of these petitioners was a fairly long one, and included two United States Senators, a Governor of a State,
two judges, an editor, and some eminent lawyers and business men.

In the class of cases where the offense was one involving
the misuse of large sums of money the reason for the pressure
was different. Cases of this kind more frequently came
before me when I was President, but they also came before
me when I was Governor, chiefly in the cases of county
treasurers who had embezzled funds. A big bank president,
a railway magnate, an official connected with some big
corporation, or a Government official in a responsible fiduci-
ary position, necessarily belongs among the men who have
succeeded in life. This means that his family are living in
comfort, and perhaps luxury and refinement, and that his
sons and daughters have been well educated. In such a case
the misdeed of the father comes as a crushing disaster to the
wife and children, and the people of the community, however
bitter originally against the man, grow to feel the most
intense sympathy for the bowed-down women and children
who suffer for the man's fault. It is a dreadful thing in life
that so much of atonement for wrong-doing is vicarious.
If it were possible in such a case to think only of the banker's
or county treasurer's wife and children, any man would
pardon the offender at once. Unfortunately, it is not right

to think only of the women and children. The very fact that in cases of this class there is certain to be pressure from high sources, pressure sometimes by men who have been beneficially, even though remotely, interested in the man's criminality, no less than pressure because of honest sympathy with the wife and children, makes it necessary that the good public servant shall, no matter how deep his sympathy and regret, steel his heart and do his duty by refusing to let the wrong-doer out. My experience of the way in which pardons are often granted is one of the reasons why I do not believe that life imprisonment for murder and rape is a proper substitute for the death penalty. The average term of so-called life imprisonment in this country is only about fourteen years.

Of course there were cases where I either commuted sentences or pardoned offenders with very real pleasure. For instance, when President, I frequently commuted sentences for horse stealing in the Indian Territory because the penalty for stealing a horse was disproportionate to the penalty for many other crimes, and the offense was usually committed by some ignorant young fellow who found a half-wild horse, and really did not commit anything like as serious an offense as the penalty indicated. The judges would be obliged to give the minimum penalty, but would forward me memoranda stating that if there had been a less penalty they would have inflicted it, and I would then commute the sentence to the penalty thus indicated.

In one case in New York I pardoned outright a man convicted of murder in the second degree, and I did this on the recommendation of a friend, Father Doyle of the Paulist Fathers. I had become intimate with the Paulist Fathers while I was Police Commissioner, and I had grown to feel confidence in their judgment, for I had found that they always told me exactly what the facts were about any man, whether he belonged to their church or not. In this case the convicted man was a strongly built, respectable old Irishman employed as a watchman around some big cattle-killing establishments. The young roughs of the neighborhood, which was then of a rather lawless type, used to try to destroy the property of the companies.   In a conflict with a watchman a member of one of the gangs was slain.   The watchman was acquitted, but the neighborhood was much wrought up over the acquittal.   Shortly afterwards, a gang of the same roughs attacked another watchman, the old Irishman in question, and finally, to save his own life, he was obliged in self-defense to kill one of his assailants.   The feeling in the community, however, was strongly against him, and some of the men high up in the corporation became frightened and thought that it would be better to throw over the watchman.   He was convicted.   Father Doyle came to me, told me that he knew the man well, that he was one of the best members of his church, admirable in every way, that he had simply been forced to fight for his life while loyally doing his duty, and that the conviction represented the triumph of the tough element of the district and the abandonment of this man, by those who should

FATHER DOYLE OF THE PAULIST FATHERS.

" I had become very intimate with the Paulist Fathers while I was Police Commissioner."

have stood by him, under the influence of an unworthy fear.   I looked into the case, came to the conclusion that Father Doyle was right, and gave the man a full pardon before he had served thirty days.

The various clashes between myself and the machine, my triumph in them, and the fact that the people were getting more and more interested and aroused, brought on a curious situation in the Republican National Convention at Philadelphia in June, 1900.   Senator Platt and the New

York machine leaders had become very anxious to get me out of the Governorship, chiefly because of the hostility of the big corporation men towards me; but they had also become convinced that there was such popular feeling on my behalf that it would be difficult to refuse me a renomination if I demanded it.   They accordingly decided to push me for Vice-President, taking advantage of the fact that there was at that time a good deal of feeling for me in the country at large.[1]   I myself did not appreciate that there was any such feeling, and as I greatly disliked the office of Vice-President and was much interested in the Governorship, I announced that I would not accept the Vice-Presidency.   I was one of the delegates to Philadelphia. On reaching there I found that the situation was complicated. Senator Hanna appeared on the surface to have control of the Convention. He was anxious that I should not be nominated as Vice-President. Senator Platt was anxious that I should be nominated as Vice-President, in order to get me out of the New York Governorship. Each took a position opposite to that of the other, but each at that time cordially sympathized with the other's feelings about me — it was the manifestations and not the feelings that differed. My supporters in New York State did not wish me nominated for Vice-President because they wished me to continue as Governor; but in every other State all the people who admired me were bound that I should be nominated as Vice-President. These people were almost all desirous of seeing Mr. McKinley renominated as President, but they became angry at Senator Hanna's opposition to me as Vice-President. He in his turn suddenly became aware that if he persisted he might find that in their anger these men would oppose Mr. McKinley's renomination, and although they could not have prevented the nomination, such opposition would have been a serious blow in the campaign which was to follow. Senator Hanna, therefore, began to waver.

Meanwhile a meeting of the New York delegation was called. Most of the delegates were under the control of Senator Platt. The Senator notified me that if I refused to

[1] See Appendix B to this chapter.

accept the nomination for Vice-President I would be beaten
for the nomination for Governor. I answered that I would
accept the challenge, that we would have a straight-out
fight on the proposition, and that I would begin it at once
by telling the assembled delegates of the threat, and giving
fair warning that I intended to fight for the Governorship
nomination, and, moreover, that I intended to get it. This
brought Senator Platt to terms. The effort to instruct the
New York delegation for me was abandoned, and Lieutenant-
Governor Woodruff was presented for nomination in my place.

I supposed that this closed the incident, and that no
further effort would be made to nominate me for the Vice-
Presidency. On the contrary, the effect was directly the reverse. The upset of the New York machine increased the
feeling of the delegates from other States that it was necessary to draft me for the nomination. By next day Senator
Hanna himself concluded that this was a necessity, and
acquiesced in the movement. As New York was already
committed against me, and as I was not willing that there
should be any chance of supposing that the New Yorkers
had nominated me to get rid of me, the result was that I was
nominated and seconded from outside States. No other
candidate was placed in the field.

By this time the Legislature had adjourned, and most of
my work as Governor of New York was over. One unexpected bit of business arose, however. It was the year of the
Presidential campaign. Tammany, which had been lukewarm about Bryan in 1896, cordially supported him in 1900;
and when Tammany heartily supports a candidate it is well
for the opposing candidate to keep a sharp lookout for election frauds. The city government was in the hands of
Tammany; but I had power to remove the Mayor, the
Sheriff, and the District Attorney for malfeasance or misfeasance in office. Such power had not been exercised by
any previous Governor, as far as I knew; but it existed, and
if the misfeasance or malfeasance warranted it, and if the
Governor possessed the requisite determination, the power
could be, and ought to be, exercised.

By an Act of the Legislature, a State Bureau of Elections

had been created in New York City, and a Superintendent of
Elections appointed by the Governor. The Chief of the
State Bureau of Elections was John McCullagh, formerly in
the Police Department when I was Police Commissioner.
The Chief of Police for the city was William F. Devery, one
of the Tammany leaders, who represented in the Police
Department all that I had warred against while Commissioner. On November 4 Devery directed his subordinates in
the Police Department to disregard the orders which Mc-
Cullagh had given to his deputies, orders which were essential if we were to secure an honest election in the city.
I had just returned from a Western campaign trip, and was
at Sagamore Hill. I had no direct power over Devery;
but the Mayor had; and I had power over the Mayor.
Accordingly, I at once wrote to the Mayor of New York, to
the Sheriff of New York, and to the District Attorney of
New York County the following letters:

STATE OF NEW YORK

OYSTER BAY, November 5, 1900.

To the Mayor of the City of New York.

Sir: My attention has been called to the official order
issued by Chief of Police Devery, in which he directs his
subordinates to disregard the Chief of the State Election
Bureau, John McCullagh, and his deputies. Unless you
have already taken steps to secure the recall of this order,
it is necessary for me to point out that I shall be obliged
to hold you responsible as the head of the city government
for the action of the Chief of Police, if it should result in
any breach of the peace and intimidation or any crime whatever against the election laws. The State and city authorities should work together. I will not fail to call to summary account either State or city authority in the event
of either being guilty of intimidation or connivance at fraud
or of failure to protect every legal voter in his rights. I
therefore hereby notify you that in the event of any wrong-
doing following upon the failure immediately to recall Chief

Devery's order, or upon any action or inaction on the part of Chief Devery, I must necessarily call you to account.

> Yours, etc.,
> THEODORE ROOSEVELT.

STATE OF NEW YORK

> OYSTER BAY, November 5, 1900.

To the Sheriff of the County of New York.

Sir: My attention has been called to the official order issued by Chief of Police Devery in which he directs his subordinates to disregard the Chief of the State Election Bureau, John McCullagh, and his deputies.

It is your duty to assist in the orderly enforcement of the law, and I shall hold you strictly responsible for any breach of the public peace within your county, or for any failure on your part to do your full duty in connection with the election to-morrow.   Yours truly,
> THEODORE ROOSEVELT.

STATE OF NEW YORK

> OYSTER BAY, November 5, 1900.

To the District Attorney of the County of New York.

Sir: My attention has been called to the official order issued by Chief of Police Devery, in which he directs his subordinates to disregard the Chief of the State Election Bureau, John McCullagh, and his deputies.

In view of this order I call your attention to the fact that it is your duty to assist in the orderly enforcement of the law, and there must be no failure on your part to do your full duty in the matter.   Yours truly,
> THEODORE ROOSEVELT.

These letters had the desired effect. The Mayor promptly required Chief Devery to rescind the obnoxious order, which was as promptly done. The Sheriff also took prompt action.   The District Attorney refused to heed my letter, and assumed an attitude of defiance, and I removed him from office.   On election day there was no clash between the city and State authorities; the election was orderly and honest.

APPENDIX A

CONSERVATION

As foreshadowing the course I later, as President, followed in this matter, I give extracts from one of my letters to the Commission, and from my second (and last) Annual Message. I spent the first months of my term in investigations to find out just what the situation was.

On November 28, 1899, I wrote to the Commission as follows:

". . . I have had very many complaints before this as to the inefficiency of the game wardens and game protectors, the complaints usually taking the form that the men have been appointed and are retained without due regard to the duties to be performed. I do not wish a man to be retained or appointed who is not thoroughly fit to perform the duties of game protector. The Adirondacks are entitled to a peculiar share of the Commission's attention, both from the standpoint of forestry, and from the less important, but still very important, standpoint of game and fish protection. The men who do duty as game protectors in the Adirondacks should, by preference, be appointed from the locality itself, and should in all cases be thorough woodsmen. The mere fact that a game protector has to hire a guide to pilot him through the woods is enough to show his unfitness for the position. I want as game protectors men of courage, resolution, and hardihood, who can handle the rifle, ax, and paddle; who can camp out in summer or winter; who can go on snow-shoes, if necessary; who can go through the woods by day or by night without regard to trails.

"I should like full information about all your employees, as to their capacities, as to the labor they perform, as to their distribution from and where they do their work."

Many of the men hitherto appointed owed their positions principally to political preference. The changes I recommended were promptly made, and much to the good of the public service. In my Annual Message, in January, 1900, I said:

"Great progress has been made through the fish hatcheries in

z   337

the propagation of valuable food and sporting fish. The laws for the protection of deer have resulted in their increase. Nevertheless, as railroads tend to encroach on the wilderness, the temptation to illegal hunting becomes greater, and the danger from forest fires increases. There is need of great improvement both in our laws and in their administration. The game wardens have been too few in number. More should be provided. None save fit men must be appointed; and their retention in office must depend purely upon the zeal, ability, and efficiency with which they perform their duties. The game wardens in the forests must be woodsmen; and they should have no outside business. In short, there should be a thorough reorganization of the work of the Commission. A careful study of the resources and condition of the forests on State land must be made. It is certainly not too much to expect that the State forests should be managed as efficiently as the forests on private lands in the same neighborhoods. And the measure of difference in efficiency of management must be the measure of condemnation or praise of the way the public forests have been managed.

"The subject of forest preservation is of the utmost importance to the State. The Adirondacks and Catskills should be great parks kept in perpetuity for the benefit and enjoyment of our people. Much has been done of late years towards their perservation, but very much remains to be done. The provisions of law in reference to sawmills and wood-pulp mills are defective and should be changed so as to prohibit dumping dye-stuff, sawdust, or tan-bark, in any amount whatsoever, into the streams. Reservoirs should be made, but not where they will tend to destroy large sections of the forest, and only after a careful and scientific study of the water resources of the region. The people of the forest regions are themselves growing more and more to realize the necessity of preserving both the trees and the game. A live deer in the woods will attract to the neighborhood ten times the money that could be obtained for the deer's dead carcass. Timber theft on the State lands is, of course, a grave offense against the whole public.

"Hardy outdoor sports, like hunting, are in themselves of no small value to the National character and should be encouraged in every way. Men who go into the wilderness, indeed, men who take part in any field sports with horse or rifle, receive a benefit which can hardly be given by even the most vigorous athletic games.

"There is a further and more immediate and practical end in

view. A primeval forest is a great sponge which absorbs and distills the rain water. And when it is destroyed the result is apt to be an alternation of flood and drought. Forest fires ultimately make the land a desert, and are a detriment to all that portion of the State tributary to the streams through the woods where they occur. Every effort should be made to minimize their destructive influence. We need to have our system of forestry gradually developed and conducted along scientific principles. When this has been done it will be possible to allow marketable lumber to be cut everywhere without damage to the forests — indeed, with positive advantage to them. But until lumbering is thus conducted, on strictly scientific principles no less than upon principles of the strictest honesty toward the State, we cannot afford to suffer it at all in the State forests. Unrestrained greed means the ruin of the great woods and the drying up of the sources of the rivers.

"Ultimately the administration of the State lands must be so centralized as to enable us definitely to place responsibility in respect to everything concerning them, and to demand the highest degree of trained intelligence in their use.

"The State should not permit within its limits factories to make bird skins or bird feathers into articles of ornament or wearing apparel. Ordinary birds, and especially song birds, should be rigidly protected. Game birds should never be shot to a greater extent than will offset the natural rate of increase. . . . Care should be taken not to encourage the use of cold storage or other market systems which are a benefit to no one but the wealthy epicure who can afford to pay a heavy price for luxuries. These systems tend to the destruction of the game, which would bear most severely upon the very men whose rapacity has been appealed to in order to secure its extermination. . . ."

I reorganized the Commission, putting Austin Wadsworth at its head.

APPENDIX B

THE POLITICAL SITUATION IN 1900

My general scheme of action as Governor was given in a letter I wrote one of my supporters among the independent district organization leaders, Norton Goddard, on April 16, 1900. It runs in part as follows: "Nobody can tell, and least of all the machine itself, whether the machine intends to renominate me next fall or not. If for some reason I should be weak, whether on account of faults or virtues, doubtless the machine will throw me over, and I think I am not uncharitable when I say they would feel no acute grief at so doing. It would be very strange if they did feel such grief. If, for instance, we had strikes which led to riots, I would of course be obliged to preserve order and stop the riots. Decent citizens would demand that I should do it, and in any event I should do it wholly without regard to their demands. But, once it was done, they would forget all about it, while a great many laboring men, honest but ignorant and prejudiced, would bear a grudge against me for doing it. This might put me out of the running as a candidate. Again, the big corporations undoubtedly want to beat me. They prefer the chance of being blackmailed to the certainty that they will not be allowed any more than their due. Of course they will try to beat me on some entirely different issue, and, as they are very able and very unscrupulous, nobody can tell that they won't succeed. . . . I have been trying to stay in with the organization. I did not do it with the idea that they would renominate me. I did it with the idea of getting things done, and in that I have been absolutely successful. Whether Senator Platt and Mr. Odell endeavor to beat me, or do beat me, for the renomination next fall, is of very small importance compared to the fact that for my two years I have been able to make a Republican majority in the Legislature do good and decent work and have prevented any split within the party. The task was one of great difficulty, because, on the one hand, I had to keep clearly before me the fact that it was better to have a split than to permit *bad* work to be done, and, on the other hand, the fact that to have that split would absolutely prevent all *good* work. The result has been that I have avoided a split and that as a net result of my two years and the two sessions of the Legislature, there has been an enormous improvement in the administration of the Government, and there has also been a great advance in legislation."

To show my reading of the situation at the time I quote from a letter of mine to Joseph B. Bishop, then editor of the *Commercial Advertiser*, with whom towards the end of my term I had grown into very close relations, and who, together with two other old friends, Albert Shaw, of the *Review of Reviews*, and Silas Mc-Bee, now editor of the *Constructive Quarterly*, knew the inside of every movement, so far as I knew it myself. The letter, which is dated April 11, 1900, runs in part as follows: "The dangerous element as far as I am concerned comes from the corporations.

The [naming certain men] crowd and those like them have been greatly exasperated by the franchise tax. They would like to get me out of politics for good, but at the moment they think the best thing to do is to put me into the Vice-Presidency. Naturally I will not be opposed openly on the ground of the corporations' grievance; but every kind of false statement will continually be made, and men like [naming the editors of certain newspapers] will attack me, not as the enemy of corporations, but as their tool! There is no question whatever that if the leaders can they will upset me."

One position which as Governor (and as President) I consistently took, seems to me to represent what ought to be a fundamental principle in American legislative work. I steadfastly refused to advocate any law, no matter how admirable in theory, if there was good reason to believe that in practice it would not be executed. I have always sympathized with the view set forth by Pelatiah Webster in 1783 — quoted by Hannis Taylor in his *Genesis of the Supreme Court* — " Laws or ordinances of any kind (especially of august bodies of high dignity and consequence) which fail of execution, are much worse than none. They weaken the government, expose it to contempt, destroy the confidence of all men, native and foreigners, in it, and expose both aggregate bodies and individuals who have placed confidence in it to many ruinous disappointments which they would have escaped had no such law or ordinance been made." This principle, by the way, not only applies to an internal law which cannot be executed; it applies even more to international action, such as a universal arbitration treaty which cannot and will not be kept; and most of all it applies to proposals to make such universal arbitration treaties at the very time that we are not keeping our solemn promise to execute limited arbitration treaties which we have already made. A general arbitration treaty is merely a promise; it represents merely a debt of honorable obligation; and nothing is more discreditable, for a nation or an individual, than to cover up the repudiation of a debt which can be and ought to be paid, by recklessly promising to incur a new and insecure debt which no wise man for one moment supposes ever will be paid.

CHAPTER IX

OUTDOORS AND INDOORS

THERE are men who love out-of-doors who yet never open a book; and other men who love books but to whom the great book of nature is a sealed volume, and the lines written therein blurred and illegible. Nevertheless among those men whom I have known the love of books and the love of outdoors, in their highest expressions, have usually gone hand in hand. It is an affectation for the man who is praising outdoors to sneer at books. Usually the keenest appreciation of what is seen in nature is to be found in those who have also profited by the hoarded and recorded wisdom of their fellow-men. Love of outdoor life, love of simple and hardy pastimes, can be gratified by men and women who do not possess large means, and who work hard; and so can love of good books — not of good bindings and of first editions, excellent enough in their way but sheer luxuries — I mean love of reading books, owning them if possible of course, but, if that is not possible, getting them from a circulating library.

Sagamore Hill takes its name from the old Sagamore Mohannis, who, as chief of his little tribe, signed away his rights to the land two centuries and a half ago. The house stands right on the top of the hill, separated by fields and belts of woodland from all other houses, and looks out over the bay and the Sound. We see the sun go down beyond long reaches of land and of water. Many birds dwell in the trees round the house or in the pastures and the woods near by, and of course in winter gulls, loons, and wild fowl frequent the waters of the bay and the Sound. We love all the seasons; the snows and bare woods of winter; the rush of growing things and the blossom-spray of spring; the yellow grain, the ripening fruits and tasseled corn, and the deep, leafy shades that are heralded by "the green dance of summer"; and the sharp fall winds that tear the brilliant banners with which the trees greet the dying year.

The Sound is always lovely. In the summer nights we watch it from the piazza, and see the lights of the tall Fall

SAGAMORE HILL.

River boats as they steam steadily by. Now and then we spend a day on it, the two of us together in the light rowing skiff, or perhaps with one of the boys to pull an extra pair of oars; we land for lunch at noon under wind-beaten oaks on the edge of a low bluff, or among the wild plum bushes on a spit of white sand, while the sails of the coasting schooners gleam in the sunlight, and the tolling of the bell-buoy comes landward across the waters.

Long Island is not as rich in flowers as the valley of the Hudson. Yet there are many. Early in April there is one

THEODORE ROOSEVELT IN WINTER RIDING COSTUME.

hillside near us which glows like a tender flame with the white of the bloodroot. About the same time we find the shy mayflower, the trailing arbutus; and although we rarely pick wild flowers, one member of the household always plucks a little bunch of mayflowers to send to a friend working in Panama, whose soul hungers for the Northern spring. Then there are shadblow and delicate anemones, about the time of the cherry blossoms; the brief glory of the apple orchards follows; and then the thronging dogwoods fill the forests with their radiance; and so flowers follow flowers until the springtime splendor closes with the laurel and the evanescent, honey-sweet locust bloom. The late summer flowers follow, the flaunting lilies, and cardinal flowers, and marshmallows, and pale beach rosemary; and the goldenrod and the asters when the afternoons shorten and we again begin to think of fires in the wide fireplaces.

Most of the birds in our neighborhood are the ordinary home friends of the house and the barn, the wood lot and the pasture; but now and then the species make queer shifts. The cheery quail, alas! are rarely found near us now; and we no longer hear the whip-poor-wills at night. But some birds visit us now which formerly did not. When I was a boy neither the black-throated green warbler nor the purple finch nested around us, nor were bobolinks found in our fields. The black-throated green warbler is now one of our commonest summer warblers; there are plenty of purple finches; and, best of all, the bobolinks are far from infrequent. I had written about these new visitors to John Burroughs, and once when he came out to see me I was able to show them to him.

When I was President, we owned a little house in western Virginia; a delightful house, to us at least, although only a shell of rough boards. We used sometimes to go there in the fall, perhaps at Thanksgiving, and on these occasions we would have quail and rabbits of our own shooting, and once in a while a wild turkey. We also went there in the spring. Of course many of the birds were different from our Long Island friends. There were mocking-birds, the most attractive of all birds, and blue grosbeaks, and cardinals and summer redbirds, instead of scarlet tanagers, and those wonderful singers the Bewick's wrens, and Carolina wrens. All these I was able to show John Burroughs when he came to visit us; although, by the way, he did not appreciate as much as we did one set of inmates of the cottage — the flying squirrels. We loved having the flying squirrels,

UNDER THE PORCH AT SAGAMORE.

father and mother and half-grown young, in their nest among the rafters; and at night we slept so soundly that we did not in the least mind the wild gambols of the little fellows through the rooms, even when, as sometimes happened, they would swoop down to the bed and scuttle across it.

One April I went to Yellowstone Park, when the snow was still very deep, and I took John Burroughs with me. I wished to show him the big game of the Park, the wild creatures that have become so astonishingly tame and tolerant of human presence. In the Yellowstone the animals seem always to behave as one wishes them to! It is always possible to see the sheep and deer and antelope, and also the great herds of elk, which are shyer than the smaller beasts. In April we found the elk weak after the short commons and hard living of winter. Once without much difficulty I regularly rounded up a big band of them, so that John Burroughs could look at them. I do not think, however, that he cared to see them as much as I did. The birds interested him more, especially a tiny owl the size of a robin which we saw perched on the top of a tree in mid-afternoon entirely uninfluenced by the sun and making a queer noise like a cork being pulled from a bottle. I was rather ashamed to find how much better his eyes were than mine in seeing the birds and grasping their differences.

When wolf-hunting in Texas, and when bear-hunting in Louisiana and Mississippi, I was not only enthralled by the sport, but also by the strange new birds and other creatures, and the trees and flowers I had not known before. By the way, there was one feast at the White House which stands above all others in my memory — even above the time when I lured Joel Chandler Harris thither for a night, a deed in which to triumph, as all who knew that inveterately shy recluse will testify. This was "the bear-hunters' dinner." I had been treated so kindly by my friends on these hunts, and they were such fine fellows, men whom I was so proud to think of as Americans, that I set my heart on having them at a hunters' dinner at the White House. One December I succeeded; there were twenty or thirty of them, all told, as good hunters, as daring riders, as first-class citizens as could be found anywhere; no finer set of guests ever sat at meat in the White House; and among other game on the table was a black bear, itself contributed by one of these same guests.

When I first visited California, it was my good fortune to see the "big trees," the Sequoias, and then to travel down into the Yosemite, with John Muir. Of course of all people in the world he was the one with whom it was best worth while thus to see the Yosemite. He told me that when Emerson came to California he tried to get him to come out and camp with him, for that was the only way in which to see at their best the majesty and charm of the Sierras. But at the time Emerson was getting old and could not go. John Muir met me with a couple of packers and two mules to carry our tent, bedding, and food for a three days' trip. The first night was clear, and we lay down in the darkening aisles of the great Sequoia grove. The majestic trunks, beautiful in color and in symmetry, rose round us like the pillars of a mightier cathedral than ever was conceived even by the fervor of the Middle Ages. Hermit thrushes sang

beautifully in the evening, and again, with a burst of wonderful music, at dawn.   I was interested and a little surprised to find that, unlike John Burroughs, John Muir cared

BEFORE THE MORNING RIDE AT SAGAMORE.

little for birds or bird songs, and knew little about them.
The hermit thrushes meant nothing to him, the trees and the
flowers and the cliffs everything.   The only birds he noticed

or cared for were some that were very conspicuous, such as
the water-ousels — always particular favorites of mine too.
The second night we camped in a snow-storm, on the edge
of the cañon walls, under the spreading limbs of a grove of
mighty silver fir; and next day we went down into the
wonderland of the valley itself.   I shall always be glad
that I was in the Yosemite with John Muir and in the
Yellowstone with John Burroughs.

Like most Americans interested in birds and books, I
know a good deal about English birds as they appear in
books.   I know the lark of Shakespeare and Shelley and the
Ettrick Shepherd; I know the nightingale of Milton and
Keats; I know Wordsworth's cuckoo; I know mavis and
merle singing in the merry green wood of the old ballads; I
know Jenny Wren and Cock Robin of the nursery books.
Therefore I had always much desired to hear the birds in
real life; and the opportunity offered in June, 1910, when I
spent two or three weeks in England.   As I could snatch but
a few hours from a very exacting round of pleasures and
duties, it was necessary for me to be with some companion
who could identify both song and singer.   In Sir Edward
Grey, a keen lover of outdoor life in all its phases, and a
delightful companion, who knows the songs and ways of
English birds as very few do know them, I found the best
possible guide.

We left London on the morning of June 9, twenty-four
hours before I sailed from Southampton.   Getting off the
train at Basingstoke, we drove to the pretty, smiling valley
of the Itchen.   Here we tramped for three or four hours,
then again drove, this time to the edge of the New Forest,
where we first took tea at an inn, and then tramped through
the forest to an inn on its other side, at Brockenhurst.   At
the conclusion of our walk my companion made a list of the
birds we had seen, putting an asterisk (*) opposite those
which we had heard sing.   There were forty-one of the
former and twenty-three of the latter, as follows :

* Thrush, * blackbird, * lark, * yellowhammer, * robin,
* wren,   * golden-crested wren,   * goldfinch,   * chaffinch,
* greenfinch, pied wagtail, sparrow, * dunnock (hedge, ac-

centor), missel thrush, starling, rook, jackdaw, * blackcap, * garden warbler, * willow warbler, * chiffchaff, * wood warbler, tree-creeper, * reed bunting, * sedge warbler, coot, water hen, little grebe (dabchick), tufted duck, wood pigeon, stock dove, * turtle dove, peewit, tit (? coal tit), * cuckoo, * nightjar, * swallow, martin, swift, pheasant, partridge.

The valley of the Itchen is typically the England that we know from novel and story and essay. It is very beautiful in every way, with a rich, civilized, fertile beauty — the rapid brook twisting among its reed beds, the rich green of trees and grass, the stately woods, the gardens and fields, the exceedingly picturesque cottages, the great handsome houses standing in their parks. Birds were plentiful; I know but few places in America where one would see such an abundance of individuals, and I was struck by seeing such large birds as coots, water hens, grebes, tufted ducks, pigeons, and peewits. In places in America as thickly settled as the valley of the Itchen, I should not expect to see any like number of birds of this size; but I hope that the efforts of the Audubon societies and kindred organizations will gradually make themselves felt until it becomes a point of honor not only with the American man, but with the American small boy, to shield and protect all forms of harmless wild life. True sportsmen should take the lead in such a movement, for if there is to be any shooting there must be something to shoot; the prime necessity is to keep, and not kill out, even the birds which in legitimate numbers may be shot.

The New Forest is a wild, uninhabited stretch of heath and woodland, many of the trees gnarled and aged, and its very wildness, the lack of cultivation, the ruggedness, made it strongly attractive in my eyes, and suggested my own country. The birds of course were much less plentiful than beside the Itchen.

The bird that most impressed me on my walk was the blackbird. I had already heard nightingales in abundance near Lake Como, and had also listened to larks, but I had never heard either the blackbird, the song thrush, or the blackcap warbler; and while I knew that all three were good singers, I did not know what really beautiful singers they were. Blackbirds were very abundant, and they played a prominent part in the chorus which we heard throughout the day on every hand, though perhaps loudest the following morning at dawn. In its habits and manners the blackbird strikingly resembles our American robin, and indeed looks exactly like a robin, with a yellow bill and coal-black plumage. It hops everywhere over the lawns, just as our robin does, and it lives and nests in the gardens in the same fashion. Its song has a general resemblance to that of our robin, but many of the notes are far more musical, more like those of our wood thrush. Indeed, there were individuals among those we heard certain of whose notes seemed to me almost to equal in point of melody the chimes of the wood thrush; and the highest possible praise for any song-bird is to liken its song to that of the wood thrush or hermit thrush. I certainly do not think that the blackbird has received full justice in the books. I knew that he was a singer, but I really had no idea how fine a singer he was. I suppose one of his troubles has been his name, just as with our own catbird. When he appears in the ballads as the merle, bracketed with his cousin the mavis, the song thrush, it is far easier to recognize him as the master singer that he is. It is a fine thing for England to have such an asset of the countryside, a bird so common, so much in evidence, so fearless, and such a really beautiful singer.

The thrush is a fine singer too, a better singer than our American robin, but to my mind not at the best quite as good as the blackbird at his best; although often I found difficulty in telling the song of one from the song of the other, especially if I only heard two or three notes.

The larks were, of course, exceedingly attractive. It was fascinating to see them spring from the grass, circle upwards, steadily singing and soaring for several minutes, and then return to the point whence they had started. As my companion pointed out, they exactly fulfilled Wordsworth's description; they soared but did not roam. It is quite impossible wholly to differentiate a bird's voice from its habits and surroundings. Although in the lark's song there are occasional musical notes, the song as a whole is not very musical; but it is so joyous, buoyant and unbroken, and uttered under such conditions as fully to entitle the bird to the place he occupies with both poet and prose writer.

The most musical singer we heard was the blackcap warbler. To my ear its song seemed more musical than that of the nightingale. It was astonishingly powerful for so small a bird; in volume and continuity it does not come up to the songs of the thrushes and of certain other birds, but in quality, as an isolated bit of melody, it can hardly be surpassed.

Among the minor singers the robin was noticeable. We all know this pretty little bird from the books, and I was prepared to find him as friendly and attractive as he proved to be, but I had not realized how well he sang. It is not a loud song, but very musical and attractive, and the bird is said to sing practically all through the year. The song of the wren interested me much, because it was not in the least like that of our house wren, but, on the contrary, like that of our winter wren. The theme is the same as the winter wren's, but the song did not seem to me to be as brilliantly musical as that of the tiny singer of the North Woods. The sedge warbler sang in the thick reeds a mocking ventriloquial lay, which reminded me at times of the less pronounced parts of our yellow-breasted chat's song. The cuckoo's cry was singularly attractive and musical, far more so than the rolling, many times repeated, note of our rain-crow.

We did not reach the inn at Brockenhurst until about nine o'clock, just at nightfall, and a few minutes before that we heard a nightjar. It did not sound in the least like either our whip-poor-will or our night-hawk, uttering a long-continued call of one or two syllables, repeated over and over. The chaffinch was very much in evidence, continually chaunting its unimportant little ditty. I was pleased to see the bold, masterful missel thrush, the stormcock as it is often called; but this bird breeds and sings in the early spring, when the weather is still tempestuous, and had long been silent when we saw it. The starlings, rooks, and jackdaws did not sing, and their calls were attractive merely as the calls of our grakles are attractive; and the other birds that we heard sing, though they played their part in the general chorus, were performers of no especial note, like our tree-creepers, pine warblers, and chipping sparrows. The great spring chorus had already begun to subside, but the woods and fields were still vocal with beautiful bird music, the country was very lovely, the inn as comfortable as possible, and the bath and supper very enjoyable after our

From the Summer House at Sagamore.

tramp; and altogether I passed no pleasanter twenty-four hours during my entire European trip.

Ten days later, at Sagamore Hill, I was among my own birds, and was much interested as I listened to and looked at them in remembering the notes and actions of the birds I had seen in England. On the evening of the first day I sat in my rocking-chair on the broad veranda, looking across the Sound towards the glory of the sunset. The thickly grassed hillside sloped down in front of me to a belt of forest from which rose the golden, leisurely chiming of the wood thrushes, chanting their vespers; through the still air came the warble

2 A

of vireo and tanager; and after nightfall we heard the flight
song of an ovenbird from the same belt of timber. Overhead an oriole sang in the weeping elm, now and then breaking his song to scold like an overgrown wren. Song-spar-
rows and catbirds sang in the shrubbery; one robin had
built its nest over the front and one over the back door, and
there was a chippy's nest in the wistaria vine by the stoop.
During the next twenty-four hours I saw and heard, either
right around the house or while walking down to bathe,
through the woods, the following forty-two birds:

Little green heron, night heron, red-tailed hawk, yellow-
billed cuckoo, kingfisher, flicker, humming-bird, swift,
meadow-lark, red-winged blackbird, sharp-tailed finch, song
sparrow, chipping sparrow, bush sparrow, purple finch,
Baltimore oriole, cowbunting, robin, wood thrush, thrasher,
catbird, scarlet tanager, red-eyed vireo, yellow warbler,
black-throated green warbler, kingbird, wood peewee, crow,
blue jay, cedar-bird, Maryland yellowthroat, chickadee,
black and white creeper, barn swallow, white-breasted
swallow, ovenbird, thistlefinch, vesperfinch, indigo bunting,
towhee, grasshopper-sparrow, and screech owl.

The birds were still in full song, for on Long Island there
is little abatement in the chorus until about the second week
of July, when the blossoming of the chestnut trees patches
the woodland with frothy greenish-yellow.[1]

Our most beautiful singers are the wood thrushes; they
sing not only in the early morning but throughout the long
hot June afternoons. Sometimes they sing in the trees immediately around the house, and if the air is still we can
always hear them from among the tall trees at the foot of
the hill. The thrashers sing in the hedgerows beyond the
garden, the catbirds everywhere. The catbirds have such
an attractive song that it is extremely irritating to know that
at any moment they may interrupt it to mew and squeal.
The bold, cheery music of the robins always seems typical of
the bold, cheery birds themselves. The Baltimore orioles
nest in the young elms around the house, and the orchard

---

[1] Alas! the blight has now destroyed the chestnut trees, and robbed our
woods of one of their distinctive beauties.

orioles in the apple trees near the garden and outbuildings. Among the earliest sounds of spring is the cheerful, simple, homely song of the song-sparrow; and in March we also hear the piercing cadence of the meadow-lark — to us one of the most attractive of all bird calls. Of late years now and then we hear the rollicking, bubbling melody of the bobolink in the pastures back of the barn; and when the full chorus of these and of many other of the singers of spring is dying down, there are some true hot-weather songsters, such as the brightly hued indigo buntings and thistlefinches. Among the finches one of the most musical and plaintive songs is that of the bush-sparrow — I do not know why the books call it field-sparrow, for it does not dwell in the open fields like the vesperfinch, the savannah-sparrow, and grasshopper-sparrow, but among the cedars and bayberry bushes and young locusts in the same places where the prairie warbler is found. Nor is it only the true songs that delight us. We love to hear the flickers call, and we readily pardon any one of their number which, as occasionally happens, is bold enough to wake us in the early morning by drumming on the shingles of the roof. In our ears the red-winged black-birds have a very attractive note. We love the screaming of the red-tailed hawks as they soar high overhead, and even the calls of the night heron that nest in the tall water maples by one of the wood ponds on our place, and the little green herons that nest beside the salt marsh. It is hard to tell just how much of the attraction in any bird-note lies in the music itself and how much in the associations. This is what makes it so useless to try to compare the bird songs of one country with those of another. A man who is worth anything can no more be entirely impartial in speaking of the bird songs with which from his earliest childhood he has been familiar than he can be entirely impartial in speaking of his own family.

At Sagamore Hill we love a great many things — birds and trees and books, and all things beautiful, and horses and rifles and children and hard work and the joy of life. We have great fireplaces, and in them the logs roar and crackle during the long winter evenings. The big piazza is for the hot, still afternoons of summer. As in every house, there are things that appeal to the householder because of their

356 THEODORE ROOSEVELT — AN AUTOBIOGRAPHY

associations, but which would not mean much to others. Naturally, any man who has been President, and filled other positions, accumulates such things, with scant regard to his own personal merits. Perhaps our most cherished possessions are a Remington bronze, "The Bronco Buster," given me by my men when the regiment was mustered out, and a big Tiffany silver vase given to Mrs. Roosevelt by the enlisted men of the battleship Louisiana after we returned from a cruise on her to Panama. It was a real surprise gift, presented to her in the White House, on behalf of the whole crew, by four as strapping man-of-war's-men as ever swung a turret or pointed a twelve-inch gun. The enlisted men of the army I already knew well — of course I knew well the officers of both army and navy. But the enlisted men of the navy I only grew to know well when I was President. On the Louisiana Mrs. Roosevelt and I once dined at the chief petty officers' mess, and on another battleship, the Missouri (when I was in company with Admiral Evans and Captain Cowles), and again on the Sylph and on the Mayflower, we also dined as guests of the crew. When we finished our trip on the Louisiana I made a short speech to the assembled crew, and at its close one of the petty officers, the very picture of what a man-of-war's-man should look like, proposed three cheers for me in terms that struck me as curiously illustrative of America at her best; he said, "Now then, men, three cheers for Theodore Roosevelt, the typical American citizen!" That was the way in which they thought of the American President — and a very good way, too. It was an expression that would have come naturally only to men in whom the American principles of government and life were ingrained, just as they were ingrained in the men of my regiment. I need scarcely add, but I will add for the benefit of those who do not know, that this attitude of self-respecting identification of interest and purpose is not only compatible with but can only exist when there is fine and real discipline, as thorough and genuine as the discipline that has always obtained in the most formidable fighting fleets and armies. The discipline and the mutual respect are complementary, not antagonistic.

During the Presidency all of us, but especially the children, became close friends with many of the sailor men.   The four bearers of the vase to Mrs. Roosevelt were promptly hailed as delightful big brothers by our two smallest boys, who at once took them to see the sights of Washington in the landau — "the President's land-ho!" as, with seafaring humor, our guests immediately styled it.   Once, after we were in private life again, Mrs. Roosevelt was in a railway station and had some difficulty with her ticket. A fine-looking, quiet man stepped up and asked if he could be of help; he remarked that he had been one of the Mayflower's crew, and knew us well; and in answer to a question explained that he had left the navy in order to study dentistry, and added — a delicious touch — that while thus preparing himself to be a dentist he was earning the necessary money to go on with his

JACK AND HIS MASTER.

studies by practicing the profession of a prize-fighter, being a good man in the ring.

There are various bronzes in the house: Saint-Gaudens's "Puritan," a token from my staff officers when I was Governor; Proctor's cougar, the gift of the Tennis Cabinet — who also gave us a beautiful silver bowl, which is always lovingly pronounced to rhyme with "owl" because that was the pronunciation used at the time of the giving by the valued friend who acted as spokesman for his fellow-members, and who was himself the only non-American member of the said Cabinet.   There is a horseman by Macmonnies, and a big bronze vase by Kemys, an adaptation or development of the pottery vases of the Southwestern Indians.   Mixed with all of these are gifts from varied sources, ranging from a brazen Buddha sent me by the Dalai Lama and a wonderful psalter from the Emperor Menelik to a priceless ancient Samurai sword, coming from Japan in remembrance of the peace of Portsmouth, and a beautifully inlaid miniature suit of Japanese armor, given me by a favorite hero of mine, Admiral Togo, when he visited Sagamore Hill. There are things from European friends; a mosaic picture of Pope Leo XIII in his garden ; a huge, very handsome edition of the Nibelungenlied ; a striking miniature of John Hampden from Windsor Castle ; editions of Dante, and the campaigns of "Eugenio von Savoy" (another of my heroes, a dead hero this time) ; a Viking cup ; the state sword of a Uganda king ; the gold box in which the "freedom of the city of London" was given me ; a beautiful head of Abraham Lincoln given me by the French authorities after my speech at the Sorbonne ; and many other things from sources as diverse as the Sultan of Turkey and the Dowager Empress of China. Then there are things from home friends : a Polar bear skin from Peary ; a Sioux buffalo robe with, on it, painted by some long-dead Sioux artist, the picture story of Custer's fight ; a bronze portrait plaque of Joel Chandler Harris ; the candlestick used in sealing the Treaty of Portsmouth, sent me by Captain Cameron Winslow ; a shoe worn by Dan Patch when he paced a mile in 1.59, sent me by his owner. There is a picture of a bull moose by Carl Rungius, which seems to me as spirited an animal painting as I have ever seen. In the north room, with its tables and mantelpiece and desks and chests made of woods sent from the Philippines by army friends, or by other friends for other reasons ; with its bison and wapiti heads ; there are three paintings by Marcus Symonds — "Where Light and Shadow Meet," "The Porcelain Towers," and "The Seats of the Mighty" ; he is dead now, and he had scant recognition while he lived, yet surely he was a great imaginative artist, a wonderful colorist, and a man with a vision more wonderful still. There is one of Lungren's pictures of the Western plains ; and a picture of the Grand Canyon ; and one by a Scandinavian artist who could see the fierce picturesqueness of workaday Pittsburgh ; and sketches of the White House by Sargent and by Hopkinson Smith.

The books are everywhere. There are as many in the
north room and in the parlor — is drawing-room a more
appropriate name than parlor ? — as in the library ; the gun-
room at the top of the house, which incidentally has the
loveliest view of all, contains more books than any of the
other rooms ; and they are particularly delightful books to

THE NORTH ROOM AT SAGAMORE.

browse among, just because they have not much relevance
to one another, this being one of the reasons why they are
relegated to their present abode.   But the books have over-
flowed into all the other rooms too.
    I could not name any principle upon which the books have
been gathered.   Books are almost as individual as friends.
There is no earthly use in laying down general laws about
them.   Some meet the needs of one person, and some of

another; and each person should beware of the booklover's besetting sin, of what Mr. Edgar Allan Poe calls "the mad pride of intellectuality," taking the shape of arrogant pity for the man who does not like the same kind of books. Of course there are books which a man or woman uses as instruments of a profession — law books, medical books, cookery books, and the like.   I am not speaking of these, for they are not properly "books" at all; they come in the category of time-tables, telephone directories, and other useful agencies of civilized life.   I am speaking of books that are meant to be read.   Personally, granted that these books are decent and healthy, the one test to which I demand that they all submit is that of being interesting.   If the book is not interesting to the reader, then in all but an infinitesimal number of cases it gives scant benefit to the reader.   Of course any reader ought to cultivate his or her taste so that good books will appeal to it, and that trash won't.   But after this point has once been reached, the needs of each reader must be met in a fashion that will appeal to those needs.   Personally the books by which I have profited infinitely more than by any others have been those in which profit was a by-product of the pleasure; that is, I read them because I enjoyed them, because I liked reading them, and the profit came in as part of the enjoyment.

Of course each individual is apt to have some special tastes in which he cannot expect that any but a few friends will share.   Now, I am very proud of my big-game library.   I suppose there must be many big-game libraries in Continental Europe, and possibly in England, more extensive than mine, but I have not happened to come across any such library in this country.   Some of the originals go back to the sixteenth century, and there are copies or reproductions of the two or three most famous hunting books of the Middle Ages, such as the Duke of York's translation of Gaston Phœbus, and the queer book of the Emperor Maximilian.   It is only very occasionally that I meet any one who cares for any of these books.   On the other hand, I expect to find many friends who will turn naturally to some of the old or the new books of poetry or romance or history to which we of the household habitually turn. Let me add that ours is in no sense a collector's library. Each book was procured because some one of the family wished to read it. We could never afford to take overmuch thought for the outsides of books; we were too much interested in their insides.

Now and then I am asked as to "what books a statesman should read," and my answer is, poetry and novels — including short stories under the head of novels. I don't mean that he should read only novels and modern poetry. If he cannot also enjoy the Hebrew prophets and the Greek dramatists, he should be sorry. He ought to read interesting books on history and government, and books of science and philosophy; and really good books on these subjects are as enthralling as any fiction ever written in prose or verse. Gibbon and Macaulay, Herodotus, Thucydides and Tacitus, the Heimskringla, Froissart, Joinville and Villehardouin, Parkman and Mahan, Mommsen and Ranke — why! there are scores and scores of solid histories, the best in the world, which are as absorbing as the best of all the novels, and of as permanent value. The same thing is true of Darwin and Huxley and Carlyle and Emerson, and parts of Kant, and of volumes like Sutherland's "Growth of the Moral Instinct," or Acton's Essays and Lounsbury's studies — here again I am not trying to class books together, or measure one by another, or enumerate one in a thousand of those worth reading, but just to indicate that any man or woman of some intelligence and some cultivation can in some line or other of serious thought, scientific or historical or philosophical or economic or governmental, find any number of books which are charming to read, and which in addition give that for which his or her soul hungers. I do not for a minute mean that the statesman ought not to read a great many different books of this character, just as every one else should read them. But, in the final event, the statesman, and the publicist, and the reformer, and the agitator for new things, and the upholder of what is good in old things, all need more than anything else to know human nature, to know the needs of the human soul; and they will find this nature and these needs set forth as nowhere else by the great imaginative writers, whether of prose or of poetry.

The room for choice is so limitless that to my mind it seems absurd to try to make catalogues which shall be supposed to appeal to all the best thinkers. This is why I have no sympathy whatever with writing lists of *the* One Hundred Best Books, or *the* Five-Foot Library. It is all right for a man to amuse himself by composing *a* list of a hundred very good books; and if he is to go off for a year or so where he cannot get many books, it is an excellent thing to choose a five-foot library of particular books which in that particular year and on that particular trip he would like to read. But there is no such thing as a hundred books that are best for all men, or for the majority of men, or for one man at all times; and there is no such thing as a five-foot library which will satisfy the needs of even one particular man on dif-

THE MISTRESS OF SAGAMORE HILL.

ferent occasions extending over a number of years. Milton is best for one mood and Pope for another. Because a man likes Whitman or Browning or Lowell he should not feel himself debarred from Tennyson or Kipling or Körner or Heine or the Bard of the Dimbovitza. Tolstoy's novels are good at one time and those of Sienkiewicz at another; and he is fortunate who can relish "Salammbo" and "Tom Brown" and the "Two Admirals" and "Quentin Durward" and "Artemus Ward" and the "Ingoldsby Legends" and

" Pickwick" and "Vanity Fair." Why, there are hundreds of books like these, each one of which, if really read, really assimilated, by the person to whom it happens to appeal, will enable that person quite unconsciously to furnish himself with much ammunition which he will find of use in the battle of life.

A book must be interesting to the particular reader at that particular time. But there are tens of thousands of interesting books, and some of them are sealed to some men and some are sealed to others; and some stir the soul at some given point of a man's life and yet convey no message at other times. The reader, the booklover, must meet his own needs without paying too much attention to what his neighbors say those needs should be. He must not hypocritically pretend to like what he does not like. Yet at the same time he must avoid that most unpleasant of all the indications of puffed-up vanity which consists in treating mere individual, and perhaps unfortunate, idiosyncrasy as a matter of pride. I happen to be devoted to Macbeth, whereas I very seldom read Hamlet (though I like parts of it). Now I am humbly and sincerely conscious that this is a demerit in me and not in Hamlet; and yet it would not do me any good to pretend that I like Hamlet as much as Macbeth when, as a matter of fact, I don't. I am very fond of simple epics and of ballad poetry, from the Nibelungenlied and the Roland song through "Chevy Chase" and "Patrick Spens" and "Twa Corbies" to Scott's poems and Longfellow's "Saga of King Olaf" and "Othere." On the other hand, I don't care to read dramas as a rule; I cannot read them with enjoyment unless they appeal to me very strongly. They must almost be Æschylus or Euripides, Goethe or Molière, in order that I may not feel after finishing them a sense of virtuous pride in having achieved a task. Now I would be the first to deny that even the most delightful old English ballad should be put on a par with any one of scores of dramatic works by authors whom I have not mentioned; I know that each of these dramatists has written what is of more worth than the ballad; only, I enjoy the ballad, and I don't enjoy the drama; and therefore the ballad is better for me, and this fact is not altered by the other fact that my own short-comings are to blame in the matter.   I still read a number of Scott's novels over and over again, whereas if I finish any-thing by Miss Austen I have a feeling that duty performed is a rainbow to the soul.   But other booklovers who are very close kin to me, and whose taste I know to be better than mine, read Miss Austen all the time — and, moreover, they are very kind, and never pity me in too offensive a manner for not reading her myself.

Aside from the masters of literature, there are all kinds of books which one person will find delightful, and which he certainly ought not to surrender just because nobody else is able to find as much in the beloved volume.   There is on our book-shelves a little pre-Victorian novel or tale called "The Semi-Attached Couple."   It is told with much humor; it is a story of gentlefolk who are really gentlefolk; and to me it is altogether delightful.   But outside the members of my own family I have never met a human being who had even heard of it, and I don't suppose I ever shall meet one.   I often enjoy a story by some living author so much that I write to tell him so — or to tell her so; and at least half the time I regret my action, because it encourages the writer to believe that the public shares my views, and he then finds that the public doesn't.

Books are all very well in their way, and we love them at Sagamore Hill; but children are better than books.   Saga-more Hill is one of three neighboring houses in which small cousins spent very happy years of childhood.   In the three houses there were at one time sixteen of these small cousins, all told, and once we ranged them in order of size and took their photograph.   There are many kinds of success in life worth having.   It is exceedingly interesting and attractive to be a successful business man, or railroad man, or farmer, or a successful lawyer or doctor; or a writer, or a President, or a ranchman, or the colonel of a fighting regiment, or to kill grizzly bears and lions.   But for unflagging interest and enjoyment, a household of children, if things go reason-ably well, certainly makes all other forms of success and achievement lose their importance by comparison.   It may be true that he travels farthest who travels alone; but the goal thus reached is not worth reaching. And as for a life deliberately devoted to pleasure as an end — why, the greatest happiness is the happiness that comes as a by-product of striving to do what must be done, even though sorrow is met in the doing. There is a bit of homely philosophy, quoted by Squire Bill Widener, of Widener's Valley, Virginia, which sums up one's duty in life: "Do what you can, with what you've got, where you are."

THE SIXTEEN COUSINS.

The country is the place for children, and if not the country, a city small enough so that one can get out into the country. When our own children were little, we were for several winters in Washington, and each Sunday afternoon the whole family spent in Rock Creek Park, which was then very real country indeed. I would drag one of the children's wagons; and when the very smallest pairs of feet grew tired of trudging bravely after us, or of racing on rapturous side trips after flowers and other treasures, the owners would clamber into the wagon. One of these wagons, by the way, a gorgeous red one, had "Express" painted on it in gilt letters, and was known to the younger children as the "'spress" wagon. They evidently associated the color with the term. Once while we were at Sagamore something happened to the cherished "'spress" wagon to the distress of the children, and especially of the child who owned it. Their mother and I were just starting for a drive in the buggy, and we promised the bereaved owner that we would visit a store we knew in East Norwich, a village a few miles away, and bring back another "'spress" wagon. When we reached the store, we found to our dismay that the wagon which we had seen had been sold. We could not bear to return without the promised gift, for we knew that the brains of small persons are much puzzled when their elders seem to break promises. Fortunately, we saw in the store a delightful little bright-red chair and bright-red table, and these we brought home and handed solemnly over to the expectant recipient, explaining that as there unfortunately was not a "'spress" wagon we had brought him back a "'spress" chair and "'spress" table. It worked beautifully! The "'spress" chair and table were received with such rapture that we had to get duplicates for the other small member of the family who was the particular crony of the proprietor of the new treasures.

When their mother and I returned from a row, we would often see the children waiting for us, running like sand-spiders along the beach. They always liked to swim in company with a grown-up of buoyant temperament and inventive mind, and the float offered limitless opportunities for enjoyment while bathing. All dutiful parents know the game of "stage-coach"; each child is given a name, such as the whip, the nigh leader, the off wheeler, the old lady passenger, and, under penalty of paying a forfeit, must get up and turn round when the grown-up, who is improvising a thrilling story, mentions that particular object; and when the word "stage-coach" is mentioned, everybody has to get up and turn round. Well, we used to play stage-coach on the float while in swimming, and instead of tamely getting up and turning round, the child whose turn it was had to plunge overboard. When I mentioned "stage-coach," the water fairly foamed with vigorously kicking little legs; and then there was always a moment of interest while I counted, so as to be sure that the number of heads that came up corresponded with the number of children who had gone down.

No man or woman will ever forget the time when some child lies sick of a disease that threatens its life. Moreover, much less serious sickness is unpleasant enough at the time. Looking back, however, there are elements of comedy in certain of the less serious cases. I well remember one such instance which occurred when we were living in Washington, in a small house, with barely enough room for everybody when all the chinks were filled. Measles descended on the household. In the effort to keep the children that were well and those that were sick apart, their mother and I had to camp out in improvised fashion. When the eldest small boy was getting well, and had recovered his spirits, I slept on a sofa beside his bed — the sofa being so short that my feet projected over anyhow. One afternoon the small boy was given a toy organ by a sympathetic friend. Next morning early I was waked to find the small boy very vivacious and re-questing a story. Having drowsily told the story, I said, "Now, father's told you a story, so you amuse yourself and let father go to sleep"; to which the small boy responded most virtuously, "Yes, father will go to sleep and I'll play the organ," which he did, at a distance of two feet from my head. Later his sister, who had just come down with the measles, was put into the same room. The small boy was convalescing, and was engaged in playing on the floor with some tin ships, together with two or three pasteboard monitors and rams of my own manufacture.

BUBBLES.

368 THEODORE ROOSEVELT — AN AUTOBIOGRAPHY

He was giving a vivid rendering of Farragut at Mobile Bay, from memories of how I had told the story. My pasteboard rams and monitors were fascinating — if a naval architect may be allowed to praise his own work — and as property they were equally divided between the little girl and the small boy. The little girl looked on with alert suspicion from the bed, for she was not yet convalescent enough to be allowed down on the floor. The small boy was busily reciting the phases of the fight, which now approached its climax, and the little girl evidently suspected that her monitor was destined to play the part of victim.

Little boy. "And then they steamed bang into the monitor."

Little girl. "Brother, don't you sink my monitor!"

Little boy (without heeding, and hurrying toward the climax). "And the torpedo went at the monitor!"

Little girl. "My monitor is not to sink!"

Little boy, dramatically: "And bang the monitor sank!"

Little girl. "It didn't do any such thing. My monitor always goes to bed at seven, and it's now quarter past. My monitor was in bed and *couldn't* sink!"

When I was Assistant Secretary of the Navy, Leonard Wood and I used often to combine forces and take both families of children out to walk, and occasionally some of their playmates. Leonard Wood's son, I found, attributed the paternity of all of those not of his own family to me. Once we were taking the children across Rock Creek on a fallen tree. I was standing on the middle of the log trying to prevent any of the children from falling off, and while making a clutch at one peculiarly active and heedless child I fell off myself. As I emerged from the water I heard the little Wood boy calling frantically to the General: "Oh! oh! The father of all the children fell into the creek!" — which made me feel like an uncommonly moist patriarch.

Of course the children took much interest in the trophies I occasionally brought back from my hunts. When I started for my regiment, in '98, the stress of leaving home, which was naturally not pleasant, was somewhat lightened by the next to the youngest boy, whose ideas of what was about to happen were hazy, clasping me round the legs with a beaming smile and saying, "And is my father going to the war ? And will he bring me back a bear ?" When, some five months later, I returned, of course in my uniform, this little boy was much puzzled as to my identity, although he greeted me affably with "Good afternoon, Colonel."

Half an hour later some-body asked him, "Where's father ?" to which he re-sponded, "I don't know; but the Colonel is taking a bath."

Of course the children an-thropomorphized — if that is the proper term — their friends of the animal world. Among these friends at one period was the baker's horse, and on a very rainy day I heard the little girl, who was looking out of the window, say, with a melan-choly shake of her head, "Oh ! there's poor Kraft's horse, all soppin' wet !"

While I was in the White House the youngest boy be-came an *habitué* of a small and rather noisome animal

Copyright by E. S. Curtis.
DAISIES.

shop, and the good-natured owner would occasionally let him take pets home to play with. On one occasion I was holding a conversation with one of the leaders in Congress, Uncle Pete Hepburn, about the Railroad Rate Bill. The chil-dren were strictly trained not to interrupt business, but on this particular occasion the little boy's feelings overcame him. He had been loaned a king-snake, which, as all nature-lovers know, is not only a useful but a beautiful snake, very friendly to human beings ; and he came rushing home to show the treasure. He was holding it inside his coat,

2 B

and it contrived to wiggle partly down the sleeve. Uncle
Pete Hepburn naturally did not understand the full import
of what the little boy was saying to me as he endeavored
to wriggle out of his jacket, and kindly started to help him
— and then jumped back with alacrity as the small boy
and the snake both popped out of the jacket.

There could be no healthier and pleasanter place in which
to bring up children than in that nook of old-time America
around Sagamore Hill. Certainly I never knew small
people to have a better time or a better training for their
work in after life than the three families of cousins at Sagamore Hill. It was real country, and — speaking from the
somewhat detached point of view of the masculine parent
— I should say there was just the proper mixture of freedom and control in the management of the children. They
were never allowed to be disobedient or to shirk lessons or
work; and they were encouraged to have all the fun possible.
They often went barefoot, especially during the many hours
passed in various enthralling pursuits along and in the waters
of the bay. They swam, they tramped, they boated, they
coasted and skated in winter, they were intimate friends
with the cows, chickens, pigs, and other live stock. They
had in succession two ponies, General Grant and, when the
General's legs became such that he lay down too often and
too unexpectedly in the road, a calico pony named Algon-
quin, who is still living a life of honorable leisure in the
stable and in the pasture — where he has to be picketed,
because otherwise he chases the cows. Sedate pony Grant
used to draw the cart in which the children went driving
when they were very small, the driver being their old nurse
Mame, who had held their mother in her arms when she
was born, and who was knit to them by a tie as close as any
tie of blood. I doubt whether I ever saw Mame really
offended with them except once when, out of pure but misunderstood affection, they named a pig after her. They
loved pony Grant. Once I saw the then little boy of three
hugging pony Grant's fore legs. As he leaned over, his
broad straw hat tilted on end, and pony Grant meditatively
munched the brim; whereupon the small boy looked up

with a wail of anguish, evidently thinking the pony had decided to treat him like a radish.

The children had pets of their own, too, of course. Among them guinea pigs were the stand-bys — their highly unemotional nature fits them for companionship with adoring but over-enthusiastic young masters and mistresses. Then there were flying squirrels, and kangaroo rats, gentle and trustful, and a badger whose temper was short but whose nature was fundamentally friendly. The badger's name was Josiah; the particular little boy whose property he was used to carry him about, clasped firmly around what would have been his waist if he had had any. Inasmuch as when on the ground the badger would play energetic games of tag with the little boy and nip his bare legs, I suggested that it would be uncommonly disagreeable if he took advantage of being held in the little boy's arms to bite his face; but this suggestion was repelled with scorn as an unworthy assault on the character of Josiah. "He

JOSIAH AND HIS MASTER.

bites legs sometimes, but he never bites faces," said the little boy. We also had a young black bear whom the children christened Jonathan Edwards, partly out of compliment to their mother, who was descended from that great Puritan divine, and partly because the bear possessed a temper in which gloom and strength were combined in what the children regarded as Calvinistic proportions. As for the dogs, of course there were many, and during their lives they were intimate and valued family friends, and their deaths were household tragedies. One of them, a large yellow animal of several good breeds and valuable rather because of psychical than physical traits, was named "Susan" by his small owners, in commemoration of another retainer, a white cow; the fact that the cow and the dog were not of the same sex being treated with indifference. Much the most individual of the dogs and the one with the strongest character was Sailor Boy, a Chesapeake Bay dog. He had a masterful temper and a strong sense of both dignity and duty. He would never let the other dogs fight, and he himself never fought unless circumstances imperatively demanded it; but he was a murderous animal when he did fight. He was not only exceedingly fond of the water, as was to be expected, but passionately devoted to gunpowder in every form, for he loved firearms and fairly reveled in the Fourth of July celebrations — the latter being rather hazardous occasions, as the children strongly objected to any "safe and sane" element being injected into them, and had the normal number of close shaves with rockets, Roman candles, and firecrackers.

One of the stand-bys for enjoyment, especially in rainy weather, was the old barn. This had been built nearly a century previously, and was as delightful as only the pleasantest kind of old barn can be. It stood at the meeting-spot of three fences. A favorite amusement used to be an obstacle race when the barn was full of hay. The contestants were timed and were started successively from outside the door. They rushed inside, clambered over or burrowed through the hay, as suited them best, dropped out of a place where a loose board had come off, got over, through, or under the three fences, and raced back to the starting-point. When they were little, their respective fathers were expected also to take part in the obstacle race, and when with the advance of years the fathers finally refused to be contestants, there was a general feeling of pained regret among the children at such a decline in the sporting spirit.

Another famous place for handicap races was Cooper's Bluff, a gigantic sand-bank rising from the edge of the bay, a mile from the house. If the tide was high there was an added thrill, for some of the contestants were sure to run into the water.

As soon as the little boys learned to swim they were allowed to go off by themselves in rowboats and camp out for the night along the Sound. Sometimes I would go along so as to take the smaller children. Once a schooner was wrecked on a point half a dozen miles away. She held together well for a season or two after having been cleared of everything down to the timbers, and this gave us the

THE OBSTACLE RACE AROUND THE OLD BARN.

chance to make camping-out trips in which the girls could also be included, for we put them to sleep in the wreck, while the boys slept on the shore; squaw picnics, the children called them.

My children, when young, went to the public school near us, the little Cove School, as it is called. For nearly thirty years we have given the Christmas tree to the school. Before the gifts are distributed I am expected to make an address, which is always mercifully short, my own children having impressed upon me with frank sincerity the attitude of other children to addresses of this kind on such occasions. There are of course performances by the children themselves, while all of us parents look admiringly on, each sympathizing with his or her particular offspring in the somewhat wooden recital of "Darius Green and his Flying Machine" or "The Mountain and the Squirrel had a Quarrel." But the tree and the gifts make up for all shortcomings.

THE SMALL BOY OF THE WHITE HOUSE.

We had a sleigh for winter; but if, when there was much snow, the whole family desired to go somewhere, we would put the body of the farm wagon on runners and all bundle in together. We always liked snow at Christmas time, and the sleigh-ride down to the church on Christmas eve. One of the hymns always sung at this Christmas eve festival begins, "It's Christmas eve on the river, it's Christmas eve on the bay." All good natives of the village firmly believe that this hymn was written here, and with direct reference to Oyster Bay; although if such were the case the word "river" would have to be taken in a hyperbolic sense, as the nearest approach to a river is the village pond. I used to share this belief myself, until my faith was shaken by a Denver lady who wrote that she had sung that hymn when a child in Michigan, and that at the present time her little Denver babies also loved it, although in their case the river was not represented by even a village pond.

When we were in Washington, the children usually went with their mother to the Episcopal church, while I went to the Dutch Reformed. But if any child misbehaved itself, it was sometimes sent next Sunday to church with me, on the theory that my companionship would have a sedative effect — which it did, as I and the child walked along with rather constrained politeness, each eying the other with watchful readiness for the unexpected. On one occasion, when the child's conduct fell just short of warranting such extreme measures, his mother, as they were on the point of entering church, concluded a homily by a quotation which showed a certain haziness of memory concerning the marriage and baptismal services: "No, little boy, if this conduct continues, I shall think that you neither love, honor, nor obey me!" However, the culprit was much impressed with a sense of shortcoming as to the obligations he had undertaken; so the result was as satisfactory as if the quotation had been from the right service.

As for the education of the children, there was of course much of it that represented downright hard work and drudgery. There was also much training that came as a by-product and was perhaps almost as valuable — not as a substitute but as an addition. After their supper, the children, when little, would come trotting up to their mother's room to be read to, and it was always a surprise to me to notice the extremely varied reading which interested them, from Howard Pyle's "Robin Hood," Mary Alicia Owen's "Voodoo Tales," and Joel Chandler Harris's "Aaron in the Wild Woods," to "Lycidas" and "King John." If their mother was absent, I would try to act as vice-mother — a poor substitute, I fear — superintending the supper and reading aloud afterwards. The children did not wish me to read the books they desired their mother to read, and I usually took some such book as "Hereward the Wake," or "Guy Mannering," or "The Last of the Mohicans" or else some story about a man-eating tiger, or a man-eating lion, from one of the hunting books in my library. These latter stories were always favorites, and as the authors told them in the first person, my interested auditors grew to know them by the name of the "I" stories, and regarded them as adventures all of which happened to the same individual. When Selous, the African hunter, visited us, I had to get him to tell to the younger children two or three of the stories with which they were already familiar from my reading; and as Selous is a most graphic narrator, and always enters thoroughly into the feeling not only of himself but of the opposing lion or buffalo, my own rendering of the incidents was cast entirely into the shade.

Besides profiting by the more canonical books on education, we profited by certain essays and articles of a less orthodox type.   I wish to express my warmest gratitude for such books — not of avowedly didactic purpose — as Laura Richards's books, Josephine Dodge Daskam's "Madness of Philip," Palmer Cox's " Queer People," the melodies of Father Goose and Mother Wild Goose, Flandreau's "Mrs. White's," Myra Kelly's stories of her little East Side pupils, and Michelson's "Madigans."   It is well to take duties, and life generally, seriously.   It is also well to remember that a sense of humor is a healthy anti-scorbutic to that portentous seriousness which defeats its own purpose.

Occasionally bits of self-education proved of unexpected help to the children in later years.   Like other children, they were apt to take to bed with them treasures which they particularly esteemed.   One of the boys, just before his sixteenth birthday, went moose hunting with the family doctor, and close personal friend of the entire family, Alexander Lambert. Once night overtook them before they camped, and they had to lie down just where they were.   Next morning Dr. Lambert rather enviously congratulated the boy on the fact that stones and roots evidently did not interfere with the soundness of his sleep; to which the boy responded, " Well, Doctor, you see it isn't very long since I used to take fourteen china animals to bed with me every night ! "

As the children grew up, Sagamore Hill remained delightful for them.   There were picnics and riding parties, there were dances in the north room — sometimes fancy dress dances — and open-air plays on the green tennis court of one of the cousin's houses.   The children are no longer children now.   Most of them are men and women, working out their own fates in the big world ; some in our own land,

others across the great oceans or where the Southern Cross
blazes in the tropic nights. Some of them have children
of their own ; some are working at one thing, some at another ;
in cable ships, in business offices, in factories, in newspaper
offices, building steel
bridges, bossing
gravel trains and
steam shovels, or lay-
ing tracks and super-
intending freight
traffic. They have
had their share of ac-
cidents and escapes ;
as I write, word
comes from a far-off
land that one of
them, whom Seth
Bullock used to call
"Kim" because he
was the friend of all
mankind, while boss-
ing a dangerous but
necessary steel struc-
tural job has had two
ribs and two back
teeth broken, and is
back at work. They
have known and they
will know joy and
sorrow, triumph and
temporary defeat.

THE FIRST GRANDCHILD AT SAGAMORE HILL.

But I believe they are all the better off because of their
happy and healthy childhood.

It is impossible to win the great prizes of life without
running risks, and the greatest of all prizes are those connected with the home. No father and mother can hope to
escape sorrow and anxiety, and there are dreadful moments
when death comes very near those we love, even if for the
time being it passes by. But life is a great adventure, and

the worst of all fears is the fear of living.   There are many forms of success, many forms of triumph.   But there is no other success that in any shape or way approaches that which is open to most of the many, many men and women who have the right ideals.   These are the men and the women who see that it is the intimate and homely things that count most.   They are the men and women who have the courage to strive for the happiness which comes only with labor and effort and self-sacrifice, and only to those whose joy in life springs in part from power of work and sense of duty.

CHAPTER X

ON September 6, 1901, President McKinley was shot by an Anarchist in the city of Buffalo. I went to Buffalo at once. The President's condition seemed to be improving, and after a day or two we were told that he was practically out of danger. I then joined my family, who were in the Adirondacks, near the foot of Mount Tahawus. A day or two afterwards we took a long tramp through the forest, and in the afternoon I climbed Mount Tahawus. After reaching the top I had descended a few hundred feet to a shelf of land where there was a little lake, when I saw a guide coming out of the woods on our trail from below. I felt at once that he had bad news, and, sure enough, he handed me a telegram saying that the President's condition was much worse and that I must come to Buffalo immediately. It was late in the afternoon, and darkness had fallen by the time I reached the clubhouse where we were staying. It was some time afterwards before I could get a wagon to drive me out to the nearest railway station, North Creek, some forty or fifty miles distant. The roads were the ordinary wilderness roads and the night was dark. But we changed horses two or three times — when I say "we" I mean the driver and I, as there was no one else with us — and reached the station just at dawn, to learn from Mr. Loeb, who had a special train waiting, that the President was dead. That evening I took the oath of office, in the house of Ansley Wilcox, at Buffalo.

On three previous occasions the Vice-President had succeeded to the Presidency on the death of the President. In each case there had been a reversal of party policy, and a nearly immediate and nearly complete change in the personnel of the higher offices, especially the Cabinet. I

From a painting by John S. Sargent.   Photograph by Frances B. Johnson.

PRESIDENT ROOSEVELT.

This portrait of Theodore Roosevelt, by John S. Sargent, is at the White House.

had never felt that this was wise from any standpoint.
If a man is fit to be President, he will speedily so impress
himself in the office that the policies pursued will be his anyhow, and he will not have to bother as to whether he is
changing them or not; while as regards the offices under
him, the important thing for him is that his subordinates
shall make a success in handling their several departments.
The subordinate is sure to desire to make a success of his
department for his own sake, and if he is a fit man, whose
views on public policy are sound, and whose abilities entitle
him to his position, he will do excellently under almost any
chief with the same purposes.

I at once announced that I would continue unchanged
McKinley's policies for the honor and prosperity of the
country, and I asked all the members of the Cabinet to stay.
There were no changes made among them save as changes
were made among their successors whom I myself appointed.
I continued Mr. McKinley's policies, changing and developing them and adding new policies only as the questions
before the public changed and as the needs of the public
developed. Some of my friends shook their heads over this,
telling me that the men I retained would not be "loyal to
me," and that I would seem as if I were "a pale copy of
McKinley." I told them that I was not nervous on this
score, and that if the men I retained were loyal to their
work they would be giving me the loyalty for which I most
cared; and that if they were not, I would change them anyhow; and that as for being "a pale copy of McKinley,"
I was not primarily concerned with either following or not
following in his footsteps, but in facing the new problems
that arose; and that if I were competent I would find ample
opportunity to show my competence by my deeds without
worrying myself as to how to convince people of the fact.

For the reasons I have already given in my chapter on the
Governorship of New York, the Republican party, which in
the days of Abraham Lincoln was founded as the radical
progressive party of the Nation, had been obliged during the
last decade of the nineteenth century to uphold the interests
of popular government against a foolish and illjudged mock-

radicalism.   It remained the Nationalist as against the particularist or State's rights party, and in so far it remained absolutely sound; for little permanent good can be done by any party which worships the State's rights fetish or which fails to regard the State, like the county or the municipality, as merely a convenient unit for local self-government, while in all National matters, of importance to the whole people, the Nation is to be supreme over State, county, and town alike.   But the State's rights fetish, although still effectively used at certain times by both courts and Congress to block needed National legislation directed against the huge corporations or in the interests of workingmen, was not a prime issue at the time of which I speak.   In 1896, 1898, and 1900 the campaigns were waged on two great moral issues: (1) the imperative need of a sound and honest currency; (2) the need, after 1898, of meeting in manful and straightforward fashion the extraterritorial problems arising from the Spanish War.   On these great moral issues the Republican party was right, and the men who were opposed to it, and who claimed to be the radicals, and their allies among the sentimentalists, were utterly and hopelessly wrong.   This had, regrettably but perhaps inevitably, tended to throw the party into the hands not merely of the conservatives but of the reactionaries; of men who, sometimes for personal and improper reasons, but more often with entire sincerity and uprightness of purpose, distrusted anything that was progressive and dreaded radicalism.   These men still from force of habit applauded what Lincoln had done in the way of radical dealing with the abuses of his day; but they did not apply the spirit in which Lincoln worked to the abuses of their own day.   Both houses of Congress were controlled by these men.   Their leaders in the Senate were Messrs. Aldrich and Hale.   The Speaker of the House when I became President was Mr. Henderson, but in a little over a year he was succeeded by Mr. Cannon, who, although widely differing from Senator Aldrich in matters of detail, represented the same type of public sentiment.   There were many points on which I agreed with Mr. Cannon and Mr. Aldrich, and some points on which I agreed with Mr. Hale.

I made a resolute effort to get on with all three and with their followers, and I have no question that they made an equally resolute effort to get on with me. We succeeded in working together, although with increasing friction, for some years, I pushing forward and they hanging back. Gradually, however, I was forced to abandon the effort to persuade them to come my way, and then I achieved results only by appealing over the heads of the Senate and House leaders to the people, who were the masters of both of us. I continued in this way to get results until almost the close of my term; and the Republican party became once more the progressive and indeed the fairly radical progressive party of the Nation. When my successor was chosen, however, the leaders of the House and Senate, or most of them, felt that it was safe to come to a break with me, and the last or short session of Congress, held between the election of my successor and his inauguration four months later, saw a series of contests between the majorities in the two houses of Congress and the President,—myself,—quite as bitter as if they and I had belonged to opposite political parties. However, I held my own. I was not able to push through the legislation I desired during these four months, but I was able to prevent them doing anything I did not desire, or undoing anything that I had already succeeded in getting done.

There were, of course, many Senators and members of the lower house with whom up to the very last I continued to work in hearty accord, and with a growing understanding. I have not the space to enumerate, as I would like to, these men. For many years Senator Lodge had been my close personal and political friend, with whom I discussed all public questions, that arose, usually with agreement; and our intimately close relations were of course unchanged by my entry into the White House. He was of all our public men the man who had made the closest and wisest study of our foreign relations, and more clearly than almost any other man he understood the vital fact that the efficiency of our navy conditioned our national efficiency in foreign affairs. Anything relating to our international relations, from Panama and the navy to the Alaskan boundary question, the Algeciras negotiations, or the peace of Portsmouth, I was certain to discuss with Senator Lodge and also with certain other members of Congress, such as Senator Turner of Washington and Representative Hitt of Illinois. Anything relating to labor legislation and to measures for controlling big business or efficiently regulating the giant railway systems, I was certain to discuss with Senator Dolliver or Congressman Hepburn or Congressman Cooper. With men like Senator Beveridge, Congressman (afterwards Senator) Dixon, and Congressman Murdock, I was apt to discuss pretty nearly everything relating to either our internal or our external affairs There were many, many others. The present President of the Senate, Senator Clark, of Arkansas, was as fearless and high-minded a representative of the people of the United States as I ever dealt with. He was one of the men who combined loyalty to his own State with an equally keen loyalty to the people of all the United States. He was politically opposed to me; but when the interests of the country were at stake, he was incapable of considering party differences; and this was especially his attitude in international matters — including certain treaties which most of his party colleagues, with narrow lack of patriotism, and complete subordination of National to factional interest, opposed. I have never anywhere met finer, more faithful, more disinterested, and more loyal public servants than Senator O. H. Platt, a Republican, from Connecticut, and Senator Cockrell, a Democrat, from Missouri. They were already old men when I came to the Presidency; and doubtless there were points on which I seemed to them to be extreme and radical; but eventually they found that our motives and beliefs were the same, and they did all in their power to help any movement that was for the interest of our people as a whole. I had met them when I was Civil Service Commissioner and Assistant Secretary of the Navy. All I ever had to do with either was to convince him that a given measure I championed was right, and he then at once did all he could to have it put into effect. If I could not convince them, why ! that was my fault, or my misfortune; but if I could convince them, I never had to think again as

to whether they would or would not support me.   There
were many other men of mark in both houses with whom
I could work on some points, whereas on others we had to
differ.   There was one powerful leader — a burly, forceful
man, of admirable traits — who had, however, been trained
in the post-bellum school of business and politics, so that his
attitude towards life, quite unconsciously, reminded me a
little of Artemus Ward's view of the Tower of London —
"If I like it, I'll buy it."   There was a big governmental job
in which this leader was much interested, and in reference
to which he always wished me to consult a man whom he
trusted, whom I will call Pitt Rodney.   One day I answered
him, "The trouble with Rodney is that he misestimates
his relations to cosmos"; to which he responded, "Cosmos
— Cosmos ?   Never heard of him.   You stick to Rodney.
He's your man !"   Outside of the public servants there
were multitudes of men, in newspaper offices, in magazine
offices, in business or the professions or on farms or in shops,
who actively supported the policies for which I stood and
did work of genuine leadership which was quite as effective
as any work done by men in public office.   Without the
active support of these men I would have been powerless.
In particular, the leading newspaper correspondents at
Washington were as a whole a singularly able, trustworthy,
and public-spirited body of men, and the most useful of
all agents in the fight for efficient and decent government.

As for the men under me in executive office, I could not
overstate the debt of gratitude I owe them.   From the
heads of the departments, the Cabinet officers, down, the
most striking feature of the Administration was the devoted,
zealous, and efficient work that was done as soon as it became
understood that the one bond of interest among all of us
was the desire to make the Government the most effective
instrument in advancing the interests of the people as a
whole, the interests of the average men and women of the
United States and of their children.   I do not think I overstate the case when I say that most of the men who did the
best work under me felt that ours was a partnership, that
we all stood on the same level of purpose and service, and

2 c

386 THEODORE ROOSEVELT — AN AUTOBIOGRAPHY

that it mattered not what position any one of us held so long as in that position he gave the very best that was in him. We worked very hard; but I made a point of getting a couple of hours off each day for equally vigorous play. The men with whom I then played, whom we laughingly grew to call the "Tennis Cabinet," have been mentioned in a previous chapter of this book in connection with the gift they gave me at the last breakfast which they took at the White House. There were many others in the public service under me with whom I happened not to play, but who did their share of our common work just as effectively as it was done by us who did play. Of course nothing could have been done in my Administration if it had not been for the zeal, intelligence, masterful ability, and downright hard labor of these men in countless positions under me. I was helpless to do anything except as my thoughts and orders were translated into action by them; and, moreover, each of them, as he grew specially fit for his job, used to suggest to me the right thought to have, and the right order to give, concerning that job. It is of course hard for me to speak with cold and dispassionate partiality of these men, who were as close to me as were the men of my regiment. But the outside observers best fitted to pass judgment about them felt as I did. At the end of my Administration Mr. Bryce, the British Ambassador, told me that in a long life, during which he had studied intimately the government of many different countries, he had never in any country seen a more eager, high-minded, and efficient set of public servants, men more useful and more creditable to their country, than the men then doing the work of the American Government in Washington and in the field. I repeat this statement with the permission of Mr. Bryce.

At about the same time, or a little before, in the spring of 1908, there appeared in the English *Fortnightly Review* an article, evidently by a competent eye witness, setting forth more in detail the same views to which the British Ambassador thus privately gave expression. It was in part as follows:

"Mr. Roosevelt has gathered around him a body of public servants who are nowhere surpassed, I question whether

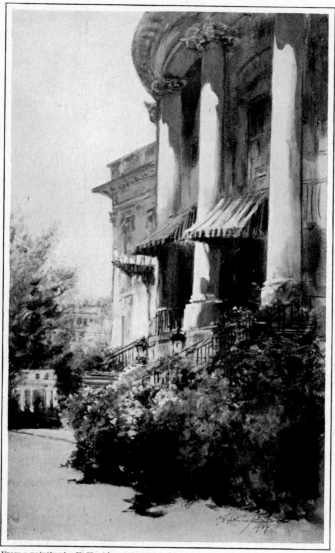

From a painting by F. Hopkinson Smith.

THE WHITE HOUSE FROM THE GARDEN.

they are anywhere equaled, for efficiency, self-sacrifice, and an absolute devotion to their country's interests. Many of them are poor men, without private means, who have voluntarily abandoned high professional ambitions and turned their backs on the rewards of business to serve their country on salaries that are not merely inadequate, but indecently so. There is not one of them who is not constantly assailed by offers of positions in the world of commerce, finance, and the law that would satisfy every material ambition with which he began life. There is not one of them who could not, if he chose, earn outside Washington from ten to twenty times the income on which he economizes as a State official. But these men are as indifferent to money and to the power that money brings as to the allurements of Newport and New York, or to merely personal distinctions, or to the commercialized ideals which the great bulk of their fellow-countrymen accept without question. They are content, and more than content, to sink themselves in the National service without a thought of private advancement, and often at a heavy sacrifice of worldly honors, and to toil on . . . sustained by their own native impulse to make of patriotism an efficient instrument of public betterment."

The American public rarely appreciate the high quality of the work done by some of our diplomats — work, usually entirely unnoticed and unrewarded, which redounds to the interest and the honor of all of us. The most useful man in the entire diplomatic service, during my presidency, and for many years before, was Henry White; and I say this having in mind the high quality of work done by such admirable ambassadors and ministers as Bacon, Meyer, Straus, O'Brien, Rockhill, and Egan, to name only a few among many. When I left the presidency White was Ambassador to France; shortly afterwards he was removed by Mr. Taft, for reasons unconnected with the good of the service.

The most important factor in getting the right spirit in my Administration, next to the insistence upon courage, honesty, and a genuine democracy of desire to serve the plain people, was my insistence upon the theory that the executive power was limited only by specific restrictions and prohibitions appearing in the Constitution or imposed by the Congress under its Constitutional powers. My view was that every executive officer, and above all every executive officer in high position, was a steward of the people bound actively and affirmatively to do all he could for the people, and not to content himself with the negative merit of keeping his talents undamaged in a napkin. I declined to adopt the view that what was imperatively necessary for the Nation could not be done by the President unless he could find some specific authorization to do it. My belief was that it was not only his right but his duty to do anything that the needs of the Nation demanded unless such action was forbidden by the Constitution or by the laws. Under this interpretation of executive power I did and caused to be done many things not previously done by the President and the heads of the departments. I did not usurp power, but I did greatly broaden the use of executive power. In other words, I acted for the public welfare, I acted for the common well-being of all our people, whenever and in whatever manner was necessary, unless prevented by direct constitutional or legislative prohibition. I did not care a rap for the mere form and show of power; I cared immensely for the use that could be made of the substance. The Senate at one time objected to my communicating with them in printing, preferring the expensive, foolish, and laborious practice of writing out the messages by hand. It was not possible to return to the outworn archaism of hand writing; but we endeavored to have the printing made as pretty as possible. Whether I communicated with the Congress in writing or by word of mouth, and whether the writing was by a machine, or a pen, were equally, and absolutely, unimportant matters. The importance lay in what I said and in the heed paid to what I said. So as to my meeting and consulting Senators, Congressmen, politicians, financiers, and labor men. I consulted all who wished to see me; and if I wished to see any one, I sent for him; and where the consultation took place was a matter of supreme unimportance. I consulted every man with the sincere hope that I could profit by and follow his advice; I consulted every member of Congress who wished to be consulted, hoping to be able to come to an agreement of action with him; and I always finally acted as my conscience and common sense bade me act.

About appointments I was obliged by the Constitution to consult the Senate; and the long-established custom of the Senate meant that in practice this consultation was with individual Senators and even with big politicians who stood behind the Senators. I was only one-half the appointing power; I nominated; but the Senate confirmed. In practice, by what was called "the courtesy of the Senate," the Senate normally refused to confirm any appointment if the Senator from the State objected to it. In exceptional cases, where I could arouse public attention, I could force through the appointment in spite of the opposition of the Senators; in all ordinary cases this was impossible. On the other hand, the Senator could of course do nothing for any man unless I chose to nominate him. In consequence the Constitution itself forced the President and the Senators from each State to come to a working agreement on the appointments in and from that State.

My course was to insist on absolute fitness, including honesty, as a prerequisite to every appointment; and to remove only for good cause, and, where there was such cause, to refuse even to discuss with the Senator in interest the unfit servant's retention. Subject to these considerations, I normally accepted each Senator's recommendations for offices of a routine kind, such as most post-offices and the like, but insisted on myself choosing the men for the more important positions. I was willing to take any good man for postmaster; but in the case of a Judge or District Attorney or Canal Commissioner or Ambassador, I was apt to insist either on a given man or else on any man with a given class of qualifications. If the Senator deceived me, I took care that he had no opportunity to repeat the deception.

I can perhaps best illustrate my theory of action by two specific examples. In New York Governor Odell and Senator Platt sometimes worked in agreement and sometimes were at swords' points, and both wished to be con-

sulted. To a friendly Congressman, who was also their
friend, I wrote as follows on July 22, 1903 :
"I want to work with Platt. I want to work with Odell.
I want to support both and take the advice of both. But
of course ultimately I must be the judge as to acting on the
advice given. When, as in the case of the judgeship, I
am convinced that the advice of both is wrong, I shall act
as I did when I appointed Holt. When I can find a friend
of Odell's like Cooley, who is thoroughly fit for the position
I desire to fill, it gives me the greatest pleasure to appoint
him. When Platt proposes to me a man like Hamilton
Fish, it is equally a pleasure to appoint him."

This was written in connection with events which led
up to my refusing to accept Senator Platt's or Governor
Odell's sugestions as to a Federal Judgeship and a Federal
District Attorneyship, and insisting on the appointment,
first of Judge Hough and later of District Attorney Stimson ;
because in each case I felt that the work to be done was of so
high an order that I could not take an ordinary man.

The other case was that of Senator Fulton, of Oregon.
Through Francis Heney I was prosecuting men who were
implicated in a vast network of conspiracy against the law
in connection with the theft of public land in Oregon. I
had been acting on Senator Fulton's recommendations for
office, in the usual manner. Heney had been insisting that
Fulton was in league with the men we were prosecuting,
and that he had recommended unfit men. Fulton had been
protesting against my following Heney's advice, particularly
as regards appointing Judge Wolverton as United States
Judge. Finally Heney laid before me a report which convinced me of the truth of his statements. I then wrote to
Fulton as follows, on November 20, 1905 : "My dear
Senator Fulton : I inclose you herewith a copy of the
report made to me by Mr. Heney. I have seen the originals
of the letters from you and Senator Mitchell quoted therein.
I do not at this time desire to discuss the report itself, which
of course I must submit to the Attorney-General. But
I have been obliged to reach the painful conclusion that your
own letters as therein quoted tend to show that you recom-

mended for the position of District Attorney B when you
had good reason to believe that he had himself been guilty

Copyright by Frances B. Johnston.   From a painting by Theobald Chartran.

MRS. THEODORE ROOSEVELT.

of fraudulent conduct; that you recommended C for the
same position simply because it was for B's interest that he

should be so recommended, and, as there is reason to believe, because he had agreed to divide the fees with B if he were appointed; and that you finally recommended the reappointment of H with the knowledge that if H were appointed he would abstain from prosecuting B for criminal misconduct, this being why B advocated H's claims for reappointment. If you care to make any statement in the matter, I shall of course be glad to hear it. As the District Judge of Oregon I shall appoint Judge Wolverton." In the letter I of course gave in full the names indicated above by initials. Senator Fulton gave no explanation. I therefore ceased to consult him about appointments under the Department of Justice and the Interior, the two departments in which the crookedness had occurred — there was no question of crookedness in the other offices in the State, and they could be handled in the ordinary manner. Legal proceedings were undertaken against his colleague in the Senate, and one of his colleagues in the lower house, and the former was convicted and sentenced to the penitentiary.

In a number of instances the legality of executive acts of my Administration was brought before the courts. They were uniformly sustained. For example, prior to 1907 statutes relating to the disposition of coal lands had been construed as fixing the flat price at $10 to $20 per acre. The result was that valuable coal lands were sold for wholly inadequate prices, chiefly to big corporations. By executive order the coal lands were withdrawn and not opened for entry until proper classification was placed thereon by Government agents. There was a great clamor that I was usurping legislative power; but the acts were not assailed in court until we brought suits to set aside entries made by persons and associations to obtain larger areas than the statutes authorized. This position was opposed on the ground that the restrictions imposed were illegal; that the executive orders were illegal. The Supreme Court sustained the Government. In the same way our attitude in the water power question was sustained, the Supreme Court holding that the Federal Government had the rights we claimed over streams that are or may be declared navigable by Congress.

Again, when Oklahoma became a State we were obliged to use the executive power to protect Indian rights and property, for there had been an enormous amount of fraud in the obtaining of Indian lands by white men. Here we were denounced as usurping power over a State as well as usurping power that did not belong to the executive. The Supreme Court sustained our action.

In connection with the Indians, by the way, it was again and again necessary to assert the position of the President as steward of the whole people. I had a capital Indian Commissioner, Francis E. Leupp. I found that I could rely on his judgment not to get me into fights that were unnecessary, and therefore I always backed him to the limit when he told me that a fight was necessary. On one occasion, for example, Congress passed a bill to sell to settlers about half a million acres of Indian land in Oklahoma at one and a half dollars an acre. I refused to sign it, and turned the matter over to Leupp. The bill was accordingly withdrawn, amended so as to safeguard the welfare of the Indians, and the minimum price raised to five dollars an acre. Then I signed the bill. We sold that land under sealed bids, and realized for the Kiowa, Comanche, and Apache Indians more than four million dollars — three millions and a quarter more than they would have obtained if I had signed the bill in its original form. In another case, where there had been a division among the Sac and Fox Indians, part of the tribe removing to Iowa, the Iowa delegation in Congress, backed by two Iowans who were members of my Cabinet, passed a bill awarding a sum of nearly a half million dollars to the Iowa seceders. They had not consulted the Indian Bureau. Leupp protested against the bill, and I vetoed it. A subsequent bill was passed on the lines laid down by the Indian Bureau, referring the whole controversy to the courts, and the Supreme Court in the end justified our position by deciding against the Iowa seceders and awarding the money to the Oklahoma stay-at-homes.

As to all action of this kind there have long been two schools of political thought, upheld with equal sincerity. The division has not normally been along political, but temperamental, lines. The course I followed, of regarding the executive as subject only to the people, and, under the Constitution, bound to serve the people affirmatively in cases where the Constitution does not explicitly forbid him to render the service, was substantially the course followed by both Andrew Jackson and Abraham Lincoln. Other honorable and well-meaning Presidents, such as James Buchanan, took the opposite and, as it seems to me, narrowly legalistic view that the President is the servant of Congress rather than of the people, and can do nothing, no matter how necessary it be to act, unless the Constitution explicitly commands the action. Most able lawyers who are past middle age take this view, and so do large numbers of well-meaning, respectable citizens. My successor in office took this, the Buchanan, view of the President's powers and duties.

For example, under my Administration we found that one of the favorite methods adopted by the men desirous of stealing the public domain was to carry the decision of the Secretary of the Interior into court. By vigorously opposing such action, and only by so doing, we were able to carry out the policy of properly protecting the public domain. My successor not only took the opposite view, but recommended to Congress the passage of a bill which would have given the courts direct appellate power over the Secretary of the Interior in these land matters. This bill was reported favorably by Mr. Mondell, Chairman of the House Committee on public lands, a Congressman who took the lead in every measure to prevent the conservation of our natural resources and the preservation of the National domain for the use of home-seekers. Fortunately, Congress declined to pass the bill. Its passage would have been a veritable calamity.

I acted on the theory that the President could at any time in his discretion withdraw from entry any of the public lands of the United States and reserve the same for forestry, for water-power sites, for irrigation, and other public purposes. Without such action it would have been impossible to stop the activity of the land thieves. No one ventured to test its legality by lawsuit. My successor, however, himself questioned it, and referred the matter to Congress. Again Congress showed its wisdom by passing a law which gave the President the power which he had long exercised, and of which my successor had shorn himself.

Perhaps the sharp difference between what may be called the Lincoln-Jackson and the Buchanan-Taft schools, in their views of the power and duties of the President, may be best illustrated by comparing the attitude of my successor toward his Secretary of the Interior, Mr. Ballinger, when the latter was accused of gross misconduct in office, with my attitude towards my chiefs of department and other subordinate officers. More than once while I was President my officials were attacked by Congress, generally because these officials did their duty well and fearlessly. In every such case I stood by the official and refused to recognize the right of Congress to interfere with me excepting by impeachment or in other Constitutional manner. On the other hand, wherever I found the officer unfit for his position I promptly removed him, even although the most influential men in Congress fought for his retention. The Jackson-Lincoln view is that a President who is fit to do good work should be able to form his own judgment as to his own subordinates, and, above all, of the subordinates standing highest and in closest and most intimate touch with him. My secretaries and their subordinates were responsible to me, and I accepted the responsibility for all their deeds. As long as they were satisfactory to me I stood by them against every critic or assailant, within or without Congress; and as for getting Congress to make up my mind for me about them, the thought would have been inconceivable to me. My successor took the opposite, or Buchanan, view when he permitted and requested Congress to pass judgment on the charges made against Mr. Ballinger as an executive officer. These charges were made to the President; the President had the facts before him and could get at them at any time, and he alone had power to act if the charges were true. However, he permitted and requested Congress to investigate Mr. Ballinger. The party minority of the committee that investigated him, and one member of the majority, declared that the charges were well founded and that Mr. Ballinger should be removed. The other members of the majority declared the charges ill founded. The President abode by the view of the majority. Of course believers in the Jackson-Lincoln theory of the Presidency would not be content with this town meeting majority and minority method of determining by another branch of the Government what it seems the especial duty of the President himself to determine for himself in dealing with his own subordinate in his own department.

There are many worthy people who reprobate the Buchanan method as a matter of history, but who in actual life reprobate still more strongly the Jackson-Lincoln method when it is put into practice. These persons conscientiously believe that the President should solve every doubt in favor of inaction as against action, that he should construe strictly and narrowly the Constitutional grant of powers both to the National Government, and to the President within the National Government. In addition, however, to the men who conscientiously believe in this course from high, although as I hold misguided, motives, there are many men who affect to believe in it merely because it enables them to attack and to try to hamper, for partisan or personal reasons, an executive whom they dislike. There are other men in whom, especially when they are themselves in office, practical adherence to the Buchanan principle represents not well-thought-out devotion to an unwise course, but simple weakness of character and desire to avoid trouble and responsibility. Unfortunately, in practice it makes little difference which class of ideas actuates the President, who by his action sets a cramping precedent. Whether he is highminded and wrongheaded or merely infirm of purpose, whether he means well feebly or is bound by a mischievous misconception of the powers and duties of the National Government and of the President, the effect of his actions is the same. The President's duty is to act so that he himself and his subordinates shall be able to do efficient work for the people, and this efficient work he and they cannot do if Congress is permitted to undertake the

The Rough Rider

With Mr. Punch's best wishes to Colonel Roosevelt, President of the United States.

Reproduced by permission of the proprietors of *Punch*.   Cartoon by Bernard Partridge.

THE ROUGH RIDER.

With Mr. Punch's best wishes to Colonel Roosevelt, President of the United States.

Punch's congratulations when Colonel Roosevelt became President.

task of making up his mind for him as to how he shall per-
from what is clearly his sole duty

One of the ways in which by independent action of the
executive we were able to accomplish an immense amount of
work for the public was through volunteer unpaid commissions appointed by the President. It was possible to
get the work done by these volunteer commissions only
because of the enthusiasm for the public service which,
starting in the higher offices at Washington, made itself
felt throughout the Government departments — as I have
said, I never knew harder and more disinterested work
done by any people than was done by the men and women
of all ranks in the Government service. The contrast
was really extraordinary between their live interest in their
work and the traditional clerical apathy which has so often
been the distinguishing note of governmental work in Washington. Most of the public service performed by these
volunteer commissions, carried on without a cent of pay to
the men themselves, and wholly without cost to the Government, was done by men the great majority of whom were
already in the Government service and already charged
with responsibilities amounting each to a full man's job.

The first of these Commissions was the Commission on
the Organization of Government Scientific Work, whose
Chairman was Charles D. Walcott. Appointed March 13,
1903, its duty was to report directly to the President "upon
the organization, present condition, and needs of the Executive Government work wholly or partly scientific in character, and upon the steps which should be taken, if any,
to prevent the duplication of such work, to co-ordinate its
various branches, to increase its efficiency and economy,
and to promote its usefulness to the Nation at large."
This Commission spent four months in an examination
which covered the work of about thirty of the larger scientific and executive bureaus of the Government, and prepared a report which furnished the basis for numerous
improvements in the Government service.

Another Commission, appointed June 2, 1905, was that
on Department Methods — Charles H. Keep, Chairman

— whose task was to "find out what changes are needed to place the conduct of the executive business of the Government in all its branches on the most economical and effective basis in the light of the best modern business practice." The letter appointing this Commission laid down nine principles of effective Governmental work, the most striking of which was: "The existence of any method, standard, custom, or practice is no reason for its continuance when a better is offered." This Commission, composed like that just described, of men already charged with important work, performed its functions wholly without cost to the Government. It was assisted by a body of about seventy experts in the Government departments chosen for their special qualifications to carry forward a study of the best methods in business, and organized into assistant committees under the leadership of Overton W. Price, Secretary of the Commission. These assistant committees, all of whose members were still carrying on their regular work, made their reports during the last half of 1906. The Committee informed itself fully regarding the business methods of practically every individual branch of the business of the Government, and effected a marked improvement in general efficiency throughout the service. The conduct of the routine business of the Government had never been thoroughly overhauled before, and this examination of it resulted in the promulgation of a set of working principles for the transaction of public business which are as sound to-day as they were when the Committee finished its work. The somewhat elaborate and costly investigations of Government business methods since made have served merely to confirm the findings of the Committee on Departmental Methods, which were achieved without costing the Government a dollar. The actual saving in the conduct of the business of the Government through the better methods thus introduced amounted yearly to many hundreds of thousands of dollars; but a far more important gain was due to the remarkable success of the Commission in establishing a new point of view in public servants toward their work. The need for improvement in the Governmental methods of transacting business may be illustrated by an actual case. An officer in charge of an Indian agency made a requisition in the autumn for a stove costing seven dollars, certifying at the same time that it was needed to keep the infirmary warm during the winter, because the old stove was worn out. Thereupon the customary papers went through the customary routine, without unusual delay at any point. The transaction moved like a glacier with dignity to its appointed end, and the stove reached the infirmary in good order in time for the Indian agent to acknowledge its arrival in these words: "The stove is here. So is spring."

The Civil Service Commission, under men like John McIlhenny and Garfield, rendered service without which the Government could have been conducted with neither efficiency nor honesty. The politicians were not the only persons at fault; almost as much improper pressure for appointments is due to mere misplaced sympathy, and to the spiritless inefficiency which seeks a Government office as a haven for the incompetent. An amusing feature of office seeking is that each man desiring an office is apt to look down on all others with the same object as forming an objectionable class with which *he* has nothing in common. At the time of the eruption of Mt. Pelée, when among others the American Consul was killed, a man who had long been seeking an appointment promptly applied for the vacancy. He was a good man, of persistent nature, who felt I had been somewhat blind to his merits. The morning after the catastrophe he wrote, saying that as the consul was dead he would like his place, and that I could surely give it to him, because "even the office seekers could not have applied for it yet!"

The method of public service involved in the appointment and the work of the two commissions just described was applied also in the establishment of four other commissions, each of which performed its task without salary or expense for its members, and wholly without cost to the Government. The other four commissions were:

Commission on Public Lands;
Commission on Inland Waterways;

2 D

Commission on Country Life; and
Commission on National Conservation.

All of these commissions were suggested to me by Gifford Pinchot, who served upon them all. The work of the last four will be touched upon in connection with the chapter on Conservation. These commissions by their reports and findings directly interfered with many place-holders who were doing inefficient work, and their reports and the action taken thereon by the Administration strengthened the hands of those administrative officers who in the various departments, and especially in the Secret Service, were proceeding against land thieves and other corrupt wrong-doers. Moreover, the mere fact that they did efficient work for the public along lines new to veteran and cynical politicians of the old type created vehement hostility to them. Senators like Mr. Hale and Congressmen like Mr. Tawney were especially bitter against these commissions; and towards the end of my term they were followed by the majority of their fellows in both houses, who had gradually been sundered from me by the open or covert hostility of the financial or Wall Street leaders, and of the newspaper editors and politicians who did their bidding in the interest of privilege. These Senators and Congressmen asserted that they had a right to forbid the President profiting by the unpaid advice of disinterested experts. Of course I declined to admit the existence of any such right, and continued the Commissions. My successor acknowledged the right, upheld the view of the politicians in question, and abandoned the commissions, to the lasting detriment of the people as a whole.

One thing is worth pointing out: During the seven and a half years of my Administration we greatly and usefully extended the sphere of Governmental action, and yet we reduced the burden of the taxpayers; for we reduced the interest-bearing debt by more than $90,000,000. To achieve a marked increase in efficiency and at the same time an increase in economy is not an easy feat; but we performed it.

There was one ugly and very necessary task. This was

to discover and root out corruption wherever it was found in any of the departments. The first essential was to make it clearly understood that no political or business or social influence of any kind would for one moment be even considered when the honesty of a public official was at issue. It took a little time to get this fact thoroughly drilled into the heads both of the men within the service and of the political leaders without. The feat was accomplished so thoroughly that every effort to interfere in any shape or way with the course of justice was abandoned definitely and for good. Most, although not all, of the frauds occurred in connection with the Post-Office Department and the Land Office.

It was in the Post-Office Department that we first definitely established the rule of conduct which became universal throughout the whole service. Rumors of corruption in the department became rife, and finally I spoke of them to the then First Assistant Postmaster-General, afterwards Postmaster-General, Robert J. Wynne. He reported to me, after some investigation, that in his belief there was doubtless corruption, but that it was very difficult to get at it, and that the offenders were confident and defiant because of their great political and business backing and the ramifications of their crimes. Talking the matter over with him, I came to the conclusion that the right man to carry on the investigation was the then Fourth Assistant Postmaster-General, now a Senator from Kansas, Joseph L. Bristow, who possessed the iron fearlessness needful to front such a situation. Mr. Bristow had perforce seen a good deal of the seamy side of politics, and of the extent of the unscrupulousness with which powerful influence was brought to bear to shield offenders. Before undertaking the investigation he came to see me, and said that he did not wish to go into it unless he could be assured that I would stand personally behind him, and, no matter where his inquiries led him, would support him and prevent interference with him. I answered that I would certainly do so. He went into the investigation with relentless energy, dogged courage, and keen intelligence. His success was

complete, and the extent of his services to the Nation are
not easily to be exaggerated. He unearthed a really appalling amount of corruption, and he did his work with such
absolute thoroughness that the corruption was completely
eradicated.

We had, of course, the experience usual in all such investigations. At first there was popular incredulity and disbelief
that there was much behind the charges, or that much
could be unearthed. Then when the corruption was shown
there followed a yell of anger from all directions, and a
period during which any man accused was forthwith held
guilty by the public; and violent demands were made by
the newspapers for the prosecution not only of the men who
could be prosecuted with a fair chance of securing conviction
and imprisonment, but of other men whose misconduct had
been such as to warrant my removing them from office,
but against whom it was not possible to get the kind of
evidence which would render likely conviction in a criminal
case. Suits were brought against all the officials whom we
thought we could convict; and the public complained bitterly
that we did not bring further suits. We secured several
convictions, including convictions of the most notable
offenders. The trials consumed a good deal of time. Public attention was attracted to something else. Indifference
succeeded to excitement, and in some subtle way the juries
seemed to respond to the indifference. One of the worst
offenders was acquitted by a jury; whereupon not a few of
the same men who had insisted that the Government was
derelict in not criminally prosecuting every man whose misconduct was established so as to make it necessary to turn
him out of office, now turned round and, inasmuch as the
jury had not found this man guilty of crime, demanded
that he should be reinstated in office! It is needless to
say that the demand was not granted. There were two or
three other acquittals, of prominent outsiders. Nevertheless the net result was that the majority of the worst offenders were sent to prison, and the remainder dismissed from
the Government service, if they were public officials, and if
they were not public officials at least so advertised as to

render it impossible that they should ever again have dealings with the Government. The department was absolutely cleaned and became one of the very best in the Government. Several Senators came to me — Mr. Garfield was present on the occasion — and said that they were glad I was putting a stop to corruption, but they hoped I would avoid all scandal; that if I would make an example of some one man and then let the others quietly resign, it would avoid a disturbance which might hurt the party. They were advising me in good faith, and I was as courteous as possible in my answer, but explained that I would have to act with the utmost rigor against the offenders, no matter what the effect on the party, and, moreover, that I did not believe it would hurt the party. It did not hurt the party. It helped the party. A favorite war-cry in American political life has always been, "Turn the rascals out." We made it evident that, as far as we were concerned, this war-cry was pointless; for we turned our own rascals out.

There were important and successful land fraud prosecutions in several Western States. Probably the most important were the cases prosecuted in Oregon by Francis J. Heney, with the assistance of William J. Burns, a secret service agent who at that time began his career as a great detective. It would be impossible to overstate the services rendered to the cause of decency and honesty by Messrs. Heney and Burns. Mr. Heney was my close and intimate adviser professionally and non-professionally, not only as regards putting a stop to frauds in the public lands, but in many other matters of vital interest to the Republic. No man in the country has waged the battle for National honesty with greater courage and success, with more wholehearted devotion to the public good; and no man has been more traduced and maligned by the wrong-doing agents and representatives of the great sinister forces of evil. He secured the conviction of various men of high political and financial standing in connection with the Oregon prosecutions; he and Burns behaved with scrupulous fairness and propriety; but their services to the public caused them to incur the bitter hatred of those who had wronged the pub-

lic, and after I left office the National Administration turned
against them.   One of the most conspicuous of the men
whom they had succeeded in convicting was pardoned by
President Taft — in spite of the fact that the presiding
Judge, Judge Hunt, had held that the evidence amply
warranted the conviction, and had sentenced the man to
imprisonment.   As was natural, the one hundred and forty-
six land-fraud defendants in Oregon, who included the foremost machine political leaders in the State, furnished the
backbone of the opposition to me in the Presidential contest
of 1912.   The opposition rallied behind Messrs. Taft and
LaFollette ; and although I carried the primaries handsomely,
half of the delegates elected from Oregon under instructions
to vote for me, sided with my opponents in the National
Convention — and as regards some of them I became convinced that the mainspring of their motive lay in the intrigue
for securing the pardon of certain of the men whose conviction Heney had secured.

Land fraud and post-office cases were not the only ones.
We were especially zealous in prosecuting all of the "higher
up" offenders in the realms of politics and finance who
swindled on a large scale.   Special assistants of the Attorney-General, such as Mr. Frank Kellogg, of St. Paul, and
various first-class Federal district attorneys in different
parts of the country secured notable results :   Mr. Stimson
and his assistants, Messrs. Wise, Denison, and Frankfurter, in New York, for instance, in connection with the
prosecution of the Sugar Trust and of the banker Morse,
and of a great metropolitan newspaper for opening its
columns to obscene and immoral advertisements ; and in
St. Louis Messrs. Dyer and Nortoni, who, among other
services, secured the conviction and imprisonment of Senator
Burton, of Kansas ; and in Chicago Mr. Sims, who raised
his office to the highest pitch of efficiency, secured the conviction of the banker Walsh and of the Beef Trust, and first
broke through the armor of the Standard Oil Trust.   It is
not too much to say that these men, and others like them,
worked a complete revolution in the enforcement of the
Federal laws, and made their offices organized legal machines

fit and ready to conduct smashing fights for the people's rights and to enforce the laws in aggressive fashion. When I took the Presidency, it was a common and bitter saying that a big man, a rich man, could not be put in jail. We put many big and rich men in jail; two United States Senators, for instance, and among others two great bankers, one in New York and one in Chicago. One of the United States Senators died, the other served his term. (One of the bankers was released from prison by executive order after I left office.) These were merely individual cases among many others like them. Moreover, we were just as relentless in dealing with crimes of violence among the disorderly and brutal classes as in dealing with the crimes of cunning and fraud of which certain wealthy men and big politicians were guilty. Mr. Sims in Chicago was particularly efficient in sending to the penitentiary numbers of the infamous men who batten on the "white slave" traffic, after July, 1908, when by proclamation I announced the adherence of our Government to the international agreement for the suppression of the traffic.

The views I then held and now hold were expressed in a memorandum made in the case of a Negro convicted of the rape of a young Negro girl, practically a child. A petition for his pardon had been sent me.

WHITE HOUSE, WASHINGTON, D. C.,
August 8, 1904.

The application for the commutation of sentence of John W. Burley is denied. This man committed the most hideous crime known to our laws, and twice before he has committed crimes of a similar, though less horrible, character. In my judgment there is no justification whatever for paying heed to the allegations that he is not of sound mind, allegations made after the trial and conviction. Nobody would pretend that there has ever been any such degree of mental unsoundness shown as would make people even consider sending him to an asylum if he had not committed this crime. Under such circumstances he should certainly be esteemed sane enough to suffer the penalty for his monstrous deed. I have scant sympathy with the plea of insanity advanced to save a man from the consequences of crime, when unless that crime had been committed it would have been impossible to persuade any responsible authority to commit him to an asylum as insane. Among the most dangerous criminals, and especially among those prone to commit this particular kind of offense, there are plenty of a temper so fiendish or so brutal as to be incompatible with any other than a brutish order of intelligence; but these men are nevertheless responsible for their acts; and nothing more tends to encourage crime among such men than the belief that through the plea of insanity or any other method it is possible for them to escape paying the just penalty of their crimes. The crime in question is one to the existence of which we largely owe the existence of that spirit of lawlessness which takes form in lynching. It is a crime so revolting that the criminal is not entitled to one particle of sympathy from any human being. It is essential that the punishment for it should be not only as certain but as swift as possible. The jury in this case did their duty by recommending the infliction of the death penalty. It is to be regretted that we do not have special provision for more summary dealing with this type of cases. The more we do what in us lies to secure certain and swift justice in dealing with these cases, the more effectively do we work against the growth of that lynching spirit which is so full of evil omen for this people, because it seeks to avenge one infamous crime by the commission of another of equal infamy.

The application is denied and the sentence will be carried into effect.

(Signed) THEODORE ROOSEVELT.

One of the most curious incidents of lawlessness with which I had to deal affected an entire State. The State of Nevada in the year 1907 was gradually drifting into utter governmental impotence and downright anarchy. The people were at heart all right; but the forces of evil had been permitted to get the upper hand, and for the time being the decent citizens had become helpless to assert themselves either by controlling the greedy corporations on the one hand or repressing the murderous violence of certain lawless labor organizations on the other hand. The Governor of the State was a Democrat and a Southern man, and in the abstract a strong believer in the doctrine of State's Rights. But his experience finally convinced him that he could obtain order only through the intervention of the National Government; and then he went over too far and wished to have the National Government do his police work for him. In the Rocky Mountain States there had existed for years what was practically a condition of almost constant war between the wealthy mine-owners and the Western Federation of Miners, at whose head stood Messrs. Haywood, Pettibone, and Moyer, who were about that time indicted for the murder of the Governor of Idaho. Much that was lawless, much that was indefensible, had been done by both sides. The Legislature of Nevada was in sympathy with, or at least was afraid of not expressing sympathy for, Messrs. Moyer, Haywood, Pettibone, and their associates. The State was practically without any police, and the Governor had recommended the establishment of a State Constabulary, along the lines of the Texas Rangers; but the Legislature rejected his request. The Governor reported to me the conditions as follows. During 1907 the Goldfield mining district became divided into two hostile camps. Half of the Western Federation of Miners were constantly armed, and arms and ammunition were purchased and kept by the union as a body, while the mine-owners on their side retained large numbers of watchmen and guards who were also armed and always on duty. In addition to these opposing forces there was, as the Governor reported, an unusually large number of the violent and criminal element, always attracted to a new and booming mining camp. Under such conditions the civil authorities were practically powerless, and the Governor, being helpless to avert civil war, called on me to keep order. I accordingly threw in a body of regular troops under General Funston. These

Cartoon by Bernard Partridge.

THE SOAP-AND-WATER CURE.

President Roosevelt : "As I recently remarked at Nashville, Tenn. : 'During the next sixteen months of my term of office this policy shall be persevered in unswervingly.'"

AMERICAN EAGLE : "JE-HOSAPHAT!"

kept order completely, and the Governor became so well satisfied that he thought he would like to have them there permanently! This seemed to me unhealthy, and on December 28, 1907, I notified him that while I would do my duty, the first need was that the State authorities should do theirs, and that the first step towards this was the assembling of the Legislature. I concluded my telegram: "If within five days from receipt of this telegram you shall have issued the necessary notice to convene the Legislature of Nevada, I shall continue the troops during a period of three weeks. If when the term of five days has elapsed the notice has not been issued, the troops will be immediately returned to their former stations." I had already investigated the situation through a committee, composed of the Chief of the Bureau of Corporations, Mr. H. K. Smith, the Chief of the Bureau of Labor, Mr. C. P. Neill, and the Comptroller of the Treasury, Mr. Lawrence Murray. These men I could thoroughly trust, and their report, which was not over-favorable to either side, had convinced me that the only permanent way to get good results was to insist on the people of the State themselves grappling with and solving their own troubles. The Governor summoned the Legislature, it met, and the constabulary bill was passed. The troops remained in Nevada until time had been given for the State authorities to organize their force so that violence could at once be checked. Then they were withdrawn.

Nor was it only as regards their own internal affairs that I sometimes had to get into active communication with the State authorities. There has always been a strong feeling in California against the immigration of Asiatic laborers, whether these are wage-workers or men who occupy and till the soil. I believe this to be fundamentally a sound and proper attitude, an attitude which must be insisted upon, and yet which can be insisted upon in such a manner and with such courtesy and such sense of mutual fairness and reciprocal obligation and respect as not to give any just cause of offense to Asiatic peoples. In the present state of the world's progress it is highly inadvisable that peoples in wholly different stages of civilization, or of wholly different types of civilization even although both equally high, shall be thrown into intimate contact. This is especially undesirable when there is a difference of both race and standard of living. In California the question became acute in connection with the admission of the Japanese. I then had and now have a hearty admiration for the Japanese people. I believe in them; I respect their great qualities; I wish that our American people had many of these qualities. Japanese and American students, travelers, scientific and literary men, merchants engaged in international trade, and the like can meet on terms of entire equality and should be given the freest access each to the country of the other. But the Japanese themselves would not tolerate the intrusion into their country of a mass of Americans who would displace Japanese in the business of the land. I think they are entirely right in this position. I would be the first to admit that Japan has the absolute right to declare on what terms foreigners shall be admitted to work in her country, or to own land in her country, or to become citizens of her country. America has and must insist upon the same right. The people of California were right in insisting that the Japanese should not come thither in mass, that there should be no influx of laborers, of agricultural workers, or small tradesmen — in short, no mass settlement or immigration.

Unfortunately, during the latter part of my term as President certain unwise and demagogic agitators in California, to show their disapproval of the Japanese coming into the State, adopted the very foolish procedure of trying to provide by law that the Japanese children should not be allowed to attend the schools with the white children, and offensive and injurious language was used in connection with the proposal. The Federal Administration promptly took up the matter with the California authorities, and I got into personal touch with them. At my request the Mayor of San Francisco and other leaders in the movement came on to see me. I explained that the duty of the National Government was twofold: in the first place, to meet every reasonable wish and every real need of the people of California or any other State in dealing with the people of

a foreign power; and, in the next place, itself exclusively
and fully to exercise the right of dealing with this foreign
power.

Inasmuch as in the last resort, including that last of all
resorts, war, the dealing of necessity had to be between
the foreign power and the National Government, it was
impossible to admit that the doctrine of State sovereignty
could be invoked in such a matter. As soon as legislative
or other action in any State affects a foreign nation, then
the affair becomes one for the Nation, and the State
should deal with the foreign power purely through the
Nation.

I explained that I was in entire sympathy with the people
of California as to the subject of immigration of the Japanese
in mass; but that of course I wished to accomplish the object
they had in view in the way that would be most courteous
and most agreeable to the feelings of the Japanese; that all
relations between the two peoples must be those of reciprocal justice, and that it was an intolerable outrage on the
part of newspapers and public men to use offensive and
insulting language about a high-spirited, sensitive, and
friendly people; and that such action as was proposed
about the schools could only have bad effects, and would
in no shape or way achieve the purpose that the Californians
had in mind. I also explained that I would use every
resource of the National Government to protect the Japanese
in their treaty rights, and would count upon the State
authorities backing me up to the limit in such action.
In short, I insisted upon the two points (1) that the Nation
and not the individual States must deal with matters of
such international significance and must treat foreign
nations with entire courtesy and respect; and (2) that the
Nation would at once, and in efficient and satisfactory
manner, take action that would meet the needs of California.
I both asserted the power of the Nation and offered a full
remedy for the needs of the State. This is the right, and
the only right, course. The worst possible course in such a
case is to fail to insist on the right of the Nation, to offer
no action of the Nation to remedy what is wrong, and yet

to try to coax the State not to do what it is mistakenly encouraged to believe it has the power to do, when no other alternative is offered.

After a good deal of discussion, we came to an entirely satisfactory conclusion. The obnoxious school legislation was abandoned, and I secured an arrangement with Japan under which the Japanese themselves prevented any emigration to our country of their laboring people, it being distinctly understood that if there was such emigration the United States would at once pass an exclusion law. It was of course infinitely better that the Japanese should stop their own people from coming rather than that we should have to stop them; but it was necessary for us to hold this power in reserve.

Unfortunately, after I left office, a most mistaken and ill-advised policy was pursued towards Japan, combining irritation and inefficiency, which culminated in a treaty under which we surrendered this important and necessary right. It was alleged in excuse that the treaty provided for its own abrogation; but of course it is infinitely better to have a treaty under which the power to exercise a necessary right is explicitly retained rather than a treaty so drawn that recourse must be had to the extreme step of abrogating if it ever becomes necessary to exercise the right in question.

The arrangement we made worked admirably, and entirely achieved its purpose. No small part of our success was due to the fact that we succeeded in impressing on the Japanese that we sincerely admired and respected them, and desired to treat them with the utmost consideration. I cannot too strongly express my indignation with, and abhorrence of, reckless public writers and speakers who, with coarse and vulgar insolence, insult the Japanese people and thereby do the greatest wrong not only to Japan but to their own country.

Such conduct represents the nadir of underbreeding and folly. The Japanese are one of the great nations of the world, entitled to stand, and standing, on a footing of full equality with any nation of Europe or America. I have the heartiest admiration for them. They can teach us much. Their civilization is in some respects higher than our own. It is eminently undesirable that Japanese and Americans should attempt to live together in masses; any such attempt would be sure to result disastrously, and the far-seeing statesmen of both countries should join to prevent it.

But this is not because either nation is inferior to the other; it is because they are different. The two peoples represent two civilizations which, although in many respects equally high, are so totally distinct in their past history that it is idle to expect in one or two generations to overcome this difference. One civilization is as old as the other; and in neither case is the line of cultural descent coincident with that of ethnic descent. Unquestionably the ancestors of the great majority both of the modern Americans and the modern Japanese were barbarians in that remote past which saw the origins of the cultured peoples to which the Americans and the Japanese of to-day severally trace their civilizations. But the lines of development of these two civilizations, of the Orient and the Occident, have been separate and divergent since thousands of years before the Christian era; certainly since that hoary eld in which the Akkadian predecessors of the Chaldean Semites held sway in Mesopotamia. An effort to mix together, out of hand, the peoples representing the culminating points of two such lines of divergent cultural development would be fraught with peril; and this, I repeat, because the two are different, not because either is inferior to the other. Wise statesmen, looking to the future, will for the present endeavor to keep the two nations from mass contact and intermingling, precisely because they wish to keep each in relations of permanent good will and friendship with the other.

Exactly what was done in the particular crisis to which I refer is shown in the following letter which, after our policy had been successfully put into execution, I sent to the then Speaker of the California lower house of the Legislature:

THE WHITE HOUSE, WASHINGTON,
February 8, 1909.

HON. P. A. STANTON,
   Speaker of the Assembly,
      Sacramento, California :

I trust there will be no misunderstanding of the Federal Government's attitude. We are jealously endeavoring to guard the interests of California and of the entire West in accordance with the desires of our Western people. By friendly agreement with Japan, we are now carrying out a policy which, while meeting the interests and desires of the Pacific slope, is yet compatible, not merely with mutual self-respect, but with mutual esteem and admiration between the Americans and Japanese. The Japanese Government is loyally and in good faith doing its part to carry out this policy, precisely as the American Government is doing. The policy aims at mutuality of obligation and behavior. In accordance with it the purpose is that the Japanese shall come here exactly as Americans go to Japan, which is in effect that travelers, students, persons engaged in international business, men who sojourn for pleasure or study, and the like, shall have the freest access from one country to the other, and shall be sure of the best treatment, but that there shall be no settlement in mass by the people of either country in the other. During the last six months under this policy more Japanese have left the country than have come in, and the total number in the United States has diminished by over two thousand. These figures are absolutely accurate and cannot be impeached. In other words, if the present policy is consistently followed and works as well in the future as it is now working, all difficulties and causes of friction will disappear, while at the same time each nation will retain its self-respect and the good will of the other. But such a bill as this school bill accomplishes literally nothing whatever in the line of the object aimed at, and gives just and grave cause for irritation; while in addition the United States Government would be obliged immediately to take action in the Federal courts to test such legislation, as we hold it to be clearly a violation of the treaty. On this point I refer you to the numerous decisions of the United States Supreme Court in regard to State laws which violate treaty obligations of the United States. The legislation would accomplish nothing beneficial and would certainly cause some mischief, and might cause very grave mischief. In short, the policy of the Administration is to combine the maximum of efficiency in achieving the real object which the people of the Pacific Slope have at heart, with the minimum of friction and trouble, while the misguided men who advocate such action as this against which I protest are following a policy which combines the very minimum of efficiency with the maximum of insult, and which, while totally failing to achieve any real result for good, yet might accomplish an infinity of harm. If in the next year or two the action of the Federal Government fails to achieve what it is now achieving, then through the further action of the President and Congress it can be made entirely efficient. I am sure that the sound judgment of the people of California will support you, Mr. Speaker, in your effort. Let me repeat that at present we are actually doing the very thing which the people of California wish to be done, and to upset the arrangement under which this is being done cannot do good and may do great harm. If in the next year or two the figures of immigration prove that the arrangement which has worked so successfully during the last six months is no longer working successfully, then there would be ground for grievance and for the reversal by the National Government of its present policy. But at present the policy is working well, and until it works badly it would be a grave misfortune to change it, and when changed it can only be changed effectively by the National Government.

THEODORE ROOSEVELT.

In foreign and domestic affairs alike the policy pursued during my Administration was simple. In foreign affairs the principle from which we never deviated was to have the Nation behave toward other nations precisely as a strong,

2 E

From a painting by John S. Sargent.

Rear Portico — The White House.

honorable, and upright man behaves in dealing with his fellow-men. There is no such thing as international law in the sense that there is municipal law or law within a nation. Within the nation there is always a judge, and a policeman who stands back of the judge. The whole system of law depends first upon the fact that there is a judge competent to pass judgment, and second upon the fact that there is some competent officer whose duty it is to carry out this judgment, by force if necessary. In international law there is no judge, unless the parties in interest agree that one shall be constituted; and there is no policeman to carry out the judge's orders. In consequence, as yet each nation must depend upon itself for its own protection. The frightful calamities that have befallen China, solely because she has had no power of self-defense, ought to make it inexcusable in any wise American citizen to pretend to patriotic purpose, and yet to fail to insist that the United States shall keep in a condition of ability if necessary to assert its rights with a strong hand. It is folly of the criminal type for the Nation not to keep up its navy, not to fortify its vital strategic points, and not to provide an adequate army for its needs. On the other hand, it is wicked for the Nation to fail in either justice, courtesy, or consideration when dealing with any other power, big or little. John Hay was Secretary of State when I became President, and continued to serve under me until his death, and his and my views as to the attitude that the Nation should take in foreign affairs were identical, both as regards our duty to be able to protect ourselves against the strong and as regards our duty always to act not only justly but generously toward the weak.

John Hay was one of the most delightful of companions, one of the most charming of all men of cultivation and action. Our views on foreign affairs coincided absolutely; but, as was natural enough, in domestic matters he felt much more conservative than he did in the days when as a young man he was private secretary to the great radical democratic leader of the '60's, Abraham Lincoln. He was fond of jesting with me about my supposedly dangerous

tendencies in favor of labor against capital.   When I was
inaugurated on March 4, 1905, I wore a ring he sent me the
evening before, containing the hair of Abraham Lincoln.
This ring was on my finger when the Chief Justice administered to me the oath of allegiance to the United States;
I often thereafter told John Hay that when I wore such a
ring on such an occasion I bound myself more than ever to
treat the Constitution, after the manner of Abraham Lincoln, as a document which put human rights above property
rights when the two conflicted.   The last Christmas John
Hay was alive he sent me the manuscript of a Norse saga
by William Morris, with the following note:

Christmas Eve, 1904.

DEAR THEODORE: In your quality of Viking this Norse
saga should belong to you, and in your character of Enemy
of Property this Ms. of William Morris will appeal to you.
Wishing you a Merry Christmas and many happy years,
I am yours affectionately,

JOHN HAY.

In internal affairs I cannot say that I entered the
Presidency with any deliberately planned and far-reaching
scheme of social betterment.   I had, however certain strong
convictions; and I was on the lookout for every opportunity
of realizing those convictions.   I was bent upon making the
Government the most efficient possible instrument in helping the people of the United States to better themselves in
every way, politically, socially, and industrially.   I believed
with all my heart in real and thoroughgoing democracy,
and I wished to make this democracy industrial as well as
political, although I had only partially formulated the methods I believed we should follow.   I believed in the people's
rights, and therefore in National rights and States' rights
just exactly to the degree in which they severally secured
popular rights.   I believed in invoking the National power
with absolute freedom for every National need; and I
believed that the Constitution should be treated as the
greatest document ever devised by the wit of man to aid a

people in exercising every power necessary for its own betterment, and not as a straitjacket cunningly fashioned to
strangle growth. As for the particular methods of realizing these various beliefs, I was content to wait and see
what method might be necessary in each given case as it
arose; and I was certain that the cases would arise fast
enough.

As the time for the Presidential nomination of 1904 drew
near, it became evident that I was strong with the rank and
file of the party, but that there was much opposition to me
among many of the big political leaders, and especially
among many of the Wall Street men. A group of these
men met in conference to organize this opposition. It was
to be done with complete secrecy. But such secrets are
very hard to keep. I speedily knew all about it, and took
my measures accordingly. The big men in question, who
possessed much power so long as they could work under
cover, or so long as they were merely throwing their weight
one way or the other between forces fairly evenly balanced,
were quite helpless when fighting in the open by themselves.
I never found out that anything practical was even attempted by most of the men who took part in the conference. Three or four of them, however, did attempt
something. The head of one big business corporation
attempted to start an effort to control the delegations from
New Jersey, North Carolina, and certain Gulf States against
me. The head of a great railway system made preparations
for a more ambitious effort looking towards the control of
the delegations from Iowa, Kansas, Nebraska, Colorado,
and California against me. He was a very powerful man
financially, but his power politically was much more limited,
and he did not really understand his own limitations or
the situation itself, whereas I did. He could not have
secured a delegate against me from Iowa, Nebraska, or
Kansas. In Colorado and California he could have made a
fight, but even there I think he would have been completely
beaten. However, long before the time for the Convention
came round, it was recognized that it was hopeless to make
any opposition to my nomination. The effort was aban-

doned, and I was nominated unanimously. Judge Parker was nominated by the Democrats against me. Practically all the metropolitan newspapers of largest circulation were against me; in New York City fifteen out of every sixteen copies of papers issued were hostile to me. I won by a popular majority of about two million and a half, and in the electoral college carried 330 votes against 136. It was by far the largest popular majority ever hitherto given any Presidential candidate.

My opponents during the campaign had laid much stress upon my supposed personal ambition and intention to use the office of President to perpetuate myself in power. I did not say anything on the subject prior to the election, as I did not wish to say anything that could be construed into a promise offered as a consideration in order to secure votes. But on election night, after the returns were in I issued the following statement: "The wise custom which limits the President to two terms regards the substance and not the form, and under no circumstances will I be a candidate for or accept another nomination."

The reason for my choice of the exact phraseology used was twofold. In the first place, many of my supporters were insisting that, as I had served only three and a half years of my first term, coming in from the Vice-Presidency when President McKinley was killed, I had really had only one elective term, so that the third term custom did not apply to me; and I wished to repudiate this suggestion. I believed then (and I believe now) the third term custom or tradition to be wholesome, and, therefore, I was determined to regard its substance, refusing to quibble over the words usually employed to express it. On the other hand, I did not wish simply and specifically to say that I would not be a candidate for the nomination in 1908, because if I had specified the year when I would not be a candidate, it would have been widely accepted as meaning that I intended to be a candidate some other year; and I had no such intention, and had no idea that I would ever be a candidate again. Certain newspaper men did ask me if I intended to apply my prohibition to 1912, and I answered that I was not thinking of 1912, nor of 1920, nor of 1940, and that I must decline to say anything whatever except what appeared in my statement.

The Presidency is a great office, and the power of the President can be effectively used to secure a renomination, especially if the President has the support of certain great political and financial interests. It is for this reason, and this reason alone, that the wholesome principle of continuing in office, so long as he is willing to serve, an incumbent who has proved capable, is not applicable to the Presidency. Therefore, the American people have wisely established a custom against allowing any man to hold that office for more than two consecutive terms. But every shred of power which a President exercises while in office vanishes absolutely when he has once left office. An ex-President stands precisely in the position of any other private citizen, and has not one particle more power to secure a nomination or election than if he had never held the office at all — indeed, he probably has less because of the very fact that he has held the office. Therefore the reasoning on which the anti-third term custom is based has no application whatever to an ex-President, and no application whatever to anything except consecutive terms. As a barrier of precaution against more than two consecutive terms the custom embodies a valuable principle. Applied in any other way it becomes a mere formula, and like all formulas a potential source of mischievous confusion. Having this in mind, I regarded the custom as applying practically, if not just as much, to a President who had been seven and a half years in office as to one who had been eight years in office, and therefore, in the teeth of a practically unanimous demand from my own party that I accept another nomination, and the reasonable certainty that the nomination would be ratified at the polls, I felt that the substance of the custom applied to me in 1908. On the other hand, it had no application whatever to any human being save where it was invoked in the case of a man desiring a third consecutive term. Having given such substantial proof of my own regard for the custom, I deem it a duty to add this comment on it. I believe that it is well to have a custom of this kind, to be generally observed, but that it would be very unwise to have it definitely hardened into a Constitutional prohibition. It is not desirable ordinarily that a man should stay in office twelve consecutive years as President; but most certainly the American people are fit to take care of themselves, and stand in no need of an irrevocable self-denying ordinance. They should not bind themselves never to take action which under some quite conceivable circumstances it might be to their great interest to take. It is obviously of the last importance to the safety of a democracy that in time of real peril it should be able to command the service of every one among its citizens in the precise position where the service rendered will be most valuable. It would be a benighted policy in such event to disqualify absolutely from the highest office a man

From the *Chronicle*, Chicago.   Cartoon by A. L. Lovey.

HIS FAVORITE AUTHOR.

"There was one cartoon made while I was President, in which I appeared incidentally, that was always a great favorite of mine. It pictured an old fellow with chin whiskers, a farmer, in his shirt-sleeves, with his boots off, sitting before the fire, reading the President's message."

who while holding it had actually shown the highest capacity to exercise its powers with the utmost effect for the public defense. If, for instance, a tremendous crisis occurred at the end of the second term of a man like Lincoln, as such a crisis occurred at the end of his first term, it would be a veritable calamity if the American people were forbidden to continue to use the services of the one man whom they knew, and did not merely guess, could carry them through the crisis. The third term tradition has no value whatever except as it applies to a third consecutive term. While it is well to keep it as a custom, it would be a mark both of weakness and unwisdom for the American people to embody it into a Constitutional provision which could not do them good and on some given occasion might work real harm.

There was one cartoon made while I was President, in which I appeared incidentally, that was always a great favorite of mine. It pictured an old fellow with chin whiskers, a farmer, in his shirt-sleeves, with his boots off, sitting before the fire, reading the President's Message. On his feet were stockings of the kind I have seen hung up by the dozen in Joe Ferris's store at Medora, in the days when I used to come in to town and sleep in one of the rooms over the store. The title of the picture was "His Favorite Author." This was the old fellow whom I always used to keep in my mind. He had probably been in the Civil War in his youth; he had worked hard ever since he left the army; he had been a good husband and father; he had brought up his boys and girls to work; he did not wish to do injustice to any one else, but he wanted justice done to himself and to others like him; and I was bound to secure that justice for him if it lay in my power to do so.[1]

---

[1] I believe I realized fairly well this ambition. I shall turn to my enemies to attest the truth of this statement. The New York *Sun*, shortly before the National Convention of 1904, spoke of me as follows:

"President Roosevelt holds that his nomination by the National Republican Convention of 1904 is an assured thing. He makes no concealment of his conviction, and it is unreservedly shared by his friends. We think President Roosevelt is right.

"There are strong and convincing reasons why the President should feel that success is within his grasp. He has used the opportunities that he found or created, and he has used them with consummate skill and undeniable success.

"The President has disarmed all his enemies. Every weapon they had, new or old, has been taken from them and added to the now unassailable Roosevelt arsenal. Why should people wonder that Mr. Bryan clings to silver? Has not Mr. Roosevelt absorbed and sequestered every vestige of the Kansas City platform that had a shred of practical value? Suppose that Mr. Bryan had been elected President. What could he have accomplished compared with what Mr. Roosevelt has accomplished? Will his most passionate followers pretend for one moment that Mr. Bryan could have conceived, much less enforced, any such pursuit of the trusts as that which Mr. Roosevelt has just brought to a triumphant issue? Will Mr.

Bryan himself intimate that the Federal courts would have turned to his projects the friendly countenance which they have lent to those of Mr. Roosevelt?

"Where is 'government by injunction' gone to? The very emptiness of that once potent phrase is beyond description! A regiment of Bryans could not compete with Mr. Roosevelt in harrying the trusts, in bringing wealth to its knees, and in converting into the palpable actualities of action the wildest dreams of Bryan's campaign orators. He has outdone them all.

"And how utterly the President has routed the pretensions of Bryan, and of the whole Democratic horde in respect to organized labor! How empty were all their professions, their mouthings and their howlings in the face of the simple and unpretentious achievements of the President! In his own straightforward fashion he inflicted upon capital in one short hour of the coal strike a greater humiliation than Bryan could have visited upon it in a century. He is the leader of the labor unions of the United States. Mr. Roosevelt has put them above the law and above the Constitution, because for him they are the American people." [This last, I need hardly say, is merely a rhetorical method of saying that I gave the labor union precisely the same treatment as the corporation.]

Senator La Follette, in the issue of his magazine immediately following my leaving the Presidency in March, 1909, wrote as follows:

"Roosevelt steps from the stage gracefully. He has ruled his party to a large extent against its will. He has played a large part in the world's work, for the past seven years. The activities of his remarkably forceful personality have been so manifold that it will be long before his true rating will be fixed in the opinion of the race. He is said to think that the three great things done by him are the undertaking of the construction of the Panama Canal and its rapid and successful carrying forward, the making of peace between Russia and Japan, and the sending around the world of the fleet.

"These are important things, but many will be slow to think them his greatest services. The Panama Canal will surely serve mankind when in operation; and the manner of organizing this work seems to be fine. But no one can yet say whether this project will be a gigantic success or a gigantic failure; and the task is one which must, in the nature of things, have been undertaken and carried through some time soon, as historic periods go, anyhow. The Peace of Portsmouth was a great thing to be responsible for, and Roosevelt's good offices undoubtedly saved a great and bloody battle in Manchuria. But the war was fought out, and the parties ready to quit, and there is reason to think that it was only when this situation was arrived at that the good offices of the President of the United States were, more or less indirectly, invited. The fleet's cruise was a strong piece of diplomacy, by which we informed Japan that we will send our fleet wherever we please and whenever we please. It worked out well.

"But none of these things, it will seem to many, can compare with some of Roosevelt's other achievements. Perhaps he is loth to take credit as a reformer, for he is prone to spell the word with question marks, and to speak disparingly of 'reform.'

"But for all that, this contemner of 'reformers' made reform respectable in the United States, and this rebuker of 'muck-rakers' has been the chief agent in making the history of 'muck-raking' in the United States a National one, conceded to be useful. He has preached from the White House many doctrines; but among them he has left impressed on the American mind the one great truth of economic justice couched in the pithy and stinging phrase 'the square deal.' The task of making reform respectable in a commercialized world, and of giving the Nation a slogan in a phrase, is greater than the man who performed it is likely to think.

"And, then, there is the great and statesmanlike movement for the conservation of our National resources, into which Roosevelt so energetically threw himself at a time when the Nation as a whole knew not that we are ruining and bankrupting ourselves as fast as we can. This is probably the greatest thing Roosevelt did, undoubtedly. This globe is the capital stock of the race. It is just so much coal and oil and gas. This may be economized or wasted. The same thing is true of phosphates and other mineral resources. Our water resources are immense, and we are only just beginning to use them. Our forests have been destroyed; they must be restored. Our soils are being depleted; they must be built up and conserved.

"These questions are not of this day only or of this generation. They belong all to the future. Their consideration requires that high moral tone which regards the earth as the home of a posterity to whom we owe a sacred duty.

"This immense idea Roosevelt, with high statesmanship, dinned into the ears of the Nation until the Nation heeded. He held it so high that it attracted the attention of the neighboring nations of the continent, and will so spread and intensify that we will soon see the world's conferences devoted to it.

"Nothing can be greater or finer than this. It is so great and so fine that when the historian of the future shall speak of Theodore Roosevelt he is likely to say that he did many notable things, among them that of inaugurating the movement which finally resulted in the square deal, but that his greatest work was inspiring and actually beginning a world movement for staying terrestrial waste and saving for the human race the things upon which, and upon which alone, a great and peaceful and progressive and happy race life can be founded.

"What statesman in all history has done anything calling for so wide a view and for a purpose more lofty?"

CHAPTER XI

THE NATURAL RESOURCES OF THE NATION

WHEN Governor of New York, as I have already described, I had been in consultation with Gifford Pinchot and F. H. Newell, and had shaped my recommendations about forestry largely in accordance with their suggestions. Like other men who had thought about the national future at all, I had been growing more and more concerned over the destruction of the forests.

While I had lived in the West I had come to realize the vital need of irrigation to the country, and I had been both amused and irritated by the attitude of Eastern men who obtained from Congress grants of National money to develop harbors and yet fought the use of the Nation's power to develop the irrigation work of the West. Major John Wesley Powell, the explorer of the Grand Cañon, and Director of the Geological Survey, was the first man who fought for irrigation, and he lived to see the Reclamation Act passed and construction actually begun. Mr. F. H. Newell, the present Director of the Reclamation Service, began his work as an assistant hydraulic engineer under Major Powell; and, unlike Powell, he appreciated the need of saving the forests and the soil as well as the need of irrigation. Between Powell and Newell came, as Director of the Geological Survey, Charles D. Walcott, who, after the Reclamation Act was passed, by his force, pertinacity, and tact, succeeded in putting the act into effect in the best possible manner. Senator Francis G. Newlands, of Nevada, fought hard for the cause of reclamation in Congress. He attempted to get his State to act, and when that proved hopeless to get the Nation to act; and was ably assisted by Mr. G. H. Maxwell, a Californian, who had taken a deep interest in irrigation matters. Dr. W J McGee was one of the leaders in all the later stages of the movement. But Gifford Pinchot is the man to whom the nation owes most for what has been accomplished as regards the preservation of the natural resources of our country. He led, and indeed during its most vital period embodied, the fight for the preservation through use of our forests. He played one of the leading parts in the effort to make the National Government the chief instrument in developing the irrigation of the arid West. He was the foremost leader in the great struggle to coördinate all our social and governmental forces in the effort to secure the adoption of a rational and farseeing policy for securing the conservation of all our national resources. He was already in the Government service as head of the Forestry Bureau when I became President; he continued throughout my term, not only as head of the Forest service, but as the moving and directing spirit in most of the conservation work, and as counsellor and assistant on most of the other work connected with the internal affairs of the country. Taking into account the varied nature of the work he did, its vital importance to the nation and the fact that as regards much of it he was practically breaking new ground, and taking into account also his tireless energy and activity, his fearlessness, his complete disinterestedness, his single-minded devotion to the interests of the plain people, and his extraordinary efficiency, I believe it is but just to say that among the many, many public officials who under my administration rendered literally invaluable service to the people of the United States, he, on the whole, stood first. A few months after I left the Presidency he was removed from office by President Taft.

The first work I took up when I became President was the work of reclamation. Immediately after I had come to Washington, after the assassination of President McKinley, while staying at the house of my sister, Mrs. Cowles, before going into the White House, Newell and Pinchot called upon me and laid before me their plans for National irrigation of the arid lands of the West, and for the consolidation of the forest work of the Government in the Bureau of Forestry.

At that time a narrowly legalistic point of view toward natural resources obtained in the Departments, and controlled the Governmental administrative machinery. Through the General Land Office and other Government bureaus, the public resources were being handled and disposed of in accordance with the small considerations of petty legal formalities, instead of for the large purposes of constructive development, and the habit of deciding, whenever possible, in favor of private interests against the public welfare was firmly fixed. It was as little customary to favor the bona-fide settler and home builder, as against the strict construction of the law, as it was to use the law in thwarting the operations of the land grabbers. A technical compliance with the letter of the law was all that was required.

The idea that our natural resources were inexhaustible still obtained, and there was as yet no real knowledge of their extent and condition. The relation of the conservation of natural resources to the problems of National welfare and National efficiency had not yet dawned on the public mind. The reclamation of arid public lands in the West was still a matter for private enterprise alone; and our magnificent river system, with its superb possibilities for public usefulness, was dealt with by the National Government not as a unit, but as a disconnected series of pork-barrel problems, whose only real interest was in their effect on the reëlection or defeat of a Congressman here and there — a theory which, I regret to say, still obtains.

The place of the farmer in the National economy was still regarded solely as that of a grower of food to be eaten by others, while the human needs and interests of himself and his wife and children still remained wholly outside the recognition of the Government.

All the forests which belonged to the United States were held and administered in one Department, and all the foresters in Government employ were in another Department. Forests and foresters had nothing whatever to do with each other. The National Forests in the West (then called forest reserves) were wholly inadequate in area to meet the purposes for which they were created, while the need for forest protection in the East had not yet begun to enter the public mind.

Such was the condition of things when Newell and Pinchot called on me. I was a warm believer in reclamation and in forestry, and, after listening to my two guests, I asked them to prepare material on the subject for me to use in my first message to Congress, of December 3, 1901. This message laid the foundation for the development of irrigation and forestry during the next seven and one-half years. It set forth the new attitude toward the natural resources in the words: "The Forest and water problems are perhaps the most vital internal problems of the United States."

On the day the message was read, a committee of Western Senators and Congressmen was organized to prepare a Reclamation Bill in accordance with the recommendations. By far the most effective of the Senators in drafting and pushing the bill, which became known by his name, was Newlands. The draft of the bill was worked over by me and others at several conferences and revised in important particulars; my active interference was necessary to prevent it from being made unworkable by an undue insistence upon States Rights, in accordance with the efforts of Mr. Mondell and other Congressmen, who consistently fought for local and private interests as against the interests of the people as a whole.

On June 17, 1902, the Reclamation Act was passed. It set aside the proceeds of the disposal of public lands for the purpose of reclaiming the waste areas of the arid West by irrigating lands otherwise worthless, and thus creating new homes upon the land. The money so appropriated was to be repaid to the Government by the settlers, and to be used again as a revolving fund continuously available for the work.

The impatience of the Western people to see immediate results from the Reclamation Act was so great that red tape was disregarded, and the work was pushed forward at a rate previously unknown in Government affairs. Later, as in almost all such cases, there followed the criticisms of alleged illegality and haste which are so easy to make after results have been accomplished and the need for the measures without which nothing could have been done has gone by. These criticisms were in character precisely the same as that made about the acquisition of Panama, the settlement of the anthracite coal strike, the suits against the big trusts, the stopping of the panic of 1907 by the action of the Executive concerning the Tennessee Coal and Iron Company; and, in short, about most of the best work done during my administration.

With the Reclamation work, as with much other work under me, the men in charge were given to understand that they must get into the water if they would learn to swim; and, furthermore, they learned to know that if they acted honestly, and boldly and fearlessly accepted responsibility, I would stand by them to the limit. In this, as in every other case, in the end the boldness of the action fully justified itself.

Every item of the whole great plan of Reclamation now in effect was undertaken between 1902 and 1906. By the spring of 1909 the work was an assured success, and the Government had become fully committed to its continuance. The work of Reclamation was at first under the United States Geological Survey, of which Charles D. Walcott was at that time Director. In the spring of 1908 the United States Reclamation Service was established to carry it on, under the direction of Frederick Hayes Newell, to whom the inception of the plan was due. Newell's single-minded devotion to this great task, the constructive imagination which enabled him to conceive it, and the executive power and high character through which he and his assistant, Arthur P. Davis, built up a model service — all these have made him a model servant. The final proof of his merit is supplied by the character and records of the men who later assailed him.

Although the gross expenditure under the Reclamation Act is not yet as large as that for the Panama Canal, the engineering obstacles to be overcome have been almost as great, and the political impediments many times greater. The Reclamation work had to be carried on at widely sepa-

Copyright by Edwin Levick.

THE ROOSEVELT DAM IN ARIZONA.

Just before the Roosevelt party arrived to dedicate the dam.

2 F

rated points, remote from railroads, under the most difficult pioneer conditions. The twenty-eight projects begun in the years 1902 to 1906 contemplated the irrigation of more than three million acres and the watering of more than thirty thousand farms. Many of the dams required for this huge task are higher than any previously built anywhere in the world. They feed main-line canals over seven thousand miles in total length, and involve minor constructions, such as culverts and bridges, tens of thousands in number.

What the Reclamation Act has done for the country is by no means limited to its material accomplishment. This Act and the results flowing from it have helped powerfully to prove to the Nation that it can handle its own resources and exercise direct and business-like control over them. The population which the Reclamation Act has brought into the arid West, while comparatively small when compared with that in the more closely inhabited East, has been a most effective contribution to the National life, for it has gone far to transform the social aspect of the West, making for the stability of the institutions upon which the welfare of the whole country rests : it has substituted actual homemakers, who have settled on the land with their families, for huge, migratory bands of sheep herded by the hired shepherds of absentee owners.

The recent attacks on the Reclamation Service, and on Mr. Newell, arise in large part, if not altogether, from an organized effort to repudiate the obligation of the settlers to repay the Government for what it has expended to reclaim the land. The repudiation of any debt can always find supporters, and in this case it has attracted the support not only of certain men among the settlers who hope to be relieved of paying what they owe, but also of a variety of unscrupulous politicians, some highly placed. It is unlikely that their efforts to deprive the West of the revolving Irrigation fund will succeed in doing anything but discrediting these politicians in the sight of all honest men.

When in the spring of 1911 I visited the Roosevelt Dam in Arizona, and opened the reservoir, I made a short speech to the assembled people. Among other things, I said to the engineers present that in the name of all good citizens I thanked them for their admirable work, as efficient as it was honest, and conducted according to the highest standards of public service. As I looked at the fine, strong, eager faces of those of the force who were present, and thought of the similar men in the service, in the higher positions, who were absent, and who were no less responsible for the work done, I felt a foreboding that they would never receive any real recognition for their achievement; and, only half humorously, I warned them not to expect any credit, or any satisfaction, except their own knowledge that they had done well a first-class job, for that probably the only attention Congress would ever pay them would be to investigate them. Well, a year later a Congressional Committee actually did investigate them. The investigation was instigated by some unscrupulous local politicians and by some settlers who wished to be relieved from paying their just obligations; and the members of the Committee joined in the attack on as fine and honorable a set of public servants as the Government has ever had; an attack made on them solely because they were honorable and efficient and loyal to the interests both of the Government and the settlers.

When I became President, the Bureau of Forestry (since 1905 the United States Forest Service) was a small but growing organization, under Gifford Pinchot, occupied mainly with laying the foundation of American forestry by scientific study of the forests, and with the promotion of forestry on private lands. It contained all the trained foresters in the Government service, but had charge of no public timberland whatsoever. The Government forest reserves of that day were in the care of a Division in the General Land Office, under the management of clerks wholly without knowledge of forestry, few if any of whom had ever seen a foot of the timberlands for which they were responsible. Thus the reserves were neither well protected nor well used. There were no foresters among the men who had charge of the National Forests, and no Government forests in charge of the Government foresters.

In my first message to Congress I strongly recommended

the consolidation of the forest work in the hands of the trained men of the Bureau of Forestry. This recommendation was repeated in other messages, but Congress did not give effect to it until three years later. In the meantime, by thorough study of the Western public timberlands, the groundwork was laid for the responsibilities which were to fall upon the Bureau of Forestry when the care of the National Forests came to be transferred to it. It was evident that trained American Foresters would be needed in considerable numbers, and a forest school was established at Yale to supply them.

In 1901, at my suggestion as President, the Secretary of the Interior, Mr. Hitchcock, made a formal request for technical advice from the Bureau of Forestry in handling the National Forests, and an extensive examination of their condition and needs was accordingly taken up. The same year a study was begun of the proposed Appalachian National Forest, the plan of which, already formulated at that time, has since been carried out. A year later experimental planting on the National Forests was also begun, and studies preparatory to the application of practical forestry to the Indian Reservations were undertaken. In 1903, so rapidly did the public work of the Bureau of Forestry increase, that the examination of land for new forest reserves was added to the study of those already created, the forest lands of the various States were studied, and coöperation with several of them in the examination and handling of their forest lands was undertaken. While these practical tasks were pushed forward, a technical knowledge of American Forests was rapidly accumulated. The special knowledge gained was made public in printed bulletins; and at the same time the Bureau undertook, through the newspaper and periodical press, to make all the people of the United States acquainted with the needs and the purposes of practical forestry. It is doubtful whether there has ever been elsewhere under the Government such effective publicity — publicity purely in the interest of the people — at so low a cost. Before the educational work of the Forest Service was stopped by the Taft Administration, it was securing the publication of facts about forestry in fifty million copies of newspapers a month at a total expense of $6000 a year. Not one cent has ever been paid by the Forest Service to any publication of any kind for the printing of this material. It was given out freely, and published without cost because it was news. Without this publicity the Forest Service could not have survived the attacks made upon it by the representatives of the great special interests in Congress; nor could forestry in America have made the rapid progress it has.

The result of all the work outlined above was to bring together in the Bureau of Forestry, by the end of 1904, the only body of forest experts under the Government, and practically all of the first-hand information about the public forests which was then in existence. In 1905, the obvious foolishness of continuing to separate the foresters and the forests, reënforced by the action of the First National Forest Congress, held in Washington, brought about the Act of February 1, 1905, which transferred the National Forests from the care of the Interior Department to the Department of Agriculture, and resulted in the creation of the present United States Forest Service.

The men upon whom the responsibility of handling some sixty million acres of National Forest lands was thus thrown were ready for the work, both in the office and in the field, because they had been preparing for it for more than five years. Without delay they proceeded, under the leadership of Pinchot, to apply to the new work the principles they had already formulated. One of these was to open all the resources of the National Forests to regulated use. Another was that of putting every part of the land to that use in which it would best serve the public. Following this principle, the Act of June 11, 1906, was drawn, and its passage was secured from Congress. This law throws open to settlement all land in the National Forests that is found, on examination, to be chiefly valuable for agriculture. Hitherto all such land had been closed to the settler.

The principles thus formulated and applied may be summed up in the statement that the rights of the public to the natural resources outweigh private rights, and must be given its first consideration. Until that time, in dealing with the National Forests, and the public lands generally, private rights had almost uniformly been allowed to over-balance public rights. The change we made was right, and was vitally necessary; but, of course, it created bitter opposition from private interests.

One of the principles whose application was the source of much hostility was this : It is better for the Government to help a poor man to make a living for his family than to help a rich man make more profit for his company. This prin-ciple was too sound to be fought openly. It is the kind of principle to which politicians delight to pay unctuous homage in words. But we translated the words into deeds ; and when they found that this was the case, many rich men, especially sheep owners, were stirred to hostility, and they used the Congressmen they controlled to assault us — getting most aid from certain demagogues, who were equally glad im-properly to denounce rich men in public and improperly to serve them in private. The Forest Service established and enforced regulations which favored the settler as against the large stock owner ; required that necessary reductions in the stock grazed on any National Forest should bear first on the big man, before the few head of the small man, upon which the living of his family depended, were reduced ; and made grazing in the National Forests a help, instead of a hindrance, to permanent settlement. As a result, the small settlers and their families became, on the whole, the best friends the Forest Service has ; although in places their ignorance was played on by demagogues to influence them against the policy that was primarily for their own interest.

Another principle which led to the bitterest antagonism of all was this — whoever (except a bona-fide settler) takes public property for private profit should pay for what he gets. In the effort to apply this principle, the Forest Service obtained a decision from the Attorney-General that it was legal to make the men who grazed sheep and cattle on the National Forests pay for what they got. Accordingly, in the summer of 1906, for the first time, such a charge was made; and, in the face of the bitterest opposition, it was collected.

Up to the time the National Forests were put under the charge of the Forest Service, the Interior Department had made no effort to establish public regulation and control of water powers. Upon the transfer, the Service immediately began its fight to handle the power resources of the National Forests so as to prevent speculation and monopoly and to yield a fair return to the Government. On May 1, 1906, an Act was passed granting the use of certain power sites in Southern California to the Edison Electric Power Company, which Act, at the suggestion of the Service, limited the period of the permit to forty years, and required the payment of an annual rental by the company, the same conditions which were thereafter adopted by the Service as the basis for all permits for power development. Then began a vigorous fight against the position of the Service by the water-power interests. The right to charge for water-power development was, however, sustained by the Attorney-General.

In 1907, the area of the National Forests was increased by Presidential proclamation more than forty-three million acres; the plant necessary for the full use of the Forests, such as roads, trails, and telephone lines, began to be provided on a large scale; the interchange of field and office men, so as to prevent the antagonism between them, which is so destructive of efficiency in most great businesses, was established as a permanent policy; and the really effective management of the enormous area of the National Forests began to be secured.

With all this activity in the field, the progress of technical forestry and popular education was not neglected. In 1907, for example, sixty-one publications on various phases of forestry, with a total of more than a million copies, were issued, as against three publications, with a total of eighty-two thousand copies, in 1901. By this time, also, the opposition of the servants of the special interests in Congress to the Forest Service had become strongly developed, and more time appeared to be spent in the yearly attacks upon it during the passage of the appropriation bills than on all other Government Bureaus put together. Every year the Forest Service had to fight for its life.

One incident in these attacks is worth recording. While the Agricultural Appropriation Bill was passing through the Senate, in 1907, Senator Fulton, of Oregon, secured an amendment providing that the President could not set aside any additional National Forests in the six Northwestern States. This meant retaining some sixteen million of acres to be exploited by land grabbers and by the representatives of the great special interests, at the expense of the public interest. But for four years the Forest Service had been gathering field notes as to what forests ought to be set aside in these States, and so was prepared to act. It was equally undesirable to veto the whole agricultural bill, and to sign it with this amendment effective. Accordingly, a plan to create the necessary National Forest in these States before the Agricultural Bill could be passed and signed was laid before me by Mr. Pinchot. I approved it. The necessary papers were immediately prepared. I signed the last proclamation a couple of days before, by my signature, the bill became law; and, when the friends of the special interests in the Senate got their amendment through and woke up, they discovered that sixteen million acres of timberland had been saved for the people by putting them in the National Forests before the land grabbers could get at them. The opponents of the Forest Service turned handsprings in their wrath; and dire were their threats against the Executive; but the threats could not be carried out, and were really only a tribute to the efficiency of our action.

By 1908, the fire prevention work of the Forest Service had become so successful that eighty-six per cent of the fires that did occur were held down to an area of five acres or less, and the timber sales, which yielded $60,000 in 1905, in 1908 produced $850,000. In the same year, in addition to the work on the National Forests, the responsibility for the proper handling of Indian timberlands was laid upon the Forest Service, where it remained with great benefit to the

Indians until it was withdrawn, as a part of the attack on the Conservation policy made after I left office.

By March 4, 1909, nearly half a million acres of agricultural land in the National Forests had been opened to settlement under the Act of June 11, 1906. The business management of the Forest Service became so excellent, thanks to the remarkable executive capacity of the Associate Forester, Overton W. Price (removed after I left office), that it was declared by a well-known firm of business organizers to compare favorably with the best managed of the great private corporations, an opinion which was confirmed by the report of a Congressional investigation, and by the report of the Presidential Committee on Department method. The area of the National Forests had increased from 43 to 194 million acres; the force from about 500 to more than 3000. There was saved for public use in the National Forests more Government timberland during the seven and a half years prior to March 4, 1909, than during all previous and succeeding years put together.

The idea that the Executive is the steward of the public welfare was first formulated and given practical effect in the Forest Service by its law officer, George Woodruff. The laws were often insufficient, and it became well nigh impossible to get them amended in the public interest when once the representatives of privilege in Congress grasped the fact that I would sign no amendment that contained anything not in the public interest. It was necessary to use what law was already in existence, and then further to supplement it by Executive action. The practice of examining every claim to public land before passing it into private ownership offers a good example of the policy in question. This practice, which has since become general, was first applied in the National Forests. Enormous areas of valuable public timberland were thereby saved from fraudulent acquisition; more than 250,000 acres were thus saved in a single case.

This theory of stewardship in the interest of the public was well illustrated by the establishment of a water-power policy. Until the Forest Service changed the plan, water-

THE ROOSEVELT DAM IRRIGATING A YOUNG ORCHARD.

powers on the navigable streams, on the public domain, and in the National Forests were given away for nothing, and substantially without question, to whoever asked for them. At last, under the principle that public property should be paid for and should not be permanently granted away when such permanent grant is avoidable, the Forest Service established the policy of regulating the use of power in the National Forests in the public interest and making a charge for value received. This was the beginning of the water-power policy now substantially accepted by the public, and doubtless soon to be enacted into law. But there was at the outset violent opposition to it on the part of the water-power companies, and such representatives of their views in Congress as Messrs. Tawney and Bede.

Many bills were introduced in Congress aimed, in one way or another, at relieving the power companies of control and payment. When these bills reached me I refused to sign them; and the injury to the public interest which would follow their passage was brought sharply to public attention in my message of February 26, 1908. The bills made no further progress.

Under the same principle of stewardship, railroads and other corporations, which applied for and were given rights in the National Forests, were regulated in the use of those rights. In short, the public resources in charge of the Forest Service were handled frankly and openly for the public welfare under the clear-cut and clearly set forth principle that the public rights come first and private interest second.

The natural result of this new attitude was the assertion in every form by the representatives of special interests that the Forest Service was exceeding its legal powers and thwarting the intention of Congress. Suits were begun wherever the chance arose. It is worth recording that, in spite of the novelty and complexity of the legal questions it had to face, no court of last resort has ever decided against the Forest Service. This statement includes two unanimous decisions by the Supreme Court of the United States (U. S. *vs*. Grimaud, 220 U. S., 506, and Light *vs*. U. S., 220 U. S., 523).

In its administration of the National Forests, the Forest Service found that valuable coal lands were in danger of passing into private ownership without adequate money return to the Government and without safeguard against monopoly; and that existing leglslation was insufficient to prevent this. When this condition was brought to my attention I withdrew from all forms of entry about sixty-eight million acres of coal land in the United States, including Alaska. The refusal of Congress to act in the public interest was solely responsible for keeping these lands from entry.

The Conservation movement was a direct outgrowth of the forest movement. It was nothing more than the application to our other natural resources of the principles which had been worked out in connection with the forests. Without the basis of public sentiment which had been built up for the protection of the forests, and without the example of public foresight in the protection of this, one of the great natural resources, the Conservation movement would have been impossible. The first formal step was the creation of the Inland Waterways Commission, appointed on March 14, 1907. In my letter appointing the Commission, I called attention to the value of our streams as great natural resources, and to the need for a progressive plan for their development and control, and said: "It is not possible to properly frame so large a plan as this for the control of our rivers without taking account of the orderly development of other natural resources. Therefore I ask that the Inland Waterways Commission shall consider the relations of the streams to the use of all the great permanent natural resources and their conservation for the making and maintenance of prosperous homes."

Over a year later, writing on the report of the Commission, I said:

"The preliminary Report of the Inland Waterways Commission was excellent in every way. It outlines a general plan of waterway improvement which when adopted will give assurance that the improvements will yield practical results in the way of increased navigation and water transportation. In every essential feature the plan recommended by the Commission is new. In the principle of coördinating all uses of the waters and treating each waterway system as a unit; in the principle of correlating water traffic with rail and other land traffic; in the principle of expert initiation of projects in accordance with commercial foresight and the needs of a growing country; and in the principle of coöperation between the States and the Federal Government in the administration and use of waterways, etc.; the general plan proposed by the Commission is new, and at the same time sane and simple. The plan deserves unqualified support. I regret that it has not yet been adopted by Congress, but I am confident that ultimately it will be adopted."

The most striking incident in the history of the Commission was the trip down the Mississippi River in October, 1907, when, as President of the United States, I was the chief guest. This excursion, with the meetings which were held and the wide public attention it attracted, gave the development of our inland waterways a new standing in public estimation. During the trip a letter was prepared and presented to me asking me to summon a conference on the conservation of natural resources. My intention to call such a conference was publicly announced at a great meeting at Memphis, Tenn.

In the November following I wrote to each of the Governors of the several States and to the Presidents of various important National Societies concerned with natural resources, inviting them to attend the conference, which took place May 13 to 15, 1908, in the East Room of the White House. It is doubtful whether, except in time of war, any new idea of like importance has ever been presented to a Nation and accepted by it with such effectiveness and rapidity, as was the case with this Conservation movement when it was introduced to the American people by the Conference of Governors. The first result was the unanimous declaration of the Governors of all the States and Territories upon the subject of Conservation, a document which ought to be hung in every schoolhouse throughout the land. A further result was the appointment of thirty-six State Conservation Commissions and, on June 8, 1908, of the National Conser-

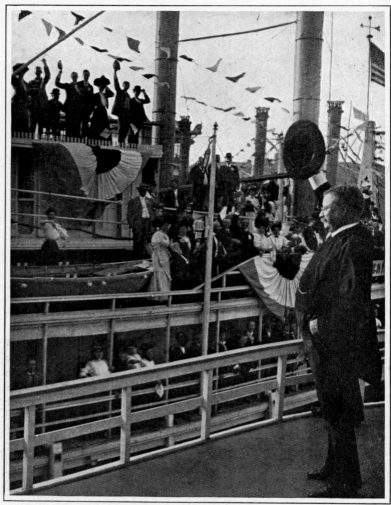

DOWN THE MISSISSIPPI.

vation Commission. The task of this Commission was to prepare an inventory, the first ever made for any nation, of all the natural resources which underlay its property. The making of this inventory was made possible by an Executive order which placed the resources of the Government Departments at the command of the Commission, and made possible the organization of subsidiary committees by which the actual facts for the inventory were prepared and digested. Gifford Pinchot was made chairman of the Commission.

The report of the National Conservation Commission was not only the first inventory of our resources, but was unique in the history of Government in the amount and variety of information brought together. It was completed in six months. It laid squarely before the American people the essential facts regarding our natural resources, when facts were greatly needed as the basis for constructive action. This report was presented to the Joint Conservation Congress in December, at which there were present Governors of twenty States, representatives of twenty-two State Conservation Commissions, and representatives of sixty National organizations previously represented at the White House conference. The report was unanimously approved, and transmitted to me, January 11, 1909. On January 22, 1909, I transmitted the report of the National Conservation Commission to Congress with a Special Message, in which it was accurately described as "one of the most fundamentally important documents ever laid before the American people."

The Joint Conservation Conference of December, 1908, suggested to me the practicability of holding a North American Conservation Conference. I selected Gifford Pinchot to convey this invitation in person to Lord Grey, Governor General of Canada; to Sir Wilfrid Laurier; and to President Diaz of Mexico; giving as reason for my action, in the letter in which this invitation was conveyed, the fact that: "It is evident that natural resources are not limited by the boundary lines which separate nations, and that the need for conserving them upon this continent is as wide as the area upon which they exist."

In response to this invitation, which included the colony of Newfoundland, the Commissioners assembled in the White House on February 18, 1909. The American Commissioners were Gifford Pinchot, Robert Bacon, and James R. Garfield. After a session continuing through five days, the Conference united in a declaration of principles, and suggested to the President of the United States "that all nations should be invited to join together in conference on the subject of world resources, and their inventory, conservation, and wise utilization." Accordingly, on February 19, 1909, Robert Bacon, Secretary of State, addressed to forty-five nations a letter of invitation "to send delegates to a conference to be held at The Hague at such date to be found convenient, there to meet and consult the like delegates of the other countries, with a view of considering a general plan for an inventory of the natural resources of the world and to devising a uniform scheme for the expression of the results of such inventory, to the end that there may be a general understanding and appreciation of the world's supply of the material elements which underlie the development of civilization and the welfare of the peoples of the earth." After I left the White House the project lapsed.

Throughout the early part of my Administration the public land policy was chiefly directed to the defense of the public lands against fraud and theft. Secretary Hitchcock's efforts along this line resulted in the Oregon land fraud cases, which led to the conviction of Senator Mitchell, and which made Francis J. Heney known to the American people as one of their best and most effective servants. These land fraud prosecutions under Mr. Heney, together with the study of the public lands which preceded the passage of the Reclamation Act in 1902, and the investigation of land titles in the National Forests by the Forest Service, all combined to create a clearer understanding of the need of land law reform, and thus led to the appointment of the Public Lands Commission. This Commission, appointed by me on October 22, 1903, was directed to report to the President: "Upon the condition, operation, and effect of the present land laws, and to recommend such changes as are needed to effect the largest practicable disposition of the public lands to actual settlers who will build permanent homes upon them, and to secure in permanence the fullest and most effective use of the resources of the public lands." It proceeded without loss of time to make a personal study on the ground of public land problems throughout the West, to confer with the Governors and other public men most concerned, and to assemble the information concerning the public lands, the laws and decisions which governed them, and the methods of defeating or evading those laws, which was already in existence, but which remained unformulated in the records of the General Land Office and in the minds of its employees. The Public Lands Commission made its first preliminary report on March 7, 1904. It found "that the present land laws do not fit the conditions of the remaining public lands," and recommended specific changes to meet the public needs. A year later the second report of the Commission recommended still further changes, and said "The fundamental fact that characterizes the situation under the present land laws is this, that the number of patents issued is increasing out of all proportion to the number of new homes." This report laid the foundation of the movement for Government control of the open range, and included by far the most complete statement ever made of the disposition of the public domain.

Among the most difficult topics considered by the Public Land Commission was that of the mineral land laws. This subject was referred by the Commission to the American Institute of Mining Engineers, which reported upon it through a Committee. This Committee made the very important recommendation, among others, "that the Government of the United States should retain title to all minerals, including coal and oil, in the lands of unceded territory, and lease the same to individuals or corporations at a fixed rental." The necessity for this action has since come to be very generally recognized. Another recommendation, since partly carried into effect, was for the separation of the surface and the minerals in lands containing coal and oil.

Our land laws have of recent years proved inefficient; yet

2 G

The First Governors' Conference at the White House.

the land laws themselves have not been so much to blame as the lax, unintelligent, and often corrupt administration of these laws. The appointment on March 4, 1907, of James R. Garfield as Secretary of the Interior led to a new era in the interpretation and enforcement of the laws governing the public lands. His administration of the Interior Department was beyond comparison the best we have ever had. It was based primarily on the conception that it is as much the duty of public land officials to help the honest settler get title to his claim as it is to prevent the looting of the public lands. The essential fact about public land frauds is not merely that public property is stolen, but that every claim fraudulently acquired stands in the way of the making of a home or a livelihood by an honest man.

As the study of the public land laws proceeded and their administration improved, a public land policy was formulated in which the saving of the resources on the public domain for public use became the leading principle. There followed the withdrawal of coal lands as already described, of oil lands and phosphate lands, and finally, just at the end of the Administration, of water-power sites on the public domain. These withdrawals were made by the Executive in order to afford to Congress the necessary opportunity to pass wise laws dealing with their use and disposal; and the great crooked special interests fought them with incredible bitterness.

Among the men of this Nation interested in the vital problems affecting the welfare of the ordinary hard-working men and women of the Nation, there is none whose interest has been more intense, and more wholly free from taint of thought of self, than that of Thomas Watson, of Georgia. While President I often discussed with him the condition of women on the small farms, and on the frontier, the hardship of their lives as compared with those of the men, and the need for taking their welfare into consideration in whatever was done for the improvement of life on the land. I also went over the matter with C. S. Barrett, of Georgia, a leader in the Southern farmers' movement, and with other men, such as Henry Wallace, Dean L. H. Bailey, of Cornell, and Kenyon Butterfield. One man from whose advice I especially profited was not an American, but an Irishman, Sir Horace Plunkett. In various conversations he described to me and my close associates the reconstruction of farm life which had been accomplished by the Agricultural Organization Society of Ireland, of which he was the founder and the controlling force; and he discussed the application of similar methods to the improvements of farm life in the United States. In the spring of 1908, at my request, Plunkett conferred on the subject with Garfield and Pinchot, and the latter suggested to him the appointment of a Commission on Country Life as a means for directing the attention of the Nation to the problems of the farm, and for securing the necessary knowledge of the actual conditions of life in the open country. After long discussion a plan for a Country Life Commission was laid before me and approved. The appointment of the Commission followed in August, 1908. In the letter of appointment the reasons for creating the Commission were set forth as follows: "I doubt if any other nation can bear comparison with our own in the amount of attention given by the Government, both Federal and State, to agricultural matters. But practically the whole of this effort has hitherto been directed toward increasing the production of crops. Our attention has been concentrated almost exclusively on getting better farming. In the beginning this was unquestionably the right thing to do. The farmer must first of all grow good crops in order to support himself and his family. But when this has been secured, the effort for better farming should cease to stand alone, and should be accompanied by the effort for better business and better living on the farm. It is at least as important that the farmer should get the largest possible return in money, comfort, and social advantages from the crops he grows, as that he should get the largest possible return in crops from the land he farms. Agriculture is not the whole of country life. The great rural interests are human interests, and good crops are of little value to the farmer unless they open the door to a good kind of life on the farm."

The Commission on Country Life did work of capital importance. By means of a widely circulated set of questions the Commission informed itself upon the status of country life throughout the Nation. Its trip through the East, South, and West brought it into contact with large numbers of practical farmers and their wives, secured for the Commissioners a most valuable body of first-hand information, and laid the foundation for the remarkable awakening of interest in country life which has since taken place throughout the Nation.

One of the most illuminating — and incidentally one of the most interesting and amusing — series of answers sent to the Commission was from a farmer in Missouri. He stated that he had a wife and 11 living children, he and his wife being each 52 years old; and that they owned 520 acres of land without any mortgage hanging over their heads. He had himself done well, and his views as to why many of his neighbors had done less well are entitled to consideration. These views are expressed in terse and vigorous English; they cannot always be quoted in full. He states that the farm homes in his neighborhood are not as good as they should be because too many of them are encumbered by mortgages; that the schools do not train boys and girls satisfactorily for life on the farm, because they allow them to get an idea in their heads that city life is better, and that to remedy this practical farming should be taught. To the question whether the farmers and their wives in his neighborhood are satisfactorily organized, he answers: "Oh, there is a little one-horse grange gang in our locality, and every darned one thinks they ought to be a king." To the question, "Are the renters of farms in your neighborhood making a satisfactory living?" he answers: "No; because they move about so much hunting a better job." To the question, "Is the supply of farm labor in your neighborhood satisfactory?" the answer is: "No; because the people have gone out of the baby business"; and when asked as to the remedy, he answers, "Give a pension to every mother who gives birth to seven living boys on American soil." To the question, "Are the conditions surrounding

hired labor on the farm in your neighborhood satisfactory to
the hired men ? " he answers : "Yes, unless he is a drunken
cuss," adding that he would like to blow up the stillhouses
and root out whisky and beer.   To the question, "Are the
sanitary conditions on the farms in your neighborhood
satisfactory ? " he answers : "No ; too careless about chicken
yards, and the like, and poorly covered wells.   In one well
on neighbor's farm I counted seven snakes in the wall of the
well, and they used the water daily : his wife dead now and
he is looking for another."   He ends by stating that the most
important single thing to be done for the betterment of
country life is "good roads"; but in his answers he shows
very clearly that most important of all is the individual
equation of the man or woman.

Like the rest of the Commissions described in this chapter,
the Country Life Commission cost the Government not
one cent, but laid before the President and the country a
mass of information so accurate and so vitally important
as to disturb the serenity of the advocates of things as they
are;   and therefore it incurred the bitter opposition of the
reactionaries.   The report of the Country Life Commission
was transmitted to Congress by me on February 9, 1909.
In the accompanying message I asked for $25,000 to print
and circulate the report and to prepare for publication
the immense amount of valuable material collected by the
Commission but still unpublished.   The reply made by
Congress was not only a refusal to appropriate the money,
but a positive prohibition against continuing the work.
The Tawney amendment to the Sundry Civil bill forbade
the President to appoint any further Commissions unless
specifically authorized by Congress to do so.   Had this
prohibition been enacted earlier *and complied with*, it
would have prevented the appointment of the six Roosevelt
Commissions.   But I would not have complied with it.
Mr. Tawney, one of the most efficient representatives of the
cause of special privilege as against public interest to be
found in the House, was later, in conjunction with Senator
Hale and others, able to induce my successor to accept their
view.   As what was almost my last official act, I replied to

Congress that if I did not believe the Tawney amendment to be unconstitutional I would veto the Sundry Civil bill which contained it, and that if I were remaining in office I would refuse to obey it. The memorandum ran in part: "The chief object of this provision, however, is to prevent the Executive repeating what it has done within the last year in connection with the Conservation Commission and the Country Life Commission. It is for the people of the country to decide whether or not they believe in the work done by the Conservation Commission and by the Country Life Commission. * * *

"If they believe in improving our waterways, in preventing the waste of soil, in preserving the forests, in thrifty use of the mineral resources of the country for the nation as a whole rather than merely for private monopolies, in working for the betterment of the condition of the men and women who live on the farms, then they will unstintedly condemn the action of every man who is in any way responsible for inserting this provision, and will support those members of the legislative branch who opposed its adoption. I would not sign the bill at all if I thought the provision entirely effective. But the Congress cannot prevent the President from seeking advice. Any future President can do as I have done, and ask disinterested men who desire to serve the people to give this service free to the people through these commissions. * * *

"My successor, the President-elect, in a letter to the Senate Commission on Appropriations, asked for the continuance and support of the Conservation Commission. The Conservation Commission was appointed at the request of the Governors of over forty States, and almost all of these States have since appointed commissions to coöperate with the National Commission. Nearly all the great national organizations concerned with natural resources have been heartily coöperating with the commission.

"With all these facts before it, the Congress has refused to pass a law to continue and provide for the commission; and it now passes a law with the purpose of preventing the Executive from continuing the commission at all. The Executive, therefore, must now either abandon the work and reject the coöperation of the States, or else must continue the work personally and through executive officers whom he may select for that purpose."

The Chamber of Commerce of Spokane, Washington, a singularly energetic and far-seeing organization, itself published the report which Congress had thus discreditably refused to publish.

The work of the Bureau of Corporations, under Herbert Knox Smith, formed an important part of the Conservation movement almost from the beginning. Mr. Smith was a member of the Inland Waterways Commission and of the National Conservation Commission and his Bureau prepared material of importance for the reports of both. The investigation of standing timber in the United States by the Bureau of Corporations furnished for the first time a positive knowledge of the facts. Over nine hundred counties in timbered regions were covered by the Bureau, and the work took five years. The most important facts ascertained were that forty years ago three-fourths of the standing timber in the United States was publicly owned, while at the date of the report four-fifths of the timber in the country was in private hands. The concentration of private ownership had developed to such an amazing extent that about two hundred holders owned nearly one-half of all privately owned timber in the United States; and of this the three greatest holders, the Southern Pacific Railway, the Northern Pacific Railway, and the Weyerhaeuser Timber Company, held over ten per cent. Of this work, Mr. Smith says:

"It was important, indeed, to know the facts so that we could take proper action toward saving the timber still left to the public. But of far more importance was the light that this history (and the history of our other resources) throws on the basic attitude, tradition and governmental beliefs of the American people. The whole standpoint of the people toward the proper aim of government, toward the relation of property to the citizen, and the relation of property to the government, were brought out first by this Conservation work."

The work of the Bureau of Corporations as to water power was equally striking. In addition to bringing the concentration of water-power control first prominently to public attention, through material furnished for my message in my veto of the James River Dam Bill, the work of the Bureau showed that ten great interests and their allies held nearly sixty per cent of the developed water power of the United States. Says Commissioner Smith: "Perhaps the most important thing in the whole work was its clear demonstration of the fact that the only effective place to control water power in the public interest is at the power sites; that as to powers now owned by the public it is absolutely essential that the public shall retain title. . . . The only way in which the public can get back to itself the margin of natural advantage in the water-power site is to rent that site at a rental which, added to the cost of power production there, will make the total cost of water power about the same as fuel power, and then let the two sell at the same price, *i.e.*, the price of fuel power."

Of the fight of the water-power men for States Rights at the St. Paul Conservation Congress in September, 1909, Commissioner Smith says:

"It was the first open sign of the shift of the special interests to the Democratic party for a logical political reason, namely, because of the availability of the States Rights idea for the purposes of the large corporations. It marked openly the turn of the tide."

Mr. Smith brought to the attention of the Inland Waterways Commission the overshadowing importance to waterways of their relation with railroad lines, the fact that the bulk of the traffic is long distance traffic, that it cannot pass over the whole distance by water, while it can go anywhere by rail, and that therefore the power of the rail lines to pro-rate or not to pro-rate, with water lines really determines the practical value of a river channel. The controlling value of terminals and the fact that out of fifty of our leading ports, over half the active water frontage in twenty-one ports was con-

PALISADES, LOOKING TOWARD SLAO ROCK IN THE NORTHEAST QUADRANT OF CRATER-CRATER, NATIONAL PARK, OREGON.

trolled by the railroads, was also brought to the Commission's attention, and reports of great value were prepared both for the Inland Waterways Commission and for the National Conservation Commission. In addition to developing the basic facts about the available timber supply, about waterways, water power, and iron ore, Mr. Smith helped to develop and drive into the public conscience the idea that the people ought to retain title to our natural resources and handle them by the leasing system.

The things accomplished that have been enumerated above were of immediate consequence to the economic well-being of our people. In addition certain things were done of which the economic bearing was more remote, but which bore directly upon our welfare, because they add to the beauty of living and therefore to the joy of life. Securing a great artist, Saint-Gaudens, to give us the most beautiful coinage since the decay of Hellenistic Greece was one such act. In this case I had power myself to direct the Mint to employ Saint-Gaudens. The first, and most beautiful, of his coins were issued in thousands before Congress assembled or could intervene; and a great and permanent improvement was made in the beauty of the coinage. In the same way, on the advice and suggestion of Frank Millet, we got some really capital medals by sculptors of the first rank. Similarly, the new buildings in Washington were erected and placed in proper relation to one another, on plans provided by the best architects and landscape architects. I also appointed a Fine Arts Council, an unpaid body of the best architects, painters, and sculptors in the country, to advise the Government as to the erection and decoration of all new buildings. The "pork-barrel" Senators and Congressmen felt for this body an instinctive, and perhaps from their standpoint a natural, hostility; and my successor a couple of months after taking office revoked the appointment and disbanded the Council.

Even more important was the taking of steps to preserve from destruction beautiful and wonderful wild creatures whose existence was threatened by greed and wantonness. During the seven and a half years closing on March 4, 1909,

more was accomplished for the protection of wild life in the
United States than during all the previous years, excepting
only the creation of the Yellowstone National Park.   The
record includes the creation of five National Parks — Crater
Lake, Oregon ; Wind Cave, South Dakota ; Platt, Oklahoma ;
Sully Hill, North Dakota, and Mesa Verde, Colorado ;
four big game refuges in Oklahoma, Arizona, Montana, and
Washington ; fifty-one bird reservations ; and the enactment of laws for the protection of wild life in Alaska, the
District of Columbia, and on National bird reserves.   These
measures may be briefly enumerated as follows :

The enactment of the first game laws for the Territory of
Alaska in 1902 and 1908, resulting in the regulation of the
export of heads and trophies of big game and putting an
end to the slaughter of deer for hides along the southern
coast of the Territory.

The securing in 1902 of the first appropriation for the
preservation of buffalo and the establishment in the Yellowstone National Park of the first and now the largest herd of
buffalo belonging to the Government.

The passage of the Act of January 24, 1905, creating the
Wichita Game Preserves, the first of the National game preserves.   In 1907, 12,000 acres of this preserve were inclosed
with a woven wire fence for the reception of the herd
of fifteen buffalo donated by the New York Zoölogical
Society.

The passage of the Act of June 29, 1906, providing for the
establishment of the Grand Cañon Game Preserve of Arizona, now comprising 1,492,928 acres.

The passage of the National Monuments Act of June 8,
1906, under which a number of objects of scientific interest
have been preserved for all time.   Among the Monuments
created are Muir Woods, Pinnacles National Monument
in California and the Mount Olympus National Monument,
Washington, which form important refuges for game.

The passage of the Act of June 30, 1906, regulating shooting
in the District of Columbia and making three-fourths of the
environs of the National Capital within the District in
effect a National Refuge.

The passage of the Act of May 23, 1908, providing for the establishment of the National Bison Range in Montana. This range comprises about 18,000 acres of land formerly in the Flathead Indian Reservation, on which is now established a herd of eighty buffalo, the nucleus of which was donated to the Government by the American Bison Society.

The issue of the Order protecting birds on the Niobrara Military Reservation, Nebraska, in 1908, making this entire reservation in effect a bird reservation.

The establishment by Executive Order between March 14, 1903, and March 4, 1909, of fifty-one National Bird Reservations distributed in seventeen States and Territories from Porto Rico to Hawaii and Alaska. The creation of these reservations at once placed the United States in the front rank in the world work of bird protection. Among these reservations are the celebrated Pelican Island rookery in Indian River, Florida ; The Mosquito Inlet Reservation, Florida, the northernmost home of the manatee ; the extensive marshes bordering Klamath and Malheur Lakes in Oregon, formerly the scene of slaughter of ducks for market and ruthless destruction of plume birds for the millinery trade ; the Tortugas Key, Florida, where, in connection with the Carnegie Institute, experiments have been made on the homing instinct of birds ; and the great bird colonies on Laysan and sister islets in Hawaii, some of the greatest colonies of sea birds in the world.

CHAPTER XII

ONE of the vital questions with which as President I had to deal was the attitude of the Nation toward the great corporations. Men who understand and practice the deep underlying philosophy of the Lincoln school of American political thought are necessarily Hamiltonian in their belief in a strong and efficient National Government and Jeffersonian in their belief in the people as the ultimate authority, and in the welfare of the people as the end of Government. The men who first applied the extreme Democratic theory in American life were, like Jefferson, ultra individualists, for at that time what was demanded by our people was the largest liberty for the individual. During the century that had elapsed since Jefferson became President the need had been exactly reversed. There had been in our country a riot of individualistic materialism, under which complete freedom for the individual — that ancient license which President Wilson a century after the term was excusable has called the "New" Freedom — turned out in practice to mean perfect freedom for the strong to wrong the weak. The total absence of governmental control had led to a portentous growth in the financial and industrial world both of natural individuals and of artificial individuals — that is, corporations. In no other country in the world had such enormous fortunes been gained. In no other country in the world was such power held by the men who had gained these fortunes; and these men almost always worked through, and by means of, the giant corporations which they controlled. The power of the mighty industrial overlords of the country had increased with giant strides, while the methods of controlling them, or checking abuses by them, on the part of the people, through the Government, remained archaic and therefore practically impotent. The courts, not unnaturally, but most regrettably, and to the grave detriment of the people and of their own standing, had for a quarter of a century been on the whole the agents of reaction, and by conflicting decisions which, however, in their sum were hostile to the interests of the people, had left both the nation and the several States well-nigh impotent to deal with the great business combinations. Sometimes they forbade the Nation to interfere, because such interference trespassed on the rights of the States; sometimes they forbade the States to interfere (and often they were wise in this), because to do so would trespass on the rights of the Nation; but always, or well-nigh always, their action was negative action against the interests of the people, ingeniously devised to limit their power against wrong, instead of affirmative action giving to the people power to right wrong. They had rendered these decisions sometimes as upholders of property rights against human rights, being especially zealous in securing the rights of the very men who were most competent to take care of themselves; and sometimes in the name of liberty, in the name of the so-called "new freedom," in reality the old, old "freedom," which secured to the powerful the freedom to prey on the poor and the helpless.

One of the main troubles was the fact that the men who saw the evils and who tried to remedy them attempted to work in two wholly different ways, and the great majority of them in a way that offered little promise of real betterment. They tried (by the Sherman law method) to bolster up an individualism already proved to be both futile and mischievous; to remedy by more individualism the concentration that was the inevitable result of the already existing individualism. They saw the evil done by the big combinations, and sought to remedy it by destroying them and restoring the country to the economic conditions of the middle of the nineteenth century. This was a hopeless effort, and those who went into it, although they regarded themselves as radical progressives, really represented a form of sincere rural toryism. They confounded monopolies with big business combinations, and in the effort to prohibit both alike, instead of where possible prohibiting one and drastically controlling the other, they succeeded merely in preventing any effective control of either.

On the other hand, a few men recognized that corporations and combinations had become indispensable in the business world, that it was folly to try to prohibit them, but that it was also folly to leave them without thoroughgoing control. These men realized that the doctrines of the old *laissez faire* economists, of the believers in unlimited competition, unlimited individualism, were in the actual state of affairs false and mischievous. They realized that the Government must now interfere to protect labor, to subordinate the big corporation to the public welfare, and to shackle cunning and fraud exactly as centuries before it had interfered to shackle the physical force which does wrong by violence.

The big reactionaries of the business world and their allies and instruments among politicians and newspaper editors took advantage of this division of opinion, and especially of the fact that most of their opponents were on the wrong path; and fought to keep matters absolutely unchanged. These men demanded for themselves an immunity from governmental control which, if granted, would have been as wicked and as foolish as immunity to the barons of the twelfth century. Many of them were evil men. Many others were just as good men as were some of these same barons; but they were as utterly unable as any medieval castle-owner to understand what the public interest really was. There have been aristocracies which have played a great and beneficent part at stages in the growth of mankind; but we had come to the stage where for our people what was needed was a real democracy; and of all forms of tyranny the least attractive and the most vulgar is the tyranny of mere wealth, the tyranny of a plutocracy.

When I became President, the question as to the *method*

by which the United States Government was to control the corporations was not yet important. The absolutely vital question was whether the Government had power to control them at all. This question had not yet been decided in favor of the United States Government. It was useless to discuss methods of controlling big business by the National Government until it was definitely settled that the National Government had the power to control it. A decision of the Supreme Court had, with seeming definiteness, settled that the National Government had not the power.

This decision I caused to be annulled by the court that had rendered it; and the present power of the National Government to deal effectively with the trusts is due solely to the success of the Administration in securing this reversal of its former decision by the Supreme Court.

The Constitution was formed very largely because it had become imperative to give to some central authority the power to regulate and control interstate commerce. At that time when corporations were in their infancy and big combinations unknown, there was no difficulty in exercising the power granted. In theory, the right of the Nation to exercise this power continued unquestioned. But changing conditions obscured the matter in the sight of the people as a whole; and the conscious and the unconscious advocates of an unlimited and uncontrollable capitalism gradually secured the whittling away of the National power to exercise this theoretical right of control until it practically vanished. After the Civil War, with the portentous growth of industrial combinations in this country, came a period of reactionary decisions by the courts which, as regards corporations, culminated in what is known as the Knight case.

The Sherman Anti-Trust Law was enacted in 1890 because the formation of the Tobacco Trust and the Sugar Trust, the only two great trusts then in the country (aside from the Standard Oil Trust, which was a gradual growth), had awakened a popular demand for legislation to destroy monopoly and curb industrial combinations. This demand the Anti-Trust Law was intended to satisfy. The Admin-

2 H

istrations of Mr. Harrison and Mr. Cleveland evidently construed this law as prohibiting such combinations in the future, not as condemning those which had been formed prior to its enactment.   In 1895, however, the Sugar Trust, whose output originally was about fifty-five per cent of all sugar produced in the United States, obtained control of three other companies in Philadelphia by exchanging its stock for theirs, and thus increased its business until it controlled ninety-eight per cent of the entire product.   Under Cleveland, the Government brought proceedings against the Sugar Trust, invoking the Anti-Trust Law, to set aside the acquisition of these corporations.   The test case was on the absorption of the Knight Company.[1] The Supreme Court of the United States, with but one dissenting vote, held adversely to the Government. They took the ground that the power conferred by the Constitution to regulate and control interstate commerce did not extend to the production or manufacture of commodities within a State, and that nothing in the Sherman Anti-Trust Law prohibited a corporation from acquiring all the stock of other corporations through exchange of its stock for theirs, such exchange not being "commerce" in the opinion of the Court, even though by such acquisition the corporation was enabled to control the entire production of a commodity that was a

OSCAR STRAUS.

[1] The case is known in the law books as U. S. vs. E. C. Knight, 156 U. S., Sept., p. 1.

necessary of life.   The effect of this decision was not merely
the absolute nullification of the Anti-Trust Law, so far as
industrial corporations were concerned, but was also in
effect a declaration that, under the Constitution, the National Government could pass no law really effective for
the destruction or control of such combinations.

This decision left the National Government, that is,
the people of the Nation, practically helpless to deal with
the large combinations of modern business.   The courts
in other cases asserted the power of the Federal Government
to enforce the Anti-Trust Law so far as transportation rates
by railways engaged in interstate commerce were concerned.
But so long as the trusts were free to control the production of commodities without interference from the General
Government, they were well content to let the transportation of commodities take care of itself — especially as the
law against rebates was at that time a dead letter; and the
Court by its decision in the Knight case had interdicted
any interference by the President or by Congress with the
production of commodities.   It was on the authority of
this case that practically all the big trusts in the United
States, excepting those already mentioned, were formed.
Usually they were organized as "holding" companies, each
one acquiring control of its constituent corporations by
exchanging its stock for theirs, an operation which the
Supreme Court had thus decided could not be prohibited,
controlled, regulated, or even questioned by the Federal
Government.

Such was the condition of our laws when I acceded to
the Presidency.   Just before my accession, a small group
of financiers desiring to profit by the governmental impotence to which we had been reduced by the Knight decision, had arranged to take control of practically the entire
railway system in the Northwest — possibly as the first step
toward controlling the entire railway system of the country.
This control of the Northwestern railway systems was to
be effected by organizing a new "holding" company, and
exchanging its stock against the stock of the various corporations engaged in railway transportation throughout that

vast territory, exactly as the Sugar Trust had acquired
control of the Knight company and other concerns. This
company was called the Northern Securities Company.
Not long after I became President, on the advice of the
Attorney-General, Mr. Knox, and through him, I ordered
proceedings to be instituted for the dissolution of the company. As far as could be told by their utterances at the
time, among all the great lawyers in the United States Mr.
Knox was the only one who believed that this action could
be sustained. The defense was based expressly on the
ground that the Supreme Court in the Knight case had
explicitly sanctioned the formation of such a company as
the Northern Securities Company. The representatives of
privilege intimated, and sometimes asserted outright, that
in directing the action to be brought I had shown a lack of
respect for the Supreme Court, which had already decided
the question at issue by a vote of eight to one. Mr. Justice
White, then on the Court and now Chief Justice, set forth
the position that the two cases were in principle identical
with incontrovertible logic. In giving the views of the dissenting minority on the action I had brought, he said:

"The parallel between the two cases [the Knight case and
the Northern Securities case] is complete. The one corporation acquired the stock of other and competing corporations in exchange for its own. It was conceded for the
purposes of the case, that in doing so monopoly had been
brought about in the refining of sugar, that the sugar to
be produced was likely to become the subject of interstate
commerce, and indeed that part of it would certainly become
so. But the power of Congress was decided not to extend
to the subject, because the ownership of the stock in the
corporations was not itself commerce."[1]

Mr. Justice White was entirely correct in this statement.
The cases were parallel. It was necessary to reverse the
Knight case in the interests of the people against monopoly
and privilege just as it had been necessary to reverse the
Dred Scott case in the interest of the people against slavery

[1] Northern Securities Company et al. vs. U. S., 156 U. S., Sept., pp. 391–2.

and privilege; just as later it became necessary to reverse the New York Bakeshop case in the interest of the people against that form of monopolistic privilege which put human rights below property rights where wage workers were concerned.

By a vote of five to four the Supreme Court reversed its decision in the Knight case, and in the Northern Securities case sustained the Government. The power to deal with industrial monopoly and suppress it and to control and regulate combinations, of which the Knight case had deprived the Federal Government, was thus restored to it by the Northern Securities case. After this later decision was rendered, suits were brought by my direction against the American Tobacco Company and the Standard Oil Company. Both were adjudged criminal conspiracies, and their dissolution ordered. The Knight case was finally overthrown. The vicious doctrine it embodied no longer remains as an obstacle to obstruct the pathway of justice when it assails monopoly. Messrs. Knox, Moody, and Bonaparte, who successively occupied the position of Attorney-General under me, were profound lawyers and fearless and able men; and they completely established the newer and more wholesome doctrine under which the Federal Government may now deal with monopolistic combinations and conspiracies.

The decisions rendered in these various cases brought under my direction constitute the entire authority upon which any action must rest that seeks through the exercise of national power to curb monopolistic control. The men who organized and directed the Northern Securities Company were also the controlling forces in the Steel Corporation, which has since been prosecuted under the act. The proceedings against the Sugar Trust for corruption in connection with the New York Custom House are sufficiently interesting to be considered separately.

From the standpoint of giving complete control to the National Government over big corporations engaged in inter-State business, it would be impossible to over-estimate the importance of the Northern Securities decision and of the decisions afterwards rendered in line with it in connection with the other trusts whose dissolution was ordered. The success of the Northern Securities case definitely established the power of the Government to deal with all great corporations. Without this success the National Government must have remained in the impotence to which it had been reduced by the Knight decision as regards the most important of its internal functions. But our success in establishing the power of the National Government to curb monopolies did not establish the right method of exercising that power. We had gained the power. We had not devised the proper method of exercising it.

HERBERT KNOX SMITH.

Monopolies can, although in rather cumbrous fashion, be broken up by law suits. Great business combinations, however, cannot possibly be made useful instead of noxious industrial agencies merely by law suits, and especially by law suits supposed to be carried on for their destruction and not for their control and regulation. I at once began to urge upon Congress the need of laws supplementing the Anti-Trust Law — for this law struck at all big business, good and bad, alike, and as the event proved was very inefficient in checking bad big business, and yet was a constant threat against decent business men. I strongly urged the inauguration of a system of thoroughgoing and drastic Governmental regulation and control over all big business combinations engaged in inter-State industry.

Here I was able to accomplish only a small part of what

I desired to accomplish.   I was opposed both by the foolish radicals who desired to break up all big business, with the impossible ideal of returning to mid-nineteenth century industrial conditions; and also by the great privileged interests themselves, who used these ordinarily — but sometimes not entirely — well-meaning "stool pigeon progressives" to further their own cause.   The worst representatives of big business encouraged the outcry for the total abolition of big business, because they knew that they could not be hurt in this way, and that such an outcry distracted the attention of the public from the really efficient method of controlling and supervising them, in just but masterly fashion, which was advocated by the sane representatives of reform.   However, we succeeded in making a good beginning by securing the passage of a law creating the Department of Commerce and Labor, and with it the erection of the Bureau of Corporations.   The first head of the Department of Commerce and Labor was Mr. Cortelyou, later Secretary of the Treasury.   He was succeeded by Mr. Oscar Straus.   The first head of the Bureau of Corporations was Mr. Garfield, who was succeeded by Mr. Herbert Knox Smith.   No four better public servants from the standpoint of the people as a whole could have been found.

The Standard Oil Company took the lead in opposing all this legislation.   This was natural, for it had been the worst offender in the amassing of enormous fortunes by improper methods of all kinds, at the expense of business rivals and of the public, including the corruption of public servants.   If any man thinks this condemnation extreme, I refer him to the language officially used by the Supreme Court of the nation in its decision against the Standard Oil Company.   Through their counsel, and by direct telegrams and letters to Senators and Congressmen from various heads of the Standard Oil organization, they did their best to kill the bill providing for the Bureau of Corporations. I got hold of one or two of these telegrams and letters, however, and promptly published them; and, as generally happens in such a case, the men who were all-powerful as long as they could work in secret and behind closed doors became powerless as soon as they were forced into the open. The bill went through without further difficulty.

The true way of dealing with monopoly is to prevent it by administrative action before it grows so powerful that even when courts condemn it they shrink from destroying it. The Supreme Court in the Tobacco and Standard Oil cases, for instance, used very vigorous language in condemning these trusts; but the net result of the decision was of positive advantage to the wrongdoers, and this has tended to bring the whole body of our law into disrepute in quarters where it is of the very highest importance that the law be held in respect and even in reverence. My effort was to secure the creation of a Federal Commission which should neither excuse nor tolerate monopoly, but prevent it when possible and uproot it when discovered; and which should in addition effectively control and regulate all big combinations, and should give honest business certainty as to what the law was and security as long as the law was obeyed. Such a Commission would furnish a steady expert control, a control adapted to the problem; and dissolution is neither control nor regulation, but is purely negative; and negative remedies are of little permanent avail. Such a Commission would have complete power to examine into every big corporation engaged or proposing to engage in business between the States. It would have the power to discriminate sharply between corporations that are doing well and those that are doing ill; and the distinction between those who do well and those who do ill would be defined in terms so clear and unmistakable that no one could misapprehend them. Where a company is found seeking its profits through serving the community by stimulating production, lowering prices or improving service, while scrupulously respecting the rights of others (including its rivals, its employees, its customers, and the general public), and strictly obeying the law, then no matter how large its capital, or how great the volume of its business it would be encouraged to still more abundant production, or better service, by the fullest protection that the Government could afford it. On the other hand, if a corporation were found seeking profit through injury or oppression of the community, by restricting production through trick or device, by plot or conspiracy against competitors, or by oppression of wage-workers, and then extorting high prices for the commodity it had made artificially scarce, it would be prevented from organizing if its nefarious purpose could be discovered in time, or pursued and suppressed by all the power of Government whenever found in actual operation. Such a commission, with the power I advocate, would put a stop to abuses of big corporations and small corporations alike; it would draw the line on conduct and not on size; it would destroy monopoly, and make the biggest business man in the country conform squarely to the principles laid down by the American people, while at the same time giving fair play to the little man and certainty of knowledge as to what was wrong and what was right both to big man and little man.

Although under the decision of the courts the National Government had power over the railways, I found, when I became President, that this power was either not exercised at all or exercised with utter inefficiency. The law against rebates was a dead letter. All the unscrupulous railway men had been allowed to violate it with impunity; and because of this, as was inevitable, the scrupulous and decent railway men had been forced to violate it themselves, under penalty of being beaten by their less scrupulous rivals. It was not the fault of these decent railway men. It was the fault of the Government.

Thanks to a first-class railway man, Paul Morton of the Santa Fé, son of Mr. Cleveland's Secretary of Agriculture, I was able completely to stop the practice. Mr. Morton volunteered to aid the Government in abolishing rebates. He frankly stated that he, like every one else, had been guilty in the matter; but he insisted that he uttered the sentiments of the decent railway men of the country when he said that he hoped the practice would be stopped, and that if I would really stop it, and not merely make believe to stop it, he would give the testimony which would put into the hands of the Government the power to put a complete check to the practice.   Accordingly he testified, and on the information which he gave us we were able to take such action through the Inter-State Commerce Commission and the Department of Justice, supplemented by the necessary additional legislation, that the evil was absolutely eradicated.   He thus rendered, of his own accord, at his own personal risk, and from purely disinterested motives, an invaluable service to the people, a service which no other man who was able to render was willing to render.   As an immediate sequel, the world-old alliance between Blifil and Black George was immediately revived against Paul Morton.   In giving rebates he had done only what every honest railway man in the country had been obliged to do because of the failure of the Government to enforce the prohibition as regards dishonest railway men.   But unlike his fellows he had then shown the courage and sense of obligation to the public which made him come forward and without evasion or concealment state what he had done, in order that we might successfully put an end to the practice; and put an end to the practice we did, and we did it because of the courage and patriotism he had shown.   The unscrupulous railway men, whose dishonest practices were thereby put a stop to, and the unscrupulous demagogues who were either under the influence of these men or desirous of gaining credit with thoughtless and ignorant people no matter who was hurt, joined in vindictive clamor against Mr. Morton.   They actually wished me to prosecute him, although such prosecution would have been a piece of unpardonable ingratitude and treachery on the part of the public toward him — for I was merely acting as the steward of the public in this matter.   I need hardly say that I stood by him; and later he served under me as Secretary of the Navy, and a capital Secretary he made too.

We not only secured the stopping of rebates, but in the Hepburn Rate Bill we were able to put through a measure which gave the Inter-State Commerce Commission for the first time real control over the railways.   There were two or three amusing features in the contest over this bill. All of the great business interests which objected to Governmental control banded to fight it, and they were helped by the honest men of ultra-conservative type who always dread change, whether good or bad. We finally forced it through the House. In the Senate it was referred to a committee in which the Republican majority was under the control of Senator Aldrich, who took the lead in opposing the bill. There was one Republican on the committee, however, whom Senator Aldrich could not control — Senator Dolliver, of Iowa. The leading Democrat on the committee was Senator Tillman, of South Carolina, with whom I was not on good terms, because I had been obliged to cancel an invitation to him to dine at the White House on account of his having made a personal assault in the Senate Chamber on his colleague from South Carolina; and later I had to take action against him on account of his conduct in connection with certain land matters. Senator Tillman favored the bill. The Republican majority in the committee under Senator Aldrich, when they acted adversely on the bill, turned it over to Senator Tillman, thereby making him its sponsor. The object was to create what it was hoped would be an impossible situation in view of the relations between Senator Tillman and myself. I regarded the action as simply childish. It was a curious instance of how able and astute men sometimes commit blunders because of sheer inability to understand intensity of disinterested motive in others. I did not care a rap about Mr. Tillman's getting credit for the bill, or having charge of it. I was delighted to go with him or with any one else just so long as he was traveling my way — and no longer.

There was another amusing incident in connection with the passage of the bill. All the wise friends of the effort to secure Governmental control of corporations know that this Government control must be exercised through administrative and not judicial officers if it is to be effective. Everything possible should be done to minimize the chance of appealing from the decisions of the administrative officer to the courts. But it is not possible Constitutionally, and probably would not be desirable anyhow, completely to abolish the appeal. Unwise zealots wished to make the effort totally to abolish the appeal in connection with the Hepburn Bill. Representatives of the special interests wished to extend the appeal to include what it ought not to include. Between stood a number of men whose votes would mean the passage of, or the failure to pass, the bill, and who were not inclined towards either side. Three or four substantially identical amendments were proposed, and we then suddenly found ourselves face to face with an

WILLIAM H. MOODY.

absurd situation. The good men who were willing to go with us but had conservative misgivings about the ultra-radicals would not accept a good amendment if one of the latter proposed it; and the radicals would not accept their own amendment if one of the conservatives proposed it. Each side got so wrought up as to be utterly unable to get matters into proper perspective; each prepared to stand on unimportant trifles; each announced with hysterical emphasis — the reformers just as hysterically as the reactionaries — that the decision as regards each unimportant trifle determined the worth or worthlessness of the measure. Gradually we secured a measurable return to sane appreciation of the essentials. Finally both sides reluctantly agreed to accept the so-called Allison amendment which did not, as a matter of fact, work any change in the bill at all. The amendment was drawn by Attorney-General Moody after consultation with the Inter-State Commerce Commission, and was forwarded by me to Senator Dolliver; it was accepted, and the bill became law.

Thanks to this law and to the way in which the Inter-

State Commerce Commission was backed by the Administration, the Commission, under men like Prouty, Lane, and Clark, became a most powerful force for good. Some of the good that we had accomplished was undone after the close of my Administration by the unfortunate law creating a Commerce Court; but the major part of the immense advance we had made remained. There was one point on which I insisted, and upon which it is necessary always to insist. The Commission cannot do permanent good unless it does justice to the corporations precisely as it exacts justice from them. The public, the shippers, the stock and bondholders, and the employees, all have their rights, and none should be allowed unfair privileges at the expense of the others. Stock watering, and swindling of any kind should of course not only be stopped but punished. When, however, a road is managed fairly and honestly, and when it renders a real and needed service, then the Government must see that it is not so burdened as to make it impossible to run it at a profit. There is much wise legislation necessary for the safety of the public, or — like workmen's compensation — necessary to the well-being of the employee, which nevertheless imposes such a burden on the road that the burden must be distributed between the general public and the corporation, or there will be no dividends. In such a case it may be the highest duty of the commission to raise rates; and the commission, when satisfied that the necessity exists, in order to do justice to the owners of the road, should no more hesitate to raise rates, than under other circumstances to lower them.

So much for the "big stick" in dealing with the corporations when they went wrong. Now for a sample of the square deal.

In the fall of 1907 there were severe business disturbances and financial stringency, culminating in a panic which arose in New York and spread over the country. The damage actually done was great, and the damage threatened was incalculable. Thanks largely to the action of the Government, the panic was stopped before, instead of being merely a serious business check, it became a frightful and Nation-wide calamity, a disaster fraught with untold misery and woe to all our people. For several days the Nation trembled on the brink of such a calamity, of such a disaster.

During these days both the Secretary of the Treasury and I personally were in hourly communication with New York, following every change in the situation, and trying to anticipate every development. It was the obvious duty of the Administration to take every step possible to prevent appalling disaster by checking the spread of the panic before it grew so that nothing could check it. And events moved with such speed that it was necessary to decide and to act on the instant, as each successive crisis arose, if the decision and action were to accomplish anything. The Secretary of the Treasury took various actions, some on his own initiative, some by my direction. Late one evening I was informed that two representatives of the Steel Corporation wished to see me early the following morning, the precise object not being named. Next morning, while at breakfast, I was informed that Messrs. Frick and Gary were waiting at the office. I at once went over, and, as the Attorney-General, Mr. Bonaparte, had not yet arrived from Baltimore, where he had been passing the night, I sent a message asking the Secretary of State, Mr. Root, who was also a lawyer, to join us, which he did. Before the close of the interview and in the presence of the three gentlemen named, I dictated a note to Mr. Bonaparte, setting forth exactly what Messrs. Frick and Gary had proposed, and exactly what I had answered — so that there might be no possibility of misunderstanding. This note was published in a Senate Document while I was still President. It runs as follows:

THE WHITE HOUSE, WASHINGTON,

November 4, 1907.

My dear Mr. Attorney-General:

Judge E. H. Gary and Mr. H. C. Frick, on behalf of the Steel Corporation, have just called upon me. They state that there is a certain business firm (the name of which I have not been told, but which is of real importance in New York business circles), which will undoubtedly fail this week if help is not given. Among its assets are a majority of the securities of the Tennessee Coal Company. Application has been urgently made to the Steel Corporation to purchase this stock as the only means of avoiding a failure. Judge Gary and Mr. Frick informed me that as a mere business transaction they do not care to purchase the stock; that under ordinary circumstances they would not consider purchasing the stock, because but little benefit will come to the Steel Corporation from the purchase; that they are aware that the purchase will be used as a handle for attack upon them on the ground that they are striving to secure a monopoly of the business and prevent competition — not that this would represent what could honestly be said, but what might recklessly and untruthfully be said.

They further informed me that, as a matter of fact, the policy of the company has been to decline to acquire more than sixty per cent of the steel properties, and that this purpose has been persevered in for several years past, with the object of preventing these accusations, and, as a matter of fact, their proportion of steel properties has slightly decreased, so that it is below this sixty per cent, and the acquisition of the property in question will not raise it above sixty per cent. But they feel that it is immensely to their interest, as to the interest of every responsible business man, to try to prevent a panic and general industrial smash-up at this time, and that they are willing to go into this transaction, which they would not otherwise go into, because it seems the opinion of those best fitted to express judgment in New York that it will be an important factor in preventing a break that might be ruinous; and that this has been urged upon them by the combination of the most responsible bankers in New York who are now thus engaged in endeavoring to save the situation. But they asserted that they did not wish to do this if I stated that it ought not to be done. I answered that, while of course I could not advise them to take the action proposed, I felt it no public duty of mine to interpose any objections.

Sincerely yours,
(Signed) THEODORE ROOSEVELT.
HON. CHARLES J. BONAPARTE,
     Attorney-General.

Mr. Bonaparte received this note in about an hour, and that same morning he came over, acknowledged its receipt, and said that my answer was the only proper answer that could have been made, having regard both to the law and to the needs of the situation. He stated that the legal situation had been in no way changed, and that no sufficient ground existed for prosecution of the Steel Corporation. But I acted purely on my own initiative, and the responsibility for the act was solely mine.

I was intimately acquainted with the situation in New York. The word "panic" means fear, unreasoning fear; to stop a panic it is necessary to restore confidence; and at the moment the so-called Morgan interests were the only interests which retained a full hold on the confidence of the people of New York — not only the business people, but the immense mass of men and women who owned small investments or had small savings in the banks and trust companies. Mr. Morgan and his associates were of course fighting hard to prevent the loss of confidence and the panic distrust from increasing to such a degree as to bring any other big financial institutions down; for this would probably have been followed by a general, and very likely a worldwide, crash. The Knickerbocker Trust Company had already failed, and runs had begun on, or were threatened as regards, two other big trust companies. These companies were now on the fighting line, and it was to the interest of everybody to strengthen them, in order that the situation might be saved. It was a matter of general knowledge and belief that they, or the individuals prominent in them, held the securities of the Tennessee Coal and Iron Company, which securities had no market value, and were useless as a source of strength in the emergency. The Steel Corporation securities, on the contrary, were immediately marketable, their great value being known and admitted all over the world — as the event showed. The proposal of Messrs. Frick and Gary was that the Steel Corporation should at once acquire the Tennessee Coal and Iron Company, and thereby substitute, among the assets of the threatened institutions (which, by the way, they did not name to me), securities of great and immediate value for securities which at the moment were of no value. It was necessary for me to decide on the instant, before the Stock Exchange opened, for the situation in New York was such that any hour might be vital, and failure to act for even an hour might make all subsequent effort to act utterly useless. From the best information at my disposal, I believed (what was actually the fact) that the addition of the Tennessee Coal and Iron property would only increase the proportion of the Steel Company's holdings by about four per cent, making them about sixty-two per cent instead of about fifty-eight per cent of the total value in the country; an addition which, by itself, in my judgment (concurred in, not only by the Attorney-General but by every competent lawyer), worked no change in the legal status

CHARLES J. BONAPARTE.

of the Steel corporation. The diminution in the percentage of holdings, and production, has gone on steadily, and the percentage is now about ten per cent less than it was ten years ago.

The action was emphatically for the general good. It offered the only chance for arresting the panic, and it did arrest the panic. I answered Messrs. Frick and Gary, as set forth in the letter quoted above, to the effect that I did not deem it my duty to interfere, that is, to forbid the action which more than anything else in actual fact saved

21

the situation. The result justified my judgment. The panic was stopped, public confidence in the solvency of the threatened institution being at once restored.

Business was vitally helped by what I did. The benefit was not only for the moment. It was permanent. Particularly was this the case in the South. Three or four years afterwards I visited Birmingham. Every man I met, without exception, who was competent to testify, informed me voluntarily that the results of the action taken had been of the utmost benefit to Birmingham, and therefore to Alabama, the industry having profited to an extraordinary degree, not only from the standpoint of the business, but from the standpoint of the community at large and of the wage-workers, by the change in ownership. The results of the action I took were beneficial from every standpoint, and the action itself, at the time when it was taken, was vitally necessary to the welfare of the people of the United States.

I would have been derelict in my duty, I would have shown myself a timid and unworthy public servant, if in that extraordinary crisis I had not acted precisely as I did act. In every such crisis the temptation to indecision, to non-action, is great, for excuses can always be found for non-action, and action means risk and the certainty of blame to the man who acts. But if the man is worth his salt he will do his duty, he will give the people the benefit of the doubt, and act in any way which their interests demand and which is not affirmatively prohibited by law, unheeding the likelihood that he himself, when the crisis is over and the danger past, will be assailed for what he has done.

Every step I took in this matter was open as the day, and was known in detail at the moment to all people. The press contained full accounts of the visit to me of Messrs. Frick and Gary, and heralded widely and with acclamation the results of that visit. At the time the relief and rejoicing over what had been done were well-nigh universal. The danger was too imminent and too appalling for men to be willing to condemn those who were successful in saving them from it. But I fully understood and expected that when there was no longer danger, when the fear had been forgotten, attack would be made upon me; and as a matter of fact after a year had elapsed the attack was begun, and has continued at intervals ever since; my ordinary assailant being some politician of rather cheap type.

If I were on a sail-boat, I should not ordinarily meddle with any of the gear; but if a sudden squall struck us, and the main sheet jammed, so that the boat threatened to capsize, I would unhesitatingly cut the main sheet, even though I were sure that the owner, no matter how grateful to me at the moment for having saved his life, would a few weeks later, when he had forgotten his danger and his fear, decide to sue me for the value of the cut rope. But I would feel a hearty contempt for the owner who so acted.

There were many other things that we did in connection with corporations. One of the most important was the passage of the meat inspection law because of scandalous abuses shown to exist in the great packing-houses in Chicago and elsewhere. There was a curious result of this law, similar to what occurred in connection with the law providing for effective railway regulation. The big beef men bitterly opposed the law; just as the big railway men opposed the Hepburn Act. Yet three or four years after these laws had been put on the statute books every honest man both in the beef business and the railway business came to the conclusion that they worked good and not harm to the decent business concerns. They hurt only those who were not acting as they should have acted. The law providing for the inspection of packing-houses, and the Pure Food and Drugs Act, were also extremely important; and the way in which they were administered was even more important. It would be hard to overstate the value of the service rendered in all these cases by such cabinet officers as Moody and Bonaparte, and their outside assistants of the stamp of Frank Kellogg.

It would be useless to enumerate all the suits we brought. Some of them I have already touched upon. Others, such as the suits against the Harriman railway corporations, which were successful, and which had been rendered absolutely necessary by the grossly improper action of the corporations concerned, offered no special points of interest. The Sugar Trust proceedings, however, may be mentioned as showing just the kind of thing that was done and the kind of obstacle encountered and overcome in prosecutions of this character.

It was on the advice of my secretary, William Loeb, Jr., afterward head of the New York Custom-House, that the action was taken which started the uncovering of the frauds perpetrated by the Sugar Trust and other companies in connection with the importing of sugar. Loeb had from time to time told me that he was sure that there was fraud in connection with the importations by the Sugar Trust through the New York Custom-House. Finally, some time toward the end of 1904, he informed me that Richard Parr, a sampler at the New York Appraisers' Stores (whose duties took him almost continually on the docks in connection with the sampling of merchandise), had called on him, and had stated that in his belief the sugar companies were defrauding the Government in the matter of weights, and had stated that if he could be made an investigating officer of the Treasury Department, he was confident that he could show there was wrongdoing. Parr had been a former school fellow of Loeb in Albany, and Loeb believed him to be loyal, honest, and efficient. He thereupon laid the matter before me, and advised the appointment of Parr as a special employee of the Treasury Department, for the specific purpose of investigating the alleged sugar frauds. I instructed the Treasury Department accordingly, and was informed that there was no vacancy in the force of special employees, but that Parr would be given the first place that opened up. Early in the spring of 1905 Parr came to Loeb again, and said that he had received additional information about the sugar frauds, and was anxious to begin the investigation. Loeb again discussed the matter with me; and I notified the Treasury Department to appoint Parr immediately. On June 1, 1905, he received his appointment, and was assigned to the port of Boston for the purpose of gaining some experience as an investigating officer. During the month he was transferred to the Maine District, with headquarters at Portland, where he remained until March, 1907. During his service in Maine he uncovered extensive wool smuggling frauds. At the conclusion of the wool case, he appealed to Loeb to have him transferred to New York, so that he might undertake the investigation of the sugar underweighing frauds. I now called the attention of Secretary Cortelyou personally to the matter, so that he would be able to keep a check over any subordinates who might try to interfere with Parr, for the conspiracy was evidently widespread, the wealth of the offenders great, and the corruption in the service far-reaching — while moreover as always happens with "respectable" offenders, there were many good men who sincerely disbelieved in the possibility of corruption on the part of men of such high financial standing. Parr was assigned to New York early in March, 1907, and at once began an active investigation of the conditions existing on the sugar docks. This terminated in the discovery of a steel spring in one of the scales of the Havemeyer & Elder docks in Brooklyn, November 20, 1907, which enabled us to uncover what were probably the most colossal frauds ever perpetrated in the Customs Service. From the beginning of his active work in the investigation of the sugar frauds in March, 1907, to March 4, 1909, Parr, from time to time, personally reported to Loeb, at the White House, the progress of his investigations, and Loeb in his turn kept me personally advised. On one occasion there was an attempt made to shunt Parr off the investigation and substitute another agent of the Treasury, who was suspected of having some relations with the sugar companies under investigation; but Parr reported the facts to Loeb, I sent for Secretary Cortelyou, and Secretary Cortelyou promptly took charge of the matter himself, putting Parr back on the investigation.

During the investigation Parr was subjected to all sorts of harassments, including an attempt to bribe him by Spitzer, the dock superintendent of the Havemeyer & Elder Refinery, for which Spitzer was convicted and served a term in prison. Brzezinski, a special agent, who was assisting Parr, was convicted of perjury and also served a term in prison, he having changed his testimony, in the trial of Spitzer for the attempted bribery of Parr, from that which he gave before the Grand Jury. For his extraordinary services in connection with this investigation Parr was granted an award of $100,000 by the Treasury Department.

District-Attorney Stimson, of New York, assisted by Denison, Frankfurter, Wise, and other employees of the Department of Justice, took charge of the case, and carried on both civil and criminal proceedings. The trial in the action against the Sugar Trust, for the recovery of duties on the cargo of sugar, which was being sent over the scales at the time of the discovery of the steel spring by Parr, was begun in 1908; judgment was rendered against the defendants on March 5, 1909, the day after I left office. Over four million dollars were recovered and paid back into the United States Treasury by the sugar companies which had perpetrated the various forms of fraud. These frauds were unearthed by Parr, Loeb, Stimson, Frankfurter, and the other men mentioned and their associates, and it was to them that the people owed the refunding of the huge sum of money mentioned. We had already secured heavy fines from the Sugar Trust, and from various big railways, and private individuals, such as Edwin Earle, for unlawful rebates. In the case of the chief offender, the American Sugar Refining Company (the Sugar Trust), criminal prosecutions were carried on against every living man whose position was such that he would naturally know about the fraud. All of them were indicted, and the biggest and most responsible ones were convicted. The evidence showed that the president of the company, Henry O. Havemeyer, virtually ran the entire company, and was responsible for all the details of the management. He died two weeks after the fraud was discovered, just as proceedings were being begun. Next to him in importance was the secretary and treasurer, Charles R. Heike, who was convicted. Various other officials and employees of the Trust, and various Government employees, were indicted, and most of them convicted. Ernest W.

Gerbracht, the superintendent of one of the refineries, was convicted, but his sentence was commuted to a short jail imprisonment, because he became a Government witness and greatly assisted the Government in the suits.

Heike's sentence was commuted so as to excuse him from going to the penitentiary; just as the penitentiary sentence of Morse, the big New York banker, who was convicted of gross fraud and misapplication of funds, was commuted. Both commutations were granted long after I left office. In each case the commutation was granted because, as was stated, of the prisoner's age and state of health. In Morse's case the President originally refused the request, saying that Morse had exhibited "fraudulent and criminal disregard of the trust imposed upon him," that "he was entirely unscrupulous as to the methods he adopted," and "that he seemed at times to be absolutely heartless with regard to the consequences to others, and he showed great shrewdness in obtaining

PAUL MORTON.

large sums of money from the bank without adequate security and without making himself personally liable therefor." The two cases may be considered in connection with the announcement in the public press that on May 17, 1913, the President commuted the sentence of Lewis A. Banks, who was serving a very long term penitentiary sentence for an attack on a girl in the Indian Territory; "the reason for the commutation which is set forth in the press being that 'Banks is in poor health.'"

It is no easy matter to balance the claims of justice and

mercy in such cases.   In these three cases, of all of which I
had personal cognizance, I disagreed radically with the views
my successors took, and with the views which many respectable men took who in these and similar cases, both while I
was in office and afterward, urged me to show, or to ask
others to show, clemency.   It then seemed to me, and it now
seems to me, that such clemency is from the larger standpoint a gross wrong to the men and women of the country.

One of the former special assistants of the district-attorney,
Mr. W. Cleveland Runyon, in commenting bitterly on the
release of Heike and Morse on account of their health,
pointed out that their health apparently became good when
once they themselves became free men, and added:

"The commutation of these sentences amounts to a direct
interference with the administration of justice by the courts.
Heike got a $25,000 salary and has escaped his imprison-
ment, but what about the six $18 a week checkers, who were
sent to jail, one of them a man of more than sixty ?   It is
cases like this that create discontent and anarchy.   They
make it seem plain that there is one law for the rich and
another for the poor man, and I for one will protest."

In dealing with Heike the individual (or Morse or any
other individual), it is necessary to emphasize the social
aspects of his case.   The moral of the Heike case, as has been
well said, is "how easy it is for a man in modern corporate
organization to drift into wrongdoing."   The moral restraints are loosened in the case of a man like Heike by the
insulation of himself from the sordid details of crime, through
industrially coerced intervening agents.   Professor Ross has
made the penetrating observation that "distance disinfects
dividends"; it also weakens individual responsibility, particularly on the part of the very managers of large business,
who should feel it most acutely.   One of the officers of the
Department of Justice who conducted the suit, and who
inclined to the side of mercy in the matter, nevertheless
writes: "Heike is a beautiful illustration of mental and
moral obscuration in the business life of an otherwise valuable member of society.   Heike had an ample share in the
guidance of the affairs of the American Sugar Company,

and we are apt to have a foreshortened picture of his responsibility, because he operated from the easy coign of vantage of executive remoteness.   It is difficult to say to what extent he did, directly or indirectly, profit by the sordid practices of his company.   But the social damage of an individual in his position may be just as deep, whether merely the zest of the game or hard cash be his dominant motive."

I have coupled the cases of the big banker and the Sugar Trust official and the case of the man convicted of a criminal assault on a woman.   All of the criminals were released from penitentiary sentences on grounds of ill health.   The offenses were typical of the worst crimes committed at the two ends of the social scale.   One offense was a crime of brutal violence; the other offenses were crimes of astute corruption.   All of them were offenses which in my judgment were of such a character that clemency towards the offender worked grave injustice to the community as a whole, injustice so grave that its effects might be far-reaching in their damage.

Every time that rape or criminal assault on a woman is pardoned, and anything less than the full penalty of the law exacted, a premium is put on the practice of lynching such offenders.   Every time a big monied offender, who naturally excites interest and sympathy, and who has many friends, is excused from serving a sentence which a man of less prominence and fewer friends would have to serve, justice is discredited in the eyes of plain people — and to undermine faith in justice is to strike at the foundation of the Republic.   As for ill health, it must be remembered that few people are as healthy in prison as they would be outside; and there should be no discrimination among criminals on this score; either all criminals who grow unhealthy should be let out, or none.   Pardons must sometimes be given in order that the cause of justice may be served; but in cases such as these I am considering, while I know that many amiable people differ from me, I am obliged to say that in my judgment the pardons work far-reaching harm to the cause of justice.

Among the big corporations themselves, even where

they did wrong, there was a wide difference in the moral obliquity indicated by the wrongdoer. There was a wide distinction between the offenses committed in the case of the Northern Securities Company, and the offenses because of which the Sugar Trust, the Tobacco Trust, and the Standard Oil Trust were successfully prosecuted under my

JAMES R. GARFIELD.

Administration. It was vital to destroy the Northern Securities Company; but the men creating it had done so in open and above-board fashion, acting under what they, and most of the members of the bar, thought to be the law established by the Supreme Court in the Knight sugar case. But the Supreme Court in its decree dissolving the Standard Oil and Tobacco Trusts, condemned them in the severest language for moral turpitude; and an even severer meed of condemnation should be visited on the Sugar Trust.

However, all the trusts and big corporations against which we proceeded — which included in their directorates practically all the biggest financiers in the country — joined in making the bitterest assaults on me and on my Administration. Of their actions I wrote as follows to Attorney-General Bonaparte, who had been a peculiarly close friend and adviser through the period covered by my public life in high office and who, together with Attorney-General Moody, possessed the same understanding sympathy with my social and industrial program that was possessed by such officials as Straus, Garfield, H. K. Smith, and Pinchot. The letter runs:

January 2, 1908.

My dear Bonaparte:

I must congratulate you on your admirable speech at Chicago. You said the very things it was good to say at this time. What you said bore especial weight because it represented what you had done. You have shown by what you have actually accomplished that the law is enforced against the wealthiest corporation, and the richest and most powerful manager or manipulator of that corporation, just as resolutely and fearlessly as against the humblest citizen. The Department of Justice is now in very fact the Department of Justice, and justice is meted out with an even hand to great and small, rich and poor, weak and strong. Those who have denounced you and the action of the Department of Justice are either misled, or else are the very wrongdoers, and the agents of the very wrongdoers, who have for so many years gone scot-free and flouted the laws with impunity. Above all, you are to be congratulated upon the bitterness felt and expressed towards you by the representatives and agents of the great law-defying corporations of immense wealth, who, until within the last half-dozen years, have treated themselves and have expected others to treat them as being beyond and above all possible check from law.

It was time to say something, for the representatives of predatory wealth, of wealth accumulated on a giant scale by iniquity, by wrongdoing in many forms, by plain swindling, by oppressing wage-workers, by manipulating securities, by unfair and unwholesome competition and by stock-jobbing, — in short, by conduct abhorrent to every man of ordinarily decent conscience, have during the last few months made it evident that they are banded together to work for a reaction, to endeavor to overthrow and discredit all who honestly administer the law, and to secure a return to the days when every unscrupulous wrongdoer could do what he wished unchecked, provided he had enough money. They attack you because they know your honesty and fearlessness, and dread them. The enormous sums of money these men have at their control enable them to carry on an effective campaign. They find their tools in a portion

of the public press, including especially certain of the great
New York newspapers.   They find their agents in some
men in public life, — now and then occupying, or having
occupied, positions as high as Senator or Governor, — in
some men in the pulpit, and most melancholy of all, in a
few men on the bench.   By gifts to colleges and universities they are occasionally able to subsidize in their own
interest some head of an educational body, who, save only
a judge, should of all men be most careful to keep his skirts
clear from the taint of such corruption.   There are ample
material rewards for those who serve with fidelity the
Mammon of unrighteousness, but they are dearly paid for
by that institution of learning whose head, by example
and precept, teaches the scholars who sit under him that
there is one law for the rich and another for the poor.   The
amount of money the representatives of the great monied
interests are willing to spend can be gauged by their recent
publication broadcast throughout the papers of this country
from the Atlantic to the Pacific of huge advertisements,
attacking with envenomed bitterness the Administration's
policy of warring against successful dishonesty, advertisements that must have cost enormous sums of money.   This
advertisement, as also a pamphlet called "The Roosevelt
Panic," and one or two similar books and pamphlets, are
written especially in the interest of the Standard Oil and
Harriman combinations, but also defend all the individuals
and corporations of great wealth that have been guilty of
wrongdoing.   From the railroad rate law to the pure food
law, every measure for honesty in business that has been
pressed during the last six years, has been opposed by these
men, on its passage and in its administration, with every
resource that bitter and unscrupulous craft could suggest,
and the command of almost unlimited money secure.   These
men do not themselves speak or write ; they hire others to
do their bidding.   Their spirit and purpose are made clear
alike by the editorials of the papers owned in, or whose
policy is dictated by, Wall Street, and by the speeches of
public men who, as Senators, Governors, or Mayors, have
served these their masters to the cost of the plain people.

At one time one of their writers or speakers attacks the rate law as the cause of the panic; he is, whether in public life or not, usually a clever corporation lawyer, and he is not so foolish a being as to believe in the truth of what he says; he has too closely represented the railroads not to know well that the Hepburn Rate Bill has helped every honest railroad, and has hurt only the railroads that regarded themselves as above the law.   At another time, one of them assails the Administration for not imprisoning people under the Sherman Anti-Trust Law; for declining to make what he well knows, in view of the actual attitude of juries (as shown in the Tobacco Trust cases and in San Francisco in one or two of the cases brought against corrupt business men) would have been the futile endeavor to imprison defendants whom we are actually able to fine.   He raises the usual clamor, raised by all who object to the enforcement of the law, that we are fining corporations instead of putting the heads of the corporations in jail; and he states that this does not really harm the chief offenders.   Were this statement true, he himself would not be found attacking us. The extraordinary violence of the assault upon our policy contained in speeches like these, in the articles in the subsidized press, in such huge advertisements and pamphlets as those above referred to, and the enormous sums of money spent in these various ways, give a fairly accurate measure of the anger and terror which our actions have caused the corrupt men of vast wealth to feel in the very marrow of their being.

The man thus attacking us is usually, like so many of his fellows, either a great lawyer, or a paid editor who takes his commands from the financiers and his arguments from their attorneys.   If the former, he has defended many malefactors, and he knows well that, thanks to the advice of lawyers like himself, a certain kind of modern corporation has been turned into an admirable instrument by which to render it well nigh impossible to get at the really guilty man, so that in most cases the only way of punishing the wrong is by fining the corporation or by proceeding personally against some of the minor agents.   These lawyers and their employers are the men mainly responsible for this state of things, and their responsibility is shared with the legislators who ingeniously oppose the passing of just and effective laws, and with those judges whose one aim seems to be to construe such laws so that they cannot be executed.   Nothing is sillier than this outcry on behalf of the "innocent stockholders" in the corporations.   We are besought to pity the Standard Oil Company for a fine relatively far less great than the fines every day inflicted in the police courts upon multitudes of push cart peddlers and other petty offenders, whose woes never extort one word from the men whose withers are wrung by the woes of the mighty.   The stockholders have the control of the corporation in their own hands. The corporation officials are elected by those holding the majority of the stock and can keep office only by having behind them the good-will of these majority stockholders. They are not entitled to the slightest pity if they deliberately choose to resign into the hands of great wrongdoers the control of the corporations in which they own the stock. Of course innocent people have become involved in these big corporations and suffer because of the misdeeds of their criminal associates.   Let these innocent people be careful not to invest in corporations where those in control are not men of probity, men who respect the laws; above all let them avoid the men who make it their one effort to evade or defy the laws.   But if these honest innocent people are in the majority in any corporation they can immediately resume control and throw out of the directory the men who misrepresent them.   Does any man for a moment suppose that the majority stockholders of the Standard Oil are others then Mr. Rockefeller and his associates themselves and the beneficiaries of their wrongdoing?   When the stock is watered so that the innocent investors suffer, a grave wrong is indeed done to these innocent investors as well as to the public; but the public men, lawyers and editors, to whom I refer, do not under these circumstances express sympathy for the innocent; on the contrary they are the first to protest with frantic vehemence against our efforts by law to put a stop to over-capitalization and stock-watering.   The apologists of successful dishonesty always declaim against any effort to punish or prevent it on the ground that such effort will "unsettle business." It is they who by their acts have unsettled business ; and the very men raising this cry spend hundreds of thousands of dollars in securing, by speech, editorial, book or pamphlet, the defense by mis- statement of what they have done ; and yet when we correct their misstatements by telling the truth, they declaim against us for breaking silence, lest "values be unsettled !" They have hurt honest business men, honest working men, honest farmers ; and now they clamor against the truth being told.

The keynote of all these attacks upon the effort to secure honesty in business and in politics, is expressed in a recent speech, in which the speaker stated that prosperity had been checked by the effort for the "moral regeneration of the business world," an effort which he denounced as "un- natural, unwarranted and injurious" and for which he stated the panic was the penalty. The morality of such a plea is precisely as great as if made on behalf of the men caught in a gambling establishment when that gambling establishment is raided by the police. If such words mean anything they mean that those whose sentiments they represent stand against the effort to bring about a moral regeneration of business which will prevent a repetition of the insurance, banking and street railroad scandals in New York ; a repetition of the Chicago and Alton deal ; a repetition of the combination between certain professional politicians, certain professional labor leaders and certain big financiers from the disgrace of which San Francisco has just been rescued ; a repetition of the successful efforts by the Standard Oil people to crush out every competitor, to overawe the common carriers, and to establish a monopoly which treats the public with the contempt which the public deserves so long as it permits men like the public men of whom I speak to represent it in politics, men like the heads of colleges to whom I refer to educate its youth. The out- cry against stopping dishonest practices among the very wealthy is precisely similar to the outcry raised against every effort for cleanliness and decency in city government because, forsooth, it will "hurt business." The same outcry is made against the Department of Justice for prosecuting the heads of colossal corporations that is made against the men who in San Francisco are prosecuting with impartial severity the wrongdoers among business men, public officials, and

GIFFORD PINCHOT.

labor leaders alike. The principle is the same in the two cases. Just as the blackmailer and the bribe giver stand on the same evil eminence of infamy, so the man who makes an enormous fortune by corrupting Legislatures and municipalities and fleecing his stockholders and the public stands on a level with the creature who fattens on the blood money of the gambling house, the saloon and the brothel.

Moreover, both kinds of corruption in the last analysis are far more intimately connected than would at first sight appear; the wrong-doing is at bottom the same. Corrupt business and corrupt politics act and react, with ever increasing debasement, one on the other; the rebate-taker, the franchise-trafficker, the manipulator of securities, the purveyor and protector of vice, the black-mailing ward boss, the ballot box stuffer, the demagogue, the mob leader, the hired bully and mankiller, all alike work at the same web of corruption, and all alike should be abhorred by honest men.

The "business" which is hurt by the movement for honesty is the kind of business which, in the long run, it pays the country to have hurt. It is the kind of business which has tended to make the very name "high finance" a term of scandal to which all honest American men of business should join in putting an end. One of the special pleaders for business dishonesty, in a recent speech, in denouncing the Administration for enforcing the law against the huge and corrupt corporations which have defied the law, also denounced it for endeavoring to secure a far-reaching law making employers liable for injuries to their employees. It is meet and fit that the apologists for corrupt wealth should oppose every effort to relieve weak and helpless people from crushing misfortune brought upon them by injury in the business from which they gain a bare livelihood and their employers fortunes. It is hypocritical baseness to speak of a girl who works in a factory where the dangerous machinery is unprotected as having the "right" freely to contract to expose herself to dangers to life and limb. She has no alternative but to suffer want or else to expose herself to such dangers, and when she loses a hand or is otherwise maimed or disfigured for life it is a moral wrong that the burden of the risk necessarily incidental to the business should be placed with crushing weight upon her weak shoulders and the man who has profited by her work escape scot-free. This is what our opponents advocate, and it is proper that they should advocate it, for it rounds out their advocacy of those most dangerous members of the criminal class,

2 K

the criminals of vast wealth, the men who can afford best to pay for such championship in the press and on the stump.

It is difficult to speak about the judges, for it behooves us all to treat with the utmost respect the high office of judge; and our judges as a whole are brave and upright men. But there is need that those who go wrong should not be allowed to feel that there is no condemnation of their wrongdoing. A judge who on the bench either truckles to the mob or bows down before a corporation; or who, having left the bench to become a corporation lawyer, seeks to aid his clients by denouncing as enemies of property all those who seek to stop the abuses of the criminal rich; such a man performs an even worse service to the body politic than the Legislator or Executive who goes wrong. In no way can respect for the courts be so quickly undermined as by teaching the public through the action of a judge himself that there is reason for the loss of such respect. The judge who by word or deed makes it plain that the corrupt corporation, the law-defying corporation, the law-defying rich man, has in him a sure and trustworthy ally, the judge who by misuse of the process of injunction makes it plain that in him the wage-worker has a determined and unscrupulous enemy, the judge who when he decides in an employers' liability or a tenement house factory case shows that he has neither sympathy for nor understanding of those fellow-citizens of his who most need his sympathy and under-standing; these judges work as much evil as if they pandered to the mob, as if they shrank from sternly repressing violence and disorder. The judge who does his full duty well stands higher, and renders a better service to the people, than any other public servant; he is entitled to greater respect; and if he is a true servant of the people, if he is upright, wise and fearless, he will unhesitatingly disregard even the wishes of the people if they conflict with the eternal principles of right as against wrong. He must serve the people; but he must serve his conscience first. All honor to such a judge; and all honor cannot be rendered him if it is rendered equally to his brethren who fall immeasurably below the high ideals for which he stands. There should be a sharp discrimination against such judges. They claim immunity from criticism, and the claim is heatedly advanced by men and newspapers like those of whom I speak. Most certainly they can claim immunity from untruthful criticism; and their champions, the newspapers and the public men I have mentioned, exquisitely illustrate by their own actions mendacious criticism in its most flagrant and iniquitous form.

But no servant of the people has a right to expect to be free from just and honest criticism. It is the newspapers, and the public men whose thoughts and deeds show them to be most alien to honesty and truth who themselves loudly object to truthful and honest criticism of their fellow-servants of the great monied interests.

We have no quarrel with the individuals, whether public men, lawyers or editors, to whom I refer. These men derive their sole power from the great, sinister offenders who stand behind them. They are but puppets who move as the strings are pulled by those who control the enormous masses of corporate wealth which if itself left uncontrolled threatens dire evil to the Republic. It is not the puppets, but the strong, cunning men and the mighty forces working for evil behind, and to a certain extent through, the puppets, with whom we have to deal. We seek to control law-defying wealth, in the first place to prevent its doing evil, and in the next place to avoid the vindictive and dreadful radicalism which if left uncontrolled it is certain in the end to arouse. Sweeping attacks upon all property, upon all men of means, without regard to whether they do well or ill, would sound the death knell of the Republic; and such attacks become inevitable if decent citizens permit rich men whose lives are corrupt and evil to domineer in swollen pride, unchecked and unhindered, over the destinies of this country. We act in no vindictive spirit, and we are no respecters of persons. If a labor union does what is wrong, we oppose it as fearlessly as we oppose a corporation that does wrong; and we stand with equal stoutness for the rights of the man of wealth and for the rights of the wage-workers; just as much so for one as for the other. We seek to stop wrongdoing; and we desire to punish the wrongdoer only so far as is necessary in order to achieve this end. We are the stanch upholders of every honest man, whether business man or wage-worker.

I do not for a moment believe that our actions have brought on business distress; so far as this is due to local and not world-wide causes, and to the actions of any particular individuals, it is due to the speculative folly and flagrant dishonesty of a few men of great wealth, who now seek to shield themselves from the effects of their own wrongdoings by ascribing its results to the actions of those who have sought to put a stop to the wrongdoing. But if it were true that to cut out rottenness from the body politic meant a momentary check to an unhealthy seeming prosperity, I should not for one moment hesitate to put the knife to the cancer. On behalf of all our people, on behalf no less of the honest man of means than of the honest man who earns each day's livelihood by that day's sweat of his brow, it is necessary to insist upon honesty in business and politics alike, in all walks of life, in big things and in little things; upon just and fair dealing as between man and man. We are striving for the right in the spirit of Abraham Lincoln when he said:

"Fondly do we hope — fervently do we pray — that this mighty scourge may speedily pass away. Yet, if God wills that it continue until all the wealth piled by the bondsmen's two hundred and fifty years of unrequited toil shall be sunk, and until every drop of blood drawn with the lash shall be paid by another drawn with the sword, as was said three thousand years ago, so still it must be said, 'The judgments of the Lord are true and righteous altogether.'

"With malice toward none; with charity for all; with firmness in the right, as God gives us to see the right, let us strive on to finish the work we are in."

Sincerely yours,

THEODORE ROOSEVELT.

HON. CHARLES J. BONAPARTE.
Attorney-General.

CHAPTER XIII

SOCIAL AND INDUSTRIAL JUSTICE

BY the time I became President I had grown to feel with deep intensity of conviction that governmental agencies must find their justification largely in the way in which they are used for the practical betterment of living and working conditions among the mass of the people. I felt that the fight was really for the abolition of privilege; and one of the first stages in the battle was necessarily to fight for the rights of the workingman. For this reason I felt most strongly that all that the government could do in the interest of labor should be done. The Federal Government can rarely act with the directness that the State governments act. It can, however, do a good deal. My purpose was to make the National Government itself a model employer of labor, the effort being to make the per diem employee just as much as the Cabinet officer regard himself as one of the partners employed in the service of the public, proud of his work, eager to do it in the best possible manner, and confident of just treatment. Our aim was also to secure good laws wherever the National Government had power, notably in the Territories, in the District of Columbia, and in connection with inter-State commerce. I found the eight-hour law a mere farce, the departments rarely enforcing it with any degree of efficiency. This I remedied by executive action. Unfortunately, thoroughly efficient government servants often proved to be the prime offenders so far as the enforcement of the eight-hour law was concerned, because in their zeal to get good work done for the Government they became harsh taskmasters, and declined to consider the needs of their fellow-employees who served under them.

The more I had studied the subject the more strongly I had become convinced that an eight-hour day under the conditions of labor in the United States was all that could, with wisdom and propriety, be required either by the Government or by private employers; that more than this meant, on the average, a decrease in the qualities that tell for good citizenship. I finally solved the problem, as far as Government employees were concerned, by calling in Charles P. Neill, the head of the Labor Bureau; and, acting on his advice, I speedily made the eight-hour law really effective. Any man who shirked his work, who dawdled and idled, received no mercy; slackness is even worse than harshness; for exactly as in battle mercy to the coward is cruelty to the brave man, so in civil life slackness towards the vicious and idle is harshness towards the honest and hard-working.

We passed a good law protecting the lives and health of miners in the Territories, and other laws providing for the supervision of employment agencies in the District of Columbia, and protecting the health of motormen and conductors on street railways in the District. We practically started the Bureau of Mines. We provided for safeguarding factory employees in the District against accidents, and for the restriction of child labor therein. We passed a workmen's compensation law for the protection of Government employees; a law which did not go as far as I wished, but which was the best I could get, and which committed the Government to the right policy. We provided for an investigation of woman and child labor in the United States. We incorporated the National Child Labor Committee. Where we had most difficulty was with the railway companies engaged in inter-State business. We passed an act improving safety appliances on railway trains without much opposition, but we had more trouble with acts regulating the hours of labor of railway employees and making those railways which were engaged in inter-State commerce liable for injuries to or the death of their employees while on duty. One important step in connection with these latter laws was taken by Attorney-General

Moody when, on behalf of the Government, he intervened in the case of a wronged employee. It is unjust that a law which has been declared public policy by the representatives of the people should be submitted to the possibility of nullification because the Government leaves the enforcement of it to the private initiative of poor people who have just suffered some crushing accident. It should be the business of the Government to enforce laws of this kind, and to appear in court to argue for their constitutionality and proper enforcement. Thanks to Moody, the Government assumed this position. The first employers' liability law affecting inter-State railroads was declared unconstitutional. We got through another, which stood the test of the courts.

The principle to which we especially strove to give expression, through these laws and through executive action, was that a right is valueless unless reduced from the abstract to the concrete. This sounds like a truism. So far from being such, the effort practically to apply it was almost revolutionary, and gave rise to the bitterest denunciation of us by all the big lawyers, and all the big newspaper editors, who, whether sincerely or for hire, gave expression to the views of the privileged classes. Ever since the Civil War very many of the decisions of the courts, not as regards ordinary actions between man and man, but as regards the application of great governmental policies for social and industrial justice, had been in reality nothing but ingenious justifications of the theory that these policies were mere high-sounding abstractions, and were not to be given practical effect. The tendency of the courts had been, in the majority of cases, jealously to exert their great power in protecting those who least needed protection and hardly to use their power at all in the interest of those who most needed protection. Our desire was to make the Federal Government efficient as an instrument for protecting the rights of labor within its province, and therefore to secure and enforce judicial decisions which would permit us to make this desire effective. Not only some of the Federal judges, but some of the State courts invoked the Constitution in a spirit of the narrowest legalistic obstruction to prevent the Government from acting in defense of labor on inter-State railways. In effect, these judges took the view that while Congress had complete power as regards the goods transported by the railways, and could protect wealthy or well-to-do owners of these goods, yet that it had no power to protect the lives of the men engaged in transporting the goods. Such judges freely issued injunctions to prevent the obstruction of traffic in the interest of the property owners, but declared unconstitutional the action of the Government in seeking to safeguard the men, and the families of the men, without whose labor the traffic could not take place. It was an instance of the largely unconscious way in which the courts had been twisted into the exaltation of property rights over human rights, and the subordination of the welfare of the laborer when compared with the profit of the man for whom he labored. By what I fear my conservative friends regarded as frightfully aggressive missionary work, which included some uncommonly plain speaking as to certain unjust and anti-social judicial decisions, we succeeded in largely, but by no means altogether, correcting this view, at least so far as the best and most enlightened judges were concerned.

Very much the most important action I took as regards labor had nothing to do with legislation, and represented executive action which was not required by the Constitution. It illustrated as well as anything that I did the theory which I have called the Jackson-Lincoln theory of the Presidency; that is, that occasionally great national crises arise which call for immediate and vigorous executive action, and that in such cases it is the duty of the President to act upon the theory that he is the steward of the people, and that the proper attitude for him to take is that he is bound to assume that he has the legal right to do whatever the needs of the people demand, unless the Constitution or the laws explicitly forbid him to do it.

Early in the spring of 1902 a universal strike began in the anthracite regions. The miners and the operators became deeply embittered, and the strike went on throughout the summer and the early fall without any sign of reaching an end, and with almost complete stoppage of mining. In many cities, especially in the East, the heating apparatus is designed for anthracite, so that the bituminous coal is only a very partial substitute. Moreover, in many regions, even in farmhouses, many of the provisions are for burning coal and not wood. In consequence, the coal famine became a National menace as the winter approached. In most big cities and many farming districts east of the Mississippi the shortage of anthracite threatened calamity. In the populous industrial States, from Ohio eastward, it was not merely calamity, but the direst disaster, that was threatened. Ordinarily conservative men, men very sensitive as to the rights of property under normal conditions, when faced by this crisis felt, quite rightly, that there must be some radical action. The Governor of Massachusetts and the Mayor of New York both notified me, as the cold weather came on, that if the coal famine continued the misery throughout the Northeast, and especially in the great cities, would become appalling, and the consequent public disorder so great that frightful consequences might follow. It is not too much to say that the situation which confronted Pennsylvania, New York, and New England, and to a less degree the States of the Middle West, in October, 1902, was quite as serious as if they had been threatened by the invasion of a hostile army of overwhelming force.

The big coal operators had banded together, and positively refused to take any steps looking toward an accommodation. They knew that the suffering among the miners was great; they were confident that if order were kept, and nothing further done by the Government, they would win; and they refused to consider that the public had any rights in the matter. They were, for the most part, men of unquestionably good private life, and they were merely taking the extreme individualistic view of the rights of property and the freedom of individual action upheld in the *laissez faire* political economies. The mines were in the State of Pennsylvania. There was no duty whatever laid upon me by the Constitution in the matter, and I had in theory no power to act directly unless the Governor of Pennsylvania or the Legislature, if it were in session, should notify me that Pennsylvania could not keep order, and request me as commander-in-chief of the army of the United States to intervene and keep order.

As long as I could avoid interfering I did so; but I directed the head of the Labor Bureau, Carroll Wright, to make a thorough investigation and lay the facts fully before me. As September passed without any sign of weakening either among the employers or the striking workmen, the situation became so grave that I felt I would have to try to do something. The thing most feasible was to get both sides to agree to a Commission of Arbitration, with a promise to accept its findings; the miners to go to work as soon as the commission was appointed, at the old rate of wages. To this proposition the miners, headed by John Mitchell, agreed, stipulating only that I should have power to name the Commission. The operators, however, positively refused. They insisted that all that was necessary to do was for the State to keep order, using the militia as a police force; although both they and the miners asked me to intervene under the Inter-State Commerce Law, each side requesting that I proceed against the other, and both requests being impossible.

Finally, on October 3, the representatives of both the operators and the miners met before me, in pursuance of my request. The representatives of the miners included as their head and spokesman John Mitchell, who kept his temper admirably and showed to much advantage. The representatives of the operators, on the contrary, came down in a most insolent frame of mind, refused to talk of arbitration or other accommodation of any kind, and used language that was insulting to the miners and offensive to me. They were curiously ignorant of the popular temper; and when they went away from the interview they, with much pride, gave their own account of it to the papers, exulting in the fact that they had "turned down" both the miners and the President.

I refused to accept the rebuff, however, and continued the

effort to get an agreement between the operators and the miners. I was anxious to get this agreement, because it would prevent the necessity of taking the extremely drastic action I meditated, and which is hereinafter described.

Fortunately, this time we were successful. Yet we were on the verge of failure, because of self-willed obstinacy on the part of the operators. This obstinacy was utterly silly from their own standpoint, and well-nigh criminal from the standpoint of the people at large. The miners proposed that I should name the Commission, and that if I put on a representative of the employing class I should also put on a labor union man. The operators positively declined to accept the suggestion. They insisted upon my naming a Commission of only five men, and specified the qualifications these men should have, carefully choosing these qualifications so as to exclude those whom it had leaked out I was thinking of appointing, including ex-President Cleveland. They made the condition that I was to appoint one officer of the engineer corps of the army or navy, one man with experience of mining, one "man of prominence," "eminent as a sociologist," one Federal judge of the Eastern District of Pennsylvania, and one mining engineer.

They positively refused to have me appoint any representative of labor, or to put on an extra man. I was desirous of putting on the extra man, because Mitchell and the other leaders of the miners had urged me to appoint some high Catholic ecclesiastic. Most of the miners were Catholics, and Mitchell and the leaders were very anxious to secure peaceful acquiescence by the miners in any decision rendered, and they felt that their hands would be strengthened if such an appointment were made. They also, quite properly, insisted that there should be one representative of labor on the Commission, as all of the others represented the propertied classes. The operators, however, absolutely refused to acquiesce in the appointment of any representative of labor, and also announced that they would refuse to accept a sixth man on the Commission; although they spoke much less decidedly on this point. The labor men left everything in my hands.

The final conferences with the representatives of the operators took place in my rooms on the evening of October 15. Hour after hour went by while I endeavored to make the operators through their representatives see that the country would not tolerate their insisting upon such conditions; but in vain. The two representatives of the operators were Robert Bacon and George W. Perkins. They were entirely reasonable. But the operators themselves were entirely unreasonable. They had worked themselves into a frame of mind where they were prepared to sacrifice everything and see civil war in the country rather than back down and acquiesce in the appointment of a representative of labor. It looked as if a deadlock were inevitable.

Then, suddenly, after about two hours' argument, it dawned on me that they were not objecting to the thing, but to the name. I found that they did not mind my appointing any man, whether he was a labor man or not, so long as he was not appointed *as* a labor man, or *as* a representative of labor; they did not object to my exercising any latitude I chose in the appointments so long as they were made under the headings they had given. I shall never forget the mixture of relief and amusement I felt when I thoroughly grasped the fact that while they would heroically submit to anarchy rather than have Tweedledum, yet if I would call it Tweedledee they would accept it with rapture; it gave me an illuminating glimpse into one corner of the mighty brains of these "captains of industry." In order to carry the great and vital point and secure agreement by both parties, all that was necessary for me to do was to commit a technical and nominal absurdity with a solemn face. This I gladly did. I announced at once that I accepted the terms laid down. With this understanding, I appointed the labor man I had all along had in view, Mr. E. E. Clark, the head of the Brotherhood of Railway Conductors, calling him an "eminent sociologist" — a term which I doubt whether he had ever previously heard. He was a first-class man, whom I afterward put on the Inter-State Commerce Commission. I added to the Arbitration Commission, on my own authority, a sixth member, in the person of Bishop Spalding, a Catholic bishop, of Peoria, Ill., one of the very best men to be found in the entire country. The man whom the operators had expected me to appoint as the sociologist was Carroll Wright — who really was an eminent sociologist. I put him on as recorder of the Com- mission, and added him as a seventh member as soon as the Commission got fairly started. In publishing the list of the Commissioners, when I came to Clark's ap- pointment, I added: "As a sociologist — the President assuming that for the pur- poses of such a Commission, the term sociologist means a man who has thought and studied deeply on social questions and has practi- cally applied his knowl- edge."

FATHER CURRAN.

The relief of the whole country was so great that the sudden appearance of the head of the Brother- hood of Railway Conduct- ors as an "eminent sociol- ogist" merely furnished material for puzzled comment on the part of the press. It was a most admirable Commission. It did a noteworthy work, and its report is a monument in the history of the relations of labor and capital in this coun- try. The strike, by the way, brought me into contact with more than one man who was afterward a valued friend and fellow-worker. On the suggestion of Carroll Wright I ap- pointed as assistant recorders to the Commission Charles P. Neill, whom I afterward made Labor Commissioner, to suc- ceed Wright himself, and Mr. Edward A. Moseley. Wilkes- Barre was the center of the strike; and the man in Wilkes- Barre who helped me most was Father Curran; I grew to know and trust and believe in him, and throughout my term in office, and afterward, he was not only my stanch friend, but one of the men by whose advice and counsel I profited most in matters affecting the welfare of the miners and their families.

I was greatly relieved at the result, for more than one reason. Of course, first and foremost, my concern was to avert a frightful calamity to the United States. In the next place I was anxious to save the great coal operators and all of the class of big propertied men, of which they were members, from the dreadful punishment which their own folly would have brought on them if I had not acted; and one of the exasperating things was that they were so blinded that they could not see that I was trying to save them from themselves and to avert, not only for their sakes, but for the sake of the country, the excesses which would have been indulged in at their expense if they had longer persisted in their conduct.

The great Anthracite Strike of 1902 left an indelible impress upon the people of the United States. It showed clearly to all wise and far-seeing men that the labor problem in this country had entered upon a new phase. Industry had grown. Great financial corporations, doing a nation-wide and even a world-wide business, had taken the place of the smaller concerns of an earlier time. The old familiar, intimate relations between employer and employee were passing. A few generations before, the boss had known every man in his shop; he called his men Bill, Tom, Dick, John; he inquired after their wives and babies; he swapped jokes and stories and perhaps a bit of tobacco with them. In the small establishment there had been a friendly human relationship between employer and employee.

There was no such relation between the great railway magnates, who controlled the anthracite industry, and the one hundred and fifty thousand men who worked in their mines, or the half million women and children who were dependent upon these miners for their daily bread. Very few of these mine workers had ever seen, for instance, the president of the Reading Railroad. Had they seen him many of them could not have spoken to him, for tens of thousands of the mine workers were recent immigrants who did not understand the language which he spoke and who spoke a language which he could not understand.

Again, a few generations ago an American workman could have saved money, gone West and taken up a homestead. Now the free lands were gone. In earlier days a man who began with pick and shovel might have come to own a mine. That outlet too was now closed, as regards the immense majority, and few, if any, of the one hundred and fifty thousand mine workers could ever aspire to enter the small circle of men who held in their grasp the great anthracite industry. The majority of the men who earned wages in the coal industry, if they wished to progress at all, were compelled to progress not by ceasing to be wage-earners, but by improving the conditions under which all the wage-earners in all the industries of the country lived and worked, as well, of course, as improving their own individual efficiency.

Another change which had come about as a result of the foregoing was a crass inequality in the bargaining relation between the employer and the individual employee standing alone. The great coal-mining and coal-carrying companies, which employed their tens of thousands, could easily dispense with the services of any particular miner. The miner, on the other hand, however expert, could not dispense with the companies. He needed a job; his wife and children would starve if he did not get one. What the miner had to sell — his labor — was a perishable commodity; the labor of to-day — if not sold to-day — was lost forever. Moreover, his labor was not like most commodities — a mere thing; it was part of a living, breathing human being. The workman saw, and all citizens who gave earnest thought to the matter saw, that the labor problem was not only an economic, but also a moral, a human problem. Individually the miners were impotent when they sought to enter a wage-contract with the great companies; they could make fair terms only by uniting into trade unions to bargain collectively. The men were forced to coöperate to secure not only their economic, but their simple human rights. They, like other workmen, were compelled by the very conditions under which they lived to unite in unions of their industry or trade, and these unions were bound to grow in size, in strength, and in power for good and evil as the industries in which the men were employed grew larger and larger.

A democracy can be such in fact only if there is some rough approximation to similarity in stature among the men composing it.   One of us can deal in our private lives with the grocer or the butcher or the carpenter or the chicken raiser, or if we are the grocer or carpenter or butcher or farmer, we can deal with our customers, because *we are all of about the same size*.   Therefore a simple and poor society can exist as a democracy on a basis of sheer individualism. But a rich and complex industrial society cannot so exist; for some individuals, and especially those artificial individuals called corporations, become so very big that the ordinary individual is utterly dwarfed beside them, and cannot deal with them on terms of equality.   It therefore becomes necessary for these ordinary individuals to combine in their turn, first in order to act in their collective capacity through that biggest of all combinations called the Government, and second, to act, also in their own self-defense, through private combinations, such as farmers' associations and trade unions.

This the great coal operators did not see.   They did not see that their property rights, which they so stoutly defended, were of the same texture as were the human rights, which they so blindly and hotly denied.   They did not see that the power which they exercised of representing their stockholders was of the same texture as the power which the union leaders demanded of representing the workmen, who had democratically elected them.   They did not see that the right to use one's property as one will can be maintained only so long as it is consistent with the maintenance of certain fundamental human rights, of the rights to life, liberty and the pursuit of happiness, or, as we may restate them in these later days, of the rights of the worker to a living wage, to reasonable hours of labor, to decent working and living conditions, to freedom of thought and speech and industrial representation, — in short, to a measure of industrial democracy and, in return for his arduous toil, to a worthy and decent life according to American standards. Still another thing these great business leaders did not see. They did not see that both their interests and the interests of the workers must be accommodated, and if need be, subordinated, to the fundamental permanent interests of the whole community. No man and no group of men may so exercise their rights as to deprive the nation of the things which are necessary and vital to the common life. A strike which ties up the coal supplies of a whole section is a strike invested with a public interest.

So great was that public interest in the Coal Strike of 1902, so deeply and strongly did I feel the wave of indignation which swept over the whole country that had I not succeeded in my efforts to induce the operators to listen to reason, I should reluctantly but none the less decisively have taken a step which would have brought down upon my head the execrations of many of "the captains of industry," as well as of sundry " respectable " newspapers who dutifully take their cue from them. As a man should be judged by his intentions as well as by his actions, I will give here the story of the intervention that never happened.

While the coal operators were exulting over the fact that they had "turned down" the miners and the President, there arose in all parts of the country an outburst of wrath so universal that even so naturally conservative a man as Grover Cleveland wrote to me, expressing his sympathy with the course I was following, his indignation at the conduct of the operators, and his hope that I would devise some method of effective action. In my own mind I was already planning effective action; but it was of a very drastic character, and I did not wish to take it until the failure of all other expedients had rendered it necessary. Above all, I did not wish to talk about it until and unless I actually acted. I had definitely determined that somehow or other act I would, that somehow or other the coal famine should be broken. To accomplish this end it was necessary that the mines should be run, and, if I could get no voluntary agreement between the contending sides, that an

2 L

Arbitration Commission should be appointed which would command such public confidence as to enable me, without too much difficulty, to enforce its terms upon both parties. Ex-President Cleveland's letter not merely gratified me, but gave me the chance to secure him as head of the Arbitration Commission. I at once wrote him, stating that I would very probably have to appoint an Arbitration Commission or Investigating Commission to look into the matter and decide on the rights of the case, whether or not the operators asked for or agreed to abide by the decisions of such a Commission; and that I would ask him to accept the chief place on the Commission. He answered that he would do so. I picked out several first-class men for other positions on the Commission.

Meanwhile the Governor of Pennsylvania had all the Pennsylvania militia in the anthracite region, although without any effect upon the resumption of mining. The method of action upon which I had determined in the last resort was to get the Governor of Pennsylvania to ask me to keep order. Then I would put in the army under the command of some first-rate general. I would instruct this general to keep absolute order, taking any steps whatever that were necessary to prevent interference by the strikers or their sympathizers with men who wanted to work. I would also instruct him to dispossess the operators and run the mines as a receiver until such time as the Commission might make its report, and until I, as President, might issue further orders in view of this report. I had to find a man who possessed the necessary good sense, judgment, and nerve to act in such event. He was ready to hand in the person of Major-General Schofield. I sent for him, telling him that if I had to make use of him it would be because the crisis was only less serious than that of the Civil War, that the action taken would be practically a war measure, and that if I sent him he must act in a purely military capacity under me as commander-in-chief, paying no heed to any authority, judicial or otherwise, except mine. He was a fine fellow — a most respectable-looking old boy, with side whiskers and a black skull-cap, without any of the outward aspect of the conventional military dictator ; but in both nerve and judgment he was all right, and he answered quietly that if I gave the order he would take possession of the mines, and would guarantee to open them and to run them without permitting any interference either by the owners or the strikers or anybody else, so long as I told him to stay. I then saw Senator Quay, who, like every other responsible man in high position, was greatly wrought up over the condition of things. I told him that he need be under no alarm as to the problem not being solved, that I was going to make another effort to get the operators and miners to come together, but that I would solve the problem in any event and get coal ; that, however, I did not wish to tell him anything of the details of my intention, but merely to have him arrange that whenever I gave the word the Governor of Pennsylvania should request me to intervene ; that when this was done I would be responsible for all that followed, and would guarantee that the coal famine would end forthwith. The Senator made no inquiry or comment, and merely told me that he in his turn would guarantee that the Governor would request my intervention the minute I asked that the request be made.

These negotiations were conducted with the utmost secrecy, General Schofield being the only man who knew exactly what my plan was, and Senator Quay, two members of my Cabinet, and ex-President Cleveland and the other men whom I proposed to put on the Commission, the only other men who knew that I had a plan. As I have above outlined, my efforts to bring about an agreement between the operators and miners were finally successful. I was glad not to have to take possession of the mines on my own initiative by means of General Schofield and the regulars. I was all ready to act, and would have done so without the slightest hesitation or a moment's delay if the negotiations had fallen through. And my action would have been entirely effective. But it is never well to take drastic action if the result can be achieved with equal efficiency in less drastic fashion ; and, although this was a minor consideration, I was personally saved a good deal of future trouble by being able to avoid this drastic action. At the time I should have been almost unanimously supported. With the famine upon them the people would not have tolerated any conduct that would have thwarted what I was doing. Probably no man in Congress, and no man in the Pennsylvania State Legislature, would have raised his voice against me. Although there would have been plenty of muttering, nothing would have been done to interfere with the solution of the problem which I had devised, *until the solution was accomplished and the problem ceased to be a problem.* Once this was done, and when people were no longer afraid of a coal famine, and began to forget that they ever had been afraid of it, and to be indifferent as regards the consequences to those who put an end to it, then my enemies would have plucked up heart and begun a campaign against me. I doubt if they could have accomplished much anyway, for the only effective remedy against me would have been impeachment, and that they would not have ventured to try.[1]

[1] One of my appointees on the Anthracite Strike Commission was Judge George Gray, of Delaware, a Democrat whose standing in the country was second only to that of Grover Cleveland. A year later he commented on my action as follows:

"I have no hesitation in saying that the President of the United States was confronted in October, 1902, by the existence of a crisis more grave and threatening than any that had occurred since the Civil War. I mean that the cessation of mining in the anthracite country, brought about by the dispute between the miners and those who controlled the greatest natural monopoly in this country and perhaps in the world, had brought upon more than one-half of the American people a condition of deprivation of one of the necessaries of life, and the probable continuance of the dispute threatened not only the comfort and health, but the safety and good order, of the nation. He was without legal or constitutional power to interfere, but his position as President of the United States gave him an influence, a leadership, as first citizen of the republic, that enabled him to appeal to the patriotism and good sense of the parties to the controversy and to place upon them the moral coercion of public opinion to agree to an arbitrament of the strike then existing and threatening consequences so direful to the whole country. He acted promptly and courageously, and in so doing averted the dangers to which I have alluded.

"So far from interfering or infringing upon property rights, the President's action tended to conserve them. The peculiar situation, as regards the anthracite coal interest, was that they controlled a natural monopoly of a product necessary to the comfort and to the very life of a large portion of the pople. A prolonged deprivation of the enjoyment of this necessary of life would have tended to precipitate an attack upon these property rights of which you speak; for, after all, it is vain to deny that this property, so peculiar in its conditions, and which is properly spoken of as a natural monopoly, is affected with a public interest.

"I do not think that any President ever acted more wisely, courageously or promptly in a national crisis. Mr. Roosevelt deserves unstinted praise for what he did."

They would doubtless have acted precisely as they acted as regards the acquisition of the Panama Canal Zone in 1903, and the stoppage of the panic of 1907 by my action in the Tennessee Coal and Iron Company matter. Nothing could have made the American people surrender the canal zone. But after it was an accomplished fact, and the canal was under way, then they settled down to comfortable acceptance of the accomplished fact, and as their own interests were no longer in jeopardy, they paid no heed to the men who attacked me because of what I had done — and also continue to attack me, although they are exceedingly careful not to propose to right the "wrong," in the only proper way if it really was a wrong, by replacing the old Republic of Panama under the tyranny of Colombia and giving Colombia sole or joint ownership of the canal itself. In the case of the panic of 1907 (as in the case of Panama), what I did was not only done openly, but depended for its effect upon being done openly and with the widest advertisement. Nobody in Congress ventured to make an objection at the time. No serious leader outside made any objection. The one concern of everybody was to stop the panic, and everybody was overjoyed that I was willing to take the responsibility of stopping it upon my own shoulders. But a few months afterward, the panic was a thing of the past. People forgot the frightful condition of alarm in which they had been. They no longer had a personal interest in preventing any interference with the stoppage of the panic. Then the men who had not dared to raise their voices until all danger was past came bravely forth from their hiding places and denounced the action which had saved them. They had kept a hushed silence when there was danger; they made clamorous outcry when there was safety in doing so.

Just the same course would have been followed in connection with the Anthracite Coal Strike if I had been obliged to act in the fashion I intended to act had I failed to secure a voluntary agreement between the miners and the operators. Even as it was, my action was remembered with rancor by the heads of the great monied interests; and as time went by was assailed with constantly increasing vigor by the newspapers these men controlled. Had I been forced to take possession of the mines, these men and the politicians hostile to me would have waited until the popular alarm was over and the popular needs met, just as they waited in the case of the Tennessee Coal and Iron Company; and then they would have attacked me precisely as they did attack me as regards the Tennessee Coal and Iron Company.

Of course, in labor controversies it was not always possible to champion the cause of the workers, because in many cases strikes were called which were utterly unwarranted and were fought by methods which cannot be too harshly condemned. No straightforward man can believe, and no fearless man will assert, that a trade union is always right. That man is an unworthy public servant who by speech or silence, by direct statement or cowardly evasion, invariably throws the weight of his influence on the side of the trade union, whether it is right or wrong. It has occasionally been my duty to give utterance to the feelings of all right thinking men by expressing the most emphatic disapproval of unwise or even immoral actions by representatives of labor. The man is no true democrat, and if an American, is unworthy of the traditions of his country who, in problems calling for the exercise of a moral judgment, fails to take his stand on conduct and not on class. There are good and bad wage-workers just as there are good and bad employers, and good and bad men of small means and of large means alike.

But a willingness to do equal and exact justice to all citizens, irrespective of race, creed, section or economic interest and position, does not imply a failure to recognize the enormous economic, political and moral possibilities of the trade union. Just as democratic government cannot be condemned because of errors and even crimes committed by men democratically elected, so trade-unionism must not be condemned because of errors or crimes of occasional trade-union leaders. The problem lies deeper. While we must repress all illegalities and discourage all immoralities, whether of labor organizations or of corporations, we must recognize the fact that to-day the organization of labor into trade unions and federations is necessary, is beneficent, and is one of the greatest possible agencies in the attainment of a true industrial, as well as a true political, democracy in the United States.

This is a fact which many well-intentioned people even to-day do not understand. They do not understand that the labor problem is a human and a moral as well as an economic problem; that a fall in wages, an increase in hours, a deterioration of labor conditions mean wholesale moral as well as economic degeneration, and the needless sacrifice of human lives and human happiness, while a rise of wages, a lessening of hours, a bettering of conditions, mean an intellectual, moral and social uplift of millions of American men and women. There are employers to-day who, like the great coal operators, speak as though they were lords of these countless armies of Americans, who toil in factory, in shop, in mill and in the dark places under the earth. They fail to see that all these men have the right and the duty to combine to protect themselves and their families from want and degradation. They fail to see that the Nation and the Government, within the range of fair play and a just administration of the law, must inevitably sympathize with the men who have nothing but their wages, with the men who are struggling for a decent life, as opposed to men, however honorable, who are merely fighting for larger profits and an autocratic control of big business. Each man should have all he earns, whether by brain or body; and the director, the great industrial leader, is one of the greatest of earners, and should have a proportional reward; but no man should live on the earnings of another, and there should not be too gross inequality between service and reward.

There are many men to-day, men of integrity and intelligence, who honestly believe that we must go back to the labor conditions of half a century ago. They are opposed to trade unions, root and branch. They note the unworthy conduct of many labor leaders, they find instances of bad work by union men, of a voluntary restriction of output, of vexatious and violent strikes, of jurisdictional disputes between unions which often disastrously involve the best intentioned and fairest of employers. All these things occur and should be repressed. But the same critic of the trade union might find equal cause of complaint against individual employers of labor, or even against great associations of manufacturers. He might find many instances of an unwarranted cutting of wages, of flagrant violations of factory laws and tenement house laws, of the deliberate and systematic cheating of employees by means of truck stores, of the speeding up of work to a point which is fatal to the health of the workman, of the sweating of foreign-born workers, of the drafting of feeble little children into dusty workshops, of black-listing, of putting spies into union meetings and of the employment in strike times of vicious and desperate ruffians, who are neither better nor worse than are the thugs who are occasionally employed by unions under the sinister name, "entertainment committees." I believe that the overwhelming majority, both of workmen and of employers, are law-abiding, peaceful, and honorable citizens, and I do not think that it is just to lay up the errors and wrongs of individuals to the entire group to which they belong. I also think — and this is a belief which has been borne upon me through many years of practical experience — that the trade union is growing constantly in wisdom as well as in power, and is becoming one of the most efficient agencies toward the solution of our industrial problems, the elimination of poverty and of industrial disease and accidents, the lessening of unemployment, the achievement of industrial democracy and the attainment of a larger measure of social and industrial justice.

If I were a factory employee, a workman on the railroads or a wage-earner of any sort, I would undoubtedly join the union of my trade. If I disapproved of its policy, I would join in order to fight that policy; if the union leaders were dishonest, I would join in order to put them out. I believe in the union and I believe that all men who are benefited by the union are morally bound to help to the extent of their power in the common interests advanced by the union. Nevertheless, irrespective of whether a man should or should not, and does or does not, join the union of his trade, all the rights, privileges and immunities of that man as an American and as a citizen should be safegurded and upheld by the law. We dare not make an outlaw of any individual or any group, whatever his or its opinions or professions. The non-unionist, like the unionist, must be protected in all his legal rights by the full weight and power of the law.

This question came up before me in the shape of the right of a non-union printer named Miller to hold his position in the Government Printing Office. As I said before, I believe in trade unions. I always prefer to see a union shop. But my private preferences cannot control my public actions. The Government can recognize neither union men nor non-union men as such, and is bound to treat both exactly alike. In the Government Printing Office not many months prior to the opening of the Presidential campaign of 1904, when I was up for reëlection, I discovered that a man had been dismissed because he did not belong to the union. I reinstated him. Mr. Gompers, the President of the American Federation of Labor, with various members of the executive council of that body, called upon me to protest on September 29, 1903, and I answered them as follows:

"I thank you and your committee for your courtesy, and I appreciate the opportunity to meet with you. It will always be a pleasure to see you or any representatives of your organizations or of your Federation as a whole.

"As regards the Miller case, I have little to add to what I have already said. In dealing with it I ask you to remember that I am dealing purely with the relation of the Government to its employees. I must govern my action by the laws of the land, which I am sworn to administer, and which differentiate any case in which the Government of the United States is a party from all other cases whatsoever. These laws are enacted for the benefit of the whole people, and cannot and must not be construed as permitting discrimination against some of the people. I am President of all the people of the United States, without regard to creed, color, birthplace, occupation or social condition. My aim is to do equal and exact justice as among them all. In the employment and dismissal of men in the Government service

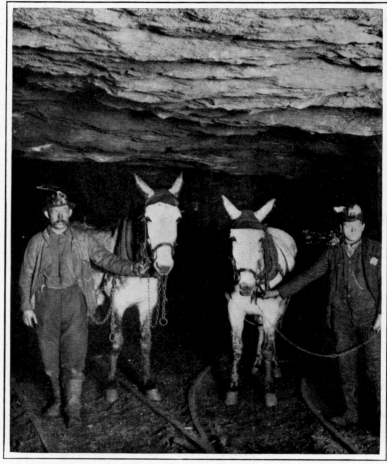

THE COAL MINERS.

I can no more recognize the fact that a man does or does not belong to a union as being for or against him than I can recognize the fact that he is a Protestant or a Catholic, a Jew or a Gentile, as being for or against him.

"In the communications sent me by various labor organizations protesting against the retention of Miller in the Government Printing Office, the grounds alleged are twofold: 1, that he is a non-union man; 2, that he is not personally fit. The question of his personal fitness is one to be settled in the routine of administrative detail, and cannot be allowed to conflict with or to complicate the larger question of governmental discrimination for or against him or any other man because he is or is not a member of a union. This is the only question now before me for decision; and as to this my decision is final."

Because of things I have done on behalf of justice to the workingman, I have often been called a Socialist. Usually I have not taken the trouble even to notice the epithet. I am not afraid of names, and I am not one of those who fear to do what is right because some one else will confound me with partisans with whose principles I am not in accord. Moreover, I know that many American Socialists are high-minded and honorable citizens, who in reality are merely radical social reformers. They are oppressed by the brutalities and industrial injustices which we see everywhere about us. When I recall how often I have seen Socialists and ardent non-Socialists working side by side for some specific measure of social or industrial reform, and how I have found opposed to them on the side of privilege many shrill reactionaries who insist on calling all reformers Socialists, I refuse to be panic-stricken by having this title mistakenly applied to me.

None the less, without impugning their motives, I do disagree most emphatically with both the fundamental philosophy and the proposed remedies of the Marxian Socialists. These Socialists are unalterably opposed to our whole industrial system. They believe that the payment of wages means everywhere and inevitably an exploitation of the laborer by the employer, and that this leads inevitably to a class war between those two groups, or, as they would say, between the capitalists and the proletariat. They assert that this class war is already upon us and can only be ended when capitalism is entirely destroyed and all the machines, mills, mines, railroads and other private property used in production are confiscated, expropriated or taken over by the workers. They do not as a rule claim — although some of the sinister extremists among them do — that this class war is a war of blood and bullets, but they do claim that there is and must be a continual struggle between two great classes, whose interests are opposed and cannot be reconciled. In this war they insist that the whole government — National, State and local — is on the side of the employers and is used by them against the workmen, and that our law and even our common morality are class weapons, like a policeman's club or a Gatling gun.

I have never believed, and do not to-day believe, that such a class war is upon us, or need ever be upon us; nor do I believe that the interests of wage-earners and employers cannot be harmonized, compromised and adjusted. It would be idle to deny that wage-earners have certain different economic interests from, let us say, manufacturers or importers, just as farmers have different interests from sailors, and fishermen from bankers. There is no reason why any of these economic groups should not consult their group interests by any legitimate means and with due regard to the common, overlying interests of all. I do not even deny that the majority of wage-earners, because they have less property and less industrial security than others and because they do not own the machinery with which they work (as does the farmer) are perhaps in greater need of acting together than are other groups in the community. But I do insist (and I believe that the great majority of wage-earners take the same view) that employers and employees have overwhelming interests in common, both as partners in industry and as citizens of the Republic, and that where these interests are apart they can be adjusted by so altering our laws and their interpretation as to secure to all members of the community social and industrial justice.

I have always maintained that our worst revolutionaries to-day are those reactionaries who do not see and will not admit that there is any need for change. Such men seem to believe that the four and a half million Progressive voters, who in 1912 registered their solemn protest against our social and industrial injustices, are "anarchists," who are not willing to let ill enough alone. If these reactionaries had lived at an earlier time in our history, they would have advocated Sedition Laws, opposed free speech and free assembly, and voted against free schools, free access by settlers to the public lands, mechanics' lien laws, the prohibition of truck stores and the abolition of imprisonment for debt; and they are the men who to-day oppose minimum wage laws, insurance of workmen against the ills of industrial life and the reform of our legislatures and our courts, which can alone render such measures possible. Some of these reactionaries are not bad men, but merely shortsighted and belated. It is these reactionaries, however, who, by "standing pat" on industrial injustice, incite inevitably to industrial revolt, and it is only we who advocate political and industrial democracy who render possible the progress of our American industry on large constructive lines with a minimum of friction because with a maximum of justice.

Everything possible should be done to secure the wage-workers fair treatment. There should be an increased wage for the worker of increased productiveness. Everything possible should be done against the capitalist who strives, not to reward special efficiency, but to use it as an excuse for reducing the reward of moderate efficiency. The capitalist is an unworthy citizen who pays the efficient man no more than he has been content to pay the average man, and nevertheless reduces the wage of the average man; and effort should be made by the Government to check and punish him. When labor-saving machinery is introduced, special care should be taken — by the Government if necessary — to see that the wage-worker gets his share of the benefit, and that it is not all absorbed by the employer or capitalist. The following case, which has come to my knowledge, illustrates what I mean. A number of new machines were installed in a certain shoe factory, and as a result there was a heavy increase in production even though there was no increase in the labor force. Some of the workmen were instructed in the use of these machines by special demonstrators sent out by the makers of the machines. These men, by reason of their special aptitudes and the fact that they were not called upon to operate the machines continuously nine hours every day, week in and week out, but only for an hour or so at special times, were naturally able to run the machines at their maximum capacity. When these demonstrators had left the factory, and the company's own employees had become used to operating the machines at a fair rate of speed, the foreman of the establishment gradually speeded the machines and demanded a larger and still larger output, constantly endeavoring to drive the men on to greater exertions. Even with a slightly less maximum capacity, the introduction of this machinery resulted in a great increase over former production with the same amount of labor; and so great were the profits from the business in the following two years as to equal the total capitalized stock of the company. But not a cent got into the pay envelope of the workmen beyond what they had formerly been receiving before the introduction of this new machinery, notwithstanding that it had meant an added strain, physical and mental, upon their energies, and that they were forced to work harder than ever before. The whole of the increased profits remained with the company. Now this represented an "increase of efficiency," with a positive decrease of social and industrial justice. The increase of prosperity which came from increase of production in no way benefited the wage-workers. I hold that they were treated with gross injustice; and that society, acting if necessary through the Government, in such a case should bend its energies to remedy such injustice; and I will support any proper legislation that will aid in securing the desired end.

The wage-worker should not only receive fair treatment; he should give fair treatment. In order that prosperity may be passed around it is necessary that the prosperity exist. In order that labor shall receive its fair share in the division of reward it is necessary that there be a reward to divide. Any proposal to reduce efficiency by insisting that the most efficient shall be limited in their output to what the least efficient can do, is a proposal to limit by so much production, and therefore to impoverish by so much the public, and specifically to reduce the amount that can be divided among the producers. This is all wrong. Our protest must be against unfair division of the reward for production. Every encouragement should be given the business man, the employer, to make his business prosperous, and therefore to earn more money for himself; and in like fashion every encouragement should be given the efficient workman. We must always keep in mind that to reduce the amount of production serves merely to reduce the amount that is to be divided, is in no way permanently efficient as a protest against unequal distribution and is permanently detrimental to the entire community. But increased productiveness is not secured by excessive labor amid unhealthy surroundings. The contrary is true. Shorter hours, and healthful conditions, and opportunity for the wage-worker to make more money, and the chance for enjoyment as well as work, all add to efficiency. My contention is that there should be no penalization of efficient productiveness, brought about under healthy conditions; but that every increase of production brought about by an increase in efficiency should benefit all the parties to it, including wage-workers as well as employers or capitalists, men who work with their hands as well as men who work with their heads.

With the Western Federation of Miners I more than once had serious trouble. The leaders of this organization had preached anarchy, and certain of them were indicted for having practiced murder in the case of Governor Steunenberg, of Idaho. On one occasion in a letter or speech I coupled condemnation of these labor leaders and condemnation of certain big capitalists, describing them all alike as "undesirable citizens." This gave great offense to both sides. The open attack upon me was made for the most part either by the New York newspapers which were frankly representatives of Wall Street, or else by those so-called —

and miscalled — Socialists who had anarchistic leanings. Many of the latter sent me open letters of denunciation, and to one of them I responded as follows:

THE WHITE HOUSE, WASHINGTON,
April 22, 1907.

Dear Sir:

I have received your letter of the 19th instant, in which you enclose the draft of the formal letter which is to follow. I have been notified that several delegations, bearing similar requests, are on the way hither. In the letter you, on behalf of the Cook County Moyer-Haywood conference, protest against certain language I used in a recent letter which you assert to be designed to influence the course of justice in the case of the trial for murder of Messrs. Moyer and Haywood. I entirely agree with you that it is improper to endeavor to influence the course of justice, whether by threats or in any similar manner. For this reason I have regretted most deeply the actions of such organizations as your own in undertaking to accomplish this very result in the very case of which you speak. For instance, your letter is headed "Cook County Moyer-Haywood-Pettibone Conference," with the headlines: "*Death* — cannot — will not — and shall not claim our brothers!" This shows that you and your associates are not demanding a fair trial, or working for a fair trial, but are announcing in advance that the verdict shall only be one way and that you will not tolerate any other verdict. Such action is flagrant in its impropriety, and I join heartily in condemning it.

But it is a simple absurdity to suppose that because any man is on trial for a given offense he is therefore to be freed from all criticism upon his general conduct and manner of life. In my letter to which you object I referred to a certain prominent financier, Mr. Harriman, on the one hand, and to Messrs Moyer, Haywood and Debs on the other, as being equally undesirable citizens. It is as foolish to assert that this was designed to influence the trial of Moyer and Haywood as to assert that it was designed to influence the suits that have been brought against Mr.

Harriman. I neither expressed nor indicated any opinion as to whether Messrs. Moyer and Haywood were guilty of the murder of Governor Steunenberg. If they are guilty, they certainly ought to be punished. If they are not guilty, they certainly ought not to be punished. But no possible outcome either of the trial or the suits can affect my judgment as to the undesirability of the type of citizenship of those whom I mentioned. Messrs. Moyer, Haywood, and Debs stand as representatives of those men who have done as much to discredit the labor movement as the worst speculative financiers or most unscrupulous employers of labor and debauchers of legislatures have done to discredit honest capitalists and fair-dealing business men. They stand as the representatives of those men who by their public utterances and manifestoes, by the utterances of the papers they control or inspire, and by the words and deeds of those associated with or subordinated to them, habitually appear as guilty of incitement to or apology for bloodshed and violence. If this does not constitute undesirable citizenship, then there can never be any undesirable citizens. The men whom I denounce represent the men who have abandoned that legitimate movement for the uplifting of labor, with which I have the most hearty sympathy; they have adopted practices which cut them off from those who lead this legitimate movement. In every way I shall support the law-abiding and upright representatives of labor; and in no way can I better support them than by drawing the sharpest possible line between them on the one hand, and, on the other hand, those preachers of violence who are themselves the worst foes of the honest laboring man.

Let me repeat my deep regret that any body of men should so far forget their duty to the country as to endeavor by the formation of societies and in other ways to influence the course of justice in this matter. I have received many such letters as yours. Accompanying them were newspaper clippings announcing demonstrations, parades, and mass-meetings designed to show that the representatives of labor, without regard to the facts, demand the acquittal of Messrs. Haywood and Moyer. Such meetings can, of

2 M

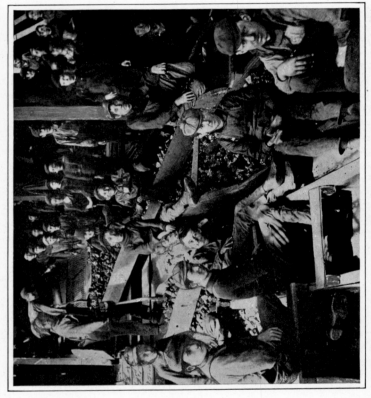

Breaker Boys.

course, be designed only to coerce court or jury in rendering a verdict, and they therefore deserve all the condemnation which you in your letters say should be awarded to those who endeavor improperly to influence the course of justice.

You would, of course, be entirely within your rights if you merely announced that you thought Messrs. Moyer and Haywood were "desirable citizens"—though in such case I should take frank issue with you and should say that, wholly without regard to whether or not they are guilty of the crime for which they are now being tried, they represent as thoroughly undesirable a type of citizenship as can be found in this country; a type which, in the letter to which you so unreasonably take exception, I showed not to be confined to any one class, but to exist among some representatives of great capitalists as well as among some representatives of wage-workers. In that letter I condemned both types. Certain representatives of the great capitalists in turn condemned me for including Mr. Harriman in my condemnation of Messrs. Moyer and Haywood. Certain of the representatives of labor in their turn condemned me because I included Messrs. Moyer and Haywood as undesirable citizens together with Mr. Harriman. I am as profoundly indifferent to the condemnation in one case as in the other. I challenge as a right the support of all good Americans, whether wage-workers or capitalists, whatever their occupation or creed, or in whatever portion of the country they live, when I condemn both the types of bad citizenship which I have held up to reprobation. It seems to be a mark of utter insincerity to fail thus to condemn both; and to apologize for either robs the man thus apologizing of all right to condemn any wrongdoing in any man, rich or poor, in public or in private life.

You say you ask for a "square deal" for Messrs. Moyer and Haywood. So do I. When I say "square deal," I mean a square deal to every one; it is equally a violation of the policy of the square deal for a capitalist to protest against denunciation of a capitalist who is guilty of wrongdoing and for a labor leader to protest against the denunciation of a labor leader who has been guilty of wrongdoing. I stand for equal justice to both; and so far as in my power lies I shall uphold justice, whether the man accused of guilt has behind him the wealthiest corporations, the greatest aggregations of riches in the country, or whether he has behind him the most influential labor organizations in the country.

I treated anarchists and the bomb-throwing and dynamiting gentry precisely as I treated other criminals. Murder is murder. It is not rendered one whit better by the allegation that it is committed on behalf of "a cause." It is true that law and order are not all-sufficient; but they are essential; lawlessness and murderous violence must be quelled before any permanence of reform can be obtained. Yet when they have been quelled, the beneficiaries of the enforcement of law must in their turn be taught that law is upheld as a means to the enforcement of justice, and that we will not tolerate its being turned into an engine of injustice and oppression. The fundamental need in dealing with our people, whether laboring men or others, is not charity but justice; we must all work in common for the common end of helping each and all, in a spirit of the sanest, broadest and deepest brotherhood.

It was not always easy to avoid feeling very deep anger with the selfishness and short-sightedness shown both by the representatives of certain employers' organizations and by certain great labor federations or unions. One such employers' association was called the National Association of Manufacturers. Extreme though the attacks sometimes made upon me by the extreme labor organizations were, they were not quite as extreme as the attacks made upon me by the head of the National Association of Manufacturers, and as regards their attitude toward legislation I came to the conclusion toward the end of my term that the latter had actually gone further the wrong way than did the former — and the former went a good distance also. The opposition of the National Association of Manufacturers to every rational and moderate measure for benefiting workingmen, such as measures abolishing child labor, or securing workmen's compensation, caused me real and grave concern;

for I felt that it was ominous of evil for the whole country to have men who ought to stand high in wisdom and in guiding force take a course and use language of such reactionary type as directly to incite revolution — for this is what the extreme reactionary always does.

Often I was attacked by the two sides at once. In the spring of 1906 I received in the same mail a letter from a very good friend of mine who thought that I had been unduly hard on some labor men, and a letter from another friend, the head of a great corporation, who complained about me for both favoring labor and speaking against large fortunes. My answers ran as follows:

April 26, 1906.

"Personal.

My dear Doctor:

In one of my last letters to you I enclosed you a copy of a letter of mine, in which I quoted from [So and so's] advocacy of murder. You may be interested to know that he and his brother Socialists — in reality anarchists — of the frankly murderous type have been violently attacking my speech because of my allusion to the sympathy expressed for murder. In *The Socialist*, of Toledo, Ohio, of April 21st, for instance, the attack [on me] is based specifically on the following paragraph of my speech, to which he takes violent exception:

We can no more and no less afford to condone evil in the man of capital than evil in the man of no capital. The wealthy man who exults because there is a failure of justice in the effort to bring some trust magnate to an account for his misdeeds is as bad as, and no worse than, the so-called labor leader who clamorously strives to excite a foul class feeling on behalf of some other labor leader who is implicated in murder. One attitude is as bad as the other, and no worse; in each case the accused is entitled to exact justice; and in neither case is there need of action by others which can be construed into an expression of sympathy for crime.

Remember that this crowd of labor leaders have done all in their power to overawe the executive and the courts of

Idaho on behalf of men accused of murder, and beyond question inciters of murder in the past."

April 26, 1906.

"My dear Judge:

I wish the papers had given more prominence to what I said as to the murder part of my speech. But oh, my dear sir, I utterly and radically disagree with you in what you say about large fortunes. I wish it were in my power to devise some scheme to make it increasingly difficult to heap them up beyond a certain amount. As the difficulties in the way of such a scheme are very great, let us at least prevent their being bequeathed after death or given during life to any one man in excessive amount.

You and other capitalist friends, on one side, shy off at what I say against them. Have you seen the frantic articles against me by [the anarchists and] the Socialists of the bomb-throwing persuasion, on the other side, because of what I said in my speech in reference to whose who, in effect, advocate murder?"

On another occasion I was vehemently denounced in certain capitalistic papers because I had a number of labor leaders, including miners from Butte, lunch with me at the White House; and this at the very time that the Western Federation of Miners was most ferocious in its denunciation of me because of what it alleged to be my unfriendly attitude toward labor. To one of my critics I set forth my views in the following letter:

November 26, 1903.

"I have your letter of the 25th instant, with enclosure. These men, not all of whom were miners, by the way, came here and were at lunch with me, in company with Mr. Carroll D. Wright, Mr. Wayne MacVeagh, and Secretary Cortelyou. They are as decent a set of men as can be. They all agreed entirely with me in my denunciation of what had been done in the Cœur d'Alene country; and it appeared that some of them were on the platform with me when I denounced this type of outrage three years ago in Butte. There is not one man who was here, who, I believe, was in any way, shape or form responsible for such outrages. I find that the ultra-Socialistic members of the unions in Butte denounced these men for coming here, in a manner as violent — and I may say as irrational — as the denunciation [by the capitalistic writer] in the article you sent me. Doubtless the gentleman of whom you speak as your general manager is an admirable man. I, of course, was not alluding to him; but I most emphatically *was* alluding to men who write such articles as that you sent me. These articles are to be paralleled by the similar articles in the Populist and Socialist papers when two years ago I had at dinner at one time Pierpont Morgan, and at another time J. J. Hill, and at another, Harriman, and at another time Schiff. Furthermore, they could be paralleled by the articles in the same type of paper which at the time of the Miller incident in the Printing Office were in a condition of nervous anxiety because I met the labor leaders to discuss it. It would have been a great misfortune if I had not met them; and it would have been an even greater misfortune if after meeting them I had yielded to their protests in the matter.

You say in your letter that you know that I am "on record" as opposed to violence. Pardon my saying that this seems to me not the right way to put the matter, if by "record" you mean utterance and not action. Aside from what happened when I was Governor in connection, for instance, with the Croton dam strike riots, all you have to do is to turn back to what took place last June in Arizona — and you can find out about it from [Mr. X] of New York. The miners struck, violence followed, and the Arizona Territorial authorities notified me they could not grapple with the situation. Within twenty minutes of the receipt of the telegram, orders were issued to the nearest available troops, and twenty-four hours afterwards General Baldwin and his regulars were on the ground, and twenty-four hours later every vestige of disorder had disappeared. The Miners' Federation in their meeting, I think at Denver, a short while afterwards, passed resolutions denouncing me. I do not know whether the *Mining and Engineering Journal* paid any heed to this incident or knew of it. If the *Journal* did, I suppose it can hardly have failed to understand that to put an immediate stop to rioting by the use of the United States army is a fact of importance beside which the criticism of my having " labor leaders " to lunch, shrinks into the same insignificance as the criticism in a different type of paper about my having "trust magnates" to lunch. While I am President I wish the labor man to feel that he has the same right of access to me that the capitalist has ; that the doors swing open as easily to the wage-worker as to the head of a big corporation — *and no easier*. Anything else seems to be not only un-American, but as symptomatic of an attitude which will cost grave trouble if persevered in. To discriminate against labor men from Butte because there is reason to believe that rioting has been excited in other districts by certain labor unions, or individuals in labor unions in Butte, would be to adopt precisely the attitude of those who desire me to discriminate against all capitalists in Wall Street because there are plenty of capitalists in Wall Street who have been guilty of bad financial practices and who have endeavored to override or evade the laws of the land. In my judgment, the only safe attitude for a private citizen, and still more for a public servant, to assume, is that he will draw the line on conduct, discriminating against-neither corporation nor union as such, nor in favor of either as such, but endeavoring to make the decent member of the union and the upright capitalists alike feel that they are bound, not only by self-interest, but by every consideration of principle and duty to stand together on the matters of most moment to the nation."

On another of the various occasions when I had labor leaders to dine at the White House, my critics were rather shocked because I had John Morley to meet them. The labor leaders in question included the heads of the various railroad brotherhoods, men like Mr. Morrissey, in whose sound judgment and high standard of citizenship I had peculiar confidence ; and I asked Mr. Morley to meet them because they represented the exact type of American citizen with whom I thought he ought to be brought in contact.

One of the devices sometimes used by big corporations to break down the law was to treat the passage of laws as an excuse for action on their part which they knew would be resented by the public, it being their purpose to turn this resentment against the law instead of against themselves. The heads of the Louisville and Nashville road were bitter opponents of everything done by the Government toward securing good treatment for their employees. In February, 1908, they and various other railways announced that they intended to reduce the wages of their employees. A general strike, with all the attendant disorder and trouble, was threatened in consequence. I accordingly sent the following open letter to the Inter-State Commerce Commission:

February 18, 1908.

"To the Inter-State Commerce Commission:

I am informed that a number of railroad companies have served notice of a proposed reduction of wages of their employees. One of them, the Louisville and Nashville, in announcing the reduction, states that " the drastic laws inimical to the interests of the railroads that have in the past year or two been enacted by Congress and the State Legislatures " are largely or chiefly responsible for the conditions requiring the reduction.

Under such circumstances it is possible that the public may soon be confronted by serious industrial disputes, and the law provides that in such case either party may demand the services of your Chairman and of the Commissioner of Labor as a Board of Mediation and Conciliation. These reductions in wages may be warranted, or they may not. As to this the public, which is a vitally interested party, can form no judgment without a more complete knowledge of the essential facts and real merits of the case than it now has or than it can possibly obtain from the special pleadings, certain to be put forth by each side in case their dispute should bring about serious interruption to traffic. If the reduction in wages is due to natural causes, the loss of business being such that the burden should be, and is, equitably distributed between capitalist and wage-worker, the public should know it. If it is caused by legislation, the public, and Congress, should know it; and if it is caused by misconduct in the past financial or other operations of any railroad, then everybody should know it, especially if the excuse of unfriendly legislation is advanced as a method of covering up past business misconduct by the railroad managers, or as a justification for failure to treat fairly the wage-earning employees of the company.

Moreover, an industrial conflict between a railroad corporation and its employees offers peculiar opportunities to any small number of evil-disposed persons to destroy life and property and foment public disorder. Of course, if life, property, and public order are endangered, prompt and drastic measures for their protection become the first plain duty. All other issues then become subordinate to the preservation of the public peace, and the real merits of the original controversy are necessarily lost from view. This vital consideration should be ever kept in mind by all law-abiding and far-sighted members of labor organizations.

It is sincerely to be hoped, therefore, that any wage controversy that may arise between the railroads and their employees may find a peaceful solution through the methods of conciliation and arbitration already provided by Congress, which have proven so effective during the past year. To this end the Commission should be in a position to have available for any Board of Conciliation or Arbitration relevant data pertaining to such carriers as may become involved in industrial disputes. Should conciliation fail to effect a settlement and arbitration be rejected, accurate information should be available in order to develop a properly informed public opinion.

I therefore ask you to make such investigation, both of your records and by any other means at your command, as will enable you to furnish data concerning such conditions obtaining on the Louisville and Nashville and any other roads, as may relate, directly or indirectly, to the real merits of the possibly impending controversy.

THEODORE ROOSEVELT."

This letter achieved its purpose, and the threatened reduction of wages was not made. It was an instance of what could be accomplished by governmental action. Let me add, however, with all the emphasis I possess, that this does not mean any failure on my part to recognize the fact that if governmental action places too heavy burdens on railways, it will be impossible for them to operate without doing injustice to somebody. Railways cannot pay proper wages and render proper service unless they make money. The investors must get a reasonable profit or they will not invest, and the public cannot be well served unless the investors are making reasonable profits. There is every reason why rates should not be too high, but they must be sufficiently high to allow the railways to pay good wages. Moreover, when laws like workmen's compensation laws, and the like are passed, it must always be kept in mind by the Legislature that the purpose is to distribute over the whole community a burden that should not be borne only by those least able to bear it — that is, by the injured man or the widow and orphans of the dead man. If the railway is already receiving a disproportionate return from the public, then the burden may, with propriety, bear purely on the railway ; but if it is not earning a disproportionate return, then the public must bear its share of the burden of the increased service the railway is rendering. Dividends and wages should go up together ; and the relation of rates to them should never be forgotten. This of course does not apply to dividends based on water ; nor does it mean that if foolish people have built a road that renders no service, the public must nevertheless in some way guarantee a return on the investment ; but it does mean that the interests of the honest investor are entitled to the same protection as the interests of the honest manager, the honest shipper and the honest wage earner. All these conflicting considerations should be carefully considered by Legislatures before passing laws. One of the great objects in creating commissions should be the provision of disinterested, fair-minded experts who will really and wisely consider all these matters, and will shape their actions accordingly. This is one reason why such matters as the regulation of rates, the provision for full crews on roads and the like should be left for treatment by railway commissions, and not be settled off hand by direct legislative action.

APPENDIX

SOCIALISM

As regards what I have said in this chapter concerning Socialism, I wish to call especial attention to the admirable book on "Marxism versus Socialism," which has just been published by Vladimir D. Simkhovitch. What I have, here and elsewhere, merely pointed out in rough and ready fashion from actual observation of the facts of life around me, Professor Simkhovitch in his book has discussed with keen practical insight, with profundity of learning, and with a wealth of applied philosophy. Crude thinkers in the United States, and moreover honest and intelligent men who are not crude thinkers, but who are oppressed by the sight of the misery around them and have not deeply studied what has been done elsewhere, are very apt to adopt as their own the theories of European Marxian Socialists of half a century ago, ignorant that the course of events has so completely falsified the prophecies contained in these theories that they have been abandoned even by the authors themselves. With quiet humor Professor Simkhovitch now and then makes an allusion which shows that he appreciates to perfection this rather curious quality of some of our fellow countrymen; as for example when he says that "A Socialist State with the farmer outside of it is a conception that can rest comfortably only in the head of an American Socialist," or as when he speaks of Marx and Engels as men "to whom thinking was not an irrelevant foreign tradition." Too many thoroughly well-meaning men and women in the America of to-day glibly repeat and accept — much as medieval schoolmen repeated and accepted authorized dogma in their day — various assumptions and speculations by Marx and others which by the lapse of time and by actual experiment have been shown to possess not one shred of value. Professor Simkhovitch possesses the gift of condensation as well as the gift of clear and logical statement, and it is not possible to give in brief any idea of his admirable work. Every social reformer who desires to face facts should study it — just as social reformers should study John Graham Brooks's "American Syndicalism." From

Professor Simkhovitch's book we Americans should learn: First, to discard crude thinking; second, to realize that the orthodox or so-called scientific or purely economic or materialistic socialism of the type preached by Marx is an exploded theory; and, third, that many of the men who call themselves Socialists to-day are in reality merely radical social reformers, with whom on many points good citizens can and ought to work in hearty general agreement, and whom in many practical matters of government good citizens can well afford to follow.

CHAPTER XIV

THE MONROE DOCTRINE AND THE PANAMA CANAL

NO nation can claim rights without acknowledging the duties that go with the rights. It is a contemptible thing for a great nation to render itself impotent in international action, whether because of cowardice or sloth, or sheer inability or unwillingness to look into the future. It is a very wicked thing for a nation to do wrong to others. But the most contemptible and most wicked course of conduct is for a nation to use offensive language or be guilty of offensive actions toward other people and yet fail to hold its own if the other nation retaliates; and it is almost as bad to undertake responsibilities and then not fulfil them. During the seven and a half years that I was President, this Nation behaved in international matters toward all other nations precisely as an honorable man behaves to his fellow-men. We made no promise which we could not and did not keep. We made no threat which we did not carry out. We never failed to assert our rights in the face of the strong, and we never failed to treat both strong and weak with courtesy and justice; and against the weak when they misbehaved we were slower to assert our rights than we were against the strong.

As a legacy of the Spanish War we were left with peculiar relations to the Philippines, Cuba, and Porto Rico, and with an immensely added interest in Central America and the Caribbean Sea. As regards the Philippines my belief was that we should train them for self-government as rapidly as possible, and then leave them free to decide their own fate. I did not believe in setting the time-limit within which we would give them independence, because I did not believe it wise to try to forecast how soon they would be fit for self-government; and once having made the promise I would have felt that it was imperative to keep it. Within a few months of my assuming office we had stamped out the last armed resistance in the Philippines that was not of merely sporadic character; and as soon as peace was secured we turned our energies to developing the islands in the interests of the natives. We established schools everywhere; we built roads; we administered an even-handed justice; we did everything possible to encourage agriculture and industry; and in constantly increasing measure we employed natives to do their own governing, and finally provided a legislative chamber. No higher grade of public officials ever handled the affairs of any colony than the public officials who in succession governed the Philippines. With the possible exception of the Sudan, and not even excepting Algiers, I know of no country ruled and administered by men of the white race where that rule and that administration have been exercised so emphatically with an eye single to the welfare of the natives themselves. The English and Dutch administrators of Malaysia have done admirable work; but the profit to the Europeans in those States has always been one of the chief elements considered; whereas in the Philippines our whole attention was concentrated upon the welfare of the Filipinos themselves, if anything to the neglect of our own interests.

I do not believe that America has any special beneficial interest in retaining the Philippines. Our work there has benefited us only as any efficiently done work performed for the benefit of others does incidentally help the character of those who do it. The people of the islands have never developed so rapidly, from every standpoint, as during the years of the American occupation. The time will come when it will be wise to take their own judgment as to whether they wish to continue their association with America or not. There is, however, one consideration upon which we should insist. Either we should retain complete control of the islands, or absolve ourselves from all responsibility for them. Any half and half course would be both foolish and disastrous. We are governing and have been governing the islands in the interests of the Filipinos themselves. If after due time the Filipinos themselves decide that they do not wish to be thus governed, then I trust that we will leave; but when we do leave it must be distinctly understood that we retain no protectorate — and above all that we take part in no joint protectorate — over the islands, and give them no guarantee, of neutrality or otherwise; that, in short, we are absolutely quit of responsibility for them, of every kind and description.

The Filipinos were quite incapable of standing by themselves when we took possession of the islands, and we had made no promise concerning them. But we had explicitly promised to leave the island of Cuba, had explicitly promised that Cuba should be independent. Early in my administration that promise was redeemed. When the promise was made, I doubt if there was a single ruler or diplomat in Europe who believed that it would be kept. As far as I know, the United States was the first power which, having made such a promise, kept it in letter and spirit. England was unwise enough to make such a promise when she took Egypt. It would have been a capital misfortune to have kept the promise, and England has remained in Egypt for over thirty years, and will unquestionably remain indefinitely; but though it is necessary for her to do so, the fact of her doing so has meant the breaking of a positive promise and has been a real evil. Japan made the same guarantee about Korea, but as far as can be seen there was never even any thought of keeping the promise in this case; and Korea, which had shown herself utterly impotent either for self-government or self-defense, was in actual fact almost immediately annexed to Japan.

We made the promise to give Cuba independence; and we kept the promise. Leonard Wood was left in as Governor for two or three years, and evolved order out of chaos, raising the administration of the island to a level, moral and material, which it had never before achieved. We also by treaty gave the Cubans substantial advantages in our markets. Then we left the island, turning the government over to its own people. After four or five years a revolution broke out,

2 N

during my administration, and we again had to intervene to restore order. We promptly sent thither a small army of pacification. Under General Barry, order was restored and kept, and absolute justice done. The American troops were then withdrawn and the Cubans reëstablished in complete possession of their own beautiful island, and they are in possession of it now. There are plenty of occasions in our history when we have shown weakness or inefficiency, and some occasions when we have not been as scrupulous as we should have been as regards the rights of others. But I know of no action by any other government in relation to a weaker power which showed such disinterested efficiency in rendering service as was true in connection with our intervention in Cuba.

In Cuba, as in the Philippines and as in Porto Rico, Santo Domingo, and later in Panama, no small part of our success was due to the fact that we put in the highest grade of men as public officials. This practice was inaugurated under President McKinley. I found admirable men in office, and I continued them and appointed men like them as their successors. The way that the custom-houses in Santo Domingo were administered by Colton definitely established the success of our experiment in securing peace for that island republic; and in Porto Rico, under the administration of affairs under such officials as Hunt, Winthrop, Post, Ward and Grahame, more substantial progress was achieved in a decade than in any previous century.

The Philippines, Cuba, and Porto Rico came within our own sphere of governmental action. In addition to this we asserted certain rights in the Western Hemisphere under the Monroe Doctrine. My endeavor was not only to assert these rights, but frankly and fully to acknowledge the duties that went with the rights.

The Monroe Doctrine lays down the rule that the Western Hemisphere is not hereafter to be treated as subject to settlement and occupation by Old World powers. It is not international law; but it is a cardinal principle of our foreign policy. There is no difficulty at the present day in maintaining this doctrine, save where the American power whose interest is threatened has shown itself in international matters both weak and delinquent. The great and prosperous civilized commonwealths, such as the Argentine, Brazil, and Chile, in the Southern half of South America, have advanced so far that they no longer stand in any position of tutelage toward the United States. They occupy toward us precisely the position that Canada occupies. Their friendship is the friendship of equals for equals. My view was that as regards these nations there was no more necessity for asserting the Monroe Doctrine than there was to assert it in regard to Canada. They were competent to assert it for themselves. Of course if one of these nations, or if Canada, should be overcome by some Old World power, which then proceeded to occupy its territory, we would undoubtedly, if the American Nation needed our

MEDAL AWARDED BY MR. ROOSE-VELT FOR TWO YEARS' CONTINUOUS SERVICE ON THE PANAMA CANAL.

help, give it in order to prevent such occupation from taking place. But the initiative would come from the Nation itself, and the United States would merely act as a friend whose help was invoked.

The case was (and is) widely different as regards certain — not all — of the tropical states in the neighborhood of the Caribbean Sea. Where these states are stable and prosperous, they stand on a footing of absolute equality with all other communities. But some of them have been a prey to such continuous revolutionary misrule as to have grown impotent either to do their duties to outsiders or to enforce their rights against outsiders. The United States has not the slightest desire to make aggressions on any one of these states. On the contrary, it will submit to much from them without showing resentment. If any great civilized power, Russia or Germany, for instance, had behaved toward us as Venezuela under Castro behaved, this country would have gone to war at once.   We did not go to war with Venezuela merely because our people declined to be irritated by the actions of a weak opponent, and showed a forbearance which probably went beyond the limits of wisdom in refusing to take umbrage at what was done by the weak; although we would certainly have resented it had it been done by the strong.   In the case of two states, however, affairs reached such a crisis that we had to act.   These two states were Santo Domingo and the then owner of the Isthmus of Panama, Colombia.

The Santo Domingan case was the less important; and yet it possessed a real importance, and moreover is instructive because the action there taken should serve as a precedent for American action in all similar cases.   During the early years of my administration Santo Domingo was in its usual condition of chronic revolution.   There was always fighting, always plundering; and the successful graspers for governmental power were always pawning ports and custom-houses, or trying to put them up as guarantees for loans.   Of course the foreigners who made loans under such conditions demanded exorbitant interest, and if they were Europeans expected their governments to stand by them.   So utter was the disorder that on one occasion when Admiral Dewey landed to pay a call of ceremony on the President, he and his party were shot at by revolutionists in crossing the square, and had to return to the ships, leaving the call unpaid.   There was default on the interest due to the creditors; and finally the latter insisted upon their governments intervening. Two or three of the European powers were endeavoring to arrange for concerted action, and I was finally notified that these powers intended to take and hold several of the seaports which held custom-houses.

This meant that unless I acted at once I would find foreign powers in partial possession of Santo Domingo; in which event the very individuals who, in the actual event deprecated the precaution taken to prevent such action, would have advocated extreme and violent measures to undo the effect of their own supineness.   Nine-tenths of wisdom is to be wise in time, and at the right time; and my whole

foreign policy was based on the exercise of intelligent forethought and of decisive action sufficiently far in advance of
any likely crisis to make it improbable that we would run
into serious trouble.

Santo Domingo had fallen into such chaos that once for
some weeks there were two rival governments in it, and a
revolution was being carried on against each. At one period
one government was at sea in a small gunboat, but still
stoutly maintained that it was in possession of the island and
entitled to make loans and declare peace or war. The
situation had become intolerable by the time that I interfered. There was a naval commander in the waters whom I
directed to prevent any fighting which might menace the
custom-houses. He carried out his orders, both to his and
my satisfaction, in thoroughgoing fashion. On one occasion, when an insurgent force threatened to attack a town
in which Americans had interests, he notified the commanders on both sides that he would not permit any fighting
in the town, but that he would appoint a certain place where
they could meet and fight it out, and that the victors should
have the town. They agreed to meet his wishes, the fight
came off at the appointed place, and the victors, who if I
remember rightly were the insurgents, were given the town.

It was the custom-houses that caused the trouble, for they
offered the only means of raising money, and the revolutions
were carried on to get possession of them. Accordingly I
secured an agreement with the governmental authorities,
who for the moment seemed best able to speak for the
country, by which these custom-houses were placed under
American control. The arrangement was that we should
keep order and prevent any interference with the custom-
houses or the places where they stood, and should collect
the revenues. Forty-five per cent of the revenue was then
turned over to the Santo Domingan Government, and fifty-
five per cent put in a sinking fund in New York for the
benefit of the creditors. The arrangement worked in capital
style. On the forty-five per cent basis the Santo Domingan
Government received from us a larger sum than it had ever
received before when nominally all the revenue went to it.

The creditors were entirely satisfied with the arrangement, and no excuse for interference by European powers remained. Occasional disturbances occurred in the island, of course, but on the whole there ensued a degree of peace and prosperity which the island had not known before for at least a century.

All this was done without the loss of a life, with the assent of all the parties in interest, and without subjecting the United States to any charge, while practically all of the interference, after the naval commander whom I have mentioned had taken the initial steps in preserving order, consisted in putting a first-class man trained in our insular service at the head of the Santo Domingan customs service. We secured peace, we protected the people of the islands against foreign foes, and we minimized the chance of domestic trouble. We satisfied the creditors and the foreign nations to which the creditors belonged; and our own part of the work was done with the utmost efficiency and with rigid honesty, so that not a particle of scandal was ever so much as hinted at.

Under these circumstances those who do not know the nature of the professional international philanthropists would suppose that these apostles of international peace would have been overjoyed with what we had done. As a matter of fact, when they took any notice of it at all it was to denounce it; and those American newspapers which are fondest of proclaiming themselves the foes of war and the friends of peace violently attacked me for averting war from, and bringing peace to, the island. They insisted I had no power to make the agreement, and demanded the rejection of the treaty which was to perpetuate the agreement. They were, of course, wholly unable to advance a single sound reason of any kind for their attitude. I suppose the real explanation was partly their dislike of me personally, and unwillingness to see peace come through or national honor upheld by me; and in the next place their sheer, simple devotion to prattle and dislike of efficiency. They liked to have people come together and talk about peace, or even sign bits of paper with something about peace or arbitration on them, but they took no interest whatever in the practical achievement of a peace that told for good government and decency and honesty. They were joined by the many moderately well-meaning men who always demand that a thing be done, but also always demand that it be not done in the only way in which it is, as a matter of fact, possible to do it. The men of this kind insisted that of course Santo Domingo must be protected and made to behave itself, and that of course the Panama Canal must be dug; but they insisted even more strongly that neither feat should be accomplished in the only way in which it was possible to accomplish it at all.

The Constitution did not explicitly give me power to bring about the necessary agreement with Santo Domingo. But the Constitution did not forbid my doing what I did. I put the agreement into effect, and I continued its execution for two years before the Senate acted; and I would have continued it until the end of my term, if necessary, without any action by Congress. But it was far preferable that there should be action by Congress, so that we might be proceeding under a treaty which was the law of the land and not merely by a direction of the Chief Executive which would lapse when that particular executive left office. I therefore did my best to get the Senate to ratify what I had done. There was a good deal of difficulty about it. With the exception of one or two men like Clark of Arkansas, the Democratic Senators acted in that spirit of unworthy partisanship which subordinates national interest to some fancied partisan advantage, and they were cordially backed by all that portion of the press which took its inspiration from Wall Street, and was violently hostile to the Administration because of its attitude towards great corporations. Most of the Republican Senators under the lead of Senator Lodge stood by me; but some of them, of the more "conservative" or reactionary type, who were already growing hostile to me on the trust question, first proceeded to sneer at what had been done, and to raise all kinds of meticulous objections, which they themselves finally abandoned, but which furnished an excuse on which the opponents of the treaty could hang adverse action. Unfortunately the Senators who were most apt to speak of the dignity of the Senate, and to insist upon its importance, were the very ones who were also most apt to try to make display of this dignity and importance by thwarting the public business.   This case was typical.   The Republicans in question spoke against certain provisions of the proposed treaty.   They then, having ingeniously provided ammunition for the foes of the treaty, abandoned their opposition to it, and the Democrats stepped into the position they had abandoned.   Enough Republicans were absent to prevent the securing of a two-thirds vote for the treaty, and the Senate adjourned without any action at all, and with a feeling of entire self-satisfaction at having left the country in the position of assuming a responsibility and then failing to fulfil it.   Apparently the Senators in question felt that in some way they had upheld their dignity.   All that they had really done was to shirk their duty.   Somebody had to do that duty, and accordingly I did it.   I went ahead and administered the proposed treaty anyhow, considering it as a simple agreement on the part of the Executive which would be converted into a treaty whenever the Senate acted.   After a couple of years the Senate did act, having previously made some utterly unimportant changes which I ratified and persuaded Santo Domingo to ratify.   In all its history Santo Domingo has had nothing happen to it as fortunate as this treaty, and the passing of it saved the United States from having to face serious difficulties with one or more foreign powers.

It cannot in the long run prove possible for the United States to protect delinquent American nations from punishment for the non-performance of their duties unless she undertakes to make them perform their duties.   People may theorize about this as much as they wish, but whenever a sufficiently strong outside nation becomes sufficiently aggrieved, then either that nation will act or the United States Government itself will have to act.   We were face to face at one period of my administration with this condition of affairs in Venezuela, when Germany, rather feebly backed by England, undertook a blockade against Venezuela to make Venezuela adopt the German and English view about

certain agreements. There was real danger that the blockade would finally result in Germany's taking possession of
certain cities or custom-houses. I succeeded, however,
in getting all the parties in interest to submit their cases to
the Hague Tribunal.

By far the most important action I took in foreign affairs
during the time I was President related to the Panama
Canal. Here again there
was much accusation about
my having acted in an "unconstitutional" manner — a
position which can be upheld
only if Jefferson's action in
acquiring Louisiana be also
treated as unconstitutional;
and at different stages of
the affair believers in a do-
nothing policy denounced
me as having "usurped
authority" — which meant,
that when nobody else could
or would exercise efficient
authority, I exercised it.

During the nearly four
hundred years that had
elapsed since Balboa crossed
the Isthmus, there had been
a good deal of talk about
building an Isthmus canal,
and there had been various

Copyright by Underwood and Underwood.
COLONEL G. W. GOETHALS.

discussions of the subject and negotiations about it in
Washington for the previous half century. So far it had
all resulted merely in conversation; and the time had come
when unless somebody was prepared to act with decision
we would have to resign ourselves to at least half a century
of further conversation. Under the Hay-Pauncefote Treaty
signed shortly after I became President, and thanks to our
negotiations with the French Panama Company, the United
States at last acquired a possession, so far as Europe was

concerned, which warranted her in immediately undertaking the task. It remained to decide where the canal should be, whether along the line already pioneered by the French company in Panama, or in Nicaragua. Panama belonged to the Republic of Colombia. Nicaragua bid eagerly for the privilege of having the United States build the canal through her territory. As long as it was doubtful which route we would decide upon, Colombia extended every promise of friendly coöperation : at the Pan-American Congress in Mexico her delegate joined in the unanimous vote which requested the United States forthwith to build the canal ; and at her eager request we negotiated the Hay-Herran Treaty with her, which gave us the right to build the canal across Panama. A board of experts sent to the Isthmus had reported that this route was better than the Nicaragua route, and that it would be well to build the canal over it provided we could purchase the rights of the French company for forty million dollars ; but that otherwise they would advise taking the Nicaragua route. Ever since 1846 we had had a treaty with the power then in control of the Isthmus, the Republic of New Granada, the predecessor of the Republic of Colombia and of the present Republic of Panama, by which treaty the United States was guaranteed free and open right of way across the Isthmus of Panama by any mode of communication that might be constructed, while in return our Government guaranteed the perfect neutrality of the Isthmus with a view to the preservation of free transit.

For nearly fifty years we had asserted the right to prevent the closing of this highway of commerce. Secretary of State Cass in 1858 officially stated the American position as follows :

"Sovereignty has its duties as well as its rights, and none of these local governments, even if administered with more regard to the just demands of other nations than they have been, would be permitted, in a spirit of Eastern isolation, to close the gates of intercourse of the great highways of the world, and justify the act by the pretension that these avenues of trade and travel belong to them and that they choose to shut them, or, what is almost equivalent, to encumber them with such unjust relations as would prevent their general use."

We had again and again been forced to intervene to protect the transit across the Isthmus, and the intervention was frequently at the request of Colombia herself. The effort to build a canal by private capital had been made under De Lesseps and had resulted in lamentable failure. Every serious proposal to build the canal in such manner had been abandoned. The United States had repeatedly announced that we would not permit it to be built or controlled by any old-world government. Colombia was utterly impotent to build it herself. Under these circumstances it had become a matter of imperative obligation that we should build it ourselves without further delay.

I took final action in 1903. During the preceding fifty-three years the Governments of New Granada and of its successor, Colombia, had been in a constant state of flux; and the State of Panama had sometimes been treated as almost independent, in a loose Federal league, and sometimes as the mere property of the Government at Bogota; and there had been innumerable appeals to arms, sometimes for adequate, sometimes for inadequate, reasons. The following is a partial list of the disturbances on the Isthmus of Panama during the period in question, as reported to us by our consuls. It is not possible to give a complete list, and some of the reports that speak of "revolutions" must mean unsuccessful revolutions:

May 22, 1850. — Outbreak; two Americans killed. War vessel demanded to quell outbreak.

October, 1850. — Revolutionary plot to bring about independence of the Isthmus.

July 22, 1851. — Revolution in four Southern provinces.

November 14, 1851. — Outbreak at Chagres. Man-of-war requested for Chagres.

June 27, 1853. — Insurrection at Bogota, and consequent disturbance on Isthmus. War vessel demanded.

May 23, 1854. — Political disturbances. War vessel requested.

June 28, 1854. — Attempted revolution.

October 24, 1854. — Independence of Isthmus demanded by provincial legislature.

April, 1856. — Riot, and massacre of Americans.

May 4, 1856. — Riot.

May 18, 1856. — Riot.

June 3, 1856. — Riot.

October 2, 1856. — Conflict between two native parties. United States force landed.

December 18, 1858. — Attempted secession of Panama.

April, 1859. — Riots.

September, 1860. — Outbreak.

October 4, 1860. — Landing of United States forces in consequence.

May 23, 1861. — Intervention of the United States forces required, by intendente.

October 2, 1861. — Insurrection and civil war.

April 4, 1862. — Measures to prevent rebels crossing Isthmus.

June 13, 1862. — Mosquera's troops refused admittance to Panama.

March, 1865. — Revolution, and United States troops landed.

August, 1865. — Riots; unsuccessful attempt to invade Panama.

March, 1866. — Unsuccessful revolution.

April, 1867. — Attempt to overthrow Government.

August, 1867. — Attempt at revolution.

July 5, 1868. — Revolution; provisional government inaugurated.

August 29, 1868. — Revolution; provisional government overthrown.

April, 1871. — Revolution; followed apparently by counter revolution.

April, 1873. — Revolution and civil war which lasted to October, 1875.

August, 1876. — Civil war which lasted until April, 1877.

July, 1878. — Rebellion.

December, 1878. — Revolt.

April, 1879. — Revolution.

June, 1879. — Revolution.

March, 1883. — Riot.

May, 1883. — Riot.
June, 1884. — Revolutionary attempt.
December, 1884. — Revolutionary attempt.
January, 1885. — Revolutionary disturbances.
March, 1885. — Revolution.
April, 1887. — Disturbance on Panama Railroad.
November, 1887. — Disturbance on line of canal.
January, 1889. — Riot.
January, 1895. — Revolution which lasted until April.
March, 1895. — Incendiary attempt.
October, 1899. — Revolution.
February, 1900, to July, 1900. — Revolution.
January, 1901. — Revolution.
July, 1901. — Revolutionary disturbances.
September, 1901. — City of Colon taken by rebels.
March, 1902. — Revolutionary disturbances.
July, 1902. — Revolution.

The above is only a partial list of the revolutions, rebellions, insurrections, riots, and other outbreaks that occurred during the period in question; yet they number fifty-three for the fifty-three years, and they showed a tendency to increase, rather than decrease, in numbers and intensity. One of them lasted for nearly three years before it was quelled; another for nearly a year. In short, the experience of over half a century had shown Colombia to be utterly incapable of keeping order on the Isthmus. Only the active interference of the United States had enabled her to preserve so much as a semblance of sovereignty. Had it not been for the exercise by the United States of the police power in her interest, her connection with the Isthmus would have been sundered long before it was. In 1856, in 1860, in 1873, in 1885, in 1901, and again in 1902, sailors and marines from United States warships were forced to land in order to patrol the Isthmus, to protect life and property, and to see that the transit across the Isthmus was kept open. In 1861, in 1862, in 1885, and in 1900, the Colombian Government asked that the United States Government would land troops to protect Colombian interests and maintain order on the

Isthmus. The people of Panama during the preceding twenty years had three times sought to establish their independence by revolution or secession — in 1885, in 1895, and in 1899.

The peculiar relations of the United States toward the Isthmus, and the acquiescence by Colombia in acts which were quite incompatible with the theory of her having an absolute and unconditioned sovereignty on the Isthmus,

Drawing for *Punch* by E. T. Reed.

"Kindred Spirits of the Strenuous Life."

(Kaiser Wilhelm II and President Roosevelt.)

are illustrated by the following three telegrams between two of our naval officers whose ships were at the Isthmus, and the Secretary of the Navy on the occasion of the first outbreak that occurred on the Isthmus after I became President (a year before Panama became independent) :

September 12, 1902.

Ranger, Panama:

United States guarantees perfect neutrality of Isthmus and that a free transit from sea to sea be not interrupted or embarrassed. . . . Any transportation of troops which might contravene these provisions of treaty should not be sanctioned by you, nor should use of road be permitted which might convert the line of transit into theater of hostility.

MOODY.

COLON, September 20, 1902.
Secretary Navy, Washington:

Everything is conceded. The United States guards and guarantees traffic and the line of transit. To-day I permitted the exchange of Colombian troops from Panama to Colon, about 1000 men each way, the troops without arms in trains guarded by American naval force in the same manner as other passengers; arms and ammunition in separate train, guarded also by naval force in the same manner as other freight.

McLEAN.

PANAMA, October 3, 1902.
Secretary Navy,

Washington, D.C.:

Have sent this communication to the American Consul at Panama:

"Inform Governor, while trains running under United States protection, I must decline transportation any combatants, ammunition, arms, which might cause interruption to traffic or convert line of transit into theater hostilities."

CASEY.

When the Government in nominal control of the Isthmus continually besought American interference to protect the "rights" it could not itself protect, and permitted our Government to transport Colombian troops unarmed, under protection of our own armed men, while the Colombian arms and ammunition came in a separate train, it is obvious that the Colombian "sovereignty" was of such a character as to warrant our insisting that inasmuch as it only existed because of our protection there should be in requital a sense of the obligations that the acceptance of this protection implied.

Meanwhile Colombia was under a dictatorship. In 1898 M. A. Sanclamente was elected President, and J. M. Maroquin Vice-President, of the Republic of Colombia.

On July 31, 1900, the Vice-President, Maroquin, executed a "coup d'état" by seizing the person of the President, Sanclamente, and imprisoning him at a place a few miles out of Bogota. Maroquin thereupon declared himself possessed of the executive power because of "the absence of the President" — a delightful touch of unconscious humor. He then issued a decree that public order was disturbed, and, upon that ground, assumed to himself legislative power under another provision of the constitution; that is, having himself disturbed the public order, he alleged the disturbance as a justification for seizing absolute power. Thenceforth Maroquin, without the aid of any legislative body, ruled as a dictator, combining the supreme executive, legislative, civil, and military authorities, in the so-called Republic of Colombia. The "absence" of Sanclamente from the capital became permanent by his death in prison in the year 1902. When the people of Panama declared their independence in November, 1903, no Congress had sat in Colombia since the year 1898, except the special Congress called by Maroquin to reject the canal treaty, and which did reject it by a unanimous vote, and adjourned without legislating on any other subject. The constitution of 1886 had taken away from Panama the power of self-government and vested it in Colombia. The *coup d'état* of Maroquin took away from Colombia herself the power of government and vested it in an irresponsible dictator.

Consideration of the above facts ought to be enough to show any human being that we were not dealing with normal conditions on the Isthmus and in Colombia. We were dealing with the government of an irresponsible alien dictator, and with a condition of affairs on the Isthmus itself which was marked by one uninterrupted series of outbreaks and revolutions. As for the "consent of the governed" theory, that absolutely justified our action; the people on the Isthmus were the "governed"; they were governed by Colombia, without their consent, and they unanimously repudiated the Colombian government, and demanded that the United States build the canal.

I had done everything possible, personally and through

Secretary Hay, to persuade the Colombian Government to keep faith. Under the Hay-Pauncefote Treaty, it was explicitly provided that the United States should build the canal, should control, police and protect it, and keep it open to the vessels of all nations on equal terms. We had assumed the position of guarantor of the canal, including, of course, the building of the canal, and of its peaceful use by all the world. The enterprise was recognized everywhere as responding to an international need. It was a mere travesty on justice to treat the government in possession of the Isthmus as having the right — which Secretary Cass forty-five years before had so emphatically repudiated — to close the gates of intercourse on one of the great highways of the world. When we submitted to Colombia the Hay-Herran Treaty, it had been settled that the time for delay, the time for permitting any government of anti-social character, or of imperfect development, to bar the work, had passed. The United States had assumed in connection with the canal certain responsibilities not only to its own people but to the civilized world which imperatively demanded that there should be no further delay in beginning the work. The Hay-Herran Treaty, if it erred at all, erred in being overgenerous toward Colombia. The people of Panama were delighted with the treaty, and the President of Colombia, who embodied in his own person the entire government of Colombia, had authorized the treaty to be made. But after the treaty had been made the Colombia Government thought it had the matter in its own hands; and the further thought, equally wicked and foolish, came into the heads of the people in control at Bogota that they would seize the French Company at the end of another year and take for themselves the forty million dollars which the United States had agreed to pay the Panama Canal Company.

President Maroquin, through his Minister, had agreed to the Hay-Herran Treaty in January, 1903. He had the absolute power of an unconstitutional dictator to keep his promise or break it. He determined to break it. To furnish himself an excuse for breaking it he devised the plan of summoning a Congress especially called to reject the canal

20

treaty. This the Congress — a Congress of mere puppets — did, without a dissenting vote; and the puppets adjourned forthwith without legislating on any other subject. The fact that this was a mere sham, and that the President had entire power to confirm his own treaty and act on it if he desired, was shown as soon as the revolution took place, for

The standard original drawing for *Punch* by E. T. Reed, Nov., 1904

CONFISCATED BY THE BERLIN POLICE. WHAT ARE THEY AFRAID OF? IS IT THIS?

The Berlin Police have confiscated from the numbers of *Punch* of Nov. 16, the page containing the caricature of the Emperor William and President Roosevelt entitled "Kindred Spirits of the Strenuous Life."

on November 6 General Reyes of Colombia addressed the American Minister at Bogota, on behalf of President Maroquin, saying that "if the Government of the United States. would land troops and restore the Colombian sovereignty" the Colombian President would "declare martial law;

and, by virtue of vested constitutional authority, when public order is disturbed, would approve by decree the ratification of the canal treaty as signed; or, if the Government of the United States prefers, would call an extra session of the Congress — with new and friendly members — next May to approve the treaty." This, of course, is proof positive that the Colombian dictator had used his Congress as a mere shield, and a sham shield at that, and it shows how utterly useless it would have been further to trust his good faith in the matter.

When, in August, 1903, I became convinced that Colombia intended to repudiate the treaty made the preceding January, under cover of securing its rejection by the Colombian Legislature, I began carefully to consider what should be done. By my direction Secretary Hay, personally and through the Minister at Bogota, repeatedly warned Colombia that grave consequences might follow her rejection of the treaty. The possibility of ratification did not wholly pass away until the close of the session of the Colombian Congress on the last day of October. There would then be two possibilities. One was that Panama would remain quiet. In that case I was prepared to recommend to Congress that we should at once occupy the Isthmus anyhow, and proceed to dig the canal; and I had drawn out a draft of my message to this effect.[1] But from the information I received, I deemed it likely that there would be a revolution in Panama as soon as the Colombian Congress adjourned without ratifying the treaty, for the entire population of Panama felt that the immediate building of the canal was of vital concern to their well-being. Correspondents of the different newspapers on theIsthmus had sent to their respective papers widely published forecasts indicating that there would be a revolution in such event.

Moreover, on October 16, at the request of Lieutenant-General Young, Captain Humphrey and Lieutenant Murphy, two army officers who had returned from the Isthmus, saw me and told me that there would unquestionably be a revolu-

[1] See appendix at end of this chapter.

tion on the Isthmus, that the people were unanimous in their criticism of the Bogota Government and their disgust over the failure of that Government to ratify the treaty; and that the revolution would probably take place immediately after the adjournment of the Colombian Congress. They did not believe that it would be before October 20, but they were confident that it would certainly come at the end of October or immediately afterwards, when the Colombian Congress had adjourned. Accordingly I directed the Navy Department to station various ships within easy reach of the Isthmus, to be ready to act in the event of need arising.

These ships were barely in time. On November 3 the revolution occurred. Practically everybody on the Isthmus, including all the Colombian troops that were already stationed there, joined in the revolution, and there was no bloodshed. But on that same day four hundred new Colombian troops were landed at Colon. Fortunately, the gunboat *Nashville*, under Commander Hubbard, reached Colon almost immediately afterwards, and when the commander of the Colombian forces threatened the lives and property of the American citizens, including women and children, in Colon, Commander Hubbard landed a few score sailors and marines to protect them. By a mixture of firmness and tact he not only prevented any assault on our citizens, but persuaded the Colombian commander to reëmbark his troops for Cartagena. On the Pacific side a Colombian gunboat shelled the City of Panama, with the result of killing one Chinaman — the only life lost in the whole affair.

No one connected with the American Government had any part in preparing, inciting, or encouraging the revolution, and except for the reports of our military and naval officers, which I forwarded to Congress, no one connected with the Government had any previous knowledge concerning the proposed revolution, except such as was accessible to any person who read the newspapers and kept abreast of current questions and current affairs. By the unanimous action of its people, and without the firing of a shot, the state of Panama declared themselves an independent republic. The time for hesitation on our part had passed.

My belief then was, and the events that have occurred since have more than justified it, that from the standpoint of the United States it was imperative, not only for civil but for military reasons, that there should be the immediate establishment of easy and speedy communication by sea between the Atlantic and the Pacific. These reasons were not of convenience only, but of vital necessity, and did not admit of indefinite delay. The action of Colombia had shown not only that the delay would be indefinite, but that she intended to confiscate the property and rights of the French Panama Canal Company. The report of the Panama Canal Committee of the Colombian Senate on October 14, 1903, on the proposed treaty with the United States, proposed that all consideration of the matter should be postponed until October 31, 1904, when the next Colombian Congress would have convened, because by that time the new Congress would be in condition to determine whether through lapse of time the French company had not forfeited its property and rights. "When that time arrives," the report significantly declared, "the Republic, without any impediment, will be able to contract and will be in more clear, more definite and more advantageous possession, both legally and materially." The naked meaning of this was that Colombia proposed to wait a year, and then enforce a forfeiture of the rights and property of the French Panama Company, so as to secure the forty million dollars our Government had authorized as payment to this company. If we had sat supine, this would doubtless have meant that France would have interfered to protect the company, and we should then have had on the Isthmus, not the company, but France; and the gravest international complications might have ensued. Every consideration of international morality and expediency, of duty to the Panama people, and of satisfaction of our own national interests and honor, bade us take immediate action. I recognized Panama forthwith on behalf of the United States, and practically all the countries of the world immediately followed suit. The State Department immediately negotiated a canal treaty with the new Republic.   One of the foremost men in securing the independence of Panama, and the treaty which authorized the United States forthwith to build the canal, was M. Philippe Bunau-Varilla, an eminent French engineer formerly associated with De Lesseps and then living on the Isthmus ; his services to civilization were notable, and deserve the fullest recognition.

From the beginning to the end our course was straightforward and in absolute accord with the highest of standards of international morality.   Criticism of it can come only from misinformation, or else from a sentimentality which represents both mental weakness and a moral twist.   To have acted otherwise than I did would have been on my part betrayal of the interests of the United States, indifference to the interests of Panama, and recreancy to the interests of the world at large.   Colombia had forfeited every claim to consideration ; indeed, this is not stating the case strongly enough : she had so acted that yielding to her would have meant on our part that culpable form of weakness which stands on a level with wickedness.   As for me personally, if I had hesitated to act, and had not in advance discounted the clamor of those Americans who have made a fetish of disloyalty to their country, I should have esteemed myself as deserving a place in Dante's inferno beside the faint-hearted cleric who was guilty of "il gran rifiuto." The facts I have given above are mere bald statements from the record.   They show that from the beginning there had been acceptance of our right to insist on free transit, in whatever form was best, across the Isthmus ; and that towards the end there had been a no less universal feeling that it was our duty to the world to provide this transit in the shape of a canal — the resolution of the Pan-American Congress was practically a mandate to this effect.   Colombia was then under a one-man government, a dictatorship, founded on usurpation of absolute and irresponsible power. She eagerly pressed us to enter into an agreement with her, as long as there was any chance of our going to the alternative route through Nicaragua.   When she thought we were committed, she refused to fulfil the agreement, with the avowed hope of seizing the French company's property for nothing and thereby holding us up. This was a bit of pure bandit morality. It would have achieved its purpose had I possessed as weak moral fiber as those of my critics who announced that I ought to have confined my action to feeble scolding and temporizing until the opportunity for action passed. I did not lift my finger to incite the revolutionists. The right simile to use is totally different. I simply ceased to stamp out the different revolutionary fuses that were already burning. When Colombia committed flagrant wrong against us, I considered it no part of my duty to aid and abet her in her wrongdoing at our expense, and also at the expense of Panama, of the French company, and of the world generally. There had been fifty years of continuous bloodshed and civil strife in Panama; because of my action Panama has now known ten years of such peace and prosperity as she never before saw during the four centuries of her existence — for in Panama, as in Cuba and Santo Domingo, it was the action of the American people, against the outcries of the professed apostles of peace, which alone brought peace. We gave to the people of Panama self-government, and freed them from subjection to alien oppressors. We did our best to get Colombia to let us treat her with a more than generous justice; we exercised patience to beyond the verge of proper forbearance. When we did act and recognize Panama, Colombia at once acknowledged her own guilt by promptly offering to do what we had demanded, and what she had protested it was not in her power to do. But the offer came too late. What we would gladly have done before, it had by that time become impossible for us honorably to do; for it would have necessitated our abandoning the people of Panama, our friends, and turning them over to their and our foes, who would have wreaked vengeance on them precisely because they had shown friendship to us. Colombia was solely responsible for her own humiliation; and she had not then, and has not now, one shadow of claim upon us, moral or legal; all the wrong that was done was done by her. If, as representing the American people, I had not acted precisely

A Gate at the Upper Lock at Gatun.

as I did, I would have been an unfaithful or incompetent representative; and inaction at that crisis would have meant not only indefinite delay in building the canal, but also practical admission on our part that we were not fit to play the part on the Isthmus which we had arrogated to ourselves. I acted on my own responsibility in the Panama matter. John Hay spoke of this action as follows: "The action of the President in the Panama matter is not only in the strictest accordance with the principles of justice and equity, and in line with all the best precedents of our public policy, but it was the only course he could have taken in compliance with our treaty rights and obligations."

I deeply regretted, and now deeply regret, the fact that the Colombian Government rendered it imperative for me to take the action I took; but I had no alternative, consistent with the full performance of my duty to my own people, and to the nations of mankind. (For, be it remembered, that certain other nations, Chile for example, will probably benefit even more by our action than will the United States itself.) I am well aware that the Colombian people have many fine traits; that there is among them a circle of high-bred men and women which would reflect honor on the social life of any country; and that there has been an intellectual and literary development within this small circle which partially atones for the stagnation and illiteracy of the mass of the people; and I also know that even the illiterate mass possesses many sterling qualities. But unfortunately in international matters every nation must be judged by the action of its Government. The good people in Colombia apparently made no effort, certainly no successful effort, to cause the Government to act with reasonable good faith towards the United States; and Colombia had to take the consequences. If Brazil, or the Argentine, or Chile, had been in possession of the Isthmus, doubtless the canal would have been built under the governmental control of the nation thus controlling the Isthmus, with the hearty acquiescence of the United States and of all other powers. But in the actual fact the canal would not have been built at all save for the action I took. If men choose to say that it would have been better not to build it, than to build it as the result of such action, their position, although foolish, is compatible with belief in their wrongheaded sincerity.   But it is hypocrisy, alike odious and contemptible, for any man to say both that we ought to have built the canal and that we ought not to have acted in the way we did act.

After a sufficient period of wrangling, the Senate ratified the treaty with Panama, and work on the canal was begun. The first thing that was necessary was to decide the type of canal.   I summoned a board of engineering experts, foreign and native.   They divided on their report.   The majority of the members, including all the foreign members, approved a sea-level canal.   The minority, including most of the American members, approved a lock canal.   Studying these conclusions, I came to the belief that the minority was right. The two great traffic canals of the world were the Suez and the Soo.   The Suez Canal is a sea-level canal, and it was the one best known to European engineers.   The Soo Canal, through which an even greater volume of traffic passes every year, is a lock canal, and the American engineers were thoroughly familiar with it; whereas, in my judgment, the European engineers had failed to pay proper heed to the lessons taught by its operation and management.   Moreover, the engineers who were to do the work at Panama all favored a lock canal.   I came to the conclusion that a sea-level canal would be slightly less exposed to damage in the event of war; that the running expenses, apart from the heavy cost of interest on the amount necessary to build it, would be less; and that for small ships the time of transit would be less.   But I also came to the conclusion that the lock canal at the proposed level would cost only about half as much to build and would be built in half the time, with much less risk; that for large ships the transit would be quicker, and that, taking into account the interest saved, the cost of maintenance would be less.   Accordingly I recommended to Congress, on February 19, 1906, that a lock canal should be built, and my recommendation was adopted. Congress insisted upon having it built by a commission of several men.   I tried faithfully to get good work out of the commission, and found it quite impossible; for a many-headed commission is an extremely poor executive instrument. At last I put Colonel Goethals in as head of the commission. Then, when Congress still refused to make the commission single-headed, I solved the difficulty by an executive order of January 6, 1908, which practically accomplished the object by enlarging the powers of the chairman, making all the other members of the commission dependent upon him, and thereby placing the work under one-man control. Dr. Gorgas had already performed an inestimable service by caring for the sanitary conditions so thoroughly as to make the Isthmus as safe as a health resort. Colonel Goethals proved to be the man of all others to do the job. It would be impossible to overstate what he has done. It is the greatest task of any kind that any man in the world has accomplished during the years that Colonel Goethals has been at work. It is the greatest task of its own kind that has ever been performed in the world at all. Colonel Goethals has succeeded in instilling into the men under him a spirit which elsewhere has been found only in a few victorious armies. It is proper and appropriate that, like the soldiers of such armies, they should receive medals which are allotted each man who has served for a sufficient length of time. A finer body of men has never been gathered by any nation than the men who have done the work of building the Panama Canal; the conditions under which they have lived and have done their work have been better than in any similar work ever undertaken in the tropics; they have all felt an eager pride in their work; and they have made not only America but the whole world their debtors by what they have accomplished.

APPENDIX

COLOMBIA: THE PROPOSED MESSAGE TO CONGRESS

The rough draft of the message I had proposed to send Congress ran as follows:

"The Colombian Government, through its representative here, and directly in communication with our representative at Colombia, has refused to come to any agreement with us, and has delayed action so as to make it evident that it intends to make extortionate and improper terms with us. The Isthmian Canal bill was, of course, passed upon the assumption that whatever route was used, the benefit to the particular section of the Isthmus through which it passed would be so great that the country controlling this part would be eager to facilitate the building of the canal. It is out of the question to submit to extortion on the part of a beneficiary of the scheme. All the labor, all the expense, all the risk are to be assumed by us and all the skill shown by us. Those controlling the ground through which the canal is to be put are wholly incapable of building it.

"Yet the interest of international commerce generally and the interest of this country generally demands that the canal should be begun with no needless delay. The refusal of Colombia properly to respond to our sincere and earnest efforts to come to an agreement, or to pay heed to the many concessions we have made, renders it in my judgment necessary that the United States should take immediate action on one of two lines: either we should drop the Panama canal project and immediately begin work on the Nicaraguan canal, or else we should purchase all the rights of the French company, and, without any further parley with Colombia, enter upon the completion of the canal which the French company has begun. I feel that the latter course is the one demanded by the interests of this Nation, and I therefore bring the matter to your attention for such action in the premises as you may deem wise. If in your judgment it is better not to take such action, then I shall proceed at once with the Nicaraguan canal.

"The reason that I advocate the action above outlined in regard to the Panama canal is, in the first place, the strong testimony of the experts that this route is the most feasible; and in the next place, the impropriety from an international standpoint of permitting such conduct as that to which Colombia seems to incline. The testimony of the experts is very strong, not only that the Panama route is feasible, but that in the Nicaragua route we may encounter some unpleasant surprises, and that it is far more difficult to forecast the result with any certainty as regards this latter route. As for Colombia's attitude, it is incomprehensible upon any theory of desire to see the canal built upon the basis of mutual advantage alike to those building it and to Colombia herself. All we desire to do is to take up the work begun by the French Government and to finish it. Obviously it is Colombia's duty to help towards such completion. We are most anxious to come to an agreement with her in which most scrupulous care should be taken to guard her interests and ours. But we cannot consent to permit her to block the performance of the work which it is so greatly to our interest immediately to begin and carry through."

Shortly after this rough draft was dictated the Panama revolution came, and I never thought of the rough draft again until I was accused of having instigated the revolution. This accusation is preposterous in the eyes of any one who knows the actual conditions at Panama. Only the menace of action by us in the interest of Colombia kept down revolution; as soon as Colombia's own conduct removed such menace, all check on the various revolutionary movements (there were at least three from entirely separate sources) ceased; and then an explosion was inevitable, for the French company knew that all their property would be confiscated if Colombia put through her plans, and the entire people of Panama felt that if in disgust with Colombia's extortions the United States turned to Nicaragua, they, the people of Panama, would be ruined. Knowing the character of those then in charge of the Colombian Government, I was not surprised at their bad faith; but I was surprised at their folly. They apparently had no idea either of the power of France or the power of the United States, and expected to be permitted to commit wrong with impunity, just as Castro in Venezuela had done. The difference was that, unless we acted in self-defense, Colombia had it in her power to do us serious harm, and Venezuela did not have such power. Colombia's wrongdoing, therefore, recoiled on her own head. There was no new lesson taught; it ought already to have been known to every one that wickedness, weakness, and folly combined rarely fail to meet punishment, and that the intent to do wrong, when joined to inability to carry the evil purpose to a successful conclusion, inevitably reacts on the wrongdoer.

For the full history of the acquisition and building of the canal see "The Panama Gateway," by Joseph Bucklin Bishop (Scribner's Sons).   Mr. Bishop has been for eight years secretary of the commission and is one of the most efficient of the many efficient men to whose work on the Isthmus America owes so much.

CHAPTER XV

THE PEACE OF RIGHTEOUSNESS

THERE can be no nobler cause for which to work than the peace of righteousness; and high honor is due those serene and lofty souls who with wisdom and courage, with high idealism tempered by sane facing of the actual facts of life, have striven to bring nearer the day when armed strife between nation and nation, between class and class, between man and man shall end throughout the world. Because all this is true, it is also true that there are no men more ignoble or more foolish, no men whose actions are fraught with greater possibility of mischief to their country and to mankind, than those who exalt unrighteous peace as better than righteous war. The men who have stood highest in our history, as in the history of all countries, are those who scorned injustice, who were incapable of oppressing the weak, or of permitting their country, with their consent, to oppress the weak, but who did not hesitate to draw the sword when to leave it undrawn meant inability to arrest triumphant wrong.

All this is so obvious that it ought not to be necessary to repeat it. Yet every man in active affairs, who also reads about the past, grows by bitter experience to realize that there are plenty of men, not only among those who mean ill, but among those who mean well, who are ready enough to praise what was done in the past, and yet are incapable of profiting by it when faced by the needs of the present.

During our generation this seems to have been peculiarly the case among the men who have become obsessed with the idea of obtaining universal peace by some cheap patent panacea.

There has been a real and substantial growth in the feeling for international responsibility and justice among the great civilized nations during the past threescore or fourscore years. There has been a real growth of recognition of the fact that moral turpitude is involved in the wronging of one nation by another, and that in most cases war is an evil method of settling international difficulties. But as yet there has been only a rudimentary beginning of the development of international tribunals of justice, and there has been no development at all of any international police power. Now, as I have already said, the whole fabric of municipal law, of law within each nation, rests ultimately upon the judge and the policeman; and the complete absence of the policeman, and the almost complete absence of the judge, in international affairs, prevents there being as yet any real homology between municipal and international law.

Moreover, the questions which sometimes involve nations in war are far more difficult and complex than any questions that affect merely individuals. Almost every great nation has inherited certain questions, either with other nations or with sections of its own people, which it is quite impossible, in the present state of civilization, to decide as matters between private individuals can be decided. During the last century at least half of the wars that have been fought have been civil and not foreign wars. There are big and powerful nations which habitually commit, either upon other nations or upon sections of their own people, wrongs so outrageous as to justify even the most peaceful persons in going to war. There are also weak nations so utterly incompetent either to protect the rights of foreigners against their own citizens, or to protect their own citizens against foreigners, that it becomes a matter of sheer duty for some outside power to interfere in connection with them. As yet in neither case is there any efficient method of getting international action; and if joint action by several powers is secured, the result is usually considerably worse than if only one Power interfered. The worst infamies of modern times — such affairs as the massacres of the Armenians by the Turks, for instance — have been perpetrated in a time of nominally profound international peace, when there has been a concert of big Powers to prevent the breaking of this peace, although only by breaking it could the outrages be stopped. Be it remembered that the peoples who suffered by these hideous massacres, who saw their women violated and their children tortured, were actually enjoying all the benefits of "disarmament." Otherwise they would not have been massacred; for if the Jews in Russia and the Armenians in Turkey had been armed, and had been efficient in the use of their arms, no mob would have meddled with them.

Yet amiable but fatuous persons, with all these facts before their eyes, pass resolutions demanding universal arbitration for everything, and the disarmament of the free civilized powers and their abandonment of their armed forces; or else they write well-meaning, solemn little books, or pamphlets or editorials, and articles in magazines or newspapers, to show that it is "an illusion" to believe that war ever pays, because it is expensive. This is precisely like arguing that we should disband the police and devote our sole attention to persuading criminals that it is "an illusion" to suppose that burglary, highway robbery and white slavery are profitable. It is almost useless to attempt to argue with these well-intentioned persons, because they are suffering under an obsession and are not open to reason. They go wrong at the outset, for they lay all the emphasis on peace and none at all on righteousness. They are not all of them physically timid men; but they are usually men of soft life; and they rarely possess a high sense of honor or a keen patriotism. They rarely try to prevent their fellow countrymen from insulting or wronging the people of other nations; but they always ardently advocate that we, in our turn, shall tamely submit to wrong and insult from other nations. As Americans their folly is peculiarly scandalous, because if the principles they now uphold are right, it means

2 P

that it would have been better that Americans should never have achieved their independence, and better that, in 1861, they should have peacefully submitted to seeing their country split into half a dozen jangling confederacies and slavery made perpetual. If unwilling to learn from their own history, let those who think that it is an "illusion" to believe that a war ever benefits a nation look at the difference between China and Japan. China has neither a fleet nor an efficient army. It is a huge civilized empire, one of the most populous on the globe; and it has been the helpless prey of outsiders because it does not possess the power to fight. Japan stands on a footing of equality with European and American nations because it does possess this power. China now sees Japan, Russia, Germany, England and France in possession of fragments of her empire, and has twice within the lifetime of the present generation seen her capital in the hands of allied invaders, because she in very fact realizes the ideals of the persons who wish the United States to disarm, and then trust that our helplessness will secure us a contemptuous immunity from attack by outside nations.

The chief trouble comes from the entire inability of these worthy people to understand that they are demanding things that are mutually incompatible when they demand peace at any price, and also justice and righteousness. I remember one representative of their number, who used to write little sonnets on behalf of the Mahdi and the Sudanese, these sonnets setting forth the need that the Sudan should be both independent and peaceful. As a matter of fact, the Sudan valued independence only because it desired to war against all Christians and to carry on an unlimited slave trade. It was "independent" under the Mahdi for a dozen years, and during those dozen years the bigotry, tyranny, and cruel religious intolerance were such as flourished in the seventh century, and in spite of systematic slave raids the population decreased by nearly two-thirds, and practically all the children died. Peace came, well-being came, freedom from rape and murder and torture and highway robbery, and every brutal gratification of lust and greed came, only when the Sudan lost its independence and passed under English rule. Yet this well-meaning little sonneteer sincerely felt that his verses were issued in the cause of humanity. Looking back from the vantage point of a score of years, probably every one will agree that he was an absurd person. But he was not one whit more absurd than most of the more prominent persons who advocate disarmament by the United States, the cessation of up-building the navy, and the promise to agree to arbitrate all matters, including those affecting our national interests and honor, with all foreign nations.

These persons would do no harm if they affected only themselves. Many of them are, in the ordinary relations of life, good citizens. They are exactly like the other good citizens who believe that enforced universal vegetarianism or anti-vaccination is the panacea for all ills. But in their particular case they are able to do harm because they affect our relations with foreign powers, so that other men pay the debt which they themselves have really incurred. It is the foolish, peace-at-any-price persons who try to persuade our people to make unwise and improper treaties, or to stop building up the navy. But if trouble comes and the treaties are repudiated, or there is a demand for armed intervention, it is not these people who will pay anything; they will stay at home in safety, and leave brave men to pay in blood, and honest men to pay in shame, for their folly.

The trouble is that our policy is apt to go in zigzags, because different sections of our people exercise at different times unequal pressure on our government. One class of our citizens clamor for treaties impossible of fulfilment, and improper to fulfil; another class have no objection to the passage of these treaties so long as there is no concrete case to which they apply, but instantly oppose a veto on their application when any concrete case does actually arise. One of our cardinal doctrines is freedom of speech, which means freedom of speech about foreigners as well as about ourselves; and, inasmuch as we exercise this right with complete absence of restraint, we cannot expect other nations to hold us harmless unless in the last resort we are able to make our own words good by our deeds.   One class of our citizens indulges in gushing promises to do everything for foreigners, another class offensively and improperly reviles them; and it is hard to say which class more thoroughly misrepresents the sober, self-respecting judgment of the American people as a whole.   The only safe rule is to promise little, and faithfully to keep every promise; to "speak softly and carry a big stick."

A prime need for our nation, as of course for every other nation, is to make up its mind definitely what it wishes, and not to try to pursue paths of conduct incompatible one with the other.   If this nation is content to be the China of the New World, then and then only can it afford to do away with the navy and the army.   If it is content to abandon Hawaii and the Panama Canal, to cease to talk of the Monroe Doctrine, and to admit the right of any European or Asiatic power to dictate what immigrants shall be sent to and received in America, and whether or not they shall be allowed to become citizens and hold land — why, of course, if America is content to have nothing to say on any of these matters and to keep silent in the presence of armed outsiders, then it can abandon its navy and agree to arbitrate all questions of all kinds with every foreign power. In such event it can afford to pass its spare time in one continuous round of universal peace celebrations, and of smug self-satisfaction in having earned the derision of all the virile peoples of mankind.   Those who advocate such a policy do not occupy a lofty position.   But at least their position is understandable.

It is entirely inexcusable, however, to try to combine the unready hand with the unbridled tongue.   It is folly to permit freedom of speech about foreigners as well as our-selves — and the peace-at-any-price persons are much too feeble a folk to try to interfere with freedom of speech — and yet to try to shirk the consequences of freedom of speech. It is folly to try to abolish our navy, and at the same time to insist that we have a right to enforce the Monroe Doctrine, that we have a right to control the Panama Canal which we

ourselves dug, that we have a right to retain Hawaii and
prevent foreign nations from taking Cuba, and a right to
determine what immigrants, Asiatic or European, shall
come to our shores, and the terms on which they shall be
naturalized and shall hold land and exercise other privileges.
We are a rich people, and an unmilitary people. In international affairs we are a short-sighted people. But I know
my countrymen. Down at bottom their temper is such
that they will not permanently tolerate injustice done to
them. In the long run they will no more permit affronts
to their National honor than injuries to their national
interest. Such being the case, they will do well to remember
that the surest of all ways to invite disaster is to be opulent,
aggressive and unarmed.

Throughout the seven and a half years that I was President, I pursued without faltering one consistent foreign
policy, a policy of genuine international good will and of
consideration for the rights of others, and at the same time
of steady preparedness. The weakest nations knew that
they, no less than the strongest, were safe from insult and
injury at our hands; and the strong and the weak alike also
knew that we possessed both the will and the ability to guard
ourselves from wrong or insult at the hands of any one.

It was under my administration that the Hague Court
was saved from becoming an empty farce. It had been
established by joint international agreement, but no Power
had been willing to resort to it. Those establishing it had
grown to realize that it was in danger of becoming a mere
paper court, so that it would never really come into being at
all. M. d'Estournelles de Constant had been especially
alive to this danger. By correspondence and in personal
interviews he impressed upon me the need not only of making
advances by actually applying arbitration — not merely
promising by treaty to apply it — to questions that were
up for settlement, but of using the Hague tribunal for this
purpose. I cordially sympathized with these views. On
the recommendation of John Hay, I succeeded in getting
an agreement with Mexico to lay a matter in dispute between the two republics before the Hague Court. This

was the first case ever brought before the Hague Court.   It was followed by numerous others; and it definitely established that court as the great international peace tribunal. By mutual agreement with Great Britain, through the decision of a joint commission, of which the American members were Senators Lodge and Turner, and Secretary Root, we were able peacefully to settle the Alaska Boundary question, the only question remaining between ourselves and the British Empire which it was not possible to settle by friendly arbitration; this therefore represented the removal of the last obstacle to absolute agreement between the two peoples.   We were of substantial service in bringing to a satisfactory conclusion the negotiations at Algeciras concerning Morocco.   We concluded with Great Britain, and with most of the other great nations, arbitration treaties specifically agreeing to arbitrate all matters, and especially the interpretation of treaties, save only as regards questions affecting territorial integrity, national honor and vital national interest.   We made with Great Britain a treaty guaranteeing the free use of the Panama Canal on equal terms to the ships of all nations, while reserving to ourselves the right to police and fortify the canal, and therefore to control it in time of war.   Under this treaty we are in honor bound to arbitrate the question of canal tolls for coastwise traffic between the Western and Eastern coasts of the United States.   I believe that the American position as regards this matter is right; but I also believe that under the arbitration treaty we are in honor bound to submit the matter to arbitration in view of Great Britain's contention — although I hold it to be an unwise contention — that our position is unsound.   I emphatically disbelieve in making universal arbitration treaties which neither the makers nor any one else would for a moment dream of keeping.   I no less emphatically insist that it is our duty to keep the limited and sensible arbitration treaties which we have already made.   The importance of a promise lies not in making it, but in keeping it; and the poorest of all positions for a nation to occupy in such a matter is readiness to make impossible promises at the same time that there is failure to keep promises which have been made, which can be kept, and which it is discreditable to break.

During the early part of the year 1905, the strain on the civilized world caused by the Russo-Japanese War became serious. The losses of life and of treasure were frightful. From all the sources of information at hand, I grew most strongly to believe that a further continuation of the struggle would be a very bad thing for Japan, and an even worse thing for Russia. Japan was already suffering terribly from the drain upon her men, and especially upon her resources, and had nothing further to gain from continuance of the struggle; its continuance meant to her more loss than gain, even if she were victorious. Russia, in spite of her gigantic strength, was, in my judgment, apt to lose even more than she had already lost if the struggle continued. I deemed it probable that she would no more be able successfully to defend Eastern Siberia and Northern Manchuria than she had been able to defend Southern Manchuria and Korea. If the war went on, I thought it, on the whole, likely that Russia would be driven west of Lake Baikal. But it was very far from certain. There is no certainty in such a war. Japan might have met defeat, and defeat to her would have spelt overwhelming disaster; and even if she had continued to win, what she thus won would have been of no value to her, and the cost in blood and money would have left her drained white. I believed, therefore, that the time had come when it was greatly to the interest of both combatants to have peace, and when therefore it was possible to get both to agree to peace.

I first satisfied myself that each side wished me to act, but that, naturally and properly, each side was exceedingly anxious that the other should not believe that the action was taken on its initiative. I then sent an identical note to the two powers proposing that they should meet, through their representatives, to see if peace could not be made directly between them, and offered to act as an intermediary in bringing about such a meeting, but not for any other purpose. Each assented to my proposal in principle. There was difficulty in getting them to agree on a common meeting

PEACE COMMISSION AT PORTSMOUTH.

place; but each finally abandoned its original contention in the matter, and the representatives of the two nations finally met at Portsmouth, in New Hampshire. I previously received the two delegations at Oyster Bay on the U. S. S. Mayflower, which, together with another naval vessel, I put at their disposal, on behalf of the United States Government, to take them from Oyster Bay to Portsmouth.

As is customary — but both unwise and undesirable — in such cases, each side advanced claims which the other could not grant. The chief difficulty came because of Japan's demand for a money indemnity. I felt that it would be better for Russia to pay some indemnity than to go on with the war, for there was little chance, in my judgment, of the war turning out favorably for Russia, and the revolutionary movement already under way bade fair to overthrow the negotiations entirely. I advised the Russian Government to this effect, at the same time urging them to abandon their pretensions on certain other points, notably concerning the southern half of Saghelien, which the Japanese had taken. I also, however, and equally strongly, advised the Japanese that in my judgment it would be the gravest mistake on their part to insist on continuing the war for the sake of a money indemnity; for Russia was absolutely firm in refusing to give them an indemnity, and the longer the war continued the less able she would be to pay. I pointed out that there was no possible analogy between their case and that of Germany in the war with France, which they were fond of quoting. The Germans held Paris and half of France, and gave up much territory in lieu of the indemnity, whereas the Japanese were still many thousand miles from Moscow, and had no territory whatever which they wished to give up. I also pointed out that in my judgment whereas the Japanese had enjoyed the sympathy of most of the civilized powers at the outset of and during the continuance of the war, they would forfeit it if they turned the war into one merely for getting money — and, moreover, they would almost certainly fail to get the money, and would simply find themselves at the end of a year, even if things prospered with them, in possession of territory they did not want, having spent enormous additional sums of money, and lost enormous additional numbers of men, and yet without a penny of remuneration. The treaty of peace was finally signed.

As is inevitable under such circumstances, each side felt that it ought to have got better terms; and when the danger was well past each side felt that it had been over-reached by the other, and that if the war had gone on it would have gotten more than it actually did get. The Japanese Government had been wise throughout, except in the matter of announcing that it .would insist on a money indemnity. Neither in national nor in private affairs is it ordinarily advisable to make a bluff which cannot be put through — personally, I never believe in doing it under any circumstances. The Japanese people had been misled by this bluff of their Government; and the unwisdom of the Government's action in the matter was shown by the great resentment the treaty aroused in Japan, although it was so beneficial to Japan. There were various mob outbreaks, especially in the Japanese cities; the police were roughly handled, and several Christian churches were burned, as reported to me by the American Minister. In both Russia and Japan I believe that the net result as regards myself was a feeling of injury, and of dislike of me, among the people at large. I had expected this; I regarded it as entirely natural; and I did not resent it in the least. The Governments of both nations behaved toward me not only with correct and entire propriety, but with much courtesy and the fullest acknowledgment of the good effect of what I had done; and in Japan, at least, I believe that the leading men sincerely felt that I had been their friend. I had certainly tried my best to be the friend not only of the Japanese people but of the Russian people, and I believe that what I did was for the best interests of both and of the world at large.

During the course of the negotiations I tried to enlist the aid of the Governments of one nation which was friendly to Russia, and of another nation which was friendly to Japan, in helping bring about peace. I got no aid from either. I did, however, receive aid from the Emperor of Germany. His Ambassador at St. Petersburg was the one Ambassador who helped the American Ambassador, Mr. Meyer, at delicate and doubtful points of the negotiations. Mr. Meyer, who was, with the exception of Mr. White, the most useful diplomat in the American service, rendered literally invaluable aid by insisting upon himself seeing the Czar at critical periods of the transaction, when it was no longer possible for me to act successfully through the representatives of the Czar, who were often at cross purposes with one another.

As a result of the Portsmouth peace, I was given the Nobel Peace Prize. This consisted of a medal, which I kept, and a sum of $40,000, which I turned over as a foundation of industrial peace to a board of trustees which included Oscar Straus, Seth Low and John Mitchell. In the present state of the world's development industrial peace is even more essential than international peace; and it was fitting and appropriate to devote the peace prize to such a purpose. In 1910, while in Europe, one of my most pleasant experiences was my visit to Norway, where I addressed the Nobel Committee, and set forth in full the principles upon which I had acted, not only in this particular case but throughout my administration.

GEORGE VON LENGERKE MEYER, AMBASSADOR EXTRAORDINARY AND PLENIPOTENTIARY TO RUSSIA.

I received another gift which I deeply appreciated, an original copy of Sully's "Memoires" of "Henry le Grand," sent me with the following inscription (I translate it roughly):

" PARIS, January, 1906.

"The undersigned members of the French Parliamentary Group of International Arbitration and Conciliation have decided to tender President Roosevelt a token of their high esteem and their sympathetic recognition of the persistent and decisive initiative he has taken towards gradually substituting friendly and judicial for violent methods in case of conflict between Nations.

"They believe that the action of President Roosevelt, which has realized the most generous hopes to be found in history, should be classed as a continuance of similar illustrious attempts of former times, notably the project for international concord known under the name of the 'Great Design of Henry IV' in the memoirs of his Prime Minister, the Duke de Sully. In consequence they have sought out a copy of the first edition of these memoirs, and they take pleasure in offering it to him, with the request that he will keep it among his family papers."

The signatures include those of Emile Loubet, A. Carnot, d'Estournelles de Constant, Aristide Briand, Sully Prudhomme, Jean Jaurés, A. Fallières, R. Poincaré, and two or three hundred others.

Of course what I had done in connection with the Portsmouth peace was misunderstood by some good and sincere people. Just as after the settlement of the coal strike, there were persons who thereupon thought that it was in my power, and was my duty, to settle all other strikes, so after the peace of Portsmouth there were other persons — not only Americans, by the way, — who thought it my duty forthwith to make myself a kind of international Meddlesome Mattie and interfere for peace and justice promiscuously over the world. Others, with a delightful non-sequitur, jumped to the conclusion that inasmuch as I had helped to bring about a beneficent and necessary peace I must of necessity have changed my mind about war being ever necessary. A couple of days after peace was concluded I wrote to a friend: "Don't you be misled by the fact that just at the moment men are speaking well of me. They will speak ill soon enough. As Loeb remarked to me to-day, some time soon I shall have to spank some little international brigand, and then all the well-meaning idiots will turn and shriek that this is inconsistent with what I did at the Peace Conference, whereas in reality it will be exactly in line with it."

To one of my political opponents, Mr. Schurz, who wrote me congratulating me upon the outcome at Portsmouth, and suggesting that the time was opportune for a move towards disarmament, I answered in a letter setting forth views which I thought sound then, and think sound now. The letter ran as follows :

OYSTER BAY, N. Y.,

September 8, 1905.

My dear Mr. Schurz: I thank you for your congratulations. As to what you say about disarmament — which I suppose is the rough equivalent of "the gradual diminution of the oppressive burdens imposed upon the world by armed peace" — I am not clear either as to what can be done or what ought to be done. If I had been known as one of the conventional type of peace advocates I could have done nothing whatever in bringing about peace now, I would be powerless in the future to accomplish anything, and I would not have been able to help confer the boons upon Cuba, the Philippines, Porto Rico and Panama, brought about by our action therein. If the Japanese had not armed during the last twenty years, this would indeed be a sorrowful century for Japan. If this country had not fought the Spanish War ; if we had failed to take the action we did about Panama ; all mankind would have been the loser. While the Turks were butchering the Armenians the European powers kept the peace and thereby added a burden of infamy to the Nineteenth Century, for in keeping that peace a greater number of lives were lost than in any European war since the days of Napoleon, and these lives were those of women and children as well as of men ; while the moral degradation, the brutality inflicted and endured, the aggregate of hideous wrong done, surpassed that of any war of which we have record in modern times. Until people get it firmly fixed in their minds that peace is valuable chiefly as a means to righteousness, and that it can only be considered as an end when it also coincides with righteousness, we can do only a limited amount to advance its coming on this earth. There is of course no analogy at present between international law and private or municipal law, because there is no sanction of force for the former, while there is for the latter. Inside our own nation the law-abiding man does not have to arm himself against the lawless simply because there is some armed force — the police, the sheriff's posse, the national guard, the regulars — which can be called out to enforce the laws. At present there is no similar international force to call on, and I do not as yet see how it could at present be created. Hitherto peace has often come only because some strong and on the whole just power has by armed force, or the threat of armed force, put a stop to disorder. In a very interesting French book the other day I was reading how the Mediterranean was freed from pirates only by the "pax Britannica," established by England's naval force. The hopeless and hideous bloodshed and wickedness of Algiers and Turkestan was stopped, and could only be stopped, when civilized nations in the shape of Russia and France took possession of them. The same was true of Burma and the Malay States, as well as Egypt, with regard to England. Peace has come only as the sequel to the armed interference of a civilized power which, relatively to its opponent, was a just and beneficent power. If England had disarmed to the point of being unable to conquer the Soudan and protect Egypt, so that the Mahdists had established their supremacy in northeastern Africa, the result would have been a horrible and bloody calamity to mankind. It was only the growth of the European powers in military efficiency that freed eastern Europe from the dreadful scourge of the Tartar and partially freed it from the dreadful scourge of the Turk. Unjust war is dreadful; a just war may be the highest duty. To have the best nations, the free and civilized nations, disarm and leave the despotisms and barbarisms with great mili-

tary force, would be a calamity compared to which the calamities caused by all the wars of the nineteenth century
would be trivial. Yet it is not easy to see how we can
by international agreement state exactly which power
ceases to be free and civilized and which comes near the line
of barbarism or despotism. For example, I suppose it
would be very difficult to get Russia and Japan to come to
a common agreement on this point; and there are at least
some citizens of other na-
tions, not to speak of their
governments, whom it would
also be hard to get together.

This does not in the
least mean that it is hopeless to make the effort. It
may be that some scheme
will be developed. Amer-
ica, fortunately, can cordially assist in such an
effort, for no one in his
senses would suggest our
disarmament; and though
we should continue to perfect our small navy and our
minute army, I do not think
it necessary to increase the
number of our ships — at
any rate as things look now

Model by G. Vigeland.

NOBEL PEACE PRIZE MEDALLION.

This is a direct reproduction of the reverse of
the medallion which measures 2¼ inches in
diameter. On the edge appeared the words
Parlamentum Norvegiæ MCMVI.

— nor the number of our soldiers. Of course our navy must
be kept up to the highest point of efficiency, and the replacing of old and worthless vessels by first-class new ones may
involve an increase in the personnel; but not enough to interfere with our action along the lines you have suggested.
But before I would know how to advocate such action, save
in some such way as commending it to the attention of The
Hague Tribunal, I would have to have a feasible and rational plan of action presented.

It seems to me that a general stop in the increase of the
war navies of the world *might* be a good thing; but I would

not like to speak too positively offhand. Of course it is
only in continental Europe that the armies are too large;
and before advocating action as regards them I should
have to weigh matters carefully — including by the way
such a matter as the Turkish army. At any rate nothing
useful can be done unless with the clear recognition that
we object to putting peace second to righteousness.

Sincerely yours,
THEODORE ROOSEVELT.

HON. CARL SCHURZ, Bolton Landing,
    Lake George, N. Y.

In my own judgment the most important service that I
rendered to peace was the voyage of the battle fleet round
the world.   I had become convinced that for many reasons
it was essential that we should have it clearly understood,
by our own people especially, but also by other peoples,
that the Pacific was as much our home waters as the Atlantic, and that our fleet could and would at will pass from one
to the other of the two great oceans.   It seemed to me
evident that such a voyage would greatly benefit the navy
itself; would arouse popular interest in and enthusiasm
for the navy; and would make foreign nations accept as
a matter of course that our fleet should from time to time
be gathered in the Pacific, just as from time to time it was
gathered in the Atlantic, and that its presence in one ocean
was no more to be accepted as a mark of hostility to any
Asiatic power than its presence in the Atlantic was to be
accepted as a mark of hostility to any European power.
I determined on the move without consulting the Cabinet,
precisely as I took Panama without consulting the Cabinet.
A council of war never fights, and in a crisis the duty of a
leader is to lead and not to take refuge behind the generally
timid wisdom of a multitude of councillors.   At that time,
as I happen to know, neither the English nor the German
authorities believed it possible to take a fleet of great battleships round the world.   They did not believe that their

own fleets could perform the feat, and still less did they believe that the American fleet could.   I made up my mind that it was time to have a show down in the matter; because if it was really true that our fleet could not get from the Atlantic to the Pacific, it was much better to know it and be able to shape our policy in view of the knowledge.   Many persons publicly and privately protested against the move on the ground that Japan would accept it as a threat.   To this I answered nothing in public.   In private I said that I did not believe Japan would so regard it because Japan knew my sincere friendship and admiration for her and realized that we could not as a Nation have any intention of attacking her; and that if there were any such feeling on the part of Japan as was alleged that very fact rendered it imperative that that fleet should go.   When in the spring of 1910 I was in Europe I was interested to find that high naval authorities in both Germany and Italy had expected that war would come at the time of the voyage.   They asked me if I had not been afraid of it, and if I had not expected that hostilities would begin at least by the time that the fleet reached the Straits of Magellan?   I answered that I did not expect it; that I believed that Japan would feel as friendly in the matter as we did; but that if my expectations had proved mistaken, it would have been proof positive that we were going to be attacked anyhow, and that in such event it would have been an enormous gain to have had the three months' preliminary preparation which enabled the fleet to start perfectly equipped.   In a personal interview before they left I had explained to the officers in command that I believed the trip would be one of absolute peace, but that they were to take exactly the same precautions against sudden attack of any kind as if we were at war with all the nations of the earth; and that no excuse of any kind would be accepted if there were a sudden attack of any kind and we were taken unawares.

My prime purpose was to impress the American people; and this purpose was fully achieved.   The cruise did make a very deep impression abroad; boasting about what we have done does not impress foreign nations at all, except

2 Q

From a painting by Henry Reuterdahl.

THE FLEET IN THE STRAITS OF MAGELLAN.

unfavorably, but positive achievement does; and the two American achievements that really impressed foreign peoples during the first dozen years of this century were the digging of the Panama Canal and the cruise of the battle fleet round the world. But the impression made on our own people was of far greater consequence. No single thing in the history of the new United States Navy has done as much to stimulate popular interest and belief in it as the world cruise. This effect was forecast in a well-informed and friendly English periodical, the London *Spectator*. Writing in October, 1907, a month before the fleet sailed from Hampton Roads, the *Spectator* said:

"All over America the people will follow the movements of the fleet; they will learn something of the intricate details of the coaling and commissariat work under warlike conditions; and in a word their attention will be aroused. Next time Mr. Roosevelt or his representatives appeal to the country for new battleships they will do so to people whose minds have been influenced one way or the other. The naval programme will not have stood still. We are sure that, apart from increasing the efficiency of the existing fleet, this is the aim which Mr. Roosevelt has in mind. He has a policy which projects itself far into the future, but it is an entire misreading of it to suppose that it is aimed narrowly and definitely at any single Power."

I first directed the fleet, of sixteen battleships, to go round through the Straits of Magellan to San Francisco. From thence I ordered them to New Zealand and Australia, then to the Philippines, China and Japan, and home through Suez — they stopped in the Mediterranean to help the sufferers from the earthquake at Messina, by the way, and did this work as effectively as they had done all their other work. Admiral Evans commanded the fleet to San Francisco; there Admiral Sperry took it; Admirals Thomas, Wainwright and Schroeder rendered distinguished service under Evans and Sperry. The coaling and other preparations were made in such excellent shape by the Department that there was never a hitch, not so much as the delay of an hour, in keeping every appointment made.

All the repairs were made without difficulty, the ship concerned merely falling out of column for a few hours, and when the job was done steaming at speed until she regained her position.   Not a ship was left in any port; and there was hardly a desertion.   As soon as it was known that the voyage was to be undertaken men crowded to enlist, just as freely from the Mississippi Valley as from the seaboard, and for the first time since the Spanish War the ships put to sea overmanned — and by as stalwart a set of men-of-war's men as ever looked through a porthole, game for a fight or a frolic, but withal so self-respecting and with such a sense of responsibility that in all the ports in which they landed their conduct was exemplary.   The fleet practiced incessantly during the voyage, both with the guns and in battle tactics, and came home a much more efficient fighting instrument than when it started sixteen months before.

The best men of command rank in our own service were confident that the fleet would go round in safety, in spite of the incredulity of foreign critics.   Even they, however, did not believe that it was wise to send the torpedo craft around.   I accordingly acquiesced in their views, as it did not occur to me to consult the lieutenants.   But shortly before the fleet started, I went in the Government yacht Mayflower to inspect the target practice off Provincetown.   I was accompanied by two torpedo boat destroyers, in charge of a couple of naval lieutenants, thorough gamecocks; and I had the two lieutenants aboard to dine one evening.   Towards the end of the dinner they could not refrain from asking if the torpedo flotilla was to go round with the big ships.   I told them no, that the admirals and captains did not believe that the torpedo boats could stand it, and believed that the officers and crews aboard the cockle shells would be worn out by the constant pitching and bouncing and the everlasting need to make repairs.   My two guests chorused an eager assurance that the boats could stand it.   They assured me that the enlisted men were even more anxious to go than were the officers, mentioning that on one of their boats the terms of enlistment of most of the crew were out, and the men were waiting to see whether or not to reënlist, as they did not care to do so unless the boats were to go on the cruise. I answered that I was only too glad to accept the word of the men who were to do the job, and that they should certainly go; and within half an hour I sent out the order for the flotilla to be got ready. It went round in fine shape, not a boat being laid up. I felt that the feat reflected even more credit upon the navy than did the circumnavigation of the big ships, and I wrote the flotilla commander the following letter :

May 18, 1908.

My dear Captain Cone:

A great deal of attention has been paid to the feat of our battleship fleet in encircling South America and getting to San Francisco; and it would be hard too highly to compliment the officers and enlisted men of that fleet for what they have done. Yet if I should draw any distinction at all it would be in favor of you and your associates who have taken out the torpedo flotilla. Yours was an even more notable feat, and every officer and every enlisted man in the torpedo boat flotilla has the right to feel that he has rendered distinguished service to the United States navy and therefore to the people of the United States; and I wish I could thank each of them personally. Will you have this letter read by the commanding officer of each torpedo boat to his officers and crew ?

Sincerely yours,

THEODORE ROOSEVELT.

LIEUTENANT COMMANDER HUTCH. I. CONE, U. S. N.,
Commanding Second Torpedo Flotilla,
Care Postmaster, San Franscico, Cal.

There were various amusing features connected with the trip. Most of the wealthy people and "leaders of opinion" in the Eastern cities were panic-struck at the proposal to take the fleet away from Atlantic waters. The great New York

598 THEODORE ROOSEVELT — AN AUTOBIOGRAPHY

dailies issued frantic appeals to Congress to stop the fleet
from going. The head of the Senate Committee on Naval
Affairs announced that the fleet should not and could not go
because Congress would refuse to appropriate the money —
he being from an Eastern seaboard State. However, I announced in response that I had enough money to take the
fleet around to the Pacific anyhow, that the fleet would certainly go, and that if Congress did not choose to appropriate
enough money to get the fleet back, why, it would stay in
the Pacific. There was no further difficulty about the
money.

It was not originally my intention that the fleet should
visit Australia, but the Australian Government sent a most
cordial invitation, which I gladly accepted; for I have, as
every American ought to have, a hearty admiration for,
and fellow feeling with, Australia, and I believe that America
should be ready to stand back of Australia in any serious
emergency. The reception accorded the fleet in Australia
was wonderful, and it showed the fundamental community
of feeling between ourselves and the great commonwealth
of the South Seas. The considerate, generous, and open-
handed hospitality with which the entire Australian people
treated our officers and men could not have been surpassed
had they been our own countrymen. The fleet first visited
Sidney, which has a singularly beautiful harbor. The day
after the arrival one of our captains noticed a member of
his crew trying to go to sleep on a bench in the park. He
had fixed above his head a large paper with some lines
evidently designed to forestall any questions from friendly
would-be hosts : "I am delighted with the Australian people.
I think your harbor the finest in the world. I am very tired
and would like to go to sleep."

The most noteworthy incident of the cruise was the reception given to our fleet in Japan. In courtesy and good
breeding, the Japanese can certainly teach much to the
nations of the Western world. I had been very sure that
the people of Japan would understand aright what the
cruise meant, and would accept the visit of our fleet as the
signal honor which it was meant to be, a proof of the high

regard and friendship I felt, and which I was certain the American people felt, for the great Island Empire. The event even surpassed my expectations. I cannot too strongly express my appreciation of the generous courtesy the Japanese showed the officers and crews of our fleet; and I may add that every man of them came back a friend and admirer of the Japanese. Admiral Sperry wrote me a letter of much interest, dealing not only with the reception in Tokio but with the work of our men at sea ; I herewith give it almost in full :

28 October, 1908.

Dear Mr. Roosevelt:

My official report of the visit to Japan goes forward in this mail, but there are certain aspects of the affair so successfully concluded which cannot well be included in the report.

You are perhaps aware that Mr. Denison of the Japanese Foreign Office was one of my colleagues at The Hague, for whom I have a very high regard. Desiring to avoid every possibility of trouble or misunderstanding, I wrote to him last June explaining fully the character of our men, which they have so well lived up to, the desirability of ample landing places, guides, rest houses and places for changing money in order that there might be no delay in getting the men away from the docks on the excursions in which they delight. Very few of them go into a drinking place, except to get a resting place not to be found elsewhere, paying for it by taking a drink.

I also explained our system of landing with liberty men an unarmed patrol, properly officered, to quietly take in charge and send off to their ships any men who showed the slightest trace of disorderly conduct. This letter he showed to the Minister of the Navy, who highly approved of all our arrangements, including the patrol, of which I feared they might be jealous. Mr. Denison's reply reached me in Manila, with a memorandum from the Minister of the Navy which removed all doubts. Three temporary piers were built for our boat landings, each 300 feet long, brilliantly lighted and decorated. The sleeping accommodations did not permit two or three thousand sailors to remain on shore, but the ample landings permitted them to be handled night and day with perfect order and safety.

At the landings and railroad station in Yokohama there were rest houses or booths, reputable money changers and as many as a thousand English-speaking Japanese college students acted as volunteer guides, besides Japanese sailors and petty officers detailed for the purpose. In Tokyo there were a great many excellent refreshment places, where the men got excellent meals and could rest, smoke and write letters, and in none of these places would they allow the men to pay anything, though they were more than ready to do so. The arrangements were marvelously perfect.

As soon as your telegram of October 18, giving the address to be made to the Emperor, was received, I gave copies of it to our Ambassador to be sent to the Foreign Office. It seems that the Emperor had already prepared a very cordial address to be forwarded through me to you, after delivery at the audience, but your telegram reversed the situation and his reply was prepared. I am convinced that your kind and courteous initiative on this occasion helped cause the pleasant feeling which was so

Copyright by Underwood and Underwood.

SENATOR LODGE.

obvious in the Emperor's bearing at the luncheon which followed the audience. X., who is reticent and conservative,
told me that not only the Emperor but all the Ministers
were profoundly gratified by the course of events. I am
confident that not even the most trifling incident has taken
place which could in any way mar the general satisfaction,
and our Ambassador has expressed to me his great satisfaction with all that has taken place.

Owing to heavy weather encountered on the passage
up from Manila the fleet was obliged to take about 3500
tons of coal.

The Yankton remained behind to keep up communication for a few days, and yesterday she transmitted the
Emperor's telegram to you, which was sent in reply to your
message through our Ambassador after the sailing of the
fleet. It must be profoundly gratifying to you to have the
mission on which you sent the fleet terminate so happily,
and I am profoundly thankful that, owing to the confidence which you displayed in giving me this command, my
active career draws to a close with such honorable distinction.

As for the effect of the cruise upon the training, discipline
and effectiveness of the fleet, the good cannot be exaggerated.
It is a war game in every detail. The wireless communication has been maintained with an efficiency hitherto unheard
of. Between Honolulu and Auckland, 3850 miles, we were
out of communication with a cable station for only one night,
whereas three [non-American] men-of-war trying recently to
maintain a chain of only 1250 miles, between Auckland and
Sydney, were only able to do so for a few hours.

The officers and men as soon as we put to sea turn to
their gunnery and tactical work far more eagerly than they
go to functions. Every morning certain ships leave the
column and move off seven or eight thousand yards as targets
for range measuring fire control and battery practice for
the others, and at night certain ships do the same thing for
night battery practice. I am sorry to say that this practice
is unsatisfactory, and in some points misleading, owing to
the fact that the ships are painted white. At Portland, in
1903, I saw Admiral Barker's white battleships under the

searchlights of the army at a distance of 14,000 yards, seven sea miles, without glasses, while the Hartford, a black ship, was never discovered at all, though she passed within a mile and a half. I have for years, while a member of the General Board, advocated painting the ships war color at all times, and by this mail I am asking the Department to make the necessary change in the Regulations and paint the ships properly. I do not know that any one now dissents from my view. Admiral Wainwright strongly concurs, and the War College Conference recommended it year after year without a dissenting voice.

In the afternoons the fleet has two or three hours' practice at battle maneuvers, which excite as keen interest as gunnery exercises.

The competition in coal economy goes on automatically and reacts in a hundred ways. It has reduced the waste in the use of electric light and water, and certain chief engineers are said to keep men ranging over the ships all night turning out every light not in actual and immediate use. Perhaps the most important effect is the keen hunt for defects in the machinery causing waste of power. The Yankton by resetting valves increased her speed from 10 to $11\frac{1}{2}$ knots on the same expenditure.

All this has been done, but the field is widening, the work has only begun.

*   *   *   *   *   *   *

C. S. SPERRY.

When I left the Presidency I finished seven and a half years of administration, during which not one shot had been fired against a foreign foe. We were at absolute peace, and there was no nation in the world with whom a war cloud threatened, no nation in the world whom we had wronged, or from whom we had anything to fear. The cruise of the battle fleet was not the least of the causes which ensured so peaceful an outlook.

When the fleet returned after its sixteen months' voyage around the world I went down to Hampton Roads to greet

it.   The day was Washington's Birthday, February 22, 1907.
Literally on the minute the homing battlecraft came into
view.   On the flagship of the Admiral I spoke to the officers
and enlisted men, as follows:

"*Admiral Sperry, Officers and Men of the Battle Fleet:*

"Over a year has passed since you steamed out of this

harbor, and over the world's rim, and this morning the
hearts of all who saw you thrilled with pride as the hulls
of the mighty warships lifted above the horizon.   You
have been in the Northern and the Southern Hemispheres;
four times you have crossed the line; you have steamed
through all the great oceans; you have touched the coast
of every continent.   Ever your general course has been
westward; and now you come back to the port from which

Copyright by D. W. Waterman.   The Return of the Fleet; entering Chesapeake Bay.

you set sail. This is the first battle fleet that has ever circumnavigated the globe. Those who perform the feat again can but follow in your footsteps.

"The little torpeo flotilla went with you around South America, through the Straits of Magellan, to our own Pacific Coast. The armored cruiser squadron met you, and left you again, when you were half way round the world. You have falsified every prediction of the prophets of failure. In all your long cruise not an accident worthy of mention has happened to a single battleship, nor yet to the cruisers or torpedo boats. You left this coast in a high state of battle efficiency, and you return with your efficiency increased; better prepared than when you left, not only in personnel but even in material. During your world cruise you have taken your regular gunnery practice, and skilled though you were before with the guns, you have grown more skilful still; and through practice you have improved in battle tactics, though here there is more room for improvement than in your gunnery. Incidentally, I suppose I need hardly say that one measure of your fitness must be your clear recognition of the need always steadily to strive to render yourselves more fit; if you ever grow to think that you are fit enough, you can make up your minds that from that moment you will begin to go backward.

"As a war machine, the fleet comes back in better shape than it went out. In addition, you, the officers and men of this formidable fighting force, have shown yourselves the best of all possible ambassadors and heralds of peace. Wherever you have landed you have borne yourselves so as to make us at home proud of being your countrymen. You have shown that the best type of fighting man of the sea knows how to appear to the utmost possible advantage when his business is to behave himself on shore, and to make a good impression in a foreign land. We are proud of all the ships and all the men in this whole fleet, and we welcome you home to the country whose good repute among nations has been raised by what you have done."

APPENDIX A

THE TRUSTS, THE PEOPLE, AND THE SQUARE DEAL

[Written when Mr. Taft's administration brought suit to dissolve the steel corporation, one of the grounds for the suit being the acquisition by the Corporation of the Tennessee Coal and Iron Company; this action was taken, with my acquiescence, while I was President, and while Mr. Taft was a member of my cabinet; at the time he never protested against, and as far as I knew approved of my action in this case, as in the Harvester Trust case, and all similar cases.]

The suit against the Steel Trust by the Government has brought vividly before our people the need of reducing to order our chaotic Government policy as regards business. As President, in Messages to Congress I repeatedly called the attention of that body and of the public to the inadequacy of the Anti-Trust Law by itself to meet business conditions and secure justice to the people, and to the further fact that it might, if left unsupplemented by additional legislation, work mischief, with no compensating advantage; and I urged as strongly as I knew how that the policy followed with relation to railways in connection with the Inter-State Commerce Law should be followed by the National Government as regards all great business concerns; and therefore that, as a first step, the powers of the Bureau of Corporations should be greatly enlarged, or else that there should be created a Governmental board or commission, with powers somewhat similar to those of the Inter-State Commerce Commission, but covering the whole field of inter-State business, exclusive of transportation (which should, by law, be kept wholly separate from ordinary industrial business, all common ownership of the industry and the railway being forbidden). In the end I have always believed that it would also be necessary to give the National Government complete power over the organization and capitalization of all business concerns engaged in inter-State commerce.

A member of my Cabinet with whom, even more than with the various Attorneys-General, I went over every detail of the trust situation, was the one time Secretary of the Interior, Mr. James R.

Garfield. He writes me as follows concerning the suit against the Steel Corporation:

"Nothing appeared before the House Committee that made me believe we were deceived by Judge Gary.

"This, I think, is a case that shows clearly the difference between destructive litigation and constructive legislation. I have not yet seen a full copy of the Government's petition, but our papers give nothing that indicates any kind of unfair or dishonest competition such as existed in both the Standard Oil and Tobacco Cases. As I understand it, the competitors of the Steel Company have steadily increased in strength during the last six or seven years. Furthermore, the per cent of the business done by the Steel Corporation has decreased during that time. As you will remember, at our first conference with Judge Gary, the Judge stated that it was the desire and purpose of the Company to conform to what the Government wished, it being the purpose of the Company absolutely to obey the law both in spirit and letter. Throughout the time that I had charge of the investigation, and while we were in Washington, I do not know of a single instance where the Steel Company refused any information requested; but, on the contrary, aided in every possible way our investigation.

"The position now taken by the Government is absolutely destructive of legitimate business, because they outline no rule of conduct for business of any magnitude. It is absurd to say that the courts can lay down such rules. The most the courts can do is to find as legal or illegal the particular transactions brought before them. Hence, after years of tedious litigation there would be no clear-cut rule for future action. This method of procedure is dealing with the device, not the result, and drives business to the elaboration of clever devices, each of which must be tested in the courts.

"I have yet to find a better method of dealing with the anti-trust situation than that suggested by the bill which we agreed upon in the last days of your Administration. That bill should be used as a basis for legislation, and there could be incorporated upon it whatever may be determined wise regarding the direct control and supervision of the National Government, either through a commission similar to the Inter-State Commerce Commission or otherwise."

Before taking up the matter in its large aspect, I wish to say one word as to one feature of the Government suit against the Steel Corporation. One of the grounds for the suit is the acquisition by the Steel Corporation of the Tennessee Coal and Iron Company;

and it has been alleged, on the authority of the Government officials engaged in carrying on the suit, that as regards this transaction I was misled by the representatives of the Steel Corporation, and that the facts were not accurately or truthfully laid before me. This statement is not correct. I believed at the time that the facts in the case were as represented to me on behalf of the Steel Corporation, and my further knowledge has convinced me that this was true. I believed at the time that the representatives of the Steel Corporation told me the truth as to the change that would be worked in the percentage of the business which the proposed acquisition would give the Steel Corporation, and further inquiry has convinced me that they did so. I was not misled. The representatives of the Steel Corporation told me the truth as to what the effect of the action at that time would be, and any statement that I was misled or that the representatives of the Steel Corporation did not thus tell me the truth as to the facts of the case is itself not in accordance with the truth. In *The Outlook* of August 19 last I gave in full the statement I had made to the Investigating Committee of the House of Representatives on this matter. That statement is accurate, and I reaffirm everything I therein said, not only as to what occurred, but also as to my belief in the wisdom and propriety of my action — indeed, the action not merely was wise and proper, but it would have been a calamity from every standpoint had I failed to take it. On page 137 of the printed report of the testimony before the Committee will be found Judge Gary's account of the meeting between himself and Mr. Frick and Mr. Root and myself. This account states the facts accurately. It has been alleged that the purchase by the Steel Corporation of the property of the Tennessee Coal and Iron Company gave the Steel Corporation practically a monopoly of the Southern iron ores — that is, of the iron ores south of the Potomac and the Ohio. My information, which I have every reason to believe is accurate and not successfully to be challenged, is that, of these Southern iron ores the Steel Corporation has, including the property gained from the Tennessee Coal and Iron Company, less than 20 per cent — perhaps not over 16 per cent. This is a very much smaller percentage than the percentage it holds of the Lake Superior ores, which even after the surrender of the Hill lease will be slightly over 50 per cent. According to my view, therefore, and unless — which I do not believe possible — these figures can be successfully challenged, the acquisition of the Tennessee Coal and Iron Company's ores in no way changed the situation as regards making the Steel Corporation a monopoly.[1] The showing as to the percentage of production of all kinds of steel ingots and steel castings in the United States by the Steel Corporation and by all other manufacturers respectively makes an even stronger case. It makes the case even stronger than I put it in my testimony before the Investigating Committee, for I was scrupulously careful to make statements that erred, if at all, against my own position. It appears from the figures of production that in 1901 the Steel Corporation had to its credit nearly 66 per cent of the total production as against a little over 34 per cent by all other steel manufacturers. The percentage then shrank steadily, until in 1906, the year before the acquisition of the Tennessee Coal and Iron properties, the percentage was a little under 58 per cent. In spite of the acquisition of these properties, the following year, 1907, the total percentage shrank slightly, and this shrinking has continued until in 1910 the total percentage of the Steel Corporation is but a little over 54 per cent, and the percentage by all other steel manufacturers but a fraction less than 46 per cent. Of the $54\frac{3}{10}$ per cent produced by the Steel Corporation $1\frac{9}{10}$ per cent is produced by the former Tennessee Coal and Iron Company. In other words, these figures show that the acquisition of the Tennessee Coal and Iron Company did not in the slightest degree change the situation, and that during the ten years which include the acquisition of these properties by the Steel Corporation the percentage of total output of steel manufacturers in this country by the Steel Corporation has shrunk from nearly 66 per cent to but a trifle over 54 per cent. I do not believe that these figures can be successfully controverted, and if not successfully controverted they show clearly not only that the acquisition of the Tennessee Coal and Iron properties wrought no change in the status of the Steel Corporation, but that the Steel Corporation during the decade has steadily lost, instead of gained, in monopolistic character.

So much for the facts in this particular case. Now for the general subject. When my Administration took office, I found, not only that there had been little real enforcement of the Anti-Trust Law and but little more effective enforcement of the Inter-State Commerce Law, but also that the decisions were so chaotic and the laws themselves so vaguely drawn, or at least interpreted in such widely varying fashions, that the biggest business men

---

[1] My own belief is that our Nation should long ago have adopted the policy of merely leasing for a term of years mineral-bearing land; but it is the fault of us ourselves, of the people, not of the Steel Corporation, that this policy has not been adopted.

2 R

tended to treat both laws as dead letters.   The series of actions by
which we succeeded in making the Inter-State Commerce Law an
efficient and most useful instrument in regulating the transportation of the country and exacting justice from the big railways without doing them injustice — while, indeed, on the contrary, securing
them against injustice — need not here be related.   The Anti-
Trust Law it was also necessary to enforce as it had never hitherto
been enforced; both because it was on the statute-books and because it was imperative to teach the masters of the biggest corporations in the land that they were not, and would not be permitted
to regard themselves as, above the law.   Moreover, where the
combination has really been guilty of misconduct the law serves a
useful purpose, and in such cases as those of the Standard Oil and
Tobacco Trusts, if effectively enforced, the law confers a real and
great good.

Suits were brought against the most powerful corporations in the
land, which we were convinced had clearly and beyond question
violated the Anti-Trust Law.   These suits were brought with
great care, and only where we felt so sure of our facts that we
could be fairly certain that there was a likelihood of success.   As a
matter of fact, in most of the important suits we were successful.
It was imperative that these suits should be brought, and very real
good was achieved by bringing them, for it was only these suits
that made the great masters of corporate capital in America fully
realize that they were the servants and not the masters of the people, that they were subject to the law, and that they would not be
permitted to be a law unto themselves; and the corporations
against which we proceeded had sinned, not merely by being big
(which we did not regard as in itself a sin), but by being guilty of
unfair practices towards their competitors, and by procuring
unfair advantages from the railways.   But the resulting situation has made it evident that the Anti-Trust Law is not
adequate to meet the situation that has grown up because of
modern business conditions and the accompanying tremendous
increase in the business use of vast quantities of corporate
wealth.   As I have said, this was already evident to my mind
when I was President, and in communications to Congress I
repeatedly stated the facts.   But when I made these communications there were still plenty of people who did not believe that
we would succeed in the suits that had been instituted against
the Standard Oil, the Tobacco, and other corporations, and it
was impossible to get the public as a whole to realize what the
situation was.   Sincere zealots who believed that all combinations

could be destroyed and the old-time conditions of unregulated
competition restored, insincere politicians who knew better but
made believe that they thought whatever their constituents
wished them to think, crafty reactionaries who wished to see on
the statute-books laws which they believed unenforceable, and
the almost solid "Wall Street crowd" or representatives of "big
business" who at that time opposed with equal violence both
wise and necessary and unwise and improper regulation of
business — all fought against the adoption of a sane, effective,
and far-reaching policy.

It is a vitally necessary thing to have the persons in control of
big trusts of the character of the Standard Oil Trust and Tobacco
Trust taught that they are under the law, just as it was a necessary
thing to have the Sugar Trust taught the same lesson in drastic
fashion by Mr. Henry L. Stimson when he was United States
District Attorney in the city of New York. But to attempt to
meet the whole problem not by administrative governmental
action but by a succession of lawsuits is hopeless from the standpoint of working out a permanently satisfactory solution. Moreover, the results sought to be achieved are achieved only in extremely insufficient and fragmentary measure by breaking up all
big corporations, whether they have behaved well or ill, into a
number of little corporations which it is perfectly certain will be
largely, and perhaps altogether, under the same control. Such
action is harsh and mischievous if the corporation is guilty of nothing except its size; and where, as in the case of the Standard Oil,
and especially the Tobacco, trusts, the corporation has been guilty
of immoral and anti-social practices, there is need for far more
drastic and thoroughgoing action than any that has been taken,
under the recent decree of the Supreme Court. In the case of the
Tobacco Trust, for instance, the settlement in the Circuit Court,
in which the representatives of the Government seem inclined to
concur, practically leaves all of the companies still substantially
under the control of the twenty-nine original defendants. Such a
result is lamentable from the standpoint of justice. The decision
of the Circuit Court, if allowed to stand, means that the Tobacco
Trust has merely been obliged to change its clothes, that none of
the real offenders have received any real punishment, while, as the
New York *Times*, a pro-trust paper, says, the tobacco concerns,
in their new clothes, are in positions of "ease and luxury," and
"immune from prosecution under the law."

Surely, miscarriage of justice is not too strong a term to apply to
such a result when considered in connection with what the Supreme

Court said of this Trust.   That great Court in its decision used language which, in spite of its habitual and severe self-restraint in stigmatizing wrong-doing, yet unhesitatingly condemns the Tobacco Trust for moral turpitude, saying that the case shows an "ever present manifestation . . . of conscious wrong-doing" by the Trust, whose history is "replete with the doing of acts which it was the obvious purpose of the statute to forbid, . . . demonstrative of the existence from the beginning of a purpose to acquire dominion and control of the tobacco trade, not by the mere exertion of the ordinary right to contract and to trade, but by methods devised in order to monopolize the trade by driving competitors out of business, which were ruthlessly carried out upon the assumption that to work upon the fears or play upon the cupidity of competitors would make success possible."   The letters from and to various officials of the Trust, which were put in evidence, show a literally astounding and horrifying indulgence by the Trust in wicked and depraved business methods — such as the "endeavor to cause a strike in their [a rival business firm's] factory," or the "shutting off the market" of an independent tobacco firm by "taking the necessary steps to give them a warm reception," or forcing importers into a price agreement by causing and continuing "a demoralization of the business for such length of time as may be deemed desirable" (I quote from the letters).   A Trust guilty of such conduct should be absolutely disbanded, and the only way to prevent the repetition of such conduct is by strict Government supervision, and not merely by lawsuits.

The Anti-Trust Law cannot meet the whole situation, nor can any modification of the principle of the Anti-Trust Law avail to meet the whole situation.   The fact is that many of the men who have called themselves Progressives, and who certainly believe that they are Progressives, represent in reality in this matter not progress at all but a kind of sincere rural toryism.   These men believe that it is possible by strengthening the Anti-Trust Law to restore business to the competitive conditions of the middle of the last century.   Any such effort is foredoomed to end in failure, and, if successful, would be mischievous to the last degree.   Business cannot be successfully conducted in accordance with the practices and theories of sixty years ago unless we abolish steam, electricity, big cities, and, in short, not only all modern business and modern industrial conditions, but all the modern conditions of our civilization.   The effort to restore competition as it was sixty years ago, and to trust for justice solely to this proposed restoration of competition, is just as foolish as if we should go back to the flintlocks of

Washington's Continentals as a substitute for modern weapons of precision. The effort to prohibit all combinations, good or bad, is bound to fail, and ought to fail; when made, it merely means that some of the worst combinations are not checked and that honest business is checked. Our purpose should be, not to strangle business as an incident of strangling combinations, but to regulate big corporations in thoroughgoing and effective fashion, so as to help legitimate business as an incident to thoroughly and completely safeguarding the interests of the people as a whole. Against all such increase of Government regulation the argument is raised that it would amount to a form of Socialism. This argument is familiar; it is precisely the same as that which was raised against the creation of the Inter-State Commerce Commission, and of all the different utilities commissions in the different States, as I myself saw, thirty years ago, when I was a legislator at Albany, and these questions came up in connection with our State Government. Nor can action be effectively taken by any one State. Congress alone has power under the Constitution effectively and thoroughly and at all points to deal with inter-State commerce, and where Congress, as it should do, provides laws that will give the Nation full jurisdiction over the whole field, then that jurisdiction becomes, of necessity, exclusive — although until Congress does act affirmatively and thoroughly it is idle to expect that the States will or ought to rest content with non-action on the part of both Federal and State authorities. This statement, by the way, applies also to the question of "usurpation" by any one branch of our Government of the rights of another branch. It is contended that in these recent decisions the Supreme Court legislated; so it did; and it had to; because Congress had signally failed to do *its* duty by legislating. For the Supreme Court to nullify an act of the Legislature as unconstitutional except on the clearest grounds is usurpation; to interpret such an act in an obviously wrong sense is usurpation; but where the legislative body persistently leaves open a field which it is absolutely imperative, from the public standpoint, to fill, then no possible blame attaches to the official or officials who step in because they have to, and who then do the needed work in the interest of the poeple. The blame in such cases lies with the body which has been derelict, and not with the body which reluctantly makes good the dereliction.

A quarter of a century ago, Senator Cushman K. Davis, a statesman who amply deserved the title of statesman, a man of the highest courage, of the sternest adherence to the principles laid down by an exacting sense of duty, an unflinching believer in democracy,

who was as little to be cowed by a mob as by a plutocrat, and moreover a man who possessed the priceless gift of imagination, a gift
as important to a statesman as to a historian, in an address delivered at the annual commencement of the University of Michigan
on July 1, 1886, spoke as follows of corporations :

" Feudalism, with its domains, its untaxed lords, their retainers,
its exemptions and privileges, made war upon the aspiring spirit of
humanity, and fell with all its grandeurs.   Its spirit walks the earth
and haunts the institutions of to-day, in the great corporations,
with the control of the National highways, their occupation of
great domains, their power to tax, their cynical contempt for the
law, their sorcery to debase most gifted men to the capacity of
splendid slaves, their pollution of the ermine of the judge and the
robe of the Senator, their aggregation in one man of wealth so
enormous as to make Crœsus seem a pauper, their picked, paid,
and skilled retainers who are summoned by the message of electricity and appear upon the wings of steam.   If we look into the
origin of feudalism and of the modern corporations — those
Dromios of history — we find that the former originated in a
strict paternalism, which is scouted by modern economists, and
that the latter has grown from an unrestrained freedom of action,
aggression, and development, which they commend as the very
ideal of political wisdom. *Laissez-faire*, says the professor, when
it often means bind and gag that the strongest may work his will.
It is a plea for the survival of the fittest — for the strongest male
to take possession of the herd by a process of extermination.   If
we examine this battle cry of political polemics, we find that it is
based upon the conception of the divine right of property, and the
preoccupation by older or more favored or more alert or richer
men or nations, of territory, of the forces of nature, of machinery,
of all the functions of what we call civilization.   Some of these
men, who are really great, follow these conceptions to their conclusions with dauntless intrepidity."

When Senator Davis spoke, few men of great power had the
sympathy and the vision necessary to perceive the menace contained in the growth of corporations ; and the men who did see the
evil were struggling blindly to get rid of it, not by frankly meeting
the new situation with new methods, but by insisting upon the
entirely futile effort to abolish what modern conditions had rendered absolutely inevitable.   Senator Davis was under no such
illusion.   He realized keenly that it was absolutely impossible to go
back to an outworn social status, and that we must abandon definitely the *laissez-faire* theory of political economy, and fearlessly

champion a system of increased Governmental control, paying no heed to the cries of the worthy people who denounce this as Socialistic. He saw that, in order to meet the inevitable increase in the power of corporations produced by modern industrial conditions, it would be necessary to increase in like fashion the activity of the sovereign power which alone could control such corporations. As has been aptly said, the only way to meet a billion-dollar corporation is by invoking the protection of a hundred-billion-dollar government; in other words, of the National Government, for no State Government is strong enough both to do justice to corporations and to exact justice from them. Said Senator Davis in this admirable address, which should be reprinted and distributed broadcast:

"The liberty of the individual has been annihilated by the logical process constructed to maintain it. We have come to a political deification of Mammon. *Laissez-faire* is not utterly blameworthy. It begat modern democracy, and made the modern republic possible. There can be no doubt of that. But there it reached its limit of political benefaction, and began to incline toward the point where extremes meet. . . . To every assertion that the people in their collective capacity of a government ought to exert their indefeasible right of self-defense, it is said you touch the sacred rights of property."

The Senator then goes on to say that we now have to deal with an oligarchy of wealth, and that the Government must develop power sufficient enough to enable it to do the task.

Few will dispute the fact that the present situation is not satisfactory, and cannot be put on a permanently satisfactory basis unless we put an end to the period of groping and declare for a fixed policy, a policy which shall clearly define and punish wrongdoing, which shall put a stop to the iniquities done in the name of business, but which shall do strict equity to business. We demand that big business give the people a square deal; in return we must insist that when any one engaged in big business honestly endeavors to do right he shall himself be given a square deal; and the first, and most elementary, kind of square deal is to give him in advance full information as to just what he can, and what he cannot, legally and properly do. It is absurd, and much worse than absurd, to treat the deliberate lawbreaker as on an exact par with the man eager to obey the law, whose only desire is to find out from some competent Governmental authority what the law is, and then to live up to it. Moreover, it is absurd to treat the size of a corporation as in itself a crime. As Judge Hook says in his opinion in the Standard Oil Case : "Magnitude of business does not alone constitute a monopoly . . . the genius and industry of man when kept to ethical standards still have full play, and what he achieves is his . . . success and magnitude of business, the rewards of fair and honorable endeavor [are not forbidden] . . . [the public welfare is threatened only when success is attained] by wrongful or unlawful methods." Size may, and in my opinion does, make a corporation fraught with potential menace to the community ; and may, and in my opinion should, therefore make it incumbent upon the community to exercise through its adminis- trative (not merely through its judicial) officers a strict supervision over that corporation in order to see that it does not go wrong ; but the size in itself does not signify wrong-doing, and should not be held to signify wrong-doing.

Not only should any huge corporation which has gained its position by unfair methods, and by interference with the rights of others, by demoralizing and corrupt practices, in short, by sheer baseness and wrong-doing, be broken up, but it should be made the business of some administrative governmental body, by constant supervision, to see that it does not come together again, save under such strict control as shall insure the community against all rep- etition of the bad conduct — and it should never be permitted thus to assemble its parts as long as these parts are under the con- trol of the original offenders, for actual experience has shown that these men are, from the standpoint of the people at large, unfit to be trusted with the power implied in the management of a large corporation. But nothing of importance is gained by breaking up a huge inter-State and international industrial organization *which has not offended otherwise than by its size,* into a number of small concerns without any attempt to regulate the way in which those concerns as a whole shall do business. Nothing is gained by depriving the American Nation of good weapons wherewith to fight in the great field of international industrial competition. Those who would seek to restore the days of unlimited and uncon- trolled competition, and who believe that a panacea for our indus- trial and economic ills to is be found in the mere breaking up of all big corporations, simply because they are big, are attempting not only the impossible, but what, if possible, would be undesirable. They are acting as we should act if we tried to dam the Mississippi, to stop its flow outright. The effort would be certain to result in failure and disaster ; we would have attempted the impossible, and so would have achieved nothing, or worse than nothing. But by building levees along the Mississippi, not seeking to dam the stream, but to control it, we are able to achieve our object and to confer inestimable good in the course of so doing.

This Nation should definitely adopt the policy of attacking, not the mere fact of combination, but the evils and wrong-doing which so frequently accompany combination. The fact that a combination is very big is ample reason for exercising a close and jealous supervision over it, because its size renders it potent for mischief; but it should not be punished unless it actually does the mischief; it should merely be so supervised and controlled as to guarantee us, the people, against its doing mischief. We should not strive for a policy of unregulated competition and of the destruction of all big corporations, that is, of all the most efficient business industries in the land. Nor should we persevere in the hopeless experiment of trying to regulate these industries by means only of lawsuits, each lasting several years, and of uncertain result. We should enter upon a course of supervision, control, and regulation of these great corporations — a regulation which we should not fear, if necessary, to bring to the point of control of monopoly prices, just as in exceptional cases railway rates are now regulated. Either the Bureau of Corporations should be authorized, or some other governmental body similar to the Inter-State Commerce Commission should be created, to exercise this supervision, this authoritative control. When once immoral business practices have been eliminated by such control, competition will thereby be again revived as a healthy factor, although not as formerly an all-sufficient factor, in keeping the general business situation sound. Wherever immoral business practices still obtain — as they obtained in the cases of the Standard Oil Trust and Tobacco Trust — the Anti-Trust Law can be invoked; and wherever such a prosecution is successful, and the courts declare a corporation to possess a monopolistic character, then that corporation should be completely dissolved, and the parts ought never to be again assembled save on whatever terms and under whatever conditions may be imposed by the governmental body in which is vested the regulatory power. Methods can readily be devised by which corporations sincerely desiring to act fairly and honestly can on their own initiative come under this thoroughgoing administrative control by the Government and thereby be free from the working of the Anti-Trust Law. But the law will remain to be invoked against wrongdoers; and under such conditions it could be invoked far more vigorously and successfully than at present.

It is not necessary in an article like this to attempt to work out such a plan in detail. It can assuredly be worked out. Moreover, in my opinion, substantially some such plan must be worked out or business chaos will continue. Wrongdoing such as was perpetrated by the Standard Oil Trust, and especially by the Tobacco Trust, should not only be punished, but if possible punished in the persons of the chief authors and beneficiaries of the wrong, far more severely than at present. But punishment should not be the only, or indeed the main, end in view. Our aim should be a policy of construction and not one of destruction. Our aim should not be to punish the men who have made a big corporation successful merely because they have made it big and successful, but to exercise such thoroughgoing supervision and control over them as to insure their business skill being exercised in the interest of the public and not against the public interest. Ultimately, I believe that this control should undoubtedly indirectly or directly extend to dealing with all questions connected with their treatment of their employees, including the wages, the hours of labor, and the like. Not only is the proper treatment of a corporation, from the standpoint of the managers, shareholders, and employees, compatible with securing from that corporation the best standard of public service, but when the effort is wisely made it results in benefit both to the corporation and to the public. The success of Wisconsin in dealing with the corporations within her borders, so as both to do them justice and to exact justice in return from them toward the public, has been signal; and this Nation should adopt a progressive policy in substance akin to the progressive policy not merely formulated in theory but reduced to actual practice with such striking success in Wisconsin.

To sum up, then. It is practically impossible, and, if possible, it would be mischievous and undesirable, to try to break up all combinations merely because they are large and successful, and to put the business of the country back into the middle of the eighteenth century conditions of intense and unregulated competition between small and weak business concerns. Such an effort represents not progressiveness but an unintelligent though doubtless entirely well-meaning toryism. Moreover, the effort to administer a law merely by lawsuits and court decisions is bound to end in signal failure, and meanwhile to be attended with delays and uncertainties, and to put a premium upon legal sharp practice. Such an effort does not adequately punish the guilty, and yet works great harm to the innocent. Moreover, it entirely fails to give the publicity which is one of the best by-products of the system of control by administrative officials; publicity, which is not only good in itself, but furnishes the data for whatever further action may be necessary. We need to formulate immediately and definitely a policy which, in dealing with big corporations that behave themselves and which contain no menace save what is necessarily potential in any corporation which is of great size and very well managed, shall aim not at their destruction but at their regulation and supervision, so that the Government shall control them in such fashion as amply to safeguard the interests of the whole public, including producers, consumers, and wage-workers. This control should, if necessary, be pushed in extreme cases to the point of exercising control over monopoly prices, as rates on railways are now controlled; although this is not a power that should be used when it is possible to avoid it. The law should be clear, unambiguous, certain, so that honest men may not find that unwittingly they have violated it. In short, our aim should be, not to destroy, but effectively and in thoroughgoing fashion to regulate and control, in the public interest, the great instrumentalities of modern business, which it is destructive of the general welfare of the community to destroy, and which nevertheless it is vitally necessary to that general welfare to regulate and control. Competition will remain as a very important factor when once we have destroyed the unfair business methods, the criminal interference with the rights of others, which alone enabled certain swollen combinations to crush out their competitors — and, incidentally, the "conservatives" will do well to remember that these unfair and iniquitous methods by great masters of corporate capital have done more to cause popular discontent with the propertied classes than all the orations of all the Socialist orators in the country put together.

I have spoken above of Senator Davis's admirable address delivered a quarter of a century ago. Senator Davis's one-time partner, Frank B. Kellogg, the Government counsel who did so much to win success for the Government in its prosecutions of the trusts, has recently delivered before the Palimpsest Club of Omaha an excellent address on the subject; Mr. Prouty, of the Inter-State Commerce Commission, has recently, in his speech before the Congregational Club of Brooklyn, dealt with the subject from the constructive side; and in the proceedings of the American Bar Association for 1904 there is an admirable paper on the need of thoroughgoing Federal control over corporations doing an inter-State business, by Professor Horace L. Wilgus, of the University of Michigan. The National Government exercises control over inter-State commerce railways, and it can in similar fashion, through an appropriate governmental body, exercise control over

all industrial organizations engaged in inter-State commerce.
This control should be exercised, not by the courts, but by an
administrative bureau or board such as the Bureau of Corporations
or the Inter-State Commerce Commission; for the courts cannot
with advantage permanently perform executive and administrative
functions.

BRASS BUDDHA.

Presented to President Roosevelt
by Dalai Lama.

APPENDIX B

THE CONTROL OF CORPORATIONS AND "THE NEW FREEDOM"

In his book "The New Freedom," and in the magazine articles of which it is composed, which appeared just after he had been inaugurated as President, Mr. Woodrow Wilson made an entirely unprovoked attack upon me and upon the Progressive party in connection with what he asserts the policy of that party to be concerning the trusts, and as regards my attitude while President about the trusts.

I am reluctant to say anything whatever about President Wilson at the outset of his Administration unless I can speak of him with praise. I have scrupulously refrained from saying or doing one thing since election that could put the slightest obstacle, even of misinterpretation, in his path. It is to the interest of the country that he should succeed in his office. I cordially wish him success, and I shall cordially support any policy of his that I believe to be in the interests of the people of the United States. But when Mr. Wilson, after being elected President, within the first fortnight after he has been inaugurated into that high office, permits himself to be betrayed into a public misstatement of what I have said, and what I stand for, then he forces me to correct his statements.

Mr. Wilson opens his article by saying that the Progressive "doctrine is that monopoly is inevitable, and that the only course open to the people of the United States is to submit to it." This statement is without one particle of foundation in fact. I challenge him to point out a sentence in the Progressive platform or in any speech of mine which bears him out. I can point him out any number which flatly contradict him. We have never made any such statement as he alleges about monopolies. We have said: "The corporation is an essential part of modern business. The concentration of modern business, in some degree, is both inevitable and necessary for National and international business efficiency." Does Mr. Wilson deny this? Let him answer yes or no, directly. It is easy for a politician detected in a misstatement to

take refuge in evasive rhetorical hyperbole.   But Mr. Wilson is
President of the United States, and as such he is bound to candid
utterance on every subject of public interest which he himself has
broached.   If he disagrees with us, let him be frank and consistent,
and recommend to Congress that all corporations be made illegal.
Mr. Wilson's whole attack is largely based on a deft but far from
ingenuous confounding of what we have said of monopoly, which
we propose so far as possible to abolish, and what we have said of
big corporations, which we propose to regulate; Mr. Wilson's own
vaguely set forth proposals being to attempt the destruction of
both in ways that would harm neither.   In our platform we use
the word "monopoly" but once, and then we speak of it as an
abuse of power, coupling it with stock-watering, unfair competition
and unfair privileges.   Does Mr. Wilson deny this ?   If he does,
then where else will he assert that we speak of monopoly as he says
we do ?   He certainly owes the people of the United States a
plain answer to the question.   In my speech of acceptance I said :
"We favor strengthening the Sherman Law by prohibiting agreements to divide territory or limit output; refusing to sell to customers who buy from business rivals; to sell below cost in certain
areas while maintaining higher prices in other places; using the
power of transportation to aid or injure special business concerns;
and all other unfair trade practices."   The platform pledges us to
"guard and keep open equally to all, the highways of American
commerce."   This is the exact negation of monopoly.   Unless
Mr. Wilson is prepared to show the contrary, surely he is bound in
honor to admit frankly that he has been betrayed into a misrepresentation, and to correct it.

Mr. Wilson says that for sixteen years the National Administration has "been virtually under the regulation of the trusts," and
that the big business men "have already captured the Government."   Such a statement as this might perhaps be pardoned as
mere rhetoric in a candidate seeking office — although it is the
kind of statement that never under any circumstances have I
permitted myself to make, whether on the stump or off the stump,
about any opponent, unless I was prepared to back it up with
explicit facts.   But there is an added seriousness to the charge
when it is made deliberately and in cold blood by a man who is at
the time President.   In this volume I have set forth my relations
with the trusts.   I challenge Mr. Wilson to controvert anything
I have said, or to name any trusts or any big business men who regulated, or in any shape or way controlled, or captured, the Government during my term as President.   He must furnish specifications

if his words are taken at their face value — and I venture to say in advance that the absurdity of such a charge is patent to all my fellow-citizens, not excepting Mr. Wilson.

Mr. Wilson says that the new party was founded "under the leadership of Mr. Roosevelt, with the conspicuous aid — I mention him with no satirical intention, but merely to set the facts down accurately — of Mr. George W. Perkins, organizer of the Steel Trust." Whether Mr. Wilson's intention was satirical or not is of no concern; but I call his attention to the fact that he has conspicuously and strikingly failed "to set the facts down accurately." Mr. Perkins was not the organizer of the Steel Trust, and when it was organized he had no connection with it or with the Morgan people. This is well known, and it has again and again been testified to before Congressional committees controlled by Mr. Wilson's friends who were endeavoring to find out something against Mr. Perkins. If Mr. Wilson does not know that my statement is correct, he ought to know it, and he is not to be excused for making such a misstatement as he has made when he has not a particle of evidence in support of it. Mr. Perkins was from the beginning in the Harvester Trust but, when Mr. Wilson points out this fact, why does he not add that he was the only man in that trust who supported me, and that the President of the trust ardently supported Mr. Wilson himself? It is disingenuous to endeavor to conceal these facts, and to mislead ordinary citizens about them. Under the administrations of both Mr. Taft and Mr. Wilson, Mr. Perkins has been singled out for special attack, obviously not because he belonged to the Harvester and Steel Trusts, but because he alone among the prominent men of the two corporations fearlessly supported the only party which afforded any real hope of checking the evil of the trusts.

Mr. Wilson states that the Progressives have "a programme perfectly agreeable to monopolies."

The plain and unmistakable inference to be drawn from this and other similar statements in his article, and the inference which he obviously desired to have drawn, is that the big corporations approved the Progressive plan and supported the Progressive candidate. If President Wilson does not know perfectly well that this is not the case, he is the only intelligent person in the United States who is thus ignorant. Everybody knows that the overwhelming majority of the heads of the big corporations supported him or Mr. Taft. It is equally well known that of the corporations he mentions, the Steel and the Harvester Trusts, there was but one man who took any part in the Progressive campaign, and that almost all the others, some thirty in number, were against us, and some of them, including the President of the Harvester Trust, openly and enthusiastically for Mr. Wilson himself. If he reads the newspapers at all, he must know that practically every man representing the great financial interests of the country, and without exception every newspaper controlled by Wall Street or State Street, actively supported either him or Mr. Taft, and showed perfect willingness to accept either if only they could prevent the Progressive party from coming into power and from putting its platform into effect.

Mr. Wilson says of the trust plank in that platform that it "did not anywhere condemn monopoly except in words." Exactly of what else could a platform consist ? Does Mr. Wilson expect us to use algebraic signs ? This criticism is much as if he said the Constitution or the Declaration of Independence contained nothing but words. The Progressive platform did contain words, and the words were admirably designed to express thought and meaning and purpose. Mr. Wilson says that I long ago "classified trusts for us as good and bad," and said that I was "afraid only of the bad ones." Mr. Wilson would do well to quote exactly what my language was, and where it was used, for I am at a loss to know what statement of mine it is to which he refers. But if he means that I say that corporations can do well, and that corporations can also do ill, he is stating my position correctly. I hold that a corporation does ill if it seeks profit in restricting production and then by extorting high prices from the community by reason of the scarcity of the product ; through adulterating, lyingly advertising, or over-driving the help ; or replacing men workers with children ; or by rebates ; or in any illegal or improper manner driving competitors out of its way ; or seeking to achieve monopoly by illegal or unethical treatment of its competitors, or in any shape or way offending against the moral law either in connection with the public or with its employees or with its rivals. Any corporation which seeks its profit in such fashion is acting badly. It is, in fact, a conspiracy against the public welfare which the Government should use all its powers to suppress. If, on the other hand, a corporation seeks profit solely by increasing its products through eliminating waste, improving its processes, utilizing its by-products, installing better machines, raising wages in the effort to secure more efficient help, introducing the principle of coöperation and mutual benefit, dealing fairly with labor unions, setting its face against the underpayment of women and the employment of children ; in a word, treating the public fairly and its rivals fairly : then such a corporation is behaving well. It is an instrumentality of civilization operating to promote abundance by cheapening the cost of living so as to improve conditions everywhere throughout the whole community. Does Mr. Wilson controvert either of these statements? If so, let him answer directly. It is a matter of capital importance to the country that his position in this respect be stated directly, not by indirect suggestion.

Much of Mr. Wilson's article, although apparently aimed at the Progressive party, is both so rhetorical and so vague as to need no answer. He does, however, specifically assert (among other things equally without warrant in fact) that the Progressive party says that it is "futile to undertake to prevent monopoly," and only ventures to ask the trusts to be "kind" and "pitiful"! It is a little difficult to answer a misrepresentation of the facts so radical — not to say preposterous — with the respect that one desires to use in speaking of or to the President of the United States. I challenge President Wilson to point to one sentence of our platform or of my speeches which affords the faintest justification for these assertions. Having made this statement in the course of an un-provoked attack on me, he cannot refuse to show that it is true. I deem it necessary to emphasize here (but with perfect respect) that I am asking for a plain statement of fact, not for a display of rhetoric. I ask him, as is my right under the circumstances, to quote the exact language which justifies him in attributing these views to us. If he cannot do this, then a frank acknowledgment on his part is due to himself and to the people. I quote from the Progressive platform: "Behind the ostensible Government sits enthroned an invisible Government, owing no allegiance and acknowledging no responsibility to the people. To destroy this invisible Government, to dissolve the unholy alliance between corrupt business and corrupt politics, is the first task of the statesmanship of the day. . . . This country belongs to the people. Its resources, its business, its laws, its institutions, should be utilized, maintained, or altered in whatever manner will best promote the general interest." This assertion is explicit. We say directly that "the people" are absolutely to control in any way they see fit, the "business" of the country. I again challenge Mr. Wilson to quote any words of the platform that justify the statements he has made to the contrary. If he cannot do it — and of course he cannot do it, and he must know that he cannot do it — surely he will not hesitate to say so frankly.

Mr. Wilson must know that every monopoly in the United States opposes the Progressive party. If he challenges this state-

2 S

ment, I challenge him in return (as is clearly my right) to name the monopoly that did support the Progressive party, whether it was the Sugar Trust, the Steel Trust, the Harvester Trust, the Standard Oil Trust, the Tobacco Trust, or any other.   Every sane man in the country knows well that there is not one word of justification that can truthfully be adduced for Mr. Wilson's statement that the Progressive programme was agreeable to the monopolies.   Ours was the only programme to which they objected, and they supported either Mr. Wilson or Mr. Taft against me, indifferent as to which of them might be elected so long as I was defeated.   Mr. Wilson says that I got my "idea with regard to the regulation of monopoly from the gentlemen who form the United States Steel Corporation."   Does Mr. Wilson pretend that Mr. Van Hise and Mr. Croly got their ideas from the Steel Corporation ?   Is Mr. Wilson unaware of the elementary fact that most modern economists believe that unlimited, unregulated competition is the source of evils which all men now concede must be remedied if this civilization of ours is to survive ?   Is he ignorant of the fact that the Socialist party has long been against unlimited competition ? This statement of Mr. Wilson cannot be characterized properly with any degree of regard for the office Mr. Wilson holds.   Why, the ideas that I have championed as to controlling and regulating both competition and combination in the interest of the people, so that the people shall be masters over both, have been in the air in this country for a quarter of a century.   I was merely the first prominent candidate for President who took them up.   They are the progressive ideas, and progressive business men must in the end come to them, for I firmly believe that in the end all wise and honest business men, big and little, will support our programme. Mr. Wilson in opposing them is the mere apostle of reaction.   He says that I got my "ideas from the gentlemen who form the Steel Corporation."   I did not.   But I will point out to him something in return.   It was he himself, and Mr. Taft, who got the votes and the money of these same gentlemen, and of those in the Harvester Trust.

Mr. Wilson has promised to break up all trusts.   He can do so only by proceeding at law.   If he proceeds at law, he can hope for success only by taking what I have done as a precedent.   In fact, what I did as President is the base of every action now taken or that can be now taken looking toward the control of corporations, or the suppression of monopolies.   The decisions rendered in various cases brought by my direction constitute the authority on which Mr. Wilson must base any action that he may bring to

curb monopolistic control. Will Mr. Wilson deny this, or question it in any way ? With what grace can he describe my Administration as satisfactory to the trusts when he knows that he cannot redeem a single promise that he has made to war upon the
trusts unless he avails himself of weapons of which the Federal
Government had been deprived before I became President, and
which were restored to it during my Administration and through
proceedings which I directed ? Without my action Mr. Wilson
could not now undertake or carry on a single suit against a monopoly, and, moreover, if it had not been for my action and for the
judicial decision in consequence obtained, Congress would be
helpless to pass a single law against monopoly.

Let Mr. Wilson mark that the men who organized and directed
the Northern Securities Company were also the controlling forces
in the very Steel Corporation which Mr. Wilson makes believe to
think was supporting me. I challenge Mr. Wilson to deny this,
and yet he well knew that it was my successful suit against the
Northern Securities Company which first efficiently established
the power of the people over the trusts.

After reading Mr. Wilson's book, I am still entirely in the dark
as to what he means by the "New Freedom." Mr. Wilson is an
accomplished and scholarly man, a master of rhetoric, and the
sentences in the book are well-phrased statements, usually incul-
cating a morality which is sound although vague and ill defined.
There are certain proposals (already long set forth and practiced
by me and by others who have recently formed the Progressive
party) made by Mr. Wilson with which I cordially agree. There
are, however, certain things he has said, even as regards matters
of abstract morality, with which I emphatically disagree. For
example, in arguing for proper business publicity, as to which I
cordially agree with Mr. Wilson, he commits himself to the following statement:

"You know there is temptation in loneliness and secrecy.
Haven't you experienced it ? I have. We are never so proper in
our conduct as when everybody can look and see exactly what we
are doing. If you are off in some distant part of the world and suppose that nobody who lives within a mile of your home is anywhere around, there are times when you adjourn your ordinary
standards. You say to yourself, 'Well, I'll have a fling this time;
nobody will know anything about it.' If you were on the Desert
of Sahara, you would feel that you might permit yourself — well,
say, some slight latitude of conduct; but if you saw one of your
immediate neighbors coming the other way on a camel, you would

behave yourself until he got out of sight. The most dangerous thing in the world is to get off where nobody knows you. I advise you to stay around among the neighbors, and then you may keep out of jail. That is the only way some of us can keep out of jail."

I emphatically disagree with what seems to be the morality inculcated in this statement, which is that a man is expected to do and is to be pardoned for doing all kinds of immoral things if he does them alone and does not expect to be found out. Surely it is not necessary, in insisting upon proper publicity, to preach a morality of so basely material a character.

There is much more that Mr. Wilson says as to which I do not understand him clearly, and where I condemn what I do understand. In economic matters the course he advocates as part of the "New Freedom" simply means the old, old "freedom" of leaving the individual strong man at liberty, unchecked by common action, to prey on the weak and the helpless. The "New Freedom" in the abstract seems to be the freedom of the big to devour the little. In the concrete I may add that Mr. Wilson's misrepresentations of what I have said seem to indicate that he regards the new freedom as freedom from all obligation to obey the Ninth Commandment.

But, after all, my views or the principles of the Progressive party are of much less importance now than the purposes of Mr. Wilson. These are wrapped in impenetrable mystery. His speeches and writings serve but to make them more obscure. If these attempts to refute his misrepresentation of my attitude towards the trusts should result in making his own clear, then this discussion will have borne fruits of substantial value to the country. If Mr. Wilson has any plan of his own for dealing with the trusts, it is to suppress all great industrial organizations — presumably on the principle proclaimed by his Secretary of State four years ago, that every corporation which produced more than a certain percentage of a given commodity — I think the amount specified was twenty-five per cent — no matter how valuable its service, should be suppressed. The simple fact is that such a plan is futile. In operation it would do far more damage than it could remedy. The Progressive plan would give the people full control of, and in masterful fashion prevent all wrongdoing by, the trusts, while utilizing for the public welfare every industrial energy and ability that operates to swell abundance, while obeying strictly the moral law and the law of the land. Mr. Wilson's plan would ultimately benefit the trusts and would permanently damage nobody but the people. For example, one of the steel corporations which has been guilty of the worst practices towards its employees is the Colorado Fuel and Iron Company. Mr. Wilson and Mr. Bryan's plan would, if successful, merely mean permitting four such companies, absolutely uncontrolled, to monopolize every big industry in the country. To talk of such an accomplishment as being "The New Freedom" is enough to make the term one of contemptuous derision.

President Wilson has made explicit promises, and the Democratic platform has made explicit promises. Mr. Wilson is now in power, with a Democratic Congress in both branches. He and the Democratic platform have promised to destroy the trusts, to reduce the cost of living, and at the same to increase the well-being of the farmer and of the workingman — which of course must mean to increase the profits of the farmer and the wages of the workingman. He and his party won the election on this promise. We have a right to expect that they will keep it. If Mr. Wilson's promises mean anything except the very emptiest words, he is pledged to accomplish the beneficent purposes he avows by breaking up all the trusts and combinations and corporations so as to restore competition precisely as it was fifty years ago. If he does not mean this, he means nothing. He cannot do anything else under penalty of showing that his promise and his performance do not square with each other.

Mr. Wilson says that "the trusts are our masters now, but I for one do not care to live in a country called free even under kind masters." Good! The Progressives are opposed to having masters, kind or unkind, and they do not believe that a "new freedom" which in practice would mean leaving four Fuel and Iron Companies free to do what they like in every industry would be of much benefit to the country. The Progressives have a clear and definite programme by which the people would be the masters of the trusts instead of the trusts being their masters, as Mr. Wilson says they are. With practical unanimity the trusts supported the opponents of this programme, Mr. Taft and Mr. Wilson, and they evidently dreaded our programme infinitely more than anything that Mr. Wilson threatened. The people have accepted Mr. Wilson's assurances. Now let him make his promises good. He is committed, if his words mean anything, to the promise to break up every trust, every big corporation — perhaps every small corporation — in the United States — not to go through the motions of breaking them up, but really to break them up. He is committed against the policy (of efficient control and mastery of the big corporations both by law and by administrative action in coöperation) proposed by the Progressives. Let him keep faith with the people; let him in good faith try to keep the promises he has thus repeatedly made. I believe that his promise is futile and cannot be kept. I believe that any attempt sincerely to keep it and in good faith to carry it out will end in either nothing at all or in disaster. But my beliefs are of no consequence. Mr. Wilson is President. It is his acts that are of consequence. He is bound in honor to the people of the United States to keep his promise, and to break up, not nominally but in reality, all big business, all trusts, all combinations of every sort, kind, and description, and probably all corporations. What he says is henceforth of little consequence. The important thing is what he does, and how the results of what he does square with the promises and prophecies he made when all he had to do was to speak, not to act.

APPENDIX C

THE BLAINE CAMPAIGN

In "The House of Harper," written by J. Henry Harper, the following passage occurs: "Curtis returned from the convention in company with young Theodore Roosevelt and they discussed the situation thoroughly on their trip to New York and came to the conclusion that it would be very difficult to consistently support Blaine. Roosevelt, however, had a conference afterward with Senator Lodge and eventually fell in line behind Blaine. Curtis came to our office and found that we were unanimously opposed to the support of Blaine, and with a hearty good-will he trained his editorial guns on the 'Plumed Knight' of Mulligan letter fame. His work was as effective and deadly as any fight he ever conducted in the *Weekly*." This statement has no foundation whatever in fact. I did not return from the convention in company with Mr. Curtis. He went back to New York from the convention, whereas I went to my ranch in North Dakota. No such conversation as that ever took place between me and Mr. Curtis. In my presence, in speaking to a number of men at the time in Chicago, Mr. Curtis said: "You younger men can, if you think right, refuse to support Mr. Blaine, but I am too old a Republican, and have too long been associated with the party, to break with it now." Not only did I never entertain after the convention, but I never during the convention or at any other time, entertained the intention alleged in the quotation in question. I discussed the whole situation with Mr. Lodge before going to the convention, and we had made up our minds that if the nomination of Mr. Blaine was fairly made we would with equal good faith support him.

INDEX

C

Act, 474–477; mutual obligations of corporations and, 477.

Italian, translation of "The Strenuous Life" into, 58.

Itchen, birds in valley of the, 350.

J

Jackson-Lincoln theory of the Presidency, 394–397, 504.

James River Dam Bill, veto of, 457.

Japan, friendliness of, in Spanish War, 237; feeling in, on settlement of Russo-Japanese War, 586; reception given American fleet in, 598–601.

Japanese, translation of "The Strenuous Life" into, 58.

Japanese in California, difficulties over, 411–417.

Jenkins, M. J., letter by, 286–287.

Jew-baiting preacher, story of the, 205–206.

Jiu-jitsu, 48.

Joint Conservation Conference, 447–448.

Jones, Sheriff Bill, 127–130, 131.

Jusserand, Ambassador, anecdote concerning, 52.

K

Keep, Charles H., 399–400.

Kellogg, Frank B., 406, 619.

Kellor, Frances, 180.

Kelly, Luther, 52, 54.

Kelly, Peter, 73–76.

Kent, General, 268.

Kettle Hill, the fight at, 258, 282, 284, 287, 290, 291.

Knight Company case, 466–467, 468, 469, 490.

Knox, Attorney-General, 468.

Kohrs, Conrad, 122.

Kruse, Assemblyman and judge, 73.

L

Labor, work in the interests of, 501–540.

Labor-saving machinery, worker's right to share in profits of, 525–526.

Labor unions, attitude toward, 221, 512, 518–523.

La Follette, quoted on author's services as President, 426–427.

Lambert, Dr. Alexander, 376.

Land fraud prosecutions, 405–406.

Lane, Inter-State Commerce Commissioner, 477.

Larks, observations of, in England, 351–352.

Law, study of and remarks on, 61–62.

Lawton, General, 243, 260.

Lee, Arthur, 216, 270.

Leonard, Captain, 55.

Leupp, Francis E., 394.

Lewi, Dr. Maurice, 207.

Lion hunting, 39–40.

Littledale, St. George, 52.

Little Missouri, life on the, 103–136.

Llewellyn, Major, 137.

Lodge, Henry Cabot, 150, 551; efforts of, in securing author's appointment as Assistant Secretary of the Navy, 224; fearlessness of, in upholding national honor and interest, 230; coöperation of, with author, before Spanish War, 233; close relations with, upon author's becoming President, 383–384.

Loeb, William, Jr., 319, 379, 484, 485, 486, 589.

Long, John, boxing-master, 33.

Lorimer, Senator, 167.

Louisville and Nashville R. R. trouble, 537–539.

Low, Seth, 587.

Ludlow, General, 268.

M

McBee, Silas, 340.

McCall, John A., 318, 320.

McCullagh, John, Chief of New York State Bureau of Elections, 334, 335.

McCullough, John, police inspector, 206.

MacFarlane, Federal District Attorney, 309.

McGee, W J, 428–429.
McIlhenny, John, 401.
McKinley, William, 150, 169, 224, 546; death of, 379.
Machine, the Republican, in New York State, 297–302.
Machines, distinction between organizations and, 164–167.
Mahan, Captain, writings of, 226.
Maine, blowing-up of the, 232.
Maine woods, camping and hunting in the, 35–36.
Marksmanship, degrees of, 36, 38; training of New York police in, 198; in the navy, 232–233.
Maroquin, J. M., Colombian dictator, 559–560, 561–563.
Marriage, remarks on, 62, 176–184; advantage of early, 216.
Marryat, books by, 20; a lesson from, 60.
Marshall, body-servant, 261.
Marshall, Vice-President, reported statement of, concerning author and battle of San Juan Hill, 280.
"Marxism versus Socialism," Simkhovitch's, 541–542.
Maxwell, G. H., 428.
Mayoralty campaign (1886), 144.
Meat inspection law, 483.
Merriam, Hart, 28, 29.
Merrifield, William J., 106, 117, 118, 127.
Mesa Verde National Park, 460.
Meyer, George von L., 587, 106, 118, 119, 120, 388.
Miles, General, 253.
Miller, printer, case of, 521, 523.
Millet, Frank, 459.
Mills, Lieutenant A. L., 261, 263, 270; letter by, 284.
Minckwitz family, Dresden, 25–26.
Mineral land laws, 449.
Mines, Bureau of, 502.
Mississippi River, trip of Inland Waterways Commission down the, 445.
Mitchell, John, 506, 507, 587.
Mitchell, Senator, 448.

Mondell, Congressman, 395, 431.
Monroe Doctrine, author's interpretation of the, 546–547; application of, in cases of Venezuela, Santo Domingo, and Colombia and Panama, 547–571.
Montauk Point, return of Cuban army to, 275.
Moody, Attorney-General, 469, 476, 483, 490, 503.
Moosehead Lake, trip to, 33.
Morgan, John, 228.
Morley, John, 536.
Morse, banker, case of, 406, 407, 487.
Morton, Captain, 265.
Morton, Paul, 473–474.
Morton Hall, political meeting-place, 63–64.
Mosquito Inlet Reservation, 461.
Mounted police, New York, 201.
Mount Olympus National Monument, 460.
Moyer, 409, 528 ff.
"Mr. Dooley," cited, 234.
Muir, John, visit to the Yosemite with, 347–349.
Muir Woods, 460.
Murdock, Congressman, 384.
Murphy, Lieutenant, 563.
Murray, Joseph, 64–70, 161.
Murray, Lawrence, 411.

N

National Association of Manufacturers, 532–533.
National Bird Reservations, 461.
National Bison Range, Montana, 461.
National Child Labor Committee, 502.
National Conservation, Commission on, 402, 445, 447.
National Guard of New York, author's service in, 250.
National Guard training, advantages and shortcomings of, 250–251.
National Monuments Act, 460.
National Parks, creation of, 460.

2 T

INDEX

Ranch life, 103–143.

Raphael, Otto, 192–193.

Reading, as a boy, 17, 19–22; choice of books for, 359–364; range of, for author's children, 375–376. *See* Books.

Rebates, railway, 473–474.

Reclamation, work of, 429 ff.

Reclamation Act, 428, 431, 432, 434, 448.

Reed, T. B., quoted, 167; mentioned, 294.

Reformers of "silk stocking" type, 96–97.

Reid, Mayne, 17, 19, 20.

Reid, New York policeman, 199.

Remington, Frederic, 103, 133; "Bronco Buster" by, given to author, 356.

Republican Administration, office-holders used by, to debauch political convention of 1912, 146.

Republican party, position of, in 1898, 297–298; in New York State, 298–303; at time of author's succession to Presidency, 381–382.

Revolution of Panama against Colombia, 564–566.

Revolutions on Isthmus of Panama, 555–558.

Reynolds, James B., 313.

Rhinoceros hunting, 40, 41.

Richards, Laura E., children's books by, 20, 376.

Rifle practice at Sagamore Hill, 36.

Riis, Jacob, 48, 70, 211, 313; author's close association and work with, 185 ff., 218–219; "How the Other Half Lives" by, 187.

Rixey, Surgeon-General P. M., 52, 55.

Robb, Hamden, 73.

Robin, the English, 352.

Robinson, Douglas, 294.

"Robinson Crusoe," reading of, 20–21.

Rock Creek, walks down, 51, 52.

Rock Creek Park, family excursions to, 365.

Rockhill, Ambassador, 388.

Roosevelt, Isaac, 3.

Roosevelt, Kermit, 40.

Roosevelt, Klaes Martensen van, 1.

Roosevelt, Martha Bulloch, 14.

Roosevelt, Mrs. Theodore, gift of silver vase to, by men of the Louisiana, 356.

Roosevelt, Robert, 15.

Roosevelt, Theodore, father of author, 8–14.

Roosevelt, Theodore, ancestry, 1–5; birth of, 6; childhood, 6 ff.; father, 8–14; mother, 14–15; relatives, 15–16; schooling, 17; early interest in natural history, 17–19, 22–24; reading as a child, 19–22; winter abroad, 23–26; preparation for college, 26–27; course at Harvard, 27–31; exercise and sports, 32 ff.; game shooting, 40–42; boxing and wrestling, 47–51; exercise while President, 51–54; breaking into politics, 62–64; election to New York Legislature, 70; experiences in the Assembly, 70 ff.; defeat for nomination as Speaker, and beneficial results, 95–97; ranch life on the Little Missouri, 103–143; unsuccessful campaign for Mayoralty of New York City, 144; appointment and work as Civil Service Commissioner, 144 ff.; service as Police Commissioner of New York City, 185–222; appointment to Assistant Secretaryship of the Navy, 224; preparation for the Spanish War, 230 ff.; appointed Lieutenant-Colonel of the Rough Riders, 238; activities in getting regiment to Cuba, 249–255; the fight at La Guasima and Kettle Hill, 256–261; battle of San Juan Hill, 261–266; round-robin incident, 267–269, 278–279; letters concerning share in battle of San Juan Hill, 279–291; election and work as Governor of New York, 293 ff.; nomination to the Vice-Presidency,

INDEX

645

Shafter, General, 253, 254, 267, 268.
Sharp, Lieutenant-Commander, 255.
Shaw, Albert, 340.
Sherman Anti-Trust Law, 463, 465, 470, 609–619.
Shields, cowboy-soldier, 271.
Shipp, Lieutenant W. E., 261.
Shooting, 36.
Simkhovitch, V. D., "Marxism versus Socialism" by, 541–542.
Simpson, "Hashknife," 122.
Simpson, Sloan, 122.
Sims, Federal District Attorney, 406, 407.
Sims, Lieutenant, 232.
Smith, F. Hopkinson, sketches of White House by, 358.
Smith, Herbert Knox, 411, 456–459, 471, 490.
Snyder, deputy sheriff, 129.
Social conditions, improvement of, as a Government duty, 174–175.
Socialism, Simkhovitch's book dealing with, 541–542.
Socialist, terming of author a, 523.
Socialists, 168; discussion and criticism of doctrines of, 523–527.
Spalding, Bishop, 509.
Spanish War, unpreparedness of America for, 223–227; preparing the navy for, 230–234; attitude of people in general at beginning of, 234–237; organization of Rough Riders, 238–240; conditions in Navy and War Departments, 240–245; equipping the Rough Riders, 245–248; embarcation for Cuba, 253–255; the Guasimas fight, 256–261; battle of San Juan Hill, 262–266; capture of Santiago, 266; round-robin incident, 267–268, 278; end of war and disbandment at Montauk Point, 275; letters concerning author's share in, 278–291.
Spectator, London, on world voyage of American battle fleet, 595.
Sperry, Admiral, 595; letter by, concerning world cruise of battle fleet, 599–602.
Spinney, George, 99.
Spitzer, dock superintendent, 485.
Spoils system, the, 144 ff.
Sprague, Henry, 73.
Spring-Rice, Cecil, 36.
Square Deal, in dealing with corporations, 477 ff., 606 ff.
Stalwart faction of Republican party, 76, 95.
Standard Oil Company, opposition of, to legislation affecting corporations, 471.
Standard Oil Company suit, 469.
Steel Corporation and the Tennessee Coal and Iron Company, 478–483, 607–609.
Steele, Lieutenant, 275.
Stelzle, Rev. Charles, 215.
Sternberg, Baron Speck von, 36.
Stetson, Francis Lynde, 85.
Steunenberg, Governor, murder of, 527.
Stevens, Captain M. J., 282; letter by, 286.
Stewart, Granville, 122.
Stimson, District Attorney, 391, 406, 486, 611.
Stockman's Association of Montana, 122.
Straus, Oscar, 471, 490, 587.
"Strenuous Life," speech and volume of essays on, 58.
"Strike" bills, in New York Legislature, 77–78, 81.
Strong, Mayor, 185, 187, 294.
Success, degrees and attainment of, 58–59; the highest type of, 378.
Suffrage, universal, 174 ff.
Sugar Trust, 406; investigation of frauds perpetrated by, 484 ff.
Sugar Trust prosecution, 466.
Sullivan, Big Tim, 206–207.
Sullivan, Jerry D., 206.
Sullivan, John L., 50–51.
Sully Hill Park, 460.
Sumner, General Samuel S., 243, 261,

d/